Theodor Hanf is Visiting Professor of Political Studies at the American University of Beirut and Honorary Professor of Political Science at the University of Freiburg.

'One of the best books to be written about the Lebanese conflict.'
**Karl Sharro**

'This massive work is an important scholarly contribution to our knowledge of Lebanon and its war. The book is a product of years of labour, and the author's tremendous knowledge is effectively woven into the narrative.'
***International Journal of Middle East Studies***

'Theodor Hanf brings a deep understanding of Lebanon, its society and its political system, explains it clearly and illustrates it judiciously using extensive interviews and survey data with a comparative perspective. If you want to read only one book on Lebanon, this is it.'
**Nadim Shehadi, Director, Fares Centre, The Fletcher School, Tufts University**

# Coexistence in Wartime Lebanon
## Decline of a State and Rise of a Nation

Theodor Hanf

Translated from German by John Richardson

The Centre for Lebanese Studies in association with
I.B.Tauris & Co Ltd Publishers

New paperback edition published in 2015 by I.B.Tauris & Co Ltd
in association with The Centre for Lebanese Studies
www.ibtauris.com

First published in 1993 by The Centre for Lebanese Studies
in association with I.B.Tauris & Co Ltd
Copyright © 1993, 2015 The Centre for Lebanese Studies

The right of Theodor Hanf to be identified as the author of this work has been asserted by the author in accordance with the Copyright, Designs and Patents Act 1988.

All rights reserved. Except for brief quotations in a review, this book, or any part thereof, may not be reproduced, stored in or introduced into a retrieval system, or transmitted, in any form or by any means, electronic, mechanical, photocopying, recording or otherwise, without the prior written permission of the publisher.

Every attempt has been made to gain permission for the use of the images in this book. Any omissions will be rectified in future editions.

ISBN: 978 1 84885 715 5

A full CIP record for this book is available from the British Library
A full CIP record is available from the Library of Congress

Library of Congress Catalog Card Number: available

Typeset by Selro Publishing Services, Oxford

The Centre for Lebanese Studies would like to thank Mr George Asseily and Mr Tony Asseily for their generous donation which made possible the printing of this book

Michel Allard
Marwan Buheiry
Malcolm Kerr
Jean Maroun
Michel Seurat
Riad Younès

in memoriam

# Contents

| | |
|---|---|
| Preface to the Paperback Edition | xv |
| Acknowledgements | xvii |
| On citation and transcription | xix |
| List of common abbreviations | xix |

ONE PEOPLE TOO MANY IN THE LEVANT?
Preliminary remarks on the roots of the conflict in Lebanon .... 1

## CHAPTER 1

CONFLICT REGULATION AND CRISES IN
MULTI-COMMUNAL STATES: THE PROLIFERATION
OF MULTI-COMMUNAL STATES IN THE TWENTIETH CENTURY .... 7

| | |
|---|---|
| Integration or coexistence? Changing perspectives in the social sciences | 11 |
| Culturalistic and economistic approaches | 14 |
| Modes of incorporation: Linking analytical approaches | 18 |
| Incorporation and conflict | 22 |
| Forms of conflict regulation and their ideologies | 26 |
| Ideologies and strategies | 32 |
| Civil war and conflict regulation | 37 |
| Multi-communal states and international crises | 38 |
| Lebanon as model | 40 |

## CHAPTER 2

THE 'LEBANESE MODEL'
COEXISTENCE IN PRE-WAR LEBANON .... 45

| | |
|---|---|
| Coexistence and history | 48 |
| The National Pact and proportionality | 71 |
| Parties, families and notables: Political interests in pre-war Lebanon | 75 |

| | |
|---|---:|
| Conflicts over power-sharing | 86 |
| Class, community and economic conflicts | 97 |
| Foreign policy as a conflict of identity | 110 |
| Use and abuse of coexistence | 113 |
| Fields of conflict and communal strategies | 130 |

## CHAPTER 3

### THE CLOUDING HORIZON
### NON-LEBANESE FACTORS OF CONFLICT 141

| | |
|---|---:|
| The pivot of Arab politics: The Arab-Israeli conflict | 143 |
| The Palestinian National Movement | 147 |
| The crisis of Arabism and the reawakening of Islamic fundamentalism | 152 |
| Oil on troubled waters | 156 |
| The end of neutrality by consent | 160 |
| Surrogate battlefield for Palestine | 175 |

## CHAPTER 4

### DANSE MACABRE 1975–1988:
### PARTIES, MASKS AND STEPS 179

| | |
|---|---:|
| Factions and their leaders | 181 |
| War on many fronts | 194 |
| War between the Palestinians and the Christian parties | 204 |
| Slide into civil war | 206 |
| Syrian intervention against partition | 210 |
| The PLO and the National Movement against the Lebanese Front | 213 |
| Syrian intervention against the PLO and the National Movement | 216 |
| The south: Palestinians against Christian Lebanese | 226 |
| Israeli invasion of southern Lebanon | 228 |
| Syria and the Lebanese Front in conflict | 231 |
| Civil war: Christians against Christians | 234 |
| Syrians and the Lebanese Front at war | 237 |
| Simmering warfare | 241 |
| War between Shi`is and Palestinians | 243 |
| Expansionist drives by the Lebanese Front | 246 |
| The Israeli–Palestinian 'Fourteen Day War' | 252 |

| | |
|---|---|
| The spread of simmering warfare | 253 |
| Israeli–Palestinian War | 256 |
| Cold War over Lebanon | 264 |
| Civil war: Druze against the Lebanese Forces | 275 |
| Shi`i resistance to Israel and estrangement from the government | 279 |
| War against the Israeli–Lebanese agreement | 282 |
| Civil war: Palestinians against Palestinians in Lebanon | 293 |
| Overtures and simmering warfare | 295 |
| Lebanese Forces: Insurrection and civil war around Sidon | 298 |
| The 'Camps War': Amal against Palestinians | 302 |
| War between Amal and the Druze militias | 304 |
| Civil war around Zahle and Tripoli | 305 |
| The fight over the Militia Agreement of Damascus | 306 |
| The 'Camps War': Beirut and the south | 312 |
| War in West Beirut: Amal against the Left | 314 |
| Shi`i civil war: Amal against Hezbollah | 315 |
| Civil war: Palestinians against Palestinians | 318 |
| Cold War over the Lebanese state | 318 |
| Simmering warfare over the 'security zone' | 320 |

## CHAPTER 5

### VIOLENCE WITHOUT VICTORY
### FORMS, COSTS AND CONSEQUENCES OF WAR     323

| | |
|---|---|
| Terror as a way of life | 324 |
| From ethnic mobilization to ethnic domination | 331 |
| Militias and armies in an uneasy stalemate | 335 |
| The toll of lives | 339 |
| Flight and expulsion | 342 |
| Migrant workers and emigrants | 347 |
| The war economy | 350 |
| Life in war | 357 |
| The equilibrium of terror | 359 |

## CHAPTER 6

### FOXES AND LIONS: POLITICIANS AND MILITIA
### LEADERS' PERCEPTIONS OF CONFLICT     361

| | |
|---|---|
| Perceptions of problems in pre-war Lebanon | 362 |

Perceptions of the causes of war 373
Digression: Views of Lebanese 'doves' 393
'We' and 'they' 401
Compromise or victory? 420

## CHAPTER 7

### COEXISTENCE IN WAR: ATTITUDES AND OPINIONS OF ECONOMICALLY ACTIVE LEBANESE 1981–1987 435

The comparability of the surveys 438
The 1987 survey 442
Psycho-social attitudes 459
Economic ethos and job satisfaction 464
Economy and society 475
Religion, family and community 480
The political system 490
Political tendencies 495
Religion and politics 513
Forms of conflict regulation 519
Prospects of coexistence 534
Coexistence under conditions of extreme crisis 540

## CHAPTER 8

### A REVOCABLE COVENANT: A PRELIMINARY SYNOPSIS 551

Lebanese against Lebanese 553
The militarization of the conflict 558
Inconclusive interventions 559
The transformation of the Lebanese factions 561
Misperceptions of the interests of foreign allies 562
The intentions of Arab neighbours 563
The demise of a consociational democracy:
    The failure of the elite and the international crisis 565

## CHAPTER 9

### THE DISINTEGRATION OF THE STATE THE ROAD TO DEPENDENCE, 1988–1990 567

Lebanon without a president 567
General Aoun's attempt to restore the state 572

| | |
|---|---:|
| Bombardment and blockade | 573 |
| Onlookers | 575 |
| Mediators | 578 |
| Taif: The hour of the foxes | 583 |
| Presidential election and assassination | 590 |
| Syria's man as Lebanon's president | 595 |
| War between the army and militia in the Christian heartland | 598 |
| Loss of credibility | 602 |
| Divided and ruled | 603 |

## CHAPTER 10

### THE TWO FACES OF THE SECOND REPUBLIC
### TRAPPINGS OF SOVEREIGNTY, 1990–1992

| | |
|---|---:|
| | 607 |
| In the shadow of the Kuwait conflict | 608 |
| Constitutional amendment | 609 |
| Aoun's defeat | 611 |
| Militia-free Beirut | 613 |
| Government of national unity | 614 |
| Disarming the militias | 615 |
| Treaty of brotherhood, cooperation and coordination with Syria | 617 |
| Filling the Chamber of Deputies | 618 |
| Disarming the PLO | 619 |
| Dereliction of the Taif Agreement | 621 |
| Gerrymandering | 625 |
| A minority to the polls | 630 |
| Evolving in dependence | 634 |

## CHAPTER 11

### THE EMERGENCE OF A NATION
### EPILOGUE AND CONJECTURES

| | |
|---|---:|
| | 637 |
| Peace and unity movements | 638 |
| The foundations of a new consensus | 640 |
| A nation too late? | 642 |
| The neighbour's uncertain future | 643 |
| 'Drifting dunes' | 645 |

| | |
|---|---:|
| BIBLIOGRAPHY | 647 |
| SELECTED ANNOTATED LITERATURE IN ARABIC ON THE CONFLICT IN LEBANON | 676 |
| QUESTIONNAIRE, 1984, 1986, 1987 | 684 |
| INDEX OF NAMES | 695 |
| INDEX OF PLACES | 701 |
| INDEX OF SUBJECTS | 705 |

# Preface to the Paperback Edition

This book was published first in 1990 in German, and then in 1993 in Arabic and English. All three versions have been out of print for a number of years.

This second edition in English comes in a paperback format, in reply to numerous requests from scholars and students addressed to the publisher as well as to the author. The English text of 1993 has been maintained without any additions or changes, for two reasons.

First, the data and material for the book were collected during the Lebanese wars, and the original manuscript was completed just after hostilities came to an end. The interviews which were conducted with political and military leaders involved in the war, as well as data extracted from opinion polls carried out between 1982 and 1987, remain valid today as sources of contemporary history.

Second, the central thesis of the book as originally published has been confirmed by post-war empirical surveys conducted by the author in 2002, 2006, 2007 and 2009, namely that the Lebanese perceive themselves as a nation united in diversity, certainly a sceptical nation, but a nation nevertheless.

The reader may wish the Lebanese a state that they desire: an independent, stable, prosperous, and democratic republic. Regrettably, being located in the midst of a conflict-ridden regional environment, their wishes may well remain frustrated for a longer time to come, leaving Lebanon in limbo.

# Acknowledgements

Every book is a joint effort, and I have been exceptionally fortunate in the advice, help and support received in gathering material, interpreting empirical data and preparing the manuscript for publication.

Three colleagues and friends, Boutros Labaki, Antoine Messarra and Salim Nasr, provided invaluable information and insights in countless discussions over the years. Labaki and Messarra put their unpublished material at my disposal and helped me in the selection of literature and documents in Arabic. Nasr constructed the random samples for the empirical surveys and bore with me in compiling the questionnaire.

Ibrahim Chebli, Eugène Makhlouf, Moshe Ma'oz and Nabil Nasrallah helped arrange interviews with representatives of political and military opinion.

Prominent personalities in Lebanon and neighbouring countries took the time for exhaustive discussions and lengthy conversations. If they are not named in the text, this is at their own request.

Angela Herrmann recorded most of these personal interviews. The Lebanese pollsters made an exceptional contribution to empirical social research in the difficult conditions of war. Petra Bauerle and Gerda Vierdag processed the data. Christel Weiland drew the maps.

The Deutsche Forschungsgemeinschaft and the German Institute for International Educational Research helped finance the surveys and field work in Lebanon. Angela and Gerhold Arnds were very kind and generous hosts in Beirut, as were the directors of the Orient Institute of the Deutsche Morgenländische Gesellschaft, Ulrich Haarmann, Gernot Rotter and Anton Heinen.

Special thanks are due to John Richardson, who provided the translation. His endeavours have made an English text out of a German one, and in the process refuted the saying, 'traduttore-traditore'.

I am greatly indebted to the Centre for Lebanese Studies, Oxford, particularly to the late Albert Hourani who read the initial manuscript and gave invaluable suggestions, and to Nadim Shehadi, Ingrid Hobby and Fida Nasrallah for their handling of the English edition. Anna Enayat of IB Tauris and Co Ltd gave professional evaluation and John Crabb helped with production. Margaret Owen painstakingly edited the manuscript and Kirsten Schulze proof-read the book and prepared the English index.

To the aforementioned and all the other people without whose cooperation this book could not have appeared go my sincere thanks. Only I am responsible for the conclusions and any mistakes and failings.

Finally, and above all, my deepest gratitude goes to Anne Marie, Dominik and Verena for their understanding and encouragement.

—Theodor Hanf
October 1993

# Citation and transcription

Quotations in languages other than English and French have been translated into English.

The English spelling of Arabic words is based on that used in English daily newspapers. Most readers are likely to be more familiar with these than with transliterated forms.

In the indexes, names of Arab persons, places and subjects have been transliterated in accordance with accepted practice in Oriental studies.

# List of Common Abbreviations

| | |
|---|---|
| ALA | Arab Lebanese Army |
| ALF | Arab Liberation Front |
| CP | Communist Party |
| MNF | Multinational Forces |
| OCAL | Organization for Communist Action in Lebanon |
| PLA | Palestine Liberation Army |
| PLO | Palestine Liberation Organization |
| NLP | National Liberal Party |
| SSNP | Syrian Social National Party |
| PSP | Progressive Socialist Party |
| UAR. | United Arab Republic |
| UNIFIL | United Nations Interim Force for Southern Lebanon |

# One People too Many in the Levant? Preliminary Remarks on the Roots of the Conflict in Lebanon

Rules of the game: There is one fewer chair than there are players. The chairs are arranged in two rows back to back. When the music starts the players walk around the chairs. When the music stops the players sit down as quickly as possible. The player left standing is eliminated.
The name of the game: musical chairs.[1]

In the Orient there is either one country too few or one people too many.
Charles Malek

The way to Jerusalem is over the Lebanon Mountains and through Jounieh.
Abu Iyad

On the eastern seaboard of the Mediterranean 'musical chairs' has been horrific reality for some decades. When the diplomatic music stops the struggle for the chairs is fought with guns. The music stopped for the first time in 1947/8, then in 1956, 1967, 1973 and 1975, and last in 1982. The first turns were taken around the Palestinian chair, since 1975 they have been around the Lebanese. As reality is not a game, none of the players obeys the rules: none will accept elimination, and no one seems prepared to share a chair with anyone else. The Israelis took the Palestinian chair. The Palestinians tried to take the Lebanese chair, as a stage,

---

[1] In German, musical chairs is called 'The Journey to Jerusalem'.

they said, on their journey to Jerusalem; many, above all Christian, Lebanese felt they wanted a substitute for the loss of their own chair.

Prior to 1975 Christians and Muslims shared the Lebanese chair in reasonable harmony; since then they have fought bitterly over every inch, each afraid of being shoved off. There have been several arbiters, some chosen, others self-appointed. None has been impartial, all have strengthened the bitter determination of all participants to secure a place at any price. For, in reality, the loss of one's chair means subjugation, expulsion, life in refugee camps or emigration — if not physical annihilation. The fear of being the ultimate loser is the supreme force in politics in the countries along the roads to Jerusalem.

Observers on the sidelines may have their particular fears: the major powers the attenuation of their spheres of influence, the middling powers damage to their economic interests. But those directly involved, both strong and weak, share a common fear: that the observers will not take their respective fears seriously.

Fear lies behind Israeli policies. Survivors of the national-socialist genocide and refugees from Arab countries, immigrants by Zionist conviction or because they had no alternative, all regard the Jewish state in Palestine as the only reliable guarantee against another holocaust or a life spent suffering discrimination.

Fear lies behind Syrian policies. For the past two decades, members of the Alawite minority have held power. After centuries of social and economic discrimination, the Alawites are, for the first time in Syrian history, enjoying the fruits of power. The fear of losing it, of once again being marginalized and reduced to insignificance, has driven them to erect a harsher, more stable system than Syria has previously known. The regime's domestic policy is rigorous and consistent: to keep power, for fear that the dominated majority will otherwise avenge itself. The regime acts ruthlessly against any opposition: to crush the Muslim Brotherhood insurrection in 1982, Syrian artillery and air force reduced to rubble the centre of Hama, the fourth largest city in the country; tens of thousands of people are thought to have perished. It also pursues a rigorous foreign policy if it thinks the circumstances warrant it. The claim of Syria's present rulers to leadership of the Arab world and control over both Lebanon and the Palestinian organizations is dictated as much by their Pan-Arab convictions as by strategy for the survival of their ethnic group. The loss of regional importance, restricting their influence to Syria alone, could be a prelude to the loss of power in Syria itself.

Fear lies behind Palestinian policies. After their flight and expulsion the political will of the Palestinians seemed utterly paralysed for two decades. Apathy was widespread in the squalid refugee camps. Those who had the means or education to escape from camp life concentrated their energies on personal advancement, either in the Arab world or abroad. Palestinian politics was reserved for the Arab states. Arab defeat in the Six Day War in 1967, the concomitant Israeli occupation of all Palestine and the consequent flood of refugees led to the Palestinians' re-awakening. The conviction that they could now neither expect nor hope for anything from the Arab states fuelled the spectacular rise of the Palestinian resistance movement and the resurgence of Palestinian national feeling. If there were doubts about the existence of a Palestinian people before 1967, subsequent events banished them. The threat to their existence as a group kindled a nascent nationhood of an intensity matched in the Third World only by the emergence of a common political consciousness among the blacks of South Africa. The rise of the Palestinian resistance simultaneously jeopardized it. Israel responded as experience had taught it, with military force: reprisals against Palestinian bases as well as against their host countries. In consequence, whatever their sympathies for the Palestinian cause, the *raison d'état* of the host countries conflicted with the freedom of action for the resistance movement. Jordanian toleration ended in bloodshed in 1970. As the Israelis remember Masada, so the Palestinians remember 'Black September'. The Palestinians feared a repetition of the Jordanian experience in what they felt was their last bastion, Lebanon. The fear of once again being reduced to the status of impotent pawns in the power games of Arab regimes, and the sense of standing with their backs to the sea, considerably influenced the actions of the Palestinians in Lebanon.

Fear lies behind the policies of Lebanese Christians as well. Like the Jordanians, and like many of their Muslim countrymen, they fear Israeli reprisals against Lebanon for Palestinian armed action launched from Lebanese soil. But the fears of Christian Lebanese are more deeply rooted. As far as they are concerned, Lebanon is the only country in the Arab world in which Christians are not *de jure* or *de facto* second-class citizens, the only country in which people of all religious communities enjoy equal rights. Almost half a million mainly Muslim Palestinians would shift the delicate balance between Christians and Muslims to their disadvantage. The presence of armed Palestinian commandos beyond the control of the Lebanese government would rock the foundations of the only liberal democracy in the Arab East.

Lebanese Christians' fear and self-assertion can only be understood against the background of the historic experience of non-Muslim minorities under Islamic rule. Traditionally, Islam does not distinguish between temporal and spiritual, between state and religion. It is the religious duty of every Muslim to promote Islamic rule whenever and wherever possible: the law has to be Islamic and the ruler has to be a Muslim. Members of the state, the people in the narrow sense, are the community of Muslim believers; 'people of the book', that is, Christians and Jews, are tolerated as 'wards' of the Islamic state, provided they submit to it. There is no equality between Muslims and other believers. In Lebanon and other

Arab states there are persistent calls for these principles to be put into practice. Such calls awaken in Christians memories of a not so distant past, when, as 'wards', they were forbidden to carry weapons, to sit in judgment on Muslims or to mount a horse; at times they had to wear prescribed dress by which they could be instantly recognized. Past perhaps; but a glance across the borders is enough to keep alive Lebanese Christian fears of Muslim majority rule. In all other Arab states Islam is the official religion, or, as in Syria, the constitutionally prescribed religion of the head of state. One may convert to Islam, but not from it; Muslim men may marry Jews and Christians, but Jewish and Christian men may not take a Muslim wife. The non-Muslim communities are effectively excluded from the majority society. As a rule, they are fairly prosperous — a common feature of marginalized minorities — but carry little weight politically, even where, like the Copts in Egypt, they are relatively numerous. In this light, it is understandable that Lebanese Christians do not relish the prospect of minority status in a largely Muslim society, preferring to cling to a Lebanon in which, for centuries, they have been able substantially to determine their own fate. Popular catchphrases — 'We're nobody's "wards"' and 'No Copting out' — express their deep fear of a future as a minority group.

Finally, fear is also a powerful force behind the policies of the Muslim communities in Lebanon. The Sunnis are not afraid of the Palestinians as such, most of whom are Sunnis too. Rather, their fear derives from a gradual, seemingly inexorable loss of power. Up to the collapse of the Ottoman Empire they were part of the majority, an undisputed pillar of the state. In the Lebanese Republic they became one minority among others, even though they were in the position to influence the fortunes of this state considerably. They have played only a marginal role in the wars; overshadowed by the now more numerous and more militant Shi`is, they have become the minority in West Beirut, the centre of Muslim power. The power of the Shi`is has increased, but so have their fears. In the south of the country as well as in the south-western suburbs of Beirut, where most of them now live, they have been caught between the Israeli devil and Palestinian sea. A quarter of a million Shi`is have had to flee several times. In the south they bear the main burden of the confrontation with Israel. Even the smallest of the Muslim communities, the Druze, acts in the final analysis out of fear. In 1983 they felt that Christian militia invading their traditional territory, the Chouf Mountains, constituted a lethal threat. Nearly half of the male Druze population took up arms, inflicted a crushing defeat on the Christian militia and drove virtually the entire Christian population out of the Chouf. The Druze thereby considerably increased their share of the 'Lebanese chair'. However, for want of people effectively to populate the conquered areas, they have subsequently been living in fear of others disputing their gains.

As a rule, conflicts are fuelled by many forces: economic interests and cleavages, ideals and ambitions, convictions, jealousy and envy; any analysis of conflict should consider these factors separately and jointly. Yet few analysts appreciate the forces unleashed by fear. Fear, be it justified or not, is the cause of much of the fierceness, bitterness and intransigence peculiar to so many conflicts.

In the present-day Levant many groups have real grounds to fear for their existence. This is particularly true of the Palestinians and the Lebanese Christians: the former want to have a homeland again, the latter do not want to lose theirs; both want to determine their own destiny. However, as explained, fear motivates not only the threatened and the relatively weak but also the strong. Fear is an important factor in both Israeli and Syrian policies. Once violent conflict has broken out, fear grips all parties to the violence, be they perpetrators or victims. Accordingly, in the Lebanese conflict there is now no group that does not fear for its existence: Sunnis, Shi`is and Druze have been just as little spared as Christians and Palestinians.

The Lebanese conflicts in recent years can be understood only against the background of the respective participants' fears of being the player left standing. What started primarily as a surrogate war over Palestine has become a conflict over coexistence between various Lebanese groups as well. This surrogate war is also a civil war.

The subject of this book is not the struggle for Palestine. It is conflict and conflict regulation in Lebanon. How were conflicts regulated peacefully in pre-war Lebanon? How could this country become the battle-field of a surrogate war and, at the same time, a civil war? How do Lebanese — political and military leaders, on the one hand, and ordinary citizens on the other — view what has happened to their country? What do they desire and what will they settle for? What are the prospects of re-establishing Lebanese coexistence?

This book has three objectives. The author hopes to show, firstly, that Lebanese conflicts were not a decisive cause of the war, but were crucial to the choice of battleground; secondly, that not only the 'game of nations', musical chairs over Jerusalem, can be deadly, but that the internal Lebanese 'game of communities' has only victims, no victors; and, finally, that fear can indeed produce a vicious circle of hate and violence, but also reason and compromise — that conflict can bring forth coexistence.

# 1

# Conflict Regulation and Crises in Multi-Communal States: The Proliferation of Multi-Communal States in the Twentieth Century

At the start of the twentieth century the international political map included vast multi-communal states: the Hapsburg, Romanov and Ottoman Empires. In domestic politics all three faced the same overriding problem: how to facilitate coexistence between groups with different origins, different religious convictions and languages and, in consequence, different self-perceptions. The universalistic and religious sources of their legitimacy were increasingly questioned by modern nationalism, a child of the French Revolution.

Nationalism took, in Hans Kohn's classic formulation, two forms: one 'subjectively political', the other 'objectively cultural'. The former concept is voluntaristic, the latter deterministic. Subjectively political nationalism is rooted in the decision of individuals to identify themselves with the nation. The nation is a community by the will of the individuals, constituted and held together by, in the words of Ernest Renan, 'a daily plebiscite'. Objectively cultural nationalism, by contrast, is impervious to individual decisions. The nation is a consequence of destiny, determined by origin, language and culture. A subjectively political nation can be created. Once a state exists with centralized organs of power, demarcated territory and a population, it can create its own nation. An objectively cultural nation cannot be created: it already exists. If it wishes to have its own state it can seek to create one.

Both forms of nationalism have proved to be dynamite for the multi-communal empires. Weakened by numerous different nationalisms before and during the First World War, two disintegrated after it.[1] The Paris Treaties defined the successor states to the Hapsburg and Ottoman Empires. The victorious powers made an effort to tailor the map of central and south-eastern Europe to fit 'objectively cultural' nations.

Their success was limited. Centuries of coexistence between ethnic, linguistic and regional groups within the supranational empires had sewn a 'patchwork quilt' of communities; the search for precise boundaries in accordance with 'objective' criteria was a hopeless task. Besides its 'core nation', large ethnic, and frequently dissatisfied, minorities were a feature of each new state, as were, in keeping with the logic of deterministic nationalism, irredentists and separatist movements too. The ruling majorities soon started shifting from a deterministic to a voluntaristic concept of nation: the minorities should abandon their particularisms and assimilate with the majority. Instead of one Hapsburg 'community dungeon', now there were a number of smaller 'community prisons'.[2]

In the eastern regions of the Ottoman Empire the victorious powers adopted a far less coherent policy than in south-eastern Europe. Here, too, a national movement of a culturally objective nature had emerged in the last decades of the nineteenth century, Arab nationalism.[3] To gain the support of the Arabs in its fight with the Ottomans, Great Britain pledged support for a large Arab state beween the Nile and the Euphrates. More or less simultaneously, Britain also promised the Jews a national homeland in Palestine, and signed an agreement with France to divide the region into two zones of influence. The dreams of an Arab Empire were dashed at the Maysalun Pass in the Anti Lebanon Mountains in 1920, when French troops defeated the Arab forces of the Emir Faisal and occupied Damascus. The Arab East came under British and French suzerainty as mandate territories of the League of Nations. The mandate powers created new states as they saw fit: Britain created Palestine, out of which Transjordan was subsequently carved, and Iraq, France the republics of Syria and Lebanon. The

---

[1] See Kemal H. Karpat, 'The Ottoman ethnic and confessional legacy in the Middle East', in Milton J. Esman and Itamar Rabinovich, eds., *Ethnicity, Pluralism, and the State in the Middle East* (Ithaca and London, 1988), pp.35–53. On Austro–Hungary see Adolph Fischhof, *Österreich und die Bürgschaften seines Bestandes* (Vienna, 1869).

[2] See John Coakley, 'National territories and cultural frontiers: conflicts of principle in the formation of the states in Europe', *West European Politics*, 5 (1982), pp.34–49.

[3] See the authoritative study by Bassam Tibi, *Vom Gottesreich zum Nationalstaat: Islam und panarabischer Nationalismus* (Frankfurt, 1987). For a brief survey, see Theodor Hanf, 'Arabismus und Islamismus', in Heinrich August Winkler, ed., *Nationalismus in der Welt von heute* (Göttingen, 1982), pp.157–76.

boundaries of these states were arbitrary: they did not demarcate nations which were either subjectively political or objectively cultural.

Instead of one state for the Arabs there were now several Arab states. And each of these states included a number of religious communities or ethnic groups that, as quasi-national groups, had exercised wide powers of self-administration within the Ottoman Empire. Like the peoples of south-eastern Europe, all these groups were strewn across wide areas in a patchwork quilt of settlements; none of the new states was the state of any one group. The conditions for the emergence of voluntaristic national feeling were the worst possible. For pan-Arabists the new states were too small; for particularists they were either too large or 'wrongly' drawn for their specific ethnic or religious groups.

The results of the dismemberment of two large multi-communal states after the First World War were similar in Europe and the Orient. Both were replaced by numerous smaller multi-communal or multi-ethnic states, with concomitant border disputes, rivalries and conflicts over hegemony. At the same time, all of them faced the same overriding domestic political problem that had torn apart the former empires: how to regulate conflicts between peoples, ethnic groups, religious and linguistic communities coexisting within one state. The fact that the new states were smaller exacerbated rather than relieved the problem.

Those responsible for creating the new states were well aware of this problem. Both the Treaty of Sèvres and the mandate treaties for the Orient contained provisions for the protection of minorities. And as long as the League of Nations existed the problems of minorities received at least some attention.

This changed at the end of the Second World War, when the United Nations replaced the League of Nations. The United Nations soon became the stage for the global triumph of the subjectively political, voluntaristic concept of nationalism. Both nation and 'people' were taken to mean simply the population of a state, regardless of cultural homogeneity. If the population of a state was not a nation, then a nation had to be created: 'nation-building' was to be a central normative concept of the international community of states for about three decades.

There were a number of reasons for this. After the Second World War the victorious powers wanted to avoid what, in their eyes, had in the interwar period been a cause of permanent instability and doubts about the established community of states. Hence, they were inclined to 'put things straight'. The flight and expulsion of millions of people in the final years of the war and the immediate post-war period left the populations in the states of central and eastern Europe far more homogeneous than they had been. What remained of the minorities was subjected to enormous pressure to assimilate and to abandon traditional particularities. In the United Nations there was no majority for international guarantees for minorities.[4]

The decolonization of large parts of Asia and Africa assured global victory for the voluntarist concept of nation. Colonial boundaries were ubiquitously more arbitrary than those drawn across the disintegrating Hapsburg and Ottoman Empires. They seldom took account of precolonial cultural and political conditions; certainly, it was more important to take account of rival colonial powers than of indigenous populations. In one place colonial boundaries were drawn through people with centuries of common tradition, in another they forced groups with equally long histories of enmity into one state. As the hour of decolonization approached, the colonial powers were disinclined to reform their creations in accordance with 'objectively cultural' conditions. Nor, with few exceptions, were the leaders of the independence movements any less so. Their nationalism sought liberation from colonial rule and economic dependence. In their view, particularisms of an ethnic, religious or linguistic nature were circumstances which the colonial rulers had exploited for their policies of divide and rule, and which distracted from the struggle for self-determination and economic change. For different reasons, old and new rulers were in complete agreement on retaining the colonial boundaries. After independence these colonial political facts had even greater weight than before. Fears that the alteration of even a single boundary might precipitate a chain reaction fed solemn declarations of the inviolability of all, as in the Charter of the Organization of African Unity.

Hence, a consequence of colonial conferences such as that of 1885 in Berlin and post-colonial conferences such as that of Addis Ababa was a multitude of multi-communal states.[5] By the mid-1960s the multi-communal state was no longer the exception in the international community of nations, but the rule.[6]

---

[4] Pierre L. Van Den Berghe analyses this in respect of Unesco: 'Unesco also attacked any kind of group discrimination whether based on racial or on ethnic criteria. It also condemned, of course, *forcible* assimilation of ethnic groups, but it implicitly approved of any policy encouraging assimilation by means short of open coercion. This ideological line also suited most of the member states. The USA was strongly assimilationist. The Western European countries were on the verge of jettisoning their colonies, and, at home, they were ruled by centralist, assimilationist governments. The Communist countries, while paying lip service to the rights of nationalities to cultural autonomy, were in fact also highly centralist. As for the so-called new nations, their ruling classes were all committed, at least verbally, to an ideology of 'national integration' which meant eradicating internal ethnic diversity. Unesco in the 1950s and early 1960s was, in short, the international mouthpiece of an ideology of minimization of both racial and ethnic distinctions'; 'The present state of comparative race and ethnic studies', in Jan Berting et al., eds., *Problems in International Comparative Research in the Social Sciences* (Oxford and New York, 1979), pp.23f.

[5] See Alfred Cobban, *The Nation-State and National Self-Determination* (New York, 1969).

[6] In 1972 Walker Connor calculated that of the then existing states only 9 per cent were ethnically homogeneous. In 28 per cent of them, the majority community made up more than three-quarters of the population; in 23 per cent the majority group formed between half and three-quarters of the population; and

## Integration or coexistence?
## Changing perspectives in the social sciences

Admittedly, in the mid-1960s the concept of the multi-communal state was foreign to political and scientific vocabularies. Although the societies in nine out of ten states were not culturally homogeneous, and although coexistence between different ethnic, religious and linguistic groups was a very real problem for most of these states, both politicians and social scientists preferred to ignore both facts and problems.

The politicians had their reasons. Many were aware that the explosive potential of concurrent and opposing interests of different groups might seek release after the successful, unifying struggle for self-determination. They hoped that playing them down could defuse them. And most were convinced that a consistent policy of nation-building would remove the problem. They usually broached the subject with the conviction of the factual power of the normative concept of voluntaristic nationalism: they had fought for their state and they would now create a nation.

The main schools of thought in social science long provided support for this normative approach, for this 'omnipotence of the idea'.[7] Normative bias pervades social science itself, of course. Take terminology. Not only is it Eurocentric: in respect of Europe, terms such as peoples, nations, nationalities or national minorities are used; in respect of Africa or Asia, the term tribe is often used. Many terms are pejorative: ethnic solidarity is called tribalism, regional and local affiliation parochialism, identification with a religious community becomes confessionalism or even sectarianism. The choice of words reveals normative attitudes: between state and nation — usually treated as synonymous — and the individual, there is no space for intermediate social units. Should they persist, they are at best classified as residual pre-modern phenomena predestined for extinction. As a rule, however, they are regarded as 'obstacles to development', to be fought and eradicated. Most of these normative attitudes are rooted in the conviction of the universality of the 'western model of development'. In accordance with this, traditional societies are destined for modernity, irrespective of the path — be it Max Weber's process of rationalization, Ferdinand Tönnies' transition from

---

in 30 per cent, that is, the largest single group, no group had an absolute majority. 'Nation-building or nation-destroying?', *World Politics*, 24/3 (1972), p.320.

[7] The following may be taken as representative: Gabriel Almond and James Coleman, *The Politics of the Developing Areas* (Princeton, 1960); Gabriel Almond and G. Bingham Powell, *Comparative Politics: A developmental approach* (Boston, 1966); Gabriel Almond and Sidney Verba, *The Civic Culture* (Princeton, 1963); David E. Apter, *The Politics of Modernization* (Chicago, 1965); Karl W. Deutsch and William Foltz, eds., *Nation-Building* (New York, 1966); S.N. Eisenstadt, *Modernization: Protest and Change* (Englewood Cliffs, N.J., 1966); Lucian Pye, *Aspects of Political Development* (Boston, 1966); Edward Shils, *Political Development in the New States* (The Hague, 1965).

community to society or Karl Marx's gigantic broom of revolution. Modernization is a powerful and irreversible historical process that will engulf the world. The emergence of uniform nation-states — be it as 'ultimate' units of social organization, be it as a transitional stage to a global society with a single political organization — is regarded as the culmination of, or an unavoidable stage in, this process. For many, what is inevitable is therefore desirable and to be furthered. Perceived facts become norms.

Of course, the founding fathers of the social sciences bear little responsibility for what was to be 'mainstream thought' for three decades — though it was in fact a secular belief in progress rather than progress in scientifically substantiated knowledge. Weber conceived of his ideal types as a system of hypotheses that could be used as coordinates to analyse concrete societies; his students misinterpreted them as prognoses. Neither Tönnies nor Marx equated their respective concepts of society with that of a culturally uniform nation-state. The emergence of one-sided or erroneous interpretations must be seen within the context in which the social sciences developed, a context which encouraged them temporarily to ignore wider historical perspectives. The social sciences emerged in relatively homogeneous western societies at a time when the concept of the nation-state enjoyed almost unquestioned acceptance in Europe, and reached the zenith of their institutional influence in the post-war USA. The predominant societal concern in Great Britain, France and Germany in the late nineteenth century and the first half of the twentieth century was the 'social question' — the relations and conflicts between strata and classes. Consequently, it was also the primary concern of social scientists. European social scientists paid scant attention to the problems of central, eastern and south-eastern European multi-ethnic states, in which the thorny questions of nations and nationalities competed with those of social stratification. After the Second World War the USA took the lead in social research. In consequence, scientific interest began to focus on questions of social integration in the greatest immigrant society yet known. The fascination roused by the integrative force of the American society gave birth to the paradigm of the USA as the 'first new nation'.[8] This paradigm contained a mixture of prognostic and normative elements. If people of the most varied origins, cultures and convictions could melt into one nation in the USA, then it could happen in other new nations. The driving force behind the scientific concept of 'nation-building' was an optimism nurtured by the American experience. This disregarded the fundamental differences between the 'first' and the other new nations. As a country of immigration, the USA has always attracted people fleeing material want or political bondage, people prepared to shake off their origins and previous

---

[8] Seymour Martin Lipset, *The First New Nation* (New York, 1963).

identities and become Americans. By contrast, people in other 'new states' have to, and most want to, remain where they are and what they are, that is, as their fathers were.

Where the respective fathers were different, the sons wanted to remain different too. Thus, the crucial social problem was not integration, but coexistence between the groups that already existed and would continue to exist.[9]

From the mid-1960s onwards the results of empirical research on societies of new states increasingly undermined the general conviction that nation-building works.[10] Even more than research results, events themselves questioned the accepted opinion. Numerous states were racked by civil war — not between social classes, but between ethnic, religious and linguistic groups. In many others, enormous tensions existed between such groups. Even in 'old' established states in the western world long-forgotten group conflicts regarded as obsolete have acquired a new virulence.[11] Even the USA has had to learn that its melting pot can also brew new ethnicity.[12] Finally, recent events in the former USSR and Yugoslavia demonstrate that even socialist multi-ethnic states have not found the 'solution' to the 'nationality question'. There is only one regional exception to this pattern: Latin America alone is not, to borrow Pierre van den Berghe's phrase, on the new 'ethnic trip'.

Regardless of the assumptions and convictions of social scientists, recent events — or the passage of history — ensure that the existence, persistence and regulation of conflicts between culturally distinct groups within a state can no longer be ignored. In 1972 Samuel P. Huntington declared that group conflicts had replaced socio-revolutionary conflicts as the predominant form of social

---

[9] See Milton J. Esman, 'Two Dimensions of Ethnic Politics: Defense of homelands, immigrant rights', *Ethnic and Racial Studies*, 8/3 (1985), pp.438–40. Karl W. Deutsch was one of the first to draw attention to these distinctions: 'we already know empirically that the rate of assimilation among a population that has been uprooted and mobilized — such as immigrants coming to America — is usually considerably higher than the rate of assimilation among the secluded populations of villages close to the soil.' *Nationalism and Social Communication: An inquiry into the foundations of nationality*, 2nd edn (Cambridge, Mass., 1962), p.126. In 1961 the same author pointed out that in homogeneous states processes of social mobilization may lead to consolidation, but in states with different linguistic and cultural groups they can produce strains, capable even of destroying the unity of the state; 'Social Mobilization and Political Development', *American Political Science Review*, 55/3 (1961), p.501.

[10] Rupert Emerson, *From Empire to Nation: The rise to self assertion of Asian and African peoples* (Cambridge, Mass., 1960), was the first influential critic. See also Walker Connor, 'Self-determination: The New Phase', *World Politics*, 20 (1967), pp.30–53.

[11] See Milton J. Esman, ed., *Ethnic Conflict in the Western World* (Ithaca, N.Y., 1977).

[12] Nathan Glazer and Daniel Patrick Moynihan, *Beyond the Melting Pot* (Cambridge, Mass., 1963); Harry H. Bash, *Sociology, Race and Ethnicity: A critique of American ideological intrusions upon sociological theory* (New York, 1979).

conflict, and predicted that their frequency and intensity would increase.[13] Since then the preoccupation with political systems in which different ethnic, religious and linguistic groups conflict, coexist or cooperate has increased enormously.[14]

What previously was the concern of ethnologists and anthropologists now attracts the attention of sociologists and political scientists. The terminology has changed, concepts with a strong normative bias are giving way to more neutral, analytically operational ones. One now speaks of fragmented, segmented, streamed or plural societies, often treating these concepts as synonymous. Finally, in the English-speaking world, the extremely wide concept of 'ethnicity' has become prevalent. This incorporates not only common origins but also common language, religion or other features of ethnic identity. In this sense, 'ethnic groups' may be people, national groups or religious communities — groups distinguishable from one another by one or more cultural markers.[15] The concept of the 'multi-ethnic' state reflects the late rediscovery by contemporary social science of the state embracing different peoples, the multi-communal state.

## Culturalistic and economistic approaches

The problem may have been identified, but there is no agreement on how to deal with it, or even on its significance. Opinions divide broadly into two diametrically opposed schools of thought, the culturalistic and the economistic.

The culturalistic school, which includes numerous social scientists who themselves come from minority groups, was long in the lee of mainstream teachings. As attention has switched to 'ethnic' phenomena so the school's importance has increased.[16] This school assumes that loyalties to people, ethnic, religious or

---

[13] Samuel P. Huntington, Preface to Eric A. Nordlinger, *Conflict Regulation in Divided Societies*, Occasional Papers in International Affairs, no. 29 (Cambridge, Mass., 1972).

[14] Good surveys of opinions and the state of research may be found in Donald L. Horowitz, *Ethnic Groups in Conflict* (Berkeley, 1985); Joseph Rothschild, *Ethnopolitics: A conceptual framework* (New York, 1981); G. Carter Bentley, 'Theoretical Perspectives on Ethnicity and Nationality', *Sage Race Relations Abstracts*, 8/2 (1983), pp.1–53; Crawford Young, *The Politics of Cultural Pluralism* (Madison, 1976). Milton J. Esman, 'The Management of Communal Conflict', *Public Policy*, 21 (1973), pp.49–78, is still an excellent brief introduction to the problem.

[15] Horowitz, *Ethnic Groups*, p.53, writes: 'ethnicity easily embraces groups differentiated by color, language, and religion; it covers "tribes", "races", "nationalities", and castes', as there is need for 'a concept of ethnicity that is somewhat elastic'.

[16] The German Romantic concept of culture as expounded by Herder initially strongly influenced anthropological thought, which regards culture as a unique way of living, as an integrated whole unique to each people and not transferable. See Bronislaw Malinowski, *A Scientific Theory of Culture* (Chapel Hill, 1944); Ruth Benedict, *Patterns of Culture* (London, 1961); Mary Douglas, *Purity and Danger* (London, 1966); E. Evans-Pritchard, *Witchcraft: Oracles and magic among the Azande* (Oxford, 1937).

linguistic groups, are *'primordial'*,[17] that is, are primeval or original, and have a more lasting influence on the behaviour of people than all other loyalties. Rooted in history, passed on by upbringing, and often embedded in a particular weltanschauung, primordial bonds are permanent realities. Even if sublimated and seldom conspicuous, given the opportunity, they resurface.

As a simplification, one may speak of two variants of the economistic school, one based on theories of modernization, the other on Marxist thought. Neither regards cultural phenomena as primordial and lasting, but rather as subject to rapid change. Both tend to take an instrumentalist view of culture and cultural characteristics or markers: one takes note of them as long as one needs them and as long as they are useful. Approaches based on theories of modernization continue to stress that the spread of industrialization, communication and urbanization increasingly promotes integration between individuals and groups of the most divergent origins. These processes proceed at different speeds in different societies, and there may even be setbacks. 'Intermediate societies' may be a temporary stage on the journey from traditional to modern society. But there can be no question about the journey; its destination is clear: sooner or later traditional particularisms will disappear, traditional barriers fall, and modern, integrated nation-states emerge. Whereas theories of modernization treat 'ethnicity' as a transitory phenomenon, Marxism interprets it either in instrumentalist terms — it veils fundamental economic contradictions — or as 'false consciousness', in that it prevents people of the same class from recognizing their economic interests and working together with others in the same position to pursue them.[18]

---

[17] Edward Shils, 'Primordial, Personal, Sacred, and Civic Ties', *British Journal of Sociology*, 8 (1957), pp.130–45, introduced the concept of primordialism into sociology. Shils himself felt that in his earlier studies he had underestimated the effect of 'primordial' ties in kinship, home and religion. Such ties are characterized by 'a state of intense and comprehensive solidarity', 'coerciveness', 'terror and passion' and 'sacredness'. Similarly Clifford Geertz, 'The Integrative Revolution: Primordial sentiments and civil politics in the new states', in Clifford Geertz, ed., *Old Societies and New States: The quest for modernity in Asia and Africa* (London, 1963). H. Isaacs, *Idols of the Tribe* (New York, 1975), speaks of 'basic group identity'. Connor, 'Nation-building', p.341, raises the criticism that all too frequently ethnic conflict is superficially attributed to differences in language, religion and customs or economic inequality. 'But what is fundamentally involved in such a conflict is that divergence of basic identity which manifests itself in the "us-them" syndrome.' Elsewhere, he argues that 'an intuitive bond felt toward an informal and unstructured subdivision of mankind is far more profound and potent than are the ties that bind them to the formal and legalistic state structure in which they find themselves'; Walker Connor, 'A Nation is a Nation, is a State, is an Ethnic Group, is a ...', *Ethnic and Racial Studies*, 1/4 (1978), p.377. Emmerich K. Francis, *Interethnic Relations* (New York, 1976), and Charles F. Keyes, 'Towards a New Formulation of the Concept of the Ethnic Group', *Ethnicity*, 3 (1976), pp.202–13, also argue on the basis of cultural determinism.

[18] For a clear exposition of the classical Marxist position see G. Rozat and R. Bartra, 'Racism and Capitalism', *Sociological Theories: Race and colonialism* (Paris, 1980), p.287: 'Marxist theory asserts that in social systems where the true motor of historical development is the class struggle, a theoretical and intellectual exercise such as the debate on race and racism can be more or less clearly identified as only one

Whereas the culturalists regard peoples and ethnic, religious and linguistic groups as the real 'stuff' of history, the economistic school sees them solely as transitory, as epiphenomena. The one group treats them as absolutes, the other reduces them to insignificance against the panorama of history. Yet, both history and the contemporary state of multi-communal states give cause to doubt the plausibility of purely culturalistic and purely economic explanations.[19]

Culturalists have difficulty in explaining why common origins, religious beliefs or language create group solidarity in some cases but not in others. Origins are of paramount significance in South Africa but far less so in Brazil. In Northern Ireland religious affiliation still plays an enormous role; this was formerly the case in the Netherlands too, though no longer. Language groups are politically far more relevant in Belgium and Canada than in Switzerland. There is evidence that markers serve to distinguish and create group consciousness only in conjunction with a particular interest, regardless of whether this interest concerns material goods, prestige or power. This means that although cultural markers may be primordial, this is not necessarily so of a distinct group consciousness based upon

---

episode in the process whereby an ideological edifice of domination is constructed and set in place by a class that we shall define as the dominant one — the bourgeoisie'. See H.M. Baron, 'Racial Domination in Advanced Capitalism: A theory of nationalism and divisions in the labor market', in R.C. Edwards, M. Reich and D.M. Gordon, eds., *Labor Market Segmentation* (Lexington, Mass., 1975), pp.173–216; M. Burawoy, 'Race, class and colonialism', *Social and Economic Studies*, 23 (1974), pp.521–60; Bernard Magubane, *The Political Economy of Race and Class in South Africa* (New York, 1979); Harold Wolpe, 'The "White Working Class" in South Africa', *Economy and Society*, 5 (1976), pp.197–240; Oliver C. Cox, *Caste, Class and Race: A study in social dynamics* (New York, 1948).

[19] Such doubts have given rise to liberal and Marxist 'revisionist' schools that try to take account of the realities of multi-communal states. The most interesting among the former is the competitive approach: 'people can choose between economic and cultural forms of identity, and different interest groups can compete politically. There are no "objective" criteria for group formation; if people define themselves as a group then they are one and can act politically ... The goal of competition is the control of resources, especially those under public control'; Abner Cohen, *Two-Dimensional Man: An essay on the anthropology of power and symbolism in complex society* (Berkeley, 1974); Leo. A. Despres, ed., *Ethnicity and Resource Competition in Plural Societies* (The Hague, 1975); Alvin Rabushka, *A Theory of Racial Harmony* (Columbia, 1974). Liberal 'deviations' from cultural determinism include: Michael Banton, *Race Relations* (London, 1967); Philip Mason, *Race Relations* (London, 1970) and *Patterns of Dominance* (London, 1970). An interesting neo-Marxist approach is Immanuel Wallerstein, 'Social Conflict in Post-independence Black Africa: The concepts of race and status-groups reconsidered', in E.Q. Campbell, ed., *Racial Tensions and National Identity* (Nashville, Tenn., 1972), pp.207–26. Wallerstein treats groups defined by cultural criteria as status groups in the Weberian sense, which compete against one another politically. However, in decisive conflicts their behaviour is determined by class. Another widely discussed approach is that of 'internal colonialism'; see Michael Hechter, *Internal Colonialism: The Celtic fringe in British national development 1536–1966* (London, 1975). The crux of the thesis is the division of labour between cultural groups as a consequence of capitalistic industrialization, in which certain regions and cultural groups were placed at a disadvantage. Common to these and other neo-Marxist approaches is an awareness of the complexity of multi-ethnic societies, which is ultimately ascribed to class conflicts.

them. Groups emerge, can be created, can be manipulated, but can also disband.[20] One lesson of history, surely, is that peoples and ethnic groups are neither divinely ordained nor everlasting: they come and they go.

Economistic schools, modernizationists and Marxists all have trouble explaining why many of their predictions have not come true. In many places processes of modernization have not reduced group differences, but emphasized and intensified them. Rapid urbanization and the emergence of metropolises[21] bring together people from different groups. They meet, but do not necessarily appreciate each other. Differences in living habits and social intercourse which are easy to tolerate at a distance, geographic or social, are often a source of irritation and dislike in close proximity and constant contact. Above all, living at close quarters inevitably leads to competition. The economistic school is inclined to overlook the fact that competition in a society comprising different groups easily becomes more than the concern of individuals, or even strata and classes; it can develop into rivalry between ethnic, religious and linguistic groups.[22] Outward group competition promotes inward group solidarity; a group's social status is instrumental in the success of its individual members. Improvements in the general level of education tend to accentuate cultural differences: better-educated people can articulate the respective differences in traditions, ways of thinking and forms of group self-perception more clearly and more antithetically.[23] In short: communication, urbanization and education frequently do not help to reduce cleavages, but rather to emphasize and intensify them. They mobilize without simultaneously integrating. Not infrequently it is precisely the process of modernization that gives cultural markers their relevance, mobilizes group consciousness and politicizes — a fact often overlooked by the culturalists too.

[20] See Fredrik Barth, ed., *Ethnic Groups and Boundaries: The social organization of cultural difference* (Boston, 1969); N.M. Srinivas, *Caste in Modern India and other Essays* (London, 1962) and *Social Change in Modern India* (Berkeley, 1967).

[21] 'In a curious way, theorists of urbanization have not sought to draw upon the empirical insights of students of urban political systems. The latter have long pointed out that the political processes of even the largest metropolitan areas provide a multiplicity of domains for ethnic political organization and strategy. Indeed, it is specifically in urban rather than rural areas that ethnic conflict is likely to be most explosive. The experiences of such cities as Algiers, Belfast, Beirut, Brussels, Jerusalem, Los Angeles, New York and Soweto attest to this observation.' Jeffrey A. Ross, 'Urban Development and the Politics of Ethnicity: A conceptual approach', *Ethnic and Racial Studies*, 5/4 (1982), p.441. See also Abner Cohen, *Urban Ethnicity* (London, 1974).

[22] The 'revisionist' schools (n.19 above) excluded.

[23] 'In the fast-growing cities to which ambitious educated men flocked, the resulting competition for jobs and housing inflamed age-old antagonisms and highlighted previously unremarked or unimportant cultural differences ... In the new arena provided by an ethnic community with its own history and identity, they hoped to find the status and power, which had eluded them in the state of the dominant community.' Anthony D. Smith, 'Nationalism: Towards a theory of ethnic separatism', *Ethnic and Racial Studies*, 2/1 (1979), p.30.

It appears to be incomparably simpler to achieve solidarity and, eventually, political mobilization on the basis of existing and recognized markers than through new or potential markers: ethnicity, religion and language are more immediate than stratum, class or ideology.[24] It is difficult to create a class consciousness that transcends the groups. This is not because, as culturalists maintain, blood is thicker than the water of material interests, but because people think even their economic interests are better looked after by members of their own ethnic group than by people of other groups in a similar situation; for example, a superior from the same group is preferable to a colleague from another. As long as individual and group interests are enmeshed, transcending ideologies have little chance against group-specific ideologies. This may be 'false consciousness'. But this categorization neither illuminates nor explains why, as historical and contemporary events in multi-ethnic and multi-communal states demonstrate, more people respond to 'false' rather than 'proper' consciousness, fight for it and die for it.

## Modes of incorporation:
## Linking analytical approaches

The inability of cultural and economic determinisms adequately to explain these phenomena raises the fundamental question of whether one-dimensional analysis is inadequate for the examination of multi-ethnic and multi-communal societies and states.[25] Juxtaposition may provide the most significant perspective in analysing international relations and conflicts; although even this is questionable in view of the differences in economic and political power within the global mesh of interrelationships. Hierarchical relationships between social strata and classes may be the most important aspect in an analysis of culturally homogeneous societies and states — although here too it may be rewarding to examine the real extent of homogeneity. In the case of culturally non-

---

[24] This is emphasized by, among others, Van Den Berghe. Such groups are 'extensions of the idiom of kinship and are therefore much more primordial and universal than all associations based on segmental interests such as professional associations, labor unions, political parties, or, more broadly, class. The relationship between class on the one hand, and ethnicity and race on the other, is complex because the degree of overlap between these fundamentally different lines of cleavage varies from situation to situation. Generally, however, people can be much more easily organized and mobilized along ethnic or racial lines than along class lines'; 'The Present State of Comparative Race and Ethnic Studies', p.34.

[25] 'The relationship between class and ethnic factors is exceedingly complex and unlikely to be explained by oversimplified theories of economic or cultural determinism.' James McKay, 'An Exploratory Synthesis of Primordial and Mobilizationist Approaches to Ethnic Phenomena', *Ethnic and Racial Studies*, 5/4 (1982), p.400.

homogeneous states it seems not only desirable but necessary to examine both the juxtaposition and the hierarchy of social formations.[26]

Social science has borrowed one of its most important concepts — stratification — from geology. The analogy can be taken further. Not every landscape is flat. In mountainous regions there are not only stratifications but fissures too, the juxtaposition of obviously different mountains and hills. There are landscapes with even stratification and others with numerous faults.

Societies are similar. If they are not flat, that is, culturally homogeneous, any adequate description will take account of stratification as well as of fissures and

---

[26] See Sammy Smooha, 'Pluralism and Conflict: A theoretical exploration', *Plural Societies*, 6/3 (1975), pp.69–87, This question is decisive for what Smooha calls the 'neo-pluralist' school. It was founded by J.S. Furnival, *Colonial Policy and Practice: A comparative study of Burma and Netherlands India* (New York, 1956) and *Netherlands India: A study of plural economy* (Cambridge, 1939). Furnival described a 'plural society' as 'in the strictest sense a medley of peoples, for they mix but do not combine. Each group holds by its own religion, its own culture and language, its own ideas and ways. As individuals they meet, but only in the market place, in buying and selling. There is a plural society, with different sections of the community living side by side, but separately, within the same political unit' (*Colonial Policy*, p.400). Later his approach was taken up by the Jamaican anthropologist M.G. Smith and developed as an ideal type for societies torn by conflict, in which one group dominates and exploits: M.G. Smith, 'Institutional and Political Conditions of Pluralism', in Leo Kuper and M.G. Smith, eds., *Pluralism in Africa* (Berkeley and Los Angeles, 1969), pp.27–66; and *The Plural Society in the British West Indies* (Berkeley, 1965). In the mid-1960s this approach was fundamentally revised and expanded to become a two-dimensional approach to understanding complex societies in terms of their cultural differences and cleavages, on the one hand, and their social and economic inequalities on the other. 'These two orders of cleavage ... should not be reduced into one another, nor assigned a priori precedence, but rather both must be examined jointly for the amount of overlap among them'; Smooha, 'Pluralism', p.72. Van Den Berghe, 'The Comparative State of Race and Ethnic Studies', points out that ethnicity cannot be reduced to class: 'Though ethnicity ... correlate[s] with, and partly determine[s] class position, class is also determined by a number of non-ethnic factors. Conversely there are many aspects of ethnicity that are independent of the relations of power and production which constitute the class order. Analytically, then, it is equally important to understand the specific relationship between class and ethnicity as it is to keep the two phenomena clearly distinct.'

The neo-pluralists share with neo-Marxists an interest in social and economic inequalities; in contrast to them, however, they do not give economic factors precedence a priori, that is, they are less deterministic. They share with neo-liberals an interest in competition between culturally and economically defined groups, but not the latters' view that cultural groups are of purely voluntary character. In contrast to Barth, Van Den Berghe (p.27) emphasizes the necessity of both objective and subjective factors in the emergence of ethnic groups. To constitute an ethnic group some subjective perception is necessary, 'some conception and consciousness of a distinction between "them" and "us"'; but 'these subjective perceptions do not develop at random; they crystallize around clusters of objective characteristics that become badges of inclusion or exclusion'. Yet whatever their characteristics, according to Van Den Berghe, all ethnic groups have one feature in common: they are ascriptive groups into which one is born, in which one grows up and, as a rule, within which one marries: 'They run in families'. This distinguishes them from other groups participating in the political competition. Real or imagined common descent widens the circle of the family and transfers the sense of 'brotherhood' or 'sisterhood' to the whole ethnic group. Van Den Berghe calls this school of thought 'radical–liberal', to distinguish it from the liberals and the neo-Marxists.

faults. In other words, it records not only the horizontally or vertically one-dimensional differences but tries to analyse social reality in both dimensions.

However, geological and social analyses differ completely in one respect. The geologist measures and describes 'objective' facts. For this he establishes criteria, usually in agreement with colleagues — metre and cubic metre, kilogram and tonne — and names different types of soil and rock. The social scientist does this too. He measures and describes — more or less in accordance with collegial convention — social stratification in terms of income, education and prestige, or combinations of these criteria. This enables him to draw a static picture of a society. However, societies are seldom static. To examine the relationships between social strata he must first establish whether those he regards as belonging to a specific stratum share this view, or whether it is others who see them in this light. Statements about social, and particularly political, relationships between 'objectively' measured social categories only make sense if the members of each such category regard themselves as such, that is, if they accept that the respective factors create common interests: in short, if they are aware of themselves as a social group.

What holds for socio-economic categories holds even more strongly for cultural categories. There is virtually no limit to the number of 'objective' criteria of cultural categorization. But, as shown above, even criteria such as common origins, religion and language do not in themselves always or automatically effect the emergence of a group. Even categories of people who display all the criteria necessary for an 'objectively cultural' nation in Kohn's sense do not constitute a nation so long as they have not developed or acquired a common national awareness based on these criteria. A nation needs a voluntaristic element — the will to awareness — to become a subject of social and political action.

Karl Marx takes account of this by distinguishing between a 'class in itself' and a 'class for itself'. The former is objective; the latter emerges only with class consciousness. This distinction is useful in analysing culturally different population groups. A society may have multifarious cultural segments, but this segmentation will have no political consequences until self-awareness develops. Thus, it seems sensible to apply the Marxian distinction by analogy to multi-ethnic or multi-communal societies and distinguish between cultural 'groups in themselves' and 'groups for themselves'.[27]

---

[27] In this connection, terminology does raise difficulties, for there is no authoritative consensus. Up to now the terms 'multi-ethnic state' or 'multi-group state' have been used. The term 'multi-national state' is an established historical concept, but does not adequately cover cultural segments conscious of their own identity without regarding themselves as 'people'. The term 'multi-group state' does not distinguish between socio-economic and cultural groups. The concept of nationality, which describes groups with a national consciousness that do not have their own state, has historically been restricted to central and eastern Europe.

In keeping with the most widely accepted usage in the literature, the term 'communities'[28] will be used for all 'peoples', 'national groups', cultural groups, ethnic, religious or language groups within a state that form 'cultural groups for themselves'. States that encompass several such communities — that is, are not only cultural 'groups in themselves' — will be referred to as multi-communal states, a term already employed above.

To grasp the reality of the social and political systems of multi-communal states it is necessary to examine both their horizontal dimensions, that is, their socio-economic stratification and class structure, and their vertical dimensions, that is, their fissures or cleavages along communal lines as well as the linkages between them. Each and every community within a multi-communal state is socio-economically stratified. This stratification may be similar in all communities; it may also be very dissimilar: in the extreme case one community alone constitutes the upper stratum and another the lower stratum. The concept of 'incorporation' has been coined for the association and inclusion of strata or classes and segments or communities.[29] In the former case one may speak of

---

In the English-speaking world 'ethnic group' has widest currency. Although used in the widest sense for numerous cultural markers, it has the disadvantage of sounding less suitable for religious or linguistic 'groups for themselves'. Another concept common to many languages is that of 'community', by which is understood ethnic, religious or linguistic communities with a clear group consciousness, that is, 'groups for themselves'. In the literature on the Near and Middle East in particular it is applied to religious communities. On 31st July, 1930, the International Court of Justice defined 'community' as follows: 'Le critérium de la notion de la communauté ... est l'existence d'une collectivité de personnes vivant dans un pays ou une localité donnée, ayant une race, une religion, une langue et des traditions qui leur sont propres, et unis par l'identité de cette race, de cette religion, de cette langue et de cette tradition dans un sentiment de solidarité à l'effet de conserver leur tradition, de maintenir leur culte, d'assurer l'instruction et l'éducation de leurs enfants conformément au génie de leur race et de s'assister mutuellement'; *Resumé Mensuel des Travaux de la Société des Nations*, 10/7 (July 1930), p.219. Finding that this definition has 'une valeur assez générale et charactérise très heureusement l'aspect social de la communauté', Pierre Rondot adopts it for a study of the religious communities in Lebanon, *Les Institutions Politiques du Liban* (Paris, 1947), p.22. In Lebanese political terminology the word for a religious community is *ta'ifa* (group), which is perceived in the sense of the definition quoted by Rondot.

[28] Max Weber emphasizes the importance of perception. A criterion of distinction 'leads naturally to a "community" only if it is subjectively felt to apply to all'. He points out that common communal ancestry is often of an imaginary nature, and that communal consciousness 'is, as a rule, determined by common political fate and not primarily by "origins"'. Hence, differences are 'also usually artificially created by the political community'; see *Wirtschaft und Gesellschaft: Grundriss der verstehenden Soziologie*, vol I(1), 5th edn (Tübingen, 1976), pp.238–41.

[29] M.G. Smith introduced the concept of incorporation. Initially, his interest attached exclusively to cases of 'differential integration', by which he understood political and economic domination by one community over others. He later extended the concept to distinguish between four different modes of incorporation: 'differential' (or hierarchical), 'equivalent', 'complex' — a hybrid between the first two or together with the fourth — and 'universalistic' incorporation; M.G. Smith, 'The Nature and Variety of Plural Units', hectographed manuscript (Yale University, New Haven, 1982), p.10. The terminology has only limited utility. 'Universalistic' incorporation is a new term for an integrated state; as a state of this nature is no longer plural, this term may be ignored in a study of plural or multi-communal states. In reality, modes

egalitarian, in the latter of inegalitarian incorporation. This contrast between ideal types offers a system of coordinates for classifying societies on the bases of empirical results. Instead of laying down a priori the relative importance of cultural and economic factors, one can empirically test whether and to what extent cultural groups perceive themselves as communities, strata perceive themselves as classes, as well as how these forms of group solidarity diverge or coincide. Few multi-communal societies correspond fully to one or other ideal type. Switzerland approximates egalitarian incorporation; South Africa in the mid-twentieth century approximated inegalitarian. In most cases the mode of incorporation is more complex, and needs to be examined more closely.

## Incorporation and conflict

The similarity between intercommunal relations in multi-communal states and international relations between states has often been remarked. Indeed, the self-awareness of communities is often very similar to that of nation-states;[30] the power and powerlessness, wealth and poverty, of communities are comparable with the differences between states. However, the fundamental distinction between a multi-communal state and the international system is the existence of a mutual state for all the communities. The state is the great incorporator. Whoever is in control of the state has real power to decide the distribution of power and of wealth among classes as well as communities.[31] The point in every state is the distribution of power and wealth among classes. By contrast, in the multi-communal state, the struggle over the distribution between communities plays a particular and characteristic role: it is a question of maintaining or changing a specific mode of incorporation.

---

of incorporation will almost always be 'complex'; purely 'differential' or purely 'equivalent' modes are rare. Accordingly, the author of this study has chosen to define two ideal types that can be used empirically to determine how differential and how equivalent a mode of incorporation is in a specific case. To underline the ideal character of the concepts, 'inegalitarian' will be used instead of 'differential', and 'egalitarian' instead of 'equivalent'. Horowitz, *Ethnic Groups*, pp.22ff makes a similar distinction between 'ranked' and 'unranked' ethnic groups. However, rank is less apposite than Smith's incorporation; only rarely are whole ethnic groups superior or inferior in rank, because 'rank' is an average and because strata and classes are found in most ethnic groups.

[30] E.g., Michael C. Hudson, *The Precarious Republic: Political modernization in Lebanon* (New York, 1968), p.9, writes about Lebanon: 'the subnational communities are compelled by the situation to act as if they were states in an international environment.' At another point (p.34) he remarks: 'Mutual deterrence and actors with devastating but relatively equal power create an uneasy perpetual truce.'

[31] 'Control of the state, control of a state, and exemption from control by others are among the main goals of ethnic conflict'; Horowitz, *Ethnic Groups*, p.5. 'The centre is not a neutral arbiter for conflicts originating elsewhere. On the contrary, the centre is itself a focal point of competition'; ibid., p.50.

Under what conditions will this distribution struggle become a conflict? It is widely assumed that conflict is especially likely in cases of extremely inegalitarian incorporation.[32] This assumption may seem plausible at first sight. If wealth and poverty attach to origins, religion or language, cultural distance may intensify social conflict, and vice versa. However, a comparative analysis of multi-communal societies shows that this assumption does not hold. While it is true that communities in societies with highly egalitarian incorporation are most likely to live in harmony, and the tensions that do exist are comparatively mild, the contrary is not true. Societies with extremely inegalitarian incorporation, such as caste-ridden India and, for a long time, South Africa with its system of apartheid, are often extraordinarily stable and resistant to crisis. In these cases, perceptions of cultural superiority and inferiority legitimize and stabilize extreme social ranking.

Critical developments are far more likely either in societies in which economic change has been blurring established social distinctions or in societies in which approximate social equality between communities has been diminishing to the advantage of one and the disadvantage of the others: in other words they are more likely when the mode of incorporation changes.

There is an obvious analogy between this and what revolution research has revealed about homogeneous societies. Revolutions seldom occur under conditions of extreme social inequality.[33] They tend to occur when the previously extremely deprived have been able to reduce the economic gap or when the previously privileged face social decline. In both cases the revolutionary crisis is precipitated not by those who are absolutely underprivileged but by those who are relatively so. The critical phenomenon of relative deprivation[34] applies not only to individuals,

---

[32] Michael Hechter, *Internal Colonialism*, p.43, and Christopher Bagley, 'Racialism and Pluralism: A dimensional analysis of forty-eight countries', *Race*, 13/3 (1972), pp.347–54. Smooha, 'Pluralism', p.82, cautions against such generalization. He points out that in cases of extremely unequal incorporation, as in Ancient Sparta, in the North African slave states, in the Indian caste system and in the early periods of colonial rule, dominance was, apart from occasional revolts, in general stable. 'The gulf in culture, structure and power is so great that no real challenge to the dominant group can be made.' As an illustration of the opposite of this he takes black-white relations in the USA: 'Blacks have achieved greater and greater socio-economic resources till they reached the point when the discrepancy between class attainments and forced segregation became intolerable and, in turn, a target for the Civil Rights movement'; ibid, p.83.

[33] In De Tocqueville's classical formulation: 'so that one may say the French found their situation the more unbearable the better it became ... If a bad situation changes for the worse this need not lead to revolution. It often happens that people who have accepted the most oppressive laws without complaint, as if they had not felt them, sweep them away as soon as their burden is reduced'; Alexis de Tocqueville, *The ancien régime and the Revolution* (Hamburg, 1969), p.153.

[34] James, C. Davies, 'Toward a Theory of Revolution', *American Sociological Review*, 27 (1962), pp.5–19, points out that Karl Marx describes a phenomenon that much later would be termed relative deprivation: 'The rapid growth of productive capital produces just as rapid a growth of wealth, luxury, social needs and social pleasures. Therefore, although the workers have greater pleasures, the social

strata or classes, but also to communities. Here, the critical potential is even greater than in homogeneous societies. Whereas the economically underprivileged must first acquire a class consciousness, familiar criteria of identification make it far easier to mobilize communal consciousness — even when not already present. The collective rise and decline of communities, or a social development perceived as such, leads to status dissonance between whole groups:[35] the respective community regards its economic and political situation as incommensurate with its sense of its own worth. To the sense of economic is added a sense of symbolic cultural deprivation: the dignity of the ethnic or religious or language group is felt to be offended.[36] One consequence of symbolic relative deprivation is that conflict is generated most easily and is most intense among economic equals belonging to different communities.

In contrast to the assumption of many theorists of modernization, it is precisely processes of modernization that intensify the sense of economic and symbolic

---

satisfaction derived from them has fallen in comparison with the capitalists' increased pleasures, which are out of the workers' reach, and in comparison with society's overall level of development. Our needs and pleasures derive from the society ... we do not measure them in terms of what they satisfy. Because they are of a social nature, they are of a relative nature'; Karl Marx and Friedrich Engels, *Werke*, vol. 6 (East Berlin, 1959), p.412. Ted Robert Gurr, *Why Men Rebel* (Princeton, N.J., 1970), develops an elaborate theory of relative deprivation. Although it does not refer specifically to multi-communal states, an analysis of its central concepts reveals its fruitful appplication to them. According to Gurr, the sense of deprivation extends to 'welfare, power, status' and 'communal values'; the latter are particularly appropriate to plural societies. 'Normative justification of violence' is easier if communal ideologies already exist. Similarly, 'dissident coercive control' can also emerge relatively more easily if structured communal organizations exist. Existing symbols of group identification make it easier to identify 'targets of violence' and consider a 'participation of violence'. According to Gurr, genuine violence helps strengthen group symbols, in whose name it started. 'Number and scope of communication media', according to Gurr a critical element in conflict, are, as a rule, greater in multi-communal states than in homogeneous states. Anthony Oberschall, *Social Conflicts and Social Movements* (Englewood Cliffs, 1973), p.119, demonstrates why social mobilization is easier in multi-communal states. He mentions as minimal conditions 'shared targets and objects of hostility held responsible for grievances, hardship, and suffering, augmented in some cases by more deeply rooted sentiments of collective oppression, common interest, and community of fate ... For sustained resistance or protest an organizational base and continuity of leadership are also necessary ... The collectivity might be integrated and organized along viable traditional lines based on kinship, village, ethnic or tribal organization ... A structural feature facilitating mobilization into protest movements is obtained when the society is not only highly stratified but segmented.'

[35] 'Dissonant conditions can prove destabilizing to a ranked system: inferior members of a superordinate group threaten the myth of its superiority, and the growth of an elite among a subordinate group sooner or later creates aspirations for mobility and recognition incompatible with strictly ascriptive hierarchy'; Horowitz, *Ethnic Groups*, pp.25f. This corresponds to the empirical finding that the most intense conflict in multi-communal states is often between people of different communities but of similar or the same class. See James Jupp, 'Ceylon and Malaysia', in Adrian Leftwich, ed., *South Africa. Economic Growth and Political Change: With comparative studies of Chile, Sri Lanka and Malaysia* (London and New York, 1974), pp.187–211.

[36] Max Weber emphasizes the particular significance of a sense of 'honour' and 'dignity'; *Wirtschaft und Gesellschaft*, p.236.

cultural deprivation and thus generate conflicts between communities. Advances in communication facilitate comparison and render it increasingly improbable that actual or perceived inequality will be accepted. Growing integration of the world market, rapid economic growth, and the resultant rural exodus and urbanization lead to the disintegration of traditional economic hierarchies, to the rise of some communities and the decline of others.[37] The groups most affected by economic change constitute the critical potential: impoverished peasants and agricultural labourers who stream to the cities to find only unskilled, badly paid work; self-employed artisans whose trades are becoming obsolete;[38] and graduates of intermediate and higher educational institutions unable to find jobs which meet their great expectations.[39] Precisely these groups tend to ascribe their individual failure not to personal inability or objective conditions, but to real or surmised discrimination against their respective communities. When perceived economic and symbolic cultural deprivation overlap, bitterness is particularly deep.

This combination also explains why the perception of inegalitarian incorporation, the sense of belonging to a discriminated community, often persists long after objective inequalities have been addressed or have disappeared. The 'time lag' between perceptions and factual changes can be a major obstacle to the success of social reform policies. Even relatively successful reforms may make little impact.[40]

The political leaders of all communities in multi-communal states are continually tempted to exaggerate their constituents' deprivation in order to gain or retain popularity — and many succumb. In consequence, initially vague perceptions of deprivation become political platforms and ideological dogmas. Political leaders who prefer to stick publicly to realistic assessments run the danger of being shouldered aside by radical demagogues. Crises deepen when moderate elites are first threatened and then replaced by 'lumpen-elites'.[41]

As a rule, acute situations of crisis come to a head when lengthy efforts to promote communal egalitarian incorporation suffer a setback. When hopes of

---

[37] 'Economic growth can significantly increase the number of losers'; Mancur Olsen, 'Rapid Growth as a Destabilizing Force', *Journal of Economic History*, 23 (1963), pp.529–52.

[38] See Oberschall, *Social Conflicts*, pp.41ff. Workers with permanent jobs in new industries do not, as a rule, belong to this potential, unless economic crises lead to a drastic fall in wages or to dismissal.

[39] On this point, see below, chapter 6.

[40] They often need time to take effect: 'The breathing space between the implementation of new policies and the expected benefits [is] more difficult to secure'; Oberschall, *Social Conflicts*, p.70.

[41] A term introduced by Val Lorwin. See Hans Daalder, 'The Consociational Democracy Theme', *World Politics*, 26/4 (1974), p.612.

reducing inequality are disappointed, this appears to confirm radical and ideologically systematized expressions of the sense of deprivation.[42]

Rapid social and economic change, rural exodus, the emergence of critical groups in the new, overcrowded cities, the ideological articulation of feelings of deprivation by intellectuals and the rise of radical leaders: these phenomena are also found in homogeneous societies. But they take other forms in multi-communal states. Social and economic change can affect communities to different degrees or with relative time-lags. In the new, overcrowded cities, uprooted rural populations may mix, but far more often congregate with people from their own region and community. Instead of just one, several critical groups materialize, each with its own ideological form of expressing discontent; and in each community radicals harry moderate political leaders. Social demands are submerged under different communities' symbolic cultural demands.[43]

Societal developments that may lead to social upheaval, the replacement of ruling elites and radical structural changes in homogeneous societies can — under the same economic conditions — lead to civil war in multi-communal states. As a rule, social revolutions end in defeat or victory, but civil wars between communities more often produce neither victors nor vanquished. Revolutions are usually over fairly quickly, but civil wars often go on for years. Privileged strata in homogeneous societies risk losing their privileges, but the communities who lose civil wars risk subjugation or the loss of their identity, if not their lives.

## Forms of conflict regulation and their ideologies

Therefore, there can be little doubt that the potential for conflict is considerably greater in multi-communal states than in culturally homogeneous states. For this reason, numerous scientists are of the opinion that multi-communal states are predestined for instability, and that conflicts can only be successfully regulated either by eliminating the variety of different communities or by resorting to undemocratic means, that is, the domination of one community over the others.[44] Other authors counter this pessimistic view by pointing to a number of states in

---

[42] According to Harry Eckstein, 'a combination of long term economic improvement and short term setbacks' is typical for situations of crisis. See Harry Eckstein, ed., *Internal War: Problems and approaches* (London, 1964), p.143. 'Revolutions are most likely when a lengthy period of real economic and social growth is followed by a short, sharp recession'; Davies, 'Toward a Theory of Revolution'. This insight can be applied by analogy to crises between communities.

[43] The latter may have greater weight: 'In many conflicts over material interests, the parties can each gain a slice of the pie without either group getting the entire pie. But symbols and principles by their very nature are indivisible goods'; Oberschall, *Social Conflicts*, p.50.

[44] E.g., Alvin Rabushka and Kenneth A. Shepsle, *Politics in Plural Societies: A theory of democratic instability* (Columbus, Ohio, 1972).

which institutional compromises regulate the coexistence of different communities and democratic stability; it is 'difficult, but not impossible'[45].

The pessimists have the weight of quantitative argument on their side. A study of different forms of conflict regulation in thirty-two historical and contemporary cases[46] in Europe, Africa and Asia concluded that armed conflict was still in progress in more than one-quarter of them, and in most of these for over a decade: even non-regulation can become a relatively permanent state. Another quarter practise one-sided conflict regulation: stable or unstable domination by one community over the others. However, stable domination exists only in states in which the ruling community forms the overwhelming majority of the population — or where power is maintained with the massive use of violence. But not even massive use of violence can guarantee stability: it often generates counter-violence. In almost one-fifth of the cases studied conflict regulation took the form of partition. Partitioning ensued peacefully only where the communities were already geographically separated — otherwise partition was the consequence of battle, with enormous casualties in fighting, massacres and expulsions. In the remaining one-fifth of the cases accommodation took the form of coexistence, the mutual recognition of different communities and compromises between them — though frequently only after bloody struggles.

The picture as a whole is sobering: lengthy, bitter, unsolved conflicts are common. One-community domination incurs high social costs and is seldom stable. Only in half the cases was there negotiated regulation, and in half of these the result was partition — that is, the mutual recognition that coexistence was impossible. And where accommodation was achieved through compromise this was usually preceded by great violence.

How then can one answer the 'democracy pessimists'? The fact is that in the world at large democracies are in a minority, not only among multi-communal but even among culturally homogeneous states. But that is a cold comfort. One section of those authors who tend to be 'democracy optimists', in particular theorists of modernization, hope that in the last instance social integration will eliminate particularisms within communities and permit nation-building. This hope is, as shown above, empirically unsubstantiated.

What remains is the consideration that the frequency of one or other type of conflict regulation tells us little about the probability and less about the possibility of a particular form of regulation in a specific case. The fact that in a few cases

---

[45] Arend Lijphart, *Democracy in Plural Societies: A comparative exploration* (New Haven and London, 1977), p.1.
[46] Theodor Hanf, 'The Prospects of Accommodation in Communal Conflicts: A comparative study', in Peter A. Döring et al., eds., *Bildung in sozio-ökonomischer Sicht* (Cologne and Vienna, 1989), pp.331–2.

peaceful and democratic forms of regulation have been found for multi-communal states means this possibility cannot be excluded. This raises the question of whether there is a connection between specific forms of conflict regulation, on the one hand, and specific ideological positions[47] on the problem of multi-communal states, on the other hand.

The power question in multi-communal states is seldom seen in crude socio-Darwinistic terms: for instance, that the possession of power justifies its exercise, that is, in terms of our concern, domination by one community. In most multi-communal states the ideological debate is rather about what actually constitutes a community, whether such communities exist at all — and, above all, whether they should exist.

The various positions in this debate can be reduced to three ideological tendencies. The first tendency is defined most precisely by the concept of Jacobinism. During the French Revolution the Jacobin Club formulated the purest and most radical form of the principle of *égalité*. Equality must be understood not only in social but also in cultural terms. Not only distinctions of class and property must be abolished, but also cultural distinctions. A revolutionary appeal urged the citizenesses of Strasbourg to turn their backs on German fashions because their hearts were French.[48] Although post-revolutionary France rejected social egalitarianism, it retained cultural egalitarianism. The Republic must remain 'une et indivisible', with a centralized administration, unilingual and free of any particularisms. A uniform educational system was introduced to eradicate minority languages and dialects. Expressed negatively, Jacobinism means the abolition of everything that stands in the way of political and cultural unity; put positively, it aims at the creation of a single, united republic by an act of will and the action of the state. In the twentieth century Jacobinism became Europe's most significant export, marketed, as a rule, as 'nation-building': the less homogeneous social reality was, the more attractive crusades under the Jacobinist banner against tribalism, particularism, confessionalism and separatism appeared. Jacobinism, in different guises, has become the predominant state ideology in the Third World.

The second tendency is the mobilization of communal identities. The conscious return to origins, history, language, religion or culture feeds the rejection of cultural uniformity and assimilation, the will to remain what one is, and the

---

[47] In the following the term 'ideology' will be understood as 'the systematic and explicit formulation of a general orientation to politics'; Gabriel A. Almond, 'Comparative Political Systems', *Journal of Politics*, 18 (1956), p.397. Its use will be restricted to politics in respect of the fundamental problems of multi-communal states.

[48] 'Proclamation des Représentants du Peuple. Les citoyennes de Strasbourg sont invitées de quitter les modes allemandes puisque leurs coeurs sont français. A Strasbourg le 25 Brumaire de l'an second de la République une et indivisible. ... Signés St Just et Lebar.'

determination to protect the interests of the community within the wider framework of the state.

There is a dialectical relationship between the mobilization of communal identities and Jacobinism. Just as in nineteenth-century Europe objectively deterministic nationalism drew its strength from the rejection of the Jacobinism exported by Napoleon, it has today become a common ideology of opposition to the subjectively voluntaristic Jacobinism of the new leadership strata. The deprived and discriminated are often mobilized by arousing the feelings of one community against other communities perceived as privileged, or simply against the privileged administrative bourgeoisie that justifies its position in terms of an abstract Jacobinistic concept of the state, while in practice tending to live off rather than for the state.

A third tendency may be termed syncretistic nationalism.[49] Its aim, too, is a nation. In contrast to Jacobinism, it does not seek to destroy already existing social and cultural formations. Instead, syncretistic nationalism regards existing, organic communities as the building blocks of a transcending nation. As a rule, this approach is rooted in a two-fold insight. On the one hand, it is unrealistic to hope that the existing communities will simply disappear, and any attempt to make them disappear would be unacceptable because of the social and cultural costs entailed: uprooting, insecurity, breakdown of social and moral norms. On the other hand, a radical mobilization of communities in a society in which communities are not segregated but live and work together would entail resettlement or expulsion that risked tearing the society apart — with unforeseeable consequences. Given these insights, syncretistic nationalism aims neither for unity nor for diversity at any cost, but for unity in diversity.

Syncretistic nationalism can take many forms, which find constitutional expression in either of two arrangements. One seeks to institutionalize the existing communities and organize their coexistence. Communal identity is politically articulated, though channelled within a federation of communities that constitute a transcending, multifarious nation. In Swiss political usage this is known as '*Konkordanzdemokratie*', for which a school of political thought has coined the neologism 'consociation'.[50]

---

[49] Esman, 'The Management of Communal Conflict', pp.58f, speaks of syncretistic integration 'as a form of politics that enables existing communal identities to submerge in favour of a new, national identity common to all'. In our text 'syncretism' will be used in its original sense of 'an alliance of two opponents against a third' or 'combined whole'. Accordingly, syncretistic nationalism should be understood as a concept of a new national entity embracing several components and distinct from its environment — as 'unity in diversity'.

[50] In Switzerland, the concept of *Konkordanzdemokratie* is part of the normal political vocabulary. Gerhard Lehmbruch introduced it into comparative political science, initially as 'proportional democracy'; see *Proporzdemokratie: Politisches System und politische Kultur in der Schweiz und in Österreich*

Remarkably, Lenin, writing on nationalities, proposes an analogous pattern of accommodation, at least as far as nationalities based on origin and language are concerned. All nationalities should have the right to become separate. Of course, this is not quite what Lenin wanted; he visualized one common state with autonomy for all component parts without any restrictions on any national minority.[51]

The second type of constitutional dispensation seeks to depoliticize communal identities. It institutionalizes and encourages cultural diversity in order to prevent symbolic cultural deprivation, thereby facilitating the political unity of the state. Canada, India and Indonesia practise such policies. The most important theoretical formulations are those of the Austrian Marxists Otto Bauer[52] and Karl Renner.[53] At the beginning of this century they proposed that the Hapsburg Empire with its 'patchwork quilt' of communities should introduce self-administrating cultural institutions based on the principle of personality, parallel

---

(Tübingen, 1967) and 'Konkordanzdemokratie im politischen System der Schweiz', *Politische Vierteljahresschrift*, 9 (1968), pp.443–59. Arend Lijphart, who initially spoke of 'accommodation' in *The Politics of Accommodation: Pluralism and democracy in the Netherlands*, 2nd edn (Berkeley, 1975), borrowed Johannes Althusius' concept of *consociatio* (community of common destiny, cooperative) as the cornerstone of an elaborate theory. See his major works, *Democracy in Plural Societies* and *Power-sharing in South Africa* (Berkeley, 1985). In the latter Lijphart deals in detail with criticisms of his theory. Whereas Lehmbruch emphasizes the importance of organic political cultures for consociational coexistence, Lijphart highlights the appropriate constitutional mechanisms. Lijphart regards his theory as more than an analytical instrument. It is also normative: given the conditions obtaining in plural societies, the only realistic choice is between consociation and no democracy at all. In states with different communities decisions by majority must inevitably be one-sided and favour the largest community. Consociation rests on conflict regulation through amicable agreement between the communities, by the involvement of all communities in the exercise of power and, consequently, by continual compromise. Consociation means the recognition of the existence of different communities and their political composition.

[51] V.I. Lenin, *Über die nationale und die koloniale nationale Frage* (East Berlin, 1960), pp.116 & 92. He also states: 'We are for the Jacobins and against the Girondists' (p.115) and declares himself against 'the national culture of the landowners, clerics and bourgeoisie' (p.141) and for an 'international culture of the workers' (p.93). To him this means 'no privileges for any nation whatsoever, for any language whatsoever! Not the least restriction, not the least injustice against a national minority' (p.93). 'Switzerland, Belgium, Norway and others are examples to us of how free nations under truly democratic conditions get on with one another or part in peace' (p.92). The latter refers to Norway's separation from Sweden in 1905. 'It is not our aim to "isolate" the nations but through complete democracy to ensure their equality and a (relatively) peaceful coexistence as in Switzerland' (pp.133f). Accordingly, Van Den Berghe has a point when he states: 'The model of consociationalism ... is not incompatible with a "people's democracy". Several socialist countries, most notably Yugoslavia and the USSR, have evolved toward consociational types of polity, that is, polities officially and legally recognizing ethnicity as a basis of political organization, representation and incorporation into the multinational state — ruled by a multi-ethnic bureaucratic and technocratic elite'; *The Ethnic Phenomenon* (New York and Oxford, 1981), p.191.

[52] Otto Bauer, *Die Nationalitätenfrage und die Sozialdemokratie*, 2nd edn (Vienna, 1924).

[53] Rudolf Springer, (Karl Renner's pseudonym), *Der Kampf der österreichischen Nationen um den Staat* (Leipzig and Vienna, 1902); Karl Renner, *Das Selbstbestimmungsrecht der Nationen, in besonderer Anwendung auf Österreich* (Leipzig and Vienna, 1918).

to the existing political units based on the principle of territoriality. Every person, regardless of where he lived, should have the possibility of joining a cultural community of his own choice. Bauer and Renner hoped that depoliticizing language, culture and education would facilitate the formation of transcultural political forces based on objective class interests.[54]

What is the relationship between particular forms of conflict regulation in multi-communal states and these three ideological tendencies? Where conflicts are regulated by stable domination the ruling community tends simply to regard the nation as homogeneous and deny the existence of other communities. Thus, in Turkey, Kurds have been declared 'Mountain Turks', and the ruling minority in Burundi plays down local ethnic differences as a colonial invention.

The situation is similar in some systems of instable domination. No Arab government is more Pan-Arab than the Syrian; it denies that the country is ruled by a minority and accuses opposition groups of practising divisive confessionalism. The Jordanian monarchy presents itself as an impartial authority that does not draw any distinction between Jordanians of Cis- and Trans-Jordanian origin. Despite changes of government that have brought other ethnic and religious groups to power, the governments of Cameroon and Chad have persisted in professing a purely Jacobinistic state ideology and react sensitively to allegations of preferential treatment for certain communities. Israel alone gets by without any integrative ideology, claiming a religious right to the land — though not for its non-Jewish inhabitants. Accordingly, the most contentious political issue in Israel is 'land for peace' — the question of whether it is better to give up a part of the country because of the inhabitants there or to retain the whole country despite the inhabitants.

It is striking that most instances of violent conflict are recorded not in states in which rival movements of mobilized communities face one another, but where groups with a Jacobinistic view of society confront others with a communal — ethnic, religious or linguistic — ideology. Admittedly, professions of Jacobinism may easily conceal a group's claims to domination. As Marxists, the formerly royalist Amharas continued to fight recalcitrant Eritreans and Oromos in the name of a single, united Ethiopia. In the name of one united Burma, Sri Lanka, Iraq, Sudan, Uganda and the Philippines the communities in power are fighting their non-Buddhist hill peoples, their Tamils, Kurds, Black Christians and

---

[54] Owing to Lenin's anathema — he would not hear of a separate Jewish cultural community — and the disintegration of the Hapsburg Empire, this idea was forgotten until recently unearthed by Marxist theorists; V.I. Lenin, 'Über die "nationalkulturelle" Autonomie', in *Über die nationale ... Frage*, pp.118–22. Above all, Lenin did not want to release centralized control of the educational system, though he was very much in favour of mother-tongue instruction. Although his politics are Jacobin, this does not extend to language and nationality.

Animists, all other tribal groups or their Muslim minority in the south. In Northern Ireland Protestants and Catholics wear Jacobinist robes of different hue — either the red, white and blue of a United Kingdom or the orange, white and green of a United Republic. Partition expresses the conviction that neither domination nor coexistence is possible.

Finally, in all cases in which coexistence of communities is practised the state ideology is syncretistic. If agreement was preceded by armed conflict, communal variety tends to be politically institutionalized, as in Switzerland, for many decades in Yugoslavia and, to take an historical case, in the Holy Roman Empire after the Treaty of Westphalia:[55] civil war can lead to long periods of accommodation in coexistence.

What is significant is that all multi-communal states with syncretistic national ideologies, whether their communities are politically institutionalized or not, recognize cultural differences. The Netherlands has a centralized administration, but leaves education and the media to the different 'pillars' — Protestants, Catholics, Liberals and Socialists. In Switzerland education is so decentralized that no cultural group has any say in education in any other. Belgium has transferred all matters of culture and language to institutions of the three language groups. Canada subsidizes the efforts of immigrant groups to retain their 'heritage language'. Indonesia decided not to make Javanese, the language of the majority, the country's official language, but Bahasa Indonesia, which virtually all citizens of the country have had to learn as their second language. In short: depoliticizing cultural cleavages by recognizing them is regarded as crucial to reducing conflict between communities.

To summarize, the three ideal types of ideologies of legitimization in multi-communal states are closely associated with specific patterns of conflict regulation. Why this should be so is explained by differences in historical conditions and constellations of interests.

## Ideologies and strategies

Politics in multi-communal states, like politics everywhere, is about the distribution of power and wealth. In every political system there are various intermediary institutions between the individual citizen and the political power centre — parties, interest lobbies, associations, trade unions and others. What distinguishes political processes in multi-communal states from those in homogeneous states is the fact that the communities and their political organs are the most important intermediaries, at least as long as they have not been

---

[55] On this point, see Günter Barudio, *Der Teutsche Krieg 1618–1648* (Frankfurt, 1985), pp.572ff.

completely depoliticized. In contrast to the political parties or trade unions in homogeneous societies, which citizens are free to choose and free to join, membership in communities is quasi-automatic, a matter of birth and upbringing.

Intermediary institutions and membership of them are important for access to desirable positions. This is best illustrated by the 'spoils system' practised in some western democracies. Immediately after the victory of an opposition party hundreds of incumbents are replaced in government and the civil service, and often in nationalized corporations as well. By contrast, in the political systems of multi-communal states access to — and exclusion from — influential and remunerative positions is on the basis of ascriptive criteria. In other words, successful communal politics brings quick rewards — one has advantages because one belongs to a certain community. Naturally, the contrary also holds: defeat for a community or an adverse position relative to power entails serious disadvantages for its members.

Interest in communities' positions of power varies considerably according to stratum as well as the phase of economic development. As a rule, interest is greatest among the leadership groups: they have the most to gain. Those who have the most to lose are the lower strata of the community in power. They do not owe their relatively privileged position to their own abilities or achievements but chiefly to their communal affiliation. Hence, they are most susceptible to mobilization policies based on communal identities — one may recall Jean-Paul Sartre's definition of anti-semitism as the 'capitalism of the small man'. Successful upwardly mobile groups in discriminated communities constitute a third group interested in mobilization. Despite their abilities and achievements they find their advancement blocked by ascriptive criteria. For this reason they tend to work for an improvement in the position of their community — or for the abolition of the system based on communal affiliation.[56]

What is good for these three critical groups is not necessarily good for the whole population. Some writers regard multi-communal states as Hobbesian societies — *homo homini lupus* — with each community ready to devour the others. Thus, Arend Lijphart[57] tends to the view that only an elite cartel of wise

---

[56] 'Already in eighteenth-century France, the universities were beginning to turn out more graduates than could be taken up by the bureaucracies and professions ... It was bad enough for graduates of the majority ethnic group congregated around the centre; how much worse was it likely to be for ambitious professionals hailing from the peripheral and minority ethnic communities! ... The point of their complaint was as much psychological as economic, cultural as well as political. It was not simply the failure to find employment, or even governmental posts, that bred discontent; it was failure to obtain a status and dignity commensurate with their educational achievements, and to have instead to settle for low-status and often unprofessional employment ill-matched to their professional diplomas'; Anthony D. Smith, 'Towards a Theory of Ethnic Separatism', *Ethnic and Racial Studies*, 2/1 (1979), p.29.

[57] *Democracy in Plural Societies*, passim.

and tolerant leaders can induce intolerant and latently hostile masses to accept coexistence between the communities. Yet this begs the question of how and why such masses should produce tolerant and open-minded leaders.

Be that as it may, there is some empirical evidence that the great majority of the population do have a clear perception of mutual interests that transcend communal interests, and, thus, a fundamental desire for coexistence.[58] There is much that speaks for the view that it is not so much the communities as such, that is, the mass of the population, that are responsible for the mobilization of communal feelings and the exacerbation of tension, as the special-interest groups identified above: the leadership groups, the upwardly mobile groups in discriminated communities and those sections of privileged communities that feel their position threatened — in other words, those groups that have something to gain or to lose. Naturally, these groups have a keen interest in equating their respective group interest with that of the community as a whole. Consequently, most 'ethnic entrepreneurs', the communal activists, are recruited from their ranks.

The identification of groups especially interested in mobilizing communal identity and solidarity already gives some indication of the specific economic and historical conditions that favour such mobilization. The mobilizing effect of modernization processes occurs above all in and through these groups. '"Previously" the groups got on well with one another' is a common refrain in almost all states with communal conflicts. There were indeed far fewer conflicts in pre-industrial and pre-bureaucratic societies. Peasant populations belonging to different communities often lived peacefully alongside one another for centuries. 'They may be different, but they don't bother us.' Bureaucratization, industrialization, urbanization and communication set the stage for harsher competition for desirable new positions. The competitors receive support and patronage mainly from members of their family, their place of origin and their community. It is no longer enough for political leaders to administer the status quo of a traditional society. They have to do more: find property and housing in new urban residential areas, find jobs for ambitious, upwardly mobile young people with great aspirations, and help civil servants get promotion. To deal with these new tasks successfully they require a wide following prepared to give them political support. Whereas the pre-industrial sense of community seldom went beyond the large family, clans or regional kinship ties, modern communal politics

---

[58] See Gerhard Lehmbruch, 'A Non-competitive Pattern of Conflict Management in Liberal Democracies: The case of Switzerland, Austria and Lebanon'. Paper delivered at the 7th World Congress of the International Political Science Association, Brussels 1967, p.7. See also Theodor Hanf, Heribert Weiland and Gerda Vierdag, *South Africa: The prospects of peaceful change* (London, 1981), pp.398ff.

requires larger associations: the larger the community the greater its chances of success. Only a numerous and strong community can avoid discrimination based on ascriptive criteria and improve its status. In short: modernization strengthens identification with the community; indeed, in many cases it creates it — through assignable common interests.

The more modern an economic system is, the more important the state's role as a redistributive agency. The distribution of power becomes more important because power and powerlessness mean wealth and poverty. The consequence is the politicization of communities.

Just as the mobilization of communities is rational in terms of their interests, so the choice of ideological positions is rational in terms of the power struggle within multi-communal states — with few exceptions. If one compares which ideology is chosen by which community under which conditions, both the rational and the instrumental character of this ideology becomes abundantly clear. As a rule, it is a rational articulation of an identifiable strategy in the best interests of the respective community. This is not to doubt the ideological convictions of the supporters of a specific ideology. But it is easier to hold convictions if they coincide with one's own interests.[59]

There is a fundamental distinction between various multi-communal states that influences the choice of both strategies and ideologies. They either contain clear majorities and minorities, or they do not. In the former case the communities tend to Jacobinism or to the mobilization of communities, depending on their respective strengths. These strategies may also be chosen in the latter, but the choice of syncretistic nationalism is far more common. The cases need to be examined separately.

Dominating majorities can afford to rule with the exclusive support of their own community. By completely excluding the minorities from power the majority maximizes its own benefits. By contrast, ruling minorities prefer to avoid the image of a minority regime. Jacobinistic ideologies are most suitable for disguising differences in communal privilege. Jacobinism avoids symbolic deprivation of the majority, which helps to minimize their opposition.

---

[59] 'It is obvious that a politician who said, `Believe this theory , for it serves my interests', would arouse only amusement and convince nobody. Therefore, he must appeal to specific principles that can win the approval of his audience ... He who wants to convince others often has to convince himself first, indeed, even if he is chiefly driven by his own interests he ends by believing that he is driven by the desire for the good of others'; Vilfredo Pareto, *Allgemeine Soziologie* (Tübingen, 1955), p.54.

**Table 1.1** Ideological strategies for clear majorities and minorities

|  | Jacobinism | Communal mobilization |
|---|---|---|
| Dominating majority | − | + |
| Dominating minority | + | − |
| Dominated majority | + | − |
| Large dominated majority | − | + |
| small dominated majority | + | − |

As a rule, dominated majorities also express their interests in Jacobinistic forms. The dominated do not demand that one form of dominance should replace another, but seek a new system without any discrimination against any group whatsoever. Were a dominated majority to opt for a strategy of communal mobilization, the dominant minority would have a choice only between capitulation and intransigence. This would inevitably strengthen their determination to retain power by any means. On the other hand, a Jacobinistic vision of future equality opens future perspectives for the minority which make it easier for them to consider giving up power.

Dominated large minorities generally opt for communal mobilization. Their chances of ever ruling alone are very slight. The better they organize themselves and the more completely they mobilize, the better their prospects of forming a 'blocking minority', without whose consent no decision can be taken. In consequence, the majority is forced to trade some of their privileges for the agreement of the minority.

Finally, small minorities show a clear preference for Jacobinism: 'If you can't beat them, join them.' Obvious majorities and obvious minorities choose their respective strategy or ideology on the basis of a rational assessment of their interests. However, when the numerical ratios and the power relationships between the communities are less clear-cut — the case in numerous multi-communal states — the choice is far more difficult. Both Jacobinism and communal mobilization are full of dangers for all sides. Jacobinism can rapidly degenerate into the illusion of equality. And a mobilized community may equally well get its way as come to grief.

Communities that favour Jacobinism usually are, or believe themselves to be, strongest in relative terms. It is not uncommon for them to equate the majority in the Jacobin principle of majority rule with the majority of their own community. Largish communities that do not believe they are or can become the majority seek to avoid permanent exclusion from power by demanding institutionalized involvement of all communities in the exercise of power. By contrast, small communities in states without clear majorities often reject an institutionalized distribution of power because they believe their own chances are better under a Jacobin system. The instrumental function of rival ideological positions is particularly well illustrated by demographic shifts that persuade communities positively and negatively affected by these shifts to change their ideological preferences.

## Civil war and conflict regulation

Armed conflict frequently arises through miscalculating the chance of one's demands being accepted.[60] In such situations the power politics of communities strongly resembles the classic, pre-nuclear power politics of nations. But, frequently, armed conflict stands at the start of the search for generally acceptable and negotiated forms of conflict regulation. Wars between states do not always end in clear victories, civil wars even less often. The chance that there will be neither victors nor vanquished is greatest in civil wars in multi-communal states in which no group has a clear majority.

And this is indeed a 'chance'. The likelihood of an agreement to coexist is greatest when all communities realize that none of them is strong enough to gain a clear victory, yet none so weak as to be permanently vanquished — in other words, in stalemate. Certainly, a stalemate alone will not guarantee peace — otherwise numerous civil wars would not have continued for years and even decades. The communities involved have to first realize that they are not in a position to achieve all their material and ideological objectives. Such a conflict can only end when all participants agree to share the goods and benefits of the country — as relative as they may be — in a suitable manner, to accept the existing distinctions between the communities and, above all, to abandon all 'pure' ideologies, whatever their nature. It is typical of conflicts of this kind that it is often easier to compromise on material issues than on symbolic or ideological issues. The best illustration of this is the frequent practice of 'burnt-earth' policies. Purely in terms of economic interests, such a policy is utterly irrational. Yet it is often practised by communities that feel — rightly or wrongly — that their very existence is threatened. Existential fears may make even the complete destruction of a country seem rational — a civil-war variant of absolute deterrence.

Hence, compromise is possible only when, apart from material prerequisites, the symbolic and ideological prerequisites for compromise exist — when each and

---

[60] 'Both sides lack full and accurate information about each other; they have misconceptions about each other's strengths and weaknesses'; Oberschall, *Social Conflicts*, p.25.

every side feels that its respective existence is no longer threatened. This is the hour of syncretistic national ideologies, far removed from pure Jacobinism and every form of exclusive communalism — the hour of national concepts that accept the existence of contradictions, inconsistencies and diversity, in which no one claims a monopoly of power and prosperity.

The Treaty of Westphalia was concluded against the background of battlefields and granted Catholics, Lutherans and members of the Reformed Churches equal rights in the same empire. The Swiss 'magic formula' emerged against a similar backdrop, enabling German-, French-, Italian-, and Romansch-speaking Catholics and Protestants to govern the country together, as did the constitution of socialist Yugoslavia, which recognized different nations within one transcending nation. Such solutions may horrify Jacobins and proponents of ideologies of exclusive identity. However, people directly affected have learnt that ideological horrors are preferable to the horrors of war. With luck they may, in the course of time, come to regard their solution as a national treasure, not as a lesser evil but as a strength.

What are the chances that such regulations will be sought without prior experience of violence and civil war, that is, the chances of preventive conflict regulation? To judge by historical and contemporary experience they are slight. Peoples and communities are not wont to learn from the history of others — they prefer the lessons and experiences of their own history, and in multi-communal states that is usually bloody.

Granted, there are exceptions. In Belgium and the Netherlands the different communities have never shot at one another. By comparison, though, these were contained and low-intensity conflicts. It is questionable whether the same could be achieved under more difficult conditions. However, a number of other states prove that armed stalemate is not necessary for political accommodation that neither ignores nor discriminates against minorities. In India and Rwanda, in Indonesia and Canada, communities politically and numerically in the overwhelming majority have adopted a policy of coexistence, less through coercion than insight and wisdom. They are examples that empirical probability need not be historical inevitability.

## Multi-communal states and international crises

The inability of multi-communal states to cope with their internal conflicts raises the danger that external influences will worsen them. The 'Eastern Question' of the nineteenth century is the classic example of this. Ethnic nationalism in the Balkan Peninsular, emancipation movements of religious communities and the national 'Arab awakening' in the Near East reduced the Ottoman Empire to the 'sick man of Europe'. The Great Powers pressured the Ottoman government into introducing reforms. But, in pursuing their own interests, they hastened the disintegration of the Empire. Czarist Russia sought access to the Mediterranean and, as protector of the Orthodox Church, supported the liberation movements in the Balkans. Great Britain wanted to safeguard the sea-route to India, so occupied Egypt and ultimately encouraged the 'Desert Uprising'. France built on its traditional position as protector of Christian minorities and acquired a foothold in the Orient. Other European powers behaved similarly. By the turn of the century economic penetration by European interests was already far advanced. The ambassadors of the 'Powers' in Constantinople and their consuls in many parts of the Empire had practically become co-regents. The First World War dealt the Empire its death-blow, and the powers grabbed their spoils.

Internal conflicts always invite foreign intervention.[61] And as conflicts are more common in multi-communal states, intervention in their affairs, both direct and indirect, is the rule. Intervention is particularly easy in the case of 'transnational' communities, that is when communal solidarity straddles state borders. Irredentist movements and separatist movements with foreign support are common. States seeking to establish regional hegemony seek clients among the communities of the multi-communal state in the hope of using them to influence the state's policies. They are often both fire-lighter and fire-fighter, precipitating crises in the hope of exercising as arbiters the greatest possible influence. Rival communities themselves often encourage foreign influence. There is a great temptation to compensate internal weakness with foreign support. Once different communities have found support among different foreign powers the internal crisis becomes an international one.

In the past quarter century the major powers have tended to avoid direct confrontation far from their respective geographic power centres, departing from this only if they fear the existing equilibrium may shift to their disadvantage. As a rule, they prefer to exercise their influence indirectly through regional or internal 'proxies'. The danger that a conflict will intensify and continue is greatest when rival aspirants to regional hegemony have the support of different foreign powers. Perpetuating the internal conflict in the multi-communal state affected serves, in turn, to preserve regional and international equilibrium.

Through continued support of the parties to the conflict, victory and defeat for any community is prevented and the conflict prolonged. Permanent conflict threatens particularly in regions of economic and geostrategic importance. The

---

[61] See Karl W. Deutsch, 'External involvement in internal war', in Eckstein, ed., *Internal War*, pp.100–10; Gerhard Lehmbruch, 'Consociational Democracy in the International System', *European Journal of Political Research*, 3/4 (1975), pp.377–91.

populations affected are saddled with the material and human 'costs' of preserving international or regional equilibrium.

The more militarized conflicts in these regions become, the greater the danger that local military disputes will rapidly escalate into global confrontations. When peoples and communities 'at the other end of the world' engage in conflict, the possibility that daily constitutionals — or civil rights marches — might eventually be endangered can no longer be excluded. It is in the interest even of states far from, and not directly involved in, a conflict to help to preserve or establish peace by working for a balance of interests, compromise and reconciliation in that conflict.

## Lebanon as model

Lebanon is a multi-communal state comprising many ethnic and religious communities. The history of their coexistence since the country's independence renders Lebanon an apposite object of empirical research. For three decades it was held to be an example of successful, peaceful and democratic coexistence, as one of the few viable cases of consociation outside Europe. In the following decade and a half it became the proverbial case of a country torn apart by bloody and internecine warfare. 'Lebanization' has become a household word of warning in other multi-communal states. Both manifestations — the initial coexistence and the subsequent conflict — are regarded as paradigmatic. Both need to be explained. How and why did the 'Lebanese Model' function in the pre-war period? Why did it break down? Was it because of its own weaknesses or because of stronger non-Lebanese forces? How did the country slide from its sheltered calm into the heart of the Middle Eastern storm? Who has been fighting for what in Lebanon? What have been the stages and what are the results of the armed struggles?

The literature on this topic is copious and useful. Studies by Kewenig,[62] Binder[63] and Hudson[64] in the 1960s analyse Lebanese coexistence in happier times. Khoury,[65] Khalaf,[66] Dubar and Nasr[67] provide important insights into social transformation in the immediate pre-war years. Beydoun[68] and Salibi[69] illuminate

---

[62] Wilhelm Kewenig, *Die Koexistenz der Religionsgemeinschaften im Libanon* (Berlin, 1965).

[63] Leonard Binder, ed., *Politics in Lebanon* (New York, London and Sydney, 1966).

[64] Hudson, *The Precarious Republic*.

[65] Fuad I. Khuri, *From Village to Suburb* (Chicago and London, 1975).

[66] Samir Khalaf, *Lebanon's Predicament* (New York, 1987).

[67] Claude Dubar and Salim Nasr, *Les Classes sociales au Liban* (Paris, 1976).

[68] Ahmad Beydoun, *Identité confessionnelle et temps social chez les historiens libanais contemporains* (Beirut, 1984).

[69] Kamal Salibi, *A House of Many Mansions: The history of Lebanon reconsidered* (London, 1988).

history and historistic ideologies that have influenced the self-awareness of the Lebanese communities and contributed to their mobilization. Barakat[70] and Messarra[71] have studied the adaptability and reformability of the Lebanese social and political system. Schemeil's[72] empirical surveys in the early 1970s were early evidence of rising social and political tensions. Kuderna[73] analysed the Christian, Johnson[74] the Sunni and Norton[75] the Shi`i communities in the pre-war period. Chamussy,[76] Goria,[77] Köhler,[78] Salibi[79] and Schiller[80] have treated the pre-history and first phases of the war. In 1979 Khalidi,[81] 1985 Rabinovich[82] and 1988 Picard[83] have published informative, precise and balanced studies of the war in Lebanon. Messarra[84] has examined the Lebanese system's prospects of surviving after all that has happened.

But what are not, or very rarely, found in the literature on the Lebanese conflict — indeed, in the literature on conflict as such — are studies on the thoughts, views and desires of those participating in and affected by the conflict. What do the political and military leaders perceive as the causes of the conflict and how do they perceive its course and the prospects of regulation? And what do the ordinary Lebanese think about these questions? It should be rewarding to look at these questions. As shown above, 'objective' factors alone do not determine whether differences between communities will evolve into conflicts, whether the potential for conflict is realized. An essential element consists of 'subjective'

---

[70] Halim Barakat, *Lebanon in Strife: Student preludes to the civil war.* Modern Middle East Series No. 2 (Austin and London, 1977).

[71] Antoine N. Messarra, *La structure sociale du parlement libanais (1920–1976)* (Beirut, 1977).

[72] Yves Schemeil, 'Sociologie du système politique libanais', Unpublished Ph.D dissertation, University of Grenoble, 1976.

[73] Michael Kuderna, *Christliche Gruppen im Libanon: Kampf um Ideologie und Herrschaft in einer unfertigen Nation* (Wiesbaden, 1983).

[74] Michael Johnson, *Class and Client in Beirut: The Sunni Muslim community and the Lebanese State 1840–1985* (London, 1986).

[75] Augustus Richard Norton, *Amal and the Shi'a: Struggle for the soul of Lebanon* (Austin, 1987).

[76] René Chamussy, *Chronique d'une guerre. Liban 1975–1977. En postface: Les doutes de l'après-guerre II* (Paris, 1978).

[77] Wade R. Goria, *Sovereignty and Leadership in Lebanon 1943–1976* (London, 1985).

[78] Wolfgang Köhler, *Die Vorgeschichte des Krieges im Libanon* (Wiesbaden, 1980).

[79] Kamal Salibi, *Crossroads to Civil War: Lebanon 1958–1976* (New York, 1976).

[80] David Th. Schiller, *Der Bürgerkrieg im Libanon: Entstehung, Verlauf, Hintergründe* (Munich, 1979).

[81] Walid Khalidi, *Conflict and Violence in Lebanon: Confrontation in the Middle East* (Cambridge, Mass., 1979).

[82] Itamar Rabinovich, *The War for Lebanon, 1970–1983* (Ithaca and London, 1984).

[83] Elizabeth Picard, *Liban, état de discorde: Des fondations aux guerres fratricides* (Paris, 1988).

[84] Antoine N. Messara, *Le modèle politique libanais et sa survie: Essai sur la classification et l'aménagement d'un système consociatif* (Beirut, 1983).

factors, perception.[85] What do the participants and those affected regard as conflicts, how seriously do they take them? Perceptions are particularly significant for the question of possible conflict regulation. And this is even more so for internal conflicts in multi-communal states.

On the one hand, this study is an attempt to fill this gap in our knowledge with empirical surveys, and then reconsider the question of possible conflict regulations. On the other hand, it is intended as a contribution to the study of perceptions and attitudes in societies living in conditions of war, and in particular of persistence and change in these perceptions and attitudes under the influence of extreme and traumatic events.

Two kinds of empirical data are used. The perceptions of political and military leaders were obtained in personal interviews, in part structured by the author and in part unstructured and recorded by a secretary. The 460 interviewees were chosen after a detailed analysis of position and reputation with the help of Lebanese journalists and social scientists. The list is representative of the full spectrum of Lebanese political and military positions as well as the most important tendencies within the Palestinian Liberation Organization. To complement this picture, Syrian, Israeli and American politicians, officers and diplomats concerned with Lebanese affairs were also interviewed.

The interviewees include seventeen Lebanese politicians who have held important positions for decades and previously granted the author interviews in 1960, 1971 and between 1979 and 1985. This has enabled a long-term comparison of political positions. Representative surveys of economically active Lebanese were conducted in 1981, 1984, 1986 and 1987. These form the basis for statements about the perceptions, attitudes and political opinions of the Lebanese people. The results allow an assessment of the possibilities of internal Lebanese conflict regulation that diverge from many previous assessments.

Book titles can epitomize situations. Even before the war Lebanon had been titled a 'precarious republic'[86] or an 'improbable nation'.[87] Since the outbreak of

---

[85] Walker Connor puts it succinctly: 'When analyzing socio-political situations, what ultimately matters is not *what is* but *what people believe is*'; 'Ethnonational Versus Other Forms of Group Identity: The problem of terminology'; paper presented to the Conference on Pluralism, Cape Town, May 1977, p.6. Ross speaks of an 'entirely reasonable phenomenological step of asking what ethnicity really means to the ethnics themselves'; 'Urban Development', p.443. Similarly, Van Den Berghe: 'As ethnicity, however, is not only a function of objective cultural differences, it is also important to take into account the subjective perceptions of cultural differences by members of various groups'; 'Pluralism', in John J. Honigmann, ed., *Handbook of Social and Cultural Anthropology* (Chicago, 1974), p.968.

[86] Hudson, *The Precarious Republic*.

[87] Leila M.T. Meo, *Lebanon. Improbable Nation: A study in political development* (Bloomington, 1965).

war the 'death of a country',[88] 'une croix sur le Liban'[89] and an 'état de discorde'[90] have been spotlighted. This book treats of 'coexistence in war'. Why, must be substantiated empirically.

---

[88] John Bulloch, *Death of a Country: The civil war in Lebanon* (London, 1977).
[89] Jean-Pierre Peroncel-Hugoz, *Une croix sur le Liban* (Paris, 1984).
[90] Elizabeth Picard, *Liban*.

# 2

## The 'Lebanese Model' Coexistence in Pre-war Lebanon

That intolerance of social freedom which is natural to absolutism is sure to find a corrective in the national diversities, which no other force could so efficiently provide. The coexistence of several nations under the same state is a test as well as the best security of its freedoms.

Lord Acton, 1862

It is imperative that the chairmanship of the Central Executive committee of the Union rotates between Russia, the Ukraine, Georgia, etc. Imperative.

V.I. Lenin
Memorandum for the Politburo, 6.10.1922

Lebanon offers numerous examples of impediments to social change and innovation which arise if an elaborate equilibrium of groups has to be preserved; but there is no reason to believe that the political systems of the Arab neighbour states are more efficient.

Gerhard Lehmbruch, 1967

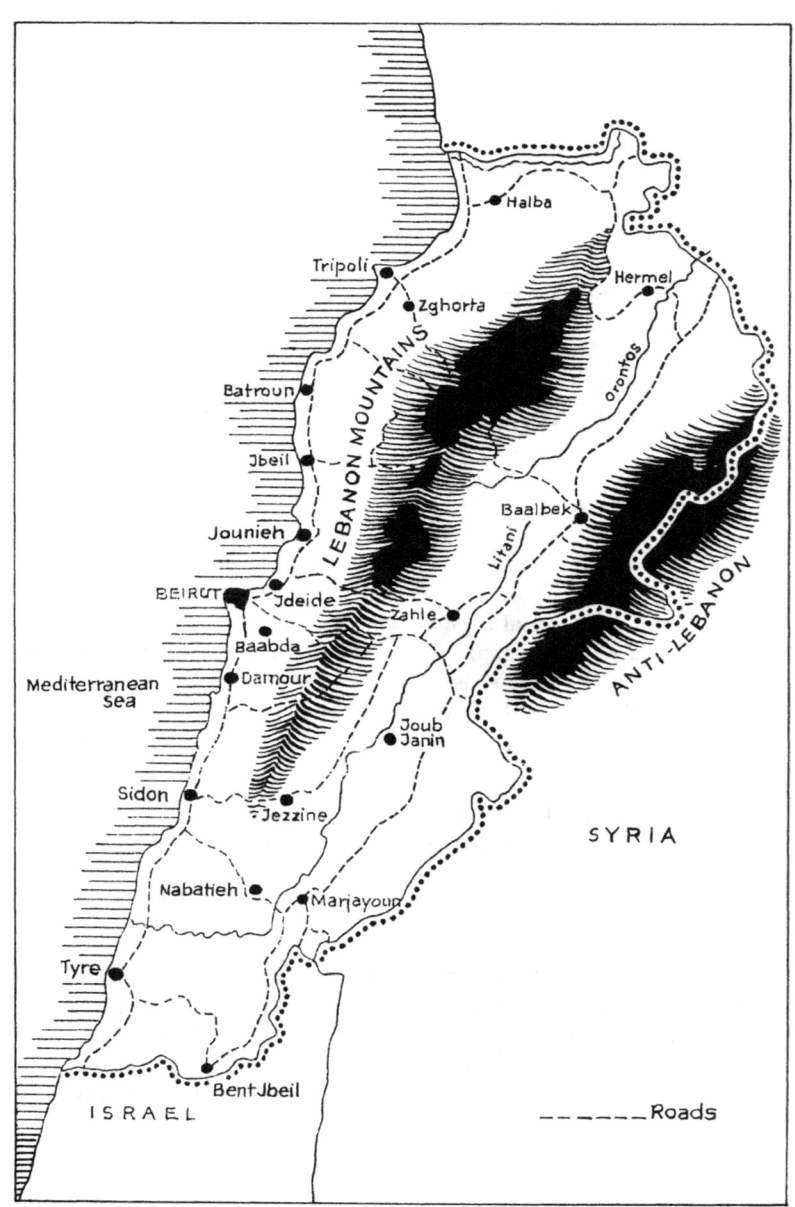

'At the western edge of the Orient lies Lebanon — a mountain range that drops to the sea.'[1] For Pierre Rondot, one of the best authorities on Lebanon, this point is crucial to an understanding of the historical and social development of this country.

> A rugged country difficult of access, Lebanon has given refuge to dissidents of all sorts. The isolation of its peaks and valleys has enabled tribes and religious groups to survive with their character intact. But the small size of the territory and the need to defend it has compelled these varied groups to practise solidarity and cooperation ... The opening to the sea has invited frequent foreign intervention, both for better and for worse. On account of its proximity, the Occident has had a strong influence, ... encouraged the development of education and emergence of new ideas. Notwithstanding this, tradition has a strong hold on this country. It remains essentially an alliance of families.[2]

Wilhelm Kewenig, too, regards geographic details as the 'key to an understanding of the outlines of Lebanese history'.[3] Kamal Salibi comes to the conclusion that in certain respects geography is just as important as history. The modern, urban Lebanese and the ancient Phoenicians have much in common. 'They live in the same cities, on the same coast of the Mediterranean and work in the same country in the same climate.'[4]

Lebanon is the smallest country in the Levant, about 210 kilometres from north to south and between 30 and 90 kilometres wide. The fertile coastal strip is 7 kilometres wide on average, and 10 kilometres in the northern Akkar plain. The largest cities lie on the coast: Tripoli in the north, the capital Beirut on a large peninsular more or less in the centre, and Sidon and Tyre in the south. To the east the coastal strip is bounded by the Lebanon Mountains, which drop gradually from the highest peaks of over 3,000 metres in the north to pass over into the hills of Galilee 160 kilometres to the south. The range is traversed by rivers flowing into the Mediterranean. Deep river valleys cleave the mountainous landscape, and each section has more in common with the corresponding coastal segment than with its mountain neighbours. Towards the east the range falls steeply to the Bekaa, the ancient Coelesyria. This valley is 160 kilometres long from north to south, but only 8 to 12 kilometres wide. The main centres are Zahle, on the edge

---

[1] Pierre Rondot, *Les institutions politiques du Liban* (Paris, 1947), p. 5.
[2] Ibid.
[3] Wilhelm Kewenig, *Die Koexistenz der Religionsgemeinschaften im Libanon* (Berlin, 1965), p. 1.
[4] Kamal S. Salibi, *A House of Many Mansions: The history of Lebanon reconsidered* (London, 1988), p. 178.

of the mountains, Chtaura in the centre and Baalbek in the north. The Litani River flows through it, before turning westwards towards the Mediterranean at the southern end of the mountain range. East of the Bekaa run the arid, and therefore virtually uninhabited Anti Lebanon Mountains, of which Mount Hermon in the south is the highest peak.

The country has no mineral resources. The coastal strip and the Bekaa are fertile, and there is enough rainfall in the mountains for terrace farming. Lebanon has two blessings. Firstly, its situation at the meeting point of three continents has turned Beirut in particular into a centre of international transport and entrepôt trade. Secondly, it has great natural beauty. Pre-war this attracted scores of tourists from Europe and, above all, the Arab world. For centuries, travellers and poets have enthused about the Mediterranean climate at the coast, the cool mountain climate in summer, the dry air of the Bekaa, the plentiful watercourses and the months of snow-covered peaks. The Lebanese themselves are no less enthusiastic. As far as this beauty and their way of life is concerned, Lebanese of all regions and groups are chauvinists, and with good reason. By common consent — and many Lebanese are very well travelled — the product of Lebanese cuisine and the pleasure of eating, of local wines, hospitality and merriness is a sweetness of life unrivalled anywhere. Thus, Lebanese of all religions will assure you that God is Lebanese.

However, this conviction in no way detracts from every Lebanese person's belief that his place of origin is God's private garden, that his particular region — pars contra totum — is to all intents and purposes Lebanon. No olives are quite so plump, no arrack so tasty, no people so generous, brave and worthy. And thus, each group think they are God's favourite children — and the others really only stepchildren. De Gaulle found a country with 360 different types of cheese difficult to govern; but what of a country with as many varieties of olive as there are villages?

The Lebanese are divided on what Lebanon was and is, whether this country should continue to exist, in what form, and under what government, and whether and what changes should be made. These differences must now be considered, as well as, in particular, the question of how, despite them, peaceful coexistence was possible and could last so long.

## Coexistence and history

Every national movement and every community calls on history to be its witness. What was should justify what is or what ought to be; multi-communal states usually have several versions of history. Lebanon is the history of religions with all their heresies and schisms, the history of ancient and more recent religious communities, the history of those who regard the Lebanese state in this century as a prize won, and the history of those who regard this state as an absurd pursuit, a detour or a stage on the way to a larger state — be it a Greater Syrian, a pan-Arab or an Islamic state. Lebanese nationalists — usually, but not exclusively, Christians — try to prove that Lebanon has existed since time immemorial, and stress its independence and uniqueness. Arab nationalists — usually, but not exclusively, Muslims — tend to present the history of what is now known as Lebanon as a provincial chapter in the history of Arab-Islamic empires. There are disputes about when which part of the country was called 'Lebanon', whether one or other of the contemporary communities was already a nation in the past, whether an autonomous principality existed from the sixteenth to the eighteenth centuries and whether it was 'Lebanese', whether bloody conflicts in the nineteenth century were religious wars or class struggles, whether the present Lebanese state is a product of the colonial scramble or of indigenous political will. Many of the sources themselves are unclear, which renders impossible unequivocal statements about various periods. On the other hand, through their sober criticism of historistic accounts, some modern Lebanese historians have been stripping away the overgrowth.[5]

It is hoped that for an understanding of present-day Lebanon it will suffice to refer to those undisputed historical facts and events that throw light on how the existing religious communities originated, how they encountered one another and how the relations between them evolved to their present state.

In the course of history many rulers have come, seen and conquered the area now known as Lebanon — and gone. Even before the first millennium BC flourishing Phoenician city-states along the coast dominated the trade of the ancient world, reaching even the Baltic Sea. In the sixth century BC they were conquered by the Persian empire, which, in turn, was destroyed by Alexander the Great two centuries later. Lebanon remained part of the Hellenistic Seleucid Empire until this fell to Rome in the last century BC. After the division of the empire, Lebanon and present-day Syria remained under Eastern Roman — Byzantine — rule until 641 AD. From then until 1918 — apart from the twelfth- and thirteenth-century interlude of the Latin Kingdoms of the Crusaders —

---

[5] Ahmad Beydoun, *Identité confessionelle et temps social chez les historiens contemporains* (Beirut, 1984); Salibi, *A House of Many Mansions* and 'L'Historiographie libanaise, histoire de vanité', *L'Orient* (25th May, 1965). Like Beydoun, the present author values Salibi's work in that he 'ne s'est pas choisi une position contemporaine de l'événement raconté, qu'il ne se tient dans les rangs d'aucune armée médiévale ... Il ne s'identifie ni aux Mamelouks ni aux chiites ni aux maronites ni aux Druzes et, à l'occasion, n'hésite point à mettre en pièces des "certitudes" communautaires jalousement défendues. Peut-être, pour avoir enfin un récit "autochtone" ainsi fait, il fallait attendre la descente sur l'arène ... d'un protestant de formation anglo-saxonne!'; Beydoun, *Identité confessionelle*, pp. 110f.

Lebanon was part of a succession of Islamic empires, of which the longest-lasting was the Ottoman Empire from 1516 onwards.

The different Christian religious communities in Lebanon emerged under Eastern Roman rule, and the present Muslim communities under the Umayyad and Fatimid dynasties. In both cases the roots of the divisions were either heresies, that is, different religious convictions, or schisms, that is, disputes over the legitimacy of religious leadership. The official religion of the Eastern and Western Roman Empires was Christianity, as summarized in the Nicene Creed promulgated in 325 AD. The first Christian divide took place at the Council of Ephesus in 431 AD. The teachings of Nestorius, alleged to deny the divine nature of Christ, were condemned as heresy. Adherents of this doctrine migrated to eastern Syria and Persia. In the thirteenth century missionaries were preaching Nestorian Christianity from southern Arabia to China. In the fourteenth century the Mongol invasions virtually obliterated it. Small communities, today known as Assyrians, survive in south-eastern Turkey, northern Iraq and Iran. Since the 1930s refugees from these countries have been settling in Beirut and Zahle.

The second parting of the Christian ways has had greater consequences for the Near East. In 451 the Council of Chalcedon decided that Christ had both a divine and a human nature. This was not accepted by the 'Monophysites', who held that there was only one — the divine — nature in the person of Christ. The Christians of Armenia, Egypt and most of Syria professed Monophysitism, and today form the Armenian Gregorian, the Coptic and the Syrian Jacobite Churches. The 'real reasons' behind this schism were 'often of a national nature' and gave 'expression essentially to emancipatory aspirations of the reawakening Near Eastern popular traditions that subsequently freed themselves ... from Hellenism'.[6] Especially 'under Islamic rule', these three Monophysitic Churches became completely identified with their ethnic groups ... whose history, culture and language they shared'.[7] Today, a large group of Gregorian Armenians and a small group of Jacobites live in Lebanon.

A further doctrinal split occurred at the Sixth Council in 680. A minority took the view that Christ had two natures but only one will. This was condemned as the 'monotheletic' heresy. Some historians surmise that the Maronites, followers of the monk Maro, who died near Antioch about 410, adhered to this doctrine —

---

[6] Burkard Spuler, *Gegenwartslage der Ostkirchen in ihrer nationalen und staatlichen Umwelt* (Frankfurt, 1968), p. 277, quoted in Klaus-Peter Hartmann, *Untersuchungen zur Sozialgeschichte christlicher Minderheiten im Vorderen Orient* (Wiesbaden, 1980), p. 21.

[7] Ibid.

which the Maronites themselves deny.[8] It is not clear just when the Maronite community migrated into the northern part of the Lebanon Mountains — some time between the late seventh and the eleventh centuries, depending on the source. What is certain, however, is that in 1182 the Maronites recognized the supremacy of the Pope in Rome. In a Papal bull of 1510 Leo X titled the Maronite community 'Rosa inter spinas' — a faithful rose among the thorns of heretics and infidels. In present-day Lebanon the Maronites are, by far, the most numerous Christian denomination.

Members of the established Byzantine Church used the term Orthodox — Greek: *orthodoxos*, that is, correct belief — to describe themselves. As supporters of the emperor they were also known as *Melchites* (literally: royalists). Melchites are found throughout the Arab Near East; in Lebanon they constitute the second largest Christian group. Of the above-mentioned Christian denominations,[9] the smaller ones are all older than Islam, and the Maronites at least as old. In pre-Islamic times specific forms of Christian belief were closely associated with tribal, ethnic or cultural communities. There is a lot to be said for the view that secessions from the state religion were motivated in part by the desire to emphasize, in religious practice too, cultural distinctions between these communities and the dominant Hellenistic cultural group in the Eastern Roman Empire.

The early history of Islam is not dissimilar to that of Christianity. Its first and most important schism occurred over the question of the succession to Muhammad. Muhammad's son-in-law, Ali, was thrice passed over for the caliphate, then elected, and murdered five years later in 661 AD. The Shi`a, literally: sect or party (that is, of Ali), insisted that the supreme authority should be a descendant of the Prophet. The majority of Muslims did not endorse this view. They called themselves the orthodox adherents of the Sunna, the body of traditional Islamic laws based on the words and acts of Muhammad and his immediate successors. The Shi`is in turn split into several sects. One of them became known as the 'Sevener Shi`is' because they recognize as imams only descendants of Ali's son Husayn. The seventh Imam was Ismail. He went into 'hiding' or seclusion. Other hidden imams followed. The Fatimid caliphs, who

---

[8] See Joseph Dibs, *Perpétuelle orthodoxie des maronites* (Awas, 1896) and *Les maronites du Liban* (Paris, 1875); Pedro Dib, *L'Église maronite* (Paris, 1930); for a critique, see Salibi, *A House of Many Mansions*, pp. 87ff.

[9] For detailed accounts see: Pierre Rondot, *Les chrétiens d'Orient* (Paris, 1955); Albert H. Hourani, *Minorities in the Arab World* (London, 1947); Robert Brenton Betts, *Christians in the Arab East. A political study* (Athens, 1975); L.C. Biegel, *Minderheden in het Midden-Oosten: Hun betekenis als politieke factor in de Arabische wereld* (Deventer, 1972); Raymond Etteldorf, *Catholic Churches in the Middle East* (New York, 1955). For a brief survey, see Theodor Hanf, 'Die christlichen Gemeinschaften im gesellschaftlichen Wandel des arabischen Vorderen Orients', *Orient*, 22/1 (1981), pp. 29–49.

ruled Tunisia and later Egypt, proclaimed themselves the re-emerged successors of Ismail. One of them was al-Hakim (996–1021), whose counsellor, al-Darazi, taught that Hakim was the ultimate incarnation of God in human history and would return in triumph when the time was ripe. The adherents of this doctrine take their name from Darazi: the Druze.[10] Persecuted by the Sunnis as heretics, they fled into the mountainous region around Hermon and into the southern part of the Lebanon Mountains.

Another, far more numerous group is the Twelver Shi`is. They hold that the twelfth, not the seventh, imam in the succession of Ali and his sons went into a cosmic 'absence'. According to their belief, injustice will reign in the world until the absent imam returns. Today, the Twelver Shi`is — or Shi`is for short — are probably the largest Muslim religious community in Lebanon, more numerous than even the Sunnis.

Just when different population groups within the borders of the present republic adopted their particular beliefs or when they migrated into this area is still disputed among historians. However, it is generally accepted that already in the eleventh century AD members of the most important of the existing religious communities were settled there:[11] Druze in the south and Maronites in the extreme north of the Lebanon Mountains, Shi`is in the southern hills, in the Bekaa and in the central section of the mountains in Kisrawan, while the coastal cities were inhabited mainly by Melchites and Sunnis, in other words, by adherents of the dominant religions of the successive empires before and after the Islamic conquest of the Near East between 635 and 637 AD.

In principle, victorious Islam had evolved fixed rules for relations both with other believers and with Muslim dissidents.[12] Other 'peoples of the book', that is, Christians, Jews and Zoroastrians, were allowed to retain and practise their beliefs and maintain their legal systems and religious hierarchies, provided that they recognized the Islamic ruler. Moreover, they had to pay a poll-tax as compensation for protection, but were freed from conscription. This tolerance went hand in hand with humiliation, but frequently with possibilities of economic improvement. Jews and Christians could escape their status as wards by converting to Islam —

---

[10] B. Carra De Vaux, 'Druzes', in H.A.R. Gibb and J.H. Kramers, eds., *Shorter Encyclopedia of Islam* (Leiden, 1953), p. 94; David Bryer, 'The Origins of the Druze Religion', *Der Islam*, 52 (1975), pp. 47–84 and 53 (1976), pp. 4–27; see also Werner Schmucker, *Krise und Erneuerung im libanesischen Drusentum* (Bonn, 1979).

[11] Salibi, *A House of Many Mansions*, pp. 12f.

[12] See D.B. MacDonald, 'Dhimma', in Gibb and Kramers, *Shorter Encyclopedia of Islam*, pp. 75f.; Louis Gardet, *La cité musulmane* (Paris' 1954), pp. 344–9; Majid Khadduri, *War and Peace in the Law of Islam* (Baltimore, 1955); Muhammad Asad, *The Principle of State and Government in Islam* (Berkeley and Los Angeles, 1961); Emile Tyan, *Histoire de l'organisation judiciaire en pays d'Islam* (Paris, 1938); Antoine Fattal, *Le statut légal des Non-Musulmans en pays d'Islam* (Beirut, 1958).

and very many did. But pressure to convert was rare, as the rulers, in general, were more interested in tax revenues than converts. The system of protection, with its vexatious regulations and harassments, was most effective in towns and villages also inhabited by Sunni Muslims. By contrast, in remote and inaccessible areas Islamic rule was restricted to the collection of taxes, either because of expected resistance or because the government of the day did not think a more direct exercise of power worth the trouble. Heterodox Muslims were far worse off legally than Christians and Jews: they were not recognized at all. They did not have to pay the poll-tax but could be conscripted. In reaction, Shi`is and Druze under Sunni rule resorted to 'dissemblance': when and where necessary they posed as Sunnis and for the rest stuck to their own beliefs and customs.

Often Christian and heterodox Muslim communities retired to remote areas where Sunni rule was least effective and tangible. This was particularly true of different mountainous regions, not least of the Lebanon Mountains. Here, such groups could survive in relative autonomy, largely cut off from the outside world. In the words of the Lebanese historian Habib Kourani, the Lebanon Mountains became the 'land of non-conformists of all ages and religions'.[13]

Whenever the central authorities felt the *de facto* autonomy of these non-conformists had got out of hand — when tax-payments were in arrears or important arteries threatened — they cracked down. At the turn of the thirteenth century the Mameluke governors launched several punitive expeditions against the Shi`is of Kisrawan, eventually expelling them from this region. In the sixteenth century the recently established Ottoman rulers undertook several military campaigns against Druze in the Chouf mountains. Regardless of the freedom the mountain inhabitants had in running their own affairs, they could not challenge the central authority of the Sunni Islamic empires with impunity, least of all the obligation to pay taxes and tribute.

The Ottoman Empire practised two different forms of dominion in different parts of the empire. The common form was direct rule. Ottoman governors ruled an area with the support of the army and a civil administration. The ancient Muslim system of 'wardship' was expanded into the 'millet system'.[14] A millet was a non-Muslim nation that recognized the sovereignty of the state but administered its own affairs. Millets chose their own leaders, but they had to be confirmed by the Sultan. Millets were not organized by territory but by personal membership of a religious community, regardless of where the people concerned

---

[13] Habib Kourani, 'Lebanon, Educational Reform', *Yearbook of Education* (London, 1949).

[14] S. Benjamin Braude and Bernard Lewis, eds., *Christians and Jews in the Ottoman Empire: The functioning of a plural society* (2 vols., New York and London, 1982); Karl Binswanger, *Untersuchungen zum Status der Nichtmuslime im Osmanischen Reich des 16. Jahrhunderts. Mit einer Neudefinition des Begriffs 'Dimma'* (Munich, 1977).

lived. Christians and Jews in the Ottoman Empire were, like Muslims, subject to the Ottoman authorities in all fiscal and criminal matters . But in all matters concerning marriage, inheritance, education and religion responsibility resided in the authorities of their respective religious community. This quasi-autonomy meant that for Christians and Jews, Ottoman rule was semi-indirect rule.

In a number of remote areas inhabited by autonomous peoples, in particular in mountainous regions, the Ottoman Empire limited its authority to indirect rule. Whether for lack of interest in direct control or because of the costs of establishing it, loyal leaders were given judicial and fiscal powers and duties. As a rule, the decisive measure for each governor was the tax-revenues. As in the rest of the empire, fiscal administration was farmed out: the tax-farmer undertook to pay the authorities a specific sum; what he collected in excess of this was his own income. In areas under indirect rule, though, the tax-farmer was not only responsible for certain aspects of public order, but also, and above all, for the administration of larger areas, which he could depute to sub-farmers. In all areas these rights and duties were generally granted for only one year, and could be renewed or withdrawn. In this manner the governor could ensure the loyalty of the tax-farmers or, if he was dissatisfied or displeased, acquire the services of others. It was a highly pragmatic system of indirect control which ensured the state a steady income at little cost.

During the time of the empire, the area of present-day Lebanon was under the jurisdiction of governors, or their subordinates, residing in either Damascus, Sidon or Tripoli and, later, Beirut. Direct rule was, for the most part, restricted to the coastal cities. The Maronites, Druze and Shi`is in the mountains were under indirect rule: they had to pay taxes, but were otherwise left in peace. From the mid-sixteenth century onwards a political and social system developed in the mountains, which, by misleading analogy with medieval Europe, is frequently termed 'feudal'. The system was not based on the ownership of land but on the right to collect taxes.[15] The tax-farmers were members of leading Druze and later Sunni and Maronite families; they depended on heads of other families to collect the taxes at the local level. These offices often remained in the respective families, so that a stratum of notables gradually developed. These prominent families used their income to extend their landholdings, often to a size which allowed them to lease out land for cash or, more usually, a share of the harvest. However, the offices were never hereditary, and their holders did not constitute a hereditary

---

[15] See the classic study of Dominique Chevallier, *La société du Mont Liban a l'époque de la revolution industrielle en Europe* (Paris, 1971), in particular pp. 80ff; see also Zvi Yehuda Hershlag, *Introduction to the Modern Economic History of the Middle East* (Leiden, 1964), pp. 9ff and Toufic Touma, *Paysans et institutions féodales chez les druzes et les maronites du Liban du XVIIème siècle à 1914* (Beirut, 1971).

# The Lebanese Model

nobility. Their influence derived from their function. Whether they retained this influence depended on whether they were able to raise the tax revenues required of them without alienating the taxpayers.

'Politics' in the seventeeth and eighteenth centuries in the Lebanon Mountains consisted chiefly of attempts by the tax-farmers to extend their areas of office and secure it for their families, and of similar attempts by tax-collectors in the individual regions to secure their prominence.

The first to include the whole of present-day Lebanon — and areas beyond — within his area of office was the Druze Prince Fakhr al-Din II (1590-1635).[16] He titled himself 'Emir of the Mountains' and tried, for a time successfully, to rule as an independent monarch. He opened the country to European trade and concluded a treaty with the Medici in Florence, created a standing army and erected fortresses. The Ottoman authorities felt he had grown too powerful and sent him into exile, but allowed him to return after a few years. When he again tried to extend his sphere of influence they sent in an army, and captured and executed him. However, the Ottoman authorities let his family, the Maan, retain the office of chief tax-farmer in the immediate environment of the mountains until they died out in 1697. Their successors until 1840 were emirs of the Chehab family. The most significant of them was Bashir II, who, like Fakhr al-Din, extended the area of his office to include the coastal strip and the Bekaa. Once again, the Ottomans disapproved and forced him into exile in 1821. Thus, during the periods of office of the Maan and Chehab families the autonomy of the Mountains was relative.[17] It included local administration, policing and jurisdiction. An independent foreign policy and, above all, a policy of expansion beyond the Mountains were not tolerated. Finally, the fiscal authority of the empire was never questioned.

The age of the emirs was characterized by several developments that were to prove momentous for the future political and social development of Lebanon. The families of tax-collecting notables gradually secured their position; the emirs had to take their counsel to ensure their collaboration. A number of these families still play a role in present-day politics. The notables exercised their office in specific territories; as officials, their religious affiliation was immaterial to themselves, the taxpayers and other people. The principle of *cuius regio, eius religio* was unknown, indeed, if anything, the contrary applied: in a number of cases the notables converted to the religion of the local people; the Druze Abi-Lama and

---

[16] The rest of this historical synopsis is based principally on the following literature: Philip Hitti, *Lebanon in History: From the earliest times to the present*, 3rd edn (London, 1967); Adel Ismail, *Histoire du Liban du XVIIème siècle à nos jours* (2 vols., Paris, 1955); Kamal S. Salibi, *The Modern History of Lebanon* (reprinted London, 1977); and *A House of Many Mansions*. Accordingly, footnotes will not be given for individual facts, dates and names in Lebanese history.

[17] Salibi, *A House of Many Mansions*, p. 109.

Sunni Chehab families became Maronites. However, these conversions are only symptoms of what may be taken as the most important development in this period, the social and political advancement of the Maronites.

Like the Druze and Shi`is, the Maronites had a tribe-like social structure: extended families and clans were the decisive social units. The particular distinction of the Maronites was an organized Church, and a Church with international connections.[18] As early as the Crusades the Maronites had established — or, in their view, restored — union with the Latin Church. With the collapse of the Latin kingdoms contact lapsed. After the fall of Constantinople in 1453 and especially with the Roman counter-reformation, Catholic Europe took renewed interest in the only Oriental Church that wished to remain in both doctrinal and hierarchical union with Rome. Franciscans and Jesuits were despatched to Lebanon and Maronite clergy went to Rome for education. In 1582 Gregory XIII founded the Maronite College in Rome.[19] Its graduates founded numerous schools in Lebanon, the beginnings of a spectacular expansion in education.[20] In 1596 the first Maronite synod, in Qannoubin, decided to reorganize and modernize the local Church. By 1736 there had been so much progress that the synod of Louweize made it local church law for every parish to maintain a school. In addition, Maronite Jesuits established Maronite colleges in Kisrawan, at Aintoura in 1734 and Ain Waraqa in 1774, the latter of which evolved into a university. Educational improvements went hand in hand with demographic and economic expansion. Originally settled in the extreme north of the Lebanon Mountains, the Maronites gradually expanded southwards. In the sixteenth century they settled in Kisrawan, from which the Mamelukes had expelled the Shi`is. From the time of Fakhr al-Din Maan onwards they were invited by Druze notables to settle in the Chouf. The emirs had become aware that numerous European firms were interested in the silk trade and consequently promoted silk production, but did not have enough labour among their own peasantry. Druze notables donated land to Maronite monasteries on condition that they recruited peasants from the north to work in silk production. The silk trade generated a number of other economic activities in intermediate trade, commissions, transport and finance, most of which were run by Maronites.

---

[18] See Iliya F. Harik, *Politics and Change in a Traditional Society: Lebanon, 1711–1845* (Princeton, 1968).

[19] See Pierre Raphael, *Le rôle du Collège Maronite Romain dans l'orientalisme aux XVIIème et XVIIIème siècles* (Beirut, 1950).

[20] For details see Theodor Hanf, *Erziehungswesen in Gesellschaft und Politik des Libanon* (Bielefeld, 1969), pp. 62ff.

## The Lebanese Model

In the course of the eighteenth century other Christian communities settled in Lebanon. In 1724 a section of the Melchite community[21] united with Rome and in 1740 a section of the Armenian community did so too. In northern Syria, in particular, these groups, henceforth known as 'Greek Catholics' and 'Armenian Catholics', met with so much enmity and persecution at the hands of their 'orthodox' brethren that many of them fled to Lebanon.

All 'Catholic' communities, that is, those in union with Rome, especially the Maronites, received encouragement and support not only from the Roman Church but also from the French state.[22] The Capitulations,[23] drawn up with the Ottoman Empire in 1740, gave France the right to intervene in favour of Catholic subjects of the empire. Under French protection numerous Christian orders began to open modern schools in Lebanon, thereby augmenting the already considerable educational efforts of the local communities.

By the late eighteenth century, the Maronites were a self-assured, ambitious, successful community, a 'unique success story in the annals of the Christians in the Muslim world'.[24] However, the two most important factors for this success — inner dynamism and foreign influence — were to cause convulsions in political and social relations in the Lebanon Mountains during the nineteenth century.

Foreign powers took note of, and began to use, the juxtaposition of the religious communities to increase their influence in the Ottoman Empire.[25] France maintained close relations with the Maronites; Russia took the Greek Orthodox, those Melchites not in union with Rome, under its wing; Austria-Hungary the Greek Catholics in union with Rome, and Great Britain tried to gain influence among the Druze. The opportunity for direct intervention was the struggle between the Viceroy of Egypt, Muhammad Ali, and the Ottoman authorities in the 1830s. France encouraged Egypt, while Russia, Austria and, especially, Great Britain supported the Sublime Porte. This international conflict caused the first severe tension between the Maronites and Druze in the Lebanon Mountains. Emir Bashir II Chehab sided with Egypt, while the Druze leaders remained loyal to the Sublime Porte. Initially, the Egyptian troops under Ibrahim Pasha were victorious, occupying all of Syria and invading Anatolia. Ibrahim was a reformer.[26] He

---

[21] See Cyrille Charon, *Histoires des patriarcats melkites* (2 vols., Rome, 1910–11).

[22] For details René Ristelhueber, *Les traditions françaises au Liban* (Paris, 1918); François Charles-Roux, *La France et les chrétiens d'Orient* (Paris, 1939).

[23] Basile Homsy, *Les capitulations et la protection des chrétiens au Proche-Orient* (Paris, 1956).

[24] Salibi, *A House of Many Mansions*, p. 106.

[25] See Alfred Schlicht, 'The role of Foreign Powers in the History of Lebanon and Syria from 1799 to 1861', *Journal of Asian History*, 14/2 (1980), pp. 97–126; Joseph Hajjar, *L'Europe et les destinées du Proche-Orient (1815–1848)* (Paris, 1970).

[26] For details see Samir Khalaf, *Persistence and Change in 19th Century Lebanon* (Beirut, 1979), pp. 45ff.

brought in efficient administration and abolished all regulations that discriminated against non-Muslims: for the first time Christians enjoyed the same rights as Muslims. They also had the same duties, including military service. High taxes to finance the war and, above all, widespread recruitment caused the people to turn against Ibrahim Pasha and, in the Lebanon Mountains, his supporter, Emir Bashir. In 1838 the Druze in the Syrian Hauran and in southern Lebanon rose against Egyptian rule. Ibrahim Pasha crushed the insurrection with — a fateful step for future relations between the Lebanese communities — the aid of Maronite troops. The consequent repressions worsened the situation. Numerous Druze notables had to go into exile and were forced to sell land in the Chouf to Christians. The almost wholly peaceful coexistence in the southern Lebanon Mountains was henceforth clouded by growing Druze bitterness.

Discontent with Ibrahim as well as Bashir spread not only among the Druze but also among the Shi`is and a section of the Christians. The decisive turn came once again through foreign intervention. In 1840 Egypt wanted to force a treaty on the Sublime Porte which gave Egypt control over Syria. However, the European powers, with the exception of France, disapproved. British and Austrian warships bombarded Beirut and landed troops in Jounieh, which were reinforced by Turkish units. In October 1840 the Egyptian Army met with a crushing defeat and retreated. Bashir II was exiled to Malta.

The Sublime Porte named another Chehab, Bashir III, as successor. However, he was unable to restore calm in the mountains. Although in the final phase of Egyptian rule Christians and Muslims, notables and peasants were united in their rejection of a regime that had heavily burdened the country with taxes and conscription, the end of the regime did not remove the tension which had emerged between the communities. The Druze notables returning from exile demanded restitution of land that had been sold under coercion or confiscated, and of their status quo ante. Many Maronites, not least the clergy, influenced by European republican ideas and impressed by the efficiency of the Egyptian administration, rejected a return to the former system, demanding instead the abolition of 'feudal privileges'. They wanted not only to prevent the restoration of the Druze notables but also to deprive incumbent Christian notables of their power. But as the immediate concern was the power of the deposed Druze notables, the ensuing clashes were not between notables and their opponents but between Druze and Maronites. In 1841 armed Druze attacked the mainly Maronite town of Deir al-Qamar in the Chouf and the Greek Catholic town Zahle. Zahle, with Shi`i support from the Bekaa, withstood the attack, Deir al-Qamar fell to the Druze, who took Bashir III captive in his palace at Beit Eddine. At this point the Ottoman authorities intervened. They deposed Bashir III and sent him into exile, abolished the emirate and appointed a non-Lebanese governor. The consequence of a few years of Maronite-Druze strife was the end of indirect Ottoman rule and the end of almost a quarter of a millennium of relative autonomy in the Lebanon Mountains.

Yet neither the communities living in the Lebanon Mountains nor the Great Powers who had engineered Ibrahim Pasha's defeat were satisfied with this solution. As a result of internal resistance, as well as European intervention, the Sublime Porte accepted a proposal by Metternich: the creation of two autonomous districts in the mountains, the northern to have a Maronite governor and the southern a Druze. But this settled little. The northern district contained many Druze, the southern a majority of Christians. By 1845 unrest in both districts had taken on shades of civil war. Once again the great powers negotiated with the Ottoman government, whose foreign minister, Chakib Effendi, devised a new *Règlement*: the governors of the two districts were to be advised by a council composed of five members, one each from the Sunni, Maronite, Druze, Greek Orthodox and Greek Catholic communities. As the Ottoman authorities did not recognize the Shi`is they were to be represented by the Sunnis. The *Règlement Chakib Effendi* was to have far-reaching consequences. For the first time in the history of the Mountains an institution was created based on a formal representation of the religious communities.

As the two councils were accorded powers to set and collect taxes, the *Règlement* undermined the traditional position of the notables, whose power derived from their function as tax-collectors. The Maronite clergy, most of whom were from the land, supported the candidacies of like people against those of the notables and large landowners. The election of Boulos Massad as Patriarch, the first patriarch not to come from a family of notables, strengthened this tendency. A new stratum of political leaders emerged, one which organized the farmers and peasants, demanded fairer apportionment of the harvests and, finally, a redistribution of land. In 1858 an uprising in the northern district, especially in Kisrawan, developed into a peasants' revolt.[27] They chased the governor out of the region and the notables out of office; many landowners were dispossessed and their lands divided among the peasants. In 1859 the revolt spread to the southern district, where Maronite peasants and farm labourers rose against Druze notables and landowners. Whereas in Kisrawan the uprising was a social revolution of Maronites against Maronites, in the south the Druze notables were able to deflect it into confessional warfare. The Maronite peasants of Kisrawan and the Chouf had originally come from the north of the country and had few or no traditional

---

[27] For details see Malcolm H. Kerr, *Lebanon in the Last Years of Feudalism: 1840–1868* (Beirut, 1959) (annotated translation of a contemporary account by Antun Hakir al-Aquigui and other documents); Yehoshua Porat, 'The Peasant Revolt of 1858–61 in Kisrawan', *Asian and African Studies*, 2 (1966), pp. 77–157; V. Lutsky, *Modern History of the Arab Countries* (Moscow, 1969), pp. 126–39; Gustav-Adolf Kriener, *Geschichte der Evangelischen Gemeinde zu Beirut* (Beirut, 1958), pp. 15–20.

ties with the notables. By contrast, the traditional extended families and clans of the Druze peasants and farm labourers were still intact. They may have had to suffer under their notables — but at the same time these were their sheikhs and tribal leaders.[28] These traditional ties proved to be stronger than their common economic interests with the Maronite peasants. What began as a social revolution became a war between Maronites and Druze in the south and ended as a general war of religion. Sunnis and Shi`is sided with the Druze; both Melchite communities sided with the Maronites. Fighting took place not only in the mountains but also in the Bekaa and in the south of the country. In the northern section of the mountains the Christian peasants were able to defend their revolution. In the south and the Bekaa the Druze, often supported by Ottoman garrisons, were victorious and massacres took place among the Christian population.[29] The spark of religious war jumped even to Damascus: Muslims, angry about the equality Christians had enjoyed since the time of Ibrahim Pasha, an equality reaffirmed by the Ottoman reforms of 1856,[30] as well as the economic rise of the Christians, plundered the Christian quarters of the city and murdered thousands of inhabitants. These events prompted France to intervene, with the approval of Great Britain, Prussia, Austria–Hungary and Italy.[31] The arrival of French troops was the salvation of the surviving Christians outside the northern district. The events of 1860 turned the cleavages between the religious communities into the pre-eminent factor of social and political life in Lebanon. Mistrust, fear and hate coloured attitudes on both sides. It was, above all, the fear of a repetition of these events that encouraged the Christian communities increasingly to look to the European powers for support.

In 1861 these powers negotiated a political reorganization with the Sublime Porte: the Ottoman authorities would create an autonomous governorate of 'Mount Lebanon' — the area of the Lebanon Mountains and the coastal strip both north and south of Beirut, though excluding the city — and the powers would

---

[28] 'Les Druzes étaient toujours dirigés par leurs notables, alors que les chrétiens étaient dirigés par des représentants élus, encouragés par principes égalitaires'; Boutros Labaki, 'Rapports de force intercommunautaires et genèse des conflits internes au Liban', paper presented at the annual meeting of the European Consortium for Political Research, Freiburg im Breisgau, 1983, p. 10

[29] Khalaf, *Persistence and Change*, pp. 64ff.

[30] Karl Marx, incensed about the turn the social revolution had taken, wrote on August 25th, 1860: 'Has Europe relinquished its privilege to protect its brothers in faith? It has relinquished it, if it ever reckoned with the implementation of the Hatt-i-Humajun of 18th February, if it ever believed that promised reforms are the same thing as implemented reforms ... This uprising was inevitable when one considers that the Christians' situation has not improved, but, on the contrary, worsened.' Karl Marx and Friedrich Engels, *Werke* (Berlin, 1961), vol. 15, pp. 148f.

[31] For details see Selim Baz, ed., *Pièces diplomatiques: Relations aux événements de 1860 au Liban*, 2nd edn (Beirut, 1978).

guarantee its autonomy.[32] A Christian, though not Lebanese, governor of 'Mount Lebanon' was appointed and an Administrative Council established, comprising representatives of all religious communities. Initially, all the communities, regardless of their numerical strength, had equal representation in the council. However, in 1864 a system of approximately proportional representation was introduced.[33] This was a fundamental change: instead of representation by community — which accorded equal political say in principal — representation would henceforth be tempered by demography. The political momentousness of this change would become apparent only very much later.

The successes of the social revolution were legalized. The privileges of the notability were abolished: salaried civil servants were put in charge of fiscal matters. The level of taxation was set by the Administrative Council, whose members were indirectly elected. The Council's budgetary powers were a source of recurrent friction between it and the governor, marking the first steps in what was to become a strong tradition of parliamentary democracy. A series of competent governors created a competent civil service: until the First World War Mount Lebanon was one of the best-administered provinces of the Ottoman Empire.

The country was opened to further western cultural influences. Numerous foreign schools were founded. The Syrian Protestant College (later the American University of Beirut) and the Jesuit Saint Joseph's University soon became the leading universities of the Near East.[34] Civil liberties in Mount Lebanon attracted writers and literati from the whole region: the *nahda*, the renaissance of the Arabic language and literature, started in the Beirut of Mount Lebanon.[35] Despite all reform, the multi-communal Ottoman state retained its theocratic character. Expressions of liberal and secular governance gradually crystallized in opposition to this: a Lebanese nationalism appeared as well as Greater Syrian and Arab versions.[36]

---

[32] On the following see Khalaf, *Persistence and Chance*, pp. 83–121; the most instructive study of this period is John P. Spagnolo, *France and Ottoman Lebanon, 1861–1914* (London, 1977).

[33] Four Maronites, three Druze, two Greek Orthodox, one Greek Catholic, one Sunni and one Shi'i respectively. John P. Spagnolo, *France and Ottoman Lebanon*, pp. 89f, comments: 'The final outcome ... was a constitutional system which proved to be of fundamental importance in shaping the political life of Mount Lebanon for decades to come. A guarantee for the preservation of the political viability of each sect, irrespective of numbers, was combined with the recognition of a hierarchy of importance according to numerical and socio-economic strength'. See also John S. Spagnolo, 'Constitutional Change in Mount Lebanon: 1861–1864', *Middle Eastern Studies*, 7/1 (1971), pp. 25–48.

[34] See Hanf, *Erziehungswesen*, pp. 66ff.

[35] See Albert Hourani, *Arabic Thought in the Liberal Age 1798–1939* (London, 1962); Carl Brockelmann, *Geschichte der arabischen Literatur* (Leiden, 1942), p. 420.

[36] George Antonius, *The Arab Awakening* (New York, 1946).

The economic and social development of Mount Lebanon was less rosy. The legalization of the social revolution recognized and furthered the emergence of a class of small landholders in one section of the Lebanon Mountains, which was unique in the Near East. However, improvements in education and hygiene led to a rapid increase in the population and a growing scarcity of land. To survive, farmers had to produce increasingly for export. Silkworm breeding became a monoculture. Half of the working population was employed in the silk sector, which accounted for 60 per cent of all production. Yet the dominance of French capital in this sector ensured that only 15 per cent of the raw silk was processed locally: exports were overwhelmingly in the form of raw material and semi-processed goods.[37] The development of local manufacturing was hampered by low tariffs and import privileges that the heavily indebted Ottoman Empire had had to grant the European states. The harmful effects culminated in the collapse in the price of raw silk in the 1880s, largely as a consequence of increased Japanese production.[38] The subsequent lengthy depression accelerated rural emigration: it is estimated that between 1861 and 1914 about one-third of the inhabitants of Mount Lebanon emigrated.[39] This ameliorated the consequences of the economic crisis; and the emigrants' remittances helped support their families at home. But besides impoverished farmers, numerous qualified people also left: doctors, engineers, architects, businessmen and journalists. The main beneficiary of this 'brain drain' was Egypt, whose modernization policies offered qualified immigrants enormous opportunities.[40]

Notwithstanding the depression, there was considerable economic progress in Mount Lebanon prior to the First World War. Beirut and Damascus were connected by road and rail and Beirut harbour — though not within the autonomous territory — was modernized. These improvements laid the groundwork for Lebanon's future as a centre of entrepôt trade. Although governed separately, political and social ties between Beirut and Mount Lebanon were so close that Beirut became *de facto* the capital of the autonomous province.[41] Its population increased rapidly, partly due to the influx of Christian refugees from the Chouf and, after the events of 1860, from Damascus. Whereas at the beginning of the

---

[37] For details see Boutros Labaki, *Introduction à l'histoire économique du Liban: Soie et commerce extérieur en fin de la période ottomane (1840–1914)* (Beirut, 1984).

[38] See Paul Saba, 'The Creation of the Lebanese Economy: Economic growth in the nineteenth and early twentieth centuries', in Roger Owen, ed., *Essays on the Crisis in Lebanon* (London, 1976), pp. 1–22.

[39] See Elie Safa, *L'émigration libanaise* (Beirut, 1960); Riad Younès, *Die libanesische internationale Migrationsbewegung: Eine Literaturstudie* (Freiburg, 1976).

[40] Hitti, *Lebanon in History*, p. 474.

[41] For details see Leila Tarazi Fawaz, *Merchants and Migrants in Nineteenth-Century Beirut* (Cambridge and London, 1983).

# The Lebanese Model

nineteenth century Beirut had had only 6,000 inhabitants, by 1861 it had 46,000 and in 1914 approximately 200,000. Its infrastructure grew apace: drinking water, gas street-lighting, trams, postal and telegraphic services. Numerous hospitals, schools, printing and publishing houses were established. In particular, the city became the seat of a growing number of manufacturing and trading companies. In contrast to other Oriental countries, most of these businesses were owned not by foreigners but by locals. High profit margins[42] enabled the formation of a new stratum of prosperous entrepreneurs. The majority of them were Christian,[43] in particular Greek Orthodox and Greek Catholic. Social distinctions began to colour relations between the religious communities, although there was still no difference at all in the standards of living of farmers and workers[44] of different denominations. Outward appearances underlined these social distinctions. Within a short time the new business class adopted European clothes and a wholly European lifestyle, soon copied by the Christian petty bourgeoisie, civil servants and traders. The Muslim bourgeoisie of Beirut behaved similarly, though with caution and discretion.

The numerous reports of gangsterism and thuggery between Christians and Muslims in Beirut after the turn of the century may well have reflected cultural irritations as well as social distinctions. However, in contrast to earlier — and later — periods, leading citizens of both religions acted to prevent these incidents escalating into open hostilities.

The First World War heralded the dismemberment of the Ottoman Empire, one of whose consequences was the creation of the Lebanese Republic within its existing borders.[45] Few regretted the departure of the Ottoman governors. In 1914 the autonomy of Mount Lebanon was suspended and the province placed under military rule. The war years were years of hunger, and of repression: literary circles and political societies in Beirut and the mountains, that had been making plans for the future of the Arab Orient, were brutally suppressed and many of their

---

[42] Labaki, *Introduction à l'histoire économique*, p. 371, calculates a margin of 37 per cent in the silk industry.

[43] See Labaki, 'Rapports de force', p. 14. By population, Christians were heavily over-represented in banking, silk-exporting and commerce. Virtually all general practitioners and pharmacists were Christians.

[44] Admittedly, 80 per cent of the working class was Christian (1912), with a markedly high proportion of Greek Orthodox and Greek Catholics; these two communities played a key role at all social and income levels of the modern economic sector.

[45] On this period see Stephen H. Longrigg, *Syria and Lebanon under French Mandate* (London, 1958); Eugénie E. Abouchidid, *Thirty Years of Lebanon and Syria (1917–1947)* (Beirut, 1948); Albert Hourani, *Syria and Lebanon: A political essay*, 3rd edn (London, 1954); Nicola Abdo Ziadeh, *Syria and Lebanon* (Beirut, 1968); Walter Z. Laqueur, *Communism and Nationalism in the Middle East* (London, 1956).

leading members were hanged in 1915 and 1916.[46] When French troops entered Beirut in 1919 the debate reopened with renewed intensity.[47] It concentrated on three mutually exclusive conceptions: Arab unity, a Greater Syrian state and an independent Lebanon. After the Emir Faisal entered Damascus, a united Arab kingdom under his rule seemed imminent. He had the support of Muslim political circles as well as some Greek Orthodox notables. Proponents of a Greater Syria were primarily secularly oriented intellectuals.[48] This state would have included present-day Syria, Lebanon and Palestine, but not the Hejaz. They rejected King Faisal because they felt progressive Syrian opinion would not accept a Bedouin ruler. However, precisely because of its secular character, this concept found support only among minorities in different communities. The idea of an 'independent Lebanon' received strongest support from the members of the Administrative Council of pre-war Mount Lebanon and also from the Maronite hierarchy, in other words, from among comparatively well-organized political forces. There were two schools of thought among these Lebanese nationalists. One wanted an independent state that consisted essentially of Mount Lebanon and Beirut, the other a 'Greater Lebanon' to include all the areas once ruled by Fakhr al-Din and Bashir II, that is, within what they now termed the 'historic' borders. This state would include not only the Lebanon Mountains and Beirut, but Tripoli and the Akkar plain in the north, the entire Bekaa and the Jabal Amel — the present South Lebanon.[49] The former school argued that a smaller state with a broad Christian majority would better serve the interests of the Christian communities, while the latter believed that the Christians — especially the Maronites — were strong enough to imprint their stamp on a larger state. The second school won the support of the Maronites and subsequently that of the French government, which initially had vacillated between the two. France did not want an independent kingdom under Faisal under any condition, and as the majority of the Maronites 'were the only people who knew exactly what they wanted',[50] they persuaded the French.[51] After the League of Nations had given

---

[46] See Nagib Dahdah, *Evolution historique du Liban*, 3rd edn (Beirut, 1967), pp. 225ff.

[47] For details Meir Zamir, *The Formation of Modern Lebanon* (London, 1985), pp. 38ff.

[48] Its champions were Shukri Ghanem and George Samné, both strongly influenced by the writings of the Belgian Jesuit Henri Lammens. See George Samné, *La Syrie*, with a preface by Chekri Ganem, Paris 1920, and H. Lammens, *L'évolution historique de la nationalité syrienne* (Alexandria, 1919). The idea of a Greater Syria found much support among leading intellectuals in the Syrian and Lebanese colonies in Egypt.

[49] The idea of a 'Greater Lebanon' had been actively propagated since the turn of the century by groups of Lebanese emigrants in Paris, New York and Cairo. During the war years they lobbied the respective governments with great efficiency.

[50] Salibi, *A House of Many Mansions*, p. 25.

France the mandate over Syria and Lebanon, General Gouraud proclaimed the creation of 'Greater Lebanon' on September 1st, 1920.

The Lebanese nationalists would have preferred immediate independence; but Greater Lebanon under mandate with the promise of independence[52] was better than no Greater Lebanon at all. For the Maronites, the new state was the culmination of their long search for liberty and independence. The French mandate was an unwelcome but acceptable stage before their destination.

For the majority of the Lebanese Muslims, however, inclusion in the new state coupled with French suzerainty — was 'a veritable trauma'.[53] After centuries of weakening it, reducing it to economic dependence and interfering directly in its governance, the European powers had finally shattered the last great Islamic state. As Arab Muslims, they had not always been happy with Turkish pre-eminence in this state; they would have preferred a federation under Ottoman rule, or better still a new Arab Islamic state, and a minority would even have preferred a secular Greater Arabia or at least an Arab Greater Syria. What they did not want on any account was a Lebanese state in which they — for the first time in their history — were no longer part of the ruling group but at worst the minority, at best one minority among others. The French mandate, by wounding their self-esteem, added insult to injury.

Initially they resisted. In South Lebanon in particular they attacked Christian villages until French punitive expeditions stopped them.[54] Civil resistance[55] lasted longer. Numerous Muslims refused to accept the designation 'Lebanese' in their identity papers. Muslims boycotted the census of 1921 and the elections for the Advisery Council in 1922 and 1925. In 1923, 1926, 1928 and 1936 their notables — muftis, judges, mayors, leading businessmen and landowners — held

---

[51] A delegation of Maronite prelates to the Paris Peace Conference, under the leadership of Patriarch Elias Hoyek, tipped the scales. Hayek negotiated on behalf and in the name of the Administrative Council.

[52] Article 22 of the Covenant of the League of Nations distinguished between three forms of mandate. So-called C mandates (South West Africa and some territories in the South Pacific) could be administered by the mandatories as parts of their own territory. B mandates (Togo, Cameroon, former German East Africa) could be administered as colonies but under supervision of the League of Nations. A mandates were a class instituted for the successor states to the Ottoman Empire: 'Certain communities formerly belonging to the Turkish Empire have reached a stage of development where their existence as independent nations can be provisionally recognized subject to the rendering of administrative advice and assistance by a Mandatory until such time as they are able to stand alone. The wishes of these communities must be a principal consideration in the selection of the Mandatory'; Great Britain, The Covenant of the League of Nations (HMSO, London, 1935).

[53] Salim Nasr, 'L'Islam politique et l'Etat libanais (1920–1975)', in Olivier Carré, ed., *L'Islam et l'état dans le monde d'aujourd'hui* (Paris, 1982), p. 33

[54] These villages were to provide the core of the militia commanded by Major Haddad and later by General Lahad that has cooperated with Israel since 1978.

[55] For details see Nasr, 'L'Islam politique', pp. 34f.

congresses in which, quoting the right of self-determination, they demanded unification with Syria. Graduates of Muslim schools and universities refused to enter the civil service so as to avoid collaboration with the authorities.

Hence, from its very foundation the new state was characterized by profound cleavages over the legitimacy of the state. Equally significant were the economic and social cleavages between the areas of the former Mount Lebanon and the other areas. Beirut already had close ties with its hinterland. By contrast, Tripoli and Sidon, two ports that catered to their Syrian hinterland, felt marginalized, the inhabitants of the Bekaa cut off from Damascus, those of South Lebanon from Haifa. Most of the small farmers in Mount Lebanon, especially in Christian areas, worked their own land, whereas the rural population in the new areas of the east and south were mostly tenants of large landowners. Since 1861 the Lebanon Mountains had had an excellent administration and been improving education rapidly. Until 1920, however, the north, south and east had been parts of peripheral and neglected Ottoman provinces, and state education was in its infancy.[56] Outside Beirut and the central mountain zone there was virtually no industry at all. Transport and infrastructure were incomparably better developed in Mount Lebanon. In short: socially and economically the new state was a classic case of the centre–periphery model.

The Christians, and especially the Maronites, had wanted Greater Lebanon. Now that it was there it was by no means certain that they would be able to form it as they wanted. In Mount Lebanon the Christians had constituted 85 per cent of the population, the Maronites alone 60 per cent. In Beirut the Christians had a two-thirds majority. But in the new areas together two-thirds of the population were Muslims. In Greater Lebanon as a whole the Christians formed a small majority, and this only on account of the influx of Armenian refugees from Cilicia in the early 1920s. Whereas the population of Mount Lebanon had comprised mainly Christians and Druze with a long mutual, albeit belligerent, history, Greater Lebanon had to face the problem of organizing coexistence between areas with very different histories, between two religious groups of approximately equal numbers, and several religious communities of which no single one had anything remotely like a majority.

In view of the complexity of this situation, the optimism and confidence with which the Christian leaders set about building the new state is remarkable. This had two roots. On the one hand, they trusted to their own modernity and

---

[56] At the outbreak of the First World War, there were only 125 state primary and three secondary schools in the Lebanese areas which had come later under direct Ottoman rule. The medium of instruction was not Arabic but Turkish. The pupils were mainly children of Ottoman civil servants and officers; a minority came from the then strongly Turkish-oriented Sunni upper stratum in the cities and towns. See Hanf, *Erziehungswesen*, p. 72.

## The Lebanese Model

dynamism, which had already turned Mount Lebanon into a model territory in the Orient; on the other hand, they had hopes of assistance from France as mandatory.[57] Long before the mandate period the Lebanese Christians had been open to European, and in particular French, cultural influences. French was already becoming their first foreign language. Many families were equally at ease in Arabic and French. This did not imply neglect of their oriental culture. On the contrary: leading authors of the Arab cultural renaissance in the nineteenth century had been bilingual,[58] and saw in European contact a challenge and stimulation for their own culture, and not, unlike many Muslims, a threat. 'Because the West is Christian, generally they do not regard it as alien. In fact, their feeling towards it is commonly one of affinity. Their tendency, on the whole, is to think of the culture of Europe as also being their own. Hence, when they Westernize, they do so without apology.'[59] For them modernization meant progress, not trauma. Acceptance of the republican ideal of equality had been an essential prerequisite for the peasants' revolt and the subsequent abolition of traditional privileges. The history of Mount Lebanon was proof that civil liberties made for a better life. On account of their nineteenth-century experiences, Lebanese Christians also saw the European powers as sources of security rather than oppression.

Although the Lebanese Christian leadership as a whole would have preferred immediate independence in 1920, they were thankful for assistance from France in building the new state. At the same time, they were self-assured enough to safeguard the peculiarities of the country and its institutions against French governors and officials not properly versed in the realities of oriental societies. The creation of a state machinery, an administrative and a judicial system on French lines was gladly accepted, as were a state-run educational system and the introduction of state curricula and examinations for the existing private schools and schools of the respective communities. But Lebanese politicians — against the Jacobin ideas of many French administrators of the mandate — did not want the fundamental rights of the communities that had evolved over centuries touched at all. At their insistence it was agreed in the negotiations on the mandate treaty that these rights would be respected.[60] However, the consequence was

---

[57] See Daniel Lerner, *The Passing of Traditional Society: Modernizing the Middle East* (Glencoe, 1958), pp. 170ff.

[58] Brockelmann, *Geschichte*, p. 420.

[59] Kamal S. Salibi, 'The Personality of Lebanon in Relation to the Modern World', in Leonard Binder, ed., *Politics in Lebanon* (New York, London and Sydney, 1966), pp. 266f.

[60] See Article 6 of the Mandate Treaty: 'The Mandatory shall establish ... a judicial system which shall ensure to natives as well as to foreigners the complete guarantee of their rights. Respect for the personal status of the various peoples and their religious interests shall be fully guaranteed'; 'The Mandate for Syria and Lebanon, 24th July 1922', *League of Nations Official Journal*, August 1922, cols. 1013–17.

equality for all communities: in 1926 the Shi`is, who had had the legal status of Sunnis under Ottoman rule, were recognized as a separate community.[61]

The most significant constitutional decisions of the mandate period feature compromises between centralistic Jacobin ideas and pragmatic acceptance of the political reality of a number of independent communities. The first of these, taken as early as 1922, established the electoral system for the Chamber of Deputies, the future parliament. The electoral law laid down that every representative would represent the nation as a whole, free of charge or condition. Yet it also determined that the seats were to be distributed in proportion to the numerical strength of the communities.[62] Thus, the delimitation of the constituencies determined the seats for specific communities, but the representatives were elected by all citizens entitled to vote, irrespective of community membership. The Chamber of Deputies, as a constituent assembly, voted unanimously to retain this system and presented its reasons in a report. Renunciation of proportional representation for the communities would destroy the equilibrium in the country and give some of them advantages at the expense of others, a potential cause of resentment and possibly unrest; parliament must mirror the physiognomy of the country, and this consists of communities with their own religious convictions, practices and traditions; in Lebanon communities took the place of political parties.[63] This electoral system was to have lasting repercussions.

The second significant decision was the promulgation of a Constitution for the Lebanese Republic, which, with some amendments, is still in force. In many respects it resembles that of the Third French Republic:[64] a parliamentary democracy with wide powers for the president.[65]

In Article 1 Lebanon is defined as a unitary state — shades of the 'république une et indivisible'. Probably uniquely among constitutions, the course of the country's frontiers is laid down in detail and the relinquishment of any territory within them is expressly forbidden: a profession of belief in Greater Lebanon. In contrast to the Jacobinistic definition of the state and the concentration of powers in the hands of the president, other articles guarantee the rights of the communi-

---

[61] Rondot, *Les institutions politiques*, p. 66.

[62] See decree no. 1307 of March 10th, 1922: 'Il est établi un quotient électoral qui s'obtient en divisant le total de la population électorale par le nombre des membres du conseil administratif à élire. Dans chaque municipe et Sandjak un siège au moins est attribué à tout rite comportant le quotient électoral ... Aucun rite ne peut avoir, pour l'ensemble des circonscriptions de l'Etat, ni plus ni moins de représentants que le nombre auquel lui donne droit le chiffre total de ses ressortissants dans l'Etat, divisé par le quotient électoral.'

[63] Report of the constitutional commission under the chairmanship of Chebl Dammous, quoted in Rondot, *Les institutions politiques*, p. 80.

[64] Various authors have pointed out similarities with the Egyptian and Belgian constitutions of the time.

[65] This and other aspects of Lebanese political institutions and politics will be treated in detail below.

ties. Article 9 guarantees not only freedom of conscience and the freedom of religion, but also gives communities the right to legislate on matters of civil status. Article 10 grants the communities the right to their own educational systems, subject to state supervision.

The Electoral Law as well as sections of the Constitution reflect the determination of the fathers of the Constitution to establish a Greater Lebanon, but also their willingness to respect the interests of all communities. As the political and administrative institutions consolidated, so the Muslims' solid rejection of the state began to crumble and they gradually edged towards *de facto* recognition. The majority of Muslims grasped the disadvantages accruing from their initial boycott of all public service and the consequent emergence of an overwhelmingly Christian civil service. And they also grasped that public policies could also serve their interests. The infrastructure and public services in the new areas were being improved and, indeed, enjoyed a certain priority.[66] This also applied to education. The state school system created during the mandate was planned along clear compensatory lines and, accordingly, benefited those areas most in which education had previously been neglected, that is, the peripheral areas. *De facto*, state schools became in the main schools for Muslims, who accounted for 80 per cent of the enrolment.

Another factor which contributed to the revision of Muslim attitudes towards the Lebanese state was the change in Arab nationalists' stance in the other newly created states in the Arab East.[67] The creation of a united Arab state was deferred until the withdrawal of mandatory powers had been effected and full independence attained. However, to achieve this for Lebanon presumed a consensus with the political forces of the Christian communities. Hence, increasingly, Lebanese Muslims began to weigh the opportunities active cooperation within the Lebanese state offered them.[68] In 1932 they took part in the census, which showed that the Christians' majority was very slight indeed. In the same year a Muslim stood for the presidency the first time. From 1934 onwards the Lebanese Muslims participated fully in politics: since then a Sunni has always held the premiership. The boycott of public services was also abandoned; henceforth, Muslims strove to occupy positions in proportion to their share of the population.

At the same time two antithetical tendencies polarized the Christian communities. The one, organized as the 'National Bloc' under the leadership of Emile Eddé, perpetuated the pre-1920 scepticism about Greater Lebanon, and regarded

---

[66] Nasr, 'L'Islam politique', p. 37.
[67] Ibid.
[68] See Najla Atiyah, 'The Attitude of the Lebanese Sunnis toward the State of Lebanon', Unpublished Ph.D. thesis, University of London, 1973.

Lebanon primarily as a homeland for Oriental Christians. By contrast, the other tendency, represented by the 'Destour' (Constitutional Party) under Beshara al-Khoury, sought the full collaboration with the Muslims in the new state, which they wanted to erect on the solid foundations of a broad Muslim-Christian alliance. Whereas the National Bloc wanted to prolong the mandate as long as possible, the Destour advocated early and full independence. It was above all the Christian and Muslim bourgeoisie in the cities who discovered that they had a lot in common. The Christian merchants were just as interested as the Muslim in trade with the Arabian hinterland, especially the states under British mandate, to which the French mandate was an obstacle. They had long collaborated in business; they now strove to cooperate in politics.

The last Muslim Congress to demand the union of the peripheral areas with Syria was held in 1936. In the same year the supporters of the three opposing forms of nationalism that had crystallized in the late nineteenth century organized themselves in three militant, uniformed organizations. Militant Lebanese nationalists formed the 'Kata'ib' or 'Phalanges Libanaises', militant Greater-Syrian nationalists the 'Syrian Social National Party' (SSNP, known in Lebanon as the Parti Populaire Syrien, or PPS) and militant Arab nationalists the *Najjadé*, but none of them was able to attract broad support. While they exercised, paraded through the streets and frequently — to slogans for their favoured dream — scuffled with the Senegalese troops of the mandatory power, intensive discussions and negotiations got underway in Beiruti town houses between notables, parliamentarians and *zu`ama* — popular political leaders — of the Sunni and Maronite communities. These discussions were often initiated by Greek Orthodox and Greek Catholic bankers and great merchants — representatives of communities and strata that had the greatest interest in a successful cooperation between Christians and Muslims. The essence was no more and no less than a grand 'historical compromise'[69]. The leading spokesmen were Riad Solh and Beshara al-Khoury, the most popular politicians of the Sunnis and Maronites respectively. Mediators and political brokers included Henri Pharaon and Michel Chiha, Greek Catholic and Chaldaean bankers respectively. Since the 1920s Chiha had been the principal spokesman of a school of thought that Boutros Labaki[70] has termed the 'Convivialists'. It sought coexistence between different groups in their diversity within a transcending unity, a type of syncretistic Lebanese nationalism.

Chiha,[71] one of the fathers of the constitution, felt that, given its people and its geography Lebanon had no other lot. 'La diversité est notre destin.' He held

---

[69] Nasr, 'L'Islam politique', p. 37.
[70] Labaki, 'Rapports de force'.
[71] See Michel Chiha, *Visage et présence du Liban* (Beirut, 1964).

coexistence to be imperative both internally and externally. Internally, coexistence could be successful only under a liberal state and externally only in close cooperation with the Arabs, above all Syria. To survive economically it was necessary to cooperate with other states and further polylingualism, while cultivating Lebanese-Arab culture. Lebanon could survive only if it traded, and not only in goods and services but also in ideas. And this was possible only if the country itself was a mine of ideas. A nationalism built on internal coexistence was the Lebanese form of 'collective self-love'.

His brother-in-law Pharaon puts these ideas in a nutshell: 'Perhaps it is true that not all our countrymen are Lebanese in their hearts, but sensible policies can ensure that they are Lebanese in their minds.'[72]

In 1943 such thoughts bore fruit in the form of Lebanon's 'historic compromise': the National Pact.

## The National Pact and proportionality

As the First World War was the death knell of the Ottoman Empire, so the Second World War brought the end of the mandate.[73] In June 1941 British and Free French troops occupied the mandated territories of Lebanon and Syria, supplanting the authorities loyal to the Vichy regime. Under British pressure General Catroux, De Gaulle's representative, proclaimed the independence of Lebanon on November 26th, 1941. However, the French authorities did what they could to postpone the proclamation from coming into force. In doing so, they unwittingly fostered among the Lebanese a degree of understanding and community that had not existed before. In the parliamentary elections in the summer of 1943 the political forces in favour of immediate independence won an overwhelming victory. Beshara al-Khoury was elected president and Riad Solh prime minister; the cabinet included representatives of the Maronites, Sunnis, Shi`is, Greek Orthodox, Greek Catholics and Druze. On November 8th, 1943, parliament unanimously passed a number of constitutional amendments, including the repeal of all articles referring to the mandate, and reaffirmed the independence of the country. The response of the French authorities was maladroit in the extreme: on November 11th, French marines and Senegalese troops arrested and incarcerated the president, the prime minister and three cabinet ministers. The reaction of the Lebanese was unanimous and vehement. The militant Lebanese and Arab

---

[72] Author's italics. Interview with the author, 1979.

[73] For the events surrounding independence see the memoirs of some of those involved: Camille Chamoun, *Crise au Moyen-Orient* (Paris, 1963); Bishara al-Khuri, *Haqa'iq lubnaniyya* (3 vols., Beirut, 1960); Georges Catroux, *Dans la bataille de le Méditerranée* (Paris, 1949); Georges Charaf, *Communautés et pouvoir au Liban* (Beirut, 1981), pp. 235–51.

nationalist organizations, Kata'ib and Najjadé, formed a joint commando, called a general strike, and demonstrated. Two cabinet ministers who had escaped arrest formed an emergency cabinet in the mountains; the members of parliament met in secret and declared that the national flag was no longer the Tricolour but the cedar of Lebanon on a red, white and red background. The Lebanese uprising together with British and American pressure forced the French government in Algiers to climb down. On November 22nd, 1943, Khoury, Solh and their co-prisoners were released and were greeted in Beirut with a frenzy of enthusiasm. Since then, November 22nd has been the country's national day. Upon their return to the capital, President Khoury and Premier Solh held a number of speeches and interviews in which they outlined the understanding on which their collaboration rested, and towards which they and colleagues had been working towards since 1936. This understanding, a gentlemen's agreement, has become known as the National Pact.[74]

The Pact comprises a number of mutual renunciations and guarantees, a compromise formulation on the identity of the country and on power-sharing between the religious communities. The Christians renounced the protection of western powers, the Muslims renounced union with Syria or other Arab states: Lebanon would be 'neither Eastern nor Western', but an independent country in its own right. It would retain its cultural and spiritual links with the West, but also collaborate closely with all Arab states, provided that they recognized Lebanese sovereignty; in intra-Arab conflicts Lebanon would remain neutral. It was defined as a country 'with Arab features and Arabic tongue', as a part of the Arab world, but with a 'special character'. All communities were to be included in the exercise of power, and the largest among them provide the highest dignitaries of the state: the Maronites the president, the Sunnis the prime minister.[75] Article 95 of the Constitution, as amended on November 8th, 1943, regulates the distribution of cabinet posts and positions in the public service: 'as a provisional measure, and in keeping with the desire for justice and harmony, the religious communities shall be adequately represented in the civil service and in the cabinet, provided that this does not harm the interests of the state'.

The Lebanese political scientist René Aggiouri, for many years one of the country's most influential political commentators, called the National Pact 'the unwritten expression of the will of the different Lebanese minorities to coexist within the structures of an independent and sovereign state'.[76] This will took

---

[74] See Fahim I. Qubain, *Crisis in Lebanon* (Washington, 1961), pp. 17f.

[75] Chamoun, *Crise au Moyen-Orient*, p. 118: 'La présidence de la République était dévolue aux chrétiens et la présidence du Conseil aux musulmans. En ce qui concerne la Chambre des Députés, tout le monde admet la proportion actuelle de six sièges chrétiens pour cinq sièges mahométans'.

[76] *L'Orient*, April 6th, 1957.

concrete form in a compromise that required concessions from all sides in crucial political questions. It is often referred to as the 'unwritten constitution' of Lebanon. In fact, it allows far less scope for politicking than the Constitution; as will be discussed below, much that is permitted under the Constitution cannot be reconciled with the principles of the National Pact. The Pact includes a definition of the country's character, guidelines for foreign policy and the fundamentals of power-sharing. Whereas the Constitution reflects the spirit of Jacobinism, and permits pure majority rule under a majority vote system, the combination of Constitution, Electoral Law and National Pact plainly made of Lebanon a consociation. The country is never governed by a simple majority, always by a grand coalition; in effect every large community has a right of veto; under Article 95 of the Constitution proportional representation applies to the executive and administration; Articles 9 and 10 guarantee the communities wide cultural autonomy. Although the Constitution permits other forms of government, the Pact institutionalized consociational democracy as constitutional reality: important decisions cannot be taken by simple majority; they require consensus and compromise.

The formulations in the Pact, themselves already compromises, allow broad scope for interpretation. Hence, politics in independent Lebanon became to a large extent disputes over the interpretation of the Pact, eventually questioning the Pact itself. From the start the link between the Pact and rigid proportionality in the executive and administration had been questionable and controversial. In politics the 'Pact' and 'proportionality' were frequently used as synonyms. Yet the fathers of the Pact, like those of the Constitution before them, had never intended this identity. In any case, it is proper to distinguish between them for analytical purposes. The fathers of the Pact agreed on the principle of general power-sharing. The practice of proportionality is considerably older than the Pact, going back, as seen, to 1864. Most of the those who were involved in the Pact have stated that it was generally understood that this practice, in agreement with the wording of the Constitution, would be provisional. Henri Pharaon, one of the principal negotiators is explicit: 'The Pact has been interpreted too rigidly. The confessional distribution of offices of state, let alone of civil service posts, was not intended to last for ever. It was thought of as provisional. It was not an essential element of the Pact. At the very least, it ought to be put into practice far more flexibly than it has been.'[77].

However, the political interests at play were not given to flexibility, and rigorous proportional representation was increasingly demanded. The communities came to regard not only offices of state, but positions in all ranks of the civil service as objects of patronage. Thus, every transfer and every promotion came to

---

[77] Interview with the author, May 10th, 1979.

involve politics. Whereas the Pact was a grand, indeed historical compromise, the linkage with rigid proportionality considerably restricted the scope for the small, daily compromises equally necessary if a system of consociation is to function.

It is remarkable that the National Pact does not mention social and economic matters. This may reflect the satisfactory economic situation during the Second World War, in contrast to the First World War. In the pre-war years Lebanese agriculture as well as industry had secured markets in the French Levant as well as beyond it. In the war years there was considerably less competition on the world markets and, in particular, a large decline in imports.[78] The Allied troops had to provision themselves locally, which involved huge expenditures. In consequence, Lebanese business prospered. The architects of the National Pact were drawn from these circles.[79] They took internal and external economic liberalism and a minimum of state intervention as a matter of course. As Michel Chiha points out, this implied 'legislative restraint and an administration that restricted itself to essential matters: a minimum of formality and the widest possible perspectives'.[80]

An even truer reflection of social circumstances at the time is the complete lack of any social perspective in the Pact. Consciously or unconsciously, demographic and social change was ignored. Much speaks for the view that it was the negotiators' intention to restrict themselves to certain fundamental principles, namely the affirmation of coexistence, the participation of all communities in the exercise of power and independence in close cooperation with the Arab world, and that it was their intention that these principles would be put into practice 'flexibly'. The most telling circumstantial evidence is the lack of any transcript. The history of independent Lebanon since then bears witness to the fact that the principles of the Pact are far less contentious than the rigid application of proportionality. Criticism of the Pact is mostly in connection with proportionality, either because the two are taken as identical or because it is believed that the latter cannot be changed without repealing the former.

As elsewhere, political argument in Lebanon concerns the distribution of political and economic power, and as in any multi-communal state, the definition of the state's identity, too. In Lebanon all these concerns take the form of arguments about the Pact and proportionality.

---

[78] See Boutros Labaki, 'L'économie politique du Liban indépendant 1943–1975', in Nadim Shehadi and Dana Haffar Mills, eds., *Lebanon: A History of Conflict and Consensus* (London, 1966), pp. 2f.

[79] On Christian entrepreneurs see Labaki, *Introduction à l'histoire économique*, pp. 46, 50, 55, 113–15; on Muslim entrepreneurs, ibid., pp. 392, 401–3; on the Muslim bourgeoisie see Michael Johnson, *Class and Client in Beirut: the Sunni Muslim Community and the Lebanese State 1840–1985* (London, 1986), in particular pp. 25f.

[80] Chiha, *Visage et présence*, p. 122.

## Parties, families and notables: Political interests in pre-war Lebanon

Who competed for political power in pre-war Lebanon? In liberal democracies political interests are usually represented by organized political parties; in Lebanon between 1943 and 1975 these played only a limited role.[81]

Three political parties are based on ideologies that reject community affiliation as a political criterion: the Communist Party of Lebanon (CP), the Syrian Social National Party (SSNP) and the Baath Party. Each combines various socio-political goals with a specific conception of nationality. Their adherents are drawn from different communities. The Lebanese CP, active since the mid-1920s, is the oldest of all Lebanese political parties.[82] Its popularity peaked when the Popular Front came to power in France in 1936, then again in the immediate post-war period, when it rode on the back of Soviet prestige in the Orient, and finally in the decade before the outbreak of war in Lebanon. Both during the mandate and after independence is was prohibited and then legalized several times. Compared to other Arab countries, even when illegal, the Communists in Lebanon enjoyed relatively unrestricted freedom of action; their newspaper, *an-Nida*, is the only Communist organ in the Orient that for decades was allowed to appear without interference. The CP was particularly active in the trade unions and has a solid basis in some federations of trade unions.[83]

During the mandate there had been a single party for Syria and Lebanon. In early 1944, after independence, a separate Lebanese CP was established. In 1959 it accepted the independence of the country, but retained its policy of solidarity with all Arab anti-imperialist efforts. Until the Communist Party of the USSR disbanded, the Lebanese CP was a faithful satellite. Many splinter-groups broke away. Since the early 1970s it has had to compete with the Organization for Communist Action in Lebanon (also known by its French initials, OACL), a formation of Arab nationalists who were attracted to Marxist ideas in the late 1960s and have since challenged the orthodox Communists for the support of the relatively few secularized Lebanese open to left-wing ideas.

---

[81] On Lebanese political parties see Lucien George and Toufic Mokdessi, *Les partis politiques* (Beirut, 1959); Labib Zuwiyya Yamak, 'Party politics in the Lebanese political system', in Binder, *Politics in Lebanon*, pp. 143–66; Michael W. Suleiman, *Political Parties in Lebanon* (Ithaca, N.Y., 1967).

[82] On the Lebanese CP see Laqueur, *Communism and Nationalism*, pp. 42ff, 117, 141–6, 161ff, 327–41; see also Jacques Couland, *Le mouvement syndical au Liban 1919–1946: son évolution pendant le mandat français de l'occupation à l'évaluation et au code travail* (Paris, 1970).

[83] The Communists have traditionally had strong union support among printers, builders and carpenters. Since the 1960s they have enjoyed considerable support among the intelligentsia.

Initially, the CP drew much of its support from recent Armenian immigrants, though later most of its members were native Lebanese. A disproportionate number of its leaders are Greek Orthodox. In the decade preceding the outbreak of war the CP had considerable success among Shi`i Lebanese. The recruiting pattern of the OACL is similar: the leadership is drawn from all communities, the mass of its members are Shi`i.

The Syrian Social Nationalist Party (SSNP) was founded in 1934 by Antoun Saadé, a Greek Orthodox teacher who had spent many years in Brazil. Upon his return he took a post as lecturer at the American University and began seeking support for the idea of a Greater Syrian nation. He attacked Pan-Arabism and Lebanese nationalism with equal vehemence: Arabism was a woolly concept, a guise for pan-Islamic hegemony, and Lebanese nationalism was essentially religious separatism. For Saadé, the Greater Syrian nation was an objective fact of geography, history, ethnicity and culture that should be realized in an independent state. Religion had nothing to do with nation and had to be strictly separated from politics. For the SSNP, Greater Syria was the entire Fertile Crescent — Iraq, Syria, Lebanon, Palestine — plus a 'star', Cyprus. Saadé was an authoritarian leader and gave the party a tightly disciplined organization; from the first it had a paramilitary wing. Hence, it is not surprising that the party has had a turbulent history. As early as 1949 it was involved in armed unrest. Saadé was arrested and after a dubious trial by a summary court, executed. Two years later his supporters took revenge by assassinating the prime minister, Riad Solh. The use of armed violence has always been disputed in the party, and often played a role in leadership crises and splits. In the early 1970s further internal differences of opinion about the party's socio-political orientation emerged: while one part of the leadership stuck to the authoritarian, even fascistic style of the early years, another was attracted to ideas of the Left. What always reunites supporters of the SSNP, despite all fissiparous tendencies, is the attraction its national concept exerts on a number of Lebanese who want neither what they see as Sunni dominated Pan-Arabism nor a Lebanon under Maronite domination. Greater Syria seems to them the best chance of creating a modern and, above all, laicized state. Like that of the CP, their membership includes many Greek Orthodox and, more recently, Shi`is — members of communities that derive no particular benefits from Lebanese proportionality. But over and above this, the SSNP appeals particularly to those intellectuals with secularized ideals — not only in Lebanon but throughout the Fertile Crescent — for whom Marxism is too alien.[84]

---

[84] See Labib Zuwiyya Yamak, *The Syrian Social Nationalist Party: An ideological analysis* (Cambridge, Mass., 1966).

The Baath Party,[85] or more precisely, the Socialist Party of the Arab Renaissance, by contrast, is an organization that combines integrative pan-Arabism with a strong state role in socio-political spheres. It was founded in Syria by a Greek Orthodox teacher, Michel Aflak, and a Sunni lawyer, Salah Bitar. Although it, too, favours a laicized state, it regards religion, that is, Islam in particular, as an important component of Arab culture. The Baath has operated in Lebanon since 1951. It gained a foothold among the Sunnis in Tripoli and later among urbanized Shi`is. The Baath is a 'national' party, that is, organized at a pan-Arab level with so-called regional commandos in individual states. In the latter half of the 1960s the party took power in both Syria and Iraq, and split; in Lebanon, too, there is a pro-Syrian and a pro-Iraqi wing.

In pre-war Lebanon all three parties with expressly ideological programmes attracted only limited, but extremely militant support. All of them had their bitter fights and concomitant splits over party policy. Their roles in Lebanese parliamentary politics remained marginal. The CP has never won a seat, partly a consequence of the not inconsiderable intervention of the strongly anti-communist state machinery.[86] The SSNP won a seat once, in a constituency in which the candidate had the backing of influential extended families.[87] A popular doctor,[88] whose social work has won him broader support than his party usually enjoys, has held a seat in Tripoli for the Baath since 1972.

As will be discussed below, the Lebanese electoral system works against political parties. Over and above this disadvantage, in pre-war Lebanon secularized manifestos like the CP, the SSNP and the Baath simply did not appeal to the Lebanese electorate, which felt their interests better represented by the traditional political attitudes of the respective religious communities. And these basic attitudes were articulated by other parties: the Kata'ib, the Najjadé and the Progressive Socialist Party (PSP).

The Kata'ib,[89] in French: Phalanges Libanaises, to which was appended 'Social Democratic Party of Lebanon', was founded in 1936 as a youth organization and transformed into a political party in 1943. It champions an unrestricted and unconditional independence for Lebanon. With this goal it took part in the

---

[85] Adeed I. Dawisha, 'The transnational party in regional politics: the Arab Ba`th Party', *Asian Affairs*, 61/1 (1974), pp. 23–31. See also Olivier Carré, 'Le mouvement idéologique ba`thiste', in André Raymond et al., eds., *La Syrie d'aujourd'hui* (Paris, 1980), pp. 185–224.
[86] In 1972 the Shi`i CP candidate Habib Saadé lost by only a few votes in the Marjayoun constituency.
[87] Assad el-Achkar was SSNP Deputy for the Metn from 1957 to 1960.
[88] Dr Abdel-Majid Rafai.
[89] See in particular John P. Entelis, *Pluralism and Party Transformation in Lebanon - Al Kata'ib 1936–1970* (Leiden, 1974); Frank Stoakes, 'The supervigilantes: The Lebanese Kata'ib Party as a builder, surrogate and defender of the state', *Middle Eastern Studies* 11/3 (1975), pp. 215–36.

struggle against the French mandate. Since 1943 it has vehemently opposed all ideas of a Greater Syria or pan-Arabism. Before the war it was by far the strongest and best organized party. Like the SSNP, it built up its own militia in the 1940s. According to its statute, the Kata'ib is open to all Lebanese irrespective of community; in practice most of its members are lower middle- and working-class Maronites in Beirut, its eastern suburbs and Kisrawan. In the 1960s it fought for social policies and played a leading role in drafting Lebanese social legislation. All in all, one can describe the Kata'ib as a populist party of Lebanese nationalists mainly supported by Maronites.[90]

Its Sunni counterpart is the Najjadé ('helpers'), the party of Arab Nationalism, also originally a youth organization. In contrast to the Baath Party, for them Arabism is closely linked with Islam. Its only stronghold is Beirut, where it has the support of the Sunni lower-middle and working classes.

The Progressive Socialist Party (PSP)[91] was founded in 1949. It champions the idea of a secularized state for an independent Lebanon, though closely aligned with the Arab world. Its social policies are very similar to those of Kata'ib, with which it closely collaborated on social policies in the 1960s. Like the SSNP, the PSP appealed to a number of intellectuals from different communities, who were attracted by its programmatic mix of secularism and moderately progressive policies. But its electoral support comes largely from a part of the Druze in the Chouf, traditional supporters of the Jumblatt family.[92]

The PSP differs from all previously mentioned parties in that is a small party whose policies transcend community interests. Yet, at the same time, it is the traditional electoral body of a family of Druze large landowners. Two other political organizations — Raymond Eddé's National Bloc and Camille Chamoun's National Liberal Party (NLP) — are also in effect electoral associations of families or political personalities, despite elements of a party structure such as formal membership and party offices. Like the Kata'ib, both

---

[90] Albert Hourani links the populism of the Kata'ib with the populist traditions of the Maronite peasants' revolt in the nineteenth century, as embodied by Tanious Shahin and Yusuf Karam: 'In a sense, the Phalanges of to-day can be seen as the heirs of this tradition'; 'Ideologies of the mountain and the city', in Owen, *Essays on the Crisis in Lebanon*, p. 37.

[91] See Kamal Jumblatt, *La démocratie économique, cénacle libanais* (Beirut, 1950) and *La démocratie sociale, cénacle libanais* (Beirut, 1953).

[92] Arnold Hottinger, 'Zu`ama' and parties in the Lebanese crisis of 1958', *Middle East Journal* 15/2 (1961), p. 131, writes: '[Jumblat] is the founder and the leader of the Lebanese Progressive Socialist Party. At the same time, he is, whether he wants it or not, the head of the Jumblati clan of the Druze in the Shuf. His "feudal" position is the source of his political strength and even of the strength of "his" political party'. The assessment of Samih K. Farsoun, 'Family structure and society in modern Lebanon', in Louise E. Sweet, ed., *Peoples and Cultures of the Middle East* (New York, 1970), vol. 2, p. 278, is similar: 'The "Progressive Socialist Party" is nothing more than a bloc: secondary Druze zu`ama' allied to a primary za`im Kamal Jumblatt.'

champion a Lebanese nationalism and are supported mainly by Maronites. In contrast to the populism of the Kata'ib, the National Bloc represents a more liberal variant of Maronite Lebanism, the NLP a more conservative one. Finally, there are the organized Armenian parties: the nationalist Tashnag, the socialist Hentshag Party and the liberal Ramgavar Party. All three were founded in old Armenia and, in terms of supporters and policies, have remained parties of one community. In Lebanon the Tashnag has had greatest success, often forming electoral alliances with the Kata'ib.

Between 1960 and 1972 the parliamentary representation of parties with primarily single-community support and policies mirroring that community's fundamental orientations increased.[93] The Kata'ib won between six and nine seats, the Najjadé one in 1960 and again in 1968, and the PSP regularly five or six. The National Bloc had between three and six representatives, the NLP between five and eleven and Tashnag a constant four. Even taking a very elastic definition of a modern political party, so as to include groupings like the PSP, the National Bloc and the NLP, these parties between them held at most one-third of all seats in the Lebanese Parliament.

By contrast, about two-thirds of the seats were held by independents, notables known as zu`ama' in Lebanese political jargon (singular za`im, meaning patron, head, prominent personality).[94] In pre-war Lebanon the zu`ama' were the most important intermediaries between individuals and the state, a sort of class of political 'brokers'. They concerned themselves not only with the political interests of their voters, but took a far more comprehensive interest in the concerns of their clients, settling difficulties with the authorities, arbitrating conflicts and arranging jobs, loans and businesses for individuals.

The strength and the persistence of this type of politician are rooted in the peculiarities of Lebanese society and its development. Even today, extended families and family clans are the most important social institution for most people in Lebanon. Urbanization and economic modernization have not lessened their importance: they have simply adapted to changing circumstances,[95] and in certain

---

[93] For a detailed analysis Antoine N. Messara, *La structure sociale du parlement libanais (1920–1976)* (Beirut, 1977),pp. 59ff, in particular p. 79.

[94] On the system of patronage in general see Ernest Gellner and John Waterbury, eds., *Patrons and Clients in Mediterranean Societies* (London, 1977). On the zu`ama' of Lebanon, see: Hottinger, 'Zu`ama' and parties' and 'Zu`ama' in historical perspective', in Binder, *Politics in Lebanon*, pp. 85–105; Samih K. Farsoun, 'Family structure', p. 306. An excellent brief analysis of the patronage system may be found in Hisham Sharabi, *Neopatriarchy: A theory of distorted change in Arab society* (New York and Oxford, 1988), pp. 45ff.

[95] See Fuad I. Khuri, *From Village to Suburb* (Chicago and London, 1975) and 'Sectarian loyalty among rural migrants in two Lebanese suburbs: a stage between family and national allegiance', in Richard

spheres are more important than ever before. In the new housing estates of the conurbations village kinship groups have regrouped. Pre-war, 40 per cent of all Lebanese lived less than a quarter of an hour on foot from relatives. Personal contact between members of the extended family 'is incredible by western standards':[96] in Lebanon people are in daily contact with parents and grandparents, married children and married grandchildren, with nephews, nieces, uncles and aunts. The extended family is more than an institution for intensive personal contact and relationships; it has economic significance. The majority of economic enterprises in Lebanon are family businesses, as are many joint-stock companies. These are often modern commercial constructions to keep the property of an extended family together and profitable. As the families are, indeed, very large, one typical problem of family businesses in western societies rarely arises, namely the dearth of skilled or qualified relations for important technical and managerial functions.[97] The extended family remains a fund of credit. Relations frequently finance studies, equip a doctor's practice or an engineer's offices or provide the capital for a business venture. The economic aspect of kinship can endure over continents and generations. Those at home provide the money for the emigrant's start; if the latter is successful, as is often the case, money can flow in the other direction, especially in times of need. The extended family's duty to look after its aged is taken for granted. In short: the continued existence of traditional extended families is based on emotional ties and on solid economic interest.

The stronger their solidarity and the larger the family, the better are their prospects of economic success. The first family associations to keep and strengthen contacts with even remote relations of extended families were already being formed at the end of the last century.[98] Family foundations to provide for the aged are frequent, and there are a considerable number of private schools in family ownership. Finally, family interests also find political expression. If the head of a family can depend on his relations following his instructions he becomes a 'key voter': by offering a candidate a parcel of votes, he can be sure of the latter's services should he be elected. Hence, a feature of 'election campaigns' in pre-war Lebanon was the efforts of candidates to win the support of key voters and, thus, a substantial body of votes. Political support was bargained in return for manifold services within the power of a municipal councillor or a parliamentary

---

Antoun and Iliya F. Harik, eds., *Rural Politics and Social Change in the Middle East* (Bloomington and London, 1972), pp. 198–213.

[96] Farsun, 'Family structure, p. 306.

[97] 'The members of the patrimonial group are in adequate number and can effectively share among themselves the responsibilities of managing the firm'; Samir Khalaf, *Lebanon's Predicament*, (New York, 1987), p. 150.

[98] Ibid., pp. 161–84.

deputy, such as procuring state contracts, assistance in the appointment or promotion of civil servants, building approval, trading licences, etc. The notables stand at the head of complex, yet economically rational bodies of clients that obey the laws of the market: you scratch my back and I'll scratch yours. A *za'im* represents not only the specific political interests of individuals, but far more comprehensive political, economic and cultural interests of whole families or clans. It is thus understandable why candidates with primarily or exclusively ideological party policies have so little chance against the *zu'ama'*. What they offer is more abstract than concrete. Abstract issues may appeal to individuals, but seldom to units of family interests.[99] Ideological politics has the greatest chance of success if a *za'im* of an established family becomes their spokesman. A Jumblatt, for instance, heir to an old political 'family business', may call himself conservative today, liberal tomorrow and socialist the day after, but he can always count on the votes of his clientèle, provided that he does not badly neglect their interests.

All members of extended families practically always belong to the same religious community. Although marriages between Christian communities have increased in recent decades, in 1970 they still accounted for less than 10 per cent of all Christian marriages.[100] Marriages between Muslims and Christians are statistically insignificant, and restricted to the upper-income and educated strata. Thus, extended families and communities are not competing, but similarly oriented social associations. Extended families may compete politically within a community, but in terms of the fundamental political options within the country their views are essentially the same: no family can afford a shadow of doubt about their allegiance to the community as a whole. Hence, the continued existence and the continued economic role of the extended families is also the basis for the continued existence of the communities as social and political entities. Nevertheless, it is precisely the traditional *zu'ama'* who value moderate formulations of the respective communities' positions that will enable compromise. Their interests are similar: to ensure for themselves and their clients a share in the exercise of power and the resultant benefits. For them the issue is one of a little more or a little less. For the Lebanese notables the traditional art of government is the continual search

---

[99] 'Families that still are of some political consequence refrain from joining ideological parties. By the same token, ideological political parties, such as the Ba`thists, the Syrian Nationalists, and the Communists, seem to appeal to young, semi-educated, and unmarried people. Many party recruits desert their parties after marriage'; Khuri, *From Village to Suburb*, p. 200.

[100] Salim Nasr, 'Les formes de regroupement traditionnel (familles, confessions, communautés régionales) dans la société de Beyrouth', in Dominique Chevallier, ed., *L'espace social de la ville arabe* (Paris, 1979), p. 169.

for compromises between the interests of individuals, groups of clients, regions and communities.

The peculiarities of Lebanese electoral law favoured the election of moderate parliamentarians willing to compromise.[101] In most constituencies there were several seats for different communities, and each voter, irrespective of community affiliation, cast one vote for each seat.[102] Hence, to ensure he had a chance, each candidate had to compete for votes not only within his own community but in other communities too. As a rule, the result was lists with candidates from different communities, each candidate on a list having an interest in persuading his respective key voters to vote for the whole list. The parliamentarians of the elected lists frequently formed regional 'blocs' — intercommunal parliamentary groups, as it were — regardless of their community affiliation. The constraints on the formation of the cabinet also worked in favour of political moderation. As cabinet seats were filled by proportionality, a parliamentarian who wished to join the cabinet concentrated on unseating an incumbent from his own community rather than one from another. In short: in pre-war Lebanon the mechanisms of patronage and of parliamentary election tended to promote competition within the communities and cooperation between them. Hence, controversies over the distribution of power did not, as a rule, take place in parliament. Decisions in parliament were seldom taken along community or religious lines.

However, as mentioned, there were fundamental differences of opinion and interest between the communities on the interpretation of the National Pact and the sharing of power. As the notables preferred to maintain discretion, these differences were increasingly articulated in extra-parliamentary institutions, in certain organizations within the communities themselves as well as political movements and parties.

---

[101] For details, Pierre Rondot, 'Quelques réflexions sur les structures du Liban', *Orient*, 2/6 (1958), pp. 28f and 'Expérience du collège unique dans le système représentif libanais', *Revue française de science politique* 7 (1957), pp. 67ff.

[102] Iliya F. Harik provides an illuminating example. The Zahrani constituency has two seats. One is reserved for a Shi`i, the other for a Greek Catholic. Each voter - Shi`i, Sunni, Maronite, Greek Orthodox or a member of any other community - can cast two votes: one for a Shi`i and one for a Greek Catholic - not for two candidates from one of these communities, nor for a candidate from any other community. 'Under these legal constraints, Shi`i candidates compete against each other and so do the Catholics. This makes the contest intrasectarian not intersectarian'; 'Lebanon', in Jacob Landau et al., eds., *Electoral Politics in the Middle East: Issues, voters and elites* (London, 1980), p. 152.

## Constituencies

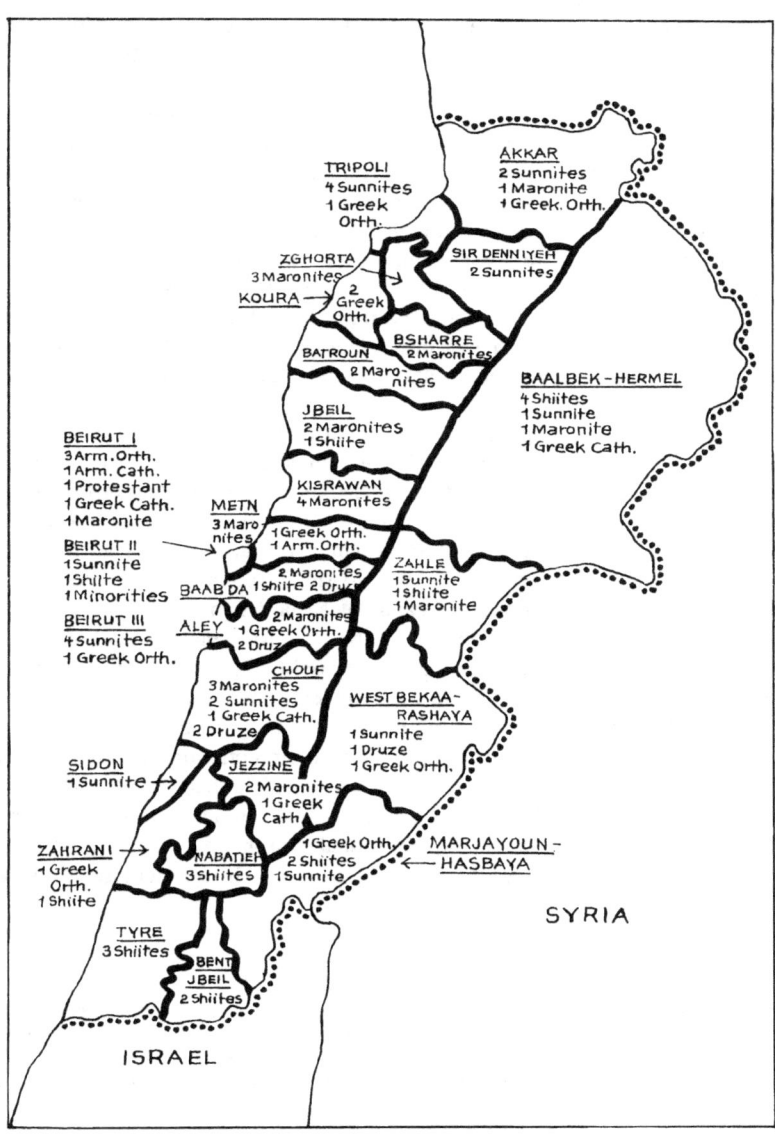

The religious heads of the communities — the Patriarchs of the Christian Churches, the Mufti of the Sunnis, since 1967 the Imam of the Shi`is, and the Sheikh Akl of the Druze — openly expressed their opinions whenever they felt the interests of their respective groups threatened in any way. For less solemn occasions various forms of gatherings served to express community interests: 'congresses' of spiritual and worldly dignitaries, a predominantly Muslim form of political manifestation; the 'Makassed', the Sunni welfare and educational institution; the 'Maronite League', a semi-political lobby; the 'Greek Orthodox Council', an elected body; and similar forums. Since independence all communities have considerably expanded their network of institutions: schools and universities, welfare associations and hospitals, youth and pupils' organizations as well as their various organs.[103] Representatives of these institutions have very much less interest than the political notables in keeping a low profile in conflicts over sharing or in ideological debates. On the contrary, the more strident their pronouncements and demands, the better they can put pressure on the notables.[104]

The same holds for the political parties. Until 1960 their activities were largely extra-parliamentary. Having minimal governmental responsibility, they could express their views as radically as they wished. For the 1960 elections the number of parliamentary seats was increased from 66 to 99, so as to draw more radical politicians of various persuasions into the ambit of parliament. The delimitation created a dozen constituencies in which single communities had such an overwhelming majority that their candidates hardly needed to bother about support from other religious groups. In these constituencies, elections became contests between traditional *zu`ama'* and party politicians of the same community. The consequence was a remarkable development: each side began to adopt the practices of the other. The *zu`ama'* felt they had to adopt strident tones and a more rigid stance on the fundamental interests of their communities, and the party politicians the methods of patronage of the *zu`ama'*. The parties became collective *zu`ama'*, above all for the interests of the urban lower-middle and working classes. Whoever had little to offer on the traditional patronage market could buy his protection here. In the rapidly expanding cities, in particular, a cleavage

---

[103] See Boutros Labaki, 'From extended family to the community in Lebanon', (forthcoming). On the political role of communal institutions see Antoine N. Messara, *Le modèle politique libanais et sa survie. Essai sur la classification et l'aménagement d'un système consociatif* (Beirut, 1983) p. 335.

[104] 'Si chaque communauté se transforme en période de crise en miniparlement, c'est que les communautés ne se sentent pas effectivement représentées à la Chambre des Députés'; Messara, *Le modèle politique libanais*, p. 337.

developed between the long-settled inhabitants, who continued to support the notables, and the new migrants, who found their home in the parties.[105]

The effects of these changes on the representation of political interests varied from community to community.[106] They were strongest among the Maronites: their parties succeeded in replacing the *zu`ama'*, particularly in Beirut and the heavily urbanized north-eastern hinterland. The Sunni notables defended their position more effectively — the electoral successes of Najjadé, Baath and smaller Nasserite groups were very limited — but at the cost of at least the verbal radicalization of the *zu`ama'*. Greek Orthodox and Greek Catholic notables remained unbeatable in elections, although Greek Orthodox, in particular, formed the core of the leadership in several extra-parliamentary parties. The traditional leader of one section of the Druze declared himself a socialist without damaging his electoral support, whereas traditionalism did not harm the leader of the other section. The developments among the Shi`is were the most complex. In the south and in the Bekaa large landowners continued to hold sway, whereas Shi`is who had migrated to Beirut started joining the CP, the Baath and the SSNP in large numbers in the late 1960s. However, as these Shi`is were not registered in Beirut but in their home towns and villages, the traditional majorities of the *zu`ama'* became narrower and narrower. At the end of the 1960s the religious head of the Shi`is, Imam Musa Sadr, involved himself in the political interests of his community, in opposition to both the *zu`ama'* and the secular parties, and with some success: in 1972 the candidates he supported were elected.

In the 1960s and the early 1970s the tendency towards stridency and populism in representing community interests gained ground in all large communities. By contrast, the Druze looked to secularist policies to protect their interests, and eventually formed an alliance with the extra-parliamentary secular parties. The moderate notables demonstrated considerable skill in resisting this general tendency — in the last parliamentary elections before the war they still managed to win two-thirds of the seats — but not even they could withstand the growing polarization indefinitely.[107]

---

[105] Khuri, 'Sectarian loyalty', pp. 207–10.

[106] Messara, *La structure sociale*, pp. 59ff.

[107] This survey of the political forces in Lebanon should have made it clear how absurd it is to apply categories of 'right' and 'left', or even 'right-wing Christian' and 'left-wing Muslim' to Lebanese politics. The Left, with support across the religious spectrum, though with mainly Christian leaders, has always been small and played only a marginal role in pre-war Lebanon. Of the established political forces, the Kata'ib, the strongest Christian party, tended to be 'left' on socio-political issues, the largely Muslim groupings generally 'right'. 'The continuing conflict can by no stretch of imagination be described as one between rival social ideologies of modern type - of the sort commonly described as "Right" versus "Left". It is, rather, a naked struggle for power between two basically confessional fronts'; Kamal S. Salibi, '"Right" and "Left" in

## Conflicts over power-sharing

As mentioned above, for a very brief period in the infancy of Mount Lebanon seats in the Administrative Council were apportioned equally between the religious communities, irrespective of numerical strength. However, in 1864 it was decided to apportion them by the numerical strength of each community, that is, to introduce proportional representation. In Mount Lebanon that caused few problems, for there was a clear-cut majority. But with the creation of Greater Lebanon clear-cut majorities were a thing of the past. In 1932, when, for the first time, a Sunni wanted to stand for the presidency, confessional statistics were the chief argument used to dissuade him. The census of 1932 was taken under the cloud of this political dispute.[108]

In a system of proportional representation, population statistics are highly political; this is particularly true of Lebanon. Given the geographic distribution of the religious communities, even a census that did not ask religious affiliation would give a good indication of the relative strengths of the communities. Thus, every statistic in Lebanon, direct or indirect, is a statistic of the strength of the communities, which raises questions about the majority and, therefore, about the distribution of power.

The census of 1932 was the last. All later figures are estimates, based on the figures of 1932. Various estimates are not free of wishful thinking. In 1973 one Christian author gives the Christians 55.1 per cent,[109] whereas two years later a Muslim author puts them at 39.9 per cent.[110] The sociologist Salim Nasr is doubtless right when he states: 'At present there are no scientific and objective statistics on the confessions.'[111] Nonetheless, it may be useful to compare the estimates of some authors, who cannot be placed in one or other camp in the Lebanese politico-demographic conflict, with the figures of the 1932 census, in order to gain some idea of the size of the differences in question.

George Samné, an author with Greater Syrian rather than Lebanese sympathies, made estimates of the population in 1920, that is, at the time of the

---

Lebanon', in Gustav Stein and Udo Steinbach, eds., *The Contemporary Middle Eastern Scene* (Opladen, 1979), p. 102.

[108] Rondot, *Les institutions politiques*, p. 29.

[109] Edmond Rabbath, *La formation historique du Liban politique et constitutionnel: Essai de synthèse* (Beirut, 1973), p. 5.

[110] Kamal Hassan, 'Le Liban de la crise', *at-Tali'a*, 11/11 (1975), p. 52, quoted in Salim Nasr, 'Pour éclairer la guerre civile au Liban. Jalons pour une position des rapports entre confessions et société libanaise', in Jean Bauberot et al., eds., *Palestine et Liban: Promesses et mensonges de l'Occident* (Paris, 1977).

[111] Ibid., p. 148.

creation of the present state.¹¹² They suggest a large Christian majority. One cannot exclude the possibility that figures like these encouraged the protagonists of Greater Lebanon. The data of the 1932 census contain two interesting sets of figures: that of the number of people resident in Lebanon, and that of all registered Lebanese nationals, whether resident or not.¹¹³ For 1943, the year of independence, there are figures on registered nationals.¹¹⁴ The data of the registration of December 31st, 1953 are also available, initially published by the German religious geographer Klaus-Peter Hartmann.¹¹⁵ The same author has also published estimates of the resident population in 1973.¹¹⁶

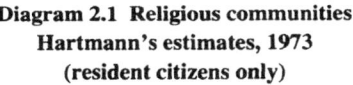

**Diagram 2.1 Religious communities Hartmann's estimates, 1973 (resident citizens only)**

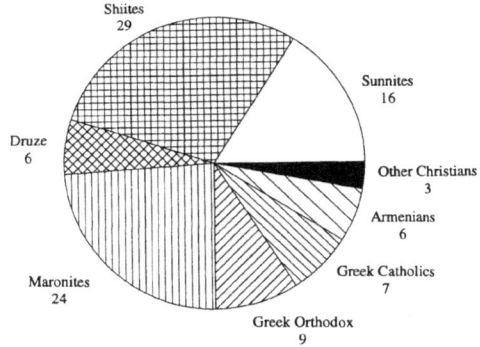

Figures in %

He himself qualifies the latter as 'approximate'. He regards the estimates for the Shi`is as the greatest factor of uncertainty; figures vary between 600,000 and

---

¹¹² George Samné, *La Syrie*, p. 285. His figures include the population of the Wadi an-Nassara, now part of Syria, which has been subtracted for our argument.
¹¹³ The latter does not include Lebanese emigrants who no longer held Lebanese nationality. See Rondot, *Les institutions politiques*, pp. 28f.
¹¹⁴ Conseil Supérieur des Intérêts Communs, *Recueil des statistiques de la Syrie et du Liban*, Beirut *1942–1943*, p. 18. See Rondot, *Les institutions politiques*, p. 29.
¹¹⁵ Hartmann, *Untersuchungen*, p. 126.
¹¹⁶ Ibid. Hartmann bases these estimates on reports in the Lebanese press and his own surveys.

900,000 — he thinks 800,000 is realistic. The sources give the following picture:[117]

**Table 2.1** Religious communities by population (%)

|  | Estimate | Census | | | | resident citizens: estimate |
|---|---|---|---|---|---|---|
|  |  | resident citizens: census | registered citizens | registration | registration |  |
|  | 1920 | 1932 | 1932 | 1943 | 1953 | 1973 |
| Maronites | 35 | 29 | 39 | 29 | 39 | 24 |
| Greek Orthodox | 17 | 10 | 11 | 10 | 11 | 9 |
| Greek Catholic | 8 | 6 | 6 | 6 | 6 | 7 |
| Armenians |  | 4 | 4 | 6 | 6 | 6 |
| Other Christians | 1 | 1 | 1 | 2 | 2 | 2 |
| All Christians | 61 | 50 | 52 | 53 | 55 | 49 |
| Sunnites | 19 | 23 | 22 | 21 | 20 | 16 |
| Shiites | 13 | 20 | 18 | 19 | 18 | 29 |
| Druze | 7 | 6 | 7 | 6 | 6 | 6 |
| All Muslims | 39 | 49 | 47 | 46 | 44 | 51 |
| Others | – | 1 | 1 | 1 | 1 | – |

If the estimates for 1920 are disregarded, then the data of the census, registrations and Hartmann all point to two important conclusions: firstly, no community forms the absolute majority, and the largest, be it Maronite or Shi`i, has not even one-third of the total population; secondly, whichever majorities existed in prewar Lebanon, be they Christian or Muslim, they appear always to have been a bare majority.

A 1971 survey by the Lebanese family-planning association established considerable differences in the fertility rates of the communities, in particular higher birth rates among the Muslims in general and among the Shi`is in particular.[118]

[117] Figures rounded up to full percentages.
[118] Association Libanaise du Planning Familial, 'La famille au Liban', (mimeograph, Beirut, 1971). The reported population growth rates are: Shi`is 3.6 per cent, Sunnis 2.8 per cent, Maronites and other

# The Lebanese Model

These differences have been confirmed by subsequent, smaller sample surveys.[119] Numerous authors have concluded on the basis of these figures that the slender Christian majority of 1932 must have given way by now to a substantial Muslim majority.[120] Yet, it is questionable whether such differences necessarily mean decisive demographic shifts in the relative weights of the communities. The estimates depend on the base population figures and on the base year chosen for extrapolations using the 1971 fertility rates. It is also questionable whether there is a fixed relationship between fertility rate and mortality rates. Hartmann assumes a lower infant and child mortality rate among Christians,[121] as does Betts.[122] A further factor of uncertainty is the rate of emigration and return. In earlier periods most emigrants were Christian. However, in recent decades Muslim emigration has risen strongly, whereas large numbers of Christian Lebanese living abroad returned to their homeland in the 1960s. The most spectacular incidence of the latter was the remigration from Egypt, after the revolutionary government introduced its policy of nationalization. After weighing up these factors Betts concludes that it is probable that prior to the outbreak of war the Christians were still in the majority.[123]

Be that as it may, neither fertility nor mortality rates based on random samples nor migration balances can replace census figures. However, the few data and the circumstantial evidence available speak against marked changes in the composition of the Lebanese population in the pre-war period. On the other hand, these also speak against any clear-cut majority. Precisely because of this, since 1932 there have been endless political debates on how to define 'Lebanese'. Muslims demand the recognition of Muslim Kurds and Bedouins as Lebanese nationals, Christians the same for Christian groups of immigrants from other Oriental countries: Assyrians, Jacobites and Chaldeans from Turkey and Iraq, Maronites,

---

Catholic communities 2.1 per cent, Druze 1.7 per cent and the Greek Orthodox 1.3 per cent. For a detailed analysis of these data see Joseph Chamie, 'Religious fertility differentials in Lebanon', Unpublished Ph.D. thesis, University of Michigan, 1976.

[119] Including the author's own surveys, see below Chapter 6.

[120] E.g., Qubain, *Crisis in Lebanon*, p. 7; much earlier, Jacques Nantet, *Histoire du Liban* (Paris, 1963), p. 304; more recent authors assume a Muslim majority of approximately 60 per cent, e.g., Thierry Desjardins, *Le martyre du Liban* (Paris, 1976), pp. 55–6; Pierre Vallaud, *Le Liban au bout du fusil: Avant-propos de Jean Lacouture* (Paris, 1976), p. 52. Desjardins and Vallaud are journalists, here reporting figures widely bandied about but unsubstantiated.

[121] Hartmann, *Untersuchungen*, p. 160.

[122] Betts, *Christians in the Arab East*, p. 85. He comes to the conclusion that 'the real birthrate of Christians and Muslims, counting only those offspring surviving infancy and childhood, is in effect identical'.

[123] Ibid. The conclusion is all the more remarkable because in his research Betts treats Oriental Christian minorities' own figures with scepticism.

Greek Orthodox and Greek Catholics from Syria.[124] The crucial issue is the Lebanese abroad. The most extreme Muslim view is to ignore them completely; the Christian counterpart is to count all as Lebanese emigrants. The inability to reach agreement on this question has precluded a census in the past half century. The debate has evolved into a ritual. Muslim politicians or institutions demand a census, Christian politicians or institutions agree, provided that all Lebanese abroad are included.[125] So long as a census in not held, each of the confessional blocs can maintain that it is in the majority and make corresponding demands with respect to the distribution of power in the state.

The demands concern essentially four institutions: the Chamber of Deputies, the presidency, the premiership and the civil service. Since 1943, seats in the Chamber of deputies have been divided in the ratio of six Christians to five Muslims.[126] Even on the basis of the 1932 figures it is difficult to justify a permanent Christian majority of 54.5 per cent. However, in parliamentary practice this discrepancy is more apparent than real, if not purely symbolic. Because of the above-mentioned peculiarities of the Lebanese electoral system there are Muslim members from constituencies with a Christian majority, and vice versa — indeed, more of the latter.[127] In the 1972 parliamentary elections, the last before the war, twelve Christian candidates were elected on lists dominated by Muslim politicians and their backers, whereas only five Muslims candidates were dependent on Christian politicians. In terms of political backing, the Muslim side of Parliament could count on 52 seats instead of only the 45 they were entitled to by law, the Christians, by contrast, on only 47 instead of a formal 54. But as decisions were rarely taken along the religious divide and parliamentary alliances tend to be temporary, the 'Muslim majority' in terms of the lists was scarcely more significant than the formal 'Christian majority' by the six:five ratio of the Electoral Law. Notwithstanding parliamentary reality, Christian politicians were quite as obdurate about their symbolic majority of parliamentary seats as their Muslim colleagues are obstinate in demanding its revision to reflect demographic changes.

---

[124] During the presidency of Camille Chamoun (1952-1958) some of these Christian immigrants as well as Christian Palestinians were granted Lebanese nationality, usually on the grounds of having Lebanese forefathers.

[125] Curiously, neither side has seriously considered including only those Lebanese abroad who still hold Lebanese nationality, in keeping with the practice of most states. The 1932 census figures and later data indicate that the difference between registered and resident nationals would not be more than a few per cent. Apparently the one side fears that their inclusion would just deprive them of the majority, and the other that it would just not be enough.

[126] Accordingly, the total number of seats was always a multiple of eleven: 44, 55, 66 and, from 1960, 99 seats. The electoral law was last amended in 1990. See Chapter 10 below.

[127] On the following see Harik, 'Lebanon', p. 153 and 'The economic and social factors in the Lebanese crisis', *Journal of Arab Affairs*, 1/2 (1982), p. 229.

## The Lebanese Model

Of far greater political import were the differences in power between the chief offices of state. The Constitution[128] gives the state president enormous powers, the prime minister far fewer. Under the Constitution the president appoints and dismisses all ministers, including the premier. He has a suspensive veto in all parliamentary decisions, which can be overruled only by an absolute majority of the Chamber. He can dissolve parliament, provided that he has the agreement of the cabinet. Constitutional reality is, of course, very different. Although most presidents have tried to use their powers to the full since 1943, as a rule these attempts provoked political crises in which they were forced to climb down. In 1952 President Beshara al-Khoury had to resign because all authoritative Sunni politicians refused to serve in a cabinet under him. On the other hand, the Lebanese system of government functions smoothly whenever a strong president chooses an equally strong prime minister — *de facto* creating a Maronite-Sunni duumvirate.[129] Since 1958 the powers of the prime minister have effectively increased. The president and the prime minister have taken to forming cabinets together, and the right to countersign laws and decrees, necessary before the president can promulgate them, has passed from the respective cabinet ministers to the prime minister, giving him in effect a right of veto. This also affects the appointment of civil servants and officers: although the constitution reserves this right to the president alone, the evolution in the practice of countersigning means that these appointments too have became subject to compromise and consensus.[130]

In spite of the considerable evolution in constitutional practice, the bicephalous disequilibrium remains: the president has the power to dismiss the prime minister. But since 1943 successive presidents have made progressively less use of it — apart from the lapse between 1970 and 1976.[131] The occasional appointment of a relatively weak or unrepresentative premier particularly angered the Sunnis and gave them cause to question the division of power between the offices of state. On the other hand, whenever the increment in the powers of the prime minister became too conspicuous, the Maronites were dissatisfied. Since 1958 they have repeatedly criticized what they see as the reduction of the presidency to the role of

---

[128] The following discussion is based on the Constitution in effect until 1990. For the 1990 amendments, see Chapter 10 below.

[129] 'Le plus souvent, tout se passe comme si les deux grandes communautés de l'Etat se satisfaisaient de voir les chefs de l'une et de l'autre associés au sommet des pouvoirs. Pour beaucoup de Libanais, le couple islamo-chrétien au sommet de l'Etat, même si les deux termes du couple ne sont pas exactement comparables, réalise un équilibre pratiquement satisfaisant'; Rondot, 'Quelques réflexions', p. 35.

[130] The office of Speaker has been reserved for a Shi`i (and the office of Deputy-Speaker for a Greek Orthodox) since 1947. Initially a largely ceremonial office, since 1964 its incumbent has exercised considerable influence on presidential elections.

[131] Beshara al-Khoury appointed nine premiers, Camille Chamoun five, Fouad Chehab four, Charles Helou three, Suleiman Franjieh six, Elias Sarkis two and Amin Gemayal two.

arbitration between the communities, while the premier uninhibitedly exploits his office to further the interests of his community. Nonetheless, Maronite political opinion is virtually unanimous that the state presidency must remain reserved for a Maronite.

The discussion of the two highest offices of state illustrates the significance of symbols: the effective shift in power to the advantage of the prime minister has embittered the Maronites without appeasing the Sunnis. The Maronites regard a Maronite in the presidency as a guarantee while the Sunnis see it as a privilege, although there is only limited truth in either view.

Finally, in the decade before the war the other communities' resentment against the entire Maronite-Sunni duumvirate grew, because it excluded them from the powerful offices of state. As the Shi`i conviction grew that they were numerically the largest community of all, certainly the largest Muslim community, they pressed ever more forcefully for a revision of the division of offices or even the abolition of the system. Druze politicians, in particular, with the solid support of the secular parties of the Left, demanded that the traditional allocations of the presidency and the premiership be abandoned. As a minimal solution they suggested rotation — of the former office among the Christian communities, of the latter among the Muslim.[132] Precisely such demands served to stabilize the existing system: if forced to choose, leading Sunni politicians, despite their longing for the presidency, prefer a bird in the hand to two in the bush. As in the question of the distribution of parliamentary seats, so here too the different interests of the communities in pre-war Lebanon produced a stalemate over the division of power at the apex of the state. In each case the existing provisions have remained in force. However, a shift in power between the offices of state is indisputable. Increasingly, the initial Maronite upper hand has given way to symbolic hegemony — as has long been the case in parliament. Conflicts over the symbols of power can be as intense as those over power itself.

The least contentious institution in pre-war Lebanon was that in which there was no hegemony, not even symbolic:[133] the cabinet. It has always been composed of an equal number of Christians and Muslims. Over the decades three trends in the composition and functioning of the government became discernible. As the number of seats in parliament increased, so did the number of ministers, in order to bind an adequate number of parliamentary blocs in governance; the number of 'preserves' — portfolios allocated to specific communities — declined;[134] and the life of cabinets increased. No cabinet was ever brought down by a vote of no-

---

[132] Information imparted to the author by a leading PSP politician, 1979.
[133] See Elie Salem, 'Cabinet politics in Lebanon', *Middle East Journal* 21/4 (1967), pp. 488–502.
[134] Ibid., p. 500.

*The Lebanese Model* 93

confidence; cabinets resigned when new parliamentary coalitions were formed. As in the government, there was, as a rule, parity on the opposition benches too — to become a minister a deputy had to replace an incumbent of his own community. As Muslim deputies were always in the minority, and there was an equal number of Muslim and Christian ministers, Muslim parliamentarians had slightly better prospects of governmental office. The government reflected in miniature of the composition of the Chamber, with one crucial distinction: parliament was elected in accordance with the contentious principle of proportional representation between Christians and Muslims, whereas the cabinet was chosen on the principle of parity, and this, as a rule, was not contentious.

A greater source of conflict than either the legislative or the executive in prewar Lebanon was the civil service. This was not a matter of symbols but of benefits. And in a system largely based on patronage the distribution of benefits is directly associated with power. As a result of the fifteen-year Muslim boycott of the Lebanese state during the mandate, there was always considerable disequilibrium in the civil service, which had been built up largely by Christians. The disequilibrium continued well into the independent republic: young civil servants appointed in the 1930s reached retiring age only in the 1960s.

The distribution of posts in the upper echelons of the civil service — secretaries of state and departmental heads, ministerial officials, heads of provincial administrations as well as diplomats — until 1958 was as follows:

**Table 2.2** Top civil service posts by community (%)

|  | 1946[135] | 1955[136] | 1958[137] |
|---|---|---|---|
| Maronites | 39 | 40 | 38 |
| Greek Orthodox | 19 | 12 | 12 |
| Greek Catholic | 3 | 9 | 11 |
| Sunnites | 29 | 27 | 26 |
| Shiites | 3 | 4 | 6 |
| Druze | 6 | 7 | 6 |

---

[135] Ralph E. Crow, Religious Sectarianism in the Lebanese Political System, in: *The Journal Of Politics*, 24 (1962)3, p. 519.
[136] Halim F. Fayyad, *The Effects of Sectarianism on the Lebanese Administration*, p. 71, quoted by Wilhelm Kewenig, op. cit. p. 83.
[137] Wilhelm Kewenig, op cit., p. 83.

In this period especially Maronites and Greek Catholics, but Sunnis too, were over-represented, 'largely at the expense of the Shi`is'.[138] The principal cause of the Shi`is' under-representation was their educational lag; until the early 1960s the community lacked the university graduates, above all lawyers, to fill the positions proportionality entitled them to.[139]

The distribution of lower and intermediate civil service posts, which did not require a university degree, was much less uneven. In 1942, 49 per cent of all posts were already held by Muslims, and 19.5 per cent by Shi`is. However, these 49 per cent received just under 41 per cent of all civil service remunerations, further evidence of under-representation in the upper, better-paid positions.[140]

As long as the Muslim communities lagged in university education — that is, until the end of the 1960s — Muslim deputies, parties and institutions were among the most zealous champions of the principle of proportionality or quotas, citing Article 95 of the Constitution, which stipulates an adequate distribution of civil service posts among the communities. Christian politicians, parties and institutions, in the knowledge of their communities' educational advantages, demanded that civil servants be appointed on merit alone, citing Article 12 of the Constitution, which stipulates that all Lebanese citizens shall have equal access to the civil service and that the only criteria of selection are merit and ability. It became a matter of the quota principle and collective justice versus the performance principle and individual justice, principles proclaimed to protect specific group interests.

The system of proportionality proved stronger. The administrative reforms of 1952/3 included a directive that if aspirant civil servants had equivalent qualifications there should be a 'concours', a competition to select the best, who would then be recruited. By 1955 political pressure was strong enough to have this directive changed. All candidates would have to sit an entry examination, but henceforth the best would not be announced. Thus, 'it was once again possible to select the candidates of the "right" religious communities from among those who had passed the examination, without evidently acting counter to the interests of the state — and thereby Article 12 of the Constitution.'[141]

---

[138] Ibid., p. 84

[139] In 1961 only one-quarter of university students were Muslim, and less than ten per cent Shi`i. At Saint Joseph's University, which, until 1960, had the only Faculty of Law in the country, ten per cent of the students were Muslim; at the American University of Beirut, approximately twenty-five per cent were.

[140] Fayyad, *The Effects of Sectarianism*, quoted by Kewenig, *Die Koexistenz*, p. 85. Kewenig comments on Fayyad's data as follows: 'Despite necessary fundamental reservations about statistical material from whatever source, it cannot be doubted but that the above survey [from which the figures in the text have been taken] are correct, as the name and denomination of each of the listed civil servants has been registered'.

[141] Kewenig, *Die Koexistenz*, pp. 96f.

In 1958 President Chehab proclaimed the introduction of the principle of strict parity: for every Christian civil servant a Muslim would also be appointed. This was realized within a few years. It meant the expansion of the civil service. And it was inevitable that the general standards of the civil service would suffer for some years. However, Chehab reckoned that the necessity of removing the legacy of disequilibrium was more important than a probably temporary problem of quality.[142] The realization of the 'fifty-fifty' principle satisfied the Muslim communities for some years; 'there were no further important domestic demands'.[143]

Only over a decade later was the question of the division of power raised anew, and with great vehemence. The bone of contention this time was a number of civil service posts that, without violating the principle of general parity at all administrative levels, had been regarded as 'preserves' of the Maronite community. Some of these were key positions: the command of the army, the directorates of military intelligence and state security, the governorship of the Central Bank and the chairmanship of the Conseil d'Etat. Others were equally prestigious, but had little political clout.[144] As in the dispute over the presidency, the Maronites argued that their incumbencies served as necessary 'guarantees' for the Christians, whereas the Muslims argued that it was a matter of unjustified privilege. Both arguments lack conviction. Only the top military and security posts can be regarded as — partial — guarantees for the Christians; on the other hand, realization of the principle of parity meant 'Maronite preserves' might well have become superfluous, but their continued existence hardly constituted privilege.

The attacks on 'privilege' were little more than effective publicity for another demand Muslims expressed with growing frequency from the late 1960s: the repeal of the quota and proportionality systems in both administration and politics. The quota system in the civil service favoured the Muslim communities as long as they suffered from an educational lag and as long as posts had to be vacated or created for them. In the late 1960s Muslim enrolment at the universities drew level with that of the Christians; in 1972/3, 53 per cent of all students were Muslims.[145] This spectacular educational advance was made possible by university expansion, above all of the state-run Lebanese University, and in particular its legal faculty, whose certificates were recognized for civil service entrance. In the 1965/6 academic year, 63 per cent of all law students were

---

[142] Interview with the author with the Minister of Justice, Fouad Boutros, 1960.

[143] Marwan Hamadé, 'L'Islam libanais, du Nassérisme à la participation', *Travaux et Jours* 53 (1974), p. 7.

[144] The rectorship of the Lebanese University, the presidency of the Appellate Division, the presidency of the Military Court of Appeal, etc.

[145] Labaki, 'Rapports de force, p. 33.

Muslims,[146] and eight years later, 64 per cent of the candidates for senior civil service posts were Muslims.[147] By this time, however, the civil service was more or less saturated. Graduates with high expectations poured into a labour market for which they were ill-prepared and ill-equipped, especially the law graduates among them.[148] Hence, all hopes were pinned on the civil service. Demands grew louder for the abolition of quotas, of 'privileges' and, eventually, of proportionality in all institutions of state. Students demonstrated against the parliamentarians, the 'ninety-nine thieves' whose potential for economic patronage was exhausted. Initially, the demonstrations were not confessional: Christian students also sensed the danger of becoming an academic proletariat. They had a common basic desire for a modern state and a modern society that could cope with the problems of the future. The intensely emotional, though politically vague bond of common interests among students of all communities broke in the early 1970s. One section joined the parties of the Left; another, larger section supported the classic demands of political Islam: a census and abolition of political and administrative proportionality. The Christian section of the student movement vacillated between progressive tendencies and the political positions of their communities.

The nature of the recrudescent conflicts over political and administrative power between independence and the outbreak of war hardly changed. The issues were the census and the conditions under which it should be held, the confessional distribution of seats in parliament, the division of powers between the president and the premier and the allocation of posts in the civil service. But there was a significant shift in the balance of real power. Between the principal offices of state a duumvirate evolved — along, as we shall see, a stormy path — in which for most practical purposes the incumbents had equal powers. In the civil service the initial Christian predominance gave way to strict parity. What remained was a Christian, and in particular Maronite, 'symbolic hegemony'. For decades the defence of this 'guarantee' against attacks on it as 'privilege' was the stuff of battles of words, both in and, especially, out of parliament. Notwithstanding this, the search for compromise and consensus was efficacious within the institutions, in which initial disequilibrium was gradually transformed into practical equilibrium. For three decades the Lebanese system of domestic political conflict regulation proved flexible and, within measure, adaptable. For a long time, the recourse to 'guarantees' and 'privileges' was little more that the respective opening tilt in

---

[146] Ibid., p. 22.

[147] 3ème catégorie (niveau licence), ibid., p. 30.

[148] Their prospects as lawyers were limited, as the established law firms preferred the better qualified graduates of Saint Joseph's University. There were plenty opportunities for legal people in the private sector. But as much of their business was international, companies wanted staff with a knowledge of foreign languages - and language courses were not very popular at the Lebanese University at this time.

bargaining over larger shares of power and the concomitant benefits. The bargaining stopped in 1975. The fault lay not in the mechanisms of the political market, but elsewhere — in conflicts of quite another nature.

## Class, community and economic conflicts

The lack of census figures stimulated not only political, but also social fantasies. And the products usually correlated with the analyst's political convictions. From the mid-1970s onwards, a number of authors more or less equated social class and community in Lebanon, and interpreted conflicts between these communities as class struggles.[149] Of course, this thesis was an effective mobilizer. It also satisfied the desire of some media for simple explanations of complex situations. The cliché of 'rich Christians' and 'poor Muslims', has had a brilliant journalistic career- and it may not be over yet.

Yet, some authors have resisted substituting convictions for census figures. Instead, they have attempted to gather reliable, if incomplete, data from numerous sources, supplement them with their own surveys and interpret them with due care. Eminent among them are Claude Dubar, Salim Nasr and Boutros Labaki.[150] Their studies provide important insights into the modes of incorporation of classes and communities, and into changes in the modes of incorporation in the pre-war period.

The creation of Greater Lebanon within the present republic's borders in 1920 united Beirut, the former province of Mount Lebanon and the peripheral areas in a state in which different governmental and economic structures quasi automatically favoured an inegalitarian incorporation of regions and — as these were inhabited by different religious communities — of communities too. In Mount Lebanon the majority of the population were small farmers. In the peripheral areas land had earlier been in village or common ethnic ownership, but in the final phase of Ottoman rule most of it had passed into the private possession of a small number of large landowners. A merchant middle class had emerged in Beirut and Mount Lebanon, a silk industry had been created and professions

---

[149] Sulaiman Taqi ad-Din, *Al-tatawwur al-tarikhi li-al-muskila al-lubnaniyya* (The historical development of the Lebanese problem) (Beirut, 1977), p. 96; M. al-Sulh, Al-maruniyya al-siyasiyya: sira dhatiyya (Political Maronitism: A personal account) (Beirut, 1978); H. Gabir, 'Al-sulta wa-al-tawazun fi Lubnan' (Domination and equilibrium in Lebanon), *Shu`un falastiniyya*, 50/51 (Beirut, n.d.). For a critique, see Yasin al-Hafiz, 'Qira'a naqdiyya li-ba`d turuhat al-harb fi Lubnan' (A critique of certain theses on the war in Lebanon), *Lubnan ad-dimuqrati al-arabi al-almani*, 8 (Beirut, 1981), pp. 1–45. See also Samir Kassir, 'L'affirmation des chiites libanais', *Le Monde diplomatique* (May, 1985), p. 12.

[150] Claude Dubar and Salim Nasr, *Les classes sociales au Liban* (Paris, 1976); Boutros Labaki, 'Structuration communautaire, rapports de force entre minorités et guerres au Liban', *Guerres mondiales at conflicts contemporains* 151 (1981), pp. 43–70.

established. Owing to their long educational tradition, the Christians were predominant in these fields:[151] about four-fifths of all merchants, silk exporters and bankers and about two-thirds of all importers and shipping merchants in Beirut were Christian, 92 per cent of the silk manufacturers,[152] most artisans and craftsmen, in 1889 every single shoemaker, 95 per cent of the tailors and cabinetmakers as well as half of the blacksmiths, and, at the outbreak of the First World War, 83 per cent of all factory workers within the borders of present-day Lebanon.[153]

These figures indicate an incorporation of considerable inequality. The Christian communities as a society provided the greater part of the merchant, industrial and professional bourgeoisie as well as the majority of tradesmen, artisans and craftsmen; moreover, the overwhelming majority of Christian farmers were independent.[154] But Christian society was not a class: it was a strongly stratified society with different classes.

The Muslim communities were also stratified. Prior to the First World War they provided 43 per cent of all merchants in the territories of present-day Lebanon, 29 per cent of the importers, 40 per cent of all insurance brokers, some bankers in Tripoli and some artisans. The vast majority of large landowners in the north, east and south of the country were Muslim, as were virtually all of their tenants and agricultural labourers. Class differences among the Muslims were far greater than among the Christians.

The two confessional societies were unequal attendants at the birth of the new state, products of the very different historical developments of central and peripheral Lebanon. Although the mandatory authorities pursued a policy of regional equalization[155] — in effect, equalization between the communities — including the introduction of state education, much of it in the peripheral regions, there were still enormous disparities on the eve of independence. Most deprived were the Shi`is and girls of all Muslim communities.[156]

The policy of social and economic equalization between the regions and communities was continued after independence, especially as Muslim insistence grew more compelling once the National Pact had given them a voice in government. Policy instruments included the system of quotas in the civil service and the infrastructural and educational policies. The most effective equalization policies

---

[151] Labaki, Ibid., p. 54.
[152] Ibid.
[153] Ibid., p. 55.
[154] Ibid., pp. 54f.
[155] Ibid., p. 56; see also Hanf, *Erziehungswesen*, pp. 74–84.
[156] République Française, *Rapport sur la situation en Syrie et au Liban à la Commission de Tutelle de la Société des Nations*, (Paris, 1926–1939), Table 3.

were introduced during President Chehab's term of office. In 1959 he commissioned a comprehensive study on the development of Lebanon from the French organization for development planning, IRFED. Chairman was the Dominican Louis-Joseph Lebret. Lebret noted that 'the differences in living standards of both regions and social strata are excessive and an enormous effort is urgently required to overcome them'.[157] A direct consequence of the Lebret study was numerous electricity, irrigation and road-building projects in less developed parts of the country. The telephone and power networks were extended to even the most remote areas and the national health system was improved. These policies met with the resistance of large Shi`i and Sunni landowners in the south and north respectively, who feared that these projects and the concomitant strengthening of state influence would weaken their own economic and political pre-eminence.[158] At the same time, the educational system was rapidly expanded, especially secondary schools, vocational schools and the Lebanese University. The consequences of this policy can be seen in the 1974 data: illiteracy among Muslims had fallen to 14 per cent, among Christians to 11 per cent.[159] Muslim and Christian enrolment at secondary schools and universities was more or less equal. The Christians' educational advantage had been reduced to certain qualitative distinctions of their educational institutions, especially intensive instruction in foreign languages. What effects did the government's policy of equalization have on the patchwork quilt of classes and communities?

Around 1960 economic stratification by community was as follows:[160] the lowest stratum consisted of seasonal and casual workers, a sort of sub-proletariat recruited mostly among non-Lebanese without an official work permit, such as Palestinians, Kurds, Alawites and Syrians. In the peripheral areas the majority of the population were agricultural labourers and tenant farmers who had virtually no economic prospects in rural areas and by 1960 were starting to drift to the cities. There, in living conditions that were hardly an improvement, they augmented the urban sub-proletariat. The overwhelming majority of the agricultural labouring class were Muslims, most of them Shi`is. Although better off than agricultural labourers, the urban working class in industry, manual labour,

---

[157] Le Rapport du Père Lebret, *Le Commerce du Levant* 1/3 (1960), p. 25.
[158] See Herwig Lechleitner, 'Konfessionsgruppen und Wirtschaftsleben im Libanon', *Geographische Rundschau* 24/6 (1972), p. 215.
[159] Yves Schemeil, 'Sociologie du système politique libanais', Unpublished Ph.D dissertation, University of Grenoble, 1976, p. 68, Table 8.
[160] For details, Hanf, *Erziehungswesen*, pp. 31–8; see also Georges Hakim, 'The economic basis of Lebanese polity', in Binder, *Politics in Lebanon*, p. 60; Ralph E. Crow, *Interest Groups in the Lebanese Political Process*, (Beirut, 1962), p. 16; *Rapport de l'IRFED*, Documents I–1–13, 38 and 36, (Beirut and Paris, 1962).

construction and services still lived in very needy circumstances — in particular those working in small firms in the services sector. At that time only about 12 per cent of all workers were members of trade unions, and their bargaining position was correspondingly weak. The majority of workers in manual jobs, construction and services were Sunnis, with smaller groups of Armenians and Maronites.

The three groups classified above constituted about half of the working population. The middle class made up most of the other half: clerks in private firms, civil servants, small farmers, traders and small manufacturers as well as independent tradesmen, artisans and professional people. Most had middle-range incomes and a large degree of independence, and many held more than one job. Apart from civil servants, the majority of the middle classes were Christian. Characteristic of the middle-class population of the mountains was a combination of agriculture — usually fruit or market-gardening — and an urban occupation in either business or the civil service; it was this agricultural activity that gave a large part of the middle class a considerable measure of independence. The upper class was very small. It was composed of large landowners, on the one hand, and industrialists and great merchants, on the other. They were drawn from all confessions, though the majority of large landowners were Muslim and the majority of industrialists Christian.

In the early 1960s the economic interests of the middle and upper classes were more or less identical. Both classes supported the established economic policies, characterized by extreme laissez-faire, indirect rather than direct taxes, and a general lack of social legislation. Hence, economic cleavages ran across the communities diagonally: the majority of Christians had middle- and upper-class interests, the majority of Muslims those of the working and agricultural labouring classes. However, as most leading Muslim politicians belonged to the upper class, workers and agricultural labourers for a long time lacked adequate articulation and representation of their interests.

Income disparities at the beginning of the 1960s were considerable.[161] The IRFED report gives the following distribution:[162]

---

[161] In a study for the ILO, Felix Paukert calculated income parities in 56 countries during the 1960s. The Gini Index varied between 0.26 (South Korea) and 0.64 (Gabon). The Index for Lebanon was 0.55, similar to that for France, 0.50; in other words, the disparities in the two countries were not very different. Figures taken from Fernand Sanan, 'Notes sur la répartition du revenu au Liban', *L'Economie des pay arabes, étude mensuelle*, 20/2 (1977), pp. 9–15.

[162] République Libanaise, Ministère du Plan, *Mission IRFED–Liban 1960–61* (Beirut), p. 93.

### Table 2.3

| Category | Average annual family income in LL | % of total population | Category as % of GNP |
|---|---|---|---|
| 'Impoverished' | 1,000 | 8.8 | 1.5 |
| 'Poor' | 2,000 | 41.2 | 16.3 |
| 'Average' | 3,500 | 32.0 | 22.2 |
| 'Well-off' | 11,000 | 14.0 | 28.0 |
| 'Wealthy' | 40,000 | 4.0 | 32.0 |

In 1973 and 1974 the French sociologist Yves Schemeil conducted empirical surveys that indicate considerable shifts in the distribution of income.[163]

### Table 2.4

| 1973 | | 1974 | |
|---|---|---|---|
| Average annual in LL | % of total population | Average annual in LL | % of total population |
| 2,000 | 23.5 | 1,850 | 20.3 |
| 3.000 | 28.1 | 2,750 | 36.7 |
| 6,150 | 25.9 | 5,500 | 23.4 |
| 8,000 | 22.2 | 7,350 | 19.5 |

By comparison with 1960, the middle-income categories had expanded considerably, and the upper-income category had decreased between 1973 and 1974.

A study carried out by Raymond Delprat in 1970 provides further evidence of some narrowing of earlier disparities. Ten years previously, Delprat had supervised the IRFED study. He used a compound index of 'quality of life', composed

---

[163] Schemeil, 'Sociologie', p. 22; Labaki deflated Schemeil's figures to 1960 prices to enable an approximate comparison. See Labaki, 'Structuration', p. 64.

of a number of individual indices: hygiene, economic and technical standards, housing, schooling and cultural and social status.[164]

**Table 2.5**

| Region | 'Quality-of-life' Index 1960 | 'Quality-of-life' Index 1970 | % increase |
|---|---|---|---|
| Central region | 2.24 | 2.59 | 15.6 |
| Northern Lebanon | 2.13 | 2.52 | 40.0 |
| Southern Lebanon | 1.53 | 2.20 | 43.8 |
| Bekaa | 1.47 | 2.00 | 36.1 |
| Rural areas overall | 1.69 | 2.23 | 32.0 |

Labaki concludes that 'the peripheral regions of Lebanon, with largely Muslim populations, have advanced most. The improvement in living standards is most marked in south Lebanon, which is 70 per cent Muslim: almost 44 per cent between 1960 and 1970.'[165]

Both overall income disparities and regional disparities in living standards have decreased since 1960. Much of this is due to the government's structural policies. But there are other factors too. The Lebanese economy has been transformed. The greatest change has taken place in agriculture. In 1959 this sector employed about half of the working population, in 1965 one-third and in 1970 only just one-fifth.[166] Independent small farmers became part-time farmers. Many large landowners sold their land to entrepreneurs, often emigrants who had made their fortune abroad and returned to establish export-oriented, capital-intensive agro-businesses. Especially in the south and in Akkar numbers of tenant farmers and agricultural labourers lost their livelihood and migrated to the cities. By 1970 Lebanon was importing 40 per cent of its food.[167] The importance of the tertiary sector — always disproportionate — became even more pronounced: in 1960 it accounted for 60 per cent of the GNP, in 1970 for over 70 per cent.[168] Banking boomed, initially on Arab capital seeking a safe haven, then on oil. But only one-

---

[164] Raymond Delprat, 'Liban: L'évolution du niveau de vie en milieu rural 1960–1970' (Beirut, 1970) (mimeographed report of the Lebanese Ministry of Planning, quoted in Labaki, 'Structuration', p. 65).
[165] Ibid.
[166] Dubar and Nasr, *Les classes sociales*, p. 93
[167] Ibid., p. 97.
[168] Ibid., p. 67.

fifth of all banking operations were transacted by institutions with Lebanese capital; branches of foreign banks dominated the market. Lebanon became the classic centre of entrepôt trade between western and Arab states: 70 per cent of its imports came from western, above all European industrial states and 60 per cent of its exports went to the Arab world.[169] Tourism grew rapidly; four-fifths of the tourists came from Arab countries. Yet, pre-war Lebanon did not live from service industries alone. Manufacturing had high rates of growth for decades: 5 per cent per year in the 1950s, 10 per cent in the 1960s and up to 12 per cent in the first half of the 1970s.[170] Small industry still predominated — 10,700 firms with fewer than twenty-five employees and only 300 with more — but there was rapid concentration in key sectors. In the 1960s the balance of payments was in surplus only because of the huge 'invisibles' account — profits from triangular trade, emigrants' transfers, etc.; the balance of trade was in chronic deficit. Yet, by 1967 exports already covered one-quarter of imports, in 1971 about one-third and in 1973 a full half.[171]

Beirut, in particular, experienced a tremendous property boom, and owners of urban property, particularly in Beirut, made fortunes or became rentiers. Alongside the old phenomenon of emigration appeared a new one of temporary migrant labour, which tapped new sources of income in the Persian Gulf. At the same time, Lebanon began importing labour: hundreds of thousands of migrant workers, above all from Syria.[172]

What were the effects of these economic changes on class structures and the economic incorporation of the communities? Using a 1970 survey of the working population by the Ministry of Planning, Claude Dubar and Salim Nasr have made the following classification of classes and strata (Table 2.6).[173]

Unfortunately, the ministry's survey did not include confessional data. However, other studies and data allow approximate classification of some strata. About one-third of all bankers and one-quarter of the owners of trading, insurance and transport companies were Muslim.[174] Of twenty-five large industrial firms, seven were controlled by Muslims and seventeen by Christians, though in most cases members of other communities had minority holdings.[175] Most new agro-businesses were in Muslim hands. All in all, probably about two-thirds of the industrial, commercial and financial bourgeoisie were Christian and one-third

---

[169] Ibid., p. 75.
[170] Ibid., p. 76.
[171] Ibid., p. 74.
[172] Ibid., p. 111.
[173] Ibid., p. 113.
[174] Labaki, 'Structuration', p. 66.
[175] Dubar and Nasr, *Les classes sociales*, p. 84.

**Table 2.6**

| Objective classes | social strata | % of working population | |
|---|---|---|---|
| Wealthy business classes (property owners, regular income, skilled non-manual work) | Heads of trading companies | 1.7 | |
| | Heads of manufacturing or service companies | 1.9 | 3.6 |
| Independent small businessmen (property owners, irregular income, skilled work) | Professions | 1.4 | |
| | Self-employed in commerce or services | 8.5 | |
| | Artisans | 11.7 | |
| | Independent farmers | 12.5 | |
| | | | 34.1 |
| Middle-class employees (no property; regular, non-manual employment) | Top-level managers and civil servants | 0.8 | |
| | Middle-level management and civil servants incl. teachers | 7.8 | |
| | Employees in commerce and services | 10.0 | |
| | Clerical staff | 7.9 | 26.5 |
| Proletariat (no property; regular manual semi-skilled employment) | Full-time, non-farm workers | 8.4 | |
| | Non-farm day labourers | 13.7 | 22.1 |
| Subproletariat (no property; irregular manual unskilled employment) | Farmworkers and tenant farmers | 5.8 | |
| | Non-permanent service jobs | 3.9 | |
| | Unemployed seeking work | 4.0 | 13.7 |

Muslim. The communal or denominational classification of the middle class is more difficult. Civil servants and employees in state-run enterprises were more or less equally divided; in the professions about one-third were Muslims.[176] A detailed 1974 survey on industrial workers by Marlène and Salim Nasr provides more precise data: 45 per cent are Christian, the majority Maronite or Armenian; 55 per cent are Muslim, of whom two-thirds are Shi`i. This finding destroys a 'particularly persistent myth' that most of the bourgeoisie and middle class, but none of the proletariat, are Christian, and the overwhelming mass of the 'common people and working class' are Muslim. 'We are able to disprove this ideological hypothesis ... the industrial proletariat is without doubt a multireligious and multiconfessional proletariat.'[177] However, Christians are over-represented among skilled workers and Muslims among semi-skilled. The sub-proletariat consists of large numbers of Shi`i agricultural and day labourers from the south and east of the country, but also landless Maronites and members of smaller Christian communities — Assyrians and Jacobites — jobbing in the service sector, as well as Armenian manual and unskilled workers in the repair trades.[178]

Deducting the approximations for the industrial, financial and commercial bourgeoisie,[179] for the civil service and state-controlled enterprises as well as the proletariat, gives the respective shares of the confessions in the rest of the middle class. One thus has a rough estimate of the distribution of confessions by class in the early 1970s (Table 2.7).

Even allowing for a reasonable margin of error, two results can hardly be disputed: both religious groups are strongly stratified, and the stratifications are similar. Although it would be an exaggeration to speak of egalitarian incorporation, inequality remains within bounds. More importantly, social and economic disparities narrowed enormously in the half century after independence.

---

[176] Labaki, 'Structuration', p. 66.

[177] Marlène and Salim Nasr, 'Morphologie sociale de la banlieue-est de Beyrouth', *Maghreb-Machrek*, 73 (1976), p. 87.

[178] Dubar and Nasr, *Les classes sociales*, p. 90.

[179] For the bourgeoisie see also the estimates of Georges Corm, *Géopolitique du conflit libanais: Étude historique et sociologique* (Paris, 1986), pp. 170f, according to whom prior to 1975 'les grandes fortunes restent largement concentrées dans les mains de la féodalité chi`ite, des grands propriétaires fonciers urbains sunnites dans leur majorité, mais aussi grec-orthodoxes. Ces derniers ont aussi une position prépondérante dans le commerce, l'industrie et la finance'. In contrast to this group, he emphasizes the emergence of a 'véritable classe moyenne d'envergure' among the Maronites, based on education rather than wealth, but he also points out that the rural exodus of a broad, deprived rural stratum over the past decades has given rise to a Maronite 'véritable couche populaire urbaine'. He sees the Maronite middle class as the 'élément moteur de la prospérité libanaise depuis le début du siècle, mais nullement détentrice du pouvoir économique véritable du pays, situé dans les autres communautés'.

The comparison of class structures in the two religious groups should not blind one to the differences within them, nor to the 'time lags' in the social and economic development of the different communities. The first to embrace modern economic practices were the urban Christian communities, the Greek Orthodox and Greek Catholics.[180] They were followed by the Sunnis, the urban Muslim community. In recent decades it was again the old-established urban communities who enjoyed the fruits of the property boom. In the 1960s and 1970s the most valuable property in Beirut belonged to Sunnis, which enabled many of them to advance rapidly: sons of craftsmen and small traders became doctors, engineers and lawyers, and many others rentiers. When the Armenians fled to Lebanon the vast majority immediately settled in the cities and have remained a predominantly urban community; only in Anjar in the Bekaa do they have a rural settlement. Maronites started moving to the cities around the turn of the century, and en masse only after the Second World War. The Shi`is were the tail end of the urbanization process: their rural exodus began only in the 1950s.[181] They had been dependent on large landowners longer than others and were the least educated group, hence had the most to catch up on and make up for. Thus, the industrial work force was drawn mainly from newly arrived Maronites and Shi`is, and those Shi`is that arrived last formed, together with those left on the land, most of the sub-proletariat.

**Table 2.7**

|  | Christian % | Total population % | Muslim % |
|---|---|---|---|
| Wealthy business classes | 4 | 6 | 2 |
| Middle classes (self-employed and salaried staff) | 67 | 60.6 | 56 |
| Proletariat | 21 | 22.1 | 23 |
| Subproletariat | 8 | 13.7 | 19 |
|  | 100 | 100 | 100 |

[180] See Fawaz, *Merchants and Migrants*, pp. 85f.
[181] In 1920 there were only about 1,500 Shi`is in Beirut. Only in the 1940s did they acquire their separate mosque. Ibid., pp. 50 and 155.

*The Lebanese Model*

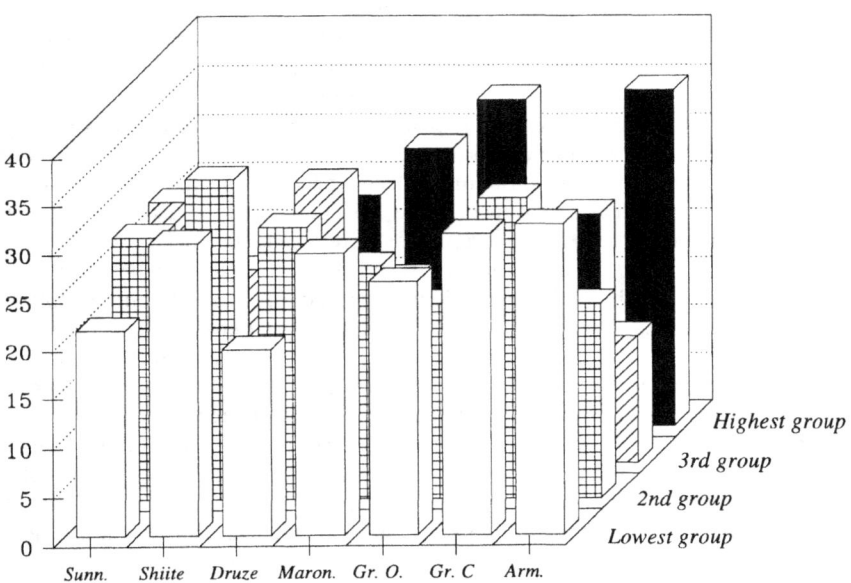

**Diagram 2.2 Religious communities by income group**

Figures in %

Hence, it is not surprising that the Shi`is have been at the centre of all social conflicts since the mid-1960s. Whereas the Sunnis, as a rule, questioned the political status quo and concentrated their economic demands on the question of quotas in the civil service, the Shi`is' concerns were primarily economic. For a long time they did not articulate these concerns as Shi`is, as members of a community, but as in inhabitants of depressed areas, as agricultural labourers and tenants exploited by large landowners, as badly paid industrial workers and as unskilled labourers without any social security. They joined parties and political movements that championed not the specific interests of one community but social and economic policies; the Baath Party, the SSNP, the Communist Party and their splinter groups, in short, the secular Left. Even when the religious institutions of the Shi`i community, concerned about the growing influence of 'atheistic' movements among their faithful, started to mobilize and organize the Shi`is as a community, they too had to voice economic grievances. The Supreme Shi`i Islamic Council was formed in 1967, and in 1969 a dynamic cleric, Imam Musa Sadr, became chairman. Musa Sadr founded the Movement of the Deprived, primarily for Shi`is, but also for other Lebanese who felt deprived. He talked not about quotas and posts in government and civil service, but about irrigation projects, dams, schools, hospitals and the price of tobacco.[182]

In the social conflicts of the last pre-war decade, Shi`is were prominent among all groups demanding economic improvements, be they trade unions, rural protest movements or left-wing parties. But this reflected primarily social, not communal, mobilization. Even when a movement of the Shi`i community began to crystallize around Sadr in the early 1970s, its grievances were essentially social.

Apart from Shi`is, the emerging social movements attracted others that felt they were victims of the rapid economic transformation, such as Sunnis in Akkar and rural Maronites. Government efforts to develop the Lebanese periphery had unforeseen consequences. The infrastructural improvements failed to attract further investment and, hence, did not bring new jobs. The new schools produced graduates who could find work only in the cities,[183] and the new roads encouraged commuting and rural exodus. A better educated population was no longer prepared to work for minimal wages or to pay landowners' excessive farm rents. Increasingly, both in the south and the north, people withdrew their political loyalty from the notables they felt were exploiting them. The poorest and the most dynamic rural inhabitants drifted to the cities, where, by the early 1970s the supply of all skills and qualifications exceeded demand.[184] After the expansion of the 1960s the civil service and the tertiary sector were more or less saturated. Over-supply depressed wages. Huge numbers of secondary-school and university graduates could not find jobs that met their expectations. Demands for the abolition of the quota system and for state employment schemes grew vociferous,

---

[182] See *an-Nahar*, 7 and 11 December 1973; see also Francis Grimblat, 'La communauté chiite libanaise et le mouvement national palestinien 1967–1986', *Guerres mondiales et conflicts contemporains* 151 (1988), pp. 74f; Hamadé, 'L'Islam libanais', p. 10. On the pre-1975 development of the Shi`is see Monika Pohl-Schöberlein, *Die schiitische Gemeinschaft des Südlibanon (Gabal `Amil) innerhalb des libanesischen konfessionellen Systems* (Berlin, 1975). See also Salim Nasr, 'Mobilisation communautaire et symbolique religieuse: L'Imam Sadr et les chi'ites du Liban (1970-1975)', in Olivier Carré et al., eds., Radicalismes islamiques, (Paris, 1985), vol. 1, pp. 119–58 (an earlier version appeared in Mourad Wahba, ed., *Youth, Violence, Religion: Secularization and de-secularization*, Cairo 1983, pp. 387–403); Augustus Richard Norton, *Amal and the Shi`a: Struggle for the soul of Lebanon* (Austin, 1987).

[183] See Schemeil, Sociologie, pp. 17ff.

[184] Dubar and Nasr, *Les classes sociales*, p. 325.

and evolved into fundamental criticism of the existing political system. The state could not solve the economic problems; the state was 'sectarian'; therefore sectarianism should go — meaning the Lebanese system of proportionality. This syllogism found wide support in intellectual circles. Despite its woolly logic, it contains a grain of truth. The Lebanese polity and its electoral system is designed to throw up deputies and ministers with many qualities, above all, moderation and readiness to compromise. An appreciation of social distress and of novel solutions is less valued. Whether Muslim or Christian, the majority of the Lebanese political élite were wealthy members of the upper strata. No matter how divided they might be on power-sharing, their economic interests were virtually identical. And these interests were best served by a liberalism untrammelled by social welfare correctives. Yet they were always prepared to violate their laissez-faire principles to preserve the interests of their own stratum. Pre-war Lebanon did not have a genuine free market economy. Cartels and even monopolies were tolerated in the import trade and certain areas of manufacturing; the beneficiaries were politicians or persons closely associated with them.[185] But they had little understanding of the economic and social concerns of the expanding working class and the new, upwardly mobile middle classes in industry and services, and even less understanding of the resurgent dissatisfaction of the rural population.

In the early 1970s social conflicts became more common and more intense. The remarkable feature was the absence of 'confessional' undertones. They were not conflicts between communities but between social and economic groups and interests.[186] In Akkar, Sunni tenants and agricultural labourers revolted against Sunni landowners. Shi'i tobacco farmers in the south protested against the practices of the state tobacco monopoly. Shi'i and Sunni workers picketed the food-processing plant of the Sunni Ghandour family for weeks. The associations of traders and importers, with members from all communities fought hard against the chamber of industry over protective tariffs and other protectionist measures. The associations of teachers, the student movement and, especially, the trade unions drew members from all communities,[187] as did the federations of industry

---

[185] For details, Salim Nasr, 'The Crisis of Lebanese Capitalism', *Merip Reports* 73 (1978), pp. 5f; see also Antoine Basile, 'Contraintes et perspectives de l'économie libanaise', in Joseph Abou Jaoude et al., *La nouvelle société libanaise dans la perception des Fa`aliyat des communautés chrétiennes*, vol. 3, Etudes et Rapports, (Kaslik, 1984), p. 271.

[186] Dubar and Nasr, *Les classes sociales*, pp. 324ff.

[187] For details, Theodor Hanf and Salim Nasr, *Gewerkschaftliche Konkordanz im Libanon. Bestimmungsfaktoren gewerkschaftlicher Einheit in einer kulturell und politisch fragmentierten Gesellschaft. Eine empirische Untersuchung. Forschungsbericht des Deutschen Instituts für Internationale Pädagogische Forschung* (Frankfurt am Main, 1982); see also Raymond Delprat, 'Blocages économiques et crise sociale au Liban', *Etudes des cahiers de l'orient contemporain* 26 (1969), p. 12.

and commerce. The leadership of the Lebanese confederation of trade unions was chosen by an informal, flexible yet efficient system of communal quotas. Between 1961 and 1975 the share of the organized workforce rose from twelve to almost 24 per cent.

In summary, between the creation of Lebanon and the outbreak of the war the enormously inegalitarian incorporation of classes and communities was considerably reduced, especially after 1960, when the government introduced its structural policies. In social terms, however, the Shi`i community remained relatively deprived. Nevertheless, the social conflict of the 1960s and early 1970s was between strata, classes and interest groups, not communities. Neither side was choosy in its methods: blockades, occupation of factories, approved and unapproved mass demonstrations, on the one hand, and lock-outs, economic reprisals and often inordinate police action on the other. However, all in all, there was little to distinguish these forms of social conflict from those in homogeneous societies in times of economic crisis. Nor were the protest movements in vain: employers conceded wage increases and improvements in working conditions; the state restricted the possibilities of arbitrary dismissal; and minimum wages were raised several times.[188] In short: Lebanon seemed to be evolving into a society in which supra-communal class conflicts were more important than cleavages between the communities, and it seemed that the class conflicts, notwithstanding their intensity, could be regulated peacefully. A leading Lebanese social scientist predicted modernization without revolution.[189]

## Foreign policy as a conflict of identity

The National Pact found formulations for compromise on the question of national identity as well as on guidelines for foreign policy. Both were vague enough for broad consensus, and interpretable enough for partiality. Yet, controversies over foreign policy always and repeatedly dragged the question of national identity into the political arena.

The controversy in the first decade of independence centred on the question of economic union with Syria, a legacy of the mandate. Muslim[190] politicians wanted to retain it, in part because it was a remnant of former dreams of unity, in part because of very real economic considerations: the largely Muslim areas of the Bekaa, Akkar and the port of Tripoli were integrated with the Syrian hinterland. The majority of Christians opposed economic association with Syria, for reasons

---

[188] Delprat, 'Blocages économiques', p. 8.
[189] Elie Salem, *Modernization without Revolution: Lebanon's experience* (Bloomington, 1973).
[190] In this section the simplifications 'Muslim' and 'Christian' will refer to the majorities of key politicians in the respective religious groups.

of principle (Lebanon should have full sovereignty) and for reasons of economic opportunity (the Syrian preference for protectionism bode ill for the service-centred Lebanese economy).[191] There was a similar divergence of views on the function and duties of the Arab League, founded in 1944. The Muslims welcomed it, though less as an inter-state organization than as a step towards integration. Christian politicians were prepared to cooperate with other states within the League, but rejected any transfer of sovereignty and any supranational powers for the League.[192]

Relations with the West were just as controversial as forms of solidarity with the Arab world. The Christians welcomed the American Point Four Program as economic aid, and the Muslims saw it as a military pact in disguise. The Christians perceived the Eisenhower Doctrine as a guarantee of Lebanese independence and help against subversion, and the Muslims felt it represented a new form of foreign protection in violation of the National Pact.[193]

Finally, there was disagreement over the form of Lebanese neutrality in intra-Arab conflicts, another stipulation of the National Pact. During the 'Arab Cold War' between a pro-Western bloc of Arab states and bloc espousing positive neutralism under Nasser's Egypt, the majority of Christians wished to preserve strict neutrality, while a minority openly sympathized with the pro-Western bloc. The Muslims took the view that the position of pro-Western Arab countries could no longer be regarded as authentically Arab; hence, neutrality was inappropriate and Lebanon should side with Egypt.[194]

The disputes over foreign policy came to a head for the first time in 1958, over the question of the relationship with the United Arab Republic, the union between Egypt and Syria. This question was crucial to the outbreak of civil war in 1958, even though there were, as shall be seen, important domestic causes too. Whereas supporters of President Chamoun insisted that Lebanon should preserve its freedom of action and sought the backing of the USA to resist Syrian and Egyptian pressure, the majority of Muslims demanded full solidarity with Gamal Abdel Nasser's policies, and a minority even that Lebanon join the Union. The civil war brought victory for neither side. After the armed struggle the only way out was retreat back to the National Pact. After 1958 extreme restraint was the keynote of Lebanese foreign policy.[195]

---

[191] See *Cahiers de l'Orient contemporain*, 1950, pp. 91ff and 219.

[192] *Cahiers de l'Orient contemporain*, 1945, pp. 244ff and 1946, p. 226.

[193] *L'Orient*, August 13th to 20th and November 26th, 1951.

[194] *L'Orient*, March 19th and April 14th, 1955.

[195] 'The political Lebanon of today may be regarded as the Lebanon giving the least possible offense to Nasser, while maintaining the most possible of her original character.' Kamal S. Salibi, 'Lebanon since the Crisis of 1958', *The World Today* 17/1 (1961), p. 42.

Consensus in foreign policy was severely tried once more during the Israeli-Arab wars of 1967 and 1973. Influential Muslim politicians and a large section of Muslim public opinion called for active Lebanese support for the Arab states, whereas Christians, drawing attention to the weakness of the Lebanese armed forces and the likely ravages Lebanon would suffer, rejected this out of hand.[196] In both cases further escalation was obviated only by the short duration of the wars.

The most serious dispute over foreign policy began in the mid-1960s: should Lebanon permit Palestinian guerrillas to operate against Israel from Lebanese territory? Neither group, Muslim or Christian, was unanimous on this question. However, most Lebanese Muslims were of the opinion that Lebanon owed the Palestinians solidarity, even at a high price, while most Christians insisted that support for the Palestinian liberation movement should be purely political and demanded that Palestinian military actions should be prevented, if necessary by force of arms. This issue was to be fateful for Lebanon. In contrast to all previous conflicts, it was not an issue that involved relations with other countries or states, but relations with a people most of whom lived in Lebanon itself: foreign politics could no longer be separated from domestic politics.

The Palestinian question was not an abstract issue. It concerned in a very immediate way the Lebanese people's understanding of themselves. One half of them did not see any contradiction between a Lebanese and an Arab-Muslim identity, whereas the other half wanted a Lebanese and only a Lebanese Lebanon. This conflict was present at the creation of the state, and was still there when peaceful coexistence between the two halves ceased. In the pre-war period it was usually clothed in one or other nationalism — either Greater Syrian or Arab, or Lebanese. The former rejected one part of the 1943 compromise, namely the 'peculiar character' of Lebanon; the latter rejected another part, namely the 'Arab features' of the country. At no time was there any lack of extreme expressions of both nationalisms. On October 3rd, 1947, quite out of the blue, posters appeared in Beirut reading: 'We are Arab. Be part of us or get out.' The next day the Kata'ib issued a manifesto: 'We are Lebanese. We are Lebanese and nothing else. And we shall stay. Our fathers and forefathers have known conquerors of all types, and they have stayed ... We shall not do otherwise. We shall fight with the pen as long as we can. But if necessary, we are ready to take up the sword.'[197]

---

[196] In 1967 Premier Karami instructed the Army Chief of Staff, Emile Boustany, to attack to relieve the hard-pressed Syrian Army. Boustany refused. The American and British ambassadors were ordered to leave the country; however, at the insistence of Christian politicians diplomatic relations were not severed. See Wade R. Goria, *Sovereignty and Leadership in Lebanon 1945–1976* (London, 1985), pp. 88f. In 1973 there were similar differences of opinion. A compromise was reached by putting the Lebanese radar station on Mount Barouk at the disposal of Syria. Ibid., p. 160.

[197] *L'Orient*, October 7th, 1947.

*The Lebanese Model* 113

These two apodeictic statements leave little room for compromise. In a famous article Georges Naccache, one of the leading intellectuals and journalists of the independence generation, put the doubts about the tenableness of the National Pact most tersely:

> The alliance between Christianity and Islam rests on a double rejection. What sort of unity can be created from such a formula? What one half of the Lebanese do not want is quite obvious, and what the other half does not want is equally obvious ... The Lebanon that has been made for us is a fatherland of two fifth columns ... For fear of being what one is, and unwilling to be one thing or the other, Lebanon is in danger of being nothing at all ... A state is not the sum of two impotences — and two negations will never bring forth a nation.[198]

Twelve years later one of the leading Sunni politicians, Premier Saeb Salam contradicted this pessimistic analysis. The Lebanese communities had much in common: the belief in one God, the experience of a common history, the experience of a common struggle for independence and, above all, the same tasks in the present. From this one must postulate: 'One single Lebanon and not two'.[199]

Naccache was writing at a time when the clouds of the first crises after independence were gathering, Salam spoke after the country had survived its first civil war and found its way back to coexistence. The Lebanese formula for coexistence has known depths that are food for pessimists and heights that are food for optimists. We must now consider why it nourishes whom when.

## Use and abuse of coexistence

To what extent 'men make history' or are a product of their social conditioning and environment is a source of perennial dispute among historians and social scientists. For those who do not accept predetermination, it is worth examining what scope political actors have and how they use it. Between 1943 and 1975 the limits to the power of Lebanese politicians varied according to economic and political circumstances as conditioned by regional or international constellations; within these limits very different use was made of purely Lebanese political power.

The first president of independent Lebanon was fortunate in that his period of office, from 1943 to 1952, was free of serious disagreement over foreign policy. In 1945 Lebanon joined the Arab League; at the same time the Arab states guaran-

---
[198] *L'Orient*, March 10th, 1949.
[199] *L'Orient*, April 18th, 1961.

teed Lebanese independence in the Protocol of Alexandria.[200] In 1947 the last French troops left. Until 1951 the president, Beshara al-Khoury, and his prime minister, Riad Solh, were evenly matched, and governed in tandem, as they had agreed to do in 1943. They frequently shuffled ministers to give all the important notables a taste of power, and to play them off against one another. The one person who did not want to lose power was President Khoury himself, and noticeably so as his period of office drew to a close. There were frequent accusations of kickbacks, nepotism and corruption against his family, in particular his brother Salim, his close advisers and political cronies. In the 1947 parliamentary elections the president resorted to electoral manipulation and fraud — through civil servants and police loyal to him personally — to ensure a broad majority. In 1948 this parliament amended the Constitution to limit the president's incumbency to six years, and re-elected Khoury. The government used its powers under the state of emergency — proclaimed because of the first Palestinian war — to cow opposition politicians and prohibit anti-government newspapers. Recruits from all communities swelled the ranks of the president's opponents. In 1951 Khoury lost his strongest pillar of support when Riad Solh was assassinated by a member of the SSNP during a state visit to Jordan. Solh's enormous popularity had helped considerably to steady Khoury's position in the face of criticism. In 1952 Khoury was toppled by the so-called 'Rosewater Revolution': premier Sami Solh resigned, and all important Sunni politicians refused to serve under Khoury; a general strike revealed the disillusionment of the population. General Chehab refused to use troops against the strikers. Thereupon Khoury resigned. The latter half of his incumbency had revealed many of the evils that were to become chronic in Lebanon: officers of state running the country 'like the family farm', as it was put at the time, irregularities in elections and, finally, manipulation of the Constitution to stay in office. But the first half showed how well the Lebanese ship of state sails if the men at the helm have the loyalty of their communities, collaborate in trust and confidence, and respect each other as equals.[201]

Khoury's successor from 1952 to 1958 was Camille Chamoun, who, together with the Druze notable Kamal Jumblatt, had been the driving force behind the opposition to Khoury.[202] At first Chamoun was very popular, especially among the Muslim population, because of his efforts for the Arab cause in the Palestine conflict as Lebanese ambassador at the UNO from 1947 to 1949. Lebanon's economic prosperity in the early years of his presidency strengthened this feeling.

---

[200] *Cahiers de l'Orient contemporain*, 1944, p. 11, including the relevant texts.

[201] On Khoury's period of office see Michael C. Hudson, *The Precarious Republic: Political modernization in Lebanon* (New York, 1968), pp. 264ff; Goria, *Sovereignty*, p. 20 (for a portrait of Beshara al-Khoury), p. 22 (on Riyad al-Solh) and 29ff.

[202] Goria, *Sovereignty*, pp. 35–48 for details on Chamoun, and pp. 30ff for details on Jumblatt.

## The Lebanese Model

Chamoun saw himself as a 'modernizer'.[203] He pinned his hopes on economic development by strengthening and improving the services sector, especially banking; a law on bank secrecy made Lebanon attractive for flight capital from neighbouring countries dabbling in socialism. But he also wanted to modernize the Lebanese system of government. He declared war on 'political feudalism', that is, the established notables, and tended to use his constitutional powers to the full in this pursuit. To weaken the position of the notables he changed the Electoral Law, breaking up a number of large constituencies in which local zu'ama' had safe majorities. He also threw the weight of his office and his government into the fray for or against particular candidates.

A number of long-established politicians lost their seats, and became his bitter enemies. As prime minister he favoured Sami Solh. However, the latter did not command the support among Sunnis his cousin, Riad Solh, had, and consequently his position vis-à-vis the president was weaker. It was not surprising that during his presidency a polemic, 'Moslem Lebanon Today',[204] posed the first serious challenge to the status quo in Lebanon. It alleged: that a census would establish that the Christians were no longer in the majority; that virtually all power was concentrated in the hands of the president, whereas the functions of the prime minister and speaker were ceremonial; that Christian parts of the country got preference and Christian private schools were subsidized, while Muslim parts and Muslim schools were neglected; that Muslims were under-represented in the civil service and that Christians were in full control of the army, the police, customs and the judiciary; and that the freeze on rents applied only to old buildings (most of which belonged to Muslims), not to new buildings (most of which belonged to Christian 'racketeers'). The polemic was a mixture of genuine grievances and imputations. But it revealed that Muslim grievances concerned not only the division of political power but also that of economic power among the communities. The polemic was prohibited, its translator deported. But its contents found fertile ground among Muslims, in particular the Sunni lower-middle class. Domestic discontent coincided with changes in the Arab environment. As part of their 'containment policy' towards the USSR, the USA propagated the Baghdad Pact[205] as a bridge between the NATO and the South Atlantic Pact. Turkey, Pakistan and the Hashemite Kingdom of Iraq joined, and other Arab states were wooed. Strongest opposition to the Pact came from Nasser, who saw no sense in

---

[203] See Pierre Rondot, 'Les couveaux problèmes de l'Etat libanais', *Revue française de science politique* 2 (1954), pp. 326ff.
[204] Reprinted by the Arab University in Beirut, 1976.
[205] See Fritz Steppat, 'Die arabischen Staaten zwischen Ost und West', in Arnold Bergstraesser and Wilhelm Cornides, eds., *Die Internationale Politik 1955. Eine Einführung in das Geschehen der Gegenwart* (Munich, 1958), pp. 619ff.

Arab membership of a pact against a country that was not hostile to the Arabs, a pact moreover that would ally the Arabs to western powers who supported the Arabs' chief enemy, Israel. Syria and Saudi Arabia shared Nasser's opinion. In Lebanon, Pierre Gemayel, leader of the Kata'ib, was for joining, as 'it was impossible to remain neutral in the present international situation'.[206] Chamoun did not express himself unequivocally against membership; but practically all Muslim politicians, Beshara al-Khoury and the Maronite Patriarch, Boulos Boutros Méouchy, opposed it. In November 1956 Israel, France and Great Britain attacked Egypt. At an Arab summit meeting in Beirut, of all Arab leaders, Chamoun alone refused to break off diplomatic relations with France and Great Britain, which provoked the resignation of Prime Minister Yafi. Chamoun appointed Sami Solh, who thereby accepted a policy most Muslims disapproved of. As foreign minister he appointed Charles Malek, a professor of philosophy known to be extremely pro-American. In March 1957 Lebanon embraced the Eisenhower Doctrine, designed to fight subversion and provide American economic aid. By so doing, Chamoun openly risked confrontation with Nasser, at a time when the Egyptian president, after his political victory in the Suez War, was a hero throughout the Arab world, and among the Lebanese Muslims too. By contrast, Chamoun had become a hero to many Christians, as a president who took no account of opposition and maintained traditional ties with the West, regardless of what 'the Arabs' might think. Chamoun turned the parliamentary elections of 1957 into an informal plebiscite on his foreign policy. He was careful not to repeat Beshara al-Khoury's mistake of open electoral fraud, but he did not baulk at gerrymandering, and Beirut constituencies were redrawn to facilitate Christian majorities. Over and above this, it was made clear to 'key voters' that they had a choice between Chamoun's favour or disfavour. The result was a drubbing for the opposition beyond the expectations of even Chamoun's most enthusiastic supporters: Jumblatt lost in the Chouf,[207] Asaad in the south, Yafi and Salam in Beirut, Franjieh in the north — results inconceivable without redelimitation, and which swelled the ranks of personal opposition to Chamoun. A little later rumour had it that Chamoun's supporters planned to amend the Constitution to enable his re-election. Chamoun himself never expressed such an intention, but never disclaimed it either. The announcement in early 1958 of the creation of the United

---

[206] *L'Orient*, March 17th, 1955.
[207] For details, Kamal S. Salibi, *Crossroads to Civil War: Lebanon 1958–1976* (New York, 1976), pp. 12f: 'Because the political following of Kamil Sham'un was numerically superior to that of Janbalat in the Shuf, it was difficult for Janbalat to win an election in the religiously mixed constituency against obstruction from Sham'un ... In 1957 ... Janbalat, who was already on bad terms with the President, had to fight his electoral campaign on his own, and lost his seat in parliament, to the wrath of the Janbalati Druzes who now marked out Sham'un as a sworn enemy.'

Arab Republic was received with trepidation by Chamoun and many Christians, but with enthusiasm by the opposition, and brought tensions to breaking point. Open rebellion broke out in May 1958.[208] The largely Christian regions of the central mountains — East Beirut and its hinterland — remained loyal to the government; the opposition gained control of West Beirut, the southern part of the mountains and most of the peripheral areas. However, the civil war did not develop into an open confessional confrontation because some influential Christians, in particular Patriarch Méouchy and the Maronites loyal to the Franjieh family in the north, joined the opposition, and others tried to form a 'third force', among them Henri Pharaon, who wanted to preserve the Lebanon of the National Pact and for this reason opposed Chamoun's re-election.

Chamoun had the backing of the Kata'ib, the SSNP (the first and only time these two groups stood together), a militia of Chamoun supporters in the Chouf, and the police. The opposition included Salam's supporters in West Beirut, Karami's in Tripoli, Franjieh's in the northern mountains and, above all, the Jumblatti Druze, and Syrian armaments. The Lebanese armed forces under the command of General Chehab remained neutral, deployed only to contain Syrian aid for the insurrectionists.

On July 14th, 1958, the Iraqi monarchy was overthrown. Enthusiasm for Pan-Arabism and Nasser's prestige were at their zenith. Chamoun appealed to the USA to intervene militarily to protect the independence of Lebanon. American troops started landing on July 15th. The American government quickly grasped the complexity of the domestic situation in Lebanon and ordered its troops to refrain from any involvement in the civil war. As neither side could gain the upper hand militarily, they agreed — with discreet American mediation — on the election of Chehab as president.

The closing stages of Chamoun's presidency were far more calamitous for the country than those of Khoury's. He repeated, less blatantly, Khoury's mistakes of electoral manipulation and attempted re-election, and lost. His style of government obeyed the letter of the Constitution rather than the spirit of the National Pact; it was a presidency rather than a duumvirate. He did not find a Riad Solh, but did not look for one either. His actions strengthened the Muslim sense that an omnipotent Maronite president held them in check politically and economically.

---

[208] The comprehensive study on this period is Qubain, *Crisis in Lebanon*. See the critique by Malcolm H. Kerr in *Middle East Journal* 16/1 (1962), pp. 96f. Of interest is the account of one at the centre of the storm, Chamoun, *Crise au Moyen-Orient*, and the critique by Michael C. Hudson in *Middle East Journal*, 18/2 (1964), pp. 245ff. See also Jean–Pierre Alem, 'Troubles insurrectionnels au Liban', *Orient* 2/6 (1958), p. 37–47, and, above all, Arnold Hottinger, 'Zu`ama' and parties'. An excellent more recent study has yet to be published: Nawaf Salam, 'L'insurrection de 1958 au Liban', doctoral thesis, University of Paris-Sorbonne, 1979.

In foreign policy he was less fortunate than his predecessor. With the creation of the United Arab Republic he had Nasser on his doorstep, and the Lebanese Muslims were carried away on a wave of Nasserite feeling. No prominent Muslim politician called for Lebanon to join the union, but many felt it should align itself with the new power of the Arab world. By contrast, Chamoun and his foreign minister Malek opted for an openly pro-western foreign policy. By maintaining diplomatic relations with the two European allies of Israel against Egypt over Suez and then by embracing the Eisenhower Doctrine, Lebanon twice antagonized the entire Arab world; neither act could be reconciled with the National Pact. In 1958 both sides acted in glaring violation of the National Pact: the insurrectionists by accepting weapons and, in the case of Jumblatt, Syrian Druze soldiers, Chamoun by calling in the Americans. Those who did respect the National Pact were the Americans, who helped to re-establish political equilibrium. Chamoun became the politician many Muslims best loved hating, and to many Christians an object of hero-worship. He tried to govern Lebanon as though it was a homogeneous society — with a narrow majority. He did not infringe the Constitution; but by going to the limits of his powers he offended against the insight that a country like Lebanon cannot be governed with the support of only one half of the population — i.e., against the insight that had produced the National Pact in the first place.

The first government under Chehab soon learnt the same lesson. Premier Karami refused to include any supporter of Chamoun in his cabinet, only opponents and members of the 'third force'. In his policy statement Karami announced the beginning of an epoch in which his comrades would reap 'the fruits of the Revolution'. This induced a 'counter-revolt' by the Kata'ib and Chamoun's supporters.[209] Those regions which had remained loyal to the former government now rose against the new one; and again the result of the fighting was inconclusive. After a month, both sides realized that the other half of the country could not govern alone. Karami and Gemayel, the protagonists of the warring factions, agreed on a 'cabinet de salut public', in which each of them would fill half the posts. The war formally ended with the slogan 'neither winners, nor losers'. After half a year of fighting and about 2,500 dead the country returned to the National Pact. Chehab's style of government was very different to those of his predecessors.[210] Like Khoury, he made a practice of appointing prime ministers with strong backing in the Sunni community; but unlike him, he strove to create a

---

[209] See Goria, *Sovereignty*, p. 44ff: 'Counter-Revolt and the Rise of Pierre Gemayel'.

[210] For an instructive, if sometimes hagiographic, account, see Georges Naccache, *Un nouveau style: Le Chéhabisme* (Beirut, 1961); see also Hudson, *The Precarious Republic*, pp. 297ff; Goria, *Sovereignty*, pp. 58ff. For a critical assessment, see Salibi, *Crossroads to Civil War*, pp. 18ff.

civil service more independent of patrimonialism. Like Chamoun, he had little time for the traditional notables, whom he contemptuously called *fromagistes* (roughly, those squabbling over the cheeseboard). But unlike him, he did not hound them out of parliament, preferring to involve as many of them as possible in governance. Above all, he addressed social grievances. To keep it out of the rough and tumble of everyday politics, he assumed direct responsibility for a programme of social development that he hoped would rectify the economic imbalances between the communities.

Chehab picked a small circle of advisers, technocrats and officers with whose assistance he established departments autonomous of the existing ministries: a planning office, a department of development, a board for the development of the Litani River, an institute of public administration and a research council. Two offices became powerful centres of coordination: the Presidial Secretariat, run by Elias Sarkis, and the Deuxième Bureau, the Office of Military Intelligence. Chehab, a professional soldier, had since independence built up a professional, apolitical army, independent of all communities, political tendencies and persons, loyal only to the state. In the political crisis of 1952 and the civil war of 1958 he had preserved strict neutrality. His intention was now to build up a similarly neutral civil service. He found a number of qualified assistants who shared his view of a gradual technocratic 'revolution from above'. To please the notables the number of seats in parliament was raised from sixty-six to ninety-nine. The cabinet was enlarged to enable as many parliamentary blocs as possible to have a presence. However, most governments of his presidency contained a hard core of ministers who shared and influenced Chehabist policies: the prime minister and a new tandem of the Kata'ib leader, Gemayel, and the PSP leader, Jumblatt. The views of Gemayel and Jumblatt on foreign policy and many other questions diverged considerably; however, they agreed in their support of Chehab's social and economic policies. As seen above, these policies produced confessional parity in the civil service and development programmes for deprived regions of the country. Of course, not everyone approved of these policies. Some Christians accused the president of going too far in his policy of 'positive discrimination' towards the Muslims, and nicknamed him 'Muhammad Chehab'[211]. Some of the notables were also dissatisfied: they might have a seat in parliament, but as the civil service, especially in the new autonomous departments, tended to ignore the *zu'ama'*, their potential for patronage diminished in equal measure. The merchant

---

[211] 'L'expérience réformiste et développementiste du président Chéhab ... fut largement combattue par l'élite politique chrétienne qui refusait ses implications autoritaires mais aussi ses effets redistributeurs'; Nasr, 'L'Islam politique', p. 39; Salibi, *Crossroads to Civil War*, p. 3, speaks of 'sullen, though inactive opposition'.

class were displeased with certain — relatively mild — measures to protect local industry. The Muslim notables in West Beirut thought that the city was being neglected at the expense of the hinterland.

The Chehabist administration responded to these criticisms not so much with arguments as with a subtle policy of weakening their opponents. This was coordinated in the Office of Military Intelligence. A large part of the notables' political 'machines' — militia-like groups, streets gangs, village and suburban associations, politicized youth groups, etc. — were given favours and subsidies, and increasingly controlled and manipulated. If opponents proved stubborn, political rivals were built up and favoured. In short: patronage undermined patronage for reasons of state. Liberal Lebanese complained about the authoritative style of government and expressed fears that Lebanon was gradually sliding into benign military dictatorship. These fears were certainly exaggerated. Neither Chehab nor his chief assistants exhibited dictatorial tendencies, only a more acute perception of the dangers to Lebanon and the conviction that a stronger state was necessary to meet them than the 'minimum of state' the Lebanese middle class thought sufficient.

At the end of 1961 the institutions of the Lebanese state were tested once again. The SSNP attempted a coup d'état, which the army crushed in two days. After this, all radical groups were stringently controlled, not least Palestinian refugees in Lebanon.[212] The previous year Chehab had already told a Palestinian delegation that the Palestinians were too powerful a group not to be kept under observation. He appreciated the tragedy of the conflict: 'Either we oppress them and are the oppressors, or we remain inactive and shall ourselves be oppressed ... but the hot blood in the veins of the Lebanese soldiers induces them to oppress rather than be oppressed'.[213]

Chehab received an extraordinarily difficult legacy in foreign policy. The withdrawal of American troops reduced tension with the United Arab Republic, but Lebanon's position on Nasser's Pan-Arabism was still unclear. In March 1959 Chehab and Nasser met at the Syrian-Lebanese frontier. Chehab assured Nasser that Lebanon would adopt a policy of strict solidarity with the Arab world. Nasser, in turn, explicitly recognized the independence and territorial integrity of Lebanon. By officially renouncing any project for 'union', Nasser helped to disperse the fears of Lebanese Christians and reduce the tensions between the communities. Chehab's foreign policy in the following years is best compared with that of Finland in the years immediately after the Second World War:

---

[212] Salibi, *Crossroads to Civil War*, p. 10.
[213] Goria, *Sovereignty*, p. 72.

Lebanon did nothing that might offend the UAR — and regained calm and freedom.

The end of Chehab's incumbency brought the first peaceful change of president. He was pressed from many sides to stay in office; he would have had the majority for a constitutional amendment. Like his predecessors, he seems to have toyed with this idea. Unlike them, he was prepared to stay only if parliament were virtually unanimous. This was not the case, so he went.

On balance, the Chehab presidency is impressive. He was able to restore peace after a civil war. Apart from the SSNP coup, Lebanon enjoyed six years without internal unrest and serious tension. The division of power between the two chief offices of state shifted: Chehab allowed his prime minister far more responsibility in everyday politics than his predecessors had. The prime minister became more visible, while the president acted as arbiter. Many of the functions of confessional representation devolved to the cabinet. However, the president kept a firm hold on security and the outlines of social and economic policy. The Muslims welcomed the latter, which in turn reconciled them to the former. Chehab was the first Lebanese president to grasp that the division of political power as agreed in the National Pact could survive only if complemented by, as it were, a social and economic pact. And he prepared the ground for it. By making solidarity the cornerstone of foreign policy he calmed tensions between the opposing forms of national definition: they were not removed, but much reduced.

By strengthening the state machinery and giving the Office of Military Intelligence powers of political control, Lebanese sovereignty had been considerably reinforced. But even under Chehab this office had occasionally abused its new powers. During the presidency of his successor they were to become the bone of contention in domestic politics.

The successor was anything but a military man. Charles Helou was an man of letters, the most educated of all Lebanese presidents. In 1958 he had belonged to the 'third force'. He had no political pressure-group of his own: he was the candidate of the parliamentary majority that would have preferred to re-elect Chehab. Most importantly, he had only limited authority over the institution that had been Chehab's 'bastion': the army. Indeed, he was so amiable Lebanese cartoonists invariably portrayed him as a clergyman.[214] He was caught in the crossfire of new and fierce disputes.

In the closing years of Chehab's presidency an old pattern had reasserted itself: all those excluded from power for whatever reason formed an opposition alliance. Among them was Camille Chamoun, whom numerous conservative Maronites continued to regard as the 'real' president, and whom Chehab, for reasons of

---

[214] Some examples have been reprinted in Hudson, *The Precarious Republic*.

foreign policy, had sidelined. Another was Raymond Eddé,[215] who had been a very successful minister of the interior in the 'cabinet de salut public', until he resigned over the encroachment of the Deuxième Bureau. A further powerful opponent was Saeb Salam,[216] who had been Chehab's prime minister in 1960, but was later antagonized for reasons that had nothing to do with politics.[217] All three disapproved of the dealings of the Deuxième Bureau. In the previous parliamentary elections Chamoun and Eddé had lost in constituencies that would normally have been considered safe and blamed their defeats, probably rightly, on the intervention of this institution. Saeb Salam was annoyed that the Chehabist administration was alienating his traditional support in West Beirut,[218] in particular a section of his militia of 1958. Once Helou had assumed office this secret service operated far more independently than it had under Chehab. Allegations of corruption were now levelled at the institution that had led the fight against patronage. The new president scarcely exercised control over its political activities. Chamoun, Eddé and Salam agreed in another point: as members of the Christian and Sunni bourgeoisie respectively, they disliked what they called Chehab's 'planned economy', including the special programmes for rural Shi`i regions. Initially the opposition was too disparate — Salam, one of the rebel leaders in 1958, and Chamoun refused to have anything to do with each other — to accomplish anything against the governing coalition, especially as the broad Chehabist coalition held. The first three years of Helou's incumbency were successfully managed by prime minister Karami and the Gemayel-Jumblatt tandem.

This tandem had been welded by Chehabist development policies and was in effect a 'social coalition'. It split in 1967 over policies towards the Palestinians. Even before the Six Day War Jumblatt was in favour of allowing Palestinians to pursue their armed struggle from bases in Lebanon. In this he broke with the consensus of Chehabist foreign policy. After the Six Day War his socio-political attitudes began to change as well. He increasingly dissociated himself from Chehabist reformism, demanded a thorough reorganization of the Lebanese system and moved closer to the parties of the Left — the Baath and the Communists. Both steps were unacceptable to Gemayel: he demanded controls on the Palestinians to avert Israeli reprisals against Lebanon; and he had little time for Jumblatt's interest in political forces he regarded as un-Lebanese and subversive.

---

[215] Salibi, *Crossroads to Civil War*, p. 7, describes Eddé as 'a liberal of the Jeffersonian school, and a firm believer in open parliamentary politics'. Goria, *Sovereignty*, pp. 60ff, draws a more detailed portrait.
[216] See Goria, *Sovereignty*, pp. 60ff.
[217] Salibi, *Crossroads to Civil War*, p. 11.
[218] The Office of Military Intelligence favoured his rivals Abdallah Yafi and Othman Dana. See Goria, *Sovereignty*, p. 67.

Gemayel's Kata'ib formed an alliance, the 'Triple Front', with Chamoun's NLP and Raymond Eddé's National Bloc. The Chehabists, the 'Democratic Parliamentary Front' led by Karami,[219] were put on the defensive. Jumblatt's left-wing bloc demanded more radical reforms and unconditional support for the Palestinians. Gemayel continued to support the Chehabist reform policies, but, together with Chamoun and Eddé, took a hard line on the Palestinians. Salam and other Muslim notables at times stood up for the Palestinians, so as not to appear less Arabist than Jumblatt; but their principal concern was to weakened Chehabism and, in particular, the Office of Military Intelligence. To this end, they collaborated with Eddé and Chamoun. The fronts in social and in foreign policy no longed overlapped but intersected. Helou was very understanding; but the more contentious the Palestinian question became, the wiser he found a less neutral stance towards the alliance of the three Maronite leaders. Thus, by 1968 Chehabism without Chehab was in a crisis.

In the parliamentary elections of 1968 the 'Triple Front' made considerable gains, becoming almost as strong as the Chehabist faction; Jumblatt's own parliamentary bloc held the balance of power. Lebanon was becoming increasingly difficult to govern.[220] In 1969 the first serious clashes occurred between the Lebanese Army and Palestinian troops, upon which Karami resigned; the country was without a government for months. Thus, it was not Lebanese politicians who negotiated a provisional and, as it proved, ineffectual compromise with the Palestinians, but the Army Chief of Staff, General Emile Boustani through the mediation of President Nasser. Parliament ratified the 'Cairo Agreement' without having seen the complete text. As the country slowly slid into its severest crisis since 1958, its leading politicians were blinkered by domestic power politics: the presidential elections of 1970. The Chehabists pinned their hopes on General Chehab — the Constitution rules out only consecutive terms of office. The 'Triple Front' wanted one of themselves. Muslim and Christian notables like Salam, Franjieh and Kamel Asaad,[221] the most influential politician in the Shi`i south who controlled a considerable bloc in parliament, knew above all what they did not want: Chehab or a Chehabist. In the end, Chehab declined to stand. He did not want to be elected with a bare majority — let alone risk defeat. His supporters agreed on Elias Sarkis, one of Chehab's closest collaborators and the governor of the Central Bank. After a long tug-of-war, Salam emerged as the kingmaker among the anti-Chehabists. He wanted neither Chamoun nor Gemayel, his opponents in 1958. He did not have any personal or political objections to Eddé;

---

[219] On Karami see ibid., pp. 68ff.
[220] See *Proche-Orient Chrétien* (1966), p. 253, and (1967), pp. 97–99 and 341f.
[221] On Kamel Assad see Goria, *Sovereignty*, pp. 73ff.

but he was the son of Emile Eddé, the president under the mandate who had cooperated most closely with France and, therefore, Salam felt, unacceptable to Muslim public opinion. Eventually he reached agreement with the 'Triple Front' on the candidacy of Suleiman Franjieh.[222]

The candidates could not have been more different. Sarkis[223] came from a humble background: his mother was a washerwoman; Franjieh[224] was the scion of an old family of large landowners in Zghorta in the Maronite north. Sarkis had worked as a clerk to finance his university studies; Franjieh was heir to his father's estates — the elder Franjieh had first been elected to parliament in 1922. Chehab had 'discovered' Sarkis, an able and incorruptible civil servant; Franjieh had inherited the family's political 'estate' after his older brother, Hamid, an established Deputy and minister, had suffered a stroke. Sarkis was a technocrat who could assess at a glance the contents of political and economic reports, Franjieh the prototype of the rural *za'im*. Above all: Sarkis represented the Chehabist concept of a strong state and a compensatory social policies, whereas Franjieh regarded Lebanese politics as a matter of extended families and their 'natural élites', which, through 'a sort of natural socialism' saw to the well-being of their adherents.[225] One could hardly have found more ideal embodiments of the strengths and weaknesses of modern and traditional Lebanon respectively.

Franjieh received one vote more than Sarkis. The deciding vote was Kamal Jumblatt's. There has been a lot of speculation on the reasons for this turn. For years Jumblatt had been a pillar of Chehabism; now he cast the die for its demolition. One reason was undoubtedly social arrogance. Jumblatt respected Chehab, not least because of his background: 'Chehab was an emir disguised as a general rather than a president.' But this respect did not extend to Chehab's assistants. 'I am no friend of Suleiman Franjieh. But he at least stands for something, whereas Mr Sarkis is only a chief clerk.'[226] But his motives were certainly more complex. Since 1967 he had aspired to more than just a reform of the Lebanese system: he wanted a different system altogether. As the last internal affairs minister under Helou, he had lifted the bans on a number of left-wing parties — parties whose cooperation he had previously sought. Furthermore, he had cultivated the role of chief spokesman for the Palestinian cause within the Lebanese establishment. Jumblatt's new allies had long been effectually controlled by the Chehabist secret security. It could not be in the interests of this new alliance to entrench security

---

[222] Author's interviews with the politicians involved, 1971 and 1979.
[223] See Goria, *Sovereignty*, pp. 120ff.
[224] Ibid., pp. 123ff.
[225] Author's interview with Suleiman Franjieh, 1979.
[226] Author's interview with Kamal Jumblatt, 1971.

interests by electing a competent and determined Chehabist president; quite the opposite. The traditionalist Franjieh was the better bet.

Nor did Franjieh disappoint the expectations of the conservatives and liberals or of the leftist anti-Chehabists. He appointed as prime minister Saeb Salam. The first spectacular step of the new government was to smash the Deuxième Bureau. A number of higher-ranking officers were arrested, and five of them sentenced to imprisonment for electoral fraud, embezzlement of public monies and contravention of army regulations. They fled to Syria, where they were granted political asylum. This was followed by numerous transfers in the civil service. Liberals, like Eddé, were jubilant: 'The Republic has been saved by one vote. Liberty reigns again'.[227] The latter is certainly correct. The freedom of expression and of the press were never greater than during Franjieh's term of office. The parliamentary elections of 1972 were the freest and cleanest in Lebanese history — the ultimate elections for what would become Lebanon's Long Parliament. The incumbency had its dark side too. Traditional patronage flourished again, coordinated development policies and large development projects were abandoned and the autonomous departments of the Chehab era lost much of their influence. Salam first formed a reform-minded cabinet of young, liberal technocrats, most of them graduates, like himself, of the American University of Beirut. It soon collapsed as one proposed reform after another was rejected: one minister resigned because his bill to tax luxury imports had to be withdrawn, another because his legislation on medicines and pharmaceutical products was blocked, two more improvements to the educational system could not find a majority.[228] Salam formed a second cabinet of veterans of notability politics, to whom such proposals were utterly foreign.

In many respects the first years of Franjieh's presidency resembled those of Beshara al-Khoury's. Both president and premier were strong personalities and very popular in their own communities. The former gave the latter a lot of scope. Both shared a liberal-conservative view of society and politics in Lebanon: 'live and let live'. And neither had any inhibitions about sharing the advantages of power with their friends and supporters. Franjieh appointed a fellow northerner and personal friend as Army Chief of Staff, and his son Tony as Minister of Posts and Telegraphs. Hence, it was not surprising that allegations of corruption became commonplace. A high-ranking American diplomat remarked maliciously: 'It's usual for Lebanese presidents to pocket something before leaving office. But now the state is being systematically looted from the start.'[229] This may be an exaggeration, but what was important politically was the fact that large parts of the

---

[227] Author's interview with Raymond Eddé, 1971.
[228] See Goria, *Sovereignty*, pp. 128ff; Salibi, *Crossroads to Civil War*, p. 57.
[229] Author's interview with an American diplomat, 1971.

Lebanese population concurred; some were cynical about it, many more were incensed.

The government might, for better or for worse, act as it did in the time of Khoury and Solh, but the people no longer reacted in the same way. What made the social and economic crises of the early 1970s so intense and so bitter was the fact that they came after a lengthy period of economic and social improvement.[230] Differentials in income and standards of living between strata, regions and communities had narrowed considerably during the Chehabist years. The crises were sparked off by objective factors like accelerating inflation and rising unemployment. But even more important was the widespread disappointment of seemingly justified expectations. Many Lebanese found that they were not going up, even slowly, but down. That the government had little understanding of social grievances, and showed it, only exacerbated feeling. Police were used to break up social and labour protests, and did so with excessive force. Tobacco farmers, agricultural labourers and industrial workers could not but gain the impression that the state sided completely with the bosses and the rich. The skittling of technocrats in Salam's first cabinet is symptomatic of the time. In a nutshell, Lebanon in the early 1970s manifested characteristic signs of a pre-revolutionary situation: the gulf between rising expectations and declining fulfilment. Schemeil's studies[231] reveal that in 1973 70 per cent of Lebanese still felt it made sense to vote, and that democracy was preferable to a military dictatorship or revolution. But 14 per cent were already in favour of military rule or revolutionary change — a view taken by one-fifth of all Sunnis and as many as one-quarter of the Shi`is. Revolutionary tendencies were strongest among unemployed secondary-school and university graduates.[232] Disaffection with the Lebanese state was extraordinarily high among university students. A good 60 per cent of them supported parties of the Left.[233] Radical attitudes among students and unemployed intellectuals are nothing unusual. 'Intellectuals dropping out'[234] may be one omen of revolutionary developments. But it is common for such attitudes to disappear as jobs reappear.

---

[230] See the views of Lebanese farmers in Thom Sicking, 'Dépérissement d'un village libanais', *Travaux et Jours* 47 (1973), p. 8.

[231] Schemeil, 'Sociologie', pp. 100 and 104.

[232] About three-quarters of the students were dissatisfied with the state. See Nafhat Nasr and Monte Palmer, 'Alienation and Political Participation in Lebanon', *International Journal of Middle East Studies* 8 (1977), p. 514.

[233] 7.8 per cent supported the PSP, 18.6 per cent the SSNP, 12.9 per cent the CP and 21.4 per cent other left-wing groups. See Theodor Hanf, 'Le comportement politique des étudiants libanais', *Travaux et Jours* 46 (1973), p. 18.

[234] See Crane Brinton, *The Anatomy of Revolution*, New York 1938.

## The Lebanese Model

However, in the Lebanon of the early 1970s there was one man who was able to articulate the disappointment and embitterment with post-Chehabist economic and social policies felt by intellectuals as well as broader groups: Kamal Jumblatt. He was uniquely placed to do so. He belonged to the Lebanese political establishment and could count on the loyalty of the greater part of the Druze community — regardless of whether these Druze agreed with his political opinions or not. In addition, he was in a position to win, with political programmes, support that reached far beyond the confines of his small community. His first attempt was the founding of the Progressive Socialist Party in 1949, but he had only moderate success. From the mid-1960s he worked consistently at a political programme for a different Lebanon: one common secular republic without privileges or quotas for communities instead of the Lebanon of the National Pact, radical reorganization by the people instead of Chehabist reformism from above. The Druze notable had become a Jacobin. His alliance with the left-wing parties rested on a common Jacobin orientation, and on the need of these parties on the edge of the political spectrum for a powerful protector who could give them legitimacy and support. After the Six Day War and the awakening of the Palestinian liberation movement Jumblatt took a decisive step: he presented himself to the Palestinian organizations as an ally and a protector as well. This was a unique opportunity for the Palestinians: identification with an important politician and his left-wing alliance. And Jumblatt won an ally who had something he lacked: armed forces. The Palestinians provided armaments and military training for the organizations of the Lebanese Left.

Before 1970 this could not have happened as it did. By smashing the Deuxième Bureau, Franjieh and Salam opened the floodgates to an unprecedented militarization of Lebanese political groups and factions: the state had no way of controlling them. The Palestinians seized their opportunity. They helped not only Jumblatt's alliance; they also 'took over' numerous other organizations and groups formerly financed, manipulated and controlled by military intelligence, especially street and district gangs that had previously acted as bodyguards and election campaigners for the zu`ama', but also gangs of smugglers. Many of these groups gave themselves a political name and received arms and money, which imparted a certain revolutionary credibility.[235]

As groups previously supervised by notables and later the Deuxième Bureau in the Muslim section of Beirut came under the protection of the Palestinian organization, a similar development was taking part in the Christian section of the capital. After the large Christian parties had learnt in 1969 that the Lebanese Army was not able to control the Palestinians, they too started to take matters into

---

[235] For a detailed analysis of this takeover see Johnson, *Class and Client*, pp. 175ff.

their own hands. Apart from Raymond Eddé's National Bloc, every party formed its own militia — the Kata'ib had always had small paramilitary units — and, with help from sections of the Lebanese Army, began to arm them.

A further spectacular incidence of militarization was Imam Musa Sadr's 'Movement of the Deprived'. The Imam founded this movement to free the Shi`i population of the south and the Bekaa from the political yoke of the large — Shi`i — landowners and to stop the drift to the non-religious parties of the Left. It was not Sadr's intention to sweep away the Lebanese system, but to win for his community an adequate say in it. Addressing a mass meeting in Baalbek in March 1974, he declared: 'Weapons are the virtue of manhood and we are for these weapons.'[236] That this was more than rhetoric only became apparent over a year later, when a bomb exploded in a training camp in the Bekaa. Sadr then announced that he had formed the militia 'Amal' (hope) as the military wing of the Movement of the Deprived. Amal received weapons and training from the Palestinians, but remained independent, as developments were to testify.[237]

The only group of traditional significance to stand aloof from the general trend towards militarization were the Sunni notables. Neither Saeb Salam nor Karami had militia stronger than a bodyguard. As tension between the Christian parties and the Palestinians mounted, the position of the Sunni *zu`ama'* became more and more difficult.[238] Their base was now as pro-Palestinian as it had been pro-Nasser in 1958. The mass of Lebanese Muslims were transported by the bravery of the fedayeen who had picked up the banner where the Arab armies had dropped it and — whether successful or not — had saved Arab honour. The myth of the unknown *fida'i* began to supersede that of Gamal Abdel Nasser.

The Sunni politicians were just as aware as their Christian colleagues of the dangers of Palestinian commando raids on Israel from bases in Lebanon. They tried to find a compromise between Christian demands that the Palestinians be brought under political control and Jumblatt's that they be actively supported. But proposals such as a 'coordination' between the Lebanese Army and the commandos were not only impracticable, they were hardly likely to carry away the Muslim masses. They found themselves in acute danger of being unseated by Jumblatt as the 'real' spokesman for the Muslims. Franjieh made their position even more

---

[236] See ibid., pp. 171ff; on Musa Sadr see Goria, *Sovereignty*, pp. 161ff.

[237] See Fouad Ajami, *The Vanished Imam; Musa al Sadr and the Shia of Lebanon* (London, 1986), pp. 168ff; Grimblat, 'La communauté chiite', pp. 72ff.

[238] 'Since 1969, the Muslim Lebanese political establishment and bourgeoisie had begun to show definite signs of impatience with the commando movement ... The Muslim Lebanese establishment, however, was politically caged by the masses on whose support it counted ... In the Muslim sectors of Beirut, the commandos were beginning to take the law into their own hands'; Salibi, *Crossroads to Civil War*, p. 54.

difficult. From 1973 onwards he returned to Chamoun's practice of appointing as prime minister not the most popular Sunni politician but one more pliable and cooperative.[239] The result was not new either. The entire Sunni community felt badly treated because of this relative loss of power, and there was nothing for their notables to do but to try not be out-Jumblatted. Thus, Jumblatt succeeded in widening his coalition of opposition or revolution: political Islam allied itself with the left-wing parties and the Palestinians.[240]

Franjieh's presidency opened to gun salutes in anticipation of what many Lebanese thought would be a return to the good old days. It ended under the barrages of war. On the whole, Franjieh had respected the National Pact. He finally turned to weak men as prime ministers primarily because he despaired of drawing up a coherent Palestinian policy with Karami or Salam, not because he wished to weaken the premiership or the position of the Sunni community.

Franjieh dismantled both the social policies and the state machinery of Chehabism. In this he had the full support of his partners, the Muslim notables. All of them wanted to get at the trough of patronage from which Chehab had increasingly barred them. And all of them underestimated the consequences. The politicians who supported Franjieh in 1970 were pragmatic, fairly tolerant and open to compromise. But they had little grasp of economic and social currents. By destroying the beginnings of a welfare state they exacerbated a social crisis, which weakened the loyalty of a broad part of the population to the Lebanese system just at the time it was needed. They did not take the rise of the political left seriously, or thought they could deal with it without incorporating it into the system. Many of them did not want to believe that Kamal Jumblatt, one of them, really meant what he said. Not one of them — with the possible exception of Jumblatt — foresaw the consequences of weakening the state, above all of smashing the Deuxième Bureau. Most of them underestimated the strength of the Palestinian organizations and their growing weight in Lebanon; and none of them had wanted it. Once it could no longer be ignored, some of them tried to exploit it to their own ends — at first Jumblatt, but later most Sunni politicians too. Unlike Chamoun, Franjieh did not neglect Arab solidarity. He was prepared to grant the Palestinians every facility in Lebanon for their political activities. In 1974 he himself addressed the General Assembly of the United Nations as spokesman for this cause.[241] But he was not prepared, as the only country in the Arab world, to run

---

[239] 'Franjieh was pleased to find a leader who, like Amin Hafez and Takieddine Solh, lacked a broader national power base'; Goria, *Sovereignty*, p. 169.

[240] The Lebanese parliament was now divided into two confessional blocks for the first time in its history; even in 1958 this had not happened. See ibid., p. 170.

[241] On this occasion the US customs used sniffer-dogs to search the president's luggage; this coloured Franjieh's attitude towards the American government.

the risk of war with Israel because of commando raids. The degree of solidarity with the Palestinians that Jumblatt demanded went far beyond anything shown by any Arab state. In this respect it was he, and not Franjieh, who violated the National Pact. Nor did Jumblatt make any secret of it: he demanded its abolition. From 1975 onwards it was no longer a question of the division of power in Lebanon, but of all or nothing. There had been many conflicts between 1943 and 1975, including one instance of open warfare, but nothing like what was to come. The 'Lebanese model' of coexistence between communities sometimes functioned well, sometimes passably and sometimes badly. The temperaments and ambitions of the men who maintained it considerably influenced its running, be it for 'better' or for 'worse'. But so did external factors. After 1967 the latter were increasingly unfavourable. But before these are examined, it is well to conclude this chapter with an analysis of the relative importance of the different fields of conflict — the conflicts over the division of power, the distribution of wealth and the definition of identity — in pre-war Lebanon.

## Fields of conflict and communal strategies

As already discussed, recrudescent conflict over the division of power was a feature of the Lebanese state from independence to the 1970s. After Chehab's election things seemed to take a turn for the better. It was almost always a question of more or less power — offices, seats, competences — but prior to the 1970s never of all or nothing. Only since then has the principle as such of sharing power, the character of Lebanon as a consociation, been questioned. There are various interpretations of the transition from disputes over more or less to a struggle for all or nothing. One thesis is that the sham conflict of the traditional political class could no longer conceal the fundamental economic contradictions in the country: it is regarded as a conflict between rich and poor. Another thesis holds that the conflict is one between a Lebanese nationalism mainly supported by Christians and an Arab nationalism with largely Muslim support: a conflict of identity. A third thesis treats it primarily as a conflict between the concept of a traditionalist, 'confessional' state and that of a modern, secular and politically integrated state: a conflict between pre-modern and modern politics. Can these theses help to clarify the conflicts in pre-war Lebanon?

As shown above, economic discontent has long played an important role. The Chehabist policies of social equalization reduced it; in the post-Chehabist era it increased again. By objective measures disparities in income and standards of living lessened and the modes of incorporation of classes and communities became less ranked. But as deranking tendencies weakened, the sense of relative deprivation grew — and was articulated politically, initially in categories of 'rich'

## The Lebanese Model

and 'poor', but increasingly of 'rich Christians' and 'poor Muslims'. Even in the issues of civil service quotas and, in particular, of 'privileges' and 'guarantees' the question of confessional discrimination dominated that of class discrimination. Still, the social crises of the 1970s cannot be unequivocally interpreted as though those affected felt they were affected — to their advantage or disadvantage — primarily because they were members of certain communities. Both the trade unions and the large strike movements expressed their respective grievances and demands in social and economic rather than in confessional categories. Class conflict seemed to have taken precedence over confessional conflict. Only in the immediate pre-war months did social protest merge with political articulation by confessional allegiance, e.g. the fishermen's demonstrations in Sidon in spring 1975. Most of the early fighting took place between poor Muslims and poor Christians, not rich and poor. Evidence suggests that in the 1940s and 1950s economic conflict was perceived primarily as confessional conflict, in the 1960s and early 1970s as non-confessional class conflict, and from the mid-1970s onwards again as confessional conflict. The conflict became most intense after a period of narrowing social distinctions between income groups and increasingly unranked incorporation, that is, when these two trends were interrupted. A sense of aggravated relative deprivation first spread through the lower classes and then through all Muslim denominations as denominations. This sense was far stronger among the Shi`is than among the Sunnis. Sunni demands and programmes gave only marginal attention to economic concerns, and even then in very general formulations. By contrast, the Shi`i demands formulated by the Supreme Shi`i Islamic Council were almost exclusively economic, indeed tantamount to a programme for economic development: quotas by denomination for posts in the public sector, execution of the Litani Project, irrigation schemes in the western part of the Bekaa, construction of schools and hospitals, higher prices for tobacco growers and development of the 'deprived' regions.[242] At the risk of some simplification: in the early 1970s the sense of relative deprivation became more acute among the entire lower strata, and then evolved among Shi`is into the feeling that their community as a whole was relatively deprived.[243]

---

[242] See Hamadé, 'L'Islam libanais', p. 10. The list of Shi`i demands contains virtually nothing that had not been part of the Chehabist plans.

[243] The development of the Shi`i community is a classic case of the emergence of relative deprivation. 'Alors que dans les années 40 les chiites étaient essentiellement une communauté marginale, rurale aux trois quarts, analphabète, dotée d'élites 'féodales', divisées et rétrogrades, ils étaient devenus dans les années 60 une communauté urbaine à plus de deux tiers ... dotées d'élites culturelles très actives, d'élites économiques montantes (émigres retournés), et d'une contre-élite politique répartie entre les divers partis marxistes ou nationalistes arabes et un mouvement propre dirigé par un leader charismatique très efficace (l'Imam Moussa Sadr)'; Nasr, 'L'Islam politique', p. 39. Because of this progress, deprivation that still existed was more acutely felt and protested about.

Arab and Lebanese nationalists have been at loggerheads since the state was created. However, it is necessary to qualify both forms of nationalism. Initially, Arab nationalism was influenced by liberal and secular ideals. Its emergence and spread owes much to members of ethnic and religious minorities. A secular nationalism held out the prospect of equal rights and recognition precluded by an Islamic theocracy. With the fall of the Ottoman Empire and the subjection of the Orient to foreign, non-Islamic powers there was a change in attitudes. The western powers were perceived as Christian, and in the struggle against them it was opportune to equate Arabism and Islam, so as to mobilize the generally apolitical masses; the secular strand was relegated.[244] After that, non-Muslim minorities were in the forefront of left-wing political movements advocating secular Arabism. After an early and committed involvement in Arab nationalism, the majority of Lebanese Christians, especially Maronites, soon began to suspect Arabism as a vehicle for the reimposition of Islamic rule, and turned to a purely Lebanese nationalism.

The Lebanese Muslims, however, had no difficulty in identifying with Arab nationalism. Among the Sunni lower classes in particular 'what really counted was the sentiment of Islamic solidarity ... To the Muslims of these classes, Arabism was little more than another name for Islam.'[245] In Lebanon, the recurrent waves of enthusiasm for the Arab cause — from union with the Arab Kingdom at the end of the First World War, through Nasserism, to identifying with the Palestinian liberation movement — were predominantly Sunni. Arabism always had a particular appeal for the Sunnis when it was a Sunni-dominated Arabism.

Lebanese nationalism is very similar. A Lebanese state is what the Maronites wanted. They wanted a Lebanon that accorded with their views. Maronite discord over the creation of the state centred on the issue of Maronite security: could Greater Lebanon be Maronite enough, or would Mount Lebanon be more reliably Maronite? At that time Maronites identified themselves with Greater Lebanon much as, and at about the same time, Czechs and Serbs identified themselves with Czechoslovakia and Yugoslavia. When faced with the real possibility of a

---

[244] 'The ordinary Moslem Arab is not conscious of belonging in one aspect of his being to the Arab community, and in another to the Islamic, but rather of belonging to a single integrated 'Arabo-Islamic' community in which he does not clearly distinguish the Arab from the Islamic elements'; Hourani, *Syria and Lebanon*, p. 103; see also Kamal S. Salibi, *Lebanon and the Middle Eastern Question* (Oxford, 1988), p. 9: 'From the very beginning there was a difference between the manner in which the Christian and Muslim Arabs conceived of Arabism. To the Christians, it involved a consciousness of a purely secular national identity which was separate and distinct from Islam as the traditional basis of Arab political life. To the Muslims, it was a consciousness of natural identity which, no matter how secular in theory, remained somehow confused with Islam.'

[245] Salibi, *A House of Many Mansions*, pp. 49f.

Lebanon that no longer corresponded to their conception of Lebanon, a considerable number of Maronites began playing with the idea of withdrawing into a smaller Lebanon, or even an enclave.

Lebanese nationalists accuse Muslims of divided loyalties, to Lebanon and to the Arab-Islamic world. This is undoubtedly true. But extreme forms of Lebanese nationalism are also a reflection of divided loyalty: to present-day Lebanon 'whilst it lasts' and to a smaller Christian Lebanon if the other no longer corresponds to their conception of it.[246] In short: the main currents of Arab nationalism in Lebanon as well as Lebanese nationalism are not so much 'Arab' and 'Lebanese' as codewords for what is best termed a Sunni and a Maronite sense of community.

The other denominational communities have been more equivocal in their support of one or other of these nationalisms. Shi`i and Druze enthusiasm for pan-Arab projects in which the Sunni element would dominate has customarily been subdued. Both groups could accept Lebanon as a fatherland, though without accepting a Lebanese nationalism that would dissociate them from the Arab and — in the case of the Shi`is — Islamic world. Greek Orthodox, Greek Catholics and Armenians were also satisfied with the state of Lebanon. But, as communities living not only in Lebanon but in other Arab states, they saw little advantage in Lebanese isolation, and — as denominations with pockets all over the country — even less in a Christian little Lebanon. Moreover, among the Greek Orthodox there were influential groups that would have preferred a Greater Syria to the existing Lebanese state and also many adherents of Arab nationalism in its purely secular form. The composition of the leadership of all left-wing parties and organizations in Lebanon indicates that a progressive and secular — non-Islamic — form of Arabism is an acceptable alternative to Lebanon for them. The Lebanese Left on the whole is secularist, but by no means unanimously Arabist. The Communist Party, for instance, has a long history of internal disputes over the issue of socialism in one country versus regional revolution. The Progressive Socialist Party has always paid lip-service to Arab solidarity; but when the chips were down what mattered — especially to its leader Jumblatt — was power in Lebanon.

Although there have been numerous conflicts between Arab and Lebanese nationalism, in the final analysis Lebanese politics cannot be reduced to this issue. Since 1943 there have been political majorities for the National Pact in all communities — in other words, not for the 'pure form' of each type of nationalism. The history of independent Lebanon until the war must be seen primarily as a

---

[246] See Fouad Ephrem Boustani, *Le problème du Liban*, 2nd edn (Kaslik, 1978), p. 37: 'C'est d'ailleurs la seule issue possible: internationalisation de la question libanaise, retour à la formule du vieux Liban: indépendence et neutralité garanties par la puissance de l'O.N.U.'

conflict between, on the one hand, the syncretistic concept of the state as a consociation of all communities and, on the other hand, forms of particularistic nationalism that serve as codewords for the interests of specific communities.

However, the syncretistic concept of the state outlined in the National Pact cannot be reconciled with the concept of a secular, socially integrated Lebanon without quotas and proportionality — the concept of a Jacobin Lebanon. This conflict too has a long history.[247] During the mandate, French governors had tried to secularize parts of the personal status law, an appropriate place to start in terms of Jacobin logic. Complete social integration, the forging of communities into one nation, cannot take place if there are legal obstacles to marriage between members of different communities. Islamic law permits marriage between Muslim men and Christian or Jewish women, but not between Muslim women and Christian or Jewish men. Integration is possible, but only down a one-way street — or, for certain communities, a dead end. In 1936 the mandatory enacted a statute extending civil jurisdiction to matters of family law.[248] The protests of religious leaders prevented it from being put into effect. Even the attempt to allow Lebanese citizens the choice between personal status under the laws of their respective communities and personal status under Lebanese civil law — which would allow civil marriage — could not realized. Even today no Lebanese can contract a civil marriage within the country.

Who are the Lebanese Jacobins? They are found among the convinced secularists of the Left and in the Kata'ib.[249] The Left wants a secular state and a secular society. Since the 1960s the Kata'ib has been willing to accept a secular state, provided that the society is also secularized, that is, that legislation allows two-way social integration. Until well into the 1970s the Left had been too weak for their position to have any realistic chance of acceptance. The Kata'ib's position was widely interpreted as a tactical move: it could espouse secularism only

---

[247] See Issam Khalife, 'A la recherche d'une politique ou d'un concept de sécularisation dans le Liban multiconfessionnel, 1958-1975', Unpublished doctoral thesis, University of Paris-Sorbonne, 1982; Jürgen Stoldt, 'Das Scheitern einer politischen Modernisierung: Säkularisierungsinitiativen im Libanon 1920–1976', Unpublished M.A. thesis, University of Freiburg im Breisgau, n.d. [1986]; Theodor Hanf, 'The "political secularization" issue in Lebanon', *Annual Review of the Social Sciences of Religion* 5 (1981), pp. 225–53.

[248] Article 14 of Law 60 of March 13th, 1936 reads: 'Les communautés de droit commun organisent et administrent librement leurs affaires dans les limites de la législation civile.' The law applied to Syria and Lebanon. After vehement protests - especially by the Muslim communities, which regarded it as incompatible with the Qur'an - its application to Muslim communities was suspended. Since then civil law regulations pertaining to personal status have been in abeyance. See Longrigg, *Syria and Lebanon*, pp. 253ff.

[249] As early as 1953 Pierre Gemayel had demanded that Lebanon become a secular state, including the extension of civil law to personal status. See Kemal H. Karpat, *Political and Social Thought in the Contemporary Middle East* (London, 1968), p. 112.

## The Lebanese Model

because it knew that the Muslims would not accept it, which, in turn, would justify the Kata'ib's insistence on the status quo of the division of power between the communities. Yet, this interpretation underestimates the extent to which Lebanese Christians — and, thus, the Kata'ib's supporters — are prepared to accept complete secularization, as will be empirically substantiated below. Be that as it may, in pre-war Lebanon complete secularization was not a relevant political issue.

But this changed with the outbreak of open warfare. In 1975 and 1976 the debate on the future political and social character of Lebanon was more serious and fiercer than any in its history.[250] It also revealed more starkly than all previous rhetoric the country's very real problems of identity.

In May 1976 the Progressive Socialist Party issued a remarkable declaration:

1. The identity of Lebanon was and still is the most distinct problem around which the successive Lebanese crises have revolved ...
2. Confessionalism has prevented the achievement of a unified national identity in Lebanon, and because of confessionalism two corresponding nationalities have emerged with two confessional situations: Lebanese Christian Maronite nationalism and Arab Islamic nationalism. These two nationalisms are tied to confessional allegiance, not to national allegiance.
3. Because of the need to unify these two conflicting nationalisms, the struggle for one national identity is always present, flaring up almost continually ...
4. The Arabism of Lebanon remained the cry of Islamic isolationists until the 60's when the Nasserite current gave this cry a dimension of belligerancy and combativeness to the point that Arabism became tied to the phrase 'liberation from imperialism.'
5. Nasserism did not face up to the social meaning of Arabism but faced only its political meaning. This prevented Nasserism from going beyond the social confessional framework.
6. Secularism attempts to abolish confessionalism, that is, abolish the social dispersion and division occurring in Lebanon. Secularism then attempts to do away with dual allegiance (to confessional community first, and to nation second) to make room for establishing one, shared allegiance — allegiance to the nation only.

---

[250] For an excellent survey of differences of opinion and arguments within the Muslim community, see Johannes Reissner, 'Säkularisierung des Libanon? Äusserungen von Muslimen zum neuen Schlagwort "Almana"', *Orient* 17/3 (1976), pp. 13–37.

7. Because secularism faces up to confessionalism (the most prominent social characteristic in Lebanon), it is forced to anchor in place a new political and social meaning for Arabism which will accomplish the following: (a) it will do away with the Utopian, emotional, confessional stamp of Arabism which was consecrated by the definitions given to it by the Islamic street and by national romantic theses (Ba`thism and Nasserism); (b) it will remove the complex of fear from the souls of Christians, because the new meaning will make Arabism a national, cultural affiliation answering to the economic and political needs of Lebanese society; (c) it will clear the way for Lebanon — subsequently — to become incorporated into a unified Arab state standing on the bases of democracy and secularism.
8. Secular Arabism differs qualitatively from Islamic Arabism because it does not focus on Islam in the following points: unity of economic interests, unity of language, unity of history and destiny, a common enemy (Israel, imperialism, Arab reactionism).
9. Secularism is the means which will make Arabism a unified national identity, shared by all Lebanese citizens, not by one group or one confessional community to the exclusion of others.
10. Secularism is not merely a collection of laws (abolition of political confessionalism, abolition of confessionalism in government posts, civil marriage, amendment of the law of inheritance, etc.), it is also the operation of transforming the culture of the society, moving it towards a culture built on reason and science.[251]

There can be no doubt: this is pure, enlightened Jacobin nationalism. Kamal Jumblatt and his party meant it seriously. In practical politics complete secularization would mean: abolition of the jurisdiction of the religious communities, extension of civil jurisdiction to the law of persons, family and inheritance, the abolition of confessional proportionality in political office and of quotas in the civil service and, for all to see, the removal of denomination from identity papers. As might be expected, the Left and some Christian parties expressed their approval. But this time it appeared as though the idea of secularization might meet with the approval of Muslims who did not belong to the Left. The Islamic Association of Makassed Graduates, whose members included a large part of the

---

[251] Author's italics. *Islamic Law and Change in Arab Society: Cemam Reports 1976*, vol. 4 (Beirut, 1978), pp. 93f. 'The bureau of information and orientation of the Progressive Socialist Party has issued the following'.

Sunni intelligentsia, declared their agreement with the concept of complete secularization, including civil law status of persons.[252]

This greatly alarmed the religious dignitaries of both the Sunni and the Shi`i communities. They feared that they were about to be overrun by the momentum of the secularist Left. The Council of Ulema in Lebanon, the higher religious body of the Lebanese Sunnis, delivered a solemn declaration.[253] Signs of fear about the disintegration of Muslim identity are unmistakeable.

What then could be the intent of uttering a call for secularism other than allowing the marriage of a Muslim girl with a non-Muslim? Those who head the call for secularism intend precisely: A. to dissolve the Islamic personality in Lebanon by marrying a Muslim girl to a non-Muslim ... B. to encourage the growth of a base generation of Christians fathers and Muslim mothers to cause fissures in Islamic family ties ... as a preparation to corrupting the authenticity of Islamic generations in the neighboring Arab world, not only in Lebanon; C. to break down the last and only barrier which protects Muslims in Lebanon from the dangers of dissolution, disintegration, and delusion to which they are exposed with persistent duress from the secularism of both the Westerners and the Marxists alike.[254]

They declared that they had no objection to the demand of the Maronite and Druze leaders for secularization in the personal status of their own communities, as long as their demands went no further. 'But if they consider secularism an appropriate solution for all, the Council objects.'[255] The Council prefaced its position and demands in that it 'announces the full mobilization of its members to face this serious danger by all means' and proceeded to decree: 'Secularism has no place in the life of a Muslim; either Islam is to exist without secularism, or secularism is to exist without Islam.'[256]

But that was not all. The Council of Ulema asked the Association of Makassed Graduates to clarify their position, earnestly requesting them 'to adhere to Islam and its current of thought, not to any other principle or current'. And it warned all presidential candidates against committing themselves to secularization, serving them notice 'that Muslims, belonging as they do to one party only — the party of God — ... will guard the rules of their religion by all means'.[257] Finally, it went on

---

[252] See *Islamic Law and Change in Arab Society, Cemam Reports 1975*, vol. 3 (Beirut, 1976), pp. 81–6.
[253] 'Declaration of the Council of Ulema in Lebanon on Secularism', *al-Anwar*, March 25th, 1976, p. 3; translation in *Cemam Reports 1976*, pp. 85–92.
[254] *Cemam Reports 1976*, p. 90.
[255] Ibid., p. 91.
[256] Ibid., pp. 90–1.
[257] Ibid.

the offensive by demanding that civil marriages contracted abroad should not be recognized.

This controversy brought home the gulf between the Left and mainstream Islam in Lebanon. As neither side wanted to destroy their political alliance, lengthy negotiations ensued. Eventually, a compromise was reached through Palestinian mediation: 'political secularization'. By this was meant the abolition of confessional proportionality in the offices of state and of quotas in the civil service; everything else had been dropped, which the Left interpreted as a temporary concession, and the other side as a matter of principle.

On closer examination, the agreement is no compromise at all. The Left had simply abandoned their position. A secularization limited to the political and administrative institutions of state is nothing else but a new name for the traditional demand of Lebanese political Islam for a redistribution of power. The Christians took this as an ultimatum to accept a fate as a tolerated minority in an Islamic state — and rejected it. In an address on July 20th, 1976, President Assad of Syria delivered the epilogue to this controversy. Jumblatt had discussed the question of secularism with him.

> I told him that the Phalangist Party is enthusiastic about secularization. When the leadership of the Phalangist Party, headed by Sheikh Pierre al-Jumayyil, visited us, I asked him in person about this matter. He told me, 'I do not accept a substitute to secularization. I insist on and cling to a secular state in Lebanon.' I raised the matter with the Moslems, with Musa al-Sadr, with certain prime ministers, and with certain speakers of the house. They rejected it because the matter deals with the essence of Islam ... The Moslems in Lebanon are the ones who do not want secularization and not vice versa ... The Phalangists cling to secularization, and Kamal Jumblat clings to secularization.[258]

The debate of 1976 serves to illuminate the basic strategies of the Lebanese communities. Arab and Lebanese nationalism are ideologies for the strategies of specific communities, and secularism the ideology for those of other communities — or of the same communities in different circumstances. The communities use ideologies to dress their interests in 'modern' clothes. The convictions of those supporting these ideologies may be genuine, but this does not alter their function. This is demonstrated by the ease with which ideologies are replaced when they no longer serve the interests of the community concerned.

---

[258] Author's italics. Itamar Rabinovich, *The War for Lebanon 1970–1983* (Ithaca and London, 1984), p. 218; for an English translation of the full text of the speech, see ibid., pp. 210–36.

Lebanese nationalism is a functional ideology for the Maronite community, as long as it ensures them a slight, or even only symbolic, advantage over others, or, in a worse case, as long as they, in conjunction with the other Christian communities, are not forced into minority status. Should this eventuality arise, the Maronites have a choice of two strategies. They can withdraw into one part of a partitioned Lebanon, and justify this in terms of a Christian Nationalism, or pursue a Jacobin state with a secularist ideology. As a powerful and dynamic community, their prospects in a completely secularized Lebanon would be good.

The Sunni community alternates between two strategies. One is union with other Arab states under the ideology of Arab nationalism, which would automatically make them part of the majority. The alternative is a redistribution of power within Lebanon under the ideology of 'political secularization'. They also have a reserve option: at a pinch they would accept the existing Lebanese system, provided that they could change places with the Maronites.

Pre-war, the Shi`i community pursued a block strategy in terms of a denominational ideology. Through better organization and mobilization they hoped to wrest an adequate share in the power and resources of the country. As the poorest of the communities, their demands were primarily economic. Only after years of warfare and in the growing conviction of being now the largest community, have the Shi`is been tempted to make a grab for power by demanding 'political secularization'.

The smaller communities have the choice between a strategy of alliance with a larger denomination, in the hope of exercising a moderating influence, and different Jacobin strategies. Most Greek Catholics have chosen the former. They support the Maronites, though themselves tone down Maronite ideologies to expressions potentially more acceptable to other groups. One section of the Greek Orthodox have chosen the same route and one section opted for Greater Syrian or Arabist Jacobisms in their purely secular versions, since only secularism can ensure them equality. The Druze under the leadership of Kamal Jumblatt best demonstrate the functional character of a Jacobin strategy pursued in terms of a secular ideology. One of the ablest and most charismatic Lebanese politicians, he aspired to greater power. But as a Druze he could attain this only in a secular system; accordingly this became his objective.

The characteristic feature of pre-war Lebanon was the generally moderate pursuit of these strategies on the part of all communities. All knew that these strategies were mutually exclusive and could be successful only with violence and at enormous cost. Hence, they were usually utilized to improve a community's relative position within the Lebanese system. Pre-war Lebanon functioned through the mutual deterrence of opposing strategies. Deterrence brought most of the politicians concerned to the insight that half a loaf was better than no bread. It was the same insight that had given birth to the National Pact, a strategy of sharing power, combined with a form of syncretistic national ideology. The Lebanese model worked most successfully during the Chehabist era. Chehab grasped better than his predecessors that this model functioned best when both the political and the economic cakes were shared equally.

At other times the model functioned less well, but it functioned. Lebanese conflicts were regulated peacefully. Conflict regulation broke down when one of the Lebanese communities or actors operated their strategy in an attempt to get more than a relative advantage, that is, control over everything. This was possible only when Lebanese actors could find non-Lebanese allies. The first instance was in 1958. Fortunately for Lebanon, two external actors neutralized each other — and were wise enough not to pursue a surrogate war in Lebanon. Equilibrium could be re-established after relatively little damage. The second time was in 1975. The external actors were already in the country, and themselves had an interest in finding Lebanese allies, not only vice versa. Jumblatt formed an alliance with the Palestinians in the hope of realizing his concept of a new Lebanon, and his role within it. By forcing the Sunni politicians into a corner in which they, in turn, had to seek an alliance with the Palestinians, Jumblatt created an extraordinarily powerful alliance. He thought victory was within his grasp, but was to be proven wrong; the other side, too, was able to find allies. And this time, in contrast to 1958, the external actors had an interest in surrogate warfare. What began in 1975 could not have done so — certainly not have been so militarized — without the external actors or without the readiness of a part of the Lebanese people to fight.

The 'Lebanese model', the Lebanon of the National Pact, had a long life, a life at times marked by sickness, but all in all a happy life. This Lebanon did not die; it was murdered. The murder victim is not guilty; but it is not innocent of complicity, either.

# 3

## The Clouding Horizon
## Non-Lebanese Factors of Conflict

'In one domain, it is true, Proporz systems seem to be less capable of effective performance of tasks: this is foreign policy.'

Gerhard Lehmbruch, 1967

I think with sadness of these civilized men who in a turbulent part of the world had fashioned a democratic society based on genuine mutual respect of the religions. Their achievement did not survive. The passions sweeping the area were too powerful to be contained by subtle constitutional arguments. As it had attempted in Jordan, the Palestinian movement wrecked the delicate balance of Lebanon's stability. Before the peace process could run its course, Lebanon was torn apart. Over its prostrate body at this writing all the factions and forces of the Middle East still chase their eternal dreams and act out their perennial nightmares.

Henry Kissinger, *Years of Upheaval*

'A quick settlement of the Palestine question ... was the only way by which the Lebanese Republic could avoid having the Arab–Israeli conflict finally resolved, in one way or another, at Lebanon's expense.'

Kamal Salibi, 1976

Lebanon is not an island. Geographically, culturally and politically it is part of that region between the Mediterranean Sea and the Persian Gulf, the Taurus Mountains and the Arabian Desert in which strategic, economic and ideological interests have clashed since the age of the Phoenicians. There were long periods of stability under the Romans, the Byzantines, the Umayyads and the Ottomans. But whenever one of the great empires was in decline or retreat, stability gave way to seemingly endless and often violent crises. In many respects, the present 'Middle East' crisis is the 'Eastern Question' of the nineteenth century in another guise. Its origins lie in the gradual decline of the Ottoman Empire, which encouraged foreign powers and local political forces to fill the emerging power vacuum. The resulting conflicts, and the fight for regional hegemony, have not yet been resolved. The armed conflicts of the present are, in the words of Georges Corm, the 'Wars of the Ottoman Succession'.[1]

There are many similarities between the patterns of conflict in the nineteenth and twentieth centuries. In the last century, British and Russian interests clashed in the Orient. British policy after Pitt's India Bill was to protect the sea route to India. Once the Romanovs gained the Ukrainian Black Sea coast in 1792, their permanent objective was access to the Mediterranean. England, Russia and other European powers sought allies in the region. They encouraged local nationalists in the Balkans and supported various minorities in the Orient. The causes of the bloody events in Lebanon between 1840 and 1860 were not only local; rivalry between the great powers played its part. Muhammad Ali's dream of Egyptian hegemony from the Nile to the Taurus Mountains was shattered by British resistance. Whereas independent nation-states succeeded Ottoman rule in the Balkans, the European powers felt they themselves were suitable successors in the Orient. At the end of the First World War two of them realized their ambitions. As League of Nations mandatories, Britain and France established their hegemony in the Orient for a good two decades.

The Russian Revolution facilitated their success, in that it isolated the country politically and diplomatically in Europe and the Orient until the victory of the anti-Hitler coalition. The pattern of superpower policies towards the Orient resembled that of the nineteenth-century Great Powers.

Like czarist Russia, the USSR sought a foothold in the Mediterranean area. Initially, this was resisted by Great Britain, then, after the Suez debacle in 1956, by the USA. The USA's influence in the region had been growing since the end of the Second World War. However, its concern was less the sea route to India than the West's oil interests in the Persian Gulf. Now, as then, the superpowers sought

---

1 Georges Corm, *Géopolitique du conflit libanais: étude historique et sociologique* (Paris, 1986), pp. 36ff.

regional allies. And just as the Ottoman Empire had sought to preserve its integrity and independence through a policy of neutrality, so its regional successors adopted various policies of neutrality, neutralism and non-alignment to preserve or improve their freedom of action vis-à-vis the superpowers. One of the driving forces behind Arab nationalism is the desire for a strong Arab nationalist political entity to fill the regional power vacuum and remove the influence of outside powers, and thereby end once and for all what was known in the nineteenth century as the 'Eastern Question' and in the twentieth as the 'Middle East crisis'.

So far, this has not happened. Indeed, the reverse is true: the Arab world is as divided as ever. The legitimacy of the states created by the Western powers is still questioned in the name of Arabism. At the same time, and also in the name of Arabism, these states are in permanent conflict over hegemony, to which Egypt, Syria, Iraq and, discreetly, Saudi Arabia all aspire. The many changes of regime in the first three of these countries since 1945 has not affected their respective claims to leadership. They see no contradiction between the *raison d'état* of individual statehood and pan-Arabism: the two are reconciled in their respective claims. As none of them has squared the circle of attaining hegemony without thereby legitimating the statehood of the existing states, the issue of the succession to the Ottoman Empire remains open and disputed.

Contentious though this issue is, it is not so divisive as another that unsettles the entire Arab family: the acceptance of the twilight child of European rule: Israel. Most Arabs regard Israel as a foreign body in the region, a Western implant and, as the leading military power in the Orient, a permanent manifestation of alien domination. Since the creation of the State of Israel in 1948 the question of policy towards Israel has crucially affected relations between the Arab world and the superpowers, relations between the Arab states and often their domestic politics as well.

## The pivot of Arab politics: The Arab-Israeli conflict

A hypothesis popular chiefly among non-Arabs holds that even without the Arab-Israeli conflict the Arab East would be just as torn and strife-ridden, as witnessed by two Gulf Wars in a decade.[2] This hypothesis cannot be tested; but all evidence

---

[2] In Lebanon this hypothesis was supported by, among others, Bashir Gemayel: 'The real Middle-East issue is now obvious: who controls the access to oil? The [first] Gulf War has suddenly made it clear that the Palestine question has only limited importance in the Middle East as a whole. Who's interested in the Palestinians today?' Interview with the author, 1980.

indicates that most Arabs see the Palestine question as the crux of Arab politics —
and Arab policies are shaped, rightly or wrongly, by this perception.[3]

This applies first of all to policies towards the superpowers. The USSR[4] supported the creation of the State of Israel and constantly advocated recognition of its existence within secure borders. It also constantly supported recognition of Palestinian rights and opposed Israel's territorial expansion. It supplied armaments to Arab states when these were particularly weak in relation to Israel. The USA[5] has repeatedly sought a peaceful settlement of the Arab–Israeli conflict. In several Arab–Israeli wars — 1956, 1973 and again in 1982 — it prevented Israel from exploiting its military advantage to the full. But it remains Israel's main source of arms and economic and political support. Its attempts to form alliances with Arab states, from the Baghdad Pact to Reagan's 'strategic consensus' have had little success. Pro-Western Arab governments have frequently accepted US aid, but since the overthrow of the Hashemite monarchy in Iraq in 1958, no Arab state has dared conclude a formal pact with the 'friend of the enemy'. But Soviet efforts were not particularly successful either. The strongest Soviet commitment was to Nasser's Egypt. And in Egypt it suffered its greatest setback when Sadat abrogated the Treaty of Friendship in 1972. Although the USSR signed treaties of friendship with Syria and Iraq, the defence clauses were pretty vague.

The relations between the Arab states and the superpowers were characterized by ambivalence. The Arab states could count on Soviet support in the Arab–Israeli conflict. But this support was finely measured, could prevent crushing defeats but not bring victory. US support for Israel was and is the chief obstacle to an Arab–American rapprochement. At the same time, the USA is the only power able to exercise a moderating influence on Israel, and even bring it to the negotiating table. In a nutshell: the relations between the Arab states and the superpowers

---

[3] On this section see Walter Z. Laqueur, ed., *The Israel–Arab Reader: A documentary history of the Middle East conflict* (New York, 1969) and *Confrontation — The Middle East War and World Politics* (London, 1974); David Hirst, *The Gun and the Olive Branch: The roots of violence in the Middle East* (London, 1977); Hisham Sharabi, *Palestine and Israel: The lethal dilemma* (New York, 1969); Trevor Nevitt Dupuy, *Elusive Victory: The Arab–Israeli Wars, 1947–74* (Indianapolis, 1977); Ronald D. McLaurin, Mohammed Mughisuddin and Abraham R. Wagner, *Foreign Policy Making in the Middle East: Domestic influences on policy in Egypt, Iraq, Israel, and Syria* (New York, 1977).

[4] See Wolfgang Berner, 'Die Nah- und Mittelostpolitik der UdSSR', in Udo Steinbach and Rüdiger Robert, *Der Nahe und Mittlere Osten. Politik, Gesellschaft, Wirtschaft, Geschichte, Kultur* (2 vols, Opladen, 1988), pp. 771–8. The USSR dissolved itself after the events described in this study.

[5] On US policy see especially William B. Quandt, *Decade of Decisions: American policy toward the Arab–Israeli conflict, 1967–1976* (Berkeley, 1977); Harold H. Saunders, *The Other Walls. The Politics of the Arab–Israeli peace process* (Washington D.C., 1985); Christian Hacke, *Amerikanische Nahostpolitik. Kontinuität und Wandel von Nixon bis Reagan* (Bonn, 1985); Haim Shaked and Itamar Rabinovich, eds., *The Middle East and the United States* (New Brunswick, 1980).

depended largely on their various assessments of how and whether one or other superpower could and would help them in their conflict with Israel.

The USSR was unswerving in its call for a global settlement of the Middle East question through international conference, provided that it participated. The USA occasionally signalled its support for such a settlement, and then tried once again to manage negotiations and the peace process on its own — that is, without the USSR. At the risk of simplification, superpower rivalry in the Middle East conflict boiled down to the USA trying to demonstrate that it alone held the key to a settlement, and the USSR demonstrating that this was not the case.

Another factor in the relationships between the Arab states is the promotion of mutually exclusive claims to hegemony. In order to justify it, each claim is presented as the best way of achieving a position of Arab strength and, hence, a favourable settlement of the Palestinian question. Much the same is true of politicians' and parties' claims to leadership within the individual Arab states. After the first Palestinian war in 1948, nascent political forces blamed the Arab governments and the disunity between them for the Arabs' defeat.[6] In the same year the parliamentary democracy underpinned by the Syrian bourgeoisie was swept away. In 1952 a bloodless coup deposed King Farouk of Egypt, in 1958 a bloody one King Faisal in Iraq. The Hashemite dynasty in Jordan survived only through the unflinching loyalty of its Bedouin troops and British help.[7]

The Arab defeat in 1956, convinced many Arab nationalists of the need to unite in one state. The charismatic leader, Gamal Abdel Nasser, who had at least retained Suez, became the idol of the masses.[8] When he spoke, traffic often came to a standstill not only in Cairo, but in Damascus, Baghdad and Beirut as well. Arab national currents that had so far kept their distance, such as the Baath Party since the 1930s and George Habash's Arab National Movement since 1948, regarded Nasser as an Arab Cavour or Bismarck. In 1958 the Arab East came closest to the 'Arab 1871' propagated by the leading theoretician of Arab nationalism, Sati al-Husri.[9] The Baath Party led Syria into union with Egypt under Nasser's leadership. In July 1958 Iraq and Lebanon seemed about to join as well. But Arabism had peaked. Arab particularisms were stronger than many

---

[6] One example among the many is Gamal Abdel Nasser's tract *Nasser: The Philosophy of the Revolution*' (Buffalo, 1959).

[7] See Arnold Hottinger, 'How the Arab bourgeoisie lost power', *Journal of Contemporary History* 3 (1968), pp. 111–28 and 'An eye-witness report on Iraq', *Swiss Review of World Affairs* 9 (1959), pp. 12–16; Miles Copeland, *The Game of Nations: The amorality of power politics* (London, 1969), pp. 28–46; Anwar Sadat, *Revolt on the Nile* (London, 1957); B. Shwadran, *Jordan: A State of Tension* (New York, 1959).

[8] George E. Kirk, *Contemporary Arab Politics: A concise history* (London, 1961), pp. 149ff.

[9] See Bassam Tibi, *Vom Gottesreich zum Nationalstaat: Islam und panarabischer Nationalismus* (Frankfurt, 1987), chapters III and IV.

foreign observers had believed and most Arab nationalists had hoped. King Hussein's regime survived in Jordan. Lebanon under Chehab adapted its foreign policy to appease Nasser, but preserved its independence. In Iraq General Kassem eliminated the Nasserite wing of the revolutionary government. In 1961 a putsch by Syrian officers from conservative middle-class backgrounds put an inglorious end to the United Arab Republic. After 1948, 1961 was the second trauma for Arab nationalism in its struggle against Israel. The dream of one common, strong state, capable of confronting Israel, was over. Arab nationalists turned to the question of the social prerequisites for national unity. It was obviously not enough just to sweep aside capitalist or monarchist 'reactionary regimes'. The idea slowly gained ground that the way to unity and to confront Israel from a position of strength was through a radical transformation of Arab society. In 1962 Nasser proclaimed the 'total revolution', which would bring about a 'democratic, cooperative socialist society'.[10] In 1963 coups d'état brought the Baath Party to power in Syria and Iraq. Like Nasser, it preached 'Arab socialism'. Both Nasser and the Baathists practised a socialism more populist than Marxist. Nasser rejected the dictatorship of the proletariat. He hoped that if workers, peasants and national capital collaborated, class differences would disappear. Baathist theorists preached similar 'visions of harmony'.[11] In practice, both Nasserite and Baathist socialism was limited to land reforms — long overdue, even in terms of non-socialist economics — the nationalization of key industries and banking, and the creation an efficient state machinery to observe and control all of society: in a nutshell, modernized dirigisme. This sort of modernization, together with the deferred goal of Arab unity, was soon seen as the best way for Arab states to match Israel in their inevitable confrontation.

However, the next round in this confrontation came much earlier than the Arab states had anticipated or desired. In 1967 Israel grasped the excuse Nasser's war-mongering gave them and delivered a crushing defeat to Egypt, Syria and Jordan in the Six Day War.

The debacle of 1967 unsettled the Arab East far more than the defeat in 1948 or the disintegration of the United Arab Republic in 1961. Since 1967 the trauma of the Arab–Israeli conflict has dominated Arab politics. This most crushing of all Arab defeats gave rise to three different, potentially incompatible developments: the Palestinian national movement, the gradual revival of Islamic fundamentalism and, finally, the rift between Arab states over superpower initiatives for a Middle

---

[10] See Fritz Steppat, 'Nasser's Revolution', *Europa-Archiv*, 17 (1962), pp. 163–73.

[11] The phrase used by Friedemann Büttner, 'Der Islam und die Entfaltung der arabischen politischen Ideen', in Karl Kaiser and Udo Steinbach, eds., *Deutsch–Arabische Beziehungen* (Munich, 1981), p. 36.

East settlement. After a sketch of each development, it will be shown how they came to clash in Lebanon.

## The Palestinian National Movement[12]

In the 1948 war the Arabs in Palestine trusted to the military might of the Arab states. When the war was over, Israel controlled far more territory than the partition plan of the United Nations had foreseen, a plan the Arab states had rejected. About half the Arab population in Palestine had either fled or been expelled from their homeland. Transjordan annexed the West Bank and East Jerusalem, which had remained in Arab hands, and renamed itself Jordan; Egypt administered the Gaza Strip. The neighbouring states settled most of the Palestinian refugees in camps, in the hope they would soon go home. But small groups of intellectuals already had doubts about the will or the ability of the Arab states to help them to return to Palestine. In 1948 George Habash founded the Arab National Movement at the American University of Beirut; in 1956 Yassir Arafat, Salah Khalaf (Abu Iyad) and Khalil Al-Wazzir (Abu Jihad) met in Gaza and founded the Palestinian National Liberation Movement — Fatah. Fatah was inspired by the Algerian liberation movement and the Syrian Baath Party. But, above all, Fatah kept up the traditions of the Muslim society of pre-Israeli Palestine: the movement appealed primarily to Sunnis. Its ideology was simple: liberate Palestine. Everything else could be discussed afterwards. By contrast, the Arab National Movement held from the start that Arab unity was essential to liberate Palestine. To achieve unity, it was necessary to overthrow reactionary Arab regimes. It was enthusiastically Nasserite until the break-up of the United Arab Republic in 1961. It then turned from pure Arab nationalism to Marxism: henceforth, Habash and his friends

---

[12] See in particular John W. Amos II, *Palestinian Resistance: Organization of a Nationalist Movement* (New York, 1980); Mosh'e Ma'oz, ed., *Palestinian Arab Politics* (Jerusalem, 1975); William W. Quandt, Fouad Jabber and Ann Mosely Lech, *The Politics of Palestinian Nationalism* (Berkeley, 1973); Walid W. Kazziha, *Palestine in the Arab Dilemma* (London, 1979); Edgar O'Ballance, *Arab Guerilla Power 1967–1972* (London, 1974); Bard O'Neill, *Revolutionary Warfare in the Middle East, Israelis versus Fedayeen* (Colorado, 1974); David Pryce-Jones, *The Face of Defeat, Palestinian Refugees and Guerillas* (London, 1974); Aaron David Miller, *The PLO and the Politics of Survival* (New York, 1983); Paul A. Jureidini and William E. Hazen, *The Palestinian Movement in Politics* (Lexington, Mass., 1976); Ehud Yaari, *Strike Terror, The story of Fatah* (New York, 1970); David Thomas Schiller, *Palästinenser zwischen Terrorismus und Diplomatie. Die paramilitärische palästinensische Nationalbewegung von 1918 bis 1981* (Munich, 1982); Shamil Sharaf, *Die Palästinenser. Geschichte der Entstehung eines nationalen Bewußtseins* (Vienna, 1983).

believed only a radical transformation of Arab society could bring change in Palestine: liberation through revolution, both in Palestine and in the Arab states.[13]

Both organizations had very small beginnings. In the first half of the 1960s their militancy and the echo they found among Palestinians and other Arabs aroused the interest of some Arab governments. Syria financed and supported Fatah's guerrilla training camps. Nasser tried to keep control of an emerging guerrilla movement and arranged for the creation of the Palestinian Liberation Organization (PLO) under the aegis of the Arab League. The Palestinians held their first national congress in Jerusalem in 1964. It elected the pro-Egyptian lawyer Ahmad Shukairi first chairman of the PLO, and passed a resolution to found a Palestinian Liberation Army (PLA). The PLA was a conventional force with brigades in Egypt, Syria and Iraq, recruited from the youth of the Palestinian camps in these countries, but under the command of the respective national armies. Independently of the PLO and PLA, though, Fatah began its own commando raids in 1965. Although the commandos came from its Syrian camps, they infiltrated Jordan to launch them. The Syrian authorities supported Fatah, but wanted to retain control over unconventional Palestinian military operations. In 1966 the Baath Congress decided to form its own guerrilla organization, Saiqa, under the command of Zuhair Mohsen, a Palestinian officer in the Syrian Army. The conflict between Palestinian independence and its instrumentalization by the Arab states arose in the early stages of the Palestinian movement and has still not been resolved.

The Six Day War was a turning point for the entire Arab world, above all the Palestinians.[14] Apart from the Egyptian Sinai Peninsular and the Syrian Golan Heights, Israel occupied the Gaza Strip and the entire West Bank: all Palestine was now under Israeli control. The crushing defeat of the Arab armies shattered any hopes that Israel might be defeated in conventional warfare, and tarnished the standing of the Arab rulers. Tens of thousands of Palestinians once again fled or were expelled. Palestinians despaired of thrice-defeated Arab states defending their cause. The hour of autonomous Palestinian nationalism had struck; it emerged and took wing.[15] The Palestinians continued to regard themselves as

---

[13] See Robert Anton Mertz, 'Why George Habbash Turned Marxist', *Mid-East Magazine* 10/4 (1970), pp. 31–6; Walid W. Kazziha, *Revolutionary Transformation in the Arab World: Habbash and his comrades from nationalism to Marxism* (London, 1975).

[14] See Bassam Tibi, 'Naher Osten — Nach dem Sechs–Tage–Krieg 1967 begann eine neue Epoche. Die regionalen und internationalen Folgen eines militärischen Konflicts', *Beiträge zur Konfliktforschung*, 17/4 (1987), pp. 69–98.

[15] 'Until 1967, the stateless Palestinians remained free-lance Arabs, trusting their cause to pan-Arab management ... Two decades of shared adversity, and countless humiliations inflicted on them by fellow Arabs ... had forged among them a sense of particularist identity ... The Palestinians, in short, had finally become a people with a separate and distinct sense of identity ... Lacking the territory to enable them to

Arabs and the entire Arab world as responsible for the Palestinian cause. But henceforth they would also see themselves as Palestinians, as the only Arab people to have suffered from the Arab-Israeli conflict. From 1967 they felt forced to take their fate into their own hands. No longer would they be exclusively dependent on the decisions of Arab governments: the goal of the Palestinian movement was to provide the organization and institutions for 'sovereign Palestinian decisions'. Palestinians would now fight autonomously for Palestine. The Arab governments were in no position to contradict the newly found will of the Palestinians. In 1968 the PLO elected Yahya Hamuda to succeed Shukairi; Hamuda was succeeded by Yassir Arafat in 1969. The PLO was now the Palestinians' independent national movement.

Ever since, the PLO has consistently claimed its dual rights on the basis of two nationalisms: Palestinian as well as Arab. As Palestinians they claim the right to decide for themselves on any matter pertaining to them; as Arabs they claim the right to support from all Arabs, including — above all — the freedom to operate unhindered from Arab territory, in any state, in their struggle for liberation. The practice of the latter soon proved incompatible with other considerations of state in those Arab areas from which Palestinians launched military activities, and led to bitter conflicts.

Initially, an armed liberation struggle was thought feasible within Palestine itself. About one million Palestinians were now living under Israeli occupation: an uprising as in Algeria or Vietnam was conceivable. Almost immediately, in June 1967, Fatah transferred its headquarters to the West Bank and started organizing underground resistance. However, as early as September of that year a general strike called in the occupied territories failed. Using the information of Jordanian archives captured in the war, the Israeli Army was able to arrest numerous Palestinian nationalists. The population was cowed and hardly dared to support the guerrillas. The guerrillas found the classic rule did not hold: they could not swim like fish in the water of the sympathizing masses; the guerrillas were like fish out of water.[16] At the end of 1967 Arafat and his staff had to withdraw from the occupied territories. It would be twenty years before another Palestinian uprising using different methods — civil disobedience and peaceful demonstrations — seriously troubled the Israeli occupiers. It continues.

At the start of 1968 the PLO had to reconsider its tactics. It chose another form of armed struggle, a hybrid of guerrilla action and conventional warfare:

---

organize themselves as a sovereign Palestinian state, the only course open to them, under the umbrella of the PLO, was to organize themselves as a sovereign revolution.' Kamal S. Salibi, *Lebanon and the Middle Eastern Question* (Oxford, 1988), pp. 13f.

[16] David Thomas Schiller, 'Entstehung und Verlauf des libanesischen Bürgerkriegs', Unpublished honours thesis, Otto Suhr Institute, Berlin, 1978, p. 93.

commando raids from bases in neighbouring countries. The consequence of these raids was Israeli reprisals against the host countries. Notwithstanding reprisals, the commandos found support, especially in Jordan. In March 1968 an Israeli 'punitive action' against Palestinians in the Jordan Valley was repelled by Palestinian guerrillas and Jordanian armoured troops with heavy losses on both sides. The 'Battle of Karameh' was a watershed for the Palestinians and for their relations with the Arab states. 'For the first time we tasted victory', as a Palestinian leader put it. 'In spite of heavy casualties, 60 per cent of our fighters, we won, because, for the first time, Arabs had not run away. For the first time, the Israeli super-soldiers appeared vincible.'[17] Karameh became a legend in the Palestinian movement and gave it self-confidence. But Karameh also awakened the Jordanian government to the fact that Palestinian commando raids involved the danger of another conventional war with Israel, a war they did not want. Therefore Jordan tried to bring the guerrillas under control.

The Palestinian movement's new-found independence was soon in jeopardy. The reactions of its member organizations varied. In the late 1960s the PLO comprised approximately twenty different groups. The strongest was Fatah. In 1967 Habash's Arab National Movement had merged with two smaller groups to form the Popular Front for the Liberation of Palestine (PFLP — known as the Popular Front). In 1968 Ahmed Jibril's Popular Front for the Liberation of Palestine-General Command (PFLP-GC — Popular Front-General Command) split away from the Popular Front, and in 1969 the Popular Democratic Front for the Liberation of Palestine (PDFLP — Democratic Front for short) was formed under the leadership of Nayef Hawatmeh. The Iraqi government founded the Arab Liberation Front (ALF) as a rival to the Syrian-sponsored Saiqa. The Popular Front-General Command was close to the Syrian government, without becoming its tool, as Saiqa was. Among the organizations that could act independently of direct government interference, the Popular Front and the Democratic Front were Fatah's real rivals. Fatah remained essentially a conservative nationalist movement of Sunni persuasion. Its most important financial backer was Saudi Arabia. Fatah wanted Palestinian independence but was quite prepared to act in coordination with, and make concessions to, Arab governments, including the Jordanian. The Popular Front and the Democratic Front drew most of their support from religious minorities — Habash has a Greek Orthodox, Hawatmeh a Greek Catholic background — and secularized Muslims. The Popular Front supported an independent, the Democratic Front a fairly orthodox, version of Marxism. The Popular Front especially took a line not only of unconditional confrontation with

---

[17] Interview with Issam Sartawi, 1979.

## The Clouding Horizon: Non-Lebanese Factors of Conflict 151

Israel, but also of revolution against reactionary and capitalist regimes in the Arab world, in particular the Jordanian, and later also the Lebanese.

Arafat tried to hold together the different factions in the PLO: the autonomous and the state-controlled, the conservative nationalists and the revolutionaries. This meant that his Fatah was frequently drawn into conflicts it would have preferred to avoid. The first occurred in Jordan. As Israeli reprisals against Jordan mounted in 1968 and 1969, about 100,000 farmers and camp people in the Jordan Valley sought refuge in the interior. The Palestinian organizations fortified their commando posts, training bases and refugee camps, creating a state within a state within a short time.[18] The Popular Front and the Democratic Front called for the overthrow of King Hussein. The first armed clashes between the Palestinians and the Jordanian Army took place in November 1968. The presence of the Palestinian guerrillas, who had started taking the law into their own hands, caused growing bitterness, especially among the indigenous population of Transjordan and those parts of the army recruited from Bedouin tribes loyal to the Hashemite dynasty. The crisis broke in September 1970, when Popular Front commandos simultaneaously hijacked aircraft of three international airlines to Sarka in Transjordan. Although Arafat and Saiqa dissociated themselves from this action, King Hussein moved to end the presence of armed Palestinian organizations on his territory, irrespective of political orientation.[19] For nine days Jordanian artillery shelled Palestinian bases and camps, the Bedouin army destroyed the Palestinian commando units and drove their remnants across the Syrian border;[20] the PLO claims about 10,000 guerrillas were killed.

Syria deported the remaining Palestinian units, followed by many civilians, to Lebanon. In 1967 Israel had crushed the Palestinian resistance within the country itself. 'Black September' in 1970 put an end to commando raids from Jordan. Syria kept a tight control on 'its' Palestinians and did not tolerate any attacks from Syrian territory. The last country the Palestinians could use for their armed struggle was Lebanon.

---

[18] The Jordanian government and its security forces lost control over whole centres and areas in the north of the country. The town of Irbid was declared the 'Hanoi of the Middle East'.

[19] See William B. Quandt, 'Lebanon, 1958 and Jordan, 1970', in Barry M. Blechman and Stephen S. Kaplan, eds., *Force without War: The use of the armed forces as a political instrument* (Washington, 1978), pp. 222–88.

[20] The Syrian government considered intervening in support of the Palestinians. After threats from Israel it restricted itself to sending the Hittin Brigade of the PLA and some Syrian armoured brigades disguised as PLA brigades; both were repelled by the Jordanian air force and armoured troops with heavy losses near Irbid.

## The crisis of Arabism and the reawakening of Islamic fundamentalism[21]

Defeat in the Six Day War plunged the Arab East into a political, intellectual and moral crisis which favoured not only the rise of the Palestinian national movement but also the emergence of religious protest movements in several Arab countries. Radical religious movements are not new to the Arab world. The modernizing currents of Arab nationalism, especially Nasserism and Baathism have always rejected Marxism as 'un-Arab' and an 'atheistic ideology'. On the other hand, as declared secular movements, they have never hesitated to use the power of the state to repress movements preaching theocratic forms of government. Nasser had thousands of supporters of the Muslim Brotherhood thrown into prison, where hundreds died. During Egypt, Syria and Iraq's pan-Arab socialist phase, Islamic fundamentalist movements were more strongly marginalized than ever. Personal popularity, and the political strength this gave him, allowed Nasser[22] to give short shrift to Islamic fundamentalist activists; efficiency and military power did the same for the Baath governments. However, secularized Arab nationalism enjoyed mass support only as long as it had something to show for itself. As discussed above, evidence suggests that popular support for Arabism generally identifies Arabness with Islam, no matter how carefully political leaders and theorists distinguish between the two. For this reason, Islamic fundamentalism is always a potential political force, waiting for a crisis to break.

Unlike earlier crises, the crisis of 1967 was more than a crisis of political leaders and regimes: it was a crisis of Arabism as such.[23] The concept of the Arab nation united in one state had proved to be an extraordinarily effective instrument for emotional mass mobilization. But it was unable to convert these emotions into political action and lasting, tangible changes in political and social structures. In terms of its own claims, Arabism had at best only partial success, be it in building

---

[21] See especially Tibi, *Vom Gottesreich zum Nationalstaat: Die Krise des modernen Islams: Eine vorindustrielle Kultur im wissenschaftlich-technischen Zeitalter* (Munich, 1981); and *Der Islam und das Problem der kulturellen Bewältigung sozialen Wandels* (Frankfurt am Main, 1985). On the crisis in the Arab world after 1967 see Fouad Ajami, *The Arab Predicament: Arab political thought and practice since 1967* (Cambridge, 1981); Udo Steinbach, 'Ideengeschichte im Zeichen von Kolonialismus, Unabhängigkeitsbewegung und Modernisierung', in Steinbach and Robert, *Der Nahe und Mittlere Osten*, pp. 164–7 and 175–82; Detlev Khalid, *Islam und politischer Extremismus: Einführung und Dokumentation* (Hamburg 1985); Werner Ende und Udo Steinbach, eds., *Der Islam in der Gegenwart* (Munich, 1984).

[22] See Amos Perlmutter, *Egypt: The pretorian state* (New Brunswick, 1974).

[23] See Fritz Steppat, 'Internationale Politik am Mittelmeer' in Karl Carstens et al., eds., *Die Internationale Politik 1966–67* (Munich, 1973), pp. 207–305 and Der Mittelostkonflikt nach dem Krieg von 1967, in Karl Kaiser et al., eds., *Die Internationale Politik 1968–69* (Munich, 1974), pp. 227–84.

a nation, resisting the economic and political penetration of foreign powers or in solving economic and social problems of development.

No matter how artificial the colonial boundaries of the post-Ottoman Arab states might be, they have shown considerable resilience. One reason is the stigma of hegemony that attaches to all attempts at union.[24] The pursued partner has always spurned advances; no state has been in a position to enforce its aspirations. Since Nasser's failure, a system of complicated multi-centric constellations has emerged among the Arab states, in which alliances keep disbanding and forming. One explanation lies in the fact that, notwithstanding their artificiality, the boundaries of the individual states demarcate historical, socio-cultural and economic distinctions in which genuine particularisms are rooted. Recourse to the glorious past awakens different feelings in Damascus, Baghdad and Cairo. Exalting the Umayyad, Abbasid and Fatimid dynasties respectively to historical ideology makes each of these cities the legitimate centre of the Arab world. The different mixes in each Arab state of the three traditional and traditionally contrary forms of life and economy in the Arab world — nomadism, riparian agriculture in the valleys and trade in the cities — have produced widely divergent social structures in the separate states. Even without suspicions of hegemony, these render union very difficult.[25] The United Arab Republic is a case in point. In recent years, economic differences have become even crasser: heavily populated poor states contrast starkly with lightly populated wealthy states.

Apart from state particularisms, ethno-religious particularisms[26] have also shown remarkable vitality — and by no means in Lebanon alone. In Iraq a Sunni and in Syria an Alawite minority is in power. Christian minorities play very different roles in Egypt, Jordan, Syria and Iraq, as well as in the Palestinian movement, from passive resignation, through collaboration with the respective strongest community, to ideological and revolutionary activism. Notwithstanding the large Sunni majority in the region as a whole, these particularisms accentuate the peculiarities of each state, though obviously not as conspicuously as the vested interests of the political and administrative leadership in each country. Whatever

---

[24] See René Aggiouri, *Les problèmes actuels du Proche-Orient* (Beirut, 1960).

[25] See Muhsin Mahdi, *Die geistigen und sozialen Wandlungen im Nahen Osten* (Freiburg im Breisgau, 1961).

[26] See Ronald D. McLaurin, ed., *The Political Role of Minority Groups in the Middle East* (New York, 1979); Nikolaos Van Dam, *The Struggle for Power in Syria: Sectarianism, regionalism and tribalism in politics 1961–1978* (London, 1979) and 'Middle Eastern Political Clichés: "Takriti" and "Sunni rule" in Iraq; "Alawi Rule" in Syria. A critical appraisal', Orient 21 (1980), pp. 42–57; Moshe Ma'oz and Avner Yaniv, eds., *Syria under Assad: Domestic constraints and regional risks* (London, 1986); cf. Theodor Hanf, 'Die christlichen Gemeinschaften im gesellschaftlichen Wandel des arabischen Vorderen Orients', Orient 22/1 (1981), pp.29–49; Erhard Franz, 'Religiöse und periphere Minderheiten', in Steinbach and Robert, *Der Nahe und Mittlere Osten*, vol. 1, pp. 67–78.

the reasons, Arabism is as far from its goal of a single state as it was after the two World Wars, and far further than it seemed to be in 1958.

Economic developments were equally uninspiring. Experiments in 'Arab socialism' were disappointing. In Egypt the attempt to create a centrally administered state economy was an utter failure. A well-meant educational policy guaranteed every university graduate who could not find any other work a job in the civil service. The staff in both the civil service and state enterprises expanded to levels which bore no relation to economic reality. Strong measures virtually rooted out once flourishing corruption, but made it virtually impossible to get anything done. Under Nasser, Egypt became a Spartan, impressively reputable but unproductive society.[27] It remained a very hierarchic society. The old grand bourgeoisie was replaced by a 'new class', the administrative petty bourgeoisie, which lived both for and from the state, controlling the means of extraction rather than the means of production. Years later, when Sadat ended austerity as part of his policy of *infitah*, the economically parasitic nature of the new class was revealed in all its ugliness, and liberalization could do little to change things. In the two other countries of the Arab East that experimented with socialism, Syria and Iraq, neither austerity nor the subsequent liberalization was pursued as consistently as in Egypt. But here too Arab socialism produced state classes whose relatively privileged positions set them apart from the masses. The people had different rulers but were ruled no differently. The fathers of Arab socialism had hoped it would transform Arab society, but the changes were minor.

Arabism's balance sheet at the start of the Six Day War showed meagre results. The depth of the crisis after the war must be seen against this background. The military defeat destroyed any illusions about the underlying political and social malaise of the Arab East. The intelligentsia brooded over the causes and reached various conclusions. A minority was more convinced than ever that the answer lay in Marxism. Others looked to the past for solutions. It is not a rare phenomenon for people and even whole peoples in crisis to seek comfort in religion. After the evident failure of secular Arabism, recourse to Islam was an obvious move for Muslim Arabs. That defeat had been inflicted by a state perceived not only as a Western intrusion in the Orient but also as a Jewish theocracy added insult to injury. Secular Arabs had branded the Jewish character of the Israeli state as a sign of backwardness. Yet this backward state had now proved its superiority. The syllogism was clear: only by re-establishing the Islamic character of Arab state-

---

[27] See W. Wym, *Nasser of Egypt: The search for dignity* (Cambridge, Mass., 1959); Hrair R. Dekmejian, *Egypt under Nasir: A study in political dynamics* (New York, 1971); Anouar Abdel Malek, *Egypte, société militaire* (Paris, 1962).

hood could Islam demonstrate the superiority it had of right. The answer to the Zionist state was, as it were, a sort of Islamic 'Zionization'.

After 1967 new political movements under new leaders sprang up all over the Arab world and threatened established regimes. Without exception, the message was simple. And it was precisely this simplicity that appealed to disoriented and desperate people.[28] Society had fallen into faithlessness, decadence and corruption as in pre-Islamic times. Politicians across the board had abandoned the true faith. A true believer could not survive as an individual in a state devoid of faith; he had to put all his energies towards the realization of the community of the faithful in accordance with the rules of the Qur'an, the traditional laws and the words and the example of the Prophet. The political leaders had to be forced to re-institute the Islamic order — or be overthrown. Some empirical data[29] are available on the cadres and supporters of these movements. The cadres were upwardly mobile members of the new lower-middle classes threatened by downward mobility in times of national crisis. The hotbed of support was among people of rural and small-town origins engulfed by the anonymous living conditions of urban spread.

As yet, none of these movements has come to power in an Arab state;[30] and only in Sudan has one, the Muslim Brotherhood, been part of a coalition government. However, in many places Islamic fundamentalism is an effective ideology of opposition. In Egypt it has been behind assassination attempts, uprisings and riots, as in Syria and Saudi Arabia. But in 1979 it came to power in Iran — not without the help of the PLO, which had trained Iranian Islamic activists at its Lebanese bases. From Iran the victorious Shi`i version of Islamic fundamentalism rebounded on the Arab world.[31] Iraq started the first Gulf War to pre-empt the fundamentalist threat from Iran. Since 1979, even before that war, pro-Iranian Lebanese Shi`is and pro-Iraqi Palestinians had been fighting each other in the suburbs of Beirut. In 1982 secular Syria allowed Iranian Pasdaran to participate in

---

[28] For a selection of texts in translation see *Sou'al* (four-monthly review), special issue, *L'Islamisme aujourd'hui* (Paris, 1985). See also Hamied N. Ansari, 'The Islamic militants in Egyptian politics', *International Journal of Middle East Studies* 16 (1984), pp. 123–44; Alexander S. Cudsi and Ali E. Hillal Dessouki, eds., *Islam and Power* (London, 1981); Saad Eddin Ibrahim, 'Anatomy of Egypt's militant Islamic studies groups', paper presented to the Middle Eastern Studies Association Annual Congress, Washington, D.C., November 1980; Gilles Kepel, *Le prophète et pharaon: Les mouvements islamistes dans l'Egypte contemporaine* (Paris, 1984); Susan E. Marshall, 'Paradoxes of change: Culture crisis, Islamic revival, and the reactivation of patriarchy', *Journal of Asian and African Studies* 19/1–2 (1984), pp. 1–17; Johannes Reissner, 'Die militant-islamischen Gruppen', in Ende and Steinbach, *Der Islam*, pp. 470–86.
[29] Ibrahim, 'Anatomy of Egypt's Militant Islamic groups'.
[30] The Islamic Salvation Front seemed set to win the Algerian elections in January 1992, until forestalled by a coup d'état.
[31] See Bassma Kodmani-Darwish, 'L'Iran, nouvel acteur fort au Liban?', in Bassma Kodmani-Darwish, ed., *Liban: espoirs et réalités* (Paris, 1987), pp. 153–64.

the war against Israel in Lebanon, and to establish a branch of the Hezbollah, the 'Party of God' there. Syria itself was mercilessly repressing the Muslim Brotherhood at home. In the aftermath of the Six Day War Lebanon was gradually turned into the battlefield of the Arab–Israeli conflict. Fifteen years later the Iranian version of Islamic fundamentalism had also marched on to this field and, as will be seen below, joined the internal battle of the Lebanese too.

It is an irony of history that since the start of the uprising in the occupied territories in 1987 there has been bitter rivalry between the PLO, the only political force in the 1960s to promote Iranian Islamic fundamentalism, and Islamic fundamentalists among the Palestinians. On the other hand, there is a certain historical logic in the fact that Islamic fundamentalism has now arrived where the decline of Arabism began, in Palestine.

## Oil on troubled waters[32]

The first reaction of the Arab states to the Israeli victory in the Six Day War was one of total rejection. At the summit conference of the Arab League in Khartoum in 1967 they solemnly proclaimed their 'three noes': no recognition of Israel, no negotiations, no peace. Israel's victory left it the military great power of the region. But the enormity of this victory made it impossible for the Arabs to accept it. In view of the explosive mood of humiliation, injured pride and anger at defeat of what was felt to be a just cause, no Arab government could dare consider negotiations. On the other hand, Israel had acquired such a sense of superiority that it never even considered offering its defeated opponents generous terms of peace. There were no signs of compromise, only omens of further conflict.

The explosive potential of perpetuating yet greater hostility in the Middle Eastern conflict jolted the superpowers: once again, war in the Middle East had raised the possibility of a direct confrontation between them. Thus, immediately after the cease-fire both the Americans and the Soviets started trying to arrange a settlement. This proved extraordinarily difficult. The respective concepts of the superpowers overlapped only in part, for each was simultaneously pursuing its own interests in the region. The USA tended to change its peace plans and proposals with its presidents, and sometimes more often. Moreover, neither Israel nor the Arab states were completely dependent on the superpowers. They might need their support, but this did not prevent them from often behaving as they saw

---

[32] See the excellent, brief review by Udo Seinbach, 'Israelisch-arabischer Konflikt', in Steinbach and Robert, *Der Nahe und Mittlere Osten*, vol. 1, pp. 639–61; Fred J. Khouri, 'The Arab–Israeli Conflict', in P. Edward Haley and Lewis W. Snider, eds., *Lebanon in Crisis: Participants and issues* (Syracuse, 1979), pp. 161–77; Quandt, *Decade of Decisions*; Saunders, *The Other Walls*; Henry Kissinger, *Years of Upheaval* (Boston, 1982) (for Lebanon, see especially pp. 787–89).

fit: not only did they reject proposals of the superpowers, in 1973 and 1982 they went to war in defiance of them.

The emergence of the PLO and its rapid rise after 1967 was another factor. The Arab states could speak on behalf of the Palestinians only conditionally; the Palestinians themselves had a voice too. While Israel was always prepared to negotiate with the Arab states, it unconditionally rejected the PLO as a negotiating partner. The unilateral refusal to negotiate, initiated by the Arabs in 1948 and reaffirmed in 1967, became bilateral and mutual: Israel would negotiate only in the absence of the PLO, whereas after 1967 the Arab states increasingly felt they could negotiate only in its presence.

The more concrete the proposed substance of negotiations, the more obvious it became that both sides would have to make concessions and compromises. Whenever a number of parties are involved in a conflict, concessions must take account of different interests and opinions. Those who have a lot to lose if the conflict continues are more likely to make concessions than those who have little or nothing to lose. The former always include front-line states, that is, those who would be directly affected if warfare resumed. In the Middle East, one state, Egypt, had much to gain: the return of the oil-rich Sinai Peninsular. States out of the line of fire, like Libya and South Yemen, had little to lose. One group had lost almost everything, and thus had almost nothing left to lose: the Palestinians in exile and their organization, the PLO.

The more concrete the perspectives of peace negotiations, the more serious the differences of opinion in the Arab world became. The rifts caused by the peace process in the 1970s were even greater than those caused by the hegemonic struggles in the 1950s and 1960s.

In November 1967 the Security Council of the United Nations passed Resolution 242. This was the beginning of the peace process. It called for the withdrawal of Israeli forces from (the) territories occupied, an end to the state of war and recognition of the sovereignty, territorial integrity and political independence of all states in the region and their right to existence within guaranteed and recognized borders.[33] Furthermore, it called for 'a just solution to the problem of refugees'. Israel, Egypt, Jordan and Lebanon voted for the resolution. Syria and the Palestinian leaders rejected it because it mentions the Palestinians merely as refugees; they demanded that the Palestinians be recognized as a people with national rights.

---

[33] The prevailing English and French texts of the resolution differ regarding the withdrawal of Israeli troops 'from territories occupied' (which does not mean *all* territories) and 'des territoires occupés' (which is unequivocal).

The PLO had even more ambitious goals. They no longer simply demanded, as in Shukairi's time, the destruction of the 'Zionist entity'. At first unofficially, and from 1970 as official policy, they demanded the creation of a 'secular democratic state' for the whole of Palestine, in which Jews, Muslims and Christians would be equal citizens. As this concept implies the dissolution of the Jewish state, Israel will not even consider it. Resolution 242 had no immediate consequences. Israel reacted promptly and harshly to Palestinian guerrilla attacks. The outcome of the 1970 confrontation between the Jordanian state and the Palestinians relieved Israel of all trouble along the longest of its borders. After its 'Black September', Fatah formed a secret organization with the same name and, emulating the Popular Front, took its struggle beyond the confines of Palestine. A series of attacks, including the assassination of the Jordanian Prime Minister, Wasfi Tell, in 1971, the murder of Israeli sportsmen at the Olympic Games in Munich in September 1972 and of American diplomats in Khartoum in March 1973, ruled out negotiations for a while.

However, a change of opinion was brought about by the October War of 1973, when Egypt and Syria surprised Israel.[34] By the time the USA and the USSR could arrange a cease-fire, Israel was on the offensive, but had paid a heavy price. The two Arab armies had fought well, and Egypt had managed to break through the Israeli defence along the Suez Canal. What the 'Battle of Karameh' had become for the Palestinians, the October War became for the Arab states. Israel may eventually have regained the upper hand, but the Arabs had regained their honour. Arab armies had destroyed the illusion of Israel's invincibility. Yet, the October War was not a harbinger of escalation; it was the bloody prelude to serious negotiations. The superpowers had once again been frightened by the possibility of direct confrontation.[35] But Arab states too were interested. Egypt especially was tired of war. In 1956 it had borne the burden alone, in 1967 the brunt; for three years until the summer of 1970 it had fought a costly war of attrition along the Suez Canal. Military expenditures weighed heavily on its weak economy. Sadat, who had succeeded Nasser in 1970, feared internal unrest if even greater sacrifices were asked of his people. On the other hand, the renown won in this war enabled him to participate in negotiations without losing face. In December 1973 the United Nations organized a peace conference in Geneva, attended by the USA, the USSR, Israel, Egypt and Jordan. Syria declined the invitation; the PLO did not get one. Although the Geneva Conference did not produce any

---

[34] See Laqueur, *Confrontation*; Chaim Herzog, *The War of Atonement* (London, 1975); Ze'ev Schiff, *October Earthquake: Yom Kippur 1973* (Tel Aviv, 1974); Lawrence C. Whetten, *The Canal War: Four-Power Conflict in the Middle East* (Cambridge, Mass., 1974).

[35] See Robert O. Freedman, *Soviet Policy toward the Middle East since 1970* (New York, 1978); Galia Goaln, *Yom Kippur and After: The Soviet Union and the Middle East crisis* (Cambridge, 1977).

concrete results, it did open the way to the shuttle diplomacy of the US Secretary of State, Henry Kissinger.

Kissinger achieved his first success in January 1974: an agreement on the disengagement of Israeli and Egyptian troops in Sinai (the so-called Sinai I). While Kissinger was shuttling between Jerusalem and Cairo the war of attrition between Syria and Israel on the Golan Heights continued. In April, Kissinger shuttled between Jerusalem and Damascus; in May a disengagement agreement was signed between Syria and Israel.

These agreements were unquestionably successes for diplomacy. But they were to prove fateful for Lebanon.[36] On three of Israel's borders, and those of the territories occupied by it, the war had *de facto* ended. Jordan had expelled the Palestinian guerrillas and did not want war; soldiers of an international peace unit, primarily American, stood between Egyptian and Israeli troops, and those of the United Nations separated the Israeli and Syrian armies. War had become practically impossible along these borders — nor have there been hostilities since then. But the disengagement agreements did not herald a general peace treaty. Neither was Resolution 242 realized nor were the Palestinians included in negotiations. The crux of the conflict was still unresolved: the Palestinian question.

If the Palestinians were not to resign, they had only one option: to 'bomb their way to the negotiation table', as Egypt and Syria had done in the October War. And they had only one territorial option: the Lebanese–Israeli border. After the Golan agreement, Lebanon became the geographic centre of the Middle Eastern conflict.

The PLO did not rely exclusively on its military option. In June 1974 Fatah abandoned its concept of a 'secular democratic state for the whole of Palestine'. It declared its willingness to participate in a peace conference, provided that the national rights of the Palestinians were also on the agenda. It announced its intention of erecting a Palestinian national authority in any liberated or vacated part of the country, and of pursuing this objective 'mainly' through armed struggle. Initially, the radical Palestinian organizations endorsed this text because they had not grasped the implications of the many qualifying clauses. In plain language, Fatah had abandoned its claim to all of Palestine, had accepted a Palestinian state in one part of the country, and would fight for its creation only if it could not achieve it by peaceful means. Once they had grasped Fatah's political about-turn, Libya, Iraq, the Popular Front, the Popular Front-General Command and the

---

[36] See Melhem Chaoul, 'Le dispositif de la guerre au Liban, fonction de réduction', in Fondation libanaise pour la paix civile permanente, ed., *Le Droit à la mémoire* (Beirut, 1988), pp. 60–39 (Arabic pagination).

Iraqi-sponsored Arab Liberation Front formed the 'Rejectionists Front' in opposition to the new goals.

Notwithstanding this, in October 1974 at the Arab summit conference in Rabat, the PLO was declared the sole representative of the Palestinian people, also in respect of negotiations over the future of the occupied territories. Even Jordan gave its consent. Yassir Arafat addressed the United Nations General Assembly and challenged Israel to choose between the gun and the olive branch, between war and peace.

But an olive branch in the form of a Palestinian state on the West Bank and in the Gaza Strip was singularly unattractive to the overwhelming majority of Israel's politicians and interest groups. The Palestinian movement, both its majority in or aligned with Fatah and the movements in the Rejectionists Front, stuck to the gun, from now on chiefly in Lebanon.

## The end of neutrality by consent

The Lebanese used to call their country 'the Switzerland of the Middle East'. There were remarkable similarities: small, mountainous, lacking in natural resources, yet — within their respective environments — prosperous from banking, trade and tourism. In the course of their histories their respective cultural, linguistic and religious groups had learnt to regulate their coexistence through forms of consociation. Both practised the rule of law, complete freedom of expression and of the press, and a policy of neutrality in foreign affairs, *de jure* in Switzerland, *de facto* in Lebanon. But there were two significant differences: regional environment and military ability to uphold neutrality.

Lebanon's environment was quite unlike Switzerland's. Since the early 1950s Lebanon had been the only parliamentary democracy in the Arab East. When Syria, Egypt and Iraq started experimenting with socialism in the 1960s, Lebanon's policies of free capital markets, strict bank secrecy and investment incentives attracted Arab flight capital. Syrian entrepreneurs, fed up with state interference at home, invested in Lebanese industry. Tens of thousands of Lebanese returned when Nasser's nationalization curbed their economic opportunities in Egypt. Hundreds of thousands of Syrians worked in Lebanon as seasonal or migrant workers for low wages — in hard currency. Neighbouring rulers regarded Lebanon as a provocative nest of capitalism, and its relative prosperity was viewed with a mixture of envy and frustration. Lebanon's toleration of a free press and free expression was a thorn in their flesh. Whoever lost in an Arab power struggle found political asylum in Lebanon. Banned parties from all Arab countries could hold their congresses in Beirut. In the cafes of Beirut, Arab intellectuals of all political hues discussed political and social concepts from

Islamic fundamentalism to communism, and made plans to overthrow regimes. Students and scientists from the entire Orient learnt, taught and researched at universities and institutes in Beirut, in an academic freedom and variety of opinion unique in the Arab world. Beirut was the region's most important publishing centre, and for many topics the only one. Between eighty and one hundred daily newspapers carried information and opinions that would have been censored in Cairo, Damascus or Baghdad, and possibly landed their authors in prison. The Arab regimes themselves exploited this freedom of the press, each of them subsidizing a newspaper to express its own opinions. Pre-war Lebanon was the intellectual and political stage of the Arab world. Everyone acted on it, though neighbouring states seldom appreciated the performance. For, freedom was, to their minds, tantamount to subversion. In an environment of authoritarian political systems Lebanon was a provocation, a country resented.

Switzerland had been in a similar situation only at the height of fascism and national socialism. To deter potential predators it had always had a policy of armed neutrality, with conscription, regular manoeuvres, an ingenious system of defences and its own armaments industry. National socialist functionaries would brag that a division of the Hitler Youth could bring Switzerland 'back to the Reich'. Swiss military preparedness helped dissuade the Third Reich from trying.

By contrast, Lebanon practised a decidedly pacifist security policy. It did not have conscription, but a professional army about 15,000 strong, with about 100 tanks and 150 artillery and anti-aircraft guns, an air force with 24 fighter aircraft and a navy of 5 patrol boats.[37] There was a slight Muslim, mainly Shi`i, majority in the ranks; 60 to 65 per cent of the officers were Christian, a left-over from the mandate; of the thirty-seven highest-ranking officers, eighteen were Muslim. There were two reasons why the army was so small. One was the desire for a balance in the army between the religions communities. The other was the conviction that weakness was the best security policy. Soldiering was not highly thought of in pre-war Lebanon. The vast majority of volunteers came from the economically backward, peripheral areas, that is, most were Shi`is. Maronite soldiers were recruited almost exclusively from some villages in Akkar and the south, and Sunnis also in Akkar, the only area with Sunni farmers. Urban recruits were few, partly because they had better prospects in other fields, and partly because most barracks were far away in the countryside. To maintain confessional parity, the military command had no option but to take all the Christians and Sunnis that volunteered and fill up the rest of the Muslim quota with Shi`is. Without putting too fine a point on it, the number of Christian volunteers determined the strength of the army. The only other feasible option was conscription. However, the major-

---

[37] Author's interviews with high-ranking Lebanese officers, 1979 and 1980.

ity of politicians of all communities would not hear of it. A strong army might, as in most Arab states, be tempted to intervene in politics — fears that Chehabism had strengthened. A weightier reason was the cost. Above all, it was generally felt that a symbolic army sufficed. This view was based on the conviction that it could not be in the interest of any power to invade Lebanon, especially as the very weakness of its armed forces meant that Lebanon could not pose a threat to anyone. The particular champions of this view were Pierre Gemayel and the Kata'ib, who preached the slogan: 'Our weakness is our strength'. Chehab took the contrary view, and had warned that 'of course an army costs a lot; but no army might cost a lot more'.[38] But even he was prepared to make do with a small, well-trained army, relying on the military secret service to control internal subversion and diplomacy to avert foreign political dangers. Although the precariousness of Lebanon's position was becoming apparent by 1970, the Deuxième Bureau was dismantled at this time. The desire of the anti-Chehabist majority to clip this institution's wings was stronger than any fear of the consequences of its impotence. As the danger mounted that the country would be drawn into the Middle East conflict and its neutrality ignored, this neutrality was practically defenceless.

The political guarantees of neutrality seemed dependable. The Lebanese Army had participated without distinction or humiliation in the first Palestinian war against Israel in 1948. The subsequent cease-fire agreement between the two countries included mutual respect of the common border. Until the mid-1960s it was Israel's most peaceful border; Israel regarded Lebanon as its 'least hostile neighbour'. The Arab states respected Lebanon's decision not to participate militarily in the struggle against Israel, and expressly recognized it at the summit conference of the Arab League in Cairo in 1964. The summit conference in Khartoum in 1967 decided that Palestinian guerrilla activities against Israel should be launched from Egypt, Syria and Jordan, but not from Lebanon.

Lebanon's de facto neutrality was not an expression of sympathy for Israel. The great majority of Lebanese politicians and of public opinion regarded Israel with mistrust, fear and dislike. Lebanon had accepted about 100,000 Palestinian refugees in 1947 and 1948. A minority had been integrated into Lebanese society. The majority lived in camps on the edge of the cities, permanent witness to the injustice Israel had wreaked on a neighbouring people. There was a widespread fear that Israel wished to expand into southern Lebanon, especially with an eye to harnessing the waters of the Litani River. Above all, Israel was regarded as the antithesis of the Lebanese state: as a state that founded its existence on confessionalism and rejected coexistence, whereas Lebanon was based on coexistence between different religions. Leading Christian intellectuals such as Michel

---

[38] Information from a former close associate of President Chehab.

## The Clouding Horizon: Non-Lebanese Factors of Conflict 163

Chiha[39] and René Aggiouri[40] pointed out that Lebanon's existence by itself proved how unwarranted the Israeli thesis was that coexistence between different groups in one state was impossible, and that for this reason Israel had an interest in destroying the Lebanese model. When the Palestinian movement developed the concept of a secular and democratic state for Jews, Muslims and Christians it was greeted with enthusiasm in Lebanon. The Lebanese politicians who espoused the Palestinian cause in international bodies after 1948 usually did this with deep conviction — up to and including President Franjieh's address to the United Nations General Assembly in 1974, in which he proposed the Lebanese model as a model for Palestine.

The Lebanese themselves were unanimous about making the country's facilities available to the Palestinian resistance for its political activities. As discussed above, the parting of minds came when Palestinian organizations began to launch commando raids from Lebanese territory.[41] Incidents between the guerrillas and the Lebanese Army became more frequent between 1965 and 1967. The Syrian government supported guerrilla actions from Lebanese territory, while keeping a tight control on those from Syrian territory.[42] The resources of the Lebanese Army and police were too few to patrol the long Syrian-Lebanese border effectively, particularly in the mountainous south-east.[43]

Up to the Six Day War activity was mainly in the form of 'transit traffic' of guerrilla commandos. They either passed through on their way from Syria to Israel or — more commonly — shelled Israeli settlements with mortars or artillery rockets ('katyushas') from along the Lebanese-Israeli border and withdrew to Syria. This changed in 1968, after Palestinian resistance in the occupied territories collapsed. The PLO began to establish bases in south-east Lebanon for guerrilla units infiltrating from Jordan and Syria, and to recruit and

---

[39] Michel Chiha, *Visage et présence du Liban* (Beirut, 1964), pp. 124ff.

[40] René Aggiouri, *Le conflit de Palestine dans le jeu des puissances* (Beirut, 1968).

[41] The Deuxième Bureau arrested guerrillas for the first time in 1964, before they could infiltrate into Israel. In 1965 a Palestinian guerrilla died in a Lebanese prison, probably after mistreatment, which provoked the first demonstrations for Palestinian freedom of action. In the same year Yassir Arafat and some of his closest collaborators were held for forty days on the grounds of deliberately trying to provoke a conflict between Lebanon and Israel through Fatah activities.

[42] In 1966 the Syrian Army arrested Arafat and released him a number of weeks later, but only after he had agreed to obey the orders of the Syrian general staff to the letter.

[43] The remainder of this section is based chiefly on an analysis of the Lebanese press. Footnotes are not provided for dates and events that can be verified in generally accessible chronicles such as *Fiches du Monde Arabe* (Beirut and Larnaka), *Middle East Reporter* (Beirut), etc. Detailed accounts of relations between Lebanon, the Palestinians and Israel may be found in Wade R. GORIA, *Sovereignty and Leadership in Lebanon 1945–1976* (London, 1985), pp. 88–172; Wolfgang Köhler, *Die Vorgeschichte des Krieges im Libanon* (Wiesbaden, 1980); and Kamal S. Salibi, *Crossroads to Civil War: Lebanon 1958–1976* (New York, 1976), passim.

train guerrillas in Lebanese refugee camps. The cycle of violence on the border started in spring 1968. After Palestinians shelled a kibbutz close to the border, the Israelis shelled Lebanese villages with heavy artillery, causing heavy damage. In May, the Lebanese and Israeli armies exchanged artillery fire. As the influx of armed Palestinians in the Arkoub hills continued through the summer and autumn 1968, the area became known as 'Fatahland'. Palestinian reinforcements and supplies came in over a mountain track soon known — by analogy with the 'Ho-Chi-Minh Trail' in Vietnam — as the 'Arafat Trail'. Attacks and counter-attacks grew more frequent; Israeli Army units, no longer content with just shelling Palestinian bases, took to invading Lebanese territory to attack them directly. The escalation of fighting along the border precipitated the first large flight of people from villages in the vicinity.

On December 26th, 1968 Palestinians hijacked an El Al airliner in Athens. Israel's harsh reprisal came two days later: Israeli commandos landed by helicopter at Beirut airport, destroyed thirteen aircraft of the Lebanese Middle East Airlines and blew up an oil-tank. The aim of the Israeli government was obviously to force the Lebanese government and Lebanese Army to 'crack down' on Palestinian guerrillas. But by attacking civil targets it aroused Lebanese anger and a wave of solidarity with the Palestinians.[44] In spring 1969 the Lebanese Army tried to get the guerrillas to withdraw from the border zone, so as not to give Israel cause for further attacks. The Palestinians resisted; there were almost daily clashes between them and the army, which could not gain the upper hand. Saiqa units crossed the Syrian border to support the hard-pressed guerrillas in Lebanon. The Palestinian organizations tightened their hold over the refugee camps, expelling the Lebanese police. But most encouraging for them was Lebanese political support. Jumblatt organized mass demonstrations in Beirut, Tripoli, Sidon and Tyre. In April an attempt by Lebanese security forces to break up a march from the Palestinian camp of Ain Helweh to Sidon ended in a battle between the army and the commandos. Armed clashes also occurred in Beirut and the Bekaa. On April 24th a state of emergency was declared. Karami declared that Lebanon was forced to preserve and defend its sovereignty. Jumblatt, in turn, attacked Karami, holding him responsible for repressive measures against the Palestinians and declaring that any obstruction of the Palestinian guerrillas 'serves the interests of only the Israeli enemy'. For the first time the alliance between the Palestinian and Lebanese Left proved astonishingly effective. Habash's Popular Front had provoked most of the incidents with the army and police, and Jumblatt put pressure on the Muslim politicians, making it difficult for

---

[44] Prime Minister Abdallah Yafi resigned. Karami formed a new government and announced a policy of consultation and coordination with the Palestinians.

them to give priority to the interests of the Lebanese state and defend them against a general public highly emotionalized since the Israeli attack on Beirut airport. On May 6th, 1969, President Helou addressed the nation on television and stated that the country could support the rightful cause of the Palestinians in so far as this did not compromise the sovereignty and security of the Lebanese Republic.[45] Only Christian politicians openly supported the president and the army; Jumblatt and his Left Front assailed them. Premier Karami no longer dared associate himself with the policies of the president and the army, and resigned. The leading Sunni politicians tried to compromise with a formula of 'coordination'; none was prepared to accept government responsibility at a critical time. For months the country was without a government because it seemed impossible to find a compromise between the two options of effectively preventing the Palestinians from fighting their war from Lebanese territory and giving them a free hand and accepting the consequences. Israel stoked this Arab fire: in August and September it resorted to air-attacks for the first time, bombing the town of Hasbaya and a number of villages in south Lebanon.

In mid-October, the army command decided, on its own responsibility, to try to restore Lebanese sovereignty. It launched an operation to cut the Palestinians' lines of supply from Syria. Initially, it had some success. But by the next day Syrian troops started massing on the border. Four days later Saiqa and PLO units attacked Lebanese border posts in the centre and north of the Bekaa. The Palestinian organizations tried to relieve the guerrillas encircled by the army in 'Fatahland' by opening other fronts: they blocked the road from Beirut to Tripoli.[46]

PLA troops occupied a number of villages in the Bekaa and, supported by Syrian artillery, attacked the town of Rashaya. The army managed to repulse the attack on Rashaya. But by the end of October it was clear that it lacked the resources to carry out a large operation in the Arkoub, preserve security in the cities and protect the border areas of the country against attacks from regular units of the PLA in Syria at the same time. Finally, there was a risk of war with Syria.

A further consideration was the enormous pressure from almost all Arab states:

> The radical Arab régimes ... openly condemned the efforts of the Lebanese Army to liquidate the Palestinian commando movement in Lebanon. Even conservative Arab régimes, under pressure from the PLO, began, one after

---

[45] See Pierre Rondot, 'Le Liban devant la résistance palestinienne', in *Revue du défence national* 25 (1969), cols. 1410–1432.
[46] In Tripoli itself the '24th of October Movement', led by Faruq Muqaddam, a populist rival of Karami, occupied several police stations and the citadel.

another, to pronounce themselves in favour of the continued existence of the commando movement in Lebanon under a minimum of controls, urging that the Palestinian armed struggle was the natural right of the Palestinian people, and that it was not necessarily incompatible with the sovereignty of such Arab States as happened to be its hosts.'[47] The decisions of previous summit conferences that had explicitly excluded Lebanon from any involvement in guerrilla warfare were forgotten. Syria procured for Palestinians that freedom of action in Lebanon that it denied them in Syria.

From November 1st to 3rd, 1969, Yassir Arafat and the commander of the Lebanese Army, General Emile Boustani, negotiated in Cairo through the offices of the Egyptian ministers of war and foreign affairs. The result was the so-called Cairo Agreement. It gave the Palestinian guerrilla organizations the right to establish and man armed units in the refugee camps and observation posts in the border zone; the Lebanese authorities bound themselves to guarantee the lines of supply from Syria and to facilitate the movement of commandos to the Israeli border in coordination with the Lebanese Army. The Palestinian organizations, for their part, undertook to maintain discipline among their troops and not to interfere in Lebanese affairs. Finally, both sides affirmed Lebanon's sovereign rights over all camps and bases.

In effect, though, the Cairo Agreement considerably compromised Lebanese sovereignty. Sovereignty over the camps as well as the bases had *de facto* passed to the PLO. The PLO could henceforth behave as 'a state within the state': it had total control over specific territories, could recruit and train soldiers and could be armed by Syria. The right of free access to the Israeli border meant that the Palestinian state within the Lebanese state could also carry on war. By this agreement Lebanon had granted the PLO far wider rights than any other Arab country had done.[48]

In essence, the Cairo Agreement documented rights the Palestinians already exercised. The Lebanese parliament ratified it without knowledge of the full text, which both sides had agreed to keep secret. One deputy, Raymond Eddé, voted against it; all the others accepted the fait accompli. 'In effect, the Cairo Agreement legitimized the armed Palestinian presence in Lebanon. It tried to reconcile and regulate this presence with Lebanese sovereignty, an exercise which turned out to resemble an attempt to square the circle.'[49]

---

[47] Salibi, *Crossroads to Civil War*, p. 42.
[48] The text of the Cairo Agreement may be found in Walid Khadduri, ed., *International Documents on Palestine* (Beirut, 1969), and in Camille Chamoun, *Crise au Liban* (Beirut, 1977).
[49] John K. Cooley, 'The Palestinians', in Haley and Snider, *Lebanon in Crisis*, pp. 30f.

As might be expected, it proved impossible to square the circle. Karami was now able to form a government, with none other than Jumblatt as interior minister. Jumblatt, the PLO's most powerful protector within the Lebanese establishment, tried to reach a practicable agreement with the PLO. Palestinian bases were to be at least one kilometre from towns and villages to spare these from Israeli reprisals; for the same reason, military training should not take place in the refugee camps. In May 1970 the government prohibited the PLO from firing rockets from Lebanese territory, from laying minefields and, above all, from bearing arms in towns and villages. Fatah and Saiqa accepted these regulations, but the Popular Front, which had already rejected the Cairo Agreement, did not. What one important Palestinian organization refused to accept the others could not agree to if they were to hold their own in the permanent rivalry between the organizations. The agreed restraint was briefly respected, and then forgotten. The Palestinian guerrillas were encouraged by the indecisive outcome of their test of strength with the Lebanese Army, and felt their position confirmed by the Cairo Agreement. Youths who had grown up in the camps on the edge of Lebanese society, treated by Lebanese with a mixture of pity and disdain, now carried weapons and felt superior, were proud and not infrequently arrogant. The refugee camps lined the access roads to virtually every Lebanese city. PLO militia frequently erected roadblocks and controlled people and vehicles, molesting, detaining or kidnapping Lebanese as well as foreigners on the ground that they constituted a danger to the Palestinian revolution. Given the number and autonomy of the Palestinian organizations, it was often unclear which was responsible for which infringement. Not used to such treatment from their own soldiers and police, infuriated Lebanese were not prepared to accept it from Palestinians. The Christian population in particular, already shocked by the Cairo Agreement, which many of them saw as a capitulation, was alarmed. If the state could not guarantee the safety of its citizens, they would have to take matters into their own hands. The Kata'ib bolstered its paramilitary units; Chamoun's National Liberal Party began to build up its 'Tiger militia'; the Franjieh clan in Zghorta armed a few hundred young men under the command of Tony Franjieh; and the most important *za`im* in Sidon, Maarouf Saad, organized his own armed group. In March 1970 the first serious clashes occurred between Palestinians and armed Christian militia. In the Maronite village of Kahhale there was an exchange of fire between locals and a Palestinian convoy escorting the coffin with the body of a fallen guerrilla to Damascus for burial, in which ten Palestinians died. The accounts are contradictory, as was to become the rule in such incidents. According to the Palestinians, they drove into a carefully laid ambush; according to the inhabitants of Kahhale, the Palestinians drove into the village shooting. The most probable explanation is that the Palestinians were firing into the air as they drove through the village 'to make an impression'; the locals, already on their guard against possible trouble from a larger Palestinian convoy, mistook the firing for an attack and, as they thought, returned it. Immediately after the Kahhale incident fighting broke out between Palestinians and Kata'ib commandos, the heaviest between the Tel al-Za`tar camp and the neighbouring, mainly Maronite suburb of Dekwaneh. On March 25th, 1970 Palestinians kidnapped Bashir Gemayel, the younger son of the Kata'ib leader, and held him for eight hours in Tel al-Za`tar until Jumblatt and Arafat arranged his release. The week of fighting ended only after the intervention of the Egyptian foreign minister.

Greater tension between Palestinians and — mainly Christian — Lebanese was not the only consequence of the Cairo Agreement; guerrilla activity against Israel, and, therefore, Israeli reprisals, increased considerably.[50] Syrian pioneers built a road through the Arkoub to facilitate commando access to the border. As countermeasures, the Israelis erected fortifications on Lebanese territory and also built an access road. Inexorably, the extreme south of Lebanon was becoming a war zone. Another wave of local refugees fled north. The inhabitants in some villages in which Palestinians had set up quarters tried to resist, but with little success.[51]

Even more than the Cairo Agreement, the bloody events of 'Black September' 1970 in Jordan raised the intensity of armed conflict on the border and within the country. Expelled from Jordan, the PLO leadership settled in Beirut. They were accompanied by the embittered survivors of the fighting[52] and tens of thousands of Palestinian civilians. There are no reliable figures for the number of new arrivals. Estimates of the total Palestinian population in Lebanon after 1970 vary from 200,000 to 500,000. At any rate, the result of the Jordanian debacle was an enormous increase in the number of Palestinian combatants and potential PLO recruits.

In many respects Beirut was an ideal base for the PLO.[53] The large camps on the periphery of the cities were under their control, and recognized by the Lebanese in the Cairo Agreement as quasi-extraterritorial. It could use the excellent Lebanese transport and communications networks for its diplomatic and informational activities. Among the Lebanese, Kamal Jumblatt and the left-wing parties were reliable allies, and they had many Muslim sympathizers. In the

---

[50] In May 1970 the Israeli Army reacted to the bombardment of Kiryat Shmona by invading Lebanese territory. Lebanese troops were caught up in the fighting and suffered heavy casualties. In the same month the Popular Front attacked an Israeli school-bus.

[51] The Lebanese Deuxième Bureau had started to form village militias in the south; this stopped after the election of Franjieh as president in August 1970.

[52] The new Salam government did not even make a pretence of hindering their expulsion from Syria.

[53] Edward W. Said has described Beirut as 'a substitute for Palestine' and 'the Lebanese period in the history of the Palestinian national movement' as 'the first truly independent period of Palestinian national history'; 'Palestinians in the aftermath of Beirut', in *Journal of Palestine Studies* 12/2 (1983), pp. 8 and 5.

aftermath of 'Black September' the Palestinian leaders engaged in an intense debate on the lessons to be drawn from the Jordanian debacle. They came to the conclusion that whatever else, the PLO had to gain broad support among the population of the host country. The small parties of the Left did not offer this. Also, the reliability of traditional politicians of the Muslim community, notwithstanding their basic sympathy for the Palestinian cause, could not be taken for granted if it came to an open conflict between Palestinian and Lebanese interests. Each Palestinian organization cultivated relations with its 'sister party': the Popular Front with the Organization for Communist Action in Lebanon, the Democratic Front with the CP, Saiqa with the pro-Syrian and the ALF with the pro-Iraqi wing of the Lebanese Baath Party. Fatah began to cultivate a network of street and city-block groups, the former clients of the Muslim *zu`ama'*, particularly after the Deuxième Bureau's control had been broken. The PLO's most powerful means of extending allegiance was financial support: generous contributions from the Arab oil-states kept their coffers full. But neither did they hesitate to use their growing power in large parts of the country to persuade recalcitrant Lebanese to change their attitudes.[54] Finally, as important as subsidies and coercion were arms for groups cooperating with the PLO. In those parts of Lebanon in which either the PLO organizations themselves or their allies held sway, might was increasingly right. Those who did not support the Palestinian cause out of conviction now had good reason to do so out of opportunism, or at least to conceal their reservations. The allied Lebanese groups were kept dependent on the PLO arms and money. Henceforth, any conflict between the Palestinians and the Lebanese state or other Lebanese groups could, with the help of these allies, at any time be turned into an intra-Lebanese conflict.

The alliance policy of the Palestinian organizations had a far-reaching sideeffect. Their most convinced allies were the left-wing parties. Armaments gave them power out of all proportion to their political significance within the country. However, the dovetailed Lebanese and Palestinian Left had objectives and strategies that went far beyond anything dreamt of by the PLO majority or, indeed, Fatah. They wanted a radical social and political reorganization of Lebanon and the whole Arab world. By contrast, Fatah was primarily concerned with consolidating its position in Lebanon and exploiting it in the struggle for Palestine. The activism of the more radical Palestinian and Lebanese organizations was to draw the entire Palestinian movement into conflicts the majority did not seek.

---

[54] To put pressure on Rashid Karami in Tripoli, they supported his opponents. In Sidon they kidnapped the Sunni leader Maarouf Saad and his son Mustapha and released them only after they had declared they would support the Palestinian cause unconditionally. Intractable inhabitants of Shi`i villages were intimidated. With their drastic methods, the PLO brought even the West Beirut underworld largely under their control.

Within a few months of 'Black September' the balance of power in Lebanon had shifted in favour of the Palestinians: they could now afford generally to ignore the Cairo Agreement. No one was in a position to restrain them, in terms of the Agreement, from 'interfering in Lebanese affairs'. The alliance policy had turned them into an essential element of these affairs. Above all, the Palestinians could not be constrained to a war zone along the Israeli border. In Beirut they planned their worldwide actions against Israeli targets. After the PLO prepared an attack for the Japanese Red Brigade on Lydda airport in late May 1972, the Israeli government announced it would hold the Lebanese government responsible for all PLO actions as Lebanon was the centre of their operations. Israeli reprisals became more frequent and fiercer.[55] In September 1972 the Lebanese Army held up an Israeli advance for forty-eight hours, after which the Israelis withdrew, destroying bridges and villages as they went. The Shi`i population in the south, initially rather hostile to the guerrillas, now blamed their losses at the hands of the Israelis on the inactivity of Lebanese government. The government pleaded with the PLO to restrain themselves out of consideration for the population. Arafat agreed to 'freeze' the operations, whereupon Habash and Jibril declared that their organizations were not bound by this promise. By the end of 1972 the majority of Israeli politicians were determined to force Lebanon to act against the Palestinians. Israeli strikes grew more frequent in early 1973. Helicopters landed paratroopers and marines near Tripoli, where they attacked two Palestinian camps. On April 10th Israeli sea-borne commandos landed in Sidon and Beirut, hit their targets — including three prominent Fatah leaders in their own apartments — and were back in their boats before the Lebanese Army had been alerted. The 'Rent-A-Car Raid' — agents had hired cars for the commandos in Beirut — unleashed a wave of anger, even among Lebanese with reservations about the Palestinian presence. While enormous demonstrations marched through Beirut, Prime Minister Salam demanded the dismissal of the army commander-in-chief, General Ghanem. President Franjieh refused to comply, and Salam resigned. Habash's Popular Front exploited this moment of acute political crisis to provoke clashes with the army.[56] On May 2nd the army took up positions around the largest Palestinian camps in Beirut; heavy fighting broke out. The Lebanese Army

[55] The reaction to the Lydda attack included land, sea and air attacks on the Palestinian camp of Rashidieh as well as on the Lebanese town of Hasbaya and villages of Dayr Ashayer and Tibnin, in which about 150 people died. After the attack during the 1972 Olympic Games in Munich, Israelis attacked not only the Nahr al Bared camp but also villages in southern Lebanon and the Bekaa.
[56] On May 14th, they blew up oil-tanks at the refinery at Zahrani near Sidon. On April 30th, four Fatah members were arrested at the airport as they were about to board a scheduled flight to Europe with suitcases of explosives. The next day five guerrillas of the Democratic Front were arrested near the American Embassy. On May 1st, members of the Popular Front and the Democratic Front abducted three Lebanese soldiers and declared they would be held as hostages until the arrested Palestinians were released.

had been humiliated once too often and was determined to get its way this time. Hundred of Palestinians outside the camp, in particular members of the Popular Front, were detained. When rockets were fired at the airport from the Bourj al-Barajneh camp the Lebanese air force bombarded it. The Palestinian organizations were put on the defensive. As in 1969, they were saved by the support of the Arab states, especially Syria. Saiqa units and the Palestinian Liberation Army crossed the Syrian-Lebanese border and occupied parts of the southern Bekaa. The Syrian government accused Lebanon of complicity in an international plot to liquidate the Palestinian resistance. It closed its borders with Lebanon to all civilian and freight traffic, putting Lebanon, as an entrepôt country, under heavy economic pressure. After two weeks of heavy fighting the political crisis came to a head in the presidential palace. President Franjieh went back and forth between two reception rooms. In one the ambassadors and special emissaries of the Arab states pressed him to order the army to cease fire; in the other officers of the general staff pleaded with him to give the army a free hand for another day or two. Eventually Franjieh gave in to the pressure of the Arab states. The fighting stopped on May 18th. An agreement was signed in the Hotel Melkart in West Beirut, which reaffirmed the terms of the Cairo Agreement. The Palestinians undertook not to make raids across the Israeli border and a joint commission of the Lebanese Army command and the Palestinian Armed Struggle Command was formed to deal with all outstanding problems.

On paper the Melkart Protocols[57] constituted a marginal improvement in the position of the Lebanese state, mirroring the relative success of the army. But it was to prove as ineffectual as the Cairo Agreement. Both sides knew that the Palestinian logic of the struggle against Israel could not be reconciled with Lebanese considerations of state. As the first two rounds in 1969 and 1973 were inconclusive, there was a general conviction that a third encounter was inevitable.

The leaders of the Christian parties finally began to grasp the full extent of the danger that they had underestimated in 1969 during their political manoeuvring in the run-up to the presidential elections. They had believed that by electing the 'tough' Franjieh as successor to the 'weak' Helou they had taken the most important step towards containing Palestinian influence. Now they were forced to admit that at the crucial moment — and despite favourable military circumstances — Franjieh was just as powerless as Helou. Similarly, for the second time they had to learn that the leading Muslim politicians were not prepared to accept government responsibility during confrontations with the Palestinians. Hence, they concluded that the Lebanese state and its army were no longer in a position adequately to protect Lebanese sovereignty and interests. They armed and trained

---

[57] The text may be found in Chamoun, *Crise au Liban*, pp. 175–84.

their militias with greater purpose, purchased armaments in Czechoslovakia, Belgium and Bulgaria and received military aid from Jordan and Saudi Arabia. They also received help from Christian officers of the Lebanese Army. Some of them were embittered by the decision of the political leadership to constrain the army from exploiting it military opportunities in 1973, and worried that the balance of power might rapidly shift in favour of the Palestinians again. So the army ordered and imported armaments that were paid for and taken up by the militias, and Christian officers took over the training of militiamen. On the other hand, 'the Palestinian commandos were now convinced that the Lebanese authorities were determined not to rest until they had brought about their final liquidation, and they were backed in this conviction by the Lebanese radicals'.[58] The Christian parties' nightmare was the Palestinians and the Lebanese Left taking power; the Palestinians' nightmare was a Lebanese 'Black September'.

The Christians' poison was meat to Kamal Jumblatt and the parties allied with him, an opportunity he would never have had without the armed presence of the Palestinians. Conservative Muslim politicians — who would have welcomed a Palestinian defeat in 1973, not least because the Palestinians' alliance policy was eroding their political base — now accepted the facts of the situation and tried to make the best of it. So as not to be outmanoeuvred by Jumblatt in the eyes of the Muslim general public, Salam and the Mufti of the Lebanese Republic, Hassan Khaled, formed a Sunni front and repackaged traditional Sunni demands under the label of 'participation', and Imam Musa Sadr, concerned about the drift of Shi`is into left-wing militias, formed his own militia, which he let Fatah arm and train.

In synopsis, a situation had been reached in which Jumblatt and the left-wing alliance hoped for the 'next round' as their break-through to power; most Muslim leaders wondered what advantage they might derive from it if it came, while hoping that the Christian communities would agree to fundamental changes in the division of power and economic benefits so as to avert the clash. Lebanon had disintegrated into three political camps distinguished for all practical purposes by their attitudes towards the Palestinian question. Lebanese politics was reduced to the question of reactions to the Middle Eastern conflict now centred on Lebanon.

Lebanon did not participate in the October War in 1973. However, Israel destroyed the radar station on Mount Barouk which Lebanon had put at the disposal of Syria for the duration of the war. In January 1974 Israel resumed its raids on southern Lebanon, precipitating yet another large influx of refugees into Beirut. In May the disengagement agreement between Syria and Israel took effect: Lebanon, which since 1970 had borne the main burden of the Palestinian-Israeli

---

[58] Salibi, *Crossroads to Civil War*, p. 69.

conflict, now had to bear it alone. In summer the confrontation grew fiercer. Whereas Syria forbade all activity whatsoever on its border with Israel, the Syrian-sponsored Saiqa publicly stated what everybody already knew, that is, that the Palestinian organizations would not accept any prohibition on armed actions from southern Lebanon: the Melkart Protocols had been declared invalid. Jumblatt demanded that the Christian militias be disarmed, though not the Palestinian organizations. In October and again in December the Israelis bombarded villages in southern Lebanon and the Chatila camp in Beirut.

Intra-Arab conflicts over policies towards Israel aggravated the situation in Lebanon. The summit conference of the Arab League in Rabat recognized the PLO as the sole legitimate representative of the Palestinian people. It also passed a resolution that no further separate accords were to be concluded with Israel. However, in November Sadat told Kissinger that he was ready for another disengagement agreement in Sinai (Sinai II). This incensed not only the Rejectionist Front, but Syria too: Sadat was about to sacrifice on the altar of purely Egyptian interests the solidarity between Egypt and Syria that had been tried and proven in the October War. Not only the Palestinians and the — remote — states of the Rejectionists Front but also Syria felt they had to disrupt the Israeli-Egyptian rapprochement where they could, and that meant in Lebanon.

In December 1974 Pierre Gemayel addressed a memorandum to President Franjieh in which he expressed his concern that the policy of the Rejectionist Front could turn Lebanon into a second Palestine. On January 7th, 1975, the Syrian and Lebanese Presidents, Assad and Franjieh, met in Chtaura. What Assad had to offer was a promise to defend Lebanon. 'In consequence, Lebanon lost whatever advantage a policy of neutrality may have had for maintaining a viable degree of external sovereignty.'[59] Lebanon had already lost much of its internal sovereignty in 1969.

A week later Israeli troops destroyed the border village of Kfar Chouba. In the same month units of two organizations in the Rejectionist Front, the Popular Front and the Iraqi-sponsored ALF, attacked the Lebanese Army at different points, including the army barracks in Tyre. In March a serious incident in Sidon meshed Lebanese social unrest and Palestinian attacks on the government for the first time. The government had granted a Japanese firm based in Sidon, the Protein Company, a concession for deep-sea fishing. Camille Chamoun had accepted the chairmanship of the board. The coastal fishermen of Sidon felt their economic existence was threatened. They organized a huge demonstration against the government, in which many Palestinians joined. During the demonstration the popular Deputy for Sidon, Maarouf Saad, was shot twice; the identity of his

[59] Goria, *Sovereignty*, p. 178.

assailants was never established. Jumblatt called for a general strike against the government in protest against the shooting. Saad's death from his injuries was the spark for further demonstrations by both Lebanese and Palestinians in Sidon, this time against the army, whose office of military intelligence was held responsible for the assassination. The demonstrators blocked the road between Sidon and Tyre. When the army moved in to clear it, armed civilians, among them Palestinians, opened fire. Five soldiers and eleven civilians died, whereupon practically all conservative government leaders joined Jumblatt in levelling accusations against the army and demanding the reorganization of the army command. Anti- and pro-army demonstrations in West and East Beirut respectively helped stamp the army as an instrument of the Christian half of Lebanon. Palestinians, Jumblatt and his allied parties and the entire Sunni establishment were ranged together for the first time, albeit for different reasons, against the 'Christian' army and the parties of the Christian communities. The 'Protein Affair' had forged for the Palestinians the broadest alliance they could possibly conceive of in Lebanon.

They found an even more important ally outside Lebanon. When Sadat announced the re-opening of the Suez Canal, Syria accepted Arafat's offer to form a joint Syrian-Palestinian supreme command. It was the core of Assad's efforts to build up an 'eastern front' to compensate for Egypt's withdrawal from the confrontation with Israel. Syria hoped that the supreme command would give it greater influence over the Palestinian organizations and at the same time more political weight in Lebanon. An eastern front was effectively restricted to Lebanon. But Assad had reason to fear that Israel, no longer faced with the threat of war on two fronts, might be tempted to attack Syria through southern Lebanon and the Bekaa.[60] Syria's objective was controllable tension with Israel, in order to prove that a peace settlement in the Middle Eastern conflict was impossible without, let alone against, Syria.

The Israeli-Egyptian negotiations over Sinai II dashed any hopes left after the Geneva Conference of 1973 of reaching a comprehensive settlement in the Middle Eastern conflict. The Palestinians could fear with justification that bilateral agreements might include scenarios for a 'solution' to their presence in Lebanon similar to Jordan's in 1970. Among Lebanese Christians the same negotiations raised fears that the Palestinian question might be solved by settling the Palestinians permanently in Lebanon, that is, by turning Lebanon into a surrogate

---

[60] Itamar Rabinovich calls Lebanon Syria's 'soft western underbelly'; 'The limits of military power: Syria's role', in Haley and Snider, *Lebanon in Crisis*, p. 57; similarly William W. Harris, 'La politique libanaise de Hafez el-Assad', in Kodmani-Darwish, *Liban*, p. 91: 'Le Liban représente sans aucun doute le plus grand danger potentiel pour le régime d'Assad. En termes géostratégiques, le Liban est une porte ouverte sur la Syrie puisqu'il juxte toute la région occidentale de la Syrie où se trouve son centre militaire, politique et économique, à savoir sa capitale, Damas, et son principal complexe industriel, Homs.'

fatherland for the Palestinians. Politicians as far apart as Franjieh and Eddé were — and remained — convinced that this was the intention of the USA and, in particular, Kissinger. Both Palestinians and Christians were dead against it. The Palestinians were convinced that the army and Christian militias were preparing for the definitive battle against them as part of their interpretation of the 'American plan'; and the Christians were equally convinced that Palestinians, the Lebanese Left and Muslims were preparing for the battle to erect a Palestinian-Lebanese, Muslim-ruled state as part of their interpretation of the 'American plan'.

Both sides were ready for what they feared would be the other's assault. On Sunday, April 13th, 1975 the incident occurred that both regarded as the signal to attack. When the Suez Canal opened on June 5th, Lebanon was already at war.

## Surrogate battlefield for Palestine

From 1975 onwards Lebanon was not the Palestinians' surrogate fatherland but Palestine's surrogate battlefield. Until 1967 the Lebanese ship of state had skirted the Middle East conflict, which had not been without its advantages. But the wind turned, and the storm slowly bore down on it. The Palestinian resistance movement emerged from Arab defeat in the Six Day War as an independent political and military force — and simultaneously as an object that Arab states desired to control and use for their own purposes. Its scope for action narrowed inexorably: Israel quickly smashed any guerrilla organization in the occupied territories; Syria kept it under tight control from the very first; and Jordan threw it out in 1970. Lebanon was the only base for operations left. The Lebanese state attempted to bring the PLO under control in 1969 and 1973, but failed, largely because of pressure from Arab states, above all Syria. After the 1973 October War the initiatives of the superpowers aggravated tension in Lebanon, because the presence of the PLO enabled any interested party to reduce or exacerbate conflict at will. No foreign power was willing to defend the interests of the Lebanese state. They stood by and watched as Lebanon's barely armed neutrality was eroded, and some purposively contributed.

There is no evidence that the USA ever had a 'plan', as Palestinians and Christian Lebanese believe. As early as 1969 the USA took the view that the Lebanese state could not effectively control the Palestinians. By abandoning the search for a comprehensive peace settlement in the Middle East in favour of a policy of step-by-step diplomacy or bilateral agreements between Israel and the Arab states, Kissinger *de facto* brought peace to Syria and Egypt, but greatly increased the risk of war in Lebanon. Kissinger's objective was gradually to reduce the risk of another conventional war in the Middle East. He regretted the fates of the Palestinians and of Lebanon, but regarded them as of secondary importance. Kissinger had suggested a policy of benign neglect towards Latin America; his policy towards Lebanon was in word benign, and in practice neglect. This attitude persisted in US foreign policy in the post-Kissinger era. Lebanon was to play a role only when, and in so far as, conflict there threatened to spill over into other states: Lebanon per se counted for little in American foreign policy.[61]

Nor did it matter much to the USSR. Although Soviet support for an overall peace settlement in the Middle East never wavered, and only such a settlement could have brought relief to Lebanon, when the likelihood of this receded, the USSR supported Syrian efforts to hinder partial solutions under American auspices.[62] For the same reason it also supported the PLO and the Lebanese Left, occasionally directly, but as a rule indirectly via Syria. However, Lebanon as such had, to borrow Stalin's phrase, too few divisions to be of much interest.

Israel's interest in Lebanon was proportional to its function as a base for the PLO. Israel presented its policy of ruthless reprisals for Palestinian attacks anywhere in the world[63] as its means of forcing the Lebanese state to control the Palestinians. As no one knew better than the successive Israeli governments that the Lebanese government was in no position to control the Palestinians, one must assume that Israel was content to incite discord between the Palestinians and Lebanese, thereby reducing the former's capacity to attack Israel.[64] Israeli reprisals were always out of all proportion to the significance of the Palestinian commando raids — instead of the Biblical 'an eye for an eye and a tooth for a tooth', Israel consistently took an arm for a finger.

Since Syrian and Lebanese independence, no Syrian government has been kindly disposed towards Lebanon, a state that, in the opinion of most Syrian politicians, should not actually exist. Nor has Syria admired Lebanon's liberal democracy, its anarchic, though comparatively successful economy and its

---

[61] 'Lebanon was not considered a significant factor in the American effort to achieve peace between Israel and the Arab states after the October 1973 War'; Robert W. Stookey, 'The United States', in Haley and Snider, *Lebanon in Crisis*, p. 229. Edward E. Azar and Kate Shnayerson, 'United States — Lebanese Relations: A pocketful of paradoxes', in Edward E. Azar et al., eds., *The Emergence of a New Lebanon: Fantasy or reality?* (New York, 1984), p. 220, reach a similar conclusion: 'The United States conceived policy in broad, regional terms in which Lebanon mattered little, if at all.'

[62] See James F. Collins, 'The Soviet Union', in Haley and Snider, *Lebanon in Crisis*, pp. 209 and 211.

[63] Yehoshafat Harkabi, *Arab Strategies and Israel's Response* (New York, 1977).

[64] 'Israel's policy of holding the Lebanese government responsible for Palestinian attacks originating from Lebanese soil had proven unworkable and had contributed to the tensions that triggered the civil war'; Lewis W. Snider et al., 'Israel', in Haley and Snider, *Lebanon in Crisis*, p. 101; 'Instead of strengthening the government, Israel's heavy-handed raids and reprisals hastened the downfall of organized political life in Lebanon by compromising the armed forces, polarizing Lebanese politics, and adding to the numbers of homeless refugees'; ibid., p. 107.

aloofness from the Arab struggle for Palestine. Since 1967 Syria has tried everything to turn Lebanon into the crucible of confrontation, and taken pleasure in pursuing this confrontation wherever and whenever possible at Lebanon's expense. The Palestinian-Lebanese conflict gave the Syrian government the opportunity to enhance its influence both over the Palestinian movement and in internal Lebanese affairs. It has done so shrewdly, solely in its own interests, at little cost to itself and without the slightest regard for Lebanese interests.

Since 1969 there has been consensus among the other Arab states that the PLO should have freedom of action; the corollary is that Lebanon must bear the brunt of the concomitant confrontations. The states of the Rejectionist Front, principally Libya and Iraq, provided the Palestinian organizations with money and armaments. Saudi Arabia, abhorring left-wing secular organizations, Palestinian or Lebanese, supported conservative Muslim politicians, Fatah and at times even Christian militias. Only Jordan, at loggerheads with the PLO since 1968, gave — limited military — assistance solely to the Christian militias. Like the superpowers, most Arab states adapted their stance to the Palestinians' role in the Middle East conflict. Some were sympathetic, others relieved that Palestinian preoccupations in Lebanon curbed their capacity to cause trouble elsewhere. They had little interest in Lebanon per se, the smallest, strangest and weakest of the Arab 'brother countries'.

Lebanon was not the Palestinian organizations' country of choice — that was Jordan — but their bastion of last resort.[65] They mercilessly exploited its weaknesses. For, in their view all Arab states were duty-bound to make every sacrifice for the Palestinian cause, a cause concerning all Arabs. The fact that Lebanon was the only country they could force to do so was no reason for them not to do so. The conclusion they drew from the Jordanian disaster was the need for popular support in the host country. They acquired it by allying themselves with the Lebanese Left and the Muslim communities, and reducing them to varying degrees of dependence, though becoming themselves in turn dependent to some degree on their allies. In doing so, they aroused the hostility of most of the Lebanese Christian communities. As will be discussed below, the conclusions the Palestinians drew from their Jordanian defeat were not the answer. On the contrary, they were the makings of their Lebanese disaster — and of disaster for the Lebanese.

The irresponsibility of the Lebanese political class prepared the ground for this disaster. An appalling social policy had raised social tension to breaking point at just the time external dangers were at their greatest. All of them underestimated the external threats, clung to unarmed neutrality in a region bristling with arms,

---

[65] See Miller, *The PLO*.

and undermined the already limited powers of the state at a perilous time. These politicians provide impressive testimony to the ineffectuality of a consociation in foreign affairs. One may speculate on whether Lebanon might not have avoided the Middle Eastern storm had its politicians been less irresponsible. It is possible that even a more homogeneous, better governed Lebanon — say, a largely Muslim Lebanon aligned with the other Arab countries, or a largely Christian Lebanon less fearful of political impotence, probably similarly aligned — could not have skirted the maelstrom simply because of its geographic situation. One may also speculate on the likelihood of a purely Lebanese civil war even if the country had remained aloof from the Middle Eastern conflict. Counterfactuals by definition do not admit of any answer.

Lebanon was not governed particularly well in the last pre-war decade, least of all with respect to security. The developments in the region, whether towards war or peace, were all to its disadvantage. Since 1968 a Palestinian-Israeli war has been fought on Lebanese territory. Fierce armed conflicts in 1969 and 1973 may be classified as surrogate war over Palestine. But at this time there was no domestic civil war in Lebanon. Even after the war broke out — April 13th, 1975 is generally taken as the fateful date — it was to take months before it became a civil war in the narrow sense. But its pre-history demonstrates that the civil war is only an epiphenomenon of the Middle Eastern conflict.

# 4

## Danse Macabre: 1975-1988
## Parties, Masks and Steps

Some countries are unfortunate in the neighbours they happen to have. Lebanon seems to be one of these, but that cannot be changed.

William B. Quandt

Au lieu de 'tout le monde dehors', le Liban se retrouvera avec 'tout le monde dedans'.

Antoine Fattal

Lebanese leaders have at times sought primacy, often with outside support, in a political setting which calls instead for balance. And inevitably the search for primacy has led to violence, weakening the role of those in Lebanon who know the fine art of bargaining and negotiating, and strengthening those who know to use a gun and are willing to die.

William B. Quandt

It is regrettable, but the course of history is set not by justice, but by the law of the jungle.

Elie Salem

In most internal wars, elements of domestic strife and of external intervention are intermingled in varying proportions. If, on both sides of such a conflict, there is a clear quantitative preponderance of local motivations, recruitment, and resources, we may speak of an authentic internal war or revolution. If outside manpower, motives, money, and other resources appear to constitute the main capabilities committed to the struggle on both sides, then we are inclined to speak of a "war by proxy" — an international conflict between two foreign powers, fought out on the soil of a third country; disguised as conflict over an internal issue of that country; and using some or all of that country's manpower, resources, and territory as means for achieving preponderantly foreign goals and foreign strategies. To be sure, these goals of foreign powers may appear wholly compatible with those of the two main domestic factions in the struggle.[1]

In the war in Lebanon elements of civil war and of surrogate war have been present in each and every phase. The proportions of the mix in each phase must now be considered: who were the principal domestic as well as foreign parties to conflict at which time? The most useful criterion for ordering the variety and layers of conflict is periodicity; for, although at times several conflicts have run simultaneously, one of them has, as a rule, predominated, and in retrospect left its stamp on that phase.

The patterns of the war in Lebanon and the Thirty Years' War of 1618–48 are not dissimilar. For Karl Deutsch the latter is the classic example of the intermingling of internal and external conflicts to the point of indistinctness. It:

> ... assumed in some of its phases the function of a proxy war between France and Spain, with the latter supporting the Catholic faction, and the former the Protestant, in what began as a religious struggle within the Holy Roman Empire. In the outcome, the religious division of Germany and of Europe remained substantially unchanged. Germany was desolated and one-third of her population perished; Spain suffered a major political setback but escaped devastation; France emerged flourishing and her historians remember the seventeenth as "the great century" — *le grand siècle* — of French history'.[2]

Historical analogies are never perfect. The war in Lebanon did not begin as one between religious groups; it became one. And only history will tell whether one of its neighbours is on the threshold of a great century. Moreover, the patterns of

---

[1] Karl W. Deutsch, 'External Involvement in Internal War', in Harry Eckstein, ed., *Internal War: Problems and approaches*, p. 102.
[2] Ibid., p. 103.

conflict in Lebanon and the Orient towards the close of the twentieth century are, if anything, more complex than those in the mid-seventeenth: the parties to the conflict, both domestic and foreign, are more numerous, their alliances less enduring. But the two wars are comparable in two respects: the external parties soberly pursued power politics, whereas the internal parties were driven by excessive fears for their existence as religious groups; and the established political and religious leaders gradually lost power to mercenary bosses.

## Factions and their leaders

Middle Eastern politics are highly personalized. To Westerners, personality cults in Arab states, parties and militias are indistinguishable from iconography or hagiography. Portraits and photographs rather than uniforms and flags show which group controls which area. Political allegiance attaches primarily to persons, and only secondarily to organizations and programmes.

Many Arabs find superpower politics[3] uncanny because it is relatively anonymous. Even politically informed Lebanese accept that 'computers' plan superpower policies. The names of Soviet politicians were seldom mentioned, understandably in view of the consistency and continuity of Soviet Middle Eastern policy. American policies are perceived as slightly more personalized, and associated with one name in particular: Kissinger, though he left office years ago. He is seen — rightly — as the mind behind the process that was to prise Egypt out of the Arab front, and — wrongly — as the mastermind of the 'plot' against Lebanon. Most Lebanese politicians wildly overestimate superpower, especially American, interest in Lebanon. They find it difficult to accept that a superpower does not have specific plans for every region of the globe, that the USA often reacts rather than acts, and when in doubt is guided by domestic political concerns. Only after seven years of war in Lebanon did the USA become directly involved, and even then almost by default. When this role became too demanding it abandoned it and returned to the domestic election campaign. As in the pre-war era, during the war the superpowers sat on the sidelines, indirect parties to the conflict in so far as they supported or tried to restrain, at any rate hindered direct clashes between, their regional representatives: Israel and Syria.

---

[3] On non-Lebanese parties to the conflict see the brief, excellent article of Melhem Chaoul, 'Le Dispositif de la guerre au Liban, fonction de réduction', in Fondation pour la paix civile permanente, ed., *Le Droit à la mémoire* (Beirut, 1988). See also P. Edward Haley and Lewis W. Snider, eds., *Lebanon in Crisis: Participants and issues* (Syracuse, 1979); Bassma Kodmani-Darwish, ed., *Liban: espoirs et réalités* (Paris, 1987); Benassar (pseudonym of Gabriel Menassa), *Anatomie d'une guerre et d'une occupation. Evénements du Liban de 1975 à 1978* (Paris, 1978).

Israel[4] has been one of the most important parties to the conflict in Lebanon ever since the Palestinian resistance movement began operating from Lebanese territory. For more than twenty years hardly a week has passed in which Israel has not attacked targets in Lebanon. Initially, its intention was to force the Lebanese government to act against the Palestinians. But the Israelis soon went over to harassing the Palestinians in Lebanon themselves, and constraining their, and since 1976 Syrian, military capabilities. Besides direct military action, the Israelis also provided armaments and training for the Palestinians' most powerful Lebanese opponents, the Christian militias. Only after peace had been concluded with Egypt did Begin's Likud government, at the instigation of the defence minister, Ariel Sharon, adopt a far more ambitious Lebanon policy. In 1982 they felt the time was ripe to eliminate the enemy's last active front in a neighbouring country, to smash the PLO in Lebanon and establish a pro-Israeli government in the country. The attempt failed, Sharon had to resign, and Israel reverted to its policy of stoking the fires between the Arabs in Lebanon.

Since the mid-1970s, and especially since its treaty with Egypt, Israel's most important antagonist in Lebanon, as in the entire Middle East, has been Syria.[5] Whereas Israel's Lebanon policy was personalized only under Begin and Sharon, Syria's Lebanon policies, like all Syrian policies, are almost exclusively the policies of one person: Syria today is Hafez Assad. Assad has been in the inner circle of power since 1966 and governed alone since 1970. He has dealt with American presidents from Nixon to Bush, Soviet secretaries-general from Brezhnev to Gorbachev and Russia's Yeltsin, Egyptian presidents from Nasser to Mubarak and Israeli prime ministers from Golda Meir to Shamir. Such political longevity is rare in this region — only King Hussein has ruled longer — and goes hand in hand with equally rare consistency and perseverance in the pursuit of foreign political objectives. Assad is the first Syrian president from the heterodox Muslim minority of the Alawites. Since the mid-1950s the Alawites, like another minority, the Druze, have risen socially and politically, and made their mark

---

[4] On Israel's Lebanon policies see Itamar Rabinovich, *The War for Lebanon 1970-1983* (Ithaca and London, 1984) and Ze'ev Schiff and Ehud Ya'ari, *Israel's Lebanon War* (London and Sydney, 1984). See also John Bulloch, *Final Conflict: The War in the Lebanon* (London, 1983); Yair Evron, *War and Intervention in Lebanon: The Israeli-Syrian deterrence dialogue* (Baltimore, 1987); Avner Yaniv, *Dilemmas of Security: Politics, strategy and the Israeli experience in Lebanon* (New York and Oxford, 1987).

[5] See Nikolaos Van Dam, *The Struggle for Power in Syria: Sectarianism, regionalism and tribalism in politics 1961-1978* (London, 1979); Moshe Ma'oz and Avner Yaniv, eds., *Syria under Assad: Domestic constraints and regional risks* (London, 1986); Adeed I. Dawisha, *Syria and the Lebanese Crisis* (London and Basingstoke, 1980); Annie Laurent and Antoine Basbous, *Guerres secrètes au Liban* (Paris, 1987) and 'Le Liban et son voisinage', unpublished doctoral thesis, Université de Droit, d'Économie et de Science Sociales, Paris, 1986.

especially in two institutions: the army and the Baath Party. The army was an opening for children of peasants and the provincial lower-middle class; the secular ideology of the Baath Party appealed to members of minorities. A *coup d'état* brought the Baath Party to power in 1963; in 1966 the military wing, dominated by Alawites and Druze, gained the upper hand, and the Alawites soon eliminated Druze influence; in 1970 Assad won a power struggle against his Alawite rival, Salah Jadid. Crucial military units have largely been recruited among the Alawites: crack special-purpose troops largely independent of the army command, the armoured brigade in Damascus and the intelligence services. Over and above this, members of Assad's family hold key positions. It is not surprising that Assad's opponents use the 'Alawite character' of his regime to rally disaffection, in the hope of cultivating the prejudices of the Sunni majority against what they regard as a heretical minority. Assad has always countered such allegations with a pure Jacobin policy: no one is more secularist and more Arabist than he — his policies are not Alawite, but Greater Syro–Arab.[6] He is an orthodox Baathist in that he recognizes different Arab states, but only one Arab people. Consequently, he regards Syrians, Lebanese and Palestinians all as part of the same people. Hence, he does not accept that one single state, be it Syria, Lebanon or any other, can pursue its own raison d'état to the detriment of the Palestinians. Israel is and remains the principal enemy. But Assad is also a pragmatist. He shuns confrontations he does not have a fair chance of winning. In 1973 he and Sadat started the October War, the first against Israel in which Arab soldiers proved their mettle. Since then he has held the view that the Arab world must achieve military parity with Israel before they can seriously negotiate over Palestine. Unlike the Rejectionist Front, he does not object to negotiations on principle, as the Golan disengagement agreement shows. On the other hand, he disapproves of piecemeal peace measures, like Sadat's policies, that ignore the Palestinian problem. The Sinai II and Camp David Agreements isolated Syria and considerably widened the imbalance between it and Israel. This increased the importance to Syria of the Palestinians in Lebanon and Lebanon itself. As shown in the previous chapter, until 1975 Assad did all he could to concentrate the confrontation with Israel on Lebanon, including an economic blockade in 1973, which he

---

[6] See in particular Gudrun Krämer, *Arabismus und Nationalstaatlichkeit: Syrien als nahöstliche Regionalmacht* (Stiftung Wissenschaft und Politik, Ebenhausen, 1987). Karim Pakradouni, *La paix manquée: Le mandat d'Elias Sarkis (1976–1982)*, 2nd edn (n.p., 1984), p. 78, reports a statement characteristic of Assad: 'La Syrie est différente de tous les autres pays arabes ... Nous avons une vocation panarabe et tout ce qui est arabe est nôtre. Nous nous distinguons part un nationalisme interventioniste. Nulle unité arabe ne se conçoit sans la Syrie. Nulle guerre non plus. Si nous avions des frontières communes avec l'Egypte, notre armée y serait certainement entrée après la visite de Sadate à Jérusalem ... La Syrie est le noeud du problème et la clé de la solution au Moyen-Orient!' For biographical details, see Patrick Seale, *Asad of Syria: The struggle for the Middle East* (London, 1988)

kept up even after the Palestinians and the Lebanese government had signed the Melkart Protocols. Lebanon had to recognize Syrian hegemony on the 'East Front' against Israel, just as the Palestinians in Syria had had to do. Assad wanted at all costs to avert being dragged by Palestinian actions into war with Israel at an inauspicious time. At the same time, the Palestinians under his control[7] were suitable instruments with which to demonstrate that peace without Syria was a chimera, and to strengthen Syria's bargaining potential. In short: Assad's objective was neither Lebanese control over the Palestinians nor Syrian control over Lebanon, but a 'balance of weakness' in Lebanon that gave Syria control over both simultaneously. Since 1975 Syria's policy towards Lebanon has pursued this objective single-mindedly. In the war in Lebanon Assad was to play the role Cardinal Richelieu did in the Thirty Years' War: the shrewd, calculating and singularly successful master of power politics. It is still too early to say whether the game has been worth the candle.

Less important Arab parties are Libya, Egypt and Iraq. Libya was a self-appointed provider to the Palestinian organizations in the Rejectionist Front as well as some Lebanese militias. It has also tried to mediate in conflicts between Syria and the PLO, with marginal success. Under Sadat Egypt, at odds with Syria over peace negotiations, supported parties variously ranged against Syria in the Lebanon conflict, initially the Christian militias, then the Palestinians, before it completely withdrew from the Lebanese stage after the Camp David Agreement. Since the mid-1960s there has been a bitter feud between the Iraqi Baath regime and its Syrian counterpart — the Syrian leadership ousted in 1966 still lives in Baghdad. Until the outbreak of the first Gulf War, and after it until the second Gulf War, Iraq consistently supported any opposition to Syria in Lebanon.

The Palestinian organizations[8] triggered off, and remained the prime object of, the conflict in Lebanon. Israel would still like to smash them, various Lebanese, in particular Christian, organizations tried to break their military power, and Syria has tried to control them. Their relations with Israel and the Lebanese nationalist groups were simple: open hostility. They have always regarded Israel as the enemy absolute, and the Christian Lebanese nationalists as at best 'isolationists' who wished to remain aloof from the common struggle of all Arabs, at worst as collaborationists of Israel. Their relationship with Syria is more complex. Although their most important ally, protector and arms supplier, Syria

---

[7] Initially, Svria exercised influence over the Palestinian movement by patronizing Saiqa and maintaining units of the Palestinian Liberation Army. But its objective was influence in the central organization of the PLO.

[8] Their social and political programmes are discussed in Chapter 2. For a particularly instructive account see Edward W. Said, 'Palestinians in the aftermath of Beirut' in *Journal of Palestine Studies* 12/2 (1983).

has also posed the greatest threat to independent Palestinian policies. In various phases of the war Palestinians fought with Syrians, against Syrians, and among themselves over the question of their relationship with Syria. The relationships between the different Palestinian organizations have never been simple either. Saiqa invariably adopted the Syrian line of the moment, the Arab Liberation Front the Iraqi line. Both the Popular Front and the Democratic Front had Libyan support, rejected negotiations on the creation of a Palestinian state in part of Palestine and, in the early years of the war, were closely allied to the Lebanese Left. Their declared goal was revolution in Lebanon, so as to erect a militant progressive regime as the first step towards radical change throughout the Arab world. Fatah, by far the strongest Palestinian organization, was considerably more moderate in its goals, in respect both of Palestine and Lebanon. Already before the war Fatah had pragmatically brought itself to substitute a Palestinian state in part of Palestine for its policy of a secular state embracing all Palestine. Though Fatah, like Syria, opposed 'step-by-step diplomacy' and bilateral agreements with Israel, it did not disapprove of negotiations per se, but of being excluded from them. Fatah was by and large satisfied with the position it had attained in Lebanon by the mid-1970s. Along the Israeli border they were able to demonstrate militarily that they were not to be ignored. Above all, independent of a weakened Lebanese government, they were able to pursue their political and diplomatic activities, eventually gaining international recognition at the Arab summit in Rabat and in Arafat's address to the General Assembly of the United Nations in 1974. Although Fatah could hardly hope for a better arrangement than they already enjoyed in Lebanon, they were not immune to thoughts of a *coup d'état* to replace a benevolent government by a supportive, or possibly even a completely dependent one. Hence, in the early war years Fatah, and thus the PLO leadership, vacillated between defending what they had already attained and actively supporting a change of power in Lebanon.

Notwithstanding their variety and contrasts, the different Palestinian organizations do have a common framework, the PLO.[9] This comprises a form of parliament, the Palestinian National Council, and a joint executive. Fatah has a broad majority in both. All the same, the majority has always made a point of seeking consensus on important matters so as to maintain the unity of the Palestinian movement. In well-established systems of government the consensus principle tends to work in favour of preservation: concessions are made to conservative

---

[9] On the PLO see in particular Rainer Buren, *Ein palästinensischer Teilstaat? Zur internen, regionalen und internationalen Dimension der Palästinafrage* (Baden-Baden, 1982). See also Naveed Ahmed, 'The Lebanese crisis: The role of the PLO', in *Pakistan Horizon* 29/1 (1976), pp. 31–46. An excellent survey of the politics of the Palestinian movement before the outbreak of war may be found in Dunia Nahas, 'L'évolution des organisations palestiniennes', in *Travaux et Jours* 52 (1974), pp. 77–99.

minorities. However, in liberation movements the principle works in favour of radicalization: as militant minorities are able to act off their own bat, the moderate majority tends to accept compromises that are more militant than actually intended. An instance of this was the alliance between the PLO and the organizations of the Lebanese Left: in crucial phases of the war the PLO was to bow to the wishes of their allies to the detriment of their own interests.

Palestinian politics are highly personalized. Notwithstanding numerous setbacks, since his election as leader of the Palestinian Liberation Organization in 1969, Yassir Arafat has been its pre-eminent personality. The general public in the West finds it difficult to appreciate the attraction Arafat holds for his countrymen, whether in Palestine or in exile, intellectuals or peasants, great or small. His personality is a rare combination of characteristics. For a quarter of a century he has represented his cause without wavering. Whereas Nasser could not get over his defeat in 1967, Arafat has repeatedly emerged from crushing blows, his spirit unbroken. In his dealings with his countrymen he exhibits a warmth and genuine sympathy which give him credibility, even if his policies may seem incomprehensible to his followers. His flexibility in dealings with politicians goes well beyond cynicism, an attitude not inappropriate to the political situation in the Middle East. He embraces friends and deadly enemies, says one thing one day and another thing the next, as long as this serves his cause. 'Politics in the Middle East is like a landscape of drifting sand dunes: one never knows in which direction they will drift. To reach one's destination one can take the direct route or a roundabout route — the important thing is not to be buried by a dune.'[10] Asked to comment on the remark of one of his many opponents that he is the greatest liar in the Orient, he replied: 'I don't know if I'm the greatest liar in the region. But if I send people to die for my cause why shouldn't I lie for this cause?' There is much to be said for the view that were it not for Arafat's flexibility the PLO would have long since have fallen victim to inter-Arab hegemonic jostling, although this could also have been the case were it not for the readiness of the majority of Palestinians to trust in him, no matter how breathtaking his political roller-coasting. His position is undisputed. The narrow circle of Fatah's leadership is homogeneous. Within the PLO as a whole George Habash represents a political alternative attractive to many. However, Habash is Greek Orthodox. Although communal allegiance plays little role within the PLO, certainly nothing like that in Lebanese politics, this is enough to ensure that he cannot seriously contest Arafat's position. The leaders of organizations associated with particular Arab governments can be taken even less seriously as rivals of the PLO leader. Every attempt to unseat Arafat has provoked bloody internecine struggles from which

---

[10] Interview with the author, 1979.

Arafat has emerged the victor. The sheer number of Palestinian organizations, their commandos and their divergent interests has meant that the PLO, despite the weight of Fatah, has often been unable to speak with one voice or, in many cases, coordinate military actions.

The Palestinians' most important allies in Lebanon were the parties and organizations that had formed the so-called National Movement (NM) under Kamal Jumblatt's leadership. These included the parties of the Lebanese Left: Jumblatt's Progressive Socialist Party (PSP), the Lebanese branches of the Syrian and Iraqi Baath Parties, the Lebanese Communist Party (CP), the Organization for Communist Action in Lebanon (OCAL) and the Syrian Social Nationalist Party (SSNP). The SSNP had the longest paramilitary tradition and at the outbreak of war had a thoroughly trained and disciplined militia. The PSP had built up a militia in the Druze areas of the Chouf; initially it was more of a civic guard, but from 1978 onwards was transformed into a body of crack troops. The pro-Syrian Baathists worked closely with Saiqa, the pro-Iraqi with the Arab Liberation Front (ALF), the CP with the Democratic Front and the OCAL with Habash's Popular Front. The military wings of the latter four Lebanese parties were largely integrated into their respective allied Palestinian organizations. Furthermore, the National Movement included a number of smaller Nasserite organizations: the Popular Nasserite Organization of Mustapha Saad, son of Maarouf Saad, the deputy assassinated in 1973; Farouk Muqaddam's '24th of October Movement' in Tripoli, a local rival of Rashid Karami; in Beirut there were no less than four Nasserite organizations,[11] though only the militia of the Independent Nasserites, Al Mourabitoun (the Vigilantes) played a prominent part in the fighting. Al Mourabitoun were headed by Ibrahim Qulaylat. One of Saeb Salam's militiamen in 1958, assisted by the Deuxième Bureau in the Chehabist era and taken under Fatah's wing after 1970, Qulaylat evolved into a popular leader in the lower middle-class Sunni areas of West Beirut. Fatah provided Al Mourabitoun with arms, training and, above all, money[12] and turned it into its most effective Lebanese auxiliaries.

These connections between organizations of the National Movement and Palestinian groups illustrate the very close relationships between Lebanese and Palestinian parties to the conflict.[13] Al Mourabitoun is the most striking example

---

[11] Nasserite Organization/Union of Popular Labour Forces (Najah Wakim and Kamal Chatila), Nasserite Organization — Corrective Movement (Issam Arab), Arab Socialist Union (Kamal Yunes) and the Independent Nasserites Movement, the Mourabitoun (Ibrahim Qulaylat).

[12] The importance of finances for militias is illustrated by the fact that, although the Mourabitoun had 'Sunni' political leanings, about 40 per cent of its recruitment was Shi`i: militia pay was often more attractive for Shi`is than for Sunnis.

[13] See Selim Accaoui and Magida Salman, *Comprendre le Liban* (Paris, 1976). They state, from a left-

of the dependence bred by PLO funds and arsenals, especially in military matters.[14] This dependence was strongest in the initial stages of the war. Later, various parties and militias found alternative sources of finance in Arab states. At the outbreak of war the National Movement enjoyed a political significance quite unwarranted by its military strength. The chief reason for this was Kamal Jumblatt,[15] who had succeeded in moulding an extremely heterogeneous coalition — the genuinely left-wing CP and OCAL, the non-Marxist left-wing nationalist Baathists, the ideologically vague Nasserites and the previously parafascist, now leftist adherents of the SSNP — into a politico-military force to be reckoned with. Jumblatt was one of Lebanon's most controversial and complex politicians. As heir to the leadership of the largest Druze clan, he had the unconditional backing of a small, but cohesive community. However, under the National Pact precisely this position debarred him from high office, which he coveted.[16] He had absorbed an enormous range of spiritual and intellectual influences: his Catholic education had for a time given him a Christian bias; he was widely read in British and French forms of democratic socialism; his admiration of Nasser had aroused his sympathy for moderate Arabism; his discovery of Indian mysticism encouraged him to practise meditation. During Chehab's presidency he had been a committed reformer, and although the gradualism of reform later made him turn to revolution, the economic and social programme of the National Movement was little more than a mild commitment to a social welfare state. The large landowner and industrialist led strikes and demonstrating workers. The Lenin prize winner let his tenants kiss his hand. The aristocratic socialist could speak of the bourgeoisie with utter contempt. In spite or because of these contradictions, Jumblatt succeeded in welding together a political movement that sought not only a redistribution of power in Lebanon, but a new republic, not a system based on confessions but a secular one. There can be no

wing point of view: 'la Résistance palestinienne joue un rôle militaire prépondérant ... Aucune décision militaire d'envergure ne peut être prise sans l'accord des différentes organisations palestiniennes' (p. 39); 'dépendance de fait des organisations libanaises à l'égard de la Résistance palestiniennes' (p. 46).

[14] 'La politique de "non-ingérence" ... adoptée par le Fatah aboutit au renforcement d'une organisation para-militaire libanaise contrôlée directement par les directions palestiniennes. Cette organisation "El-Mourabitoun" participe aux combats dans tous les secteurs "chauds" de Beyrouth. Dans les batailles décisives de grande envergure, des combattants du Fatah rejoignent les rangs des "Mourabitoun" et combattent sous une couverture politique libanaise, afin de préserver l'aspect "proprement libanais du conflict"'; ibid., p. 53.

[15] See his autobiography, ed. Philippe Lapousterle, *Pour le Liban* (Paris, 1978). Pakradouni, *La paix manquée*, pp. 15ff, provides a detailed characterization of Jumblatt. On the National Movement see Aziz al-Azmeh, 'The Progressive Forces', in Roger Owen, ed., *Essays on the Crisis in Lebanon* (London, 1976), pp. 59–72. See also *Merip Report* no. 61, 'The Lebanese National Movement': interviews with Fawaz Traboulsi (OCAL) and Abdullah Sa'adeh (SSNP) as well as the programme of the Patriotic Christian Front.

[16] As interior minister he signed papers as 'Administrative Governor of Lebanon', a spurious title.

doubt but that he envisioned himself at its head. He saw the alliance with the armed power of the Palestinians as his historic chance. He not only grasped it; he did everything in his power to arrange it.

Kamal Jumblatt was assassinated in 1977. His son Walid succeeded him not only as Druze leader, but also as head of the Progressive Socialist Party and the National Movement. This succession may not say much about father and son, but it speaks volumes about the personnel and political weaknesses of the Lebanese Left without a Jumblatt. Politically, Walid Jumblatt had stood in the shadow of his father; his abilities were widely underestimated: he quickly became an influential politician in his own right. Unlike his father, he is no melancholy visionary filled with a personal mission. The younger Jumblatt is given to irony and self-irony, and carefully and soberly weighs all facts. Yet, he is through and through a power-conscious political leader of his community, his party, his militia, and also the conglomerate National Movement.

Before the war the National Movement also included the Shi`i 'Movement of the Deprived' and its militia, Amal.[17] With the outbreak of war its leadership decided to remain neutral. At a later phase it would attain a crucial role in the conflict, both militarily and politically. For, since 1979 at the latest it has been the pre-eminent organization of the Shi`i community. The movement was founded in 1970 by Imam Musa Sadr,[18] a cleric of Lebanese descent born and educated in Iran. Sadr settled in Lebanon in 1960 and began to organize the Shi`is religiously, socially and politically with considerable astuteness.[19] In 1969 he organized the Supreme Shi`i Council for his community, and was immediately elected its president. With a Greek Catholic bishop, Monseigneur Gregoire Haddad, he had co-founded the 'Social Movement', a self-help organization for the rural population in southern Lebanon. Towards the end of the 1960s he began to support Shi`i candidates open to developmental and social policies against *zu`ama'* and large landowners, while simultaneously combatting the Shi`i drift towards left-wing parties.[20] To improve the lot of his community he strengthened his international

---

[17] See Augustus Richard Norton, *Amal and the Shi`a: Struggle for the soul of Lebanon* (Austin, 1987); Jean Aucagne, 'L'Imam Moussa Sadr et la communauté chiite', in *Travaux et Jours* 53 (1974), pp. 31-51.

[18] See Fouad Ajami, *The Vanished Imam: Musa al Sadr and the Shia of Lebanon* (London, 1986); Werner Ende, 'Imam Mûsa as-Sadr', *Orient* 14/3 (1973), p. 103.

[19] He was supported in this by the Chehabist bureaucracy, which hoped that new social movements would stimulate development in peripheral regions.

[20] 'Les masses laborieuses migrantes se partagent entre les partis de gauche et la Résistance d'une part, et le Mouvement des Déshérités d'autre part ... Le mouvement de l'imam Sadr a sapé le développement des partis de gauche au moment où ils pensaient bénéficier de l'existence de la révolution palestinienne et de l'accumulation des problèmes sociaux pour se développer'; Fadia Kiwan, 'Stratification sociale et identification politique à Bourj el Barajneh', *L'Afrique et l'Asie modernes* 115/4 (1977), p. 26.

contacts, both with his country of birth, Iran, and with the Alawite leadership in Syria.[21] In Lebanese politics Musa Sadr's position was unequivocally reformist. He wanted the Shi`is to receive their rightful share of prosperity and power. As mentioned, Shi`i demands were primarily economic and social.

Sadr was an impressive person, a man of charisma and charm. In him the Lebanese Shi`is had for the first time a leader who was recognized and respected. Hence, his disappearance without trace in Libya in September 1978 was a tremendous shock. His fate has never been convincingly explained, and he has since become a symbolic politico-religious figure, ranked in legend redolent with traditional Shi`i teachings on the 'hidden imam'.

Sadr's position was unique. Powers he held in personal union have devolved separately. Sheikh Mohammed Mahdi Shamseddin became acting chairman of the Supreme Shi`i Council; Imam Sadr officially remains chairman until his fate is cleared. Hussein Husseini, member of an old family and a man of the political centre, elected Speaker of the Chamber of Deputies in 1986, was interim leader of Amal until succeeded in 1980 by Nabih Berri,[22] one of the most influential Lebanese politicians. Berri personifies the new Shi`i middle class. Born the son of Lebanese immigrants in Sierra Leone and trained as a lawyer, he amassed a fortune in West Africa and the USA before returning to Lebanon, where he became one of Musa Sadr's closest confidants. Husseini and Berri transformed Amal into a Shi`i popular movement. Amal first resorted to armed conflict in 1979 — four years after the outbreak of war — initially against the Palestinians. In time it became involved in numerous other confrontations, until it was to be found at the centre of most strife on Lebanese territory. Its proclaimed objectives are now those of the incipient National Movement: the introduction of a majority-vote system followed by thorough reorganization of the Lebanese political system.

From the outbreak of war the principal opposition to the armed presence of the Palestinian organizations as well as to changes in power and in the Lebanese system was a coalition of militant Christian parties and groups known since 1976 as the Lebanese Front.[23] Most important members were the Kata'ib and the National Liberal Party (NLP). Both had built up militias in the pre-war period. Allied with them in the first two years of warfare were the Marada brigade,

---

[21] In the Supreme Shi`i Council, Sadr delivered a doctrinal statement confirming the status of Alawites as true-believing Muslims. This buttressed Assad's position. For, under the Syrian constitution, the president must be Muslim, and the Sunni religious leaders were divided on the question of whether Alawites were true believers.

[22] See Detlev Khalid, 'Nabih Berri (Nabîh Birrî)', *Orient* 26 (1985), pp. 141–6.

[23] This coalition initially called itself the 'Kafur Front', from a monastery in which its leaders met, then the 'Front for the Liberty of Man' and finally the 'Lebanese Front'. For the sake of simplicity, the latter term will be used throughout.

President Franjieh's militia in the Christian areas in the north of the country, and two smaller groups, the Tanzim (the Organization) and the Guardians of the Cedars.

In times of peace the Kata'ib drew the support of only a small section of the Lebanese Christians, although by the 1960s it was already had the largest membership and best organization of all Lebanese parties. Most Christians preferred to be represented by independent notables. But from 1958 the Kata'ib had enjoyed an upsurge of support in times of crisis. Many Christian citizens who in normal circumstances had little liking for rigid party discipline or populist policies felt they could depend on the Kata'ib when Lebanon in general, and the Christian communities in particular, were under threat. One reason for this trust was Kata'ib's paramilitary wing, which had existed since the party was founded. Among Christians it was widely thought that this body would offer protection even — and precisely — when the powers of the state could not. After the confrontations between the army and the Palestinian organizations in 1969 and 1973 other Christian political groups adopted this course. The NLP organized its Tiger militia. In the Zghorta region, the stronghold of the Franjiehs, where neither of the large Christian parties was effectively represented, the Franjiehs formed the Marada as a local militia. A number of Christian intellectuals, mistrustful of the fighting abilities of the party militias, founded the Tanzim in 1973. This was not so much a fighting force as an organization for training guerrillas; with the help of sympathizers within the army, hundreds of youths received basic military training. The Guardians of the Cedars[24] were a marginal group with a particularly radical rhetoric founded to liberate Lebanon from foreigners.

The political leaders of the Lebanese Front were the party leaders of the Kata'ib and the National Liberals, Pierre Gemayel and Camille Chamoun. The leadership also included three 'wise men': the historian Jawad Boulos, the orientalist Fouad Ephrem Boustani, former rector of the Lebanese University, and the philosopher Charles Malek, foreign minister during Chamoun's presidency. A further member was Father Charbel Qassis, president of the Maronite Order of Monks, whose position in the Front was later taken by Father Boulos Naaman.[25] As will be seen below, this intellectual and spiritual collaboration left its mark on the Lebanese

---

[24] Their leader, Etienne Sakr, adopting Palestinian practice, took a nom de guerre, Abou Arz (father of the cedars). For a time the chief ideologist of this group was the poet Said Akl.

[25] During the war the Maronite hierarchy under the leadership of Patriarch Khreish took a very moderate political line so as not to give the conflict the character of a religious war. The influential Maronite Order of Monks took a different stance: it regarded the war as primarily a threat to Christianity in Lebanon and therefore felt itself duty-bound to commit itself politically and socially. The order withdrew from politics only in the mid-1980s, not without prodding from the Vatican.

Front.

The characters of the two political leaders of the Lebanese Front could hardly have been more different. Pierre Gemayel was the antithesis of the adroit, flexible broker of traditional Lebanese politics. Basically a simple soul, unswerving to the point of intransigence and utterly incorruptible, he stood for a pure and uncompromising Lebanese nationalism. In matters of principle, opportunism fell by the wayside. He opposed everyone who questioned Lebanese independence: the French during the mandate, the Greater Syrian nationalists of the SSNP, the supporters of union with the United Arab Republic and the Palestinian organizations and their allies. On the other hand, he had a deep emotional attachment to the Lebanon of the National Pact, and in the interests of this nationalism was always ready to find a modus vivendi with Muslim Lebanon. Even in very old age Camille Chamoun[26] remained a brilliant and elegant man of the world and consummate politician, not without an eye to the main chance, extremely flexible and venturesome to the point of foolhardiness. As president he managed to alienate a considerable part of the political establishment and turn his former political comrade, Kamal Jumblatt, into a mortal enemy. As Lebanese ambassador to the United Nations he was an eloquent advocate of the Palestinian cause. Shortly afterwards, he unnecessarily aroused Nasser's enmity; one enemy more or less mattered little to him. He had far fewer scruples than Pierre Gemayel about accepting Israeli assistance, or of using Lebanese partition as a political card after the outbreak of war. For all Gemayel's obduracy and Chamoun's civility, in crucial matters the former tended to be the dove and the latter the hawk.

Yet, for tenacity and intransigence neither could equal Suleiman Franjieh, the third of Christian Lebanon's three great survivors of the National-Pact generation. He, more than any other Christian politician, upheld the Maronite right to the presidency and the powers of this office. The roots of his disagreements with Gemayel and Chamoun were twofold: his confidence in President Assad, based on a long-established personal friendship, and his rejection of any cooperation whatsoever with Israel. These were the root cause of the alienation that developed between Franjieh and the Lebanese Front in the second year of the war.

However, serious cracks appeared in the Christian front only when the Kata'ib militia began to insist on the overall command of the Christian militias; when it resorted to duress they became irreparable. The ensuing intra-Christian strife resulted in a single militia called the Lebanese Forces[27], which gradually grew

---

[26] In the early years of the war Chamoun wrote two volumes of memoirs: Camille Chamoun, *Crise au Liban* (Beirut, 1977) and *Mémoires et souvenirs* (Beirut, 1979). Informative sketches of Gemayel and Chamoun may be found in Pakradouni, *La paix manquée*, pp. 98ff.

[27] See Lewis W. Snider, 'The Lebanese Forces: Wartime origins and political significance', in Edward E. Azar et al., eds., *The Emergence of a New Lebanon: Fantasy or reality?* (New York, 1984), pp. 117–

independent of and eventually usurped the political role of the Lebanese Front in the Christian heartland of Lebanon. The man responsible for this development was Pierre Gemayel's younger son, Bashir Gemayel. He had joined the Kata'ib militia as a youth. At twenty-three he commanded militia units in the first clashes with Palestinian guerrillas in 1970. In 1976 he assumed command of the whole militia after his predecessor had fallen. Whereas his older brother Amin had embarked on a parliamentary career and acquired a reputation as an accommodating politician who enjoyed the wrangling and give and take of traditional politics — a modern *za'im* so to speak — Bashir was acquainted with other Lebanese political realities. Bashir belonged to a new generation of politico-military leaders. 'The day the Lebanese realize that two and two make four and nothing else we'll have a new country.'[28] Indeed, in Lebanon's traditional political culture of compromise two and two were seldom four, sometimes a little more, sometimes a little less, always negotiable. Like his fiercest political opponents in the parties of the Left, Bashir thought the system of proportionality was the root of the country's evils. 'National Pact' to him was a term of abuse. Like Kamal Jumblatt, he favoured a pure Jacobin nationalism, though of course with very different ideas about whose voice should be heard in a Jacobin Lebanon. He became the idol of the younger generation of Christians who had not had the opportunity to know or appreciate coexistence.

Kamal Jumblatt's Jacobinism was one of the decisive generators of war, and its evolution into civil war. The war brought new Jacobins to the fore, from Bashir Gemayel to Nabih Berri. The Lebanese parties to the conflict after the outbreak of war were essentially the same as those before. But their leaders were now harder, as ready to take but less ready to give.

The majority of the elected Lebanese politicians belonged to none of these parties. Most of the Maronite, Sunni and Shi'i notables, and virtually all the Greek Orthodox and Greek Catholic, showed some understanding for their respective protagonists, even if perhaps only a reflection of their speculations on the outcome of the war. But they were against the war, thought a decisive victory for one or other group improbable and certainly not worth the sacrifice, and used every break in the fighting to resume their business of searching for a compromise. Rashid Karami, Saeb Salam and Raymond Eddé tried repeatedly to prevent new outbreaks of fighting and restore coexistence. But of the ninety-nine Deputies elected in 1972 only seventy-two were alive at the end of 1988. Karami had been

---

161.
[28] Interview with the author, 1980. Pakradouni, *La paix manquée*, p. 242 reports Chamoun's assessment: 'Bachir est honnête et croyant comme son père, mais lui ne prend pas l'Evangile au pied de la lettre.'

assassinated, Salam lives in Switzerland, Eddé in Paris. 'Only the soldier counts, the honest citizen is scorned'[29] in Lebanon after 1975.

## War on many fronts

At the outbreak of war the adherents of the various conflicting parties did not live in, or the respective militia control, clearly demarcated blocks of territory. There were Palestinians in the north, the east and the south as well as in Beirut. The strongholds of two broad Lebanese coalitions, the National Movement and the Lebanese Front, naturally respected the broad confessional divide between Christian and Muslim communities: Christians in the northern and central mountains, Muslims in the peripheral regions, especially the areas adjoined in 1920 to create Greater Lebanon. Though broadly true, this simplification conceals a feature crucial to the character of the war. In virtually all parts of the country there were 'allogeneous pockets of population',[30] that is, communities whose denomination differed from that of the surrounding population. This geographic distribution of communities resembled a patchwork quilt. The same applied to the capital. The neighbourhoods east of the street leading from the city centre to Damascus were predominantly Christian, those to the west predominantly Muslim. But neither half was homogeneous. The peculiarities of settlement of both the Palestinians and the Lebanese communities were a major determinant of the character of the war. Because there were many 'boundaries' between areas inhabited by different groups, there were many fronts. The existence of 'allogeneous pockets of population' accounted for particular features of the fighting: conflicting parties frequently held such pockets hostage to exert pressure on the other side, or they expelled them so as to consolidate and homogenize their respective areas of control. For a better understanding of the course of the war and certain phenomena of violence, it is useful briefly to sketch the pattern of both Lebanese and Palestinian patches.

In and after 1948 Palestinian refugee camps were erected in the vicinity of towns and cities. Estimates put the proportion living outside the camps in urban residential areas at about one-third, in Beirut at over half.[31] But it was in the

---

[29] Friedrich Schiller, 'Prologue to Wallenstein', in *Robbers and Wallenstein*, trans. F.J. Lanport (Harmondsworth, 1979), p. 167.

[30] The term is borrowed from Pierre Rondot, *Les institutions politiques du Liban* (Paris, 1947), p. 27.

[31] See the estimates in John K. Cooley, 'The Palestinians', in Haley and Snider, *Lebanon in Crisis*, p. 24, and Salim Nasr, 'Les formes de regroupement traditionnel (familles, confession, communautés régionales) dans la société de Beyrouth', in Dominique Chevallier, ed., *L'Espace social de la ville arabe* (Paris, 1979), pp. 148f.

camps, accorded quasi-territorial status in the Cairo Agreement of 1969, that the Palestinian organizations established their main bases.[32] Two large camps north of Tripoli lay on the highway to Syria. Around 13,000 refugees from northern Palestine, whom Syria had refused to accept, lived in the Nahr el-Bared camp. Another 7,000 lived in the neighbouring Badawi camp. The Popular Front, the Democratic Front and Fatah had headquarters in both. Wavell camp near Baalbek in the northern Bekaa, with about 4,000 inhabitants, was used by the Popular Front for military training. A string of smallish camps overlooks the town of Nabatieh in the hills of southern Lebanon. As Nabatieh lies only fourteen kilometres from the Israeli border, these camps have been favoured targets of Israeli attacks. Three camps in the vicinity of Tyre took refugees from northern Palestine: Rashidieh (13,000 inhabitants), Bourj el-Shemali (over 9,000) and el-Buss (about 4,500).[33] Rashidieh in particular was regarded as a stronghold of the guerrilla organizations. The largest refugee camp was Ain al-Helweh, south-east of Sidon, with an estimated population of 25,000 at the outbreak of war in 1975. Just east of the city lies the small Mieh-Mieh camp (2,000 people). A further 20,000 Palestinians lived in Sidon itself. The Sidon area was the Palestinians' most important stronghold after Beirut.[34]

The camps around Beirut were erected beyond the then incipient suburbs. By 1975 the latter had spread up to or around, and at some points even merged with, the camps. Bourj al-Barajneh in the south-west of the city, along the road to the airport, contained an estimated 20,000 people in 1975. Nearby, adjoining the western Beirut suburb of Sabra, is Chatila, with up to 15,000 inhabitants at the outbreak of war. The headquarters of the Popular Front were in Chatila, while Sabra became, as it were, the seat of the PLO government. Tel al-Za`tar in the south-east of the city, east of the Beirut-Damascus highway, had a population of approximately 20,000 in 1975; overlooking it was the smaller camp (2,500 in 1976) of Jisr al-Pasha. A largish number of Palestinians also lived in the East Beirut district of Nabaa, north-west of Tel al-Za`tar and in the slum district of

---

[32] For greater detail on the following see Cooley, 'The Palestinians', pp. 25ff. Unless otherwise specified, the figures are for refugees officially registered with the United Nations Relief and Works Agency for Palestine Refugees (UNRWA) in 1977. In view of the waves of refugees during the 1970s the true numbers of Palestinians in Lebanon are probably considerably higher.

[33] The people in el-Buss originally came from Haifa and Acre and were mainly Christians.

[34] The majority of the camp population in Lebanon originally came from areas included in Israel in 1948. Thus a Palestinian state restricted to the territories occupied in 1967 would hardly redress their wrongs. This helps explain their preference for radical solutions rather than compromise. See Elisabeth Stemer-Picard, 'Le Liban et la résistance palestinienne', *Revue française de science politique*, 25 (1975), p. 22.

## Palestinian camps in Lebanon, 1975

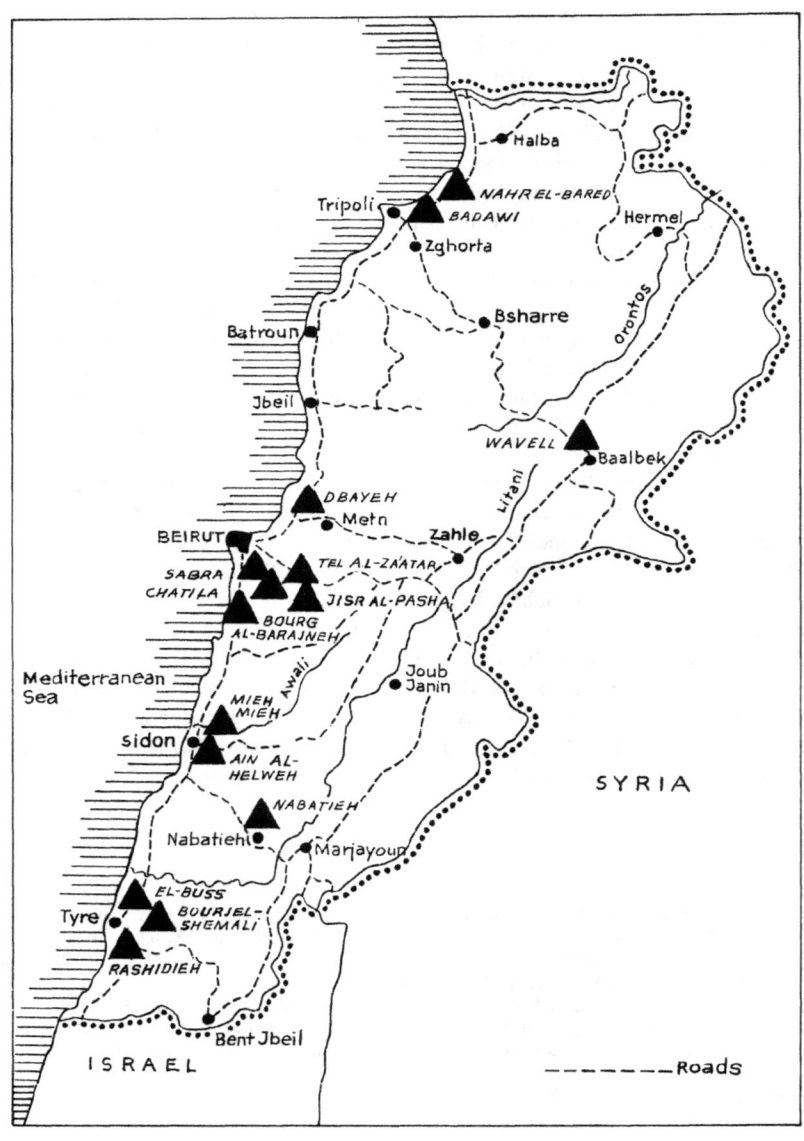

Karantina adjacent to the harbour.[35] North-east of Beirut, along the road to Jounieh, lay Dbayeh camp, housing about 3,000 predominantly Christian inhabitants at the outbreak of war. From the early 1970s onwards a number of camps were fortified with bunkers and other installations. Tel al-Za`tar in particular was converted into a military stronghold with an elaborate system of underground bunkers, casemates and trenches.[36] When the camps were established in 1948 no one imagined their positioning could one day have military significance. However, this aspect became clear in the first Palestinian–Lebanese confrontation of 1969. Once armed, the camps presented a threat to the most important Lebanese cities and towns. Beirut was surrounded by them: one camp commanded the access road to the airport, those to the east of the city commanded all roads connecting East Beirut with its Christian hinterland. Only a few kilometres separated the camps to the south-west and Tel al-Za`tar: had they linked up, East Beirut would have been encircled.

The confessional patchwork quilt in Lebanon was an arrangement of large patches each with various smaller patches. The Shi`is had huge majorities in the south and in the northern Bekaa. Sunnis predominated in the coastal cities of Tripoli, Sidon and Tyre. The northern part of the Lebanon Mountains and the adjoining coastal strip up to the Beirut–Damascus highway was mostly Christian. Jezzine, in the southern mountains east of Sidon, was also a compact Christian area. In the mountainous area south of the Damascus highway the population of the Aley region and the Chouf was evenly divided between Christians, on the one hand, and Druze and Sunnis on the other. In Akkar in the north, Christians and Sunnis were equally balanced. In the south-east of the country Christians, Druze and Muslims each formed approximately one-third of the population. Within these areas were 'allogeneous pockets': some Shi`i villages in the mountains behind Jbeil, Greek Catholic villages in the northern Bekaa, Maronite villages in the extreme south near the Israeli border. On the whole, there was a greater spread of Christian communities than Muslim. Less than half of all Lebanese Christians lived in the Christian heartland prior to the war. A number of important towns and larger villages lie outside this area: Jezzine, Deir al-Qamar in the Chouf, Zahle in the Bekaa, Kobayat in Akkar, as well as numerous smaller villages. 'Islands' were in the main Christian islands, most of them difficult or impossible to defend for any length of time and, therefore, ideal targets for 'big hostage hunters'.

---

[35] The name derives from the former quarantine station of the port of Beirut.
[36] An anti-aircraft unit of the Syrian was also stationed here.

## Distribution of the religious communities by area in pre-war Lebanon

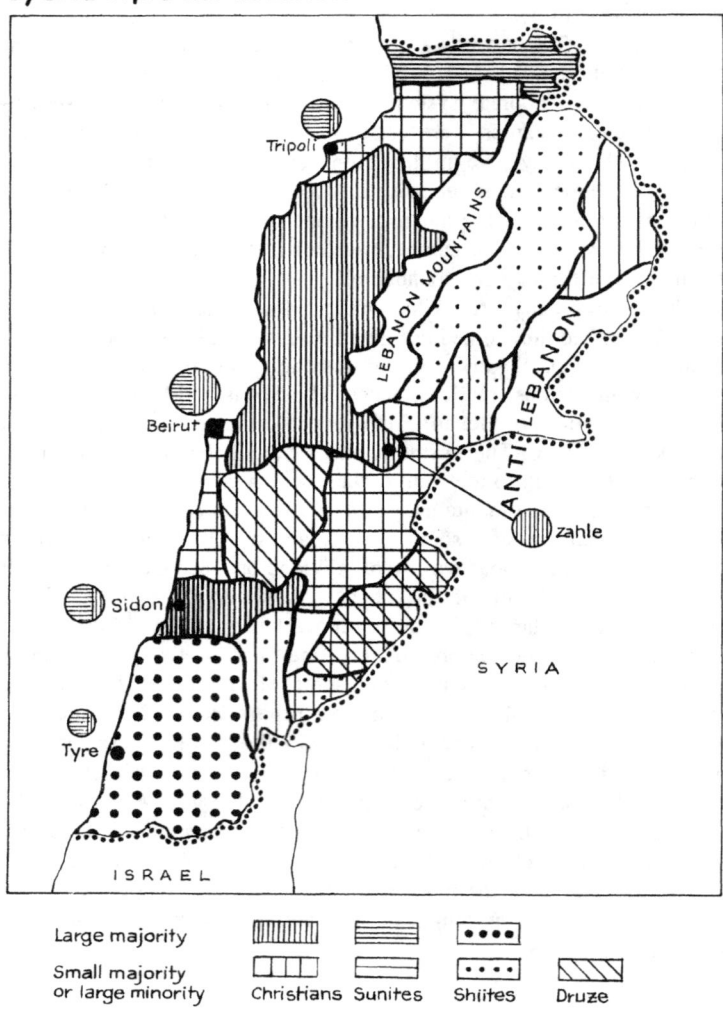

Large majority
Small majority or large minority

Christians  Sunites  Shiites  Druze

*Source*: Adapted from Eugen Wirth, 'Zur Sozialgeographie der Religionsgemeinschaften im Orient', *Erdkunde*, 14 (1965) p. 4, Appendix XII (detail), with the kind permission of the author.

If all Lebanon was the theatre of war, the centre stage in most acts was the capital, Beirut.[37] In the one and a half decades before the war the population of Beirut had doubled. One in two Lebanese lived ·in Beirut and its environs. Economic growth and the demand for labour in and around the capital had attracted not only Lebanese but vast numbers of foreigners. Kurdish migrant workers accounted for one-twentieth, Palestinian one-sixth and Syrian one-quarter of the city's population: a full 45 per cent were non-Lebanese. Beirut was not only a multi-denominational but literally a multi-ethnic city. Yet such influx seems to have exceeded the integrating potential of even this exceptionally open and integrating city, perhaps not economically, but socially and politically.

Economically, Beirut was a melting pot. Certainly, the longer established sectors tended to be concentrated in the hands of certain communities: the food industry, upstream and downstream, was largely Sunni, textiles were Greek Orthodox. Communities that urbanized later sought niches: the Armenians in money-changing and the repair trades, Maronites in international triangular transactions, Shi`is in trade with Africa and ready-to-wear clothing. But modernization is a great leveller; as modern economic sectors expanded, the demand for greater technical skills gradually eroded traditional specialization by confession. With time all denominations were represented in finance and commerce, and in the professions, as well as among factory workers. Specialization by confession came increasingly to reflect the length of urbanization of the different communities. The industrial labour force was mainly Maronite and Shi`i, communities that had moved to Beirut in great numbers only in the recent decades. The Sunnis, Greek Orthodox and Greek Catholics, long-urbanized communities, had moved to the more attractive sectors. And as they had long owned most of the land in Beirut, they also benefited most from the pre-war property boom. Social disparities were less marked between the Muslim and Christian confessions than between prosperous long-established residents of Beirut and the considerably poorer recent arrivals.

However, the picture is quite different if one includes the foreign inhabitants of Beirut. A minority of Palestinians had worked their way into the economic world of the Lebanese middle classes. But half of the Palestinians, most Kurds and the Syrian migrant labourers, formed a sub-proletariat. These foreign Beirutis were employed in menial jobs in the construction trades, road building and small industries, for the most part without social or medical insurance or trade-union rights. Lebanese society in the capital was fairly stratified, but increasingly regarded

---

[37] On Beirut in war see Nasr, 'Les formes de regroupement traditionnel'; André Bourgey, 'Beyrouth, ville éclatée', *Hérodote* 17/1 (1980), pp. 5–30; Theodor Hanf, 'Beirut: Konflikt und Koexistenz in einer geteilten Stadt', *Geographische Rundschau* 37/9 (1985), pp. 454–61.

itself as middle-class. Underneath it existed impoverished masses whose status as refugees or aliens was an effective barrier to upward mobility. In view of the growing prosperity of the Lebanese as a whole, it was inevitable that these masses became increasingly discontent with their fate. To a considerable degree, Beirut's social problem was a problem of foreigners.

Despite their many differences, economic development was gradually breaking down barriers in the working lives of Lebanese. However, there were no such forces at work in the social sphere, neither among the foreigners nor among the Lebanese. People worked together, coexisted alongside each other, but did not mix and continued to live in separate communities.

### Religious communities in Beirut, ca. 1945

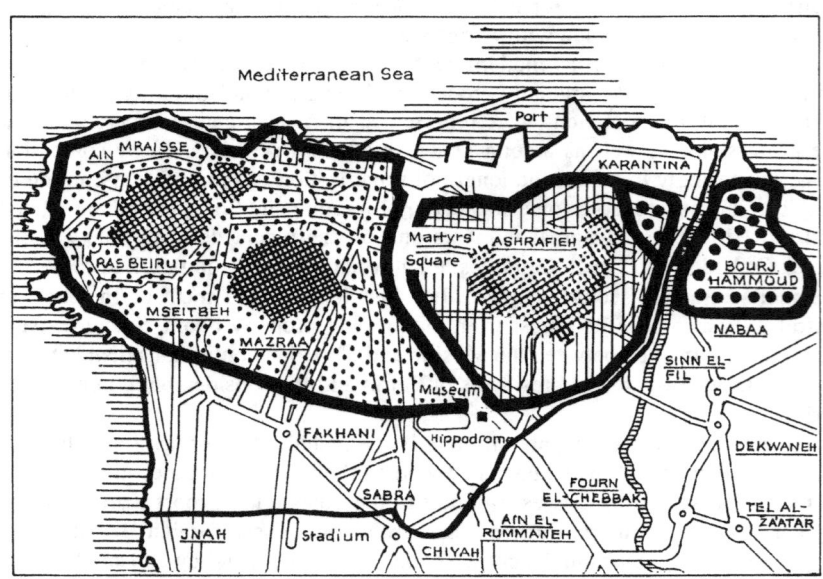

 Sunnites   Maronites   Greek Orthodox   Armenian   Boundary of the Municipality of Beirut

This had always applied to the long-established residents of Beirut. The Sunnis had always lived in the old districts west of the Beirut–Damascus highway which divides the city. The Greek Orthodox had some smaller neighbourhoods in the west but since the mid-nineteenth century had also settled on the Ashrafieh hill to the east of the highway. The Lebanese migrants in the first half of this century followed this practice. Around the turn of the century Maronites began to settle around the orthodox heart of Ashrafieh. When the Armenians arrived after the First World War they settled to the north of Ashrafieh along the Beirut River. The first Shi`is settled immediately to the west of the Damascus highway.

As the rural exodus of Maronites and Shi`is accelerated in the 1950s, new residential areas sprang up on the periphery of old Beirut, again voluntarily segregated by community. Christians settled in the east and south-east of the city, Muslims in the south-west. Old Maronite villages in the vicinity of the airport became islands in a Shi`i sea; Nabaa, between Maronites and Armenians in the north-east, was a Shi`i island. Within these new neighbourhoods the inhabitants often grouped by region and even village of origin: existing village societies transplanted to an urban environment. In a nutshell, old Beirut was a city of Sunnis and Greek Orthodox, new Beirut one of Maronites and Shi`is, and Beirut as a whole a segregated multi-ethnic city. Yet, there was one remarkable exception. In the west of the old city, in the quarter embracing Kantari, Hamra and Ras-Beirut, Christians, Muslims, Lebanese and foreigners lived together. It was a society of upper-middle strata and intellectuals that mixed socially, sent their children to the same schools, attended the same theatres and read and discussed the same books and periodicals, and occasionally even married across the confessional divide. For many Lebanese who knew it, life in this quarter was a paradigm for a future Lebanon.

Alongside the old and the new there was a third, even less integrated Beirut, that of the camps and migrant workers. The Palestinian refugee camps were set up between the new suburbs and adjoining them. Although the camps came outwardly to resemble the new suburbs, as concrete replaced canvas, wood and sheet-metal, the pervading atmosphere was that of a slum. The Lebanese districts of Chiyah, Ain al-Rummaneh, Dekwaneh, Sin el-Fil and Nabaa enclosed or intersected Beirut's 'belt of misery': Sabra and Chatila, Bourj al-Barajneh, Jisr al-Pasha, Tel al-Za`tar, Karantina and Maslakh.[38] Here Palestinians, Kurds and

---

[38] Tewfik Khalaf, 'The Phalange and the Maronite community: From Lebanonism to Maronitism', in Owen, *Essays on the Crisis in Lebanon* (London, 1976), p. 43, points out similarities between the slum belt and the newer suburbs: 'Another belt upon which this "belt of misery" was superimposed: the belt inhabited by Maronites of Sin-el-Fil, Hadath, Dekwaneh, Karm-al-Zaytoun, Siufi, Furn-el-Chebbak, Ain-el-Remaneh and Haret-Horeik. These areas too were inhabited by people who had to leave their villages to seek work in Beirut: these people too were victims of the centripetal economy of the country which made

Syrian seasonal labourers, as well as Shi`i refugees from the south without other accommodation, lived in crowded, squalid conditions.[39]

In pre-war Lebanon the level of integration decreased from the city centre outwards. In the markets, banks and department stores of the business centre, economic rationale effected cooperation. Residential areas were segregated, the newer the area, the greater the segregation. Whereas the old Beirutis had long experience of coexistence, most of the inhabitants of the newer districts had moved from homogeneous villages to an equally homogeneous urban environment. They kept a greater distance between themselves and the 'others' — who were also their competitors for jobs — than did old Beirutis, who had learnt to live with distinctions. They felt closer to a rich man of their own community than to a poor man from another community — the former was not quite so strange. Nevertheless, they were all Lebanese, most of them had jobs and some prospects of betterment. In contrast to both old and new Lebanese Beirutis, the inhabitants of the slum belt derived only marginal benefits from Lebanon's economic development. Central Beirut with its restaurants and shops selling everything the West could offer — at prices they could never afford — was an alien and hostile world. The Palestinians disliked Lebanon, where good living had precedence over the liberation of their fatherland. The Shi`i refugees could not reconcile this extravagance with the inability to protect their villages. The Syrians in Beirut had only temporary residence permits anyway. To all of them this prosperous and cosmopolitan Beirut was a symbol of un-Arab westernization and decadence.

Thus, even pre-war Beirut was a city of fissures. When war broke out Beirut soon broke up. The major faults ran between the camps-cum-slum belt and the rest, and between Christian and Muslim residential areas. Life and business in the city centre continued for some months after fighting had already disrupted the suburbs. And then Beirut broke asunder, into East Beirut and West Beirut.

---

the whole of Lebanon a "belt of misery" around Beirut'.

[39] The population of the camps had doubled in quarter of a century. Nearly two-thirds were under twenty. Sixty per cent of the houses lacked running water, 35 per cent lacked electricity. Almost 60 per cent of the inhabitants were illiterate; school enrolment was officially 64 per cent. The working population was employed mainly as casual unskilled labour in the manufacturing, agricultural and service sectors. Traditional *zu`ama'* exercised a certain authority in the camps until the early 1970s, since when 'the fedayeen (commando) leaders ... have surpassed all previous leaders of opinion in the camps ... For the Palestinians, these leaders have liberated them from years of frustration and helplessness and showed the way to become masters of their own fate'; Bassem Sirhan, 'Palestinian refugee camp life in Lebanon', *Journal of Palestine Studies* 4/2 (1975), p. 106. See Rosemary Sayigh, 'The struggle for survival. The economic conditions of Palestinian camp residents in Lebanon', *Journal of Palestinian Studies* 72 (1978), pp. 101–19.

## New suburbs and Belt of Misery, pre-1975

 Palestinians
 Shiites
 Armenians
 Maronites

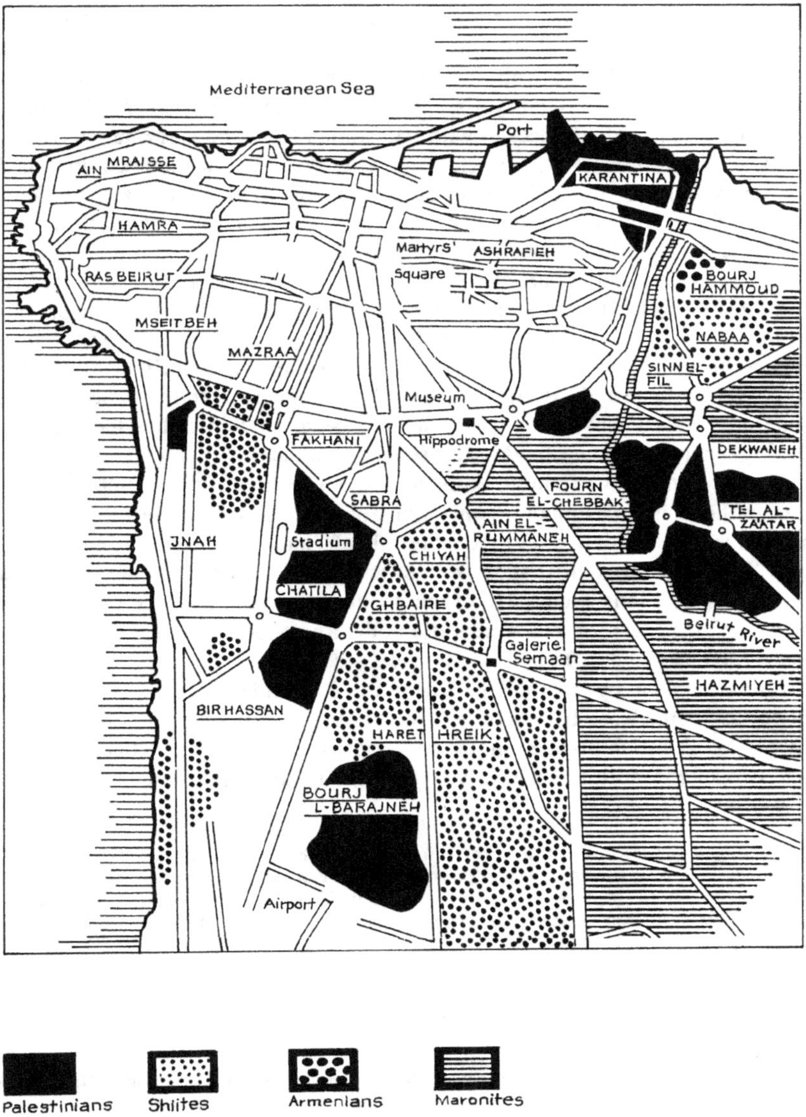

## War between the Palestinians and the Christian parties[40]

The Lebanese equivalent of the Defenestration of Prague took place on April 13th, 1975. Pierre Gemayel was attending the inauguration of a new church in the Maronite suburb of Ain al-Rummaneh. Shots were fired into the congregation from a passing car, later identified as belonging to the Democratic Front. Among those killed was one of Gemayel's bodyguards. A few hours later a bus passed through the same suburb, decked with Palestinian flags and carrying guerrillas of the Arab Liberation Front, from festivities in West Beirut commemorating the first anniversary of the Palestinian attack on Kiryat Shmona, back to Tel al-Za`tar.[41] Kata'ib militiamen, on edge after the earlier shooting, opened fire, killing twenty-seven Palestinians and injuring many more.

A provocation on the part of one or other — or perhaps a third — party? Abu Iyad later[42] accused the Military Intelligence of the Lebanese Army of planning the incident. The immediate reaction of the Palestinians and Kata'ib was to blame one another. Arafat spoke of Phalangist gangs conspiring with Zionism; Gemayel held 'undisciplined and extremist elements' of the Palestinian resistance responsible. Be that as it may, each side had long been convinced that the other was plotting against it, and each was prepared for an attack.

That evening heavy fighting erupted between the Palestinian camps and Shi`i quarters housing Palestinian organizations or allied groups on one side, and the neighbouring Christian suburbs on the other,[43] and continued for a number of days. The first Christian islands were stormed by Palestinians: Haret Hreik and the Chiyah were looted and most of the population driven out. The most active of the Palestinian organizations were those in the Rejectionist Front. There were also clashes and shooting in Tripoli, Sidon and Tyre.

Kamal Jumblatt openly took the side of the Palestinians and called for a political boycott of the Kata'ib, which, in turn, aroused a wave of support for this party among the Christian population. Gemayel adopted a conciliatory line and turned over two of the militiamen involved in the Ain al-Rummaneh incident to the

---

[40] The following discussion of the war from 1975 to 1988 is based primarily on analysis of the Lebanese press. Dates and events found in generally accessible chronicles will not be annotated. Detailed accounts of the first two years of the war may be found in the works of John Bulloch, René Chamussy, Wade R. Goria, Walid Khalidi and David Thomas Schiller and others cited above. For the years to 1985, see Rabinovich, *The War for Lebanon*.

[41] It has never been cleared up why the bus took the route through Ain al-Rummaneh, a district notorious for its antipathies towards all Palestinian organizations. For years it had been the custom of Palestinian transports between camps to the east and west of Beirut to make a detour around Ain al-Rummaneh.

[42] Interview with the author, 1979.

[43] Tel al-Za`tar against Dekwaneh and Mukallis, Chiyah against Ain al-Rummaneh, Nabaa against Sinn el-Fil. The road northwards from Ashrafieh came under fire from the Karantina.

police. He and Chamoun demanded that the army be sent in to restore order. When the Premier, Rashid Solh, who favoured Jumblatt's line, refused, the Kata'ib ministers resigned from the government, soon followed by four other Christian members. This rendered Solh's position untenable and he too resigned.[44] In the hope of strong government, President Franjieh appointed a cabinet of military men under a retired Sunni general, Nureddine Rifai. The united opposition of Muslim leaders of every political opinion forced Rifai to resign a few days later. Rashid Karami was asked to form a government. This proved extremely difficult because of Jumblatt's veto against the Kata'ib, on the one hand, and the refusal of most Christian politicians to serve in a cabinet without the Kata'ib, on the other.

While Karami negotiated, the fighting spread. Christians were driven out of one suburb in Tripoli, and Palestinian guerrillas were advancing on Zghorta, President Franjieh's stronghold. Fatah and Saiqa, supported by SSNP and CP adherents, tried to take the Greek Catholic village of Qaa in the northern Bekaa. When they failed they destroyed the irrigation network, and thus the economic basis for the villagers, who were mostly fruit-farmers. A local Shi`i clan took part in the attack on Qaa. Imam Musa Sadr, who had already dissociated himself from the Shi`is fighting in the East Beirut suburb of Nabaa, started a hunger strike as protest against the war. Kamal Jumblatt poured oil on the flames. He accused the Kata'ib of working together with Israel and the CIA and called for the abrogation of the National Pact.

Two and a half months after the outbreak of war various lines of conflict were emerging. The military struggle was primarily between Palestinians and militias of the Christian parties. The Palestinians' Lebanese allies had taken little part in the fighting. In many aspects the clashes were similar to those of 1969 and 1973, though with Christian militiamen instead of the Lebanese Army. As in 1969 and 1973, Arab states tried to mediate: Syria as well as Egypt, Saudi Arabia and the Arab League. In June Arafat and Franjieh met to negotiate a cease-fire. Jumblatt had also supported the Palestinians in 1969 and 1973. But this time his concern was not so much a settlement of a Palestinian–Lebanese conflict as radical changes to the Lebanese system. However, the established leaders of the Lebanese communities continued their efforts to revive the existing system.

At the end of June Karami managed to form a government. This had been preceded by a reconciliation between himself and Chamoun, with whom he had not spoken since 1958. Chamoun was appointed Interior Minister, which circumvented the Kata'ib boycott Jumblatt had called for. Muslim politicians had not

---

[44] In a stormy session of parliament Solh charged the Kata'ib with responsibility for the outbreak and continuance of fighting.

approved of Jumblatt's call, but none had dared join a government with Kata'ib ministers. The Kata'ib felt itself adequately represented by Chamoun and abandoned its claim to a cabinet post. Karami's new cabinet was a demonstration of the will to coexist. Three of the six ministers had served in the government which proclaimed Lebanon's independence and the National Pact in 1943.[45] In the vote of confidence on 15 July the government received 83 votes, with none against; there were 16 abstentions: Jumblatt's supporters. But the announcement of the new cabinet a fortnight previously had already led to a cease-fire.

## Slide into civil war

The lull lasted barely two months. In July and August the Palestine question raised tensions between the Arab states: Kissinger was once again shuttling between Israel and Egypt. On September 1st they initialled another disengagement agreement, Sinai II. Egypt's bilateral diplomacy weakened the positions of Syria and Jordan, which facilitated a rapprochement between them. Syria tried to pressure the PLO into joint political coordination. The states in the Rejectionist Front, distrusting both Egyptian and Syrian policies, tried to prevent just this. Arafat encouraged the Palestinians to oppose American interests in the Middle East. Both the Palestinians and the Lebanese Christians believed more strongly than ever in their conspiracy theories: the further a solution to the Palestine question receded, the more the former feared liquidation and the latter a Palestinian take-over in Lebanon.

All sides used the lull in fighting to arm themselves for the next round of fighting, which they regarded as unavoidable. The Palestinian organizations made a concentrated effort to mobilize their Lebanese allies. The Christian militias frenetically trained new volunteers — and had many trained in Israel. And Kamal Jumblatt formulated his demands for changes in the Lebanese system more precisely: abolition of political proportionality, changes in the electoral law, reorganization of the army and the naturalization of Kurds and Bedouins living in Lebanon — a programme for a complete change of power.

This programme was unacceptable to most Christian Lebanese. The initial two and a half months of war had shown that they could hardly win an armed struggle against the Palestinians. They were outnumbered approximately three to two, were not as well armed, and had miscalculated about army intervention. Although the fronts around their heartland had held, the Christian islands outside this area had been in dire straits. Jumblatt's demands, and the fact that Muslim politicians did

---

[45] Apart from Camille Chamoun, these were the Shi`i Adel Usayran and the Druze Majid Arslan. The other two members were the Greek Catholic Philippe Takla, son of a former cabinet minister, and the Greek Orthodox Ghassan Tuéni, a liberal publicist.

not contradict them, strengthened Christian suspicions that, besides the Palestinians, the majority of Lebanese Muslims were their opponents as well. These hardened when an explosion in a training base in the Bekaa blew the cover on Amal, the Shi`i militia Imam Musa Sadr had been building up in secret. Christians began openly to consider whether partition of the country might not be preferable to a shift in power in favour of the Palestinians and the Lebanese Muslims. Even if many of Jumblatt's remarks had been intended as tactical, the demand for the abolition of the National Pact system drew as Christian response the threat of partition. A change of power was a civil war concept — since the outbreak of war Jumblatt had been indulging in what amounted to verbal civil war — and partition was another. But the civil war was not to remain verbal.

At the end of August a row in a pin-ball hall in Zahle, which had nothing to do with politics, culminated in fighting between the Christians of the city and Shi`is of the suburbs and neighbouring villages. Palestinian guerrillas came to the aid of the Shi`is. Both sides sustained heavy losses. The strife fanned smouldering social tensions. Christians in Zahle owned large capital-intensive plantations in the central Bekaa. Shi`is and Palestinians destroyed artesian wells and irrigation systems, ruining approximately four-fifths of the irrigation network in a few days. A little later, a similarly banal incident — a traffic argument — led to renewed hostilities between Tripoli and Zghorta. Muslims from Tripoli abducted Maronites from Zghorta, whereupon militiamen from Zghorta abducted Muslims. A youth from Zghorta, whose brother had died in the clashes, stopped a bus on the Beirut-Tripoli motorway and shot dead twelve Muslim passengers in retaliation. Fighting now engulfed the whole of northern Lebanon. Muslims and Palestinian guerrillas attacked Zghorta, supported by artillery. In Tripoli shops and offices belonging to Christians were looted or blown up. Sunnis in Akkar attacked Christian villages, overran the Maronite village of Beit Millat and murdered a large part of its inhabitants. Most of the Christians in Akkar fled to the Christian heartland: the first of the confessionally mixed regions in the country had been violently 'homogenized'. Numerous Christians were driven out of Tripoli as well, including members of the long-settled Greek Orthodox community, which had kept aloof from the fighting.

As the fighting between Tripoli and Zghorta escalated, Karami, who came from Tripoli, and Franjieh, who came from Zghorta, agreed to deploy the army to separate the adversaries.[46] The army succeeded in creating a buffer zone between the two centres. Hardly had the situation quietened in the north when the war in

---

[46] To obtain Karami's consent, Franjieh agreed to replace the army commander General Iskandar Ghanem, a close ally, with the politically uncontentious Colonel Hanna Said.

Beirut re-erupted.[47] This time it was not restricted to the periphery, the camps and the new suburbs. The Kata'ib bombarded the souks in the centre of the old city, completely destroying much of the quarter. This act of war had enormous symbolic significance. This was the quarter in which both Christians and Muslims went about their business; it was the most visible manifestation of those common economic interests that held the communities in Lebanon together. The destruction of this quarter demonstrated the resolve of the Christian militias to subordinate common interests, indeed, even the business interests of their own community, to their own political survival if necessary. They made it clear that they would prefer a scorched earth policy rather than acceptance of demands they interpreted as capitulatory. Mid-September 1975 removed any lingering doubts that the Christian parties and their militias regarded the war as a struggle for survival. Pierre Gemayel declared that the Christians were losing their faith in the Lebanese system of coexistence. The Syrian government was very concerned about the growing acceptance of partition in Christian circles. Partition in a neighbouring country was a dangerous example to a country that resorted to rigorous Arab Jacobinism to paper over cleavages and tensions between its own religious communities. Above all, the Syrian rulers feared that a Christian Smaller Lebanon would automatically ally itself with Israel, and a Palestinian and Muslim rump state would generate a revolutionary dynamism that might draw Syria into a confrontation with Israel at a time the Syrians thought inauspicious. The Syrian Foreign Minister, Khaddam, travelled to Beirut and arranged the creation of a National Dialogue Committee, which included moderate and militant political leaders of both the Muslim and Christian communities.

Thus, a few weeks after the war between the Palestinians and Christian militias had degenerated into a Lebanese civil war, all the crucial, disputed questions of Lebanese coexistence were once again discussed, heatedly but precisely. The various positions were clear, and the opposition to each. Gemayel and Chamoun took the view that it was necessary to end the war before reforms could seriously be discussed. Jumblatt insisted that the fighting could be ended only by fundamentally changing the nature of the state as he demanded. Saeb Salam and Raymond Eddé, who represented moderate, liberal Sunni and Maronite opinion respectively, called for the resignation of President Franjieh, whom they blamed for the country's slide towards war. Salam emphasized that Jumblatt was not entitled to speak for the Muslim communities. Eddé held Gemayel responsible for the murder of innocent Muslims and for 'killing Lebanon'. Gemayel replied that Lebanon had been destroyed by those who had undermined the army. But the crux of the

---

[47] Jumblatt called for a general strike to protest against the deployment of the army. As the trade unions refused to support the call and most Muslim politicians rejected it, Jumblatt eventually called off the strike.

debates in the National Dialogue Committee was the identity of Lebanon and the nature of its political system. The former Prime Minister Yafi called for a constitutional definition of Lebanon as 'an independent Arab country'. The Kata'ib and its allies objected on the ground that as long as Arabism was equated with Islam, Lebanon could not be defined as Arab. This was the quintessential Lebanese question: that of secularism.[48] The Kata'ib agreed to accept the abolition of confessional proportionality, provided that the state was completely secularized, in particular the personal status law, in order to enable complete social integration. Jumblatt and the parties of the Left accepted this. However, the Sunni politicians objected to complete secularization on the ground that it was irreconcilable with Islam. Edmond Rabbath, a professor of constitutional law and representative of the Syrian Catholic minority on the National Dialogue Committee, proposed as a compromise that the acceptance of secularized laws be facultative. But this too was unacceptable to the Muslim representatives. Jumblatt and the Left, who were primarily interested in change in the system and, hence, power, eventually agreed to a purely 'political' secularization, which to the Christians was no secularization. What Jumblatt overlooked was the readiness of Muslim notables like Karami and Salam to accept less than a complete reorganization of the state, that is, a modification of the National Pact to their advantage. This soon became apparent.

The National Dialogue Committee disbanded without tangible results. At the end of October Karami made a desperate attempt to force a compromise. He declared he would remain in the Serail — the official residence of the prime minister — until the dialogue produced results. But within a few days, only one member of the committee was still with him, the Greek Orthodox Minister, Tuéni. In the meantime, renewed fighting had broken out in Zahle and along many fronts in Beirut. For the first time the Mourabitoun played a prominent role, in the city centre. The Palestinian organizations, content with the slide into civil war and with little military interest in the city centre, remained on the sidelines, giving the Mourabitoun more or less discreet logistic support. Heavy fighting between the Mourabitoun and the Kata'ib took place in the hotel district, along the West Beirut sea front and in the confessionally mixed residential area of Kantari.

As the internal Lebanese dialogue came to a fruitless close and shooting resumed in Beirut, regional and international efforts to mediate increased. Saudi Arabian, Kuwaiti and Egyptian efforts to organize a conference on Lebanon in Cairo met with resistance by Syria, the PLO and Franjieh to an 'Arabization' of the Lebanon crisis. Together with the Syrian government, Franjieh and Karami were searching for a compromise which would satisfy the Muslim communities without disaffecting the Christian. The objective of both president and prime

---

[48] See Chapter 2, pp. 135ff.

minister was a limited modification of the National Pact. In this they had the support of international mediators like the Vatican emissary, Cardinal Bertoli, and the French Foreign Minister, Couve de Murville. At the end of November, Franjieh and Karami announced that agreement was imminent. On December 6th, Pierre Gemayel flew to Damascus at the invitation of President Assad to present his views on the possibility of a new National Pact.

There were forces on both sides who disapproved of such a development, and still hoped to achieve their own — conflicting — goals. Neither Muslim nor Christian militia leaders, nor the more militant Palestinian organizations, had much to gain from a compromise between conservative Sunni and Maronite notables, from a 'tribal reconciliation', as Jumblatt put it. The day before Gemayel's departure, Palestinian units in the Druze town of Aley began to bombard the Maronite village of Kahhale. And on the day of his trip the bodies of four young Kata'ib members were discovered in the Metn. In a brutal act of vengeance Christian militias murdered around 200 unarmed Muslims, most of them workers and clerks at the docks. Two days after 'Black Saturday' the Mourabitoun launched an offensive against the Kata'ib positions in the city centre and the hotel district.[49] They drove the Kata'ib back to Martyrs Square in the city centre and overran Kata'ib positions in the Phoenicia and St. Georges hotels. In both East and West Beirut the number of 'identity-card victims' mounted, civilians abducted or murdered solely because of the denomination recorded on their Lebanese identity card.

## Syrian intervention against partition

In December, Christian militias began attacking 'allogeneous pockets of population' in their heartland. They expelled the inhabitants of a Shi`i settlement adjoining Antelyas to the north of Beirut, which had a strong local CP group, as well as a group of Bedouins settled in the hills east of Beirut. At the same time Palestinian guerrillas occupied the Christian village of Taalabaya in the Bekaa and drove out the inhabitants. The Christian militias' use of similar tactics aroused Syrian suspicions that preparations were being made to partition Lebanon and forestall a Syrian compromise formula for Lebanon as a whole. Up to this point the Syrian government had restricted its involvement to armaments for Palestinians and the National Movement. It now decided to intervene directly and despatched units of the Palestinian Liberation Army (PLA) under the command of Syrian officers, that is, regular troops. On December 20th, 3,000 men of the

---

[49] In interviews with the author Palestinian leaders subsequently explained that they had encouraged the Mourabitoun assault to prevent retributive acts against Christian civilians in West Beirut.

Yarmouk Brigade of the PLA crossed the Lebanese frontier and besieged Zahle. Simultaneously, the city was shelled from Syrian positions in the Anti Lebanon Mountains.

However, the Christian militias continued their offensive in Beirut. In early January, they attacked the Palestinian camps Jisr al-Pasha and Tel al-Za`tar. On the order of the Interior Minister, Chamoun, troops of the internal security forces, a garrisoned police force, joined the offensive. In a relief offensive, Palestinian guerrillas from camps in West Beirut attacked the Christian suburb of Hazmiyeh, between Bourj al-Barajneh and Tel al-Za`tar. On January 14th, Christian militiamen occupied the Dbayeh camp; on the 19th, they stormed the slum districts of Maslakh and Karantina. They took no prisoners; hundreds of civilians died in the massacre and the survivors were herded to West Beirut. The Palestinian organizations took their revenge on a number of Christian villages in Akkar and the Bekaa, at the same time appealing to Syria for immediate support. Syria responded.[50] Strong contingents of Saiqa and the PLA supported PLO troops besieging the Christian towns of Jiyeh and Damour. Both fell on January 20th, and four days later Saadiyat, just outside Damour, where Chamoun had his private

---

[50] In a speech broadcast by Radio Damascus on July 20th, 1976 President Assad explained in detail the circumstances of his intervention in Lebanon: 'One day the front of the parties in Lebanon and the front of the Palestinian resistance collapsed. They were unable to stand on their own feet. They sent us cries for help, so we tried and exerted greater efforts. One day — in the middle of January, if I remember correctly — the foreign minister contacted me and said that they had contacted him by phone from the 'Aramun summit. I do not know Beirut well, but as far as I know, 'Aramun is a place which includes the house of the Mufti, where meetings were held by the Mufti, the Imam, prime ministers, other Islamic personalities, and certain party leaders, including Kamal Junblatt. They contacted the foreign minister and pleaded with him to ask me to contact President Suleiman Faranjiyya so that he would stop the fighting, because the situation was very bad. ... Less than fifteen minutes later, he ... said that they had contacted him again to say that their situation was very bad and certain quarters had fallen. The Phalangist gunmen were storming the houses, and everything was falling before them. ... I wondered at such requests, because I knew ... that the resistance and the nationalist parties — and not only the Phalangists and the national liberals — had arms that did not belong to the Lebanese Army. The resistance and the parties had a lot more arms and ammunition than the Phalangists, the national liberals, and the Lebanese Army put together. The Lebanese Army was not in the battle ... Indeed, reports reached us on the fall of al-Maslakh, al-Karantina, and other places. They said then, If you do not make quick contact, the Phalangists will outflank western Beirut. The road is open before them. ...At this point I said, "Poor western sector." ... I contacted President Faranjiyya ... We finally agreed on a cease-fire ... After this, reports came to say that fighting was escalating and that matters were going from bad to worse. I ... began to think of what we could do to save the situation. We exerted political efforts. We gave arms and ammunition ... and yet it was not enough to save the situation. Hence, we had no choice but to intervene directly ... We thus said we must go in to save the resistance. We decided to go in under the name of the PLA ... President Suleiman Faranjiyya contacted me ... He told me that Syrian forces were entering Lebanon ... I told him that our stand toward the Palestinians was consistent and that as far as the Palestinians were concerned, there was a red line that we would absolutely not allow anyone to go beyond'; Rabinovich, *The War for Lebanon*, p. 209ff. For the text of the whole speech, see ibid., pp. 201-236.

residence.[51] The population of Saadiyat, including Chamoun, could be evacuated by helicopter and boat. But the vengeance wreaked on Christians when Damour fell matched that in Karantina.

In early January the Syrian Foreign Minister, Khaddam, had made a remarkable statement: Syria would not accept any partitioning of Lebanon; in this event, Syria would annex Lebanon, in its view historically part of Syria. Syrian intervention under the guise of the PLA forced the leaders of the Christian parties to accept a political regulation under the aegis of Syria. Their militias lifted the siege of Tel al-Za'tar. On February 7th, Franjieh and Karami journeyed to Damascus. Agreement was reached on a document that Franjieh presented as a new National Pact on February 14th, 1976.

The Damascus Agreement[52] reaffirmed the traditional distribution of the offices of state. Beyond this, seats in parliament should be divided equally between Christians and Muslims instead of in a ratio of six to five; the prime minister should be elected by a simple majority of the deputies; the enactment of laws should require the signatures of both the president and the prime minister; proportionality in the civil service should apply only to the highest category; and the law of naturalization should be amended. Concerning the Palestinians, the letter of the Cairo Agreement and the Melkart Protocols were to be respected. All in all, the agreement was tantamount to a redistribution of power between the communities, not a change in power. The Sunnis gained in that the position of the prime minister was enhanced. The existing *de facto* duumvirate was to be constitutionally entrenched, and the premier's election by parliament would make him more independent of the president. The re-apportionment of parliamentary seats was a symbolic expression of equality. The Christians had guarantees against domination in the legislative, the executive and the upper echelons of the civil service. Nor did the agreement affect the army. A further partial success for them was the reaffirmation of the earlier agreements on the Palestinians; in addition, enforcement of these should henceforth be guaranteed by Syria. In synopsis: the agreement represented a tangible gain in power and prestige for the Sunni establishment. Although the Christians had to make concessions, these did not endanger their position as self-determining communities. However, by dint of a brief, indirect intervention, the Syrian government appeared to have managed a compromise which gave it the role of arbiter in Lebanon.

---

[51] Saiqa and PLA troops in the north of the country had simultaneously attacked Zghorta, but been repulsed with heavy losses by the Marada militia and Lebanese soldiers defending the city.

[52] For exerpts in English see Walid Khalidi, *Conflict and Violence in Lebanon: Confrontation in the Middle East* (Cambridge, Mass., 1979), pp. 189–91.

## The PLO and the National Movement against the Lebanese Front

The principal beneficiaries of the compromise were the Muslim politicians who had remained aloof from the war, yet unexpectedly drew advantages from it. One of the parties to the conflict was prepared to live with it: the militant Christians. However, two other groups in the armed conflict felt cheated of their success: the Palestinian organizations and their Lebanese allies in the National Movement. Acceptance of the conditions of the Cairo Agreement and Melkart Protocols would have meant for the Palestinians the loss of much of the freedom of movement they had won since 1973 and especially since the outbreak of war. Fatah suspected that Syria was planning to keep the PLO on a far tighter political rein than it had so far been able to. Rumours spread that Syria intended to replace Arafat as PLO chairman with Zuhair Mohsen, the chairman of Saiqa. The Rejectionist Front, with the Golan disengagement agreement in mind, suspected Syria of further complicity in the American peace plans. The Damascus Agreement was an even greater disappointment for the Lebanese Left. Instead of a secular state, or even 'political secularization', the existing informal denominational distribution of the offices of state was to be entrenched in the constitution. In their eyes this was regression, not progress. Proposals to augment the powers of the premier would benefit those conservative Muslim notables who had already dissociated themselves from all left-wing tendencies in the National Dialogue Committee. To the militias of the National Movement, it seemed that they had fought simply to achieve approximate parity between premier and president and provide a seat in parliament for a few more Muslim *zu`ama'*. Kamal Jumblatt, in particular, was disappointed beyond measure. He had thought the leadership of a new republic was within his grasp, and now appeared to have been put in his place as leader of a small community — with at best the power of one minister among many. Over and above this, as an independent-minded Lebanese patriot he felt it an ignominy that Syria seemed to have practically dictated the new Lebanese formula. He thought it over for ten days, and then rejected the Damascus Agreement.[53]

An opportunity to obstruct the implementation of the agreement soon presented itself: the disintegration of the Lebanese Army. The army had seldom intervened in the fighting up to this point because the prime minister disapproved. Militant Christian leaders had repeatedly called for its deployment — and thereby strengthened the impression that it was a 'Christian army'. It had been employed

---

[53] Jumblatt seems to have hoped for at least a new provision that would have reserved the presidency for members of any Christian denomination and the premiership for members of any Muslim denomination; even if not president, he might then still become prime minister. (Information from a high-ranking PSP official.)

in some difficult missions — to create a buffer zone between Tripoli and Zghorta, to separate the opposing militias fighting in the hotel district, to assist the besieged in Damour — but always with reservations, too late, with too few means and with few clear objectives. Karami and the commander-in-chief, General Said, feared that if the army were to take vigorous action it might split. And now the split was taking place even without such action. In January 1976 a Sunni lieutenant stationed in the south, Ahmed Khatib, mutinied and proclaimed he was founding a Lebanese Arab Army (LAA). A few hundred Muslim recruits declared in his favour. The army command hesitated to act against the mutineers.[54] The Palestinian organizations, still fearful that the army might be employed against them, celebrated Khatib as a hero and gave him financial and logistic support. Yet it took another incident to turn him into a credible force. On March 11th, the commander of the Beirut barracks, Brigadier-General Aziz Ahdab occupied the radio and television station in Beirut, declared himself provisional military governor of Lebanon and called for the resignation of President Franjieh and early elections of a new president by parliament.[55] Franjieh responded immediately; he would not be made a scapegoat for the war and would only leave the presidential palace before completion of his full constitutional term of office in a coffin. A majority of deputies signed a petition for his early resignation. But Chamoun, who had refused to bow to similar pressure in 1958, and Gemayel, after briefly hesitating, and above all President Assad encouraged him to stay in office. It quickly became obvious that Ahdab had acted with little effective military backing. Lieutenant Khatib made it known that he supported Ahdab's demands, but exploited the general confusion surrounding the 'TV coup' to take control of barracks in the Lebanese periphery. Within a few days the LAA had grown to a few thousand men, and had control of the major part of the army's heavy armaments.[56] Christian soldiers in the barracks that went over to Khatib fled to garrisons in the Christian area,[57] or went home. Three days after General Ahdab's attempted coup Lieutenant Khatib and Jumblatt met. Jumblatt saw an opportunity

[54] The Lebanese air force had reported to the armed forces command that Khatib was advancing on Hasbaya-Masnaa with fifteen transporters and two tanks from his garrison in Kaukaba. However, they did not receive any order to act.

[55] A number of observers assumed that Fatah had encouraged Ahdab to stage his coup d'état, or possibly used him as their front-man. Others, including Christian officers of the general staff, deny this categorically, insisting that Ahdab, a member of a respected Tripoli family, was a convinced Chehabist and had acted to halt the disintegration of the army. (Interviews by the author.)

[56] Most heavy armaments were stored in barracks in the periphery which had gone over to Khatib: Tyre (tanks), Nabatiyeh (sappers), Marjayoun (infantry and atrillery), Sidon (infantry, tanks and artillery), Tripoli (tanks and artillery) and Baalbek (artillery and infantry).

[57] Barracks of Fayadiye, Yarze (seat of the general staff) and Sarba near Jounieh as well as the military academy.

## Dance Macabre: 1975–1988

of realizing his goals and radically reorganizing the Lebanese state, notwithstanding the Damascus Agreement. He managed to persuade the PLO leadership to join an alliance for a major offensive against the Christian heartland.[58] The PLO, the Lebanese Arab Army and the militias of the National Movement united to form the 'Joint Forces' under a joint command.

Three months previously the 'Lebanese Front' — the coalition of the Christian parties and militias — had gained the upper hand, thereby precipitating Syria's intervention. In the 'Joint Forces' it now had an opponent superior in both numbers and fire power. The first target of the 'Joint Forces' was the presidential palace at Baabda. The attack was repulsed with difficulty by soldiers of the Fayadiye barracks — only because the Syrian government ordered Saiqa and PLA units to engage PLO and LAA troops advancing on Baabda. However, Palestinians and the Mourabitoun, supported by LAA artillery, quickly overran the remaining Kata'ib positions in the hotel district, including the strategic Holiday Inn. This completed the division of the capital into East and West Beirut along the 'green line', which ran from Ain al-Rummaneh and Chiyah along the Damascus highway through Martyrs Square to the west gate of the harbour, a division that was to endure.

The heavy artillery captured by the Lebanese Arab Army was now used to bombard East Beirut and the presidential palace at Baabda. Franjieh fled to Kafur in the Christian hinterland. In the last week of March a huge offensive of the Joint Forces brought the Lebanese Front to the verge of military collapse. This was largely the work of Fatah troops under the command of Abu Musa — who later rebelled against Arafat. In a thrust into the mountains of the upper Metn they took the villages of Mtein, Tarchiche and Aintoura and advanced towards Bikfaya, Gemayel's home town. This 'Mountain War' caused virtual panic in the Christian heartland. In a dramatic appeal on radio Gemayel urged all able-bodied Christian men and women to defend their homeland. Whether the Christians' situation was quite as desperate as they and their opponents believed is disputed.[59] Once they

---

[58] Opinions were divided within the Fatah leadership. Some military commanders thought a quick military victory would present Syria with a fait accompli, and ensure greater independence for the PLO. Others were sceptical and cautioned against committing Palestinian troops in a struggle unrelated to either Palestine or the camps. The decisive factor seems to have been the consideration that Jumblatt and the LAA would strike anyway, and one could not abandon one's best ally. As one high-ranking PLO leader put it: 'We did Jumblatt a favour' (interview with the author).

[59] The commanders of the Palestinian units in the Metn believed that Arafat's vacillation — his concern over Syria's reaction — had cost them victory. Officers of the Lebanese general staff estimated that it would have needed two divisions each of six brigades to reach Jounieh through terrain defended by knowledgeable locals with anti-tank munition — a strength the attackers lacked. (Interviews by the author.) Kamal Jumblatt has published his view of his role and objectives in this 'Mountain War'. He described himself: 'inspiré par la nécessité de prendre à revers les isolationnistes sur leur propre terrain, dans des combats infiniment moins coûteux que ceux qui étaient engagés à Beyrouth. Connaissant bien l'histoire et al

had recovered from their surprise, Christian units of the army, supported by militiamen, were able to stop the offensive of the Joint Forces. On the crest of the wave Abu Iyad declared that the road to Jerusalem ran through Uyun Al-Siman, Bikfaya and Jounieh, and Kamal Jumblatt talked of inviting people to breakfast in Bikfaya. But President Assad gave Jumblatt an ultimatum, in the form of an invitation, to come to Damascus; the meeting was to alter the course of the conflict in Lebanon.

## Syrian intervention against the PLO and the National Movement

Assad and Jumblatt respected but disliked one another. Both were members of minority groups. But whereas Jumblatt had been born with a silver spoon in his mouth, Assad had worked his way up.[60] Jumblatt had inherited power; Assad had worked for his. Jumblatt played politics with bravura; Assad is the most cautious political actor on the Middle Eastern stage. Jumblatt never concealed his contempt for the petit bourgeois current in the Baath Party; Assad regards himself as the most responsible politician in the Levant. Jumblatt opposed any vassalage for Lebanon and was irritated that Syrian leaders had always assumed 'airs of a wali' (an Ottoman governor), 'just as Egyptians assume those of a pharaoh'; Assad regarded Lebanon, whatever its form, really as a part of Syria.[61]

Assad had saved Jumblatt and his Palestinian allies from defeat in January; but there was a price. Assad explained his position to Jumblatt at length, later repeated it to Arafat and made it public in a remarkable speech on July 20th, 1976.[62] The constitutional document drawn up under his aegis fulfilled practically all of Jumblatt's demands, yet the latter had supported the attempted *coup d'état* and unleashed a new round of fighting. Assad now wanted to know what Jumblatt wanted. Jumblatt told him he wanted a secular state. Assad replied that this was blocked not by the Kata'ib but by the Lebanese Muslims. The crux of the disagreement between the two men was Jumblatt's desire for a decisive military victory over the Maronites; this did not tie in with Assad's plans. While Jumblatt saw an historic opportunity to break the Maronites' political power, Assad saw an historic opportunity to win over the Maronites for Syria, by letting them understand that their salvation no longer lay with France or the West, but with the

---

géographie de mon pays, j'ai moi-même été l'instigateur de cette campagne, qui avait pour but de raccourcir la guerre. Au bout de deux semaines, nos objectifs semblaient sur le point de se réaliser. ... Nous attendions la reddition et la paix à Reyfoun ou à Beit Mery'; *Pour le Liban*, pp. 215f.

[60] On Assad's personality see Pakradouni, *La paix manquée*, pp. 71–4; for biographical details, see Seale, *Asad of Syria*.

[61] Jumblatt, *Pour le Liban*, p. 171.

[62] For an English translation see Rabinovich, *The War for Lebanon*, pp. 210–36.

Arabs.

Jumblatt's long-standing dislike of Maronites verged on hate. 'In earlier times the Maronites were good writers, scholars, historians and poets, at the same time excellent labourers, good businessmen and farmers, and that was it. The mandate put all political power in their hands. That was a gift they did not deserve — as they have shown ... As we Druze say: Maronites make bad rulers, for they have neither a sense of tradition nor of government (the Turks take much the same view).'[63] Jumblatt found even President Chehab 'too Maronite'.[64] He suggested to Assad: 'Let us discipline them. We must have decisive military action. They have been governing us for 140 years, and we want to get rid of them.'[65] Assad commented: 'At this point, I realized that all the masks had fallen. Therefore, the matter was not as we used to say it was and not as we were told. The matter was not between right and left or between a progressive and a reactionary. It was not between a Moslem and a Christian. The matter was one of vengeance, a matter of revenge, which dates back 140 years.'[66]

Jumblatt asked Assad to allow him 'three to four days, a week, at the most two' to force his opponents to capitulate.[67] Assad warned him once again of choosing a path that could serve only the 'conspiracy', that is, Israeli interests. Jumblatt left Damascus under the impression that Syria wanted to maintain equilibrium between the conflicting parties in Lebanon, and Assad was convinced that Jumblatt wanted to continue the war.

Assad was sceptical about the efficacy of 'decisive military action'.[68] He thought a decisive military victory in Lebanon impossible because the issue did not depend solely upon might. It would entail the oppression of a part of the country, and the world would sympathize with the oppressed, and the most likely result would be partition. And partition would create 'a state full of rancour', 'a state more dangerous and more hostile than Israel', but not because its inhabitants would be 'Israelis or aliens'. They would be 'an essential part of our people', and precisely because of this, oppression would make them more hostile than Israel.

The day after Jumblatt's visit Assad received Yassir Arafat and cogently explained the dangers of Palestinian participation in Jumblatt's military undertaking. 'I cannot understand what the connection is between the fighting of Palestinians in the highest mountains of Lebanon and the liberation of Palestine ...

---

[63] Jumblatt, *Pour le Liban*, p. 96.
[64] Interview with the author, 1971.
[65] Quoted from President Assad's radio address, in Rabinovich, *The War for Lebanon*, p. 218.
[66] Ibid., pp. 218–19. According to various sources, President Assad had a tape-recording made of his meeting with Jumblatt and sent a copy to every Arab head of state.
[67] Jumblatt, *Pour le Liban*, p 184.
[68] Assad, as cited in Rabinovich, *The War for Lebanon*, pp. 219ff.

The Palestinian fighting in Jabal Lubnan is definitely not fighting for Palestine. He wants to liberate Jounieh and Tripoli and does not want to liberate Palestine, even if he so claims.'[69] Arafat agreed to withdraw from the fighting. Within Fatah, opinion was split on whether to bow to Syrian pressure or not. Jumblatt insisted on continuing their joint effort. The fighting continued, albeit less fiercely.

The Syrian leadership decided to intervene again in the Lebanon conflict. Their initial intervention had prevented a victory of the Christian parties and militias, or at least a partial victory that might have led to partition. They were not prepared to countenance a victory of the Palestinian-National Movement coalition. Such a victory would raise the spectre of Israeli intervention — or the emergence of a militant politico-military bastion of completely independent Palestinian organizations and Lebanese like Jumblatt, whom the Syrians regarded as a political buccaneer. The latter eventuality would leave Syria sitting precariously between the militant and antagonistic Baath regime in Iraq to the east and an incalculable Lebanon to the west. The efforts of Jumblatt and Arafat to gain Egyptian assistance increased Syrian fears of losing control over events in Lebanon.[70]

Syria's first step was to impose an arms embargo on the Jumblatt–PLO coalition. It then sought assurances from the USA and — through American intermediaries — Israel that they would not oppose another Syrian intervention in Lebanon. An understanding was reached during a Middle East mission of Dean Brown, the American Under-Secretary of State. Israel informed the USA that it would not resist the deployment of Syrian troops, provided that they did not move south of the 'Red Line'. The USSR let Jumblatt and Arafat know that they felt the Syrian desire for a cease-fire was justified. But Jumblatt and Arafat, though less defiant, let the shooting continue. They refused to believe that Syria really did intend to act against them. Later Jumblatt wrote: 'We did not accurately calculate the risk. We counted on Europe, the USA, France, on the Arabs, on the Syrians themselves to stop President Assad taking the salute and sending in his army. We did not believe there was a danger of military intervention, perhaps because we were unaware of the relations then existing between Damascus and Washington and of Washington's pressure on Israel. That was a huge error of judgment!'[71]

Syria did intervene, gradually and cautiously, each step followed by further negotiations. At the beginning of April, regular Syrian troops crossed the

---

[69] Ibid., p. 221.

[70] In March Arafat had already requested Sadat to despatch the Ain Jalloud Brigade of the PLA to Lebanon. The arrival of Saiqa and Syrian-sponsored PLA units had forestalled this.

[71] Jumblatt, *Pour le Liban*, p. 216.

Lebanese border and took up positions in the Bekaa. At the same time, the Syrian government and Lebanese politicians of all colours were negotiating an early presidential election as a solution to the political impasse. On April 9th, the Lebanese parliament amended Article 73 of the Constitution to enable this. While fighting continued in the mountains and Beirut the deputies were trying to agree on candidates. Elias Sarkis, narrowly beaten by Franjieh in 1970, gained the support not only of the old Chehabist alliance, but also of many Christian deputies who had previously voted against him. There was no doubt that he was a Lebanese patriot through and through. He was also regarded as Syria's preferred candidate, since he had the enormous advantage of standing aloof from the warring parties. Jumblatt and his adherents were as strongly against Sarkis now as in 1970. When Jumblatt realized his election could not be prevented he supported Eddé's candidacy. Eddé stood 'on principle'. In 1958 he had stood against Chehab because he disapproved on principle of military men in politics. His 1976 candidacy was a protest against electoral manipulation from abroad, and his prospects were just as futile. Thus, the exponent of liberal Lebanon became the candidate of the Left — and lost. On May 8th, Elias Sarkis was elected president with an overwhelming majority.[72]

This election was a political defeat for the National Movement. To the Palestinian organizations it symbolized the potential restoration of the Lebanese state, which, this time with Syrian backing, might again try to restrict their freedom of movement. The allies still hoped to retain the power they had gained over the larger part of Lebanese territory by force of arms. On the other hand, the Lebanese Front had quickly recovered from the shock of the offensive in the upper Metn and started a counter-offensive in which it had already taken several villages previously held by the National Movement. Heavy artillery duels continued along the Beirut fronts. Franjieh declared that in view of the situation in the country he would not consider resigning before the end of his term of office.

Since Jumblatt's meeting with Assad, relations between the Syrian government and the National Movement had been strained. Tensions now arose between Syria and the Palestinians. Arafat sought support from other Arab states. Libya sent its Prime Minister, Jalloud, to Damascus to mediate, but in vain. Egypt warned Syria against further interference in Lebanon. For very different reasons, the states of

---

[72] Sarkis received the votes of 66 of the 69 deputies present. While the PLO and the National Movement tried to prevent a quorum, Saiqa and the PLA guarded the Mansour Palace, the provisional seat of parliament for the election, and provided escorts for deputies who came out for Sarkis. After his election, Sarkis was almost captured by a Mourabitoun commando in the Carlton Hotel, his residence since 1975. He was saved by Saiqa, who secured the hotel after several hours of fighting. Deputy Suleiman Ali from Syrian-occupied Akkar, who had initially come out in favour of Eddé, declared he would be voting for Sarkis 'sur la demande de nos amis syriens'.

the Rejectionist Front and Egypt wanted to curb Syria's influence on the PLO. Arafat went to Libya to drum up support.[73] The USSR had close relations with both Syria and the PLO, and was interested in averting a confrontation between its two main allies in the Middle East. On June 1st, Prime Minister Kosygin visited Damascus.

On the same day the Syrian government despatched further troops as well as tank units to Lebanon. This time they did not halt in the Bekaa but advanced on Tripoli from the north, on Sidon through Jezzine and along the Damascus–Beirut highway in Central Lebanon. In Akkar and the Bekaa they lifted the sieges of Christian villages that had appealed for Syrian help.[74] In the Bekaa they clashed with troops of the PLO and the National Movement, which responded by turning on Saiqa and PLA units in Beirut: the Syrian–Palestinian war began as an internal Palestinian conflict. Some PLA troops joined their attackers, the others were decimated. Saiqa suffered heavy losses.[75] Fatah stormed the bases of the pro-Syrian Baath and Syrian-sponsored groups in the National Movement; soldiers of Syrian anti-aircraft batteries stationed in the Palestinian camps were taken captive. Within a few hours Beirut had been cleaned of pro-Syrian fighting units. Libyan and Algerian mediation secured the release of their leaders.

In response, Syria raised its troop strength in Lebanon to 12,000 men. On June 7th, Syrian troops reached the summer resort of Sofar on the Beirut highway and Sidon in the south. But when Syrian armoured reconnaissance cars entered the city, Palestinians and soldiers of the LAA inflicted heavy casualties and forced them to withdraw.[76] The Syrian Army retaliated with lengthy bombardments of Palestinian camps in Sidon, West Beirut and Tripoli.[77] The eruption of the Syrian–Palestinian confrontation roused the Arab world far more than earlier phases of the war. Iraq concentrated troops on the Syrian border.[78] The Libyan

---

[73] Syria refused to let him enter its territory. As Beirut airport was closed after Christian army units opened fire to prevent the Palestinians from receiving supplies by air, he had to find another way of leaving Lebanon.

[74] The Syrian government used these acts to legitimize their intervention. In some cases telegrams ostensibly arrived from villages that did not have a telegraph office. The villages of Kobayat and Andakat had been attacked by troops of the Lebanese Arab Army — Palestinian sources claim at Syrian instigation. On Syrian intervention, see also Khalidi, *Conflict and Violence*, pp. 58ff.

[75] The head of Saiqa, Zuhair Mohsen, first fled to East Beirut and thence to the Syrian troops. He was murdered by unknown assailants in Cannes in 1979.

[76] One of the Syrians who fell was a nephew of President Assad. His body was dismembered and the pieces sent to his family in Latakia.

[77] At Syrian insistence planes from the Lebanese air force base at Rayak in the Bekaa flew sorties against PLO troops on the Beirut–Damascus highway.

[78] Iraqi volunteers were fighting on the Palestinian side in the ranks of the Arab Liberation Front. Iraq closed the oil pipeline of the Iraq Petroleum Company, which ran across Syria, depriving Syria of considerable revenue.

*Dance Macabre: 1975–1988* 221

## Beirut: fighting, 1975/76

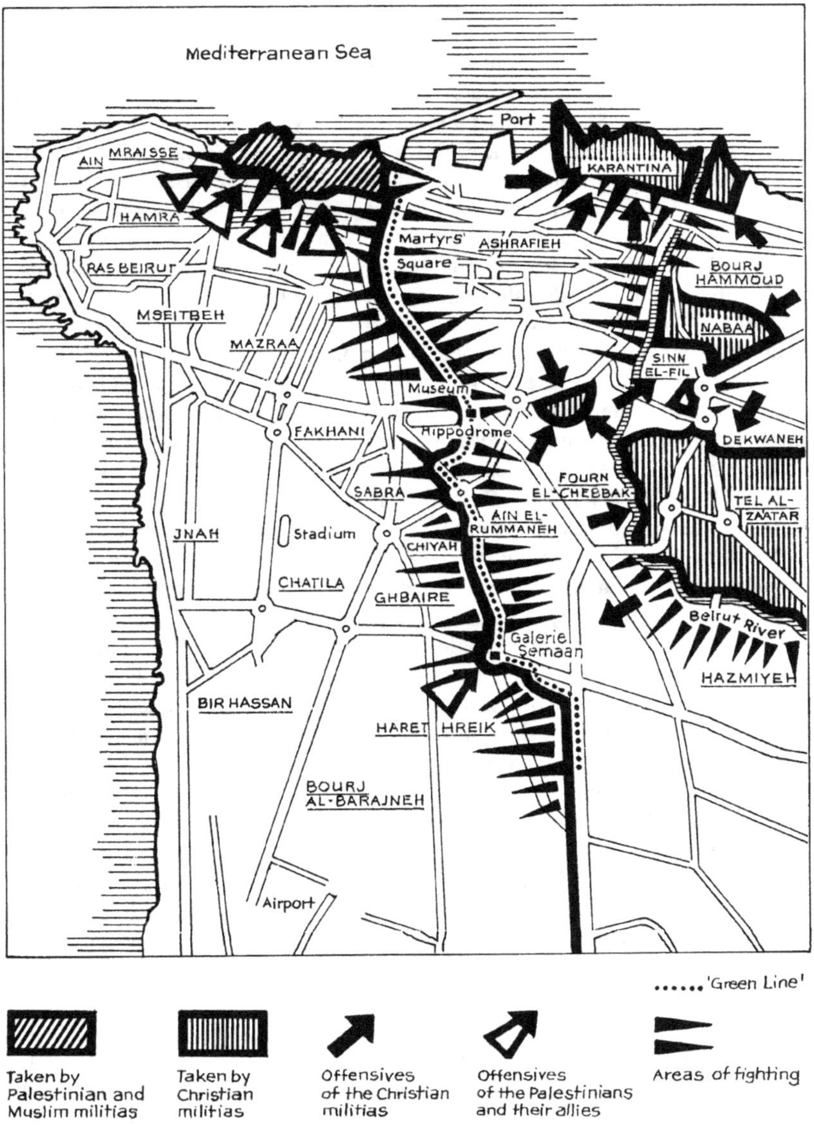

 Taken by Palestinian and Muslim militias

 Taken by Christian militias

 Offensives of the Christian militias

 Offensives of the Palestinians and their allies

 'Green Line'

 Areas of fighting

premier tried to mediate in Beirut. The foreign ministers of the Arab League conferred in Cairo. They called for a cease-fire and decided to despatch an Arab peace force to Lebanon: 2,000 Sudanese arrived soon after, followed by a Libyan contingent.

Militias of the Lebanese Front and Christian units of the Lebanese Army chose this moment to launch a fierce attack on the Palestinian camps on the eastern outskirts of Beirut. Six months previously the Syrian Army had intervened to counter precisely this. This time it did nothing: for the Syrian Army the attack represented very welcome pressure on the PLO. The assault was led by Chamoun's 'Tiger militia' and regular troops. The Kata'ib hesitated initially, joining in only later. Units of the Lebanese Army bore the brunt of the fighting. After its disintegration it had been reconstructed, and this was its first action. On the evening of the first day the Palestinian positions on the Tel al-Mirr, a hill overlooking Tel al-Za`tar, were taken. Eight days later, on July 1st, troops of the Lebanese Front stormed the Jisr al-Pasha camp.

In keeping with their earlier practice, the Palestinians sought to relieve pressure on their camps by attacking Christian 'pockets' elsewhere. However, this time their choice was limited. Syrian troops were stationed in Akkar, the Bekaa and Jezzine; enclaves in Palestinian-controlled areas had been eradicated in January. Their choice fell on Deir al-Qamar in the Chouf. However, Jumblatt refused to allow them to operate in this region. He had never wanted any Palestinian presence in 'his' region; up to now it had not been touched by the war and he wished to keep it that way. Hence, the Palestinians carried out their diversionary attack in the north. They advanced south from Tripoli into the Koura region where the SSNP had some strongholds and could assist them. They took the coastal town of Chekka, with the by now usual attendant circumstances of looting, burning and massacres. The Lebanese Front immediately launched a counter-offensive, once again with the support of Christian troops of the regular army, including tanks.[79] They advanced to the outskirts of Tripoli. The Palestinians in the city and camps were now surrounded by Syrian troops to the north and those of the Lebanese Front to the east and south.

At about this time the Syrian Army shifted its pressure on the PLO. It withdrew from the vicinity of Sidon into the mountains around Jezzine. But it simultaneously cut all lines of communication between the Palestinian guerrillas in the upper Metn and Beirut. Here too they were now caught between the Syrians and the Lebanese Front.

---

[79] The Palestinians blamed their defeat at Chekka on Kamal Jumblatt, because he had deprived them of certain victory over the lightly defended Deir al-Qamar. From this point onwards relations between Jumblatt and the PLO gradually deteriorated.

In the light of this deterioration in their military position the PLO leadership agreed to negotiate with the Syrians through Libyan mediation. The parties agreed to a cease-fire, 'non-interference' in Lebanese affairs, observance of the Cairo Agreement and recognition of the role Syria was playing 'in defence of the Palestinian cause'. What Fatah regarded as an unavoidable concession was unacceptable to the Palestinian organizations in the Rejectionist Front and to the National Movement. On the other hand, the Lebanese Front, in turn, was uneasy about what seemed to be a new rapprochement between the Syrians and the Palestinians. They tightened their military grip on the remaining Palestinian positions in East Beirut. On August 6th, they occupied the Shi`i-Palestinian district of Nabaa; prior to this Imam Musa Sadr had negotiated the evacuation of the Shi`i population of Nabaa. This left Tel al-Za`tar as the last Palestinian bastion in East Beirut. Here the organizations in the Rejectionist Front were particularly strong. Since the start of the siege they had tried desperately to breach the ring from West Beirut. They repeatedly launched attacks from Bourj al-Barajneh and Chiyah two and a half kilometres away, in the hope of advancing east of Ain al-Rummaneh through the area known as 'Galerie Semaan', after a local furniture factory. Libyan and Iraqi soldiers supported them. Their opponents were cadets of the Lebanese Military Academy and militiamen of the Tanzim and the Kata'ib. All Palestinian efforts were in vain.[80] After a siege lasting fifty-three days, heavy bombardments, advances by the besiegers and sallies by the besieged, Tel al-Za`tar fell. After Karantina, Damour, and Chekka — and many 'small' massacres of 'pockets of population' — Tel al-Za`tar was another appalling massacre. The PLO leadership had a superb press and information service. It provided publicity worldwide on the struggle for Tel al-Za`tar, turning it into a symbol of Palestinian resistance. Apart from the camp and its military significance to the PLO, the publicity of its defence was also an attempt to gain the support of Arab and other states as a counterweight to Syrian pressure. The Arab as well as the international general public was incensed. But no one came to the aid of the Palestinians.

The Christian Lebanese Front was triumphant. In March they had been facing possible collapse. Now victory no longer seemed impossible. They were the undisputed rulers of an area from the mountains of Zghorta and the outskirts of Tripoli in the north to the green line in the south; and the ring of camps around East Beirut had been broken. While some of their leaders began to contemplate the 'complete liberation' of the country, Kamal Jumblatt, further than ever from his goals, declared that the only remaining option was an out and out fight with Syria. The PLO leadership was far more realistic and would have none of that. They

---

[80] The Palestinians refused to allow the Red Cross to evacuate the civilian population of the camp, agreeing only to the removal of the wounded.

tried to gain time through negotiations, but were not prepared to bow to Syrian pressure. They still held strong positions in Sidon, Tripoli, West Beirut and the mountains east of Beirut and saw little reason to capitulate. Syria had learnt in Sidon that it could be a costly exercise for regular troops to take a city defended by guerrillas prepared to go to any lengths. Hence it suited the Syrian leadership very well that the Lebanese Front had inflicted a few defeats on the Palestinians at no cost to the Syrians.

Only after the fall of Tel al-Za`tar, when the Palestinians still refused to accept Syrian domination and shooting between the two halves of Beirut continued without pause, did the Syrian Army start to move again. It increased pressure on the Palestinians encircled in the upper Metn and gradually advanced along the Beirut–Damascus highway.

On September 23rd, Franjieh's term of office expired and Elias Sarkis became President.[81] Because of fighting in Beirut, his inauguration took place in Chtaura in the Syrian-controlled Bekaa. He had previously cleared his message to the Lebanese nation[82] with the governments in Damascus and Cairo. He wished to reach a compromise between all parties: there would be no partition of the country; Lebanon would support the Palestinian cause, but the PLO had to respect the Cairo Agreement; and he would tackle both constitutional and social reform. Above all, he did what Franjieh and his government had always avoided doing: he stated that the Syrian Army was in the country at Lebanon's invitation. To Assad the Arab cause was legitimation enough to march in; now his action had the seal of Lebanese approval.

The guns were silent for three days; Sarkis' accession to office seemed to have the psychological effect many Lebanese had hoped for — in vain — at the time of his election four months previously. But it did not last long. Three days later Palestinian guerrillas of an Iraqi-sponsored organization attacked the Semiramis Hotel in Damascus and held a number of people hostage. Syrian security troops stormed the hotel and hanged the surviving Palestinians in public. Two days after this the Syrian Army in Lebanon moved. The last Palestinians and militiamen of the National Movement in the upper Metn were driven out. Troops of the Lebanese Front tried in turn to cross the Damascus highway to take the town of Aley. To their surprise, artillery of the Syrian Army prevented them from doing so. The Syrian leadership had obviously come to the conclusion that the Christian forces had gained enough terrain in the summer; further gains would upset the

---

[81] For an instructive account of Sarkis' presidency by a 'partial observer' see Pakradouni, *La paix manquée*. Pakradouni was the president's political adviser.

[82] For exerpts in English see Khalidi, *Conflict and Violence*, pp. 193–5.

delicate internal Lebanese balance they hoped to maintain.[83] The Syrian Army would take care of any outstanding matters. On October 13th, they took the town of Bhamdoun in the mountains above Beirut against strong Palestinian resistance and simultaneously advanced again on Sidon. The PLO could hardly have doubted Syria's determination this time. However, the Syrian Army had suffered considerable casualties in taking Bhamdoun, and although it was clear that they could eventually defeat the PLO forces, the cost would be enormous. Thus, when on October 15th the Saudi government[84] invited the heads of state of Syria, Egypt and Lebanon as well as the PLO leader Arafat to attend a summit conference in Riyadh, even Syria accepted. On October 16th, a new cease-fire came into effect. The Syrian–Palestinian war was over.

On October 18th, the summit conference of Riyadh took a number of decisions. An Arab peace force of 30,000 men, the Arab Deterrent Forces, under the authority of President Sarkis, was created to re-establish and maintain peace and order in Lebanon.[85] The Syrian troops in Lebanon would henceforth be a contingent of the Arab Deterrent Forces, and by far the largest.[86] The Palestinians would withdraw to the areas accorded them by the Cairo Agreement of 1969. They, and all other belligerent parties in Lebanon, would hand over their heavy armaments to the Arab Deterrent Forces. On October 25th, the decisions of the Riyadh conference were accepted at a summit conference of the whole Arab League in Cairo; only Iraq and Libya dissented.

Syria could be satisfied. It had successively deprived both war coalitions of victory by intervening in support first one and then the other. The second intervention had involved some sacrifice. But by leaving the burden of the heavy fighting to the Lebanese Front, and by advancing slowly and cautiously — 'no blitzkrieg, just the slow progress of a steam-roller; few direct clashes, just heavy bombardments'[87] — the Syrian Army had been able to limit its own losses. Syria had foregone a total military victory. But its contingent in the Arab Deterrent

---

[83] Another reason was the massacre of numerous Druze inhabitants of the mountain village of Salima when Christian militiamen retook it, to avenge the earlier expulsion of its Christian inhabitants.

[84] The Saudi government had suspended its financial aid to Syria. This loss of income and the cost of the intervention in Lebanon forced Syria to cut its 1976 budget by a third. After the cease-fire and the Riyadh conference Saudi Arabia resumed payments. 'Thus it was the Saudis who were responsible for ending the civil war'; Adeed I. Dawisha, 'The impact of external actors on Syria's intervention in Lebanon', *Journal of South Asian and Middle Eastern Studies*, 2/1 (1978), p. 40.

[85] On the Riyadh conference, Pakradouni, La paix manquée, pp. 45ff. See also Walter Bödigheimer, 'Die arabischen Gipfelkonferenzen von Riad und Kairo. Ein Versuch zur Lösung der Libanonkrise', *Europa-Archiv*, 32/2 (1977), pp. D48–D54.

[86] 25,000 men; other contingents from the United Arab Emirates, Saudi Arabia, North Yemen and Sudan together numbered 5,000 men.

[87] Réne Chamussy, *Chronique d'une guerre. Liban 1975–1977. En postface: les doutes de l'après-guerre II* (Paris, 1978), p. 185.

Forces was the strongest military power in the country. Its military presence in the country had been legally recognized by the Lebanese government, approved by the Arab League, and would be financed by the Arab oil-states.[88] The Palestinians had little choice but to accept Syrian predominance in Lebanon. They had lost some of their best fortified strongholds, and been forced back to the political and military status quo ante of 1973. For a while the dream of a Lebanese government in power largely through their goodwill had seemed about to come true; they had had a rude awakening. But they had retained their hard-won legal status of 1969; it had been reaffirmed, and this time guaranteed by the Arab states. They had suffered considerable losses, but their military power had not been broken. The Lebanese state had been given a reprieve. Sarkis did not have his own army, but did have nominal command of an Arab military force. The two losers of Riyadh were the National Movement and the Lebanese Front, the two civil war coalitions. They had to accept — the Lebanese Front with great reluctance — the stationing of the Arab Deterrent Forces in areas they had controlled. On November 14th, 1976, about 6,000 Syrian troops wearing the green helmets of the peace forces entered both halves of Beirut without a shot being fired.

## The south: Palestinians against Christian Lebanese

Asked why he stood for the presidency in 1976, Elias Sarkis answered: 'I believed the war was drawing to a close and we could start rebuilding the country. I did not feel I was unequal to the task. What I neither knew nor suspected was that the war was just beginning.'[89] Sarkis set to work with guarded optimism. The Arab troops had been deployed without incident. A cabinet of non-political technocrats under Selim al-Hoss, a professor of economics, began to draw up plans for the recovery of the country. Officers who had remained largely aloof from the civil war coalitions formed the core of a new army.

The hopeful beginnings applied only to the country north of the 'red line'. Israel would not permit any Arab troops, let alone Syrian, to be stationed south of it.[90] Here the war had never ended, and gradually escalated after hostilities ceased in other parts of the country. In 1975 and 1976 events in the south had taken much the same turn as in other areas of the Lebanese periphery. There had been intermittent tension between the inhabitants of the few Christian villages and the Shi`i majority; occasionally 'Christian pockets' had been hard-pressed by Palestinian guerrillas. Israel had introduced its policy of the 'good fence': southern Lebanese might enter Israel for medical treatment and shopping, and a limited

---

[88] At the cost of approximately $180 million per annum.
[89] Interview with the author, 1981.
[90] Yigal Allon in an interview with the author, 1980.

number found employment in Israeli border villages at harvest time. The situation became more tense in the spring of 1976. After the Lebanese Army split, the Lebanese Arab Army took control of the garrison in Marjayoun, the most important centre in the border area. A relatively large number of Christian soldiers from border villages in the south and in Akkar decided to go home. The Lebanese general staff assigned a major from Marjayoun, Saad Haddad, the task of regrouping these soldiers into a unit loyal to the army command. Haddad was a suitable choice for this task: he was a Greek Catholic and local southern patriot with a large family in Marjayoun. But he was essentially a simple person and utterly apolitical — a 'soldat perdu' (*Le Monde*) in the complicated political situation in which he was to find himself. He disliked the Palestinians who had brought disruption and war to his homeland, and had already fought against them in 1969 and 1973. Given the choice of being caught in the Israeli–Palestinian crossfire or of facing only one enemy he opted for the latter, both out of conviction and on orders: he should defend the south where possible against the Palestinians. He had nothing against the southern Lebanese Shi`is, provided that they did not support the Palestinians. Many of them shared his concept of the enemy, organized themselves into village militias and collaborated with him. As supplies from Beirut could not reach Haddad's troops and their ammunition was running low, after much hesitancy he accepted Israeli assistance, at first discreetly and then openly. As long as war was raging throughout the country, events in the extreme south attracted little attention. That changed in November 1976. Before the Arab Deterrent Force entered Beirut and Sidon, the PLO command moved considerable numbers of Palestinian guerrillas to areas south of the 'red line'. As the decisions of the Riyadh conference obliged the peace troops to confiscate the heavy weaponry of all warring parties, the Palestinians took the major part of theirs into the south with them. The 'Mesopotamia' of Lebanon, the area between the Litani and Zahrani Rivers, was soon bristling with arms. Since Syria prevented them from extending the territory under their control, the militias of the Lebanese Front, thirsting for action after their summer successes, had been kicking their heels. They, too, decided to send units into the border strip controlled by Haddad. Soon the Palestinians and the Lebanese Front had resumed in miniature the war which Syria had stopped in the north. On October 8th, Haddad's troops and their new reinforcements took Marjayoun. The Palestinians and their Lebanese allies avenged this by destroying the isolated Christian village of Aichieh.

Haddad was unhappy with the behaviour of the militiamen who had come to his assistance. He was prepared to fight the Palestinians. But the militiamen from the north did not distinguish war from civil war: they harassed the local Shi`i population Haddad was trying to win over to his cause. He eventually managed to get them withdrawn to Beirut.

The 'red line' had originally been conceived of and instituted by American diplomacy to avoid a confrontation between Syria and Israel.[91] But it had the unforeseen effect of perpetuating a lower-key war between the Palestinians and the Christian Lebanese. Over and above this, it opened the prospect of a confrontation between the Palestinians and Israel. The Palestinians were not unhappy with this development. The south became an extension of 'Fatahland', from which they could continue their military actions and keep themselves in the world's eye. Israel preferred to deal with guerrillas along its borders rather than the Syrian Army. Haddad and the Christian population opted for an alliance with the stronger forces: Israel's.

## Israeli invasion of southern Lebanon

The year 1977 brought with it hopes of peace not only in Lebanon, despite the situation in the south, but in the whole of the Middle East. After President Carter had taken office, the USA renewed its interest in some form of regulation for the Palestine conflict. In February 1977 an American president admitted for the first time the necessity of a 'homeland' for the Palestinian refugees 'after years and years of suffering'. The secretary of state, Vance, visited the region twice. He obtained Israeli agreement to negotiations with an Arab delegation including representatives of the Palestinians. Hence, the PLO had good reason to moderate their stance. In July President Sarkis and Arafat reached agreement on more precise definitions of provisions of the Cairo Agreement. The PLO promised not to take up positions within a ten kilometre wide strip along the Israeli border and, above all, to desist from raids and artillery fire across it.

On October 1st, the USA and the USSR published a joint declaration that appeared to open the way to a comprehensive peace agreement. Normal peaceful relations should be established between all the states involved and the rights of the Palestinian people should be recognized and taken into account. A new Geneva Conference seemed imminent. However, on November 9th, President Sadat presented his alternative peace initiative,[92] which immediately exposed all the Arab rifts over the Palestine question. He declared he was prepared to go to Jerusalem to open bilateral negotiations with Israel. The Israeli government promptly issued an invitation. On November 19th, Sadat arrived in Jerusalem and

---

[91] The 'red line' was not precisely defined. When Syrian troops entered Nabatiyeh in January 1977, Israel protested. The Syrians withdrew, with the consequence that Nabatiyeh became an important Palestinian stronghold. See Pakradouni, La paix manquée, pp. 113–15.

[92] The first confidential contacts had taken place in August through the mediation of the Roumanian government. Both Begin and Sadat visited Ceaucescu, and there had been meetings between high-ranking Israeli and Egyptian officials.

addressed the Knesset. This was the beginning of the bilateral rapprochement between Israel and Egypt. Sinai II had prepared the groundwork, and it was to culminate in a separate peace treaty between these two countries. Sadat himself not only preferred a bilateral solution, but assumed he would find one that the Palestinians could also accept. The Israelis, on the other hand, grasped the prospects Sadat's initiative offered of neutralizing the strongest state in the Arab front against Israel, at no cost in the Palestine question. In the summer of 1977 Begin had won the Israeli elections and become Prime Minister. Even before negotiations started he made his stance clear. In December he declared there was no question of refugees in the neighbouring countries returning. The subsequent development was inevitable: peace for Egypt implied war for Lebanon.

It was finally clear to Syria that it could no longer count on Egypt. The threat of war had been the most effective means of pressuring Israel into making concessions on the Palestinian question. Without Egypt war with Israel was not a serious prospect. Syria's only option was to demonstrate that without Syria there could be no lasting peace. And for this Syria needed the PLO. The Palestinians in exile realized that a Israeli–Egyptian peace treaty would disregard their interests. Once again, it appeared that operations against Israel from Lebanese territory were the only means they had of demonstrating that peace over their heads had its price. Finally, Israel had two strings to its bow. The one shot was a serious attempt to make peace with Egypt, and the other was an equally serious attempt to smash the PLO — peace to the south and war to the north.

Syria and the PLO, bitter enemies just a year before, found a rapprochement in their mutual interests. Each deeply mistrusted the other. Syria's interest lay in restricting the Palestinians' scope for action: it did not wish to be drawn into a war with Israel which it could not win. But it also had an interest in a low-key war between Palestinians and Israelis on the Lebanese border to demonstrate the dubiousness of bilateral peace agreements. The PLO, in turn, wanted to avoid being treated as a Syrian lackey; it needed to prove itself as an independent force to be reckoned with. In the light of these regional developments, the agreement Sarkis and Arafat had concluded in the summer was obsolete by the autumn. Syria no longer had any interest either in disarming the Palestinians or in preventing war in the south — for which the 'red line' afforded them a suitable excuse.

Incidents on the border mounted. The new Israeli government was determined to retaliate more harshly than the previous one. On March 14th, 1978, a Palestinian commando hijacked a bus on the motorway near Haifa. By the time Israeli soldiers overpowered them, thirty-four passengers had been murdered and several more injured. The reprisal three days later took the form of a military invasion:[93]

---

[93] See Khalidi, *Conflict and Violence*, pp. 123ff.

Israeli troops occupied the whole of southern Lebanon up to Litani River. For the first time Israel and the Palestinians were involved in regular warfare.

The intention obviously was to drive Palestinian troops out of southern Lebanon rather than to smash the PLO. All the regular tactical features of Israeli warfare were missing: pincer movements, paratroopers behind enemy lines and rapid advances. 'Operation Litani' opened with systematic bombardments, before Israeli troops advanced northwards along a broad front, skirting only the Palestinian camp near Tyre. The Palestinian troops were inferior in numbers and equipment, but despite many casualties they were able to withdraw in fairly good order. Large numbers of Palestinian and Lebanese civilians — estimates run to a quarter of a million people — fled with them. At the end of the operation the Israelis had occupied about one-tenth of Lebanon's territory.

On June 19th, the Security Council of the United Nations passed Resolution 425. Israel was called upon to withdraw from Lebanon; a United Nations Interim Force for Southern Lebanon (UNIFIL) was created and despatched.[94] Israel accepted these conditions and withdrew in stages. However, on June 12th, it presented both the United Nations and the Lebanese government with a fait accompli: a ten kilometre wide strip along the border was not handed over to UNIFIL units but to troops under the command of Major Haddad instead. He resisted attempts to station UNIFIL troops in this strip.

The results of the first Israeli–Palestinian war were not conclusive. The Palestinians' experience was reminiscent of the Battle of Karameh. They had at least delayed the Israeli advance before they had been defeated, but not destroyed. They retreated across the Litani, where they regrouped. Israel had acquired a double buffer zone along its border: first Major Haddad's small army and then UNIFIL forces. These zones may have rendered Palestinian operations more difficult, but by no means impossible. The UNIFIL units were neither willing nor appropriately armed to prevent infiltration.[95] PLO fighters soon learnt to skirt round their positions. Haddad's soldiers were more effective: as the Palestinians equated them with the Israeli enemy, they were fighting for their lives. Haddad was more dependent on Israel than ever before. In the ensuing skirmishing his soldiers were

---

[94] Initially UNIFIL comprised contingents of Canadian, French, Iranian, Norwegian and Swedish troops. They were later joined by contingents from Nepal, Senegal, Nigeria, Fiji, Ireland and the Netherlands.

[95] Initially the French UNIFIL unit saw their role in an active light. After sustaining heavy casualties in clashes with Palestinians — the French commanding officer was seriously injured — they became far more circumspect. The most active and reliable units — in terms of their assignment — were those from states least involved in the Middle Eastern conflict: the Nepalese and Fijian. The Lebanese experience of the Fijian contingent was to have an unexpected spill-over effect. In 1987 its commander, Colonel Rabuka, carried out a coup d'état in his own country to preserve the position of the autochthonous Melanesians against the growing power of the immigrant Indian population.

cannon-fodder for their powerful ally.

## Syria and the Lebanese Front in conflict

Since late 1976 the pax Syriana had held sway north of the 'red line'. Its nature had always been that of a tense, imposed cease-fire rather than proper peace. Kamal Jumblatt used every opportunity — in word and writing, at home and abroad — to attack what he regarded as Syrian occupation. On March 17th, 1977, he was assassinated by unknown assailants not far from a Syrian control-post near his home in the Chouf.[96] Most Lebanese politicians, especially Muslims, interpreted this killing as a warning not to take an open stand against the Syrian position. Jumblatt's vehement opponents in the Christian Front were also horrified. Much as they opposed Jumblatt's ambitions, they nevertheless regarded him as a Lebanese patriot, and perceived his death as a blow to Lebanese independence.[97]

The leaders of the Lebanese Front were soon disillusioned with the alliance with Syria. With great reluctance they had accepted the stationing of Syrian troops in East Beirut. Bashir Gemayel, commander of the Kata'ib militias since the fight for Tel al-Za`tar, was restrained with difficulty from resisting the Syrian entry with force. In the eyes of many Christians, the consequences of the Syrian presence appeared with hindsight to justify Bashir's reservations. Civilian populations soon find any occupation, even the most peaceful, a burden. But the political implications were more serious. Syrian control points were decorated with pictures of President Assad, Syrian flags and posters with slogans of the Baath Party. Had the Christians resisted Palestinian control simply to come under the Syrian yoke? The Syrians had the al-Hoss government introduce press censorship. Was this the beginning of the end of civil liberties in Lebanon? Might the Syrians, welcomed as saviours against the Palestinians, not constitute a greater threat to Lebanese sovereignty?

Moreover, the question of the Palestinians in Lebanon had not been settled at all. At the Riyadh conference Sarkis had reiterated Lebanese acceptance of the Cairo Agreement. However, in May 1977, the leaders of the Lebanese Front demanded that this agreement be declared void. They went further: the 200,000

---

[96] In retribution, between 130 and 180 Christians were murdered in a number of Chouf villages. Kamal's son Walid tried to prevent the murders as 'the Christians didn't murder my father'. Partly in explanation and partly in excuse, he added: 'Still, Kamal Jumblatt is not murdered every day.' Interview with the author, 1979.

[97] Another leading Lebanese politician who had vehemently condemned the 'Syrian mandate over Lebanon' chose to go into exile in Paris in 1977: Raymond Eddé. In 1976 he had narrowly escaped a number of attempts on his life, one ascribed to the Kata'ib, the others to Saiqa.

Palestinian civilians who had entered the country illegally should be distributed among the other Arab countries. Only when this had been accomplished could there be serious talks on internal Lebanese reconciliation.

These demands were unacceptable to the Syrian government. It was one thing to subordinate the PLO politically, it was quite another thing to deprive it of all power in Lebanon. Sadat's journey to Jerusalem ruined the prospects of a comprehensive peace settlement in the Middle East. Consequently, Syria saw in the PLO a potential ally. It was not going to let the Lebanese Front thwart a rapprochement.

Faced with Syria's unreliability, the Lebanese Front itself began to seek new allies. The traditional hopes Christian Lebanese placed in western European countries or the USA had been dashed during the first two years of war. Karl Marx's question of 1860 — 'Has Europe abandoned its brothers in faith?'[98] — had to be answered a century later with a resounding 'Yes', difficult though it was for Lebanese Christians to accept that 'Christian Europe' no longer existed. But there was a Jewish Israel, from whom understanding for other non-Muslim minorities in the Levant could be expected. It had an interest in cultivating the enemies of its enemies, as military aid in the form of armaments and training had demonstrated since the outbreak of war. However, both sides had considerable reservations about an alliance. Among the Christians, Franjieh would not hear of it. Pierre Gemayel was extremely sceptical: in his opinion the roots of Lebanon's misery lay in the creation of Israel and the subsequent expulsion of the Palestinians. He foresaw a rupture with the entire Arab world, and believed that only the aversion of greater peril could justify a 'pact with the devil'. By contrast, Bashir Gemayel, his son, and Camille Chamoun were soon convinced that a confrontation with Syria was inevitable and saw in Israel their only possible ally.

That sections of the Lebanese Front should turn to Israel was by no means dictated solely by opportunism. The Front's think-tank, the research centre at the University of the Holy Spirit in Kaslik, was coming up with radical solutions to fundamental questions on the future of the Christian communities in Lebanon.[99] The National Pact of 1943 was a tragi-comedy.[100] Lebanon, an association of communities, had caught the 'virus of mistrust'; in such a case the best solution was to disband the association.[101] If a limb is gangrenous, amputation is the only solution.[102] The only feasible solution was the Mount Lebanon formula — independent, neutral and guaranteed by the superpowers — or at best a confed-

---

[98] Karl Marx and Friedrich Engels, *Werke*, vol 15, p. 148.
[99] Fouad Ephrem Boustany, *Le problème du Liban*, 2nd edn (Kaslik, 1978).
[100] Ibid., p. 25.
[101] Ibid., p. 19.
[102] Ibid., p. 50.

eration on the Swiss model.[103]

These views had first been published in early 1976, and were reprinted in 1978. One of the authors, Fouad Ephrem Boustani, was a member of executive committee of the Lebanese Front.[104] Their reception in Israel was favourable. The idea of a Levant splintered into confessional mini-states had always appealed to many Israelis. The thought that the first of these states was about to emerge in Lebanon was particularly attractive. As long as the Labour Party had governed in Israel, greater involvement in Lebanon had been viewed with suspicion. However, in June 1977 the Likud Bloc, under Prime Minister Begin, came to power, and a new attitude prevailed. Begin believed that the Christians in Lebanon faced genocide and he was determined to prevent it. Although the Israeli military command had its reservations, the government opted for closer cooperation with the Lebanese Front.

Against this background of reconciliation between Syria and the Palestinians, on the one hand, and closer contacts between the Lebanese Front and Israel, on the other hand, a conflict between Syria and the Lebanese Front could hardly be avoided. An incident on February 8th considerably strained relations, although the Lebanese Front was not directly involved. The Syrian Army erected a roadblock right in front of the sentries of the Lebanese Military Academy at the Fayadiye barracks. When ordered by a captain to move the roadblock, the Syrian soldiers refused and were arrested by Lebanese police. The Syrians responded by shelling the barracks. The trainees at the officers' school attacked the Syrian artillery emplacement and destroyed a Syrian company, leaving 220 dead and 30 wounded. Four attempts by Syrian reinforcements to take the barracks failed. The fighting spread. Syrian troops stationed in the Rizk Tower, a skyscraper in the East Beirut district of Ashrafieh, bombarded the Christian suburbs. Heavy artillery was used against Fayadiye as well as the headquarters of the Lebanese Army in Yarze. In East Beirut street-fighting broke out between Syrians and Christian militias. Losses were high on both sides. Within a few days a banal incident had developed into violent fighting. After a week it died down. The Syrian Army demanded that the Christian commanding officer of Fayadiye and his Muslim deputy be handed over. The Lebanese Army refused on the grounds that Lebanese soldiers had not provoked the incident. Sarkis and the Syrian government found a solution that

---

[103] Ibid., p. 51.
[104] The publications of 1975 and 1976 do not mention authors: *Témoignages vivants sur la crise qui traverse le Liban* (1975); *Note sur la question libanaise* (1975); *Lumières franches sur la question libanaise* (1975); *La crise libanaise dans ses principales dimensions* (1976); *Note explicative sur la situation au Liban*, 2nd edn (1976); *Liban 1975–1976. Qu'avons-nous fait et que faire?* (1976); *Génocide au Liban* (1976); *Rapport analytique sur l'attitude des musulmans du Liban depuis le 13 avril 1975* (1976).

allowed both sides to keep face. A joint Syrian and Lebanese military tribunal was created — the case was never closed.

However, the Fayadiye incident had abruptly revealed new realities and cleavages. President Sarkis may have been nominal commander of the Arab peace forces in Lebanon, and, hence, also of the Syrian contingent. But the Syrian Army would not hesitate to act without the knowledge of this commander against the commander's own Lebanese Army, and, when worsted, shell residential areas in revenge. The Syrian information minister declared that the Syrian Army would remain in Lebanon until its mission was completed, and would brook no unrest. On behalf of the Lebanese Front, Chamoun declared that the Syrian Army could not remain in Lebanon indefinitely. The nature of the Syrian troops in Lebanon was changing from that of a peacekeeping force to that of a party to the conflict. In April 1978, shortly after the end of the Israeli invasion of the south, fighting broke out again in Beirut's suburbs. This time Christian militias faced Palestinians and Syrian troops. Syria's reversal of allegiance was explicit: it was now allied with the Palestinians. Sarkis managed yet again to find a compromise. Saudi and Sudanese units of the Arab Deterrent Force took up positions between Chiyah and Ain al-Rummaneh and put an end to the fighting. Once again the Lebanese parliament tried to extract Lebanon from its fateful involvement in the Israeli–Arab conflict. At the end of April the seventy-four deputies present unanimously passed a resolution that called on the Palestinians and 'other parties' on Lebanese territory to cease armed actions, forbade any armed presence other than the legitimate Lebanese armed forces, and affirmed that 'Lebanese law should apply to all Lebanese and all persons on Lebanese territory without exception'. However, neither the president nor parliament had the power to enforce their decisions. Syria was determined to use its old and new allies, the Palestinians, as surrogates in its contest with Israel. On the other hand, the Lebanese Front was determined to conclude a pact 'with the devil' to drive both the Syrians and the Palestinians, if not out of Lebanon, at least out of the Christian heartland.

## Civil war: Christians against Christians

The growing understanding with Israel was not to the liking of all parties in the Lebanese Front. Suleiman Franjieh, the former state president, stuck to his view that the interests of the Lebanese in general and the Christians in particular were better safeguarded by the Syrians than by the Israelis. Since the 1950s there had been a very cordial relationship between the Franjieh and Assad families; they also had common business interests. In Lebanon itself Suleiman Franjieh had always been one of the most resolute defenders of Maronite interests. But contrary to many other Maronites, he had always seen himself as an Arab and Lebanon as an integral part of the Arab world. An alliance with Israel was anathema to him.

There were also social strains and organizational rivalry between Franjieh's adherents and those of the Kata'ib. Franjieh was one of the last Maronite *zu`ama'* whose political influence was rooted in patriarchal family traditions and land ownership. The peasants' revolts of the nineteenth century had not affected the north of the Maronite mountainous area, unlike the Kisrawan and Metn regions. By contrast, the Kata'ib was a modern party. Its roots lay not in traditional loyalties to a family or clan, but in a political programme and organized representation of working and lower-middle class interests. The war years had widened the populist appeal of the Kata'ib. Its militias found many recruits among the urban youth of humble backgrounds, in whom the levelling appeal of modernization, radicalization and ideological mobilization struck a chord. Franjieh's supporters were rural middle-class and farming people, all from the same region; his militia was essentially a civil guard recruited on kinship and local attachments. The Kata'ib perceived itself as a national movement pursuing specific social and political objectives at a national level; its militia was trying to turn itself into a regular army.

In the early course of the war the Kata'ib had become immensely popular among sections of the population beyond its own strongholds in East Beirut, the Metn and Kisrawan. It had a particular appeal for all those who had derived only marginal benefit from the traditional patronage system: agricultural labourers, small freeholders and smallholders, clerks and workers who commuted between their rural homes and urban jobs. Since 1976 it had expanded into northern Lebanon. To Franjieh's traditional political attitudes, this was an unseemly and improper interference in the affairs of a region whose interests only he and other respected families could legitimately and adequately represent. The Kata'ib took a different view. It was only natural that northern Lebanese too should finally break with political 'feudalism' and join a modern party and national movement.

The conflicts came to a head over money. Since 1975 both Franjieh's Marada militia and the Kata'ib militias had been financing themselves largely through levies imposed on commercial and manufacturing firms. The Marada and the Kata'ib started disputing one another's right to raise levies in the heavily industrialized region around Chekka, south of Tripoli.

The political disagreements — Syrian or Israeli alliance, *zu`ama'* or populist party, rights to levies — strained relations to breaking point in May 1978. Franjieh reconciled himself with Rashid Karami, the representative of established Sunni Islam in Tripoli.[105] Since Karami also favoured the Syrians, a pro-Syrian alliance emerged in the north of the country just as the Lebanese Front was

---

[105] They met in a Syrian officers' mess in Tripoli at the invitation of a high-ranking Syrian officer.

recovering from heavy fighting with the Syrians in Beirut. A few days later a leading Kata'ib member in Chekka, a bank director, was murdered. Despite the mediation of the Maronite patriarch, incidents between the two militias continued. Units of the Lebanese Army were deployed along the coastal road to prevent further fighting.

On June 14th, Kata'ib militiamen in the surrounding mountains shelled Ehden, a summer resort above Zghorta, Franjieh's stronghold. Among the dead was Franjieh's eldest son, Tony, his daughter-in-law and their baby. At noon on the same day Syrian troops occupied Ehden.

Partition of the area controlled by the Christian parties, 1978

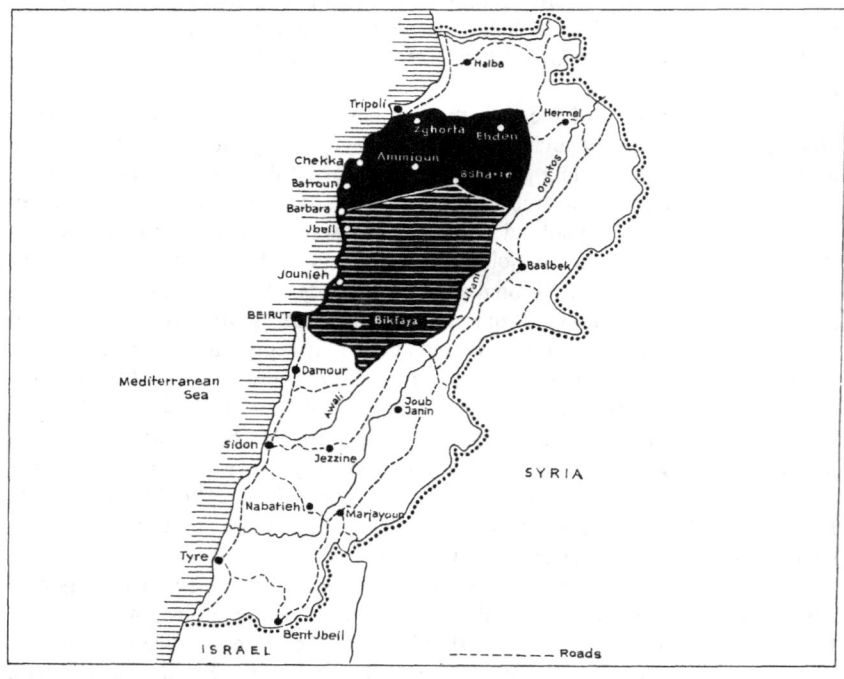

In the eyes of Franjieh's supporters, the attack was a cold-blooded assassination. The Kata'ib explained that they had obtained documents with the names of people who were to be murdered by Franjieh hit men. As the civil authorities had taken no action on previous murders, friends and relations of the murdered men had themselves tried to abduct the murderers who were holed up in Ehden. No one knew that Tony Franjieh and his family were in Ehden at the time. Kata'ib leaders later declared that their militiamen had panicked after their — northern Lebanese — commander, Samir Geagea, had been badly wounded and transported to Beirut. Bashir Gemayel, commander of the Kata'ib's forces, spoke of a 'regrettable individual initiative' that in the final analysis had its roots in the 'various difficulties the Franjieh clan had caused the people of the region'.

The Kata'ib's explanations were not convincing, and less so their expressions of regret. Members in the lower ranks made no attempt to conceal their satisfaction that the deviants in the north had been taught a lesson and regretted only that the 'main traitor', Suleiman Franjieh, was not among the victims. If the action had been intended to prevent rifts in the common front of the Christian political forces, its effect was just the opposite. The Christian north broke irrevocably with the Lebanese Front. Franjieh declared a feud against the Gemayel family, and in particular Bashir. A traditionalist of his sort could not conceive of the Ehden murder other than as a family vendetta. He gave the members of the Kata'ib in the north an ultimatum to hand in their weapons and resign from the party — or to leave the region by the end of the month.

Syrian troops now occupied the Christian mountains in the north, the Koura district, the town of Batroun and the entire coastal strip to the Madfoun Bridge, forty-five kilometres south of Tripoli. Approximately one-third of the area formerly held by Christian militias was now under Syrian control. The writ of the Lebanese Front extended over an enclave embracing only about 10 per cent of all Lebanese territory. A new frontier ran through the Christian heartland. The civil war between the Christian communities had weakened them more than all the previous attacks of Lebanese and foreign foes.

## Syria and the Lebanese Front at war

Once again, two parties were convinced that a confrontation between them was imminent. The Syrian leadership was angered by the assault on its allies and determined to deal severely with any further insubordination. The leaders of the Lebanese Front, in particular Camille Chamoun and Bashir Gemayel, were not prepared to recognize Syrian ascendancy. The menace of Syrian troops in the Christian heartland was as unsettling to them as the Palestinian camps on the outskirts of East Beirut had been. They wanted the Syrians out of this area.

## Syrian offensive against the Christian militias, 1978

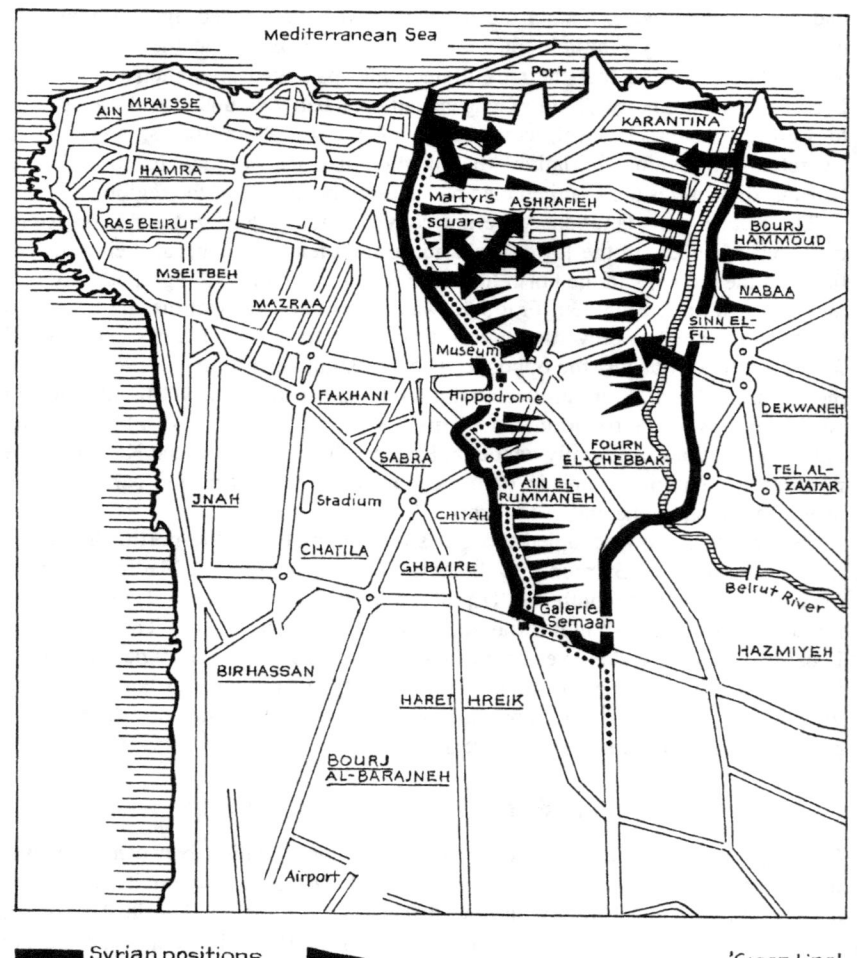

But before anything happened, the Lebanese Christians were reminded yet again that actions by Christian militias in the heartland had consequences for the Christian population outside this area. On June 29th, the Greek Catholic village of Qaa in the northern Bekaa, that is, in a Syrian-controlled part of the country, and two other villages of the same denomination, were occupied by 'armed elements'. Forty young men were arrested. That evening twenty-six of them were found murdered in a river-bed close by. The others were beaten up and released; they refused to answer any questions or make statements.

The Supreme Council of the Greek Catholic community called for a day of national mourning. It dawned with a Syrian bombardment of Ain al-Rummaneh. President Sarkis ordered the Syrian troops to stop shooting — in vain: the commander of the 'peace forces' was not in command. For the first week of July the Syrian army shelled East Beirut and the eastern suburbs without interruption. The Christian militias, in turn, attacked the Syrian troops stationed in this district. Syrian sallies against Ain al-Rummaneh and the Rizk Tower were beaten off; but the Syrian infantry was able to cut off virtually every road leading out of East Beirut.

On July 7th, President Sarkis tendered his resignation as he was unable to stop the fighting. The American administration also called for a cease-fire. The Syrian president asked Sarkis to remain in office: his resignation would have deprived the Syrian presence in Lebanon not only of any fiction of Lebanese legitimacy but also — according to the decision of the Riyadh conference — of Arab legitimacy. The Syrian Army broke off its bombardment, and Sarkis withdrew his resignation on July 18th. By the end of the month new clashes had erupted in some suburbs, and Syria resumed its blanket shelling of East Beirut at the beginning of August. Tens of thousands of civilians fled into the mountains. The militiamen, however, remained and assailed isolated Syrian positions.

A cease-fire was arranged after ten days. The Syrian troops withdrew from their positions in the centre of Ashrafieh and at the bridges on the roads to the north. This partial withdrawal was mainly tactical: the Syrians were abandoning positions difficult to hold and reducing the risk of shelling their own troops.

In early September the Israelis and Egyptians began negotiating at Camp David. The peace treaty was concluded on September 18th. As so often before, a step towards peace elsewhere in the Middle East was followed by a step towards war in Lebanon. On September 23rd ferocious Syrian shelling of East Beirut resumed. The Lebanese gendarmerie recorded 2,000 hits in Ashrafieh daily. The Syrians did not even pretend to aim at military targets; residential areas were randomly shelled, and schools, hospitals and factories systematically destroyed. As most of the civilian population had fled, there was little loss of life. But the Syrians did not have it all their own way. One of their crack units in Ashrafieh was encircled; attempts to enter the town with tanks failed. Transport by sea rendered a food blockade of East Beirut ineffectual. The Syrians then took to bombarding the Christian hinterland: Bikfaya, Beit Meri, Broumanna and even Jounieh.

Destruction on this scale was purely repressive. By mid-October it was clear that the Syrian war against the Christian militias had not achieved its objectives. At the beginning of July the Syrian minister of information had declared that if the Christian militias did not subordinate themselves they would be destroyed. After several bombardments, each heavier than the previous, swathes of Christian Beirut lay in ruins and much of the technical and industrial infrastructure shattered. But the militias had neither subordinated themselves nor been destroyed. The Christian population identified themselves with them more strongly than ever.

Full accounts of the new war in Beirut only reached the outside world in October 1978. Regardless of who was responsible for this conflict — the French Foreign Minister de Giringeau accused Chamoun and his militia of having provoked the Syrians — the Syrian choice of method was widely condemned. Shelling residential areas for weeks on end was a strange way for a peace force to keep peace.

The Security Council passed a resolution that called for all parties to the conflict to cease firing. The Christian militias interpreted this as a form of *de facto* international recognition. Saudi Arabia worked out a compromise, which enabled all sides to keep face. The Riyadh decisions were reaffirmed at a conference in Beit Eddine: the mandate of the 'Arab Deterrent Forces' was extended and Sarkis' command confirmed. The Syrian troops in East Beirut were replaced by Saudi units.

The confrontation with Syria had inflicted a lot of damage on the Christian population, but the Lebanese Front made some political gains and had slightly improved its military position. Syria's behaviour had forced Sarkis closer to the Front. At the Beit Eddine conference the fiction of his position as a president for peace and reconstruction, supported by Arab peace troops, had been plausibly resurrected, but only with difficulty.

The causes of the conflict had not been removed. Syria was still determined to break Christian militia resistance to its political ascendancy, and sought new, cheaper and less risky ways of doing so. The Lebanese Front, for their part, were more firmly convinced that they needed to get rid of the Syrians — and that their salvation lay in close ties with Israel.

## Simmering warfare

The first two war years may be seen as a sequence of conflicts between changing opponents and allies, each of them stamping one phase of the war. After 1978 the situation became more complex: conflicts ran congruently or overlapped; instead of one war, there were now several. As a purely chronological or periodic approach might present the nature of an individual conflict inadequately, important conflicts and confrontations after 1978 will be analysed successively, with brief reference to temporal and structural parallels and overlapping.

The year 1978 was marked by the Christians' civil war and the first heavy confrontation between Syria and the Lebanese Front. It was also a year of simmering warfare, either continuance of old conflicts or the start of new ones that would also drag on.

After the Israeli invasion of southern Lebanon the Palestinian organizations resumed their commando raids, albeit under more difficult conditions. Within a few months they had thoroughly infiltrated the buffer-zone controlled by UNIFIL troops. Palestinian guerrillas clashed with Norwegian and French UNIFIL units, after which both sides tried to avoid further fighting. The guerrillas quickly learnt to move in smaller groups and more discreetly. The international troops, ill-equipped for serious military confrontations, became more cautious, concentrated their efforts on fixed positions and learnt to turn a blind eye sometimes. Haddad's soldiers and militiamen to the south of them were far more militant, not least because of Palestinian animosity. They were also defending their own villages. The Lebanese and Syrian governments were agreed in principle that control of the extreme south would lie with the regular Lebanese Army. After President Sarkis took office in 1976 the army, which had disintegrated in the previous spring, had been reconstructed.[106] A number of officers who had cooperated with militias of one or other party to the civil war were retired. The Minister for Defence and army commander, Victor Khoury, tried with some success to build up a force of Lebanese patriots on the basis of strict confessional parity. However, Lebanese troops still stationed in the Bekaa had collaborated closely with the Syrian Army ever since its first intervention. The officers of this so-called 'vanguard' of the Lebanese Army enjoyed the trust of the Syrians, unlike — since the Fayadiye incidents — Lebanese units stationed in the Fayadiye barracks and in the vicinity of the presidential palace and the Ministry of Defence. The Syrian government

---

[106]'The threat to the army posed by its disintegration was overcome, and by late 1976 the army was, for the most part, again an integral, though still unused, unit, weakened by its reduced size ... but prepared to fight if ordered to do so ... the senior Sunni officer corps remained loyal to the state, to the government, and to the army'; R.D. McLaurin, 'Lebanon and its army: Past, present, and future', in Azar, *The Emergence of a New Lebanon*, p. 95.

insisted that units of the 'vanguard' be sent to the south. Both Major Haddad and Israel objected. When the 'vanguard' advanced into the south at the beginning of August, Haddad opened fire on them near the village of Kaukaba and forced them into a fairly disorderly retreat. Another 'pro-Syrian' Lebanese battalion was despatched to the south in April 1979, and again checked by Haddad's troops. Haddad was incensed. Up to this point he had considered himself and his force as part of the Lebanese Army, and could not see any reason why the south should be handed over to what in his eyes were unreliable troops.[107] He responded with open rebellion and proclaimed 'Free Lebanon'. He also demanded of Sarkis that he stop being a 'captive of the Syrians' and come to the south, from where he should 'liberate Lebanon'. As he had been stripped of his rank and dishonourably discharged, Israel agreed to pay his troops. No further attempts were made to station troops of the Lebanese Army in the south. But the petty war between Palestinians and 'Free Lebanon' simmered on. Palestinian troops fortified the old crusader stronghold, Beaufort Castle, from which they could regularly shell Haddad's 'capital', Marjayoun. Commando raids and reprisals became a permanent feature along and within the entire ten kilometre wide border strip.

Another simmering war, albeit with interruptions, broke out in the middle of Beirut and along the green line in the suburbs. After hostilities flared up between the Syrians and the Lebanese Front, relations between the Syrians and the Palestinian organizations had improved. There was also a gradual rapprochement between Syria and the organizations in the 'National Movement', whose antagonism towards Syria had reached its climax after the assassination of Kamal Jumblatt. The militias of the PLO, units of the Palestinian Liberation Army, the Mourabitoun and PSP troops were now permitted to take up positions on the western side of the green line; the Syrian Army withdrew to a few strategically important positions, including the Murr Tower, a skyscraper facing the Rizk Tower in East Beirut. Christian militias occupied positions along the east side of the green line, as did units of the regular Lebanese Army from 1979; deployment in West Beirut was refused them. There were a number of crossing places between the two parts of the city.[108] Sometimes these were safe, sometimes snipers made any crossing deadly, and sometimes they were closed. The old city on both sides, between Martyrs Square and the harbour, was left completely to the militias. Most nights they fired at each other with machine-guns, rocket-propelled grenades and field artillery; sometimes they fired during the day as well. From early 1979, a

---

[107] Interview with the author, 1980.

[108] In the harbour at the docks themselves, at the Museum and east of the city centre on the Damuscus highway, the 'Ring' — a city motorway between Ashrafieh and the old city in West Beirut — and in the suburbs, the roads from Chiyah to Hazmiyeh and from Bourj al-Barajneh to Hadath.

similar nightly routine developed between the districts of Chiyah and Ain al-Rummaneh. At times the shooting was politically motivated. Whenever the mandate of the 'peace forces' was about to expire or when emissaries of the major powers were travelling between Middle Eastern capitals, intensified shelling served as a reminder that there was a war going on, even if only in the form of trench warfare. But even the most fanciful political observers were at a loss to explain other escalations. For one party this simmering warfare in Beirut did serve some purpose. By allowing it to continue, Syria could demonstrate to the Lebanese on both sides of the green line that only a pax Syriana had a chance of lasting. This demonstration cost Syria little: after 1978 the Syrians usually let others fight for them.

In early 1980 Syria further reduced costs. Syrian troops withdrew completely from the coastal road south of Beirut and from the dividing line between the two sectors of the city, apart from one garrison, and took up positions in the mountains overlooking Beirut. Their positions in or close to the city were handed over to units of the Palestinian Liberation Army commanded by Syrian or pro-Syrian officers. One consequence of the Syrian withdrawal from West Beirut was a third, and extremely irregular, petty war between different Palestinian and Lebanese organizations. It was one that practically never concerned politics. The militias fought each other for control of different districts or even single streets, disputed each other's right to collect protection money and started shooting over traffic incidents or quarrels between individuals. Frequently West Beirut was saved from sinking into chaos only by the intervention of the military police of the PLO. As a rule, though, they intervened only when local shoot-outs threatened to escalate. While these inconclusive wars continued, two politically more significant conflicts were brewing in 1979 and 1980: one between Lebanese Shi`is and Palestinians, the other between the Lebanese Front and the Syrians. They would be fought independently of one another, but more or less simultaneously.

## War between Shi`is and Palestinians[109]

The Lebanese Christians were the first to resist the presence of armed Palestinians in Lebanon. Not they, however, but the Shi`is suffered most from their presence and its consequences. In the pre-war period between 1969 and 1975 the Shi`is had directed their anger alternately against the Palestinians and, more vehemently, against the Lebanese state, which was neither willing nor in a position to protect

---

[109] See on the following Francis Grimblat, 'La communauté chiite libanaise et le mouvement national palestinien 1967–1986', *Guerres mondiales et conflits contemporains* 151 (1988), especially pp. 80ff.; Augustus Richard Norton, 'Harakat Amal', in Azar, *The Emergence of a New Lebanon*, pp. 184ff.

them, the innocent victims of the Palestinian–Israeli confrontations. In the Beirut suburbs, Shi`is, especially those with left-wing sympathies, had fought alongside the Palestinians against the Christian militias in 1975 and 1976. However, since the outbreak of war, Imam Musa Sadr and his Amal had adopted a far more cautious policy. Amal remained neutral for the most part, and Sadr tried to mediate. When the Christian militias overran the eastern section of the Beirut 'belt of misery', Sadr negotiated the withdrawal of the Shi`i population in Nabaa without a fight. When the Syrians intervened against the Palestinians and the National Movement, Sadr openly supported the Syrians. The Palestinian organizations took offence at both actions.

After mid-1976 tensions between Shi`is and Palestinians became more strained. After their expulsion from the camps in East Beirut, the Palestinians moved into the already overcrowded south-western suburbs of Beirut. Simultaneously, the Shi`i population was swollen by the former inhabitants of Nabaa and, after the 1978 Israeli invasion, tens of thousands of refugees from the south. The Palestinians were far better armed and organized. In effect they dominated the western suburbs, to the growing irritation of the Shi`is — who, like the Christians some years previously, began to regard the Palestinians as an occupation force.[110] This feeling was stronger in the area south of the Israeli 'red line', which, since 1976, the Palestinians saw as a second 'Fatahland'. The local population was predominantly Shi`i. Numerous Shi`i villages had tried to remain neutral in the fighting between the Palestinians, and also in the fighting between the Israelis and Haddad's troops. In practice, 'neutral' meant objecting to Palestinian billets. Conversely, the Palestinians strove to melt into the local population to avoid easy identification by the Israeli armed forces. Besides Palestinian billeting, requisitioning and transgressions, the Shi`is also had to suffer Israeli reprisals. Powerless to resist either, they grew more and more embittered.[111]

---

[110] Khalidi, *Conflict and Violence*, p. 115, speaks of 'high-handedness and misconduct by certain Palestinian factions and their Lebanese allies in the south'. The traditionally pro-Palestinian Sunnis in Sidon too were increasingly disenchanted with the Palestinian presence; ibid., p. 116.

[111] Even John Bulloch, who shows great sympathy for the Palestinian cause, writes in *Final Conflict*, p. 41: 'The Palestinians themselves appeared not to realise just how isolated they were, or to understand the damage they had done by their actions in Lebanon ... It was ... particularly in the south, that the Palestinians had made themselves so unpopular. By regularly firing rockets into Upper Galilee from Beaufort Castle and other strong points, they immediately drew Israeli counter-fire, which invariably killed Lebanese villagers or damaged Lebanese homes and crops without hurting the Palestinians. That was bad enough, but the Palestinians went further: they extorted money, they meted out rough and provocative 'justice', they seized what they needed, they sited their guns near villages, they sought shelter near the border, and they made little contribution to the welfare of the area.' One of the highest Shi`i spiritual leaders, Muhammad Jawad Mughniyya, who died in 1979, expressed himself similarly: 'Palestinian leaders declare that whatever happens, they will not leave the Lebanese South. This means that they provoke Israel so that Israel destroys and occupies the South ... Knowing Israel's aggressive and expansionist goals, is that not a

Two events precipitated a rapid and extensive mobilization of the Shi`is in both Beirut and the south. In September 1978 Imam Musa Sadr disappeared without trace in Libya, and in January 1979 Shi`i revolutionaries overthrew the Shah of Iran. The former enormously augmented the Shi`is' bitterness, the latter was an extraordinary encouragement. A close colleague of Musa Sadr's, Mustapha Chamran, who had been director of a technical school founded by the Imam in southern Lebanon, became Minister of Defence in Teheran.[112] For the first time in their history the Lebanese Shi`is had, in revolutionary Iran, a foreign protector and ally.

First under the Deputy Husseini and then — from April 1980 onwards — Nabih Berri, Amal began to articulate Shi`i interests. The Amal leaders feared that the consequence of the Israeli–Palestinian confrontation in the south would be the expulsion of the Shi`i population and the creation of a *de facto* Palestinian state in their homeland. They demanded the withdrawal of Palestinian guerrillas from all residential areas — and the deployment of the regular Lebanese Army. While the militias of the National Movement denied this army access to West Beirut and the Christian militias in East Beirut saw in it a rival, the Shi`is became its convinced political supporters. The army, in turn, channelled arms to Amal and provided trainers. The PLO intensely disapproved. But it, and the Fatah leadership in particular, did not want to risk an open conflict with the Shi`is. Accordingly, they made many gestures of goodwill, without giving an inch on the crux of the matter: control over the suburbs of West Beirut and ascendancy in the south.

The Lebanese National Day in November 1979 was celebrated in West Beirut as an unusual demonstration against all non-Lebanese forces in the country. The city was a sea of cedar flags. The Sunni population, tired of the militias' chaotic rule, closed ranks with the Shi`is.

In early 1980, tensions worsened between Palestinians and the Shi`is. The Iran–Iraqi War cast its shadow before it. Before it erupted in the Gulf in September 1980 it had already begun in the suburbs of Beirut. Amal and the Iraqi-sponsored Arab Liberation Front were locked in a bitter struggle, while Fatah tried to mediate. Despite numerous cease-fires the fighting continued. From Beirut it spread to southern Lebanon. Unnoticed by the rest of the world, fighting for control over a good dozen villages continued without interruption until mid-1982.

---

strange Palestinian logic! As if you would tell the peaceful inhabitants of a quiet house: I want to blow up your house over your heads not for any other purpose than to prove my existence in the world'; *Tajarib* (Trials) (Beirut, 1980), quoted in Chibli Mallat, *Shi`i Thought from the South of Lebanon* (Oxford, 1988), p.21.

[112] Chamran was killed while on a military operation in Khuzistan in the summer of 1981.

After the war between the Palestinians and the Christian militias ended, a war less conspicuous and less spectacular, yet no less grim and horrific, broke out between the Palestinians and another Lebanese community. It would, with lulls, become the most persistent. Since late 1979 there has been little to choose between the way Shi`i politicians and militia leaders speak of Palestinians and the way Gemayel and Chamoun did between 1969 and 1976.[113] In 1976, with great sacrifices and even greater brutality, the Lebanese Christians were able to rid themselves of Palestinians in their regions. The struggle between the Shi`is and the Palestinians would be no less brutal, but would last considerably longer.

## Expansionist drives by the Lebanese Front

The result of the confrontation with Syria in 1978 had left the leaders of the Lebanese Front under the impression that in the medium term it was not impossible to force Syria to withdraw its troops from Lebanon. Certainly, they were not under any illusions about Syria's military superiority. But the fighting in 1978 had revealed that Syria hesitated to pay the price in lives and material needed to break the resistance of the Christian militias. Their hopes were strengthened by Assad's domestic problems. Since 1978 the regime had faced growing opposition from the Sunni fundamentalist Muslim Brotherhood, an organization as cavalier in its methods as Assad's regime itself. In 1979 the Muslim Brotherhood murdered dozens of Alawite trainee officers in Aleppo, and Assad himself narrowly escaped an assassination attempt in 1980. The government had hundreds of Muslim Brothers hanged and harshly suppressed demonstrations by the opposition. The Lebanese Front assessed the partial Syrian withdrawal from Beirut in 1980 as a success. But it was almost certainly a reorganization rather than a withdrawal. The Syrian Army was concentrating its forces on what it regarded as essential: a strong contingent in the Bekaa, where an Israeli attack would be most likely; a garrison in West Beirut that was not involved in daily skirmishes, but strong enough to demonstrate, if necessary, to both the Palestinians and the National Movement who had the final say; and strategic positions in the mountains to control the Beirut–Damascus highway and shell any part of Beirut if necessary. Notwithstanding this, the partial withdrawal of the Syrians was greeted with relief by Christians in the zones controlled by the Lebanese Front. The Syrian check-points on the access roads to East Beirut and between the Christian suburbs and Ashrafieh were dismantled. For the first time since the

---

[113] Pakradouni, *La paix manquée*, pp. 106f., reports a remark Musa Sadr made in June 1977: 'La Résistance palestinienne ... n'est pas une révolution car elle n'a pas le sens du martyre. C'est une machine militaire qui terrorise le monde arabe. Grâce aux armes, Arafat extorque de l'argent et grâce à l'argent il soudoie la presse, puis grâce à la presse, il impressionne l'opinion mondiale.'

Syrians had marched in in the autumn of 1976, Christian militias exercised control over an undivided territory.

The militias organized 'their' region. They instituted a number of para-statal services, in particular an efficient system of taxation to finance their operations: levies on businessman and home-owners; sales taxes on petrol stations and restaurants; customs duties at the quay controlled by the Kata'ib militia in Beirut harbour. These revenues enabled the militias to maintain a permanent force and a military staff, and to purchase armaments. The militias became more professional. Their ranks included officers and soldiers who had left the regular army after 1976. But the nature of the Lebanese Front itself detracted from its military efficiency. It was a coalition of different groups running four different militias: the Kata'ib, the 'Tigers' of the NLP, the 'Guardians of the Cedars' and the Tanzim. There was a joint command; but it was better at coordinating than commanding.[114]

Once Syrian troops had withdrawn, friction and local clashes between the Christian militias became more frequent. Social tensions played a part: belligerent sons of 'good families' tended to join the 'Tigers' of the National Liberals, whereas the Kata'ib militia recruited widely among the lower strata. But the clashes were essentially a consequence of boredom, of rivalries between competing organizations of young people with little to do once pressure on the Christian heartland had let up. As all of them were armed both on duty and off, brawls frequently ended in shooting and numerous casualties. Militia and party leaders were constantly mediating between and reconciling antagonistic groups.[115]

Bashir Gemayel, commander of the Kata'ib militia — the strongest by far — was increasingly disenchanted with negotiations and mediation. Ever since the storming of Tel al-Za`tar, when deficient planning had resulted in Christian militiamen shooting at each other, he had striven for a tightly disciplined, properly led, unified commando. Once he had come to the conclusion that this would not be achieved by agreement, he resolved to use violence. On July 7th, 1980, he launched an attack on the offices and barracks of the Tiger militia, a

---

[114] Khalaf, 'The Phalange', p. 50, points out that the Kata'ib militia gradually increased its influence at the expense of the political leadership. It further enhanced it by collaborating with the 'maximalists' in the other Christian militias. See also John P. Entelis, 'Ethnic conflict and the reemergence of radical Christian nationalism in Lebanon', in Michael Curtis, ed., *Religion and Politics in the Middle East* (Boulder, 1981), pp. 227–45.

[115] Short-lived hostilities also erupted between the Kata'ib and the militia of the Armenian Tashnag Party in May and September 1979. Although the policies of this party were similar to those of the Kata'ib, it had remained aloof from most of the fighting in 1975/6. Only in July 1976, after Armenians in the Beirut districts of Nabaa and Bourj Hammond had been attacked, did it join in the fighting against the Palestinians. The extremists in the other Christian militias took offence at the Armenians' preference for neutrality. The conflict was eventually settled amicably.

quick, extremely brutal and successful operation. About one hundred 'Tigers' died. The rest accepted his authority. For three months those in Ain al-Rummaneh retained their autonomy because units of the regular army separated the spheres of influence. Then Gemayel removed this rival remnant too, and the army units in this district at the same time.[116] Bashir Gemayel was now the sole commander of a unified militia, henceforth known as the 'Lebanese Forces'. The Lebanese Forces were a powerful military body of around 6,000 regular militiamen and about 10,000 reservists on short call. They soon introduced compulsory military training for all youths in their sphere of influence.

Unlike the conflict between the Kata'ib and Franjieh, the bloody unification of the militias did not provoke deep political dissension. Camille Chamoun was deeply shocked at the destruction of his party's militia. But in contrast to his son Dany, who had commanded the Tigers and now withdrew from politics, he regarded the political unity of the Lebanese Front as paramount and remained its chairman. The Front adopted the formula 'political pluralism — military unity'. Political pluralism was not difficult because Chamoun and Bashir Gemayel were unanimous on all important political questions. Gemayel admired Chamoun's resoluteness and experience, and the latter saw in the former a young successor. Together they charted the Front along a daring course: they risked a calculated challenge to Syria and tried to get Israel to raise its commitment to Lebanon.

Certain changes at the regional and international levels seemed to favour such a course. In May 1980 Weizmann, the former air force commander, had resigned as Israeli defence minister and Premier Begin had assumed this portfolio; Begin was not averse to greater support for the Lebanese Christians. In October, Syria concluded a treaty of friendship and defence with the USSR, which made it seem even more beholden to the Eastern superpower. In November, Ronald Reagan won the American presidential elections and named General Haig as his prospective foreign minister. Both were known to view regional conflicts in the context of the global East-West confrontation.

In December, the Lebanese Front published a detailed manifesto titled 'The Lebanon we want to build',[117] which outlined its domestic and foreign policies in plain language. Lebanon must be seen as a federation of communities. Discrimination between the Lebanese is not acceptable; there may be no privileges for the Christians, or for any other community, either. Liberty, security and 'the possibility of self-determination'[118] for the Christians in Lebanon may 'not be dependent

---

[116] There was one exception: the Kata'ib militia of the Metn under the command of Bashir's brother Amin retained a measure of autonomy right up to October 1988.

[117] 'Le Liban que nous voulons batir'(n.p., n.d.) [23rd December, Deir Aoukar].

[118] Ibid., p. 6.

on any demographic fact or political orientation'.[119] The Pact of 1943 should be revised as 'a formula for decentralization, for federation or for confederation'. The country must be liberated from the 'dual occupation'. Permanent settlement of the Palestinians in Lebanon must be categorically rejected. The position on Syria is unequivocal: 'The Syrian occupation must end.'[120]

In accordance with this objective the Lebanese Front attempted to expand the territory under its control. Since the beginning of the war the city of Zahle had been cut off from the Christian heartland. Zahle lies on the eastern slopes of the Lebanon Mountains in a river valley that opens towards the Bekaa, not far both from the Beirut–Damascus highway and the road between the highway and Baalbek. Before the war Zahle, with around 180,000 inhabitants, had been the most important business centre in the Bekaa. Most of the inhabitants are Greek Catholics, though there are large communities of Greek Orthodox and Maronites as well. Until the outbreak of hostilities the parties of the Lebanese Front had not had much of a foothold in Zahle. The inhabitants' own militia had defended the city against Palestinian attacks in 1975 and 1976, and they had welcomed the Syrian intervention with relief. This attitude changed in the course of 1980, when Syrian troops controlling communications between Zahle and the outside world, through the Bekaa as well as the mountains, started harassing civilians. In reaction, Kata'ib's popularity grew considerably. The local branch of the Lebanese Forces recruited enough young people to become the largest armed body in the city. As a counterweight, the Syrians armed members of the 'Tigers' who had fled Beirut.[121] There were exchanges of fire between the two militias in November and December 1980. Syrian soldiers supported the Tigers and suffered casualties: one officer and five soldiers killed. In retaliation, Syrian artillery in the surrounding mountains shelled Zahle throughout Christmas Week. Thereupon most of the Tiger militiamen went over to the Lebanese Forces. The Syrians had to abandon their checkpoints in the city, and continued shelling. An effectual cease-fire was arranged only after weeks. However, the Syrian Army kept up its blockade of Zahle.

The Lebanese Forces in the city now numbered 5,000 militiamen and were firmly established. Their next move was to link Zahle with the Christian areas to the west, to which purpose they started to build a road through the mountains which would break the Syrian blockade. This was a perfectly legitimate undertaking in the eyes of the inhabitants. And to the leadership of the Lebanese Forces

---

[119] Ibid., p. 5.
[120] Ibid., p. 9.
[121] The 'Tiger' commander in Ain al-Rummaneh, Hannash, came from the Zahle region. After his defeat in the capital he tried to establish a new power-base in Zahle.

it was a non-military step towards extending the territory under their control. The Syrians took a contrary view. Such a road had serious strategic implications. As the Front was cooperating ever more openly with Israel, the Syrians feared the possibility of Israeli troops advancing unhindered along this road into the central Bekaa. They would be in a position to attack the Syrian flank and threaten Damascus.

Syrian troops tried to prevent work on the road, initially in vain. In March they resumed the shelling of Zahle. The Lebanese Forces inflicted heavy casualties on Syrian troops in a suburb of Zahle; the Syrians retaliated with even heavier bombardments. Syrian artillery also started firing rockets and shells into the Christian areas of Beirut. Among their targets were positions of the regular Lebanese Army. In reaction, Lebanese soldiers stormed a Syrian barracks close to the demarcation line.

The Syrian approach was a repetition of that used in 1978: unable to hold their own in the field, they tried to force the enemy to yield by shelling residential areas in Zahle as well as Beirut. As in 1978, the enemy stood firm. And as in 1978, the war against civilians caused an international outcry. The American Secretary of State, Haig, in Jerusalem at the time, spoke of the need to stop the Syrian actions against the Lebanese Christians, and Begin announced that he would not stand by and watch the Christians being massacred. The fact that precisely Haig and Begin spoke in such terms strengthened Syrian suspicions that Zahle was more than just a local conflict with the Lebanese Forces. To stop the construction of the road to Zahle they brought in heavier military equipment. On April 26th, they employed helicopter gunships for the first time, against which the Christian militia were defenceless. The Syrians were able to take a strategic position on Mount Sannine north-west of Zahle; this was the 'Chambre des Français', a fortification dating from the mandate. This ended the attempt of the Lebanese Forces to break the isolation of Zahle. Even worse for them was the fact that from Sannine the Syrians could threaten the Christian heartland.

The Lebanese Forces' military defeat turned out to be a political gain. When Israel promised the USA not to resist Syrian intervention in Lebanon, it did so on two conditions. One was that the Syrians would respect the 'red line'; the other was that the Syrians would not employ their air force. Moreover, in 1978, the Israeli government had promised the Christian militias that it would not tolerate Syrian air attacks. Leaders of the Lebanese Front now called on Israel to keep its word. On April 28th, Israeli jets shot down two Syrian helicopters. The next day Syria escalated the conflict: it stationed SAM–2 and SAM–6 ground-to-air missiles in the Bekaa. This gave the conflict between the Lebanese Front and

Syria an international dimension.[122]

Later it became known that unfavourable weather conditions alone had hindered an immediate Israeli attack on the missile positions. The superpowers, concerned at the prospect of a Syrian–Israeli war, used this fortuitous delay for diplomatic intervention. The Soviet ambassador in Beirut declared that the defence treaty with Syria pertained only to Syrian, not Lebanese territory. The American administration despatched its special envoy, Philip Habib, to negotiate an amicable settlement of the 'missile crisis'. The Israeli government postponed its planned attack — it was election time — to give Habib time for his mission. Habib encouraged the Saudi Arabian government to mediate in the Zahle crisis.

At the beginning of June, as fighting continued in Zahle and Beirut, the foreign ministers of Saudi Arabia, Syria and Kuwait and the secretary-general of the Arab League met in Beit Eddine to confer with the Lebanese president, prime minister and foreign minister. Bashir Gemayel was also present. The emissaries from the Arab states demanded that he dissociate himself from Israel. Gemayel, in turn, demanded guarantees that the crisis in Lebanon as a whole would be settled, and declared that if he received them he would break with Israel. The Lebanese representatives, including the Sunni Premier, Wazzan, presented their programme: the Lebanese Front would break all contacts with Israel, the Palestinians would apply the provisions of the Cairo Agreement strictly and the Syrian Army would withdraw in stages by August 1st, 1982.[123] The Syrian Foreign Minister, Khaddam, rejected these terms.

But Saudi Arabian diplomacy did achieve a cease-fire and the lifting of the blockade of Zahle. The hundred or so militiamen who did not come from Zahle left the city under Saudi escort. In East Beirut they were given a hero's welcome.

Still, the Lebanese Front could hardly speak of victory. Their attempt to expand their territory had failed. The status quo was re-established in Zahle, after heavy losses and great damage. However, the militia of the Lebanese Front had fought well against a far more powerful adversary and again demonstrated to the Syrians that terror bombardment alone would not force a resolutely defended city to capitulate. Nor had the Lebanese Front succeeded in embroiling Israel in the conflict. The Israeli government kept its promise to act against Syrian air-attacks against Lebanese targets, though only after strategic positions of the Lebanese Front in the mountains had fallen. This demonstrated that it would intervene to maintain the status quo, but not to help the Christians to improve their position.

[122] See Thomas Mayer, 'Lebanese Politics and the "Missile Crisis"', in Colin Legum, et al., eds., *Middle East Contemporary Survey, Vol. V 1980–81* (New York and London, 1982), pp. 675–6.

[123] The remarkable point is Prime Minister Wazzan's support for this programme. For the first time since the outbreak of war the Lebanese president and premier were in complete agreement on a matter of vital interest. See also Pakradouni, *La paix manquée*, pp. 234ff.

Neither the Israeli connection nor the willingness to break it in the interests of an 'Arab solution' had brought the Lebanese Front much gain. The heroes' welcome disguised disappointment.

This confrontation between the Lebanese Front and Syria had one unexpected side-effect. When attacked, the Lebanese Army — both Christian and Muslim soldiers — had not hesitated to return the Syrian fire. President Sarkis, his Prime Minister, Wazzan, and Foreign Minister, Boutros, accepted that the Syrian government was no longer acting in good faith. As Sarkis turned his mind to the question of his successor, he began discreetly to canvass support for Bashir Gemayel. He advised the leader of the Lebanese Forces to rely on the USA rather than Israel, and arranged for Gemayel to be received for political discussions in Washington in August 1981.

## The Israeli–Palestinian 'Fourteen Day War'

In the meantime, the war in southern Lebanon had simmered on — a cycle of Palestinian commando raids and shelling across the border and Israeli reprisals, mostly air-attacks. In April 1981, during the fighting in Zahle, it reached a new level of intensity. The Israeli Army was becoming uneasy about the much improved equipment of the PLO and their declared intention of raising units of regular troops; Israel feared a costly war of attrition along the border.[124] On July 10th, the Israeli air force attacked Palestinian artillery and rocket positions near Sidon and Nabatiyeh. The Palestinians retaliated by shelling the border area controlled by Haddad, and Israeli villages in Upper Galilee. The Israeli air force tried in vain to take out the Palestinian batteries. For fourteen days the inhabitants of northern Israel were forced to sleep in air-raid shelters and most people in Kiryat Shmona fled southwards. On July 17th, Israeli aircraft attacked offices of various Palestinian organizations in the heavily populated Beirut district of Fakhani. Although the attack lasted only a few minutes, it left hundreds dead and over a thousand wounded, most of them civilians. In the south the shelling continued until special envoy Habib, assisted by Saudi diplomats, arranged a cease-fire in separate negotiations with Israel and the PLO.

Palestinian — and especially Lebanese — losses were much greater than Israel's in this 'Fourteen Day War'. But the Palestinians had demonstrated that even while the Israelis were taking preventive action they could continue to shell and thoroughly disrupt life in Upper Galilee. For the first time, Israel was forced to negotiate — even if indirectly — a cease-fire with the PLO. In political terms,

---

[124] See Bulloch, *Final Conflict*, p. 44: 'The UN men proved incapable of stopping the Palestinians from infiltrating into Upper Galilee, and were powerless to prevent PLO gunners from firing rockets over their heads into Israeli territory.'

this cease-fire was a victory for the Palestinians and a defeat for Israel. The Israeli government put a good face upon it because it did not want to endanger the imminent implementation of the Egyptian–Israeli peace treaty. But nobody believed that Israel would leave it at that.

## The spread of simmering warfare

The cease-fires arranged through international mediation were respected both around Zahle and in the border zone. But elsewhere the fighting continued, or new petty wars broke out. The Syrian presence had lost whatever aura it had had as a peacekeeping mission. Syria was now regarded as a party to the conflict, like the others but larger. Lebanon had disintegrated into various zones of military influence; there was always sporadic fighting on one or other demarcation line. More serious were the armed clashes within those pieces of territory not unequivocally dominated by one military force alone — and that was most of them. Order was maintained best in the area controlled by the regular Lebanese Army, a narrow strip running from Yarze and Baabda into the Beirut suburbs, and in the territory of the Lebanese Forces, which under Bashir Gemayel's leadership formed a disciplined body mostly kept in barracks, and, finally, in those Palestinian camps dominated by Fatah. Almost all other areas were disputed by different military forces.

In late 1981, it was simpler to say who was not fighting whom than who was. There was no fighting between Lebanese Christians and Muslims, between Christians and Palestinians — and between Palestinians and Israelis. Roughly speaking, the warring groups were, on the one hand, non-Lebanese against non-Lebanese, that is, Syrians against Palestinians and, on the other hand, and with increasing frequency, various Lebanese groups against Syrians or Palestinians.

Relations between the Syrian troops and the Palestinian resistance organizations had been problematical since 1976. The most important Palestinian camp in the Beirut area had resisted Syrian control, even after the invasion — an elementary condition for the Palestinians' political autonomy. Although formally allied again since late 1976, the different bodies of Palestinian troops in West Beirut remained wary of each other. However, they managed to avoid serious friction. This was not the case in the north of the country. Syria increasingly tended to regard this region — and the Bekaa to the east — as its own preserve and wanted to establish complete control, above all in Tripoli, the second largest city in the country. The Palestinians refused to acquiesce. Street fighting, involving artillery and rocket-propelled grenades, erupted in early 1982. The local Sunni militia gave the Palestinians support; the Syrians sent in their own soldiers as well as a

## Zones of military influence, 1976 – 1982

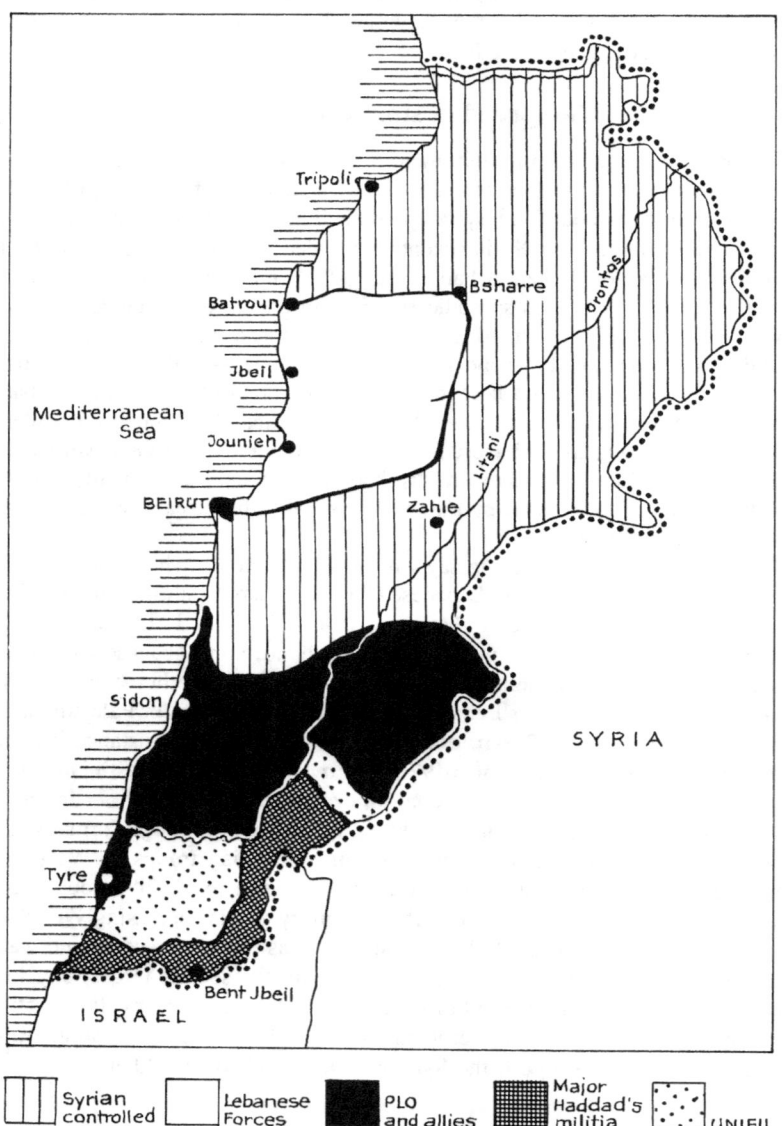

paramilitary group composed of Lebanese and Syrian Alawites. The subsequent Syrian tactics resembled those employed in the fighting with the Christian militias of Beirut and Zahle. The regular Syrian Army withdrew to the heights on the edge of the city and bombarded 'hostile' residential areas. Months of fighting through numerous cease-fires caused hundreds of civilian casualties.

As in Tripoli, dislike of the Syrian occupation mounted among Sunnis in West Beirut. But here there was a stronger Syrian presence and less dissension between them and the Palestinians. Notwithstanding this, Sunni militiamen and Syrian troops clashed in March and April 1982. At the same time, relations between Syrian units, on the one hand, and the Lebanese Army and the Christian militia, on the other hand, were tense. At irregular intervals Syrian artillery shelled positions of the Lebanese Army in the upper reaches of the mountains and along the demarcation line in the city. And the nightly duels between PLA troops and the Lebanese Forces in their respective sections of the old city continued unabated.

Syrians against Palestinians, Syrians against Lebanese Muslims as well as Christians: a more significant development in the early months of 1982 was the fighting between Lebanese Muslims and Palestinians. Since 1979 such clashes had been common in the south-western suburbs of Beirut and the region between the Litani and Zahrani Rivers. In spring 1982 they spread to the heart of West Beirut. Much of the fighting was between Amal and the Iraqi-patronized Arab Liberation Front. The latter was supported by small but tough Communist organizations. In the eyes of Amal, imbued with the spirit of Shi`i regeneration, these adversaries were particularly reprehensible, 'atheists lapsed from their Shi`i beliefs', and therefore deserving of little quarter. In April the fighting escalated to artillery exchanges between the Shi`i suburbs and the neighbouring Palestinian camps. Simultaneously, the simmering Shi`i-Palestinian warfare in the south escalated into heavier fighting in Tyre and Nabatieh. These clashes served to kindle hostilities between other organizations: in mid-May bloody clashes erupted between Sunni Nasserite militias and Fatah in Sidon.

With the exception of Syrian–Palestinian conflicts, the general aggravation of the simmering warfare in various parts of the country had a common denominator: growing Lebanese disenchantment with both Syrian and Palestinian domination. Among Christian groups this was an established pattern. But the Muslims, too, were becoming aware of their position, namely, that the Lebanese were bearing the brunt of the Arab struggle against Israel. Disillusionment with their Arab brothers spread. For generations there had been a body of Muslim Lebanese opinion that called for union with Syria; now not a single Muslim politician of the first rank would even consider it.[125] Prominent Muslim spiritual leaders accused

---

[125] Walid Jumblatt stressed this change in an interview with the author.

the Palestinians of disregarding elementary interests of the Lebanese. Moderate politicians prominent in the pre-war period began to regain some of their lost prestige, while militias and parties allied to the Palestinians — and since the death of Kamal Jumblatt even more dependent on them — found their adherents drifting away. This shift in opinion was impressively demonstrated in early 1982. The National Movement announced elections for Beirut urban district councils, a move intended to brake the growing popularity of the old zu`ama', in particular Saeb Salam's. The zu`ama' and religious leaders made common cause against the elections: their mass demonstrations in March brought far more supporters on to the streets of Beirut than their opponents' did. With the exception of Syrian–Palestinian conflicts, the general aggravation of the simmering warfare in various parts of the country had a common denominator: growing Lebanese disenchantment with both Syrian and Palestinian domination. The militias had the guns, but the old, moderate politicians had most of the people. The patent senselessness and pointlessness of the petty wars and the manifest chaos produced by all the fighting lent growing urgency to demands for the regular Lebanese Army to march into West Beirut and re-establish the rule of law. The phenomenon first observed on the National Day in 1979 had become a daily national observance: thousands of cedar flags, on mosques and schools, in front of shops and on motor-cars, private houses and ruins. Wherever Muslim Lebanese were able to do so they took up the protest — either militarily or symbolically — against what they felt was foreign occupation.[126]

## Israeli–Palestinian War[127]

Prior to 1982, Israeli–Arab wars had been preceded by brief political crises, and their outbreak had taken one or the other by surprise. From 1981, however, all sides had been anticipating a serious confrontation between Israel and the PLO in Lebanon. There were grounds enough. The missile crisis between Israel and Syria had not been settled. The 'Fourteen Day War' in July 1981 had shown Israel that

---

[126] Nawaf Salam, *The Agony of Lebanon: Scenarios and solutions*, photocopied typescript (Harvard University, Centre for Internaional Affairs, Cambridge, Mass., 1982), p. 17f, observed at this time an 'increasing Lebanese belief in a common country ... Since 1979, Flag Day has constituted a repeated outburst of "Lebanonism" among all religious segments. This new Lebanonism expresses increasing Moslem disenchantment with both the Palestinians and Syrians and with the Arab handling of the Lebanese conflict in general. It similarly expresses the growing Christian disillusionment with the West'.

[127] See especially the balanced account in Rabinovich, *The War for Lebanon*, pp. 121ff, and the detailed, albeit committed, study by Schiff and Ya'ari, *Israel's Lebanon War* (which makes of Bashir Gemayel and the Phalangists scapegoats par excellence). For a precise account of the military aspects see Moshe Gammer, 'The war in Lebanon: The course of hostilities, in Colin Legum et al., eds., *Middle East Contemporary Survey, Vol. VI, 1981–82* (New York and London, 1984, pp. 128–57. See also Bulloch, *Final Conflict*.

the PLO could shell northern Israel to a standstill. The PLO was openly building up a quasi-regular army in southern Lebanon, and Syria had embarked on an ambitious military build-up. Israel had grounds for concern: a potential war of attrition on the northern border; the question-mark over lasting peace with Egypt since the assassination of President Sadat in October 1981; and the divergence between the Egyptian and American and the Israeli positions in the negotiations over the second stage of the Camp David Accords, that is, autonomy for the Palestinians.

The second Likud government, in which Ariel Sharon was Minister of Defence, debated at length ways and means of meeting these dangers. They were unanimous on two points: no real concessions in respect of the West Bank, and measures to protect the northern region against a war of attrition. Part of the cabinet and the military command — as well as the opposition Labour Party — favoured a pragmatic 'limited solution': the creation of a forty kilometre wide security zone in Lebanon to obviate long-range shelling. Others, especially Sharon, favoured a 'broad solution'. Their conception was indeed ambitious. To their thinking, a crushing blow against the PLO was a prerequisite for a solution to the West Bank question favourable to Israel. To achieve this, it was necessary simultaneously to expel the Syrians from Lebanon and prepare the ground for the formation of a strong, pro-Israeli Lebanese government. 'Operation Litani' had demonstrated that a 'limited solution' would be ineffectual. Furthermore, the circumstances for a broad solution were favourable: Israel need not have any immediate fear of the Egyptian reaction, Iraq had its hands tied in its war with Iran, and the Syrian military build-up did not yet pose a serious threat. In 1982, a new Lebanese president had to be elected, and Bashir Gemayel was a suitable pro-Israeli candidate. Finally, American approval would probably be forthcoming. Reagan and Haig's policy for the Middle East was one of 'strategic consensus', of collaboration between all the pro-Western forces of the region, in which Israel played a major role. Weakening the PLO and stabilizing the situation in Lebanon accorded with this policy. In April 1982, a high-ranking Israeli officer informed Haig about the Israeli plans. The response was that they should wait until the final stage of the withdrawal from Sinai, so as not to jeopardize peace with Egypt.[128] In May, Sharon himself met Haig and obtained the sought-after consent, if not encouragement.[129] It is still not known whether Sharon informed Haig of his plans in their entirety. The agreement of the desired Lebanese allies was a more complicated matter. Doubtless, Bashir Gemayel wanted to become president. Doubtless,

---

[128] Ze'ev Schiff, 'The Green Light', *Foreign Policy* 50(1983), p. 79.
[129] Haig's attitude was not shared by all members of the American administration. The Defence Secretary, Weinberger, and the National Security Adviser, Clark, took a different view.

he welcomed without reservation a crushing Israeli blow against both the PLO and the Syrians in Lebanon: he regarded both the Palestinians and the Syrians as greater dangers to Lebanese sovereignty than Israel, and any help against these dangers was viewed positively by him. Nor can there be any doubt that he envisaged himself as a strong president and was convinced that Lebanon needed an undivided central government and a strong fighting army. But he was just as convinced that Lebanon could not be governed against the will of half the Lebanese, and that a Maronite president could be strong only if he did not offend the fundamental convictions and feelings of the Muslims. He was certain that the majority of the Muslims wanted to be rid of both the Palestinians and the Syrians. The growing open rejection on the part of both Shi`is and Sunnis strengthened him in this belief. But he was equally certain that the Christians would not be able to do this for their Muslim compatriots; if anyone could, as a sort of 'force majeure', it would be the Israelis.[130] Sharon expected of Bashir Gemayel and his Lebanese Forces that in the event of an Israeli invasion they would assume the task of storming and 'clearing' West Beirut of Palestinians, evidence of his ignorance of the true nature of the situation in Lebanon. Quite apart from purely military considerations — the Lebanese Forces were incapable of accomplishing this: militias are highly efficient defence forces, but seldom suited to offensive actions — this would have been political suicide; the Israeli Army would withdraw someday, but the Lebanese Christians had to live with their Muslim compatriots. Attacks on Palestinian camps: possibly; an offensive against Muslim West Beirut: never. For this reason, the Lebanese Forces never acceded to Sharon's proposal that they support the Israeli Army should it attack West Beirut. Sharon, however, acted in the belief that at the crucial moment they would accede. The response to his suggestion that Israeli troops land in Jounieh and attack Beirut in a pincer movement from north and south was clearer: the condition would be that the Israeli Army would remain in Lebanon to afford the Christians lasting protection against Syria and the rest of the Arab world.[131]

In the final analysis, the misunderstandings between Sharon and Bashir Gemayel were a reflection of far deeper misunderstandings between many Israelis and Lebanese Christians. The Israeli side had the impression that the Lebanese Christians wanted Israel 'to do their dirty work' for them. The Christians held the Israelis ultimately responsible for the expulsion of the Palestinians and all the misfortune pursuant on this in Lebanon,[132] and thought it only right that Israel should do something to mitigate this misfortune. An even more fundamental

---

[130] Interview with the author, 1981.
[131] Schiff and Ya'ari, *Israel's Lebanon War*, p. 50.
[132] Pierre Gemayel, for one, never tired of expressing this view.

misunderstanding was the Israeli belief that a predominantly Maronite regime could be erected in Lebanon — and that the Maronites wanted one. Certainly, many Maronites did take the view that their community deserved a special and prominent role in Lebanon. Yet, with the possible exception of a few militant Utopians, none of them believed that might alone might be right, or such rule even desirable. This included Bashir Gemayel: he believed in strong leadership because he was convinced that this was the desire of all Lebanese, including the Muslims. He believed the Maronites had a special role to play, but did not see it as ascendancy in the nature of the Alawites in Syria or the Hashemites in Jordan. A further Israeli misunderstanding concerned the willingness of Lebanese Christians to break with the rest of the Arab world by openly consorting with Israel. The Christians knew they could expect little sympathy and less help from the Arabs. But they also knew that they were part of the Arab world — regardless of the nature of the relationship — and that for economic reasons alone they could not afford a break.[133]

When Sharon unleashed the war in 1982, his strategic calculations proved correct. However, his erroneous interpretation of the Lebanese situation was to make of a military victory a political disaster both for Israel and, even more so, for Lebanon. The timing of the war was set before its outbreak: after completion of the withdrawal from Sinai on April 25th — to fulfil the Americans' condition for the 'green light' — and before September, the last date for the Lebanese presidential elections. From the end of April the Israelis waited for an excuse. The PLO dissident group under Abu Nidal provided one: the attempted assassination of the Israeli ambassador to the Court of St. James. The mainstream of the PLO was innocent; indeed, Abu Nidal's splinter group made a practice of murdering moderate Palestinians as a contribution to the struggle against Israel. However, in retaliation the Israeli air force bombed PLO targets in Beirut. This broke the cease-fire negotiated by Habib in 1981. The PLO responded by shelling northern Israel. On June 6th, 1982, the Israeli Army marched into southern Lebanon.

At this point the Israeli government was still undecided on the scale of the operation. Initially, the objective appeared to be a forty kilometre deep security zone north of the border; however, Sharon and his chief of staff, Eitan, did not halt the advance.[134]

In three days the Israeli Army advanced along the coast to Damour, skirting strong Palestinian positions in the camps near Tyre and Sidon. For days the

---

[133] In an interview the author asked Dory Chamoun, a son of the former president, whether, in the event of a partition of Lebanon and an alliance between the Christians and Israel, a liberal democracy in the Christian part could survive. He replied: 'We shall never know; before we could know we should have starved to death or emigrated.'

[134] See the assessment of Rabinovich, *The War for Lebanon*, pp. 132ff.

encircled PLO units resisted desperately, until bombed and shelled into submission by air force and artillery, with great loss of life and damage to property. Simultaneously, the Israelis advanced through Jezzine and the Chouf in the centre and on the west through the southern Bekaa northwards. Through American diplomatic channels the Israelis had let the Syrians know that their sole objective was the PLO, that they wished to avoid war with Syria. But as Syrian troops were stationed in the Bekaa and adjoining hills, for a few days there was heavy fighting between Syrian and Israeli forces. By June 10th, the war had been decided in military terms: the Israelis destroyed the Syrian missile system in Lebanon and much of the Syrian air force. The losses inflicted on the Syrians by previously unknown Israeli military technology included not only missiles and aircraft but half of Syria's fighter pilots as well. Despite Israeli air supremacy, hard-pressed Syrian ground troops in the Bekaa and surrounding hills continued to resist.

As so often in the past, the superpowers, frightened by the prospect of a full-scale war between Syria and Israel, took action. The Syrians appealed to the Soviets, the Soviets to the Americans, and the Americans put pressure on the Israelis. On June 11th, a Syrian–Israeli cease-fire came into effect, before the Israeli Army had reached the Beirut–Damascus highway. This cease-fire was remarkable in many ways. For the second time the USSR demonstrated that the Syrian–Soviet defence agreement did not extend to Syrian troops in Lebanon. The Americans made it clear that their consent to an Israeli blow against the Palestinians was not tantamount to approval of a Syrian rout in Lebanon. The alacrity with which the superpowers arranged a cease-fire in favour of the Syrians, but to the exclusion of the Palestinians, reaffirmed that their prime concern was the danger of war between their client states, not other acts of war in Lebanon. Syria accepted a separate cease-fire. The Syrian troops had resisted when and wherever they had been attacked. Despite Israel's technical and numerical superiority, they had succeeded in retarding the Israeli advance. Israel had not managed to reach the Beirut–Damascus highway. When the cease-fire took effect on June 11th, Syrian units were still in position in the mountains south-east and east of Beirut; at this point Beirut had not yet been encircled. The Israeli Army failed to keep the cease-fire and continued fighting towards Beirut. On June 13th, when a second cease-fire came into effect, Israeli troops had already reached the highway in the vicinity of Baabda and Yarze — the seats of the Lebanese president and Lebanese military command respectively — establishing a territorial link with the Lebanese Forces. The Israelis did not respect the second cease-fire either. They advanced eastwards on both sides of the highway until, finally, on June 24th, they forced the Syrians to withdraw from Aley and Bhamdoun. The Palestinians and a Syrian brigade in West Beirut were now separated from the main Syrian forces by a broad strip of Israeli-occupied territory. Israeli units took up positions to the east of the green

## The Israeli invasion, 1982

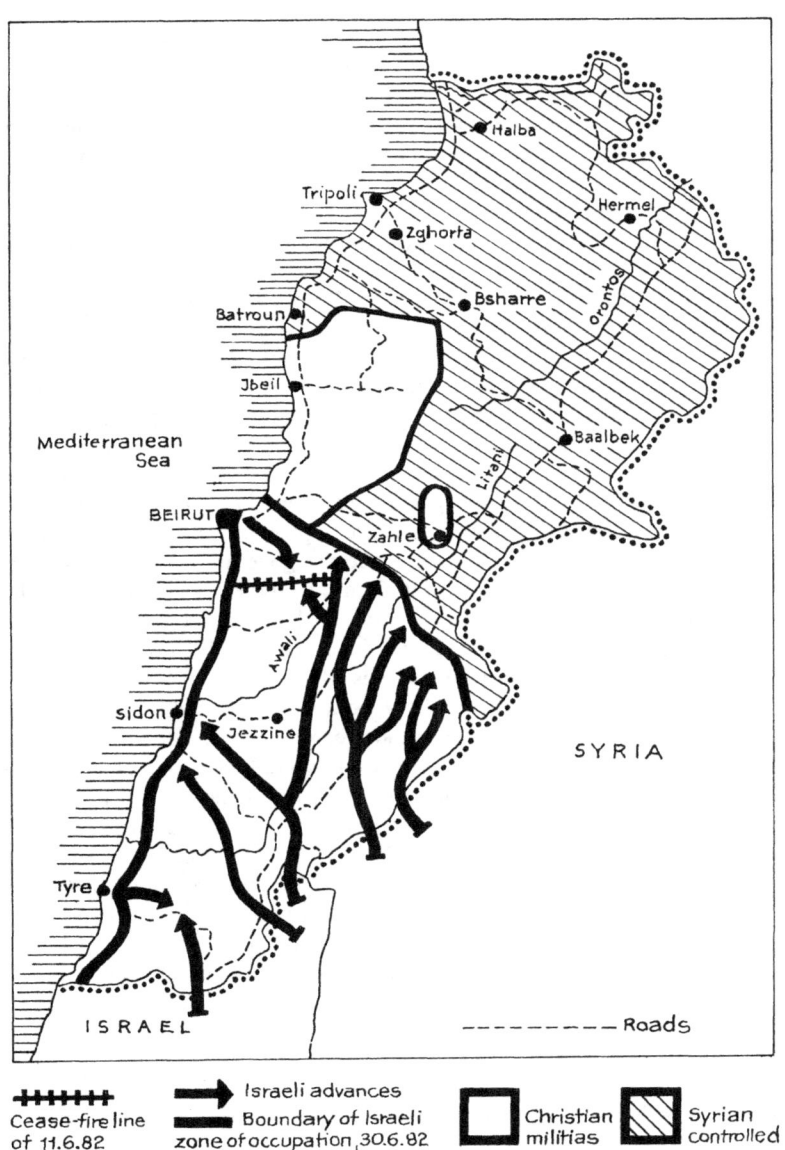

line in Beirut, while the Israeli navy imposed a blockade: West Beirut was entirely besieged.

To all practical purposes, the Syrian–Israeli war on Lebanese soil was over. It had been a by-product of the Israeli war against the PLO, and Israel had succeeded in dislodging all those Syrian troops that obstructed their drive against the Palestinians. In so far as the Israeli leaders had more ambitious plans — Sharon certainly did[135] — these could not be realized. Although the Syrian Army, and especially the air force, had suffered heavy losses, it had not been routed. When the Israelis finally deigned to respect the cease-fire, Syria was still in firm control of the northern Bekaa, the entire northern part of the country, the greater part of the Beirut–Damascus highway and, above all, the upper Metn in the central section of the Lebanon Mountains. Beirut was still within range of the Syrian batteries in the upper Metn.

But this is anticipating developments. The Israeli–Palestinian War over West Beirut began in earnest. It took place at two levels, the military and the diplomatic. Once the Israeli Army had invaded West Beirut and prepared for the siege, a controversy erupted in Israel over the objectives of the war. Although the Israeli cabinet had approved the invasion of Lebanon, it had remained split on the issue of scale and never set precise geographic objectives. Almost daily Sharon confronted the cabinet with a new fait accompli. Once the army stood on the outskirts of Beirut, he was able to convince the government to grasp the opportunity for a decisive blow against the PLO in the city. However, opinion in Israeli political and military circles divided on the method. And the gulf widened from day to day as the well-represented international mass media, especially television, reported to the world the horrific realities of the siege of a densely populated metropolis. A majority in the military command objected to any attempt to conquer and occupy the city because they feared heavy casualties. Many Israeli leaders hoped that the Lebanese Forces would spare Israeli soldiers this unpleasant task — a vain hope, for reasons mentioned. Consequently, the Israelis had to move, and chose the tactics the Syrians had used against Beirut in 1978 and Zahle and Beirut in 1981: blockade and shelling. The Israeli bombardments of 1982 were fiercer than any previously experienced: not only from the ground, but from the sea and, above all, from the air. The Israelis had to learn the same lesson as the Syrians: the victims were less the intended enemy — the guerrillas were relatively protected in their air-raid shelters and underground bunkers — than

---

[135] Sharon later accused the USA of sabotaging Israeli efforts 'by pushing Israel into a cease-fire hours before Syrian forces in Lebanon would have been decisively defeated ... With an additional few hours we would have cut the Syrian Army in the Bekaa in the area of Shtaura, Zahle'; *International Herald Tribune*, March 2nd, 1984.

Lebanese and Palestinian civilians. Like the Syrian government in its time, the Israeli government had to face international protests, but unlike the Syrians, protests from its own population and from within the ranks of its own army as well. A brigade commander tendered his resignation as he could not shell Beirut in good conscience, let alone storm the city. A 'Committee against the war in Lebanon' was formed at the end of June, and on July 3rd, over 100,000 people heeded its call to demonstrate in Tel Aviv for negotiations with the Palestinians. The Begin government refused to lift the siege, but at the same time declared that it was prepared to accept an offer of the USA to send special envoy Philip Habib to negotiate a solution.

Similar controversies to those in Israel had arisen in the American government and political public. The Reagan administration had accepted, even if not unanimously, a quick strike against the PLO. But it did not want this to escalate into war with Syria and had therefore pressured Israel to accept the partial cease-fire. Nor was it prepared to condone a long siege of West Beirut, with one exception: the Secretary of State, Haig. On June 25th, Reagan accepted Haig's resignation. For various reasons there had long been tension between Haig and other members of the administration; his unswerving support for Israel's actions in Lebanon had been the last straw. He was succeeded by George Shultz, reputed to enjoy the esteem of the Saudi Arabian government. Shultz set about reordering the priorities of American Middle East policy. The concept of 'strategic consensus' was abandoned, and with it the privileged consideration of Israeli interests. The 'regionalists' upstaged the 'globalists', and Washington began to construct a new peace initiative for the Middle East.

The shuffle in the American administration had immediate and unexpected consequences in Beirut. The PLO took courage and sought to exact the highest political price for its last bastion. When the Israelis reached Beirut the Palestinian leadership believed that the storming of the camps and the PLO headquarters was imminent. As the days passed in waiting, so their hopes grew that international pressure might indeed save them from capitulation. For, they believed, with good reason, that they would be able to survive even a long siege. They had a strong body of troops in West Beirut, reinforced by units that had managed to retreat from the south in time. They had ample supplies of guns and ammunition. They were thoroughly acquainted with the terrain, and had long experience in fighting from street to street and house to house. The civilian population would have to bear the brunt of the siege, but that was an advantage in political terms; for, as a rule, the aggressor is held responsible for civilian casualties and suffering. Soon the Palestinians were talking of turning Beirut into a 'second Stalingrad'.

Thus began a period of Israel's tightening grip and Habib's dogged negotiations between the Israeli government, on the one hand, and — through the mediation of the Lebanese Prime Minister, Wazzan, as well as Saeb Salam — Arafat, on the other. Israeli pressure on the besieged city mounted inexorably: water and electricity was cut off, the circle of defence was tightening in the south of the city, and Israeli sorties became more frequent. The negotiations dragged on. Only at the end of July did the PLO agree in principle to an evacuation of their troops. But Arafat was still bargaining for favourable conditions, either the simultaneous withdrawal of the Israeli troops or American recognition of the PLO. The cumulative effects of another round of heavy Israeli bombing and a further shrinking of the Palestinian circle of defence, greater American pressure on Israel, the PLO's recognition that the civilian population was almost at the end of its tether and renewed fears that Sharon would eventually storm the city, gradually rewarded Habib's efforts. The PLO was practically isolated, both regionally and internationally. This, at least, had been demonstrated by the siege. Not one Arab government had come to the Palestinians' assistance — and the only useful gesture had come from King Hussein of all people: he granted Palestinian soldiers in the Jordanian Army leave to volunteer in Lebanon. Qaddafi advised the Palestinians in Beirut to fight to the last man. Initially, not one Arab country was prepared to offer asylum to PLO guerrillas evacuated from Beirut. It took Habib's persistent diplomatic shuttling to prod a number of states between South Yemen and Tunisia into doing so. The USSR offered to evacuate Arafat and his staff on their warships.

Eventually, the USA devised a solution that gave the PLO retreat the trappings of honour. A multinational force of American, French and Italian troops entered Beirut, and Israel gave an assurance that it would not occupy the city. On August 21st, the evacuation began by sea of approximately 15,000 guerrillas and Palestinian civilians,[136] and by land of 6,500 Syrians and PLA soldiers. By September 1st, the last Palestinian guerrilla had left West Beirut.[137]

## Cold War over Lebanon

On the same day, President Reagan announced a new initiative on the Palestinian issue. The 'Reagan Plan' consisted of proposals to give substance to those articles of the Camp David accords pertaining to the Palestinians. Its objective was autonomy for the Palestinians on the West Bank and in the Gaza Strip 'in association with Jordan'. The first stage would require the Israelis to freeze the number of

---

[136] The PLO combattants were distributed among several Arab countries; the PLO headquarters were transferred to Tunis.

[137] The American contingent withdrew on September 10th, 1982, the Italian on the 11th and the French on the 13th — that is, before September 20th, the date agreed on with the Lebanese government — for reasons discussed below.

Jewish settlements in the occupied territories. Reagan declared that Israel's military successes in Lebanon had demonstrated that Israel was the strongest power in the region, but that force alone could not bring peace. His intention was to seek a solution that reconciled Israel's legitimate desire for security with the Palestinians' legitimate rights.

The Reagan Plan appealed to neither the Israeli nor the Syrian government. The leading members of the Likud government had no intention of loosening their hold on the West Bank. The invasion of Lebanon to smash the PLO had been one tactic in the wider strategy of dashing the hopes the Palestinians in the occupied territories had placed in the PLO, so that they would resign themselves to Israeli domination. The Reagan Plan threatened to thwart this. Begin rejected the Reagan Plan out of hand. In presenting his plan Reagan had not even mentioned Syria. In the Syrian view, a 'Jordanian solution' was a thinly veiled bilateral peace treaty, and just as suspect and unacceptable as the Camp David Agreement, an attempt to make decisions without and against Syria. However, American foreign policy experts assessed Syria in autumn 1982 as a country militarily weakened and financially dependent on Saudi Arabia, a side figure. The Americans had largely overlooked the fact that both Syria and Israel still occupied large portions of Lebanese territory and could at any time exploit their respective positions to undermine the American peace initiative. The Secretary of State, Shultz, declared that the events in Lebanon had demonstrated that America had a special responsibility to bring peace to the region; no other party had the credibility and, hence, the ability to establish the decisive contacts between all sides.

Once again a Middle Eastern peace initiative was to bring war, not peace, to Lebanon. For six months, though, this belligerence was more in the nature of a cold war. The period began with high hopes among the Lebanese.

The Lebanese were not leading actors in the Israeli war against the PLO, only extras — the victims. Most of them hoped that, whatever the result, it would at last bring peace to the country. The Lebanese government protested against the Israeli invasion, appealed to the United Nations Security Council, and ordered the Lebanese Army not to offer resistance. In mid-June the government had abrogated the treaty under which the Arab Deterrent Forces were stationed in the country and asked the Syrians to leave. The withdrawal of all foreign forces — Israeli, Syrian and Palestinian — became the official goal of Lebanese policy. Given the new equilibrium of terror, the goal did not seem unrealistic initially. The Shi`i militia Amal had bravely resisted the Israelis and suffered heavy casualties, alongside Palestinians with whom they had been locked in struggle shortly before.[138] But once the siege began, Amal too laid down their arms to avert the destruction of Shi`i suburbs. Walid Jumblatt ordered his Druze militia to offer 'passive resistance', which meant in practice that the Druze did not take up arms for their long-standing Palestinian allies, and saved the Chouf from the ravages of this war. The Lebanese inhabitants of West Beirut had no choice: they were hostages of the warring parties. Initially, Israeli bombing bred solidarity as all suffered together. Soon, however, West Beirut Muslim leaders were calling for the Palestinians to leave: what the Palestinians had started thinking about — making a 'Stalingrad' of Beirut — was to them unthinkable. Saeb Salam, in particular, did not mince his words; he told the Palestinians that their time as an armed force in Beirut had run out, that solidarity ended when existence itself was at stake. At the same time, he appealed to the American negotiators to arrange for them to withdraw with honour, knowing full well that this was the only way to spare his city utter devastation. The Christian Lebanese Forces did not resist as Israeli troops occupied East Beirut in order to close their ring around West Beirut. But Bashir Gemayel dashed the hopes many Israelis had placed in him — as well as the fears of many of his Muslim compatriots. He explained that the blame for the Israeli invasion lay with the Palestinians and Syrians, and simultaneously made it quite clear to his followers that this was not their war. Israel was not in Lebanon to save them but to pursue its own objectives. The withdrawal of all Palestinians and Syrians might be an interest common to Israelis and Lebanese, but Lebanese interests also included a speedy Israeli withdrawal. The best thing for Lebanon was for all foreign troops to get out so that Lebanon could reassert its sovereignty.

Thus, the Israeli invasion nourished an incipient development: all important Lebanese political forces agreed on the need to re-establish Lebanon's unity, and independence.

On the date set for the completion of the Palestinian withdrawal from Beirut — September 1st, 1982 — President Sarkis' term of office expired. The Lebanese Republic may have been impotent for years, but its institutions survived, and their rules were obeyed with remarkable tenacity. The parliament elected in 1972 had regularly extended its term of office, because the events of war rendered it impossible to hold elections. Since 1972 eight of the ninety-nine deputies had died naturally or been assassinated; the quorum was therefore sixty-two. Within the period set by the constitution the speaker of the Chamber of Deputies, Kamel Assad, announced a session to elect a new president. The evacuation of the PLO troops from West Beirut had just begun and there was still sporadic fighting between the Syri-

---

[138] Their most spirited resistance had been in Tyre. In the rural areas of southern Lebanon the Amal village militias had remained neutral. Amal resistance to the Israeli advance on Beirut was strongest in Chiyah, Ouzai and Ghobeiri. See Norton, 'Harakat Amal', p. 193.

ans and the Israelis in the Bekaa. Many deputies, in particular Sunnis with seats in West Beirut, argued that the election should be postponed; others declared it impossible to vote under Israeli guns. However, the majority recalled that in 1976 Sarkis had been elected under foreign — at that time Syrian — guns. Fundamentally, it was not a matter of guns but of candidates. On July 25th, during the siege of West Beirut, Bashir Gemayel had formally announced his candidacy. He had the support of most Christian deputies; the most important exceptions were Suleiman Franjieh and Raymond Eddé. Jumblatt, Berri and the majority of the Sunni deputies were opposed to him. In the eyes of the former group, Bashir Gemayel was a national hero; in the others of the latter he was an extremist candidate of a warring faction with the blood of numerous opponents, and former allies, on his hands. The former desired a 'strong man' to whom could be entrusted the task of re-establishing the authority of the state. The latter preferred a compromise candidate who would be a president open to compromise. The strongest opposition to Bashir Gemayel came from Syria. The organ of the ruling party accused him of treason and warned that 'the day of judgment was near'.[139] The Palestinians took leave of their long-standing arch-enemy by shelling the Villa Mansour, the provisional parliament on the demarcation line, thereby forcing postponement of the electoral session. The assembly was called into session on August 23rd, this time at the Lebanese Military Academy in the Fayadiye Barracks. It took hours before parliament had a quorum. On the second ballot Bashir Gemayel was elected by fifty-seven of the sixty-two deputies present: the opposition had stayed away. Almost every Maronite and Greek Catholic deputy was present, but only half the Greek Orthodox and one-quarter of the Sunnis. The election was decided by the Shi`is, two-thirds of whom attended, and the Druze, one of whom, Emir Majid Arslan, a traditional rival of the Jumblatts, voted for Gemayel. The flats or houses of those West Beirut deputies who had braved all threats were set on fire. A divisive candidate, not one of consensus, had been elected in a crucial vote taken under enormous pressure from both sides. It seemed that the new-found, fragile Lebanese consensus was about to shatter, that the new president was the president of only one part of Lebanon.

Within a few weeks opinion had turned.[140] The last Palestinian was scarcely

[139] Radio Damascus, July 26th, 1982, quoted from Yosef Olmert, 'Lebanon', in Legum, *Middle East Contemporary Survey, Vol. VI*, p. 719.

[140] In his book, *Le Proche-Orient éclaté: De Suez à l'invasion du Liban 1956–1982* (Paris, 1983), pp. 224f., George Corm, an author consistently critical of the Kata'ib and the Lebanese Forces, describes the change of mood as follows: 'le président libanais parvient en vingt jours à conquérir le coeur de toutes les communautés libanaises. Dans ses apparitions quotidiennes à télévision, Bachir parlera dans le langage le plus simple et le plus direct, loin des formules savantes et ampoulées le l'arabe classique, de son rêve: celui d'un peuple uni et fort, celui d'une administration d'où la corruption aura été chassée, celui d'une société où la promotion ne se fera que par la compétence et non plus par la fortune ou l'allégeance familiale et

out of Beirut when the Beirut Sunnis announced their readiness to cooperate with Bashir Gemayel. This was not primarily a reflection of their regained freedom of expression — that too — but a reaction to the president-elect's own statements. He declared that he wanted to be a president of all Lebanese. He gained credibility by dissociating himself more openly from Israel. In particular, he rejected a separate peace treaty with Israel. His popularity among the Muslims improved at one stroke when it became known that at a meeting with Begin he had stated that he had no intention of becoming a Lebanese Karmal Babrak. On September 11th, he conferred with Saeb Salam: the Lebanese consensus was holding up.

On September 14th, a bomb exploded in a meeting hall of the Kata'ib in Ashrafieh, leaving twenty-six dead, among them Bashir Gemayel — before he could take office. Even in a country in which violent death was an everyday occurrence this murder caused deep shock. A second followed on September 17th and 18th: the massacre in the Sabra and Chatila camps. Immediately after the Bashir Gemayel's assassination, and in contravention of the agreement with Philip Habib, the Israeli Army occupied West Beirut, though not the Palestinian camps. The Israeli commanders suspected that a number of Palestinian guerrillas had remained behind in the camps; the number bandied about was 2,000. They wanted to remove any remnants of the PLO military presence in Beirut, but did not wish their own soldiers to carry out this operation. After the murder of Bashir Gemayel they had no difficulty in finding commanders of the Lebanese Forces willing to do it for them. The predictable happened. Christian militiamen — many from Damour, where Palestinians had massacred Christians in 1976 — not only hounded armed Palestinians, but murdered hundreds of unarmed men, women and children, whether Palestinian or — mainly Shi`i — Lebanese. After years of fighting with little quarter given or taken, and innumerable other horrors and massacres, of which the world had taken little notice, many Lebanese had grown insensitive to such incidents. Despite these political, but not moral 'mitigating circumstances', the new Lebanese consensus was again in jeopardy. The massacre in Sabra and Chatila was not preceded by fierce fighting; it was cold-blooded murder of mostly defenceless people: it carried the stigma of cowardice. It also lacked even the most superficial rational justification. The brutalities against

---

confessionnelle, celui d'un pays que l'étranger devra respecter parce qu'il aura enfin une armée forte et und diplomatie musclée.

Stupéfaite, la population de Beyrouth-Ouest qui, la veille encore, saluait dans les larmes le départ d'une révolution introuvable, trouve enfin un héros libanais, jeune, fier et fougueux. Du coup brille à l'horizon la possibilité d'effacer toutes le humiliations ... de même s'estompe l'image partisane et violente que le jeune chef d'État avait donnée au cours des années de troubles 1975 à 1980 ... Bachir Gemayel apparaît alors comme le sauveur charismatique que tout un peuple a si longtemps attendu ... Assassiné le 14 septembre, neuf jours avant son entrée officielle en fonction, il est pleuré par toute la population.'

civilians in Karantina, Damour and Tel al-Za`tar all accompanied drives by one group to expel what they regarded as an antagonistic group, a threat to themselves. The inhabitants of Sabra and Chatila, however, were surrounded on all sides. They could not be expelled, only killed. And above all, the Christian militiamen had willingly acted as Israeli accomplices.

The reaction of the Lebanese Muslim leaders was a blend of cynicism about the fate of the now unwelcome Palestinians and political wisdom: they, like the Christian leaders, condemned the massacre and declared Israel solely responsible. The Kata'ib, the strongest political formation in the Lebanese Front, absolved the Lebanese Forces of all complicity. The parties of the Lebanese Left adopted the same position. Lebanese across the political spectrum decided for different reasons simply to ignore the shocking reality. Although the Israelis bore part of the responsibility for what had taken place, they were not the perpetrators. But they were the apposite scapegoat in a situation in which the Lebanese were, above all, seeking to avoid dissension.

Two days after the massacre parliament met and elected, with an exceptionally large majority,[141] Amin Gemayel as successor to his brother Bashir. This time most of the Sunni deputies were also present. Amin Gemayel found it easier than his younger brother to present himself as a president of national consensus. He had a reputation as a politician who enjoyed discussing and compromising. Since the outbreak of war he had never lost contact with Syrian and Palestinian leaders. Nor had he been involved in his party's negotiations with Israel, and was therefore not compromised in the eyes of his Muslim compatriots. Virtually all Lebanese political factions declared their willingness to cooperate with him, including his brother's arch-enemies, the supporters of Franjieh and Jumblatt. The return of a multinational force of Americans, French and Italians to Beirut was an additional source of optimism. Within a few days the divided capital was united for the first time since 1975. There was a mood of euphoric reconstruction. A Sunni multi-millionaire financed a campaign to remove rubble and clear the streets. Former militiamen drove bulldozers instead of armoured cars, shouldered shovels instead of machine guns. On November 22nd, the National Day, the Lebanese Army paraded through both parts of Beirut.

The USA announced a two-year programme to rebuild the army, including trainers and modern weapons. The army's first 'assignment', however, was singularly demoralizing: to eject 'squatters' and unlicensed hawkers from what had once been the 'better quarters' and promenades of West Beirut. Most of the squatters were destitute refugees from southern Lebanon; the hawkers were former

---

[141] Of the eighty deputies present (as against sixty-two at his brother's election), seventy-seven voted for Amin Gemayel, one against him and two abstained.

shopkeepers whose premises in the old bazaar district of the city centre had been destroyed in the fighting at the start of the war. This time they were not expelled by hostile militias but by their own army; and the government made no effort to find alternative accommodation or business premises for them. The new government's disinterest in social problems was as crass as that of any pre-war government; many of the hopes placed in it were proving premature.

Amin Gemayel also let pass the opportunity to form a broad coalition of all important political groups in the country. He retained Sarkis' last Prime Minister, Chafiq Wazzan, who had the confidence of the Beirut Sunnis. But for the rest, his ministers, like Franjieh's in the early 1970s, though competent technocrats, were politically unrepresentative light-weights. He did not seriously try to involve Amal leaders in government, although for years no group had demonstrated so great a loyalty towards the Lebanese state as this Shi`i movement.[142] He also overlooked Walid Jumblatt, who became the first important opponent of the new administration, though for reasons that had more to do with the Lebanese Forces than with Amin Gemayel. The Amal leadership soon followed his lead. Amin Gemayel thought he could govern without Amal and without Jumblatt. He banked on the traditional Shi`i *zu`ama'*, who had voted for the Gemayels, regaining their importance, and on the Arslan clan in the Druze community. This was to prove a misjudgment of social developments in both the Shi`i and Druze communities. On the other hand, the new president felt that foreign policy should have priority over domestic policy. This was not unrealistic since most of the country was still controlled by non-Lebanese arms. But by failing to nurture the incipient national consensus embodied in his election, Gemayel bears much responsibility for its fracturing when international conflicts again tested the country.

In foreign policy, Amin Gemayel had various options. But whatever his choice, he would have to walk a tightrope. The 'Syrian option' implied that he would have to accept the presence of Syrian forces in Lebanon, and the risk that Israel would entrench itself in that part of the country it occupied. The 'Israeli option' was a mirror image, otherwise analogous. Towards the end of 1982, the political nightmare of many Lebanese was a tacit understanding between Syria and Israel to simply sit tight in their respective zones of occupation. Gemayel, encouraged by

---

[142] See William W. Harris, 'La politique libanaise de Hafez el-Assad', in Kodmani-Darwish, *Liban*, p. 96. Norton, 'Harakat Amal', p. 199, comes to a similar conclusion: 'Unfortunately, President Amin al-Gemayel has seemed to be much more comfortable dealing with the established zu`ama than with their challengers in Amal... Over time, the Shi`as have come to believe that they are serving as the whipping boys for a president who cares more for his weak Maronite constituency ... Thus, it should hardly be surprising that the Shi`as came to lose patience.' See also Clinton Bailey, 'Lebanon's Shi`is after the 1982 war', in Martin Kramer, ed., *Shi`ism, Resistance, and Revolution* (Boulder and London, 1987), pp. 222ff.

his advisers,[143] sought what he took to be an 'American option' as a way out of this dilemma.[144] It was an option his predecessor, Sarkis, had been strongly recommending to Bashir Gemayel since 1981. It was very tempting to avoid choosing between unpleasant neighbours by approaching the Western superpower. With its help Lebanon might also extract itself from its neighbours' clutches.

On a visit to Washington in October 1982, Amin Gemayel gained the impression that the USA was prepared to accept the role as Lebanon's new protector. In the previous months American troops had twice landed in Lebanon — before the withdrawal of the Palestinians and after the massacre in Sabra and Chatila — to protect the Palestinians. President Reagan gave assurance that this time the American troops would remain in Lebanon until all other foreign troops had left the country and the authority of the Lebanese government had been re-established over all Lebanese territory, an assurance reiterated over the next year.

For the first time Lebanon was given priority in American Middle East policy. Reagan repeatedly declared that the Lebanese question had to be settled before the Palestinian question could be dealt with.[145] Special envoy Habib was appointed to mediate between Lebanon and its neighbours. An Israeli withdrawal should be negotiated first, and only then a Syrian withdrawal — another new priority. No cogent reason for the linkage between the Lebanese and Palestinian questions was ever given. The most plausible explanation is that American diplomats felt that the Lebanese question was less complicated, and hoped that the solution of this question would have positive effects on the Palestinian question. However, Habib did explain[146] why Israeli — rather than simultaneous — withdrawal was given priority in his Lebanese negotiations. As Israel had won the war in Lebanon, it was in the stronger position. If agreement were reached with Israel, it would only be necessary to make Israeli withdrawal dependent on Syrian withdrawal to achieve both. In any case, the threat of further Israeli strikes would encourage an already weakened Syria to compromise. These two priorities were practically an

---

[143] Two of them have published accounts of their experiences: Wadi D. Haddad, *Lebanon. The politics of revolving doors* (New York, 1985), and Ghassan Tuéni, *Une guerre pour les autres* (Paris, 1985). Haddad was Gemayel's security adviser, Tuéni his political adviser. The former president published a book towards the end of his incumbency: Amin Gemayel, *L'offense et le pardon* (Paris, 1988).

[144] Premier Wazzan agreed with the president on this point: 'nous avons estimé que la seule option réaliste qui s'imposait était l'option américaine'; *Le Monde*, May 31st, 1983.

[145] For a concise and brilliant study of American policy in Lebanon from 1982 to 1984 see William B. Quandt, 'Reagan's Lebanon policy: trial and error', *Middle East Journal* 38/2 (1984), pp. 237–54. The Begin government continued to reject the 'Reagan Plan' because their interpretation of autonomy as limited self-government excluded any form of territorial jurisdiction for the Palestinians; the Syrians were equally adamant because they were still not taken seriously.

[146] At a Ditchley conference in May 1983.

invitation to Israel and Syria to sabotage American policy on Palestine and Lebanon at every opportunity.[147] A cold war began in Lebanon.

As Israel rejected the Reagan Plan for the occupied territories, and as Reagan wanted a Lebanese settlement first, the obvious step was either to protract or block a Lebanese settlement. Moreover, the Israeli government itself had several reservations about political developments in Lebanon. As long as Bashir Gemayel was alive, they had not abandoned hopes of his establishing a regime that would in effect amount to 'Maronite domination', one dependent on Israeli support and strong enough eventually to sign a formal peace treaty between Israel and Lebanon — as second Arab state after Egypt. But they did not feel that Amin Gemayel was capable of establishing a strong regime, and they knew that he was not prepared to sacrifice his relations with the Arab world for a peace treaty with Israel. Indeed, the new president shared the view of most Lebanese politicians that the dictates of internal unity required his country to let all other Arab countries lead the way.[148] Accordingly, while the Israeli 'hawks' were doing all they could to force a settlement on their terms on the Lebanese president, more and more 'doves' were demanding an end to the Lebanese adventure and a quick withdrawal of the Israeli Army. The massacre in Sabra and Chatila had thrown Israel into a crisis of conscience. They had believed they needed to protect the Lebanese Christians from genocide; instead Christians had massacred others with the complicity of the Israeli Army. Their honour was stained. The 'hawks' had accused the Lebanese Forces of having funked fighting the Palestinians; now the 'doves' accused this militia of having wilfully drawn the Israeli Army into cold-blooded murder. In Lebanon a military court was charged with the investigation of the massacre, and produced an inconclusive report; in Israel pressure was mounting to have all aspects of the affair examined in detail. The stronger the criticism in Israel, the more the government wanted tangible results to justify its actions. Even before the Lebanese–Israeli negotiations started, Sharon put pressure on the Lebanese. In December 1982, he threatened the Kata'ib leader, Pierre Gemayel, saying that his son would be no more than mayor of Baabda — the seat of the presidential palace — if he continued to rely on the USA alone and did not accede to the concessions Israel demanded.[149] While the governments negotiated, the Israelis gave weight to their threats. In their zone of occupation

---

[147] See Quandt, 'Reagan's Lebanon policy', pp. 241f.; Paul A. Jureidini, 'Lebanon's regional politics', in Azar, *The Emergence of a New Lebanon*, p. 212: 'linking the withdrawal process in Lebanon to the peace process was a disaster'.

[148] In 1977 Elias Sarkis had already stated: 'Le Liban ne sera pas le second État arabe à conclure un accord avec Israël, mais le dernier'; Pakradouni, La paix manquée, p. 124.

[149] Sharon: 'I told Pierre Gemayel: "Don't follow the Americans' advice. No one will help you"'; *International Herald Tribune*, March 2nd, 1984.

they pursued the classic colonial policy of divide and rule. They allowed Haddad considerably to expand the area controlled by his militia and armed Shi`i groups, and even small Palestinian militias in the camps in the south. Above all, the Israeli Army simply stood by as a new internal Lebanese conflict erupted, that between the Lebanese Forces and the Druze militias in the Chouf, the subject of the next section. Finally, the Israelis were instrumental in inciting Christian opposition to Amin Gemayel. After the death of their militant leader, Bashir, the Lebanese Forces had accepted his more flexible brother with reserve. They now reproached him for the policy his brother had initiated, that is, dissociation from Israel; this, they felt, was costing them the fruits of the Israeli victory, which they erroneously claimed as their own, that is, Christian ascendancy in Lebanon. Briefly: the militant Christian commanders took it amiss that the president was not realizing the dreams they associated with the person of his deceased brother. And they were only too gullible as their Israeli middlemen and advisers extolled the advantages of an 'Israeli option', which by this time had little credence in Israel itself. Muslim Lebanese, on the other hand, held the president responsible for what the Christian militia did and said, although they were completely independent of him. As the Israeli–Lebanese negotiations dragged on, the Americans became impatient. They had few means of pressuring Israel, so instead they pressured the Lebanese to relent. At last, on May 17th, 1983, the agreement was initialled. The Lebanese concessions, especially on its sovereignty in southern Lebanon,[150] were such that, apart from the official designation, there was little to distinguish the agreement from a proper peace treaty.[151]

Israel had won the first round of the cold war. As early as April 10th, King Hussein had announced that his attempt to reach agreement with the PLO on a basis for negotiations over the occupied areas had failed. With that the Reagan Plan was a dead letter. Israeli victory was simultaneously a Syrian victory. Syria,

---

[150] Provisions of the agreement included: an end to the hostilities; mutual recognition of independence, sovereignty and inviolability of borders; prohibition on hostile activities and propaganda; opening of missions with diplomatic status; and the abrogation of all treaties whose provisions contradicted those of the Israeli–Lebanese agreement (which patently applied to the mutual Arab Defence Pact of 1950, of which Lebanon was a member). The major part of the agreement's text was concerned with security matters. A security zone should be created in southern Lebanon (south of a line running from Sidon to Rashaya). Responsibility for security in the northern section of this zone should be assumed by a brigade of the Lebanese Army alone, but in the southern section by a 'territorial brigade' as well, formed from units of the 'Army of Free Lebanon' (in terms of a separate protocol Major Saad Haddad should be given command of this territorial brigade). Mount Barouk, with the destroyed radar station of the Lebanese Army, should be demilitarized. 'Joint security teams' (eight in all), composed of equal numbers of Israelis and Lebanese, should regularly inspect the security zone.

[151] A former secretary of state in the Lebanese foreign ministry qualified the provisions of this agreement, which went beyond the cease-fire agreement of 1949 as 'plus proches d'un traité de paix que d'une convention d'armistice'; Kesrouan Labaki, *Des idées pour le Liban* (Antelias, 1984), p. 141.

for which the plan had not foreseen any role at all, had disliked it as much as Israel. It helped to thwart Reagan's initiative by encouraging elements within the PLO opposed to an understanding with Hussein. The Israeli–Lebanese agreement itself gave Syria the ultimate say in the cold war over Lebanon: the agreement would take effect when Syria agreed to withdraw its troops.[152] On May 6th, the American Secretary of State, Shultz, was told in Damascus that Syria had no intention of withdrawing: it regarded the restrictions the agreement imposed on Lebanese sovereignty as unacceptable, and even more so the fact that it equated the presence of Syrian troops, sent with the consent of the Lebanese government and the approval of the Arab League, with that of those of, in its eyes, the Israeli aggressors.[153] With that the Israeli–Lebanese agreement also became a dead letter. Had Philip Habib initially believed fear of Israel would coerce Syria into agreement or — as he still believed in May 1983 — at least into negotiations, protraction had robbed this assumption of any basis it might have had. During the negotiations Syria had been well rearmed by the USSR.[154] In addition, the USSR installed its most modern missile system in Syria and provided around 5,000 technicians to operate and maintain it.[155] In consequence, an Israeli military strike against Syria would have carried far greater risks than a few months previously. Over the same period, but independent of developments in Syria, events in Israel itself had ruled out further military adventures: the Kahan Commission published its report on the massacre in Sabra and Chatila.[156] Ariel Sharon had to resign as Minister of Defence. More importantly, it nourished a widespread mood of 'never

---

[152] In a letter to the American government the Israeli government stated that for the treaty to become effective certain conditions had to be fulfilled: the release of Israeli soldiers held captive by the Syrians and Palestinians, the withdrawal of Palestinian troops from Lebanon and the simultaneous withdrawal of Syrian and Israeli troops. It is evident that the Lebanese government could not enforce fulfilment of these conditions.

[153] 'Syria perceived the conclusion of the May 17 accord as a separate peace agreement similar to Camp David' and 'as an attempt to isolate it and to exclude it from the mainstream of regional diplomacy. In addition, several of the clauses of the May 17 accord were considered as a direct threat to Syria's strategic and security interests in Lebanon'; Nawaf Salam, *Prospects for Lebanon; An essay on political opportunities and constraints* (Oxford, 1987), pp. 18f.

[154] Armaments included MiG 23s, T 62 and T 72 tanks, helicopters, ground-to-ground SCUD (with a range of about 350km) and FROG missiles (50–60km).

[155] SAM 5 ground-to-air missiles, as well as SAM 2, 6, 8 and 11 missiles to protect the batteries. It also stationed two early warning aircraft in Syria. During a visit to Beirut in May 1983 a member of the Soviet Central Committee declared that the USSR took its treaty of friendship with Syria seriously and warned Israel against aggression against Syria. See Laurent and Basbous, 'Le Liban et son voisinage', p. 1146.

[156] *The Beirut Massacre: The complete Kahan Commission Report, with an introduction by Abba Eban* (Princeton and New York, 1983). See also, *Israel in Lebanon: Report of the International Commission to enquire into reported violations of international law by Israel during its invasion of the Lebanon* (London, 1983).

again', both among the general public and in the army: in future Israel's armed forces were to be used only to defend the country and not for politico-military interventions in neighbouring states. Sharon's successor, Moshe Arens, was not less of a 'hawk' than Sharon, but, truer to the term, prudent and balanced. He soon realized that Israel could hope for little in return for its withdrawal from Lebanon. He reduced his policy to securing the border by cementing local alliances in southern Lebanon. In August 1983, the first stage of the Israeli withdrawal began without any quid pro quo.

Syria was the clear winner of the second round in the cold war over Lebanon. The Lebanese–Israeli agreement remained ineffective and the Reagan Plan had failed. The USA could no longer count on Israel for surrogate deterrence in the region. But Syria soon succeeded in finding surrogates in Lebanon whose unconventional and conventional methods would make life a misery for both the Israeli and the Western multinational forces in Lebanon. The first attacks on American and French soldiers took place in March. In April a bomb exploded in the US embassy, killing leading CIA experts on the Middle East. These were portents of the transition from the cold to another round of hot war. The PLO may have been thrown out of Beirut, but the city and the country as a whole remained the battlefield of the Middle East conflict: internal Lebanese divisions were no more difficult to exploit in 1983 than at any other time since 1969. And as in the previous half decade, several conflicts were being fought simultaneously.

## Civil war: Druze against the Lebanese Forces[157]

Before the war, more or less equal numbers of Druze and Christians lived in the Chouf and in Aley, the district immediately to the north. There was also a small Sunni minority. Many villages were confessionally mixed. An historical name for the Chouf was 'Jabal Druze' — the Druze Mountains — and the Druze have always regarded them as such. Even if they were not an absolute majority, it was the one region in the country where they could feel as though they were. In 1975 Kamal Jumblatt wanted war, but never war in the Chouf. He never allowed the Palestinians to settle there or to use the region for military purposes, even in their common interest. Christian militias had no say in the Chouf; the Druze militia controlled the region, though they had to accept a Syrian presence from 1976 onwards. Christians were murdered after the assassination of Kamal Jumblatt in 1977, but this was an isolated incident. All the same, members of parties in the

---

[157] The Middle East Council of Churches has produced two exemplary reports on the Chouf war: Georges Assaf, 'Rapport sur la situation dans les deux districts du Chouf et d'Aley depuis l'invasion israélienne' (Beirut, 1983) and 'Septembre 1983: "Bain de sang' dans la Montagne à la suite du brusque retrait des troupes israéliennes' (Beirut, 1983) (both mimeographs).

Lebanese Front feared for their safety and most of them moved. Many Christian inhabitants of the Chouf worked in Greater Beirut and commuted. After the outbreak of war they had to pass a number of militia checkpoints, which encouraged further Christian migration. By the late 1970s, the Christian villages and Christian sections of villages were mainly inhabited by women, children and old people. Despite the numerical imbalance, the communities continued to live by and large in peaceful coexistence, and the Druze remained lords of this land, as they had been a century before.

In 1982, when the Israelis occupied the Chouf without a fight, the Lebanese Forces thought the time had come to reverse this situation. Immediately after the Israelis had taken Aley and driven back the Syrian Army, Kata'ib members who had left the town returned and opened a party office. Militiamen of the Lebanese Forces established themselves in Aley and Souk al-Gharb and advanced deeper into the Chouf, setting up checkpoints along the way. They often harassed Druze and arbitrarily arrested people. Sporadic fighting soon broke out between them and the Druze militia. The Israelis often intervened to mediate and settle differences. Eventually, Bashir Gemayel, who wanted the support of the Druze deputies in his bid for the presidency, ordered his militiamen to retreat. However, immediately after his death the Lebanese Forces again tried to establish control over the Chouf. They justified this with the need to guarantee the security and equality of the Christians living in the Chouf. But it was an open secret that militant circles in the Christian militia, and also in the Lebanese Front, had other objectives. To keep a safe land link with the Israeli allies it was thought necessary to control the southern section of the mountains as well. In the hands of the Druze the Chouf remained a potential barrier between the Christian heartland and Israel; the Chouf barrier would have to be surmounted. To these military considerations the militant Christians added the conviction that this time the old formula of 'neither victors nor vanquished' was not enough; there would be a victor — meaning, of course, themselves.

The Druze were alarmed: they felt their existence threatened. Were they to lose control of the Chouf, their position would be that of the numerically comparable Greek Catholic community: a minority in all parts of Lebanon without a territorial basis for independent political action. This fear for their existence mobilized the Druze as the 'Mountain War' had mobilized the Christians in the spring of 1976. This community of barely one-quarter of a million people put 30,000 men under arms. Besides the PSP militia, a body known as 'Ibrahim's Forces' was formed by Druze sheikhs. In their behaviour towards the Druze the Lebanese Front had failed to distinguish between supporters of Jumblatt and those of Arslan, although the latter had supported Bashir Gemayel's candidacy and voted for him. This facilitated a common front between these rival Druze clans. If a further incentive to mobilize was needed, it came on December 1st, 1982: an attempt to assassinate Walid Jumblatt, which he survived with minor injuries. In December 1982, there was fighting in many places in the Chouf, while Israeli troops tried to keep the peace.

Druze leaders went on the diplomatic offensive,[158] with remarkable astuteness. They succeeded in winning both Israeli and Syrian support. As bridges, they had Druze communities in Israel and Syria, which had retained close links with the Lebanese Druze.[159] The Israeli Druze have a unique position in Israel: they are the only Arab community in Israel to provide soldiers for the Israeli Army, and the Israeli command holds their dependability and fighting spirit in high esteem. Hence, consideration for their own Druze soldiers alone was reason enough for the Israeli Army to avoid conflict with the Lebanese Druze in the course of their invasion of Lebanon. Over and above this, the Israeli Druze are well organized politically. At the first signs of conflict in the Chouf they took to lobbying intensively for the Lebanese Druze. The latter were the only Lebanese community with a political lobby in Israel.[160] Finally, the Druze have a positive, even somewhat romantic image in Israel: that of a small, proud, warrior community. When Israelis speak about a new order in the Middle East and the possibility of creating new states for ethno-religious minorities, the Druze are frequently at the back of their minds. As Israeli disenchantment with the Maronites grew, starting with their aloofness during the battle for Beirut and culminating in the election of the, in Israeli eyes, Arabophile Amin Gemayel, so did the attractiveness of the Druze as an alternate ally.[161]

The Druze's fight against the Lebanese Forces was also in the interests of the Syrian government; it allowed Syrian Druze to join the militia in the Chouf. However, the Druze benefited not only from the remarkable transnational solidarity but also from a partial coincidence of Syrian and Israeli interests. To render an Israeli-Lebanese agreement ineffective the Syrians needed Lebanese allies; the Druze were the most obvious choice. Israel, on the other hand, saw in the Chouf conflict an opportunity to put pressure on the Lebanese government. It could reward good behaviour by separating the hostile militias and enabling the regular Lebanese Army to move into the Chouf, thereby extending the authority of the

---

[158] Shimon Peres had visited Walid Jumblatt at the latter's seat in Mukhtara at a time when Jumblatt was very reticent about his contacts with Israel. The visit was interpreted as a meeting between two chairmen of the Socialist International. Subsequent contacts with Syrian leaders were far more discreet.

[159] From the summer of 1982 onwards there was a lot of travelling back and forth by Israeli Druze visiting the Chouf and Lebanese Druze visiting Israel.

[160] A study by Aribert Ziegler should appear shortly.

[161] Moshe Arens, Sharon's successor as minister of defence, had recognized the Druze as potentially more interesting allies than the Maronites much earlier. Interview with the author, 1980.

legal government to an area bordering on Greater Beirut. Or it could punish bad behaviour by leaving the Chouf in the hands of the Druze. This coincidence of interests between Israel and Syria could not endure. But it lasted long enough for the Druze to establish good relations with both states and benefit from them.

By the spring of 1983 the Druze had an unequivocal military advantage in the Chouf. Mobilization and Syrian reinforcements ensured them numerical superiority. And Israeli troops did not hinder supplies of arms and ammunition from Syrian forces still in the upper Metn.

The units of the Lebanese Forces were much weaker; some of their supplies from the Christian heartland had to pass through Druze-controlled territory, possible only with active Israeli assistance. They were utterly dependent on Israeli goodwill. Above all, they had a front line they could not hold. At the outset they had concentrated on occupying as many Christian villages as possible, many of them virtually isolated. To improve communications they were rapidly building roads, but many links remained tenuous. The 'front' was long and snaking, and forces were stationed at large intervals. For a while Israeli troops prevented serious clashes, though not shelling and retaliatory shelling, kidnap and murder, which were particularly prevalent in April and May 1983. Both sides were waiting to see what would happen when the Israelis withdrew, and in the meantime contented themselves largely with political demands. The Druze again called for a secular state in Lebanon. If that were impossible, they wanted a second chamber of parliament, a senate with a Druze speaker, so that the Druze would have an office of state equivalent to those of the Maronites, Sunnis and Shi`is. In any event, the Lebanese Forces had to get out of Druze territory. Samir Geagea, commander of the Lebanese Forces in the Chouf, expressed his hopes of creating 'sociologically homogeneous regions within a federal system'. It was his opinion that the Druze had 'no right to rule the Mountains as in recent years', that the Lebanese Forces absolutely rejected 'Druze hegemony' and the 'foreign presence in Aley and the Chouf, represented by the PSP'.[162]

The Chouf conflict was a civil war between two Lebanese communities, even if Syrian and Israeli interests did play a role. Both the Druze and the Lebanese Forces sought to establish their hegemony by violent means over a central part of the country. Whereas the Druze understood how to exploit their Syrian and Israeli connections to their material, strategic and political advantage, the leaders of the Lebanese Forces were blind to the fact that they had manoeuvred themselves into a hopeless situation. They believed that on their own they were a match for the Druze, hoped for support from the Lebanese Army and trusted to the Israelis not

---

[162] *An-Nahar*, August 28th, 1983.

to abandon them in need.[163] All these assumptions proved false. At the beginning of August 1983 Walid Jumblatt announced: 'It will be a carnival, a bloody carnival.'[164] The prophet was in the position to ensure his prophecy would be fulfilled.

## Shi`i resistance to Israel and estrangement from the government

The Lebanese invasion was a shock for the Shi`i population in southern Lebanon, but a shock which put an end to the long hated domination by Palestinian guerrillas. The Israeli soldiers were welcomed as liberators in a few villages, though as a rule, people remained aloof; there was very little animosity. People hoped that once the Palestinians had been driven out of Beirut the occupation would quickly end.[165]

As the Israeli–Lebanese negotiations dragged on, uncertainty mounted. When it finally became known the agreement provided for a lengthy Israeli presence in this region, fears spread that southern Lebanon might become a 'North Bank', a permanent zone of Israeli influence. For, in the meantime the Shi`is had learnt to fear the dark side of Israeli rule. The economy in the south was in deep recession. For reasons of security, the Israelis had introduced restrictions on trade with the rest of the country; in trade with Israel the Lebanese could not compete on equal terms. Unemployment was rising rapidly. The practices accompanying occupation were soon hated. Houses and people were constantly being searched for weapons; incidents were punished with collective measures; and the recruitment of informants and collaborators unsettled people. Within a short time the Israelis were regarded as arrogant and rude. Israeli disrespect for religious feelings incensed the population: soldiers forced their way into Shi`i mosques to search for weapons, and did not even shrink from interrupting the solemn procession of the Ashoura, the greatest Shi`i religious festival.

In Lebanon the Israeli Army acted as it did on the West Bank, where its methods had been successful; in Lebanon they provoked resistance. The Lebanese were not as easily cowed into accepting humiliations as the Palestinians on the West Bank had been, and they were better prepared to rebel.[166]

---

[163] 'Les Forces Libanaises font preuve d'une absence incroyable de maturité politique et d'une grande crédulité à l'égard d'Israël'; Laurent and Basbous, 'Le Liban et son voisinage', p. 1240. This assessment is remarkable because Antoine Basbous was put in charge of the Lebanese Forces Paris office in 1988.
[164] L'Orient-Le Jour, August 4th, 1983.
[165] L'Orient-Le Jour, August 4th, 1983.
[166] See W. Andrew Terrill, 'Low intensity conflict in Southern Lebanon: Lessons and dynamics of the Israeli–Shi'ite war, Conflict Quarterly, 7/3 (1987), pp. 22–35. See also the chapter 'Making Enemies in South Lebanon', in Norton, Amal and the Shi`a, pp. 107ff., and Bailey, 'Lebanon's Shi`is', pp. 219–36.

In spite of searches, innumerable weapons escaped the Israelis' notice, and the locals knew how to use them. For years the Lebanese had been practising and refining the tactics of resistance against superior forces: ambushes, rocket assaults on convoys and the mining of roads and terrain. Those who had been badly treated knew how to avenge themselves, and did. The Israeli soldiers were not trained to deal with such attacks, suffered considerable casualties and losses, and responded with harsher reprisals. The policy was self-defeating: it created a fertile ground for organized militancy. Small organizations of the Lebanese Left found new outlets for their activities; Muslim activists did not want to be outdone by the Left; eventually, to retain its influence, Amal, the largest, comparatively moderate Lebanese Shi`i movement, had to resort to attacks on the occupying forces.

The appearance of a new actor on the Lebanese stage accelerated this development: Khomeini's Iran.[167] In June 1982, during the Israeli invasion, Syria had agreed to the despatch of a few hundred 'Revolutionary Guards' (Pasdaran) to Lebanon. They had established themselves in Baalbek and throughout the northern Bekaa. A section of the Amal movement led by the teacher Hussein Moussavi split off from the main body of Amal led by Nabih Berri and, as 'Islamic Amal', allied itself to the Islamic fundamentalists. They proclaimed an 'Islamic Republic of Baalbek-Hermel', prohibited alcohol and obliged women to wear the chador. On the Lebanese National Day cedar flags were ripped down and the green flag of the Islamic fundamentalists hoisted. The Christian minority in the Bekaa was thoroughly intimidated. When the Greek Catholic Archbishop, Zoghbi, protested, he was kidnapped. There were numerous attacks on the Lebanese Army. Islamic activists started training as fighters at camps in the northern Bekaa.

For years the Syrian government had been combatting Sunni fundamentalism at home, and, therefore, had reservations about this development. However, its alliance with Iran was an important element in its struggle against the Iraqi Baath regime, and brought it an economic advantage in preferential prices for Iranian oil. Moreover, the methods the Islamic fundamentalists chose to reach their objectives also had advantages for Syria. One of Syria's goals was the withdrawal of all other foreign troops from Lebanon. Shi`i death-squad attacks on American, French and Israeli bases precipitated their respective withdrawals, without any blame directly attaching to Syria.

---

[167] See Bassma Kodmani-Darwish, 'L'Iran, nouvel acteur fort au Liban?', in Bassma Kodmani-Darwish, *Liban*, pp. 153–64.

In the Islamic fundamentalists Amal had serious rivals. Hezbollah,[168] the 'Party of God', established itself both in southern Lebanon and in the Shi`i suburbs of Beirut as a radical counter-movement to Amal. Although personally religious, the men leading Amal tended to favour a secular state. By contrast, the men behind Hezbollah were Shi`i clergymen in close contact with their Iranian colleagues.[169] The upholders of a pure and radical doctrine put the Amal pragmatists on the defensive. Sheikh Shamseddin, acting chairman of the Supreme Shi`i Council, and Berri, the president of Amal, would have welcomed an end to the Israeli occupation without further warfare. Several times they implored the Israeli and Lebanese negotiators to make haste; ultimately they found themselves forced by developments to call for the liberation of the south.

Amal also came under pressure because of its attitude to Amin Gemayel and the Wazzan government. The Shi`i population of Beirut was increasingly dissatisfied with the politics of the legal government. Even more strongly than in prewar Lebanon, the Shi`is felt disadvantaged and deprived. One-quarter of the victims of the massacre in Sabra and Chatila had been Shi`is, and no one had been called to account. The manner in which the Lebanese Army proceeded to eject squatters and refugees from their wretched accommodation was degrading. The Lebanese Forces in East Beirut were allowed to keep their arms and barracks, the militias in West Beirut were first disarmed and then proscribed. The Lebanese Forces took to raids into West Beirut, arresting political opponents and holding them in their own prisons.

Berri and his colleagues were well aware than neither President Gemayel nor Premier Wazzan exercised effective authority over the Lebanese Forces. But they reproached them for the unequal treatment of the militias in East and West Beirut. They began to doubt the goodwill of both the president and his prime minister.

---

[168] See Martin Kramer, *The Moral Logic of Hizballah. Occasional Papers 101* (Shiloah Institute, Tel Aviv, 1987); Shimon Shapira, 'The origins of Hizballah', *Jerusalem Quarterly* 46 (1988), pp. 115–30.

[169] On the relationships between the Lebanese, Iraqi and Iranian ulema, see Mallat, *Shi`i Thought*, pp. 9ff. Their connections went back to their common training in the Shi`i holy cities of Najaf and Karbala in southern Iraq. Since 1958 the Sidon journal *al-`Irfan* had been a mouthpiece for the religious and political teachings of southern Iraqi religious leaders: Lebanese freedom of the press allowed publication of views suppressed by successive Iraqi military regimes. Ayatollah Khomeini spent many years of his exile in Najaf, where he established close ties with prominent Shi`i scholars in Lebanon, in particular Muhammad Mahdi Shamseddin and Muhammad Hussein Fadlallah. Others had close ties with Shariat Madari, in consequence of which the differences of opinion between Khomeini and Madari were reflected among the Lebanese Shi`i ulema. Many of these concerned the legal and political powers the Shi`i clerical hierarchy should exercise in a state. But there were also differences concerning the question of Lebanese nationalism versus pan-Islamic tendencies. Mallat, *Shi`i Thought*, p. 26, stresses 'the significant split ... between the two dominant military groups in terms of this nationalist–internationalist paradigm, with the Amal movement prone to a 'Lebanese-nationalist' stance, and the Hizbullahis ... appearing to put nationalist allegiance second to an Islamic form of internationalism centred on Iran'.

Had the president not been a leader of the Kata'ib, and was he not playing the same game between state and Christian militia in different guises? Had not the prime minister sent in the legal army — to which Amal had been pledging support for years — against Shi`is and to the advantage of the Sunni bourgeoisie? In its efforts to represent Shi`i interests, Amal found itself being driven into a corner by Hezbollah militancy. The first clashes between Amal and the Lebanese Army occurred in March 1983, after the army had detained numerous Shi`is on flimsy charges. A general strike called by Amal in June, on the first anniversary of the Israeli occupation, was widely followed. In July, Amal resisted an attempt by the army to clear a school in Wadi Abu Jamil, the old Jewish quarter, of Shi`i refugees, after a wealthy Sunni had bought the building. Berri declared that he would not let Shi`is in Lebanon be treated 'like Blacks in South Africa' and demanded Wazzan's resignation.

Dissatisfaction with the legal government and pressure from militant Islamic fundamentalists encouraged militancy in the largest Shi`i organization.[170] In 1983, Berri went beyond Musa Sadr's position in domestic politics. Instead of an adequate share of power for the Shi`is, he demanded a pure majority-vote democracy. Druze and Shi`is now had a common political goal. When the Israeli–Lebanese negotiations were eventually concluded and it became known just what concessions the Lebanese government was prepared to make to Israel in southern Lebanon, Berri and Amal rejected the agreement. Jumblatt and the Druze were opposed to the agreement because they needed Syrian support against the Lebanese Forces in the Chouf. Berri and Amal, however, opposed the agreement in the interests of their own community. The Syrian government had gained another ally; it would prove to be its most reliable and trustworthy. Before 1982, the Shi`is had been the most resolute proponents of a stronger Lebanese state. Henceforth, they would be in opposition to this state. They remained in favour of the state, provided that it became their state.

## War against the Israeli–Lebanese agreement

The agreement was initialled on May 17th, 1983. The Syrian government had already rejected what they regarded as tantamount to capitulation, refusing even negotiations on the withdrawal of its troops. In Zghorta, in the presence of a high-

---

[170] See Elisabeth Picard, 'Political identities and communal identities: Shifting mobilization among the Lebanese Shi`a through ten years of war, 1975–1985', in Dennis L. Thompson and Dov Ronen, eds., *Ethnicity, Politics, and Development* (Boulder, 1986, pp. 159–78 and 'From "Community–Class" to Patriotic Struggle: An attempt at an analysis of the role and significance of the Shi`a in the Lebanese political system (1970–1984)'; paper presented the Middle Eastern Studies Association Annual Congress, San Francisco, 1984; on criticism of Berri's compromising attitude see especially p. 14.

ranking Syrian officer, several Lebanese politicians met: Franjieh, Karami, representatives of the PSP, the SSNP, the Baath Party and the CP — all traditional Syrian allies. Amal issued its official reaction three weeks later. On June 10th, lingering doubts about the seriousness of the opposition to the agreement disappeared: East Beirut, Jounieh and Bikfaya were shelled from the Druze part of the Chouf and Syrian batteries in the upper Metn.

The Lebanese parliament met on June 14th. Seventy deputies were present; of those absent most represented constituencies in areas under Syrian control. Saeb Salam declared that the overwhelming majority of the Lebanese, and in particular of the Muslims, were in favour of the agreement.[171] Those in favour argued that the Israelis could be removed only by making concessions. The former Amal president, Hussein Husseini, made the crucial rejoinder: the agreement was worthless so long as the Syrians were not prepared to withdraw. Eventually parliament approved the agreement by sixty-four votes to two, with four abstentions.[172] This left the final decision in the hands of the president and the government: ratification. Gemayel and Wazzan procrastinated in the hope that Syria might yet come round. But no one was willing or able to persuade Syria. In May, Secretary of State Shultz had stated that the USA had contributed by mediating between Israel and Lebanon; it was now up to Lebanon to reach an understanding with Syria. Habib had counted on the support of Saudi and Kuwaiti diplomacy; but in view of Syria's adamant rejection these governments remained aloof. Israel had 'lost its deterrence capacity vis-à-vis Syria in Lebanon'.[173] For domestic reasons, Israel could no longer consider open hostilities with Syria. Ratification of the agreement would have given the war a certain post-hoc justification in the eyes of the Israeli public. But the Defence Minister, Arens, and the newly appointed coordinator of Israel's policies in Lebanon, the ambassador Uri Lubrani, were far less interested in this aspect than Sharon, the driving force behind the war. Arens and Lubrani had no illusions that, given the weakness of the Lebanese government and the growing strength of the opposition Syria was coordinating against it, Israel would gain negligible advantage from the agreement. Constant harassment and mounting Israeli casualties finally persuaded them to abandon Sharon's more ambitious objectives. Their prime objective was to secure the Israeli border, and here, they felt, the Druze and the Shi`is could be more helpful than a government with no authority beyond Beirut. In short: the Lebanese government stood alone against Syria's determination to wreck the agreement.

---

[171] *L'Orient-Le Jour*, June 16th, 1983.
[172] Forty of 50 Christian and 24 of 41 Muslim deputies voted in favour.
[173] Rabinovich, *The War for Lebanon*, p. 195.

On July 23rd, 1983, the Lebanese opposition to the treaty organized themselves into a 'National Salvation Front'. Each member of the front had his own, domestic political reasons to oppose Gemayel and Wazzan. Despite Bashir Gemayel's death, Franjieh persisted in pursuing his vendetta against the Gemayel clan and the Kata'ib. Karami was discontented because the Sunni establishment in Beirut, represented by Wazzan and Salam, had displaced him in his community. Jumblatt saw an opportunity of gaining Lebanese support for his struggle in the Chouf, thereby adding a national political dimension to a regional conflict for hegemony. The parties of the Left at last had the chance to join a broad front and regain some of their lost significance. The extreme Islamic fundamentalist groups and Amal did not formally join the 'Front'. By actively opposing the agreement, the Islamic fundamentalists could gain political respectability; if Amal then remained aloof, it would run the risk of apparent collaboration. The common denominator of the new opposition was not internal political goals but each member's ties with Syria. Each of them wanted another Lebanon, but none of them wanted the same. Their simultaneous opposition to the agreement made them a powerful coalition. The Shi`is in Beirut rose against the government, the Druze fought the Lebanese Forces and then the regular army, radical Shi`i groups attacked the Americans and the French. The Syrian government could restrict its actions to covering fire, both literally and figuratively.

In August, the Druze and the Syrians resumed intense shelling of Beirut: the airport, the presidential office and the positions of the multinational Western peace force. The French government spokesman declared that France did not want to become involved in a Lebanese civil war, the first sign of irresolution about their support for the Lebanese government. At the end of August, Shi`is rose in Beirut. Within a few hours the government had lost control over the south-western suburbs; Amal, the Mourabitoun and PSP militiamen together stormed the city centre of West Beirut. Ayatollah Khomeini's picture appeared on state-controlled television, to the horror of the Sunni business classes. The army quickly regained control of the city centre, deploying thousands of soldiers intended to take over Israeli positions as they withdrew from the Chouf. But it was unable to re-establish its authority in the suburbs.

A few days later, on September 3rd, the Israeli Army withdrew from the Aley–Chouf region. The most reliable units of the Lebanese Army had their hands full in West Beirut. Other units advanced along the Beirut–Damascus highway to Kahhale and into the north-western foothills of the Chouf Mountains as far as Souk al-Gharb.[174] In the other areas vacated by the Israelis a full-scale war broke

---

[174] The two LAF brigades en route to the Shuf had to be diverted to Beirut, where, although they distinguished themselves in difficult urban fighting, they were tied down. Thus, as Israel withdrew, no LAF

out between the Druze and the Lebanese Forces. It did not last long. The Druze, supported by Palestinian troops from the Bekaa calling themselves the 'army of return', attacked the town of Bhamdoun with tank units and inflicted a crushing defeat on the Christian militia. After that, the hopelessly inferior Lebanese Forces could fight only rearguard actions as they retreated to the largest Christian town in the Chouf, Deir al-Qamar, where they were surrounded by the Druze.[175] The Christian civilian population also fled, terrified by reports of Druze massacres. The Lebanese Forces found the time to massacre the Druze inhabitants of three villages in the line of their retreat. The victorious Druze had far more time: they perpetrated dozens of massacres as they occupied one village after another. They drew no distinction between Maronites, Greek Orthodox and Greek Catholics, or between supporters and opponents of Jumblatt's Progressive Socialist Party. The inhabitants of the village of Bireh had a long socialist tradition and felt no harm would come to them; hardly anyone survived. Within a fortnight the Chouf, with the exception of Deir al-Qamar, had been cleaned of Christians. Around sixty villages had been devastated, thousands of civilians had been murdered, tens of thousands had been driven out or had fled. The spiritual leader of the Druze, Sheikh Abu Shakra, summed up this phase of civil-war brutality, then unsurpassed anywhere in Lebanon: 'A page has turned in the book of history: Christians will never again live in the Druze Mountains'. In September the victorious Druze militias concentrated all their energies on the positions of the Lebanese Army in Souk al-Gharb, who were soon in grave difficulty. The Druze objective was to link the Chouf with the Amal-controlled Shi`i suburbs of Beirut. At the same time, the Druze and Syrian artilleries continued shelling Beirut and its Christian hinterland. The multinational forces were also hard-pressed, especially the American marines stationed around Beirut airport, who drew the fire of batteries in the nearby hills and in the Shi`i districts bordering on the airport.

The American government was in a predicament. They did not want to get involved in a Lebanese civil war; on the other hand, they wanted to prevent Syria from using the civil-war coalition to wreck American policy in Lebanon. By withdrawing from the Chouf, Israel had demonstrated that it did not intend to act as a counterweight to Syria in Lebanon, underwriting Amin Gemayel's political survival — he had still not signed the agreement — with Israeli soldiers. Neither in numbers nor in equipment was the American — or French, Italian and tiny

units were available for deployment to the Shuf'; Paul A. Jureidini and R.D. McLaurin, 'Lebanon after the war of 1982', in Azar, *The Emergence of a New Lebanon*, p. 24.

[175] The siege of Deir al-Qamar lasted until shortly before Christmas 1983. Through Israeli mediation the militiamen of the Lebanese Forces and most of the refugees were then able to leave the town. Of those left in the town, most were elderly.

British — contingent in the multinational forces prepared for serious fighting; they had been despatched on the assumption that a symbolic presence of the Western superpower and its allies would in itself be enough to create respect.[176] It was a naive attitude: all the players on the Lebanese stage, state and otherwise, had long since learnt to respect only effectually employed might. For months various militias had been testing the resolve of the Western troops and discovered that they could be attacked with impunity.

The USA was now faced with the choice of bowing to Syrian pressure, and presenting the spectacle of a superpower humbled by militias, or of giving their military involvement credibility by strengthening it. As a way out of this dilemma they intervened in the war by deploying naval ordnance to shell the hills around Souk al-Gharb. American battleships offshore, including the largest in the world, the 'New Jersey', fired on Druze positions; the noise of the ships' cannon made a far greater impact than their missiles.

The hard-pressed Lebanese Army managed to hold the line at Souk al-Gharb.[177] But it had to abandon positions in West Beirut, and on September 28th Shi`i, militiamen ejected the Christian population of Mreij, the last non-Shi`i enclave in this part of Beirut. Amal also attacked army positions along the old demarcation line between Chiyah and Ain al-Rummaneh.

On September 26th, the American special envoy Robert McFarlane — successor to Philip Habib, to whom the Syrians had refused to speak — arrived in Damascus. With Saudi mediation he negotiated a cease-fire. The announcement was made by the Syrian Foreign Minister, Khaddam, a clear demonstration that Syria, mauled and humiliated a year before, was once again playing an important role in Lebanon, and that the USA recognized this. Syria agreed to recognize Amin Gemayel as the legitimate President of Lebanon. McFarlane consented to persuade Gemayel to make concessions to the opposition and 'broaden the base of his government'. This was the start of months of misunderstanding. The American government expected Gemayel to make — unspecified — concessions to the opposition while sticking to the Israeli–Lebanese agreement. One part of the opposition wanted 'concessions' that paved the way for a change of power in Lebanon; another part, in particular Franjieh, rejected such concessions as

---

[176] All in all — Americans, French, Italians and Britons — the multi-lateral troops numbered 5,500 soldiers with light armaments. 'The Marines ... were there in a peacekeeping role, a symbol of the US commitment to Lebanon, but they were not a significant combat force. The position they occupied at the Beirut airport was exposed, difficult to defend from artillery shelling from the Druze-inhabited hills above and sniper fire from the nearby Shia-inhabited areas. By staying out of the fighting, the Marines avoided casualties, but they also seemed irrelevant'; Quandt, 'Reagan's Lebanon policy', p. 246.

[177] It had less than a full brigade. 'This unit had ... limited organic firepower, and was effectively surrounded ... Under these extremely harrowing conditions ... the LAF performed extraordinarily well'; Jureidini and McLaurin, 'Lebanon after the war of 1982', p. 34, n. 28.

adamantly as Gemayel. What the entire opposition and, behind the scenes, the Syrian government, wanted more than anything was what the Americans sought to avoid: official abrogation of the unratified agreement. The Syrian government went further, and called for the withdrawal of the multinational troops, denouncing their presence in Lebanon as unacceptable foreign interference. In brief: Gemayel was pressured by his American ally, on whose commitment he had risked everything, to do what he neither wanted nor could benefit from, and to desist from doing what Syria demanded of him. Yet, the USA had neither wanted nor was able to take the only step that could have saved the agreement, namely, to give the Lebanese government adequate military support. At the same time Syria's allies were raising their stakes: on October 23rd, suicide commandos blew up the American and French headquarters in Lebanon, killing hundreds of soldiers.

Following this escalation, Syrian and Saudi intermediaries arranged a Lebanese conference of 'National Reconciliation', which met in Geneva on October 31st.[178] Amin Gemayel presided, Franjieh, Jumblatt and Karami represented the opposition, Camille Chamoun and Pierre Gemayel the Lebanese Front, Saeb Salam the Sunnis and Adel Usayran — a minister of many years' standing and Speaker — the Shi`is. Syria had vetoed the participation of Prime Minister Wazzan: as a Sunni who had called for the withdrawal of the Syrian troops and a driving force behind the agreement with Israel, he was *persona non grata* for the Syrians. Acceptance of this veto and the presence of the Syrian Foreign Minister, Khaddam, at the conference were further signs of Syria's growing influence.

The Geneva conference did not bring progress on the question of Lebanese constitutional reform.[179] The conference agreed on a formula expressing the Arab nature of Lebanon, but not on anything remotely approaching a change of power. Suleiman Franjieh of all people took the hardest — the classic Maronite — line: true to himself, he argued for a close association with Syria and against any arrangement with Israel, and refused to compromise on the position of the Christians in Lebanon. Franjieh's compromise proposal on the Israeli–Lebanese agreement was accepted: the conference charged President Gemayel with renegotiating the agreement with American support.

On December 1st, Gemayel learnt in Washington that there could be no question of amending the agreement. However, he was urged to seek an understanding with the Druze and the Shi`is. The two sides were still talking at cross-

---

[178] For details, Tuéni, *Une guerre pour les autres*, pp. 31ff.

[179] The principal sticking point was *not* internal reforms; rather it was the May 17 agreement with Israel (presumably because this was the major issue raised by Syria, which backed the opposition to the government)'; Jureidini and McLaurin, 'Lebanon after the war of 1982', p. 25.

purposes.[180] However, the American administration, after consulting Israel, decided on a show of strength against Syria.

American planes bombed Syrian positions in the mountains, while the French bombed a Shi`i base in the Bekaa. Two American planes were shot down, one pilot killed and another captured; eight American marines died in a Syrian artillery attack. The sortie of the French Super-Etendards — the pride of the French air force — cost the life of one Lebanese cowherd. Neither the Syrians nor the Shi`is were awed. It was brought home to the Lebanese government yet again that the Western armada and its modern aircraft off its shores could not help it on land.

This unhappy attempt to put Syria in its place did have one far-reaching consequence: it fuelled criticism of the American involvement in Lebanon. Prominent conservative senators demanded the withdrawal of the American marines. 1984 was election year in the USA, and barely a decade after the scramble out of Vietnam there was hardly one American politician prepared to defend in public American involvement in wars abroad. President Reagan himself, about to seek a second term, seemed to waver. So far he had consistently taken the view that in Lebanon the USA was protecting vital interests in the global East-West confrontation. This view was not shared by all members of his cabinet, and had never been by most American experts on the Middle East. Above all, Defence Secretary Weinberger was convinced that the USA did not have an operable military option in Lebanon. In mid-December, Reagan spoke for the first time of a possible withdrawal from Lebanon, in the event of a 'breakdown of order'. But he rallied, and as late as early February declared that an American withdrawal would mean the end of Lebanon; neither he nor his allies would think of retreating; he was not prepared to capitulate to Syrian pressure.[181]

A few days prior to the American president's statement President Assad of Syria, speaking to an American diplomat, had put his assessment of US policy in a nutshell: 'The United States loses interest quickly.'[182] It did.

The cease-fire negotiated in Geneva collapsed within a few days. Another followed in mid-December, to be succeeded by bombardments and fighting at

---

[180] See Quandt, 'Reagan's Lebanon policy', p. 248: 'The message from Reagan to Gemayel was a puzzling one. Nothing could be done to change the May 17 accord, but Gemayel should nevertheless press ahead with political reconciliation, especially with the Druze and the Shia. He should also deal directly with the Israelis to work out some understandings concerning what next steps might be taken in southern Lebanon to expand the authority of the Lebanese government. Finally, the USA and Israel gave the impression of being ready to take a tougher stand toward Syria, which led some Lebanese officials to believe that a significant increase in US military involvement was in the offing. On balance, however, the Lebanese left Washington both confused and disappointed.'

[181] *Wall Street Journal*, February 3rd, 1984.

[182] *Le Monde*, January 26th, 1984.

Christmas. In mid-January 1984 Shi`i militias sniped at the Lebanese Army and French troops. On January 18th, Malcolm Kerr, the President of the American University of Beirut, was murdered by unknown assailants. At the end of January, Jumblatt and Berri called for Gemayel's resignation on the ground that he had neglected to discharge his obligation accepted at Geneva, that of negotiating a new agreement with Israel.

On January 29th, the Druze started a new offensive against the army in Souk al-Gharb. From February 1st, the army tried to advance into the southern suburbs to cut communications between the Shi`i militias in West Beirut and the Druze in the Chouf. On February 5th, the army started to shell southern Beirut, causing heavy civilian casualties and extensive damage. Events took a dramatic turn. The Wazzan government resigned and Nabih Berri appealed to the Shi`i soldiers in the Lebanese Army not to shoot at their brothers. He stated that he could no longer cooperate with Amin Gemayel as the latter was responsible for the massacre in the Shi`i suburbs. Walid Jumblatt went further: Gemayel should be 'bumped off'.[183] On February 6th, Amal and Druze militiamen went on the offensive in West Beirut. The Sixth Brigade of the Lebanese Army, composed mainly of Shi`is, followed Berri's call and deserted to Amal. On February 7th, the last regular soldiers fighting in West Beirut, most of them Christian, pulled back to the eastern sector of the city. Beirut was once again divided along the green line.

One feature of this development was new: for the first time the Lebanese themselves had divided their capital. Syria had forged and constantly assisted the coalition against the agreement, and the Palestinians had assisted the Druze take Bhamdoun and the Shi`is take West Beirut. But it was primarily the Druze and the Shi`is who had fought against the government. They may have been opposed to the agreement, but other reasons were more pertinent. The Druze saw the Lebanese Forces in the Chouf as a threat to their existence as a community and felt — rightly or wrongly — that the government was conniving with the Lebanese Forces. Developments in Lebanon after the Israeli invasion aroused Shi`i fears of once again being neglected by a coalition of Christian and Muslim notables, including those of their own community. Moreover, their hopes that the Israelis would soon leave the south were dashed by the riders to the agreement. Islamic fundamentalist militiamen may have been inspired by the Iranian Revolution and organized by Iranian cadres; but it was Lebanese Shi`is who attacked Israeli and Western troops with a fierceness and efficiency beside which earlier Palestinian commando raids paled. The president, the government and the army command all misjudged the Shi`is' mood and militancy, and their communal

---

[183] 'Ce n'est plus qu'un type à abattre'; statement heard by the author on French radio, February 7th, 1984.

## Religious communities in Beirut by area, 1984

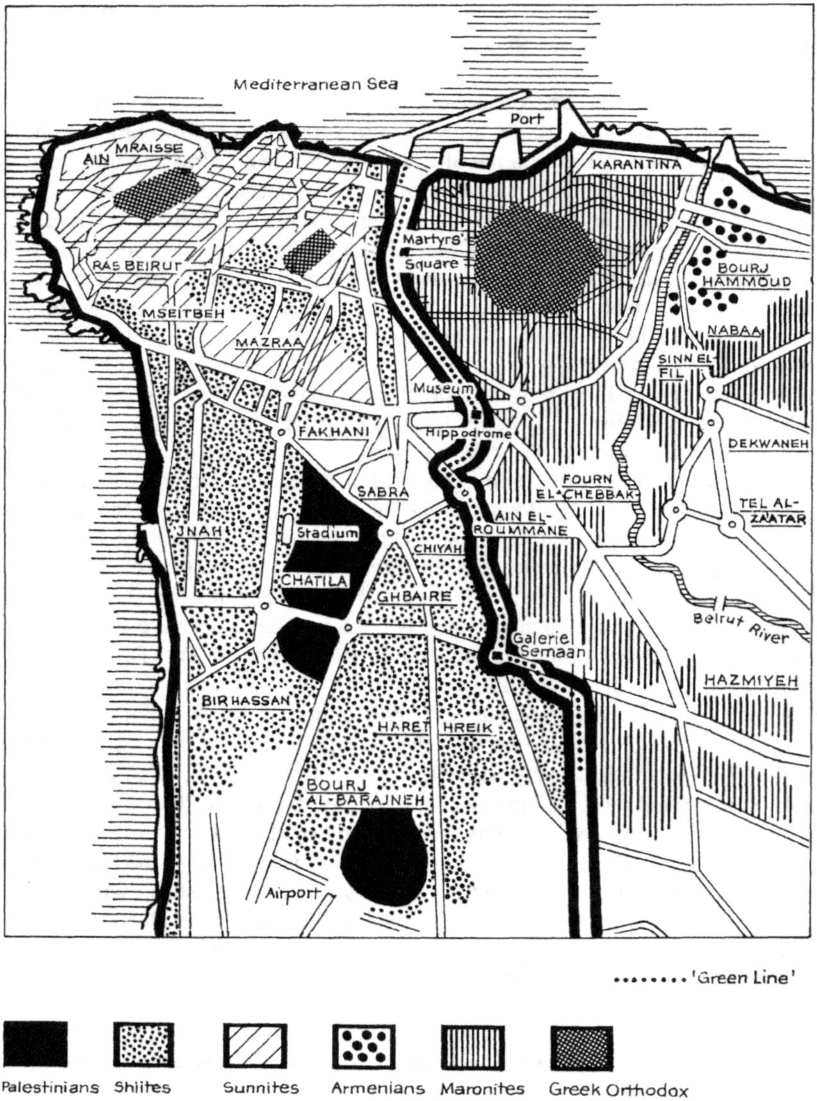

......... 'Green Line'

 Palestinians  Shiites  Sunnites  Armenians  Maronites  Greek Orthodox

## Dance Macabre: 1975–1988

solidarity. To have expected of regular Shi`i soldiers — and they were half the ranks — that they would pulverize Shi`i residential areas was as absurd as the idea that Maronite soldiers in the same army would shell Ashrafieh. The Sunnis held to the government as long as possible. When civil war flared up in Beirut, they retired or if armed, like the Mourabitoun, sided with the victors in West Beirut. Whatever role outsiders played — Syria's, certainly, was significant — on February 7th, 1984, Lebanon was not only at war against the Israeli–Lebanese treaty but in a state of civil war between Lebanese communities.

The states that had provided contingents for the multinational forces grasped the opportunity to do what they had considering for some months. On February 7th — there was still sporadic fighting in West Beirut — the American administration announced that its marines were 'redeploying' and pulling back to the ships off the Lebanese coast.[184] The Britons withdrew on February 8th, the Italians on the 20th. France had a greater sense of dignity, even in a defeat for which it was not responsible but had shared. It asked for UN units to replace the multinational forces. Only after this proposal had been rejected by the Security Council,[185] and the last American soldier had left Lebanese soil, did the French withdraw on March 31st, leaving a number of soldiers in Lebanon as cease-fire observers.[186] The Americans did not depart without emptying the guns of the USS New Jersey on to suspected Syrian positions. William Quandt reports the analogy a Lebanese drew between Reagan's exit and 'the gunslinger in a Western movie who, six-shooters blazing, backs out of the saloon brawl through the swinging doors and disappears into the night'; Quandt's comment: 'All the sound and fury could not disguise the fact, however, that Reagan's Lebanon policy lay in ruins, along with much of the city of Beirut'.[187]

On February 15th, the last hopes that the Lebanese Army might be able to turn the course of events disappeared. One brigade still stood in the coastal region of

---

[184] 'Very few predicted that Washington would not have any influence on the situation. After it had mobilized the entire Administration and pledged its credibility, at the beginning of 1984 America admitted its defeat and got ready to withdraw its marines from Beirut — claiming that the Gulf was more important for the West than the whole of Lebanon'; Bassma Kodmani-Darwish, 'Frankreich, ein zuverlässiger Verbündeter Libanons', *Beiträge zur Konfliktforschung* 14/3 (1984), p. 89.

[185] The USSR vetoed it on March 1st, 1984.

[186] 'The French were the first to intervene in Lebanon and the last to leave. In contrast to the Americans, Paris tried to prepare the withdrawal of its contingent very carefully, both technically and politically, so as not to create the impression that France had lost interest in Lebanon'; Kodmani-Darwish, 'Frankreich', p. 89.

[187] Quandt, 'Reagan's Lebanon policy', p. 250. See also Eric Hammel, *The Root: The Marines in Beirut August 1982 — February 1984* (San Diego, 1985). Two hundred American marines were interviewed on what they thought their tour had achieved: 'About half answered, we bought the Lebanese people more time. The responses of the other half amounted to "Nothing".' Hammel comments: 'As time passes, "Nothing" looks more and more like the correct assessment'; p. 426.

the Chouf. If it advanced south-west of Beirut, avoiding the suburbs, it could cut West Beirut off from the Chouf. However, before the brigade could go into action, it was attacked by the PSP militia, and disintegrated virtually without a fight. The Muslim soldiers marched to Beirut, the Christians fled to the south or by sea to East Beirut.[188] Amin Gemayel's military options against the Druze and Shi'i rebellion were exhausted.

The civil war over the agreement was not only a civil war. On February 29th, Amin Gemayel travelled to Damascus and told President Assad that he was prepared to abrogate the agreement. Gemayel did not go in sackcloth and ashes; he was received with full military honours, brotherly kisses and a state banquet. The Syrian government was, after all, welcoming back a prodigal son. On March 5th, the Lebanese government officially abrogated the Israeli–Lebanese agreement. Syria had succeeded in harnessing a largely internal Lebanese war to defeat the agreement and compel the Americans and their Western allies to pull out of Lebanon.[189]

It was a humiliating defeat for the USA. Domestically, the withdrawal from Lebanon was well received: Reagan brought the 'Marines' home from a bloody war that was incomprehensible to the American voter, and went on to re-election. His action reaffirmed the primacy of domestic politics in the American system, and the chronic inability of this superpower to pursue with military means what its leaders regard as its interests in Middle Eastern countries. Contrary to all solemn declarations, the USA had abandoned a government that had relied on it completely. Other states in the region henceforth understood that they should not take American promises at face value.[190] Israel had not achieved its objective of establishing a friendly government in Lebanon. Once Israel realized that Amin Gemayel, secure in the belief of American support, was following a course that, though not anti-Israeli, would leave him independent of Israel, it lost interest in the agreement. Its interest turned to wrecking the Reagan Plan for the Palestinians by procrastinating over the negotiations, and to finding reliable local allies who would protect its border. It succeeded well in the former, but only partially in the latter, as will be seen below. Amin Gemayel got no help from the Israelis, which

---

[188] When the Druze advanced on Damour, the units of the Lebanese Forces stationed in the town retreated southwards. About 15,000 Christian civilians fled from the coastal region of the Chouf to the Israeli-occupied area.

[189] Gemayel's last hope was that Syria would accept a Saudi plan that proposed sending UN troops to replace the multi-lateral forces. But Syria and its Lebanese allies rejected it.

[190] The President of the United Arab Emirates, Sheikh Zaid, accused the USA of deserting its allies, who, he said, were now worse off than before the American intervention. In Washington, President Mubarak of Egypt called the withdrawal of the American contingent from Lebanon a catastrophe that would cost Washington the trust of all its friends in the Middle East; *Neue Zürcher Zeitung*, February 17th, 1984. King Hussein, too, sharply criticized American policy in the Middle East.

some of his rivals could turn to their advantage, as in the Chouf. Israel's resignation and the USA's defeat encouraged Syria to try again for ascendancy in Lebanon.

Syria's Lebanese allies had profited. The Druze controlled a wider area than at any time since the eighteenth century. The Shi`is were in control of West Beirut. But neither had realized their more fundamental objectives. When Syria affirmed its recognition of Gemayel as President, Jumblatt and Berri withdrew their demand for his resignation. A 'conference of national reconciliation' met in Lausanne from March 12th to 20th. As at the Geneva Conference, Suleiman Franjieh obstructed any attempt radically to reorganize the political system in Lebanon.[191] A new government was formed under the old rules: Rashid Karami was appointed Prime Minister, and his cabinet included Chamoun and Pierre Gemayel, Jumblatt and Berri. In so far as the war against the agreement was a civil war, it ended 'without victors and without vanquished', and with all parties more dependent on Syria than ever before.

## Civil war: Palestinians against Palestinians in Lebanon

While the war against the agreement was being fought out in Beirut and its hinterland, another civil war broke out in the north-east and east of the country — a struggle between two tendencies within the PLO. Syria took an interest in this conflict too, and was kindly disposed towards one of the parties.

Just as after the Israeli invasion, Syria never lost sight of its goal of compelling the Lebanese government to tow the Syrian line on the Middle East and, in particular, Israel, so too did it still desire similarly to instruct the PLO. In 1982 Syria had been the only Arab country to go to the aid of the Palestinians in their war against Israel, and its sacrifices had been considerable. After this war, its attitude towards PLO aspirations to independent action was as critical as towards Lebanese. Once the dust had settled on the evacuation from Beirut, Arafat began to explore the possibilities of a peaceful regulation of the Palestine question. Tunis, new seat of the PLO, afforded him an autonomy he had not previously enjoyed. He renewed contacts with Egypt, Syria's main rival in crucial questions

---

[191] Franjieh is said to have stated: 'I shall never allow the role of the Maronite head of state to be reduced to that of a secretary'; *Neue Zürcher Zeitung*, March 23rd, 1984. The conference eventually agreed on a cease-fire and a commission on the constitution. Jumblatt and Berri had demanded other things: a senate in which the communities would be represented, the deconfessionalization of the chamber of deputies, and a three-year term of office for the president. Pierre Gemayel and Chamoun, for their part, wanted Lebanon to become a federal state. For a detailed account of the Lausanne Conference see Haddad, *Lebanon*, pp. 121–33.

of Middle East policy.[192] He also let it be understood that he was not utterly opposed to the Reagan Plan — which, as seen above, was quite unacceptable to Syria.

In the spring of 1983 relations worsened within the PLO as well as between Syria and the PLO leadership. In April, Issam Sartawi, a confidant of Arafat and prominent proponent of a peaceful attempt at settlement, was murdered by PLO dissidents during a conference of the Socialist International in Lisbon. On May 3rd, Assad and Arafat met in Damascus, but could not agree on a common policy. On May 12th, Fatah troops stationed in the Bekaa mutinied against Arafat's leadership. Within the PLO there had always been disagreements between Fatah and other organizations; and even within Fatah there were fierce arguments over policy. This time, however, popular officers of the PLO's crack troops demanded a change of leadership. Their leader was Colonel Abu Musa. He had commanded the Palestinians resisting the Syrian Army in Sidon in 1976 and played a prominent role in defending West Beirut during the Israeli siege in 1982. This time he came out in favour of Syria, demanding that all negotiations with the USA, Egypt and Jordan should cease and that the Palestinians should join the struggle to liberate Lebanon from Israeli occupation. But first, with Syrian support, he attacked Palestinian units in the Bekaa loyal to Arafat. The beaten remnants of the Arafat adherents retreated to Tripoli. On June 26th, Arafat again travelled to Damascus to try to reach an amicable agreement. Instead of being received by government officials, he was ordered to leave the country and deported.

The Arafat group in the PLO were now worried about losing their last strongholds around Tripoli and searched for allies. They found them among the Sunni fundamentalists led by Sheikh Said Shaban, who had formed an organization called Tawheed.[193] PLO money and training helped Tawheed form a powerful militia. The Syrians also mobilized their supporters in Tripoli: the pro-Syrian branch of the Lebanese Baath Party, the SSNP and the 'Arab Democratic Party', a predominantly Alawite militia known as the 'Pink Panthers' because of their colourful battle-dress.

On September 16th, Yassir Arafat appeared in Tripoli and assumed command of the Palestinians loyal to the PLO leadership. The Syrian government viewed this as a direct provocation. What followed was essentially a repetition of the events of 1982 in Beirut, except that Syrians, not Israelis, were besieging Palestinians in a large Lebanese city. The Syrian navy blockaded the ports of

---

[192] In the Cairo newspaper *al-Ahram* Arafat called for the readmission of Egypt to the Arab League. In February 1983 he negotiated with King Hussein on coordinating Jordanian and PLO policies.

[193] See Michel Seurat, 'Identité communautaire, violence urbaine, déréliction du politique: Un quartier populaire de Tripoli au Liban', in Salim Nasr and Theodor Hanf, eds., *Urban Crisis and Social Movements: Arab and European perspectives* (Beirut, 1987), pp. 193–8.

Tripoli and Chekka to sever Palestinian supply lines. From the hills above the city Syrian batteries pounded the refugee camps on the outskirts as well as the city centre. In Tripoli itself Palestinians and Tawheed militiamen fought against the Arab Democratic Party, the SSNP and other left-wing groups. The fundamentalists used the opportunity to murder hundreds of 'atheist Communists', whether combatants or not. In early November, the fighting took on overtones of civil war between the Sunni majority and the Alawite minority. At this point the Syrian Army and the Syrian-commanded Palestinian Liberation Army intervened. Shortly before Christmas the Palestinian camps capitulated. Arafat was evacuated from Lebanon a second time, on Greek ships escorted by French warships. The Syrian government had gained complete control over the Palestinians on Lebanese territory under their domination — and even before the Lebanese government had bowed to Syrian will.

## Overtures and simmering warfare

Initially, Syria was satisfied with the results of the Lausanne Conference. But the internal Lebanese problems the war against the agreement had so manifestly laid bare were still unsettled. Karami had taken until April to form the new government. Now the warlords congregated at the cabinet table — which did not change their respective views on the future of the country. It was not unusual for dissension in the cabinet to be accompanied by fighting between the militias of the ministers concerned. Until June there was frequent fighting along the green line and at Souk al-Gharb.

Accordingly, the president and prime minister concentrated their efforts on the so-called security plan, re-establishing law and order in Beirut: the militias should be withdrawn and replaced by units of the regular army. This proposal was well-received by the population, above all in West Beirut, where various militias were struggling for influence and increasingly making life a misery for the populace. Fundamentalists were trying violently to enforce their views, from a prohibition on alcohol to compulsory chador, views the majority of Beirut Muslims by no means shared. The Christian minority were being intimidated: businesses and shops were looted or bombed, a church in the Hamra district was set alight, and thoroughly apolitical people were kidnapped and murdered. But the Sunnis, too, were very uneasy. Rural Shi`is were moving into their residential areas in large numbers, and militiamen were requisitioning flats and houses. In March the Druze militias had defeated the Mourabitoun, the only Sunni militia. Hence, nothing appealed more to the Sunnis than Premier Karami's plan to restore public order.

This depended on the support of the regular army. It had disintegrated in the February fighting. However, in contrast to the aftermath of the split in the spring of 1976, this time units had largely abstained from shooting at each other. Another difference from 1976 lay in deployment: this time several intact brigades amounting to almost half the army were stationed in areas under government control. These brigades had most of the heavy armaments — artillery, tanks and helicopters. Although predominantly Christian, the ranks included a considerable number of Sunnis.[194] The commander and almost all troops of the Sixth Brigade in West Beirut were Shi`i.[195] The security plan proposed the deployment of predominantly Christian units in East Beirut and the Sixth brigade in West Beirut. The plan was accepted after the installation of a new army command council, in which Maronites, Greek Orthodox, Greek Catholic, Sunnis, Shi`is and Druze each had one representative, and agreement on a new commander in chief: General Michel Aoun, commander of the Souk al-Gharb front. Aoun was popular among Muslim as well as Christian soldiers, politically inclined to the Chehabist tradition of an authoritative state, and no friend of militias.

The security plan took effect on July 3rd. The militias withdrew and the army took up positions in both sections of Beirut. The harbour and airport, closed for months, were reopened. The barricades on the green line were cleared away at the end of July. The council of ministers began a series of 'conclaves' to consider political reforms. In mid-October Hussein Husseini, former chairman of Amal, was elected speaker of the house, with the votes of the Kata'ib deputies as well, another step in the rapprochement between the warring parties. Gemayel and Karami were making a serious effort to turn the imposed 'Syrian option' in foreign policy to the advantage of domestic reconciliation. The Syrian demands had been satisfied, and the Syrian government had again demonstrated that after the correction in foreign policy they had little interest in the ascendancy of one of the parties to the civil war. For the time being there was a military stalemate. Neither the Druze-Shi`i coalition, nor the Christians, nor the different parts of the army had any prospect of victory. Developments seemed to be working in favour of the moderate political leaders of the Lebanese communities, and Amin Gemayel and Rashid Karami were doing what they could to make the best of this opportunity.

But some forces were still in a position to spike their guns. The regular army might have more or less normalized the situation in Beirut, but the various militias had not disbanded. None of them was satisfied with the result of the

---

[194] The brigades in the 'east' numbered approximately 11,000 men, among them 3,500 Sunnis recruited predominantly in Akkar.

[195] The other brigades were deployed out of Beirut, in the Bekaa, Tripoli and Sidon; a small unit in Hamana (Chouf) was composed entirely of Druze.

Lausanne conference, or happy with the successive bits of compromise negotiated in the ministerial conclaves. Nor had any abandoned hope of perhaps someday helping their cause to victory. None had demobilized; only the perpetuation of tension held promise of greater power, prestige, and money. As in earlier phases of the war, so in the second half of 1984: the stalemate in the central conflict fuelled a series of clashes within the two camps. Some of these simmered on into autonomous, parallel and recrudescent conflicts.

The first clashes between Amal and Palestinians occurred in the Beirut camps in June and July 1984. These were the first exchanges in the 'Camps War', which would drag on for years. At the same time, the Muslim civil war in Tripoli flared up again; it would reach its climax in 1985. In the summer of 1984 Franjieh's Marada militia fought that of the SSNP for control of Koura, until Syria reproved its two allies. In July and August, Druze militias, and in January, Amal, attacked the Mourabitoun, before they combined forces in April and defeated it;[196] its leader, Ibrahim Qulaylat, fled into exile. In February 1985, Shi`i militias came to blows for the first time: the rivalry between Amal and Hezbollah would deepen and eventually, in 1988, degenerate into open warfare. Tension also ran high in the region under control of the Lebanese Forces. The Lebanese Forces had brusquely rejected the abrogation of the Israeli–Lebanese agreement. Some of the influential monks at Kaslik continued to support the 'Israeli option'. The Lebanese Forces were grateful to the Israeli Army for enabling their troops to leave Deir al-Qamar in December 1983, where they had been trapped since their defeat in the Chouf. In May 1984, they opened a liaison office in Jerusalem, and in June branded as 'heresy' Amin Gemayel's policies of accommodation with Syria and national reconciliation.

Initially, Amin Gemayel outmanoeuvred his Christian opposition. He ensured the support of a broad majority in the Kata'ib; the party looked askance at the growing political — as opposed to purely military — role of the Lebanese Forces and their radicalization. Many Kata'ib politicians held the Lebanese Forces responsible for the disastrous consequences of the Chouf war. In Ashrafieh the view gained ground that the war was too serious a matter to leave to self-appointed armed forces. The president also received moral support from the Vatican and Father Boulos Naaman, president of the Maronite Order of Monks, both of whom advised greater political restraint. After a cabinet meeting on August 29th, Pierre Gemayel died. Notwithstanding the vehemence with which he defended Christian interests, Pierre Gemayel had consistently adhered to the principle of coexistence in a Lebanese entity, and, hence, supported his son's policies after the Lausanne Conference. His death at this point was a serious

---

[196] Shi`i militias used the opportunity to loot a few Sunni districts of Beirut.

setback for domestic rapprochement. The Kata'ib chose Elie Karami as his successor. This urbane, cultivated Greek Catholic doctor, a convinced liberal democrat, also supported the president's policies. In October 1984, Fouad Abi Nadar, Amin Gemayel's nephew, was chosen as commander of the Lebanese Forces. It seemed as though the president had succeeded in winning over all of Christian Lebanon to his conciliatory policies. At the beginning of November, the Lebanese Forces relinquished control over Quay 5 in Beirut harbour — one of the state's major sources of revenue — to the regular army.

Gemayel and Karami now turned their attention to the task of implementing the security plan in those areas of the country from which the Israelis were withdrawing.

## Lebanese Forces: Insurrection and civil war around Sidon

In September 1984 the Labour Party and Likud formed a government of 'National Unity' in Israel, but were still at variance over Israel's Lebanon policy. Prime Minister Peres preferred as quick a withdrawal as possible, whereas Defence Minister Rabin sought to cultivate, without much success, suitable partners for some security arrangement in southern Lebanon. In July 1984, Syria had finally rejected indirect dealings with Israel. Amal indicated clearly enough that it would not countenance further guerrilla raids from Lebanese territory as southern Lebanon had already suffered enough in the Palestinian cause. But it would not have any contacts or make any arrangements with Israel. Israeli efforts to create village militias did not get very far for fear of the stigma of collaboration. The remaining option was Saad Haddad's troops; he had understood how to mobilize the local patriotism of Christian border villagers as well as some of the local Shi`is. Haddad had died in January 1984. He was succeeded by a Maronite general from the Chouf, Antoine Lahad.[197] In the course of 1984 the spiral of violence in all Israeli-occupied regions of Lebanon twisted tighter and tighter — attacks against Israeli soldiers drew reprisals, which drew retaliations, which drew retributory actions — and no amount of security could stop Israeli casualties mounting. Finally, the Israeli government decided on unilateral withdrawal in several stages; only in the south would it retain a 'security zone' policed, with Israeli support, by General Lahad's strengthened militia, to be called the 'South Lebanese Army'. Between 1977 and 1982 simmering warfare had never ceased in

---

[197] See Harald List's brief biography of Antoine Lahad, *Orient* 29/2 (1988), pp. 179–87. In 1975/6 he had commanded the Lebanese troops in the Bekaa. He was close to Chamoun and considered an opponent of Syrian intervention in Lebanon. In 1983 he was one of the two generals whose rank made them eligible for the command of the Lebanese Army; when Michel Aoun was appointed, Lahad, as is custom, tendered his resignation.

this region; as a 'security zone' it would be no more peaceful. Indeed, as soon as the Israeli Army had pulled back from the Awali River, the Sidon region and the western Bekaa, another round in the region's bloody civil war ensued.

Whether people can learn from history will probably always be disputed. The war in the region of Sidon demonstrates that it is enough for one party to a conflict not to learn, for thousands to suffer misery that could have been avoided. What took place in Iklim al-Kharroub, the southern strip between the coast and the Chouf, and in the hinterland of Sidon was a repetition of the Chouf war with consequences just as catastrophic. There were a number of Christian villages in Kharroub, and around predominantly Sunni Sidon a circle of Christian suburbs and villages that stretched to Jezzine, the hilly region to the south of the Chouf.

After the Chouf war and the flight of the Lebanese Forces from Damour, some units of the Christian militia had established themselves in these villages. Even before the Israelis had withdrawn south of the Awali River, Lebanese Forces and Druze had clashed in villages in Kharroub, but because of the proximity of the Israelis, the Druze exercised caution. The government sought to avert a repetition of the Chouf events. After long negotiations with all concerned — Jumblatt, the Nasserite militias in Sidon and the Christian deputies of the region — it was decided to send a predominantly Muslim battalion of the Lebanese Army into the region. On January 9th, 1985, the Israelis started pulling back, and the battalion advanced according to plan and without serious incident.

On February 17th, President Gemayel and Premier Karami visited liberated Sidon together. They were welcomed by jubilant crowds. The fighting in Sidon in 1975 had signalled the outbreak of war; the city wanted now to celebrate its end. The next day, however, thousands of Islamic fundamentalists travelled from Beirut to Sidon and demonstrated for an Islamic Republic of Lebanon. The army did not intervene. Islamic fundamentalists abducted a few Christians, and Christians abducted a few Muslims in return, and isolated clashes occurred in the suburbs of Sidon.

The Lebanese Forces accused the government and the army of doing nothing to protect Christians in Sidon; should this not change they would take matters into their own hands.

In early March relations between the Lebanese Forces, on the one hand, and the government and the Kata'ib, on the other hand, became very strained for reasons initially unrelated to Kharroub and Sidon. The government ordered the Lebanese Forces to remove a roadblock at Burbara in the north of the Christian-controlled area. At the roadblock the Lebanese Forces levied a toll on all travellers, their major source of income since returning Quay 5 in the port of Beirut to the government. The roadblock was manned by militiamen from the north of the country, under the command of Samir Geagea, the leader of the fateful expedition against the Franjiehs in Ehden in 1978 and commander of the Lebanese Forces in the Chouf war of 1983. Geagea refused to comply. On March 11th, he was expelled from the Kata'ib.

On March 12th, Geagea started a putsch-like rebellion within the Lebanese Forces. His supporters gained control of the most important barracks of the Lebanese Forces north of Beirut, then the headquarters in Ashrafieh. Fighting broke out between the rebels and militiamen loyal to the Kata'ib leadership, and the army had to separate the two groups. However, Geagea and the 'head of military intelligence' in the Lebanese Forces, Elie Hobeika, had the overwhelming support of the militia. Only the units in the centre of Ashrafieh and in the Metn, the Gemayels' native region, stood by the party and the president.

The leaders of the 'rebellion' declared that they wanted to prevent a sell-out of the country to Syria. It was unacceptable that the president and party should continually make concessions at the expense of the Christians. Let the president be president, and as such arbiter in compromises, but as such he could not simultaneously speak 'on behalf of the Christian people'.[198] The rebel leaders also disputed the right of the Kata'ib to speak on behalf of most Christians and demanded the creation of a 'Christian' council, a sort of parliament for Christian Lebanon. What was needed was an 'independent Christian decision'; it was clear they believed that they could implement this themselves.

Neither Geagea nor his close circle specified which of Gemayel's concrete decisions or concessions they disapproved of. But their statements, and more so the tone, encapsulated a widespread uneasiness among Christians over developments as a whole since the death of Bashir Gemayel. All those who had dreamt of establishing or re-establishing Christian ascendancy with the help of Israel, who had erroneously imagined themselves victorious, who still believed in an 'Israeli option', were dissatisfied with Amin Gemayel's realistic policy of making the best of the situation. This mood was sustained by a cult glorifying the dead Bashir, whose shadowy silhouette plastered walls and roofs in all streets and squares in areas controlled by the Lebanese Forces. Many Christians held it against Amin Gemayel that he was not his brother Bashir. Some leaders of the Lebanese Forces seemed incapable of grasping that, after the massacre in Sabra and Chatila and the partial eclipse of Sharon in Israel, the 'Israeli option' was invalid in Israel, and that the 'American option' was a thing of the past as well. The Kata'ib leadership was far more aware of these circumstances and the political possibilities.[199] But they had prevaricated, equally aware that a Christian population confronted with the unpleasant realities would be prey to resignation.

---

[198] Samir Geagea in an interview with the author, 1985.
[199] Author's interview with Elie Karami, 1984.

Samir Geagea regarded himself as Bashir Gemayel's true heir. He came closer to the stereotype of the new political leader in Lebanon than any other militia commander. From a poor rural background — whence his opponents' nickname for him: the goatherd — he had to interrupt his medical studies at the American University of Beirut at the outbreak of war, later completing them at the University of St Joseph, though he never practised. He took part in all the major battles, and defeats, of the Christian militia, from the intra-Maronite war in northern Lebanon, through Zahle to the Chouf. The backbone of his power in the Lebanese Forces was a group of about 1,500 militiamen from the Franjieh-controlled north, who — like him — could not return to their native areas; their home was their barracks. Geagea was the only influential politician who had never been out of the country. His horizon was limited to war, and especially civil war. For him the greatest good was 'security of the Christian people'. If he could have led his people to another land he would have; as he could not he wanted to provide this security for them in Lebanon. He thought the anguish of resettlement involved in creating homogeneous regions better 'than a life of dependence, as hostages, and permanently open to blackmail'.[200] He held that the old Lebanon with its formula for coexistence was a sham existence that was invalid in the face of war; a new coexistence was conceivable only on the basis of an equilibrium of power. Like Bashir Gemayel, though with the keener edge of an almost puritanical disdain for material concerns, he had nothing but contempt for the 'political brokers'. Geagea in a monk's habit would have been a Lebanese Savonarola.

Hence, it is not surprising that Lebanese Christians vacillate between admiration of his uncompromising determination and fear of the armed prophet, between the desire for a strong community and the acceptance of the need to compromise.

Initially, the rebellion was against 'concessions' to Syria. Yet its first consequence was an absurd military adventure in the Sidon region. Local commanders of the Lebanese Forces in the south joined the rebellion. They were reinforced by a few hundred militiamen from the north, equipped with heavy arms. They shelled Muslim suburbs of Sidon and harassed the Sunni population; over 20,000 Sunnis fled. They also shelled units of the regular army stationed between the Palestinian camp of Mieh-Mieh and the eponymous village; when the soldiers fled into the camp this, too, was shelled.

The Nasserite Sunni militia in Sidon, the predominantly Sunni regular soldiers and the Palestinians in the camp, who had rearmed quickly after the Israeli withdrawal, formed an alliance against the Lebanese Forces and went on the offensive before the government and army command could put into effect plans to deploy Shi`i army units between the combatants.

[200] Interview with the author, 1983.

What followed was a repeat of the Chouf war. The Lebanese Forces shelled and withdrew. One village after another in the Christian ring around Sidon fell; the population fled in panic into Jezzine and the Israeli-occupied south; those who remained were driven out. On April 24th, the non-local militiamen, with their heavy artillery, boarded ships for Beirut. Thereupon Druze militias advanced from the Chouf into Iklim al-Kharroub and expelled all Christians. The advance of the Palestinians and Sunnis was only stopped at the village of Kfar Falous, halfway between Sidon and Jezzine, by the troops of Lahad's South Lebanon Army. For the Christians the escapade was a disaster of a similar magnitude to that in the Chouf: about fifty Christian villages were taken and approximately 85,000 people fled or were ejected. The villages of the Kharroub were razed to the ground,[201] probably for fear of Shi`is moving into the abandoned houses: the Druze community itself lacked the numbers to populate the conquered territory. No convincing explanation has ever been offered of why the Lebanese Forces provoked the fighting and then pulled out. The Israeli Army dropped leaflets from helicopters, inviting the population to settle in the security zone in the south, 'ruled by local forces with the help of our army'.[202] If the intention was to bolster the Christian population in the 'security zone' with refugees, these expectations were disappointed: the vast majority of the exiled Christians removed to the Christian heartland. Geagea and his colleagues in Beirut protested that they bore no responsibility for the actions of the Lebanese Forces in the south. That may be so. However, they did not dissociate themselves in any way, as the Kata'ib did — unequivocally and before the defeat. Shortly before the rebellion, a leading Kata'ib politician had expressed his misgivings: 'I fear that we shall have to pay dearly for the dreams of Bashir and his epigones'.[203] His fears were soon fulfilled. For the second time the Lebanese Forces, regardless of the group responsible, had recklessly unleashed civil war in a part of the country, and for the second time the consequence was a mass exodus of Christians.

Another consequence of the rebellion and war in the south was that Gemayel and Karami's efforts to effect reconciliation stalled. In May there was renewed shooting along the green line, and other, parallel conflicts in different parts of the country worsened.

## The 'Camps War': Amal against Palestinians

In 1984 armed Palestinians began drifting back to Beirut and into the south. As early as 1983 guerrillas in the Popular Front and the units commanded by the

---

[201] With the equipment of the Lebanese Ministry of Transport; Walid Jumblatt held the portfolio.
[202] *Neue Zürcher Zeitung*, April 19th, 1985.
[203] Interview with the author.

Fatah dissident, Abu Musa, had fought with the Druze against the Lebanese Forces in the Chouf. With the collapse of the Lebanese Army on February 6th, 1984, the barrier between the Chouf and the south-western suburbs of Beirut fell, and the way was open for Syrian-sponsored Palestinians to enter the camps of Beirut. But the Arafat wing of the PLO also returned: after the Israeli withdrawals they could use the Druze-controlled port of Khalde and later the port of Sidon. In early 1985, rumours circulated of huge sums of money being deposited in Beirut bank accounts, which temporarily strengthened the Lebanese pound; the PLO was recruiting in the camps.

The Amal leadership watched this development with growing anxiety. Berri declared that under no circumstances would he tolerate a return to the situation before 1982, with the PLO an armed state within the state. The Shi`is' fear was one factor behind the 'Camps War'; another was Syria's interest, having expelled Arafat from Lebanon, in preventing his comeback. On May 20th, 1985, Amal militiamen, supported by the Sixth Brigade of the Lebanese Army, laid siege to Sabra, Chatila and Bourj al-Barajneh. By early June Sabra had been completely destroyed and overrun, in Chatila the PLO were trapped in a tiny area around a mosque. Bourj al-Barajneh, however, resisted fiercely. The fall of Sabra and Chatila was accompanied by horrific massacres, perpetrated this time not by Christian but by Shi`i militiamen. Nor was there a Kahan Commission to investigate them. The fighting produced unexpected realignments. In the camps, Arafat and Abu Musa supporters, antagonists in the intra-Palestinian civil war, closed ranks against the Shi`i attack. During the war against the Israeli–Lebanese agreement, the batteries manned by troops of Abu Musa and the Popular Front in the Chouf hills had shelled the Christian suburbs; their guns were now trained on the Shi`i suburbs to relieve the hard-pressed camps. Conversely, the Shi`i Sixth Brigade attacked under the covering fire of its Christian tank battalion stationed on the east side of the green line. Palestinians stood by Palestinians and Lebanese by Lebanese, regardless of ideological and confessional divides.

The Camps War was fought with extraordinary bitterness. The camps and the neighbouring Shi`i suburbs had been at war from 1979 to 1982, had suffered terribly during the Israeli invasion in 1982, and in 1984 been shelled by the Lebanese Army in their abortive attempt to regain control. These events had bred hatred between the Shi`is and the Palestinians. Although superior in numbers, as a fighting force the Amal militias were nothing in comparison with the hard core of professional Palestinian guerrillas that defended the camps and, after the initial massacre, knew full well what awaited them should they capitulate. The Bourj al-Barajneh camp did not capitulate. Amal was forced to resort to a siege. The camp was sealed off; anyone attempting to get in or out was shot.

The longer the siege endured, the greater Amal's political embarrassment. The organization could depend on Syrian approval. But the rest of the Arab world took umbrage at the Palestinians' fate. In mid-June the Arab League met and called for the siege to be lifted. Iran had little sympathy for Amal's course of action and offered to mediate. Hezbollah disregarded Amal's war, preoccupied with its own against Israel and any Western presence, in which all means were fair. In June 1985, a TWA airliner was hijacked to Beirut airport. This incident and the growing number of hostages from Western and other countries strained relations between Hezbollah and Amal. Amal sought to protect its image as legitimate representative of the Shi`i community, a 'pillar of the Lebanese state', and viewed with apprehension the gradual equation of 'Shi`i' with 'terrorist' in the public mind.

The Camps War ended only in late 1988. Cease-fires, all temporary, gave the PLO breathing-spaces they used to take money and material into the camps, and fresh fighters. Throughout 1985 and 1986 Amal and the Sixth Brigade were unable to break Palestinian resistance. The front between the camp and the Shi`i district of Bourj al-Barajneh became as permanent as the 'classic fronts' like the green line and the front between the army and the Druze at Souk al-Gharb.

## War between Amal and the Druze militias

The Druze had enabled the Palestinians to return to Beirut. When Amal launched their assault on the camps, the PSP militia remained neutral. In April the allies in the war against the Israeli–Lebanese agreement had combined forces to wipe out the Mourabitoun. The first clashes between them occurred in June 1985. What followed was a grim struggle for control of West Beirut. Amal no longer trusted the PSP because of their connections with Arafat's group. In turn, the PSP gained the support of all forces in West Beirut afraid of Shi`i dominance, especially Communist and Sunni Kurds. Kurds as well as other Lebanese Sunnis enrolled in the PSP militia; others built up a new militia, the 'Sixth of February Movement'. Palestinian and Libyan money found its way into the pockets of most anti-Shi`i groups.

Throughout June there were clashes between Amal and the PSP, towards the end of the month also between the Sixth Brigade and the PSP. Most of the Sunni populace of inner West Beirut went on strike to protest against the fighting; the Sunni Minister, Al-Hoss, demanded that all militias leave the city. In August the Syrian government tried to mediate. To their satisfaction, Syrian officers were stationed in Beirut as cease-fire observers for the first time since the Israeli invasion in 1982. By the end of July it had become obvious where Syria's sympathies lay: the Syrian Army provided Amal with fifty tanks, the Sixth Brigade with thirty and the PSP with none.

At times in the second half of 1985 Amal was simultaneously fighting the Palestinians in the camps and the Druze in West Beirut. In September Premier Karami and Minister Al-Hoss sent their first request to the Syrian government to redeploy troops in West Beirut — the most evident sign of Sunni despair: rather the Syrian Army than the chaos of Druze and Shi`i militias. At the same time the West Beiruti populace went on strike again to protest against this chaos, to little effect.

Unknown Shi`i groups attacked offices of what they called the 'atheist parties', the SSNP and the Communist Party. Four Soviet diplomats were abducted; one was murdered and the others were released through Syrian mediation.

The Druze-Shi`i struggle reached an initial climax in the so-called Flag War in November 1985. On the Lebanese National Day soldiers of the Sixth Brigade hoisted the cedar flag on all public buildings. PSP militiamen tore them down and replaced them with their party banner. Thereupon, on November 21st, Shi`i soldiers and militiamen, on the one hand, and Druze militiamen, on the other, tore into one another with tanks and artillery in the middle of West Beirut. On that one day sixty-five people were killed and over 400 abducted. After this shock the Shi`is and Druze suspended their fighting, but only for a few months.

## Civil war around Zahle and Tripoli

While Shi`is were shooting at Palestinians and Druze simultaneously or alternately, and vice versa, in Beirut, civil warfare erupted in another two Lebanese cities. The pattern was the same in both: fighting between Lebanese of different communities, calls for Syrian help and, finally, the entry of Syrian troops.

By comparison with past experience, the fighting in Zahle was light. On August 11th, 1985, Shi`i militias started shelling the city. The Lebanese Forces in the city responded by shelling neighbouring Shi`i villages. Christian notables mediated: the Lebanese Forces withdrew on August 31st, and Syrian troops entered the city on September 7th to re-establish the pax Syriana.

The fighting in Tripoli was the worst the city had experienced. When Arafat and his adherents were forced by Syria to leave the city at the end of 1983 they left behind huge stocks of armaments. Their local allies, the Sunni fundamentalist Tawheed, used them to maintain control over the city, with the exception of the Alawite quarter of Baal Mohsen, which the 'Pink Panthers' of the Arab Democratic Party held. A considerable part of the Tawheed cadres and militiamen were not Lebanese, but recruited among Syrian Sunni fundamentalists who had fled to Tripoli in 1981 and 1982 after revolts had been crushed in Hama. They established a local crypto-Islamic republic. The consumption of alcohol was prohibited, schoolboys and schoolgirls sat in separate classrooms, and the 'godless' were fair game. Dozens of communists and other left-wingers died violent deaths. In September 1985, a coalition of Alawites, Communists, Baathists and SSNP supporters turned on the fundamentalists. Approximately a quarter of a million civilians fled the city. After heavy shelling, Tawheed capitulated. On October 7th, 1985, 20,000 Syrian soldiers entered the city — the pax Syriana.

It was evident that in both Zahle and Tripoli pro-Syrian groups had started the fighting and equally evident that the Syrian government gladly responded to the appeals for help. Notwithstanding this, it was just as evident that broad sections of the local populace preferred Syrian order to simmering warfare between local militias. As described above, the mood in West Beirut was similar. The Syrian government decided that the time was ripe to regulate the conflict in Lebanon in their own best interests.

## The fight over the Militia Agreement of Damascus

The time seemed ripe because most Lebanese parties to the conflict were weakened. Zahle and Tripoli had accepted the Syrians as arbiters. Palestinians, Druze and Shi`is were doing their mutual best to weaken each other, and none seemed likely to win. Lebanese central authority was attenuated: neither president, government nor army had been able to prevent renewed fighting in any part of the country; the prime minister felt compelled to request Syrian intervention to deal with it. Finally, the Christian militia was also weakened. Whether Geagea was wholly or partially responsible for the catastrophe that overwhelmed the Christians in the south or not, populace, parties and even elements within the Lebanese Forces blamed him for it.

Even before the last militiamen had been evacuated from the south, a second rebellion took place within the Lebanese Forces. It was led by their head of military intelligence, Elie Hobeika. The background to this palace intrigue was complicated, even by Lebanese standards. President Gemayel had Geagea ordered to sign a written declaration in which he bound himself to recognize the legal institutions of the state, to hand over ports and militia checkpoints to the army, and to support the foreign policy of the government. The intermediary between Gemayel and Geagea was Karim Pakradouni. Pakradouni had mediated between the Kata'ib and Syria in 1975/6, was political adviser to President Sarkis and now adviser to the Lebanese Forces, and by far their best political mind. Geagea signed. On May 12th, 1985, the command council of the Lebanese Forces met. Hobeika attacked Geagea for signing the declaration. The command council decided that Geagea should remain as chief of staff, that is, in future he would be concerned solely with military matters, and elected Hobeika as new commander of the Lebanese Forces.

Like Geagea, Elie Hobeika made his name in and through the war. There the similarity ends; the two were very different in temperament and character. Although Hobeika also came from a simple background, his was urban, not rural. Most of his militia support was drawn from the lower classes of Beirut. He was trained in Israel, and was long regarded as Israel's man in the Lebanese Forces. Above all, he proved a brilliant autodidact in all matters relating to military intelligence, with a talent for private business, too. In contrast to Geagea, he was extremely witty and absolutely unscrupulous. His treatment of opponents earned him the nickname 'the butcher' among Israeli officers. It has often been surmised that his was the mind behind the first massacre in Sabra and Chatila; however, statements and considerations to the contrary within the context of that week cannot be dismissed.[204] He was a person of extraordinary political flexibility. The man once taken for an Israeli agent, who with Geagea rejected Amin Gemayel's 'pro-Syrian' policies, then toppled Geagea because the latter accepted Gemayel's course, had excellent contacts in Syria. In September 1985, four months after his move, he was invited to talks in Damascus.[205]

At the end of September the leaders of the three most powerful militias — Jumblatt, Berri and Hobeika, or their representatives — met in Damascus to negotiate a comprehensive peace settlement for Lebanon.[206] Berri opened the meeting by presenting the Christians with two alternatives: either the abolition of the system of proportionality or a census as the basis of revised proportions. After lengthy and tough negotiations the militias agreed on the main features of a new constitution, which would, after a reasonable period of transition, replace the system of proportionality.

All forms of partition, federalism, confederalism, cantons and decentralization of security were rejected. A second chamber, a senate, would be created, with the power to decide on constitutional amendments and confessional personal status regulations; the document makes no mention of secularization in this connection. The powers of the president would be curtailed in favour of those of the prime minister and the cabinet. The prime minister would, as a rule, chair cabinet

---

[204] These are based on Hobeika's position: he was responsible for the personal safety of Bashir Gemayel. After the assassination he was — in his very own interest — too preoccupied with tracing the perpetrators to organize a massacre.

[205] Walid Jumblatt, rather shocked by this Syrian volte face, asked Khaddam, the Syrian Foreign Minister, why he was negotiating 'with this murderer'. Khaddam's answer is worthy of note: 'Who in Lebanon is not a murderer? He, at least, is a son of the people' — a barb against Jumblatt.

[206] On the following, see *Middle East Reporter* 48/438 (1985), pp. 2f, 49/439 (1985), p. 2 and 50/440 (1985), pp. 2f.

meetings, the president only in specific cases; executive authority would reside in the cabinet; and the president would have only a suspensive veto.

During the period of transition Christians and Muslims would have an equal number of seats in parliament, as would the three largest communities. Deputies would be appointed rather than elected to vacant and new seats. The quota system in the civil service would be restricted to the highest category, where confessional parity would obtain without specific posts being reserved to specific communities.[207] A two-thirds majority would be necessary to end the transition period after four years, 55 per cent of the votes cast after eight years and 51 per cent after twelve years. There were only two substantial differences between the constitutional provisions for the period of transition in the Militia Agreement and previous proposals for reform. One was the new senate, patently to give the Druze an office of state; the other was confessional parity instead of denominational quotas at the most senior level of the civil service. The limitations on the period of transition were broad enough to allow them to be questioned later.

Far more problematic, though, was the second section of the Militia Agreement, that regulating relations between Syria and Lebanon. As one commentator pointed out, in contrast to the 'clear legal prose' of the constitutional principles in the first part, the second part was written in a style 'the Baath ideologists use in their theoretical writings, a pompous language laced with big words and elastic concepts ... From the style it would seem that that part of the document was not negotiated but dictated to the negotiators by the Syrians.'[208]

The Agreement defined the goal of relations between the two countries as 'strategic complementarity'.[209] It stated that Lebanon's Arabism found its true expression in its distinctive relationship with Syria. History and geography provided 'crucial causes' for these relations. These relations had to be 'translated in each of the two countries into legal frameworks' so as to place them above the 'whims of any political faction', above 'caprice and interests' and above 'regional influences'. In foreign policy the Agreement called for 'complete and firm coordination' on 'all issues — Arab, regional and international'. On military relations the text reads: 'The crucial conflict being waged by Syria against Israel, in its attempt to establish a strategic balance in face of Israel as a result of well-known

---

[207] The logic of provisions relating to the abolition of quotas in all other categories is questionable: 'In order to ensure the justness of the application of this principle [i.e., abolition], the rights of unfairly treated communities will be settled within six months'; *Middle East Reporter* 49/439 (1985) p. 19; in other words: quotas to abolish quotas.

[208] Arnold Hottinger, 'Syrische Wünsche nach Gleichschaltung im Libanon', *Neue Zürcher Zeitung*, January 8th, 1986; see also Daniel Pipes, 'Damascus and the claim to Lebanon', *Orbis* 30/4 (1987), pp. 663–81, especially pp. 675–6.

[209] For quotes from this part of the Agreement, see *Middle East Reporter*, 49/439 (1985), pp. 21ff.

Arab circumstances, including Egypt's exit from the arena of the conflict and creation of Arab-Palestinian axes to confuse Syria politically and on security and military levels, imposes on Lebanon that it should not be the door through which Israel can deal a blow to Syria or threaten it.' To realize this would require an agreement on the deployment of Syrian troops in Lebanon and a 'joint definition of the main threats to the security, independence and regimes of the two countries'.

The Lebanese Army would be 'rehabilitated with Syrian aid' on the basis of a 'genuine fighting creed that distinguished the real enemy from the true friend', and withdrawn from all areas 'except those of military confrontation with the Israeli occupation'.

A joint ministerial committee would supervise the realization and enforcement of the contents of the Agreement.

The contents of the draft provoked an outcry, above all the provisions of the section on relations with Syria. Hobeika tried to suppress criticism: he stopped publication of the Kata'ib's daily newspapers, gave the party an ultimatum to hand over their headquarters, and declared in the command council of the Lebanese Forces that if the Agreement were not signed, shelling of the Christian enclave would be renewed. This did not stifle broad, vocal opposition. The Kata'ib declared that Hobeika was a threat to the liberty of the Christian region, and the Agreement a threat to the liberty of the whole country; signing would mean they had spent ten years fighting for nothing. Chamoun and Franjieh spoke out against the draft, and the Maronite bishops 'for all measures that guarantee Lebanon's independence'. Sunni politicians sent their Christian colleagues messages asking them to do what they, fearing for their own safety, could not: stop the Agreement. The army command had little desire to be 'rehabilitated' by Syrian officers; they carried out manoeuvres with Christian brigades to demonstrate their will to resist. A wave of attempted assassinations worsened the confrontation: Chamoun, Elie Karami and other leaders of the Lebanese Front escaped with injuries; Hobeika and Amin Gemayel were spared injury because they were not in their vehicles when they were attacked. In spite of mounting opposition, Hobeika signed the Agreement on December 28th, 1985.

Only then was President Gemayel officially informed of the contents of the Agreement in Damascus. He refused his consent, expressly on the ground that an agreement among militias could not prejudice decisions of constitutional organs: they, and they alone, were empowered to take decisions on the constitution and conclude or abrogate international treaties.

Hobeika tried to put pressure on the president. He let units of the Lebanese Forces attack militias loyal to the Kata'ib and the president. Thereupon the Lebanese Forces split. A majority in the command council came out against the

Agreement. Samir Geagea played the crucial role. He and his troops attacked Hobeika, who, after heavy fighting was isolated in his headquarters in Karantina. The army command, with the support of the Maronite patriarch, mediated an end to the fighting without further bloodshed. Hobeika resigned as commander of the Lebanese Forces and was flown out in an army helicopter. Geagea returned to his former position; his deputy was Pakradouni. The change of command in the Lebanese Forces meant that the Militia Agreement was invalidated.

The other signatories and the Syrian government were outraged. They announced political and military sanctions, the most important of which was a boycott of the state president: there would be no further dealings with Gemayel. Cabinet meetings were suspended, the continuance of what had, in effect, been practised in the previous months. Not only Jumblatt and Berri but also moderate Sunni politicians like Karami and Al-Hoss joined the boycott, evidently for fear of offending the Syrian leaders. The government continued to function as an administrative body. Civil servants prepared decrees, obtained government approval from each minister in turn and put them into effect. But at the symbolic level the boycott expressed the disintegration of the consensus system. One year after their triumphant welcome in Sidon, president and premier no longer met. In so far as there was any consensus, it was clandestine. The military sanctions against the rejectionists were relatively mild. At the beginning of February there was shooting along the green line and in Souk al-Gharb. The Syrian artillery irregularly shelled East Beirut. In the second half of February the SSNP militia, with Syrian support, attempted to advance in the direction of Bikfaya, the home of the Gemayels, but were easily stopped by Lebanese Army troops. Syrian troops along the northern boundary of the Christian heartland also tried to advance, again without success.[210] For some months the situation remained 'normal': shooting along the demarcation line.[211]

In early summer Christian and Muslim Lebanon made tentative contact. A new Maronite Patriarch had been elected in April, Monseigneur Nasrallah Sfeir, a man known for his moderate political opinions.[212] In June, the Patriarch met the Sunni Mufti in West Beirut. Christian and Muslim ministers resumed consultations, not as a cabinet presided over by the president but in what was called a political

---

[210] Two attacks were launched in the Metn, one in Douar, the other on the road between Baskinta and Bikfaya. In the north the fighting lasted just a day: Franjieh's Marada militia had no enthusiasm for a fight against other Christians. The Lebanese Army had redeployed its troops from the green line to the presidential palace in Baabda and the upper Metn. Along the green line the militias took to shooting at each other.

[211] In April the French cease-fire observers left Beirut. They had suffered heavy casualties. Once it became apparent that the cease-fire was not being taken seriously, their mission was redundant.

[212] The Lebanese Forces had run a sort of election campaign for a more militant-minded prelate. The majority of the Bishops' Synod disapproved of this interference in their field of competence.

'dialogue'. Their venue was symbolic of the divisions in the country: the racecourse in the heart of Beirut; the green line bisected the hippodrome.

The final battle in the war over the Militia Agreement broke out unexpectedly at the end of September. After his defeat, Elie Hobeika spent a brief exile in France, then returned to Lebanon via Damascus. With Syrian assistance he gathered his adherents in the Lebanese Forces who had dispersed to West Beirut and the Bekaa. He still had numerous sympathizers among militiamen in East Beirut, in particular in military intelligence, the branch he had built up and led for years. On September 29th, Hobeika and his followers tried to retake East Beirut. The attack was launched from West Beirut across the green line. This implies that the militias in control there must have, if not actually given support, at least turned a blind eye. This was a novelty. The demarcation line established in the aftermath of the fight for the hotel district in 1976 had the nature of a permanent divide; shooting along it might have become 'normal', but no one had seriously considered carrying war across it. This move was possible only because the insurgents had an intimate knowledge of the terrain they were entering — it was, after all, their own — and accomplices who knew in the terrain from which they launched their assault. Geagea and his followers were taken completely by surprise. Hobeika's men advanced as far as the centre of Ashrafieh. Eventually they were stopped not by rival militiamen but by units of the Lebanese Army, whose command did not want East Beirut to fall into the hands of a group unreservedly aligned with Syria. Faced by the Lebanese Army, Hobeika beat a quick retreat. The attempt to impose the Militia Agreement by violence had failed. The victims of this attempt were Hobeika militiamen who did not flee quickly enough. A few hundred of them were murdered by their former comrades; 'liquidations' were still being carried out days later. Mistrust was rampant within the victorious wing of the Lebanese Forces, and not without reason: Hobeika almost certainly enjoyed clandestine support. Reciprocal shelling along the green line signalled the return to 'normality' in October.

The Militia Agreement was Syria's second attempt to impose a settlement of the conflict in Lebanon by treaty. The first agreement, the Damascus Agreement of 1976, foundered on the opposition of the Lebanese Left and the PLO, the second on that of the Christians. The first unleashed a civil war, the second a power struggle among the political and military forces in Christian Lebanon. Although the section of the Militia Agreement dealing with domestic political matters was not undisputed, its broad outlines were acceptable to many Lebanese of different political tendencies: strict parity between Christians and Muslims, and gradual transition to a majority-vote democracy. What was unacceptable to the majority of Christians and many Muslims was that section of the Agreement on future relations with Syria. Here, for the first time, the Syrian government — or an influential body within it — explicitly stated its objectives in Lebanon: not 'annexation', but complete 'coordination' in all aspects of foreign and security policy, moreover, coordination enshrined in law. Many Lebanese, including Christians, would have accepted voluntary 'Finlandization', in so far as this only involved adapting Lebanese foreign policy to Syrian, analogous to the relationship between Chehabist and Egyptian foreign policy in the 1960s. However, the Militia Agreement went far beyond voluntary restraint. Formulations such as the 'rehabilitation' of the Lebanese Army 'with Syrian help' intimated an intention to reduce Lebanon to a satellite state. This impression was hardened by the disdain for Lebanese constitutional institutions: president, prime minister and parliament were first excluded from the negotiations and then presented with a fait accompli.

Numerous Muslim politicians indicated surreptitiously that they disapproved of the Agreement and hoped that the Christians would wreck it. None of Syria's Lebanese allies wanted actually to fight for it. Hence, the civil strife over the Agreement was largely verbal; the only serious attempt to turn the tables was Hobeika's assault on East Beirut. The heart of the resistance to Syria's imposition was the Lebanese Army brigades stationed in the Christian heartland. They contained invasion attempts in the Metn and the north, and put an end to Hobeika's venture. The only political movement and militia which identified completely with the Agreement and with Syria's role as protector was Amal. Amal, and the Shi`i community as a whole, had good reasons. No other movement was so in need of Syrian aid because no other movement was involved in anything like the number of violent conflicts Amal was. The wars in Lebanon between 1986 and 1988 were, for the most part, Amal's wars. The more inextricable Amal's position became, the more it relied on Syrian support.

## The 'Camps War': Beirut and the south

In March and April of 1986 there had been renewed fighting over the Palestinian camps in Beirut. As always, the Arafat wing of the PLO had almost inexhaustible financial means and the unyielding loyalty of the majority of the Palestinians in the camps. And as always, the money was extremely useful in finding new allies. After the demise of the Mourabitoun, a new Sunni militia formed, and took its name from the date of the West Beirut uprising in 1984: 'the Sixth of February Movement'. Most of its recruits were Sunnis from Iklim al-Kharroub living in the Beirut district of Tarik al-Jadideh, and equipped and financed by the Arafat wing of the PLO. Amal soon saw the new organization as a menace to its control over West Beirut. In early June, Amal launched an assault on Tarik al-Jadideh. After unusually fierce street-fighting, the Sixth of February Movement and PSP units supporting it were beaten. The victors also suffered heavy casualties, and avenged themselves on the population of the district, not least by rape. The Sunni and Shi`i Muftis exchanged uncordial statements, and Berri called for Syrian troops to enter West Beirut. But Berri and the Syrian government did not see eye to eye over the camps. The Syrians sought to bring the camps under the control of the Abu Musa faction of the PLO. Berri took the view that differences between the different Palestinian factions were but nuances: 'An Abu Musa supporter in Damascus quickly becomes an Arafatist in Beirut.' He accused all Palestinians of wanting 'to get back to Lebanon rather than back to Palestine'. At the end of June Sunni units of the Lebanese Army, backed up by a battalion of Syrian soldiers, were deployed around Chatila and Bourj al-Barajneh, and the adversaries took a break.

Amal's struggle to prevent the re-emergence of a Palestinian 'state within the state' received a setback in the second half of 1986. The Lebanese conflict had its fair share of shifting alliances, but the new alliance was remarkable even for Lebanon: between the Arafat wing of the PLO and the Lebanese Christians. The violent conflict in Lebanon may have begun between the Palestinians and the Christians, and from 1983 Amal's stance towards the Palestinians may have resembled that of the Christians from 1969 onwards. For the Christians in 1986, though, the most serious foreign adversary was not the PLO but Syria. The Syrians' closest ally and the Christians' chief Lebanese adversary since the Militia Agreement was Amal. The enemy of the Christians' Syrian and Shi`i enemies was the PLO. Thus, by the laws of opportunism the PLO became the Christians' new ally, though neither partner willingly admitted it. President Gemayel renewed 70,000 aliens' passports for Palestinians in Lebanon, and the Lebanese Forces helped transport armaments and fighters for the PLO into the camps in Beirut and in the south.

Amal had grudgingly to accept that it could not gain complete control over the camps in Beirut. But the least Berri and other Amal leaders wanted was to prevent the PLO from using the camps in southern Lebanon as bases for their war against Israel, for that would inevitably bring new misery to the Shi`is in the south. In October 1986, Amal laid siege to Rashidieh near Tyre. For a month Shi`is fought Palestinians, but the camp did not capitulate. On the contrary: on November 24th, PLO guerrillas in the camp near Sidon launched an offensive and occupied the strategically situated village of Maghdousheh, south-west of Sidon. The next day Amal retook the village, and the day after that, the PLO restormed it. In the same period the Israeli air force bombed Palestinian positions, creating the impression of coordination — and, hence, collaboration — between Amal and Israel. Angry Shi`is started hunting down Palestinians living outside the camps, which served to strengthen the resolve of those in the camps not to capitulate on any account. In December, fighting resumed between Shi`is and Palestinians in the Beirut camps.

At the end of 1986, Amal did not have much to show for its fight against the PLO. In 1984 and 1985, Amal had taken and destroyed parts of the Beirut camps; the PLO had dug themselves in and held Bourj al-Barajneh and a corner of Chatila. In 1986, the PLO had returned to the south in force and even won and retained positions outside the camps there. Amal had not succeeded in preventing the camps from rearming and the PLO from recovering.

## War in West Beirut: Amal against the Left

Support for the PLO against Amal came not only from the Lebanese Forces but also from the Druze militias, who facilitated the movement of material and new Palestinian recruits to the south. In early 1987, after yet another futile attempt to storm the Beirut camps, Amal militiamen, embittered by the fruitlessness of their long struggle, turned on PLO sympathizers in West Beirut: the PSP and the communists.[213] By this time the PSP in Beirut was no longer an exclusively Druze militia; former members of the Mourabitoun and the Sixth of February Movement had joined it, as well as Kurdish groups previously allied to the PLO. In Beirut, one factor united Druze, Sunnis and the Left:[214] their aversion to Amal control over the entire western section of the city. In mid-February this rivalry erupted in an armed confrontation worse than any West Beirut had experienced. Heavy armaments were deployed in street-fighting at short range. The devastation equalled that during the Israeli siege of 1982. After five days the Left gained the upper hand. Amal's headquarters in the Murr Tower were overrun; the PSP took the business district around Hamra; Amal fighters were trapped at two points[215] and in a hopeless situation.

The Syrian government had been waiting for such a situation: one that justified renewed intervention in Beirut, an intervention also necessary to protect Syrian interests. Appeals from the West Beirut populace, who felt that only the Syrians could end this brutal civil war, were justification enough. The necessity arose from the precarious position of Syria's most reliable ally in Lebanon: Amal was in danger of decisive and final defeat in a simultaneous struggle against the Palestinians, the Druze and Lebanese Left.

On February 22nd, 1987, two Syrian brigades entered West Beirut. The Amal troops pulled back to the south-western suburbs. The Syrian Army forbade

---

[213] A number of leading communist intellectuals were murdered by Amal supporters, including the philosopher Hassan Hamdat, who, because of his Shi'i background, had been branded an 'atheist traitor' and was especially hated.

[214] In the summer of 1976 the SSNP had split into a pro-PLO (Libyan-patronized) and a pro-Syrian faction; the two were locked in bitter rivalry, with no quarter given or taken.

[215] Close to the Commodore Hotel, favoured by western journalists, and at the American University Hospital.

militiamen from carrying arms on the street, and cracked down on any resistance; twenty-three Hezbollah fighters who ignored the warnings were shot dead. Barely five years after Israel had compelled the Syrian Army to leave Beirut it was back in the Lebanese capital.

In 1976, the Syrian army had marched into Beirut to end a civil war between Christians and Muslims, in 1987 to end a war among the Muslims, and both times to bring both Lebanon and the PLO under its control. In 1976 it had come on an understanding with President Sarkis; in 1987 President Gemayel protested, while Al-Hoss, Berri and Jumblatt perforce paved the way for its intervention. In 1976 the main loser had been Kamal Jumblatt, whose hopes of victory Syria's action dashed; in 1987 it was his son Walid. Syria's intervention deprived him not only of the fruits of his victory in West Beirut, but also of full enjoyment of the fruits of his earlier victories over the Lebanese Forces in 1983 and 1985, namely unchallenged ascendancy in his enlarged 'Druze canton'. The Syrians occupied the road between Sofar and Khalde and the coastal road south of Beirut.[216] This rendered it impossible for Jumblatt to pursue policies independently of Syria. The most telling evidence of the subsequent resignation among the Druze and their left-wing allies was the revelation in September 1987 that about 1,000 Druze militiamen and 300 fighters of left-wing organizations had been recruited as mercenaries by Qaddafi to fight in the Chad War — with the approval of their respective leaders.[217]

Amal was saved by Syrian intervention, and thus became more dependent on Syria than ever. Until January 1988, Amal militiamen sporadically attacked the Palestinian camps in the south and Beirut; most of the time, however, they contented themselves with maintaining the blockade. On January 18th, Amal finally lifted the blockade: the Palestinians on the West Bank had started their intifada. In the eyes of the Arab world, continued pressure on the camps would have cast the Syrian government as well as Amal in very awkward roles as Israeli accomplices. Amal had another, even weightier reason to suspend its struggle against the Palestinians: a confrontation with a new adversary.

### Shi'i civil war: Amal against Hezbollah

The 'Party of God' had emerged in 1982, after Syria had allowed Iranian 'Revolutionary Guards' into the Bekaa to fight the Israeli invasion. They were too late for that war, but not for guerrilla warfare against the Israeli occupation of

---

[216] This placed the 'Druze port' of Khalde under Syrian control. The PSP militia seems to have been involved in a number of strikes against the Syrian Army in West Beirut. In June 1987 Jumblatt was forced to hand over to the Syrians a number of those involved, including his 'security chief'.

[217] The respective organizations receive a share of the pay of these new foreign legionnaires.

southern Lebanon from 1983 onwards. Under the name Hezbollah, Lebanese Shi`is carried out a number of suicide raids, becoming the terror of the troops in the Western multinational forces and considerably demoralizing the Israeli Army. Some of these commandos called themselves the 'Islamic Jihad'. Indiscriminate hostage-taking[218] became another 'trademark' of this political tendency; any Westerner was fair game. Hezbollah is not a monolithic organization, but a conglomeration of various groups with two features in common. Firstly, their goal is an Islamic Republic of Lebanon, for which Iran is the model; secondly, the Iranian government has a strong influence, due to common politico-religious convictions and enormous material support.

In 1982 Amal still appeared radical in comparison with the following of the traditional Shi`i notables. By 1983 it was under growing pressure from a far more radical movement. For years it had doggedly struggled against left-wing groups whose programmes had attracted many Shi`is in pre-war Lebanon; its new rivals were right-wing, inspired by Khomeini. Amal and Hezbollah had different policies towards Israel. Amal wanted to see the last of the Israelis in southern Lebanon, though without inflicting further suffering on the local population. For this reason it had embarked on a long struggle against the Palestinians: their resurgence was likely to attract renewed Israeli punitive measures. By contrast, Hezbollah, like the radical Palestinians, took up the banner of relentless struggle against Israel 'all the way to Jerusalem'.[219]

The two Shi`i organizations also differed fundamentally in their views on the future of Lebanon. In April 1987, fundamentalist Iranian and Lebanese clerics presented a draft constitution for an Islamic Republic of Lebanon closely modelled on Iran: all legislation would accord with Islamic law; an Islamic council — composed of Shi`is alone — would draw up a new order for the country; the 'various minorities' in the country would be granted autonomy in areas where they formed the majority.[220]

The Amal leadership dissociated itself from this concept. Berri repeatedly stressed that most of Amal's members were devout Shi`is who admired the

---

[218] There is no consensus in Hezbollah itself on whether hostage-taking is justified by the struggle. Musawi, the leader of the 'Islamic Jihad', declared that 'spies or military personnel' may legitimately be taken hostage. Muhammad Hussein Fadlallah, the most influential religious figure in the Hezbollah movement (he will not be seen as its leader), has defined kidnapping and hostage-taking as 'inhuman and irreligious' and an 'un-Islamic method', though he has not issued a formal ruling (fatwa) to this effect. Hezbollah leaders 'continue to debate among themselves the morality and legality of the means to that elusive end' (i.e. the creation of an Islamic republic in Lebanon); Kramer, *The Moral Logic of Hizballah*, pp. 21ff.

[219] See Mallat, *Shi`i Thought*, pp. 35f.

[220] Arnold Hottinger, 'Verfassungsentwurf Teherans für Libanon — über die Ausbreitung der iranischen Revolution', *Neue Zürcher Zeitung*, May 6th, 1987.

Iranian revolution. However, Lebanon and Lebanese politics were a matter for the Lebanese, and had to take account of the peculiarities of Lebanon and its numerous communities. He rejected a revival of the National Pact. Berri wanted 'majority democracy', in which the Shi`is would play a leading role, not an Islamic state.

The rivalry was as marked at the humdrum level, especially over recruitment. Hezbollah's coffers were regularly replenished by Iran; it could afford higher pay and tried to entice away Amal fighters. Amal's leaders spoke of the 'Petro Party', though contempt and suasion were not always effective antidotes to Hezbollah's tangible attractions.

In September 1987, clashes occurred between the two militias in southern Lebanon. The Shi`i civil war proper broke out in April 1988. The political divide often ran through families, one cause of the ferocity that exceeded even that of other conflicts in the long course of the war. Amal won the first round: Hezbollah was roundly defeated in the south. Berri spoke of a victory 'against radicalism, kidnapping and terrorism'. But Hezbollah won the second round. In early May, the fundamentalist militia, with the support of Iranian Revolutionary Guards, launched assaults on Amal positions in all the southern suburbs of Beirut. Nor was it all heavy fighting. Iranian arms were effective, but more effectual were Iranian alms: a number of Amal positions were taken with offers that local commanders and militiamen found irresistible. After a fortnight Hezbollah controlled about four-fifths of the Shi`i suburbs. Amal held only Chiyah, and even there was in worsening straits.

This placed the Syrian government in a predicament. Amal was again in danger of being run out of the capital. On the other hand, direct Syrian intervention in support of Amal incurred the risk of an open break with Iran, Hezbollah's protector. Iran was also Syria's most powerful ally in the region and a good trading partner that sold it oil at preferential prices. It was very tricky for Syria to act against an Iranian protégé in Lebanon. To save Amal without actually attacking Hezbollah, Syria decided to assume control of the south-west suburbs. The Syrian Army first called on both Amal and Hezbollah to withdraw to specific barracks and declared that it would not attack either party, but that Syrian soldiers had orders to crack down on any armed resistance. After several days of announcements and repeated warnings the Syrian troops entered the Shi`i suburbs without a fight on May 17th.[221]

---

[221] One Hezbollah commando shot an anti-tank grenade at a car carrying four high-ranking Syrian officers. As the vehicle was armour-plated there were no casualties. The Syrians reacted with yet another warning.

This action contained, but did not end the Shi`i civil war. Neither Hezbollah nor Amal accepted their defeats in the south and Beirut respectively. Nor had the Syrians disarmed either of the militias. The militiamen simply disappeared from the streets. Instead of open fighting, there were reciprocal kidnappings and murders. In September 1988, the Amal commander in southern Lebanon, Daoud Daoud, and two colleagues were murdered. In the same month Amal and Hezbollah militiamen clashed in the Bekaa, in the south and again in southern suburbs of Beirut. Despite Syrian mediation, heavy fighting erupted in the Beirut suburbs in early December; this time it was inconclusive. It took until the spring of 1989 to arrange a cease-fire under the auspices of Syria and Iran. The Shi`i civil war was back on the slow burner.

## Civil war: Palestinians against Palestinians

In the face of the Amal onslaught, Palestinians of all political hues and organizations had stood by each other. Hardly had the pressure on the Palestinian camps in Beirut eased — by May 1988 Amal was pre-occupied with its war against Hezbollah — than Palestinians were gunning for Palestinians within the camps. The Syrian-sponsored guerrillas commanded by Abu Musa thought their chance had come to eliminate Arafat's supporters. For around two months the Beirut 'misery belt' was the scene of parallel wars: while the Shi`is made war in the suburbs, the Palestinians made war in the camps between or alongside them. This round in the Palestinian civil war was conclusive, at least for the time being. Backed by Syrian logistics, Abu Musa's troops took Chatila in June and, finally on July 8th, Bourj al-Barajneh.

Although modest compared to the pre-1982 heyday, it had been Arafat's power base in Beirut, and Arafat had lost it once again. The Palestinians in northern, eastern and central Lebanon were now under Syrian control. In the south, in the camps around Sidon and Tyre, Fatah was still dominant. The struggle to control the Palestinians in Lebanon was not over.

## Cold war over the Lebanese state

The hot wars of the years 1986–1988 were largely fought within the former civil war camps: Hobeika's Lebanese Forces against Geagea's; Amal against the entire left wing, against Palestinians and Hezbollah; finally, Palestinians among themselves. Common to all of these conflicts was the Syrian element: Syrian allies fought against forces seeking to remain independent of the neighbouring country.

The confrontation between the civil war camps had virtually ground to a halt. The last fighting along the green line had taken place in May 1987. In March 1988, there had been brief flare-up along the demarcation line in the upper Metn.

SSNP units, covered by Syrian artillery, had launched an assault on soldiers of the regular army defending the Christian heartland. The SSNP militiamen were predominantly Christians from Akkar, the Lebanese soldiers Sunnis also from Akkar, some of them from the same villages. Once the troops on both sides realized their common origins they had no desire to slaughter each other, and the fighting ceased abruptly.

But what never ceased was the cold war over the institutions of the Lebanese state. It had begun with the collapse of the Militia Agreement of Damascus in January 1986. Jumblatt and Berri, both signatories to the Agreement and ministers in Karami's cabinet of 'national unity', called for the resignation of the state president. As a means to this end, they decided to 'boycott' cabinet meetings presided over by Gemayel. The prime minister joined the boycott, and for months the cabinet did not meet at all. In September, ministers started meeting again, not as the government, but informally as a 'committee of reconciliation' to discuss political reforms. However, they could not reach agreement. The Christian ministers, above all Chamoun, now called on Karami either to end the boycott of the state president, so that the government might resume its normal functions, or resign. Karami did neither one nor the other.

The cabinet met again only in April 1987, to consider the dramatically worsening economic situation, but to little effect. On May 4th, Karami unexpectedly announced his resignation. His explanations were in their way the opening shots in the campaign for the presidential election due a year later. Karami, who had once previously, in 1970, announced his candidacy for this office, felt that in future the presidency should not be reserved for a Maronite but be open to Lebanese of any community. The Muslims, he felt, were the majority. They were prepared to share power equally with the Christians, but no longer prepared to accept Christian preponderance. The Minister of Justice, Berri, went further, disparaging the National Pact as 'a sterile system incapable of revision or improvement'; it should be abolished. If it was impossible to agree on a new political system it would be impossible to elect a president either. The minister of transport, Jumblatt, was less circumspect: Amin Gemayel, the 'Shah of Baabda', should be chased out of office at gunpoint immediately.

The exchange remained verbal. Wars with the Left and the Palestinians tied the hands of Berri's Amal. Jumblatt's own militia was causing him difficulties: its intelligence branch had been involved in hit-and-run attacks against Syrian troops and he was compelled to hand those responsible over to Syria. None the less, Karami's resignation initiated a development that gradually unfolded into a constitutional crisis which, a year later, threatened to wreck the Lebanese state.

On June 1st, 1987, Karami was assassinated by a bomb planted in an army helicopter; it was never established who was responsible. In early August,

Mohammed Shukair, the liaison between Gemayel and the Beirut Sunni establishment, was also murdered by unknown assailants.[222] Saeb Salam retired to Switzerland. Camille Chamoun, who had survived an assassination attempt at the beginning of the year, died in the same month. Murder, exile and age decimated the circle of veterans who had worked to forge the National Pact and, regardless of all differences, sought to keep it working.

In this light, the efforts of the surviving politicians who remained in the country to uphold the political traditions and institutions of the Lebanese Republic were remarkable. Despite enormous disparities in interests and objectives, the cold war over the state was fought exceedingly legalistically. After Karami's death, President Gemayel asked the Minister of Education, Selim al-Hoss, to act as Prime Minister. Although the cabinet never met, it passed decrees by circulating them to all members; ministers retained contact either by telephone or through top-ranking civil servants. The parliamentary committees worked harder than ever, becoming the principal organs in the process of consensus. In the autumn of 1987 the presidential election due in summer 1988 began to cast its shadow. No less than fifty-nine names were mentioned as possible candidates, all Maronites; even Walid Jumblatt nominated a Maronite member of his party.

More than a dozen years of war, the fact that about 90 per cent of the country was controlled by foreign troops, and the virtual powerlessness of the presidency had not dissuaded the vast majority of Lebanese politicians that this office was worth campaigning for. The cold war over the state was manifestly the sign of a deep, perhaps desperate, belief in the future of this state; such belief is a prerequisite for the determination to contest largely symbolic power.

The decision of greatest symbolism — and at the same time of greatest desperation — was that taken by the Lebanese parliament in May 1987: it simultaneously abrogated the Cairo Agreement of 1969, and withdrew its consent to the 1983 Agreement with Israel. By this decision the Lebanese legislature dissociated itself from two agreements to which it had consented in order to avert worse in the shape of war and civil war, but which had brought just that. The decision was symbolic because it demonstrated the end of divergent opinions between Christians and Muslims over Lebanese policies towards the Palestinians and Israel. The decision was desperate, because in the meantime Lebanon had lost the ability to shape its own destiny.

---

[222] Shukair, a cultivated and successful businessman, had never had any personal political ambitions. He had excellent personal contacts in both sections of Beirut, was a close friend of the former Prime Minister, Takieddine Solh, but also on very good terms with eminent Maronites. Convinced of the need for Muslim-Christian understanding, he had altruistically offered his services as intermediary, for which he was murdered: the fate of a Lebanese patriot in 1987.

## Simmering warfare over the 'security zone'

Late 1988 was the twentieth anniversary of virtually uninterrupted violence and counter-violence in the extreme south of Lebanon. The Palestinian guerrilla raids had started here; Israeli reprisals and 'preventive intervention' had followed; and the vicious circle had not been broken.

Israel's unilaterally defined 'security zone' was barely larger than Major Haddad's pre-invasion 'Free Lebanon' of 1982. General Lahad's 'South Lebanese Army' of between 2,000 and 2,500 men exercised control by dint of Israeli assistance.[223] Lahad's troops were also defending Jezzine, the last homogeneous Christian enclave in the south. Israeli guarantees did not cover Jezzine. The extreme south was largely self-contained: the only regular connection with the Christian heartland was the ship between Naqqoura and Jounieh. The economic situation was worse than in the rest of the country; the largest employer was the UNIFIL brigade, and a few hundred commuters worked in Israel.

Two-thirds of Lahad's soldiers were Christian, the others Druze and Shi`i. In 1986 and 1987 numerous Shi`i soldiers went over to Amal and Hezbollah. After that recruitment stabilized. The zone patrolled by UNIFIL to the north of the 'security zone' was as open as it ever was. But the militiamen changed. As before, they included Palestinian guerrillas. The Hezbollah commandos were more recent. In their wake, to share the fame and prestige in the struggle against Israel, came Amal. Fighters of the small left-wing parties also took part in raids. Militiamen of both Hezbollah and the Left carried out suicide raids, a form of warfare unknown before 1982.

In late 1986 the attacks increased; in 1987, various positions of the South Lebanon Army were overrun. The Israeli Army retaliated with strikes against villages and guerrilla bases north of the security zone, from 1988 increasingly from the air. In October 1988, they pounded the Palestinian camp of Mieh-Mieh. Shortly before Christmas an Israeli commando raid launched from ships and helicopters just south of Beirut met with heavy resistance.

From the Israeli point of view, the security zone policy was moderately successful. Although the odd rocket hit northern Galilee and the occasional commando crossed the border, the number of civilian casualties fell. Limited military losses in the security zone were considered acceptable: for instance, the eight Israeli soldiers killed in a suicide bomb-attack in October 1988. Losses among the Lahad troops were higher, and General Lahad himself was injured in an attempt on his life in December 1988.

---

[223] On the following see Harald List's careful study, 'Die südlibanesische Armee und ihr Territorium' (Freiburg, 1988) (typescript, publication intended).

Two decades after the guerrilla war began in the south, and one decade after the first major Israeli invasion of Lebanon, the war simmered on. The initial objective of the 1978 invasion was to establish a buffer zone, that of the 1982 war to extend it. The price Israel had to pay was high, the costs borne by Lebanon, however, incomparably higher.

# 5

## Violence without Victory
## Forms, Costs and Consequences of War

Sixteen years of waste,
Of plunder and of misery have sped,
A dull fermenting mass the world still lies,
No distant hope of peace can yet be glimpsed.
The Empire is a raging battlefield,
Its towns a desolation, Magdeburg
In ruins, trade and industry abandoned;
Only the soldier counts, the honest citizen
Is scorned, and insolence may go unpunished,
And savage hordes encamp, made rough and wild
By years of war upon the ravaged earth.

Schiller, *Wallenstein*

Wild beasts, when at bay, fight desperately. How much more is this true of men! If they know there is no alternative, they will fight to the death.

Sun Tzu, *The Art of War*

The Christians are cowards, I agree. But are they more cowardly than cats? A cat cornered can fight like a tiger.

Fouad Chehab to Kamal Jumblatt, 1958

> Everywhere in the Middle East armies are gaining more and more political influence because they fight the wars .... But almost everywhere these forces are now so big that none is likely to win a decisive victory. So war goes on, mainly to prevent the other side from winning, and there is no end in sight. This also serves to keep the respective, in effect military, regimes in power.
>
> Arnold Hottinger, 1987

As the war in Lebanon entered its sixteenth year in the spring of 1990, victory still eluded the adversaries, internal and external. The spiral of internal violence had shifted, from conflict between to conflict within the communities. The cycle of external violence in the south was back at square one. And nine-tenths of Lebanon's territory was patrolled by non-Lebanese troops: the country had been commandeered as the battleground of the surrogate war for Palestine, and even though this war stagnated, the belligerents seemed determined to remain.

None of the original causes of the war — regional or Lebanese — had been eliminated, and new ones had arisen; there was no end in sight. The forms and the costs of the war produced social, economic and political realities whose consequence was a self-sustaining and self-perpetuating spiral of violence.

## Terror as a way of life

At no time had the war in Lebanon not been a 'pursuit of politics by other means', admittedly in a peculiarly Lebanese way. Episodes in which military means were employed to subject adversaries were the exception. As a rule, military force was used to cow the respective opponents, to weaken them to the point where they were willing to make political concessions. Nobody — with the possible exception of Kamal Jumblatt in the spring of 1976 — wanted 'total victory'; all parties sought relative victories. And all regarded it as a relative victory — that is, achievable — if they could give their opponents a thorough fright.

There is much to support the view that none of the Lebanese factions and none of their leaders — again, with the exception of Jumblatt — ever believed any party to the internal Lebanese struggle could achieve a total victory on their own.

The external parties to the conflict could have forced a decision, a complete victory over their respective Lebanese adversaries. But the fear of a violent confrontation with the respective adversary's foreign protector — or, as in the case of Israel in 1982, the political pressure of a superpower that feared just such a confrontation — cautioned each to stay its hand. Moreover, the foreign powers indirectly involved in the Lebanon conflict are burnt children: a military victory might be possible, but inordinately costly, and all dread paying the price.

Whatever their reasons, the regular Syrian and Israeli armies ultimately behaved like the Lebanese militias: they were less intent on a conventional military victory than on terrorizing their adversaries by military means in order to coerce political concessions from them.

All conflicting parties, internal and external, made errors of judgment.[1] At the beginning of the war the Palestinian organizations and their ally Jumblatt took the Christians for soft, interested only in living well, and thought they would bolt or grovel. The Kata'ib assumed that it would be enough for the Lebanese army to act against the Palestinians to force them to capitulate. The Syrian leaders thought intensive bombardments of urban areas an adequate means of forcing the Christian militias to recognize Syrian ascendancy. Israel thought — and thinks — that air-raids on Palestinian camps and punitive measures against Lebanese villages would discourage commando raids. The Americans hoped ships' guns would deter the Druze militias. All militias believed that various forms of individual and collective terror would promote their objectives.

The list of errors of judgment is long. They all arise from a fundamental error. Whereas the threat of violence may be an effective means of attaining political goals, once the spiral of violence is set in motion, people lose sight of the original goal. 'It is the fear of being marginalized, assimilated, or banished that accentuates the intensity of hostility between the warring communities. The more threatened communities become, the more they resort to violence to preserve their endangered identities, and the more apprehensive they become about the prospects of resolving the conflict, lest they lose whatever minimal gains they have made thus far. '... violence becomes both protracted and insoluble. It is a form of self-entrapment that blocks all avenues of creative peaceful change.'[2]

People accepted the terror because they feared even worse terror if they yielded; they became determined to endure terror and to terrorize. For more than fifteen years, reciprocal terror in all its facets was part of everyday life in Lebanon.

The first shellings in 1975 were justified on the grounds that the respective other side needed to be 'taught a lesson'. The aim of the lesson was political concessions. The lesson the victim learnt was counter-shelling. Reciprocity became the law of terror. If artillery on one side shelled a beach on the other, a blood bath on the beach of the former soon followed. However, precise targets were the exception rather than the rule. This was partly because all militias lacked trained artillerymen, but mainly because 'random shelling' was intentional. All

---

[1] 'All through the Lebanese crisis one can pinpoint errors of judgement made by the various politicians and political parties, errors which may be seen as so many turning points leading to a further escalation of violence ...', Tewfik Khalaf, 'The Phalange and the Maronite Community: From Lebanonism to Maronitism', in Roger Owen, ed., *Essays on the Crisis in Lebanon* (London, 1976), pp. 54f.
[2] Samir Khalaf, *Lebanon's Predicament*, op. cit., p. 239.

sides were well aware that it had little military impact in urban areas: the other side's troops were safely under cover. But indiscriminate bombardments pounded the civilian population in enemy territory and could bring civilian life to a standstill. And that created terror.

Cannonades were frequently attendant phenomena of political or diplomatic activities. When negotiations were pending or envoys of the major powers visited an Arab capital, the warring parties reminded the world of their existence. Occasionally they came out of the blue, for instance, when a militia decided to test new guns or rockets.

Lebanon is a small country. In the course of the war military technology brought ever greater swathes of territory within striking distance and increasingly blurred the distinction between 'the front' and 'behind the lines'. Beirut and its environs always constituted a single front. People cannot live indefinitely in bunkers, cellars and air-raid shelters. Business went on, schools and universities remained open, relations and friends visited one another. Only a minority lived and worked in the shrinking regions of relative security. The majority had to learn to live in fear of the next shell — until it exploded in a school, a factory, a church or a mosque. If it was the start of a new bombardment, another wave of people flowed into the hinterland. As the bombardment ebbed away, the wave flowed back to homes and jobs. Radio stations kept up a running commentary on the fighting, shelling and areas affected and recommended possible detours and escape routes — as elsewhere road and weather reports, and in much the same tone. Terror became banal; there was no other choice.

Banality in the immediate surroundings of the demarcation lines was another matter. Here, there was a greater variety of forms of terror. Heavy exchanges of short-range fire were far more frequent than the 'artillery duels' in the hinterland. The favoured weapons were machine-guns and anti-tank rockets. Snipers were a lethal danger. Whenever they felt like it they picked off whomever happened to come into their sights. Consequently, heavy barricades of concrete walls, embankments of sand, burnt out buses and railway trucks stretched along either side of all demarcation lines. Containers filled with sand protectively lined sidestreets along which enemy snipers could peer.

There was no such protection at the checkpoints between zones controlled by opposing forces. Whenever one of the belligerents wished to restrict or stop traffic or contact, snipers murdered a few people in no man's land. Yet, Lebanese on all sides never stopped using the checkpoints for long.

Every crossing of a demarcation line entailed an effort to overcome warranted fears. Any Lebanese outside of the area in which he lived and was known had very real grounds for fear. Whenever militiamen sought to avenge their losses, there was a chance that they would take revenge on members of any community they happen to regard as opponents, whether they had been involved in the actual fighting or not. The infamous identity-card murders were particularly common in the first two years of the war.³ Lebanese identity papers record confession — and the holder's name usually betrays it anyway. Hundreds of Muslims were killed simply because they were Muslims and hundreds of Christians simply because they were Christians.⁴ Even membership of a party in the National Movement — Baathist or Communist — could not save many Christians from this fate.⁵ Often such murders were the climax of torture and mutilation. They triggered off the flight of Muslims and Christians respectively from areas under the control of militias of the other confession, paving the way for the 'homogenizing' of other areas in Lebanon.

As discussed above, homogeneity could be efficaciously pursued through military operations against 'allogeneous pockets of population'. In all such operations one side was so obviously superior that there could be no doubt about the outcome. The only exception was the well fortified and heavily defended Tel al-Za`atar; moreover, until its fall there was always the possibility that the camps in west Beirut would mount a successful relief offensive. But this was the only instance of long and heavy fighting. The other 'pockets' on both sides fell without much heroism. The pattern was much the same everywhere: captives were not taken, the population was driven out, usually expedited by massacring civilians.⁶ Once again, there was one exception: the evacuation of the Shi`is from Nabaa through the mediation of Imam Musa Sadr was accomplished without a massacre.

Although the Christian populations of many smaller towns and villages in the Akkar and the Bekaa neither presented a plausible military threat nor tried to defend themselves, they too were eventually driven out. A few murders, requisitions of houses, destruction of crops and irrigation systems, etc. achieved the same end, gradually but inexorably. After 1984 the majority of Christians in west Beirut

---

³ The victims were all men. 'Sur les barrages confessionnels, les femmes ne sont jamais arrêtées ni exécutées; elles ne sont pas considérées comme dangereuses, ni reconnues comme représentatives de leur confession.' Selim Accaoui and Magida Salman, *Comprendre le Liban* (Paris, 1976), pp. 67f.

⁴ '... les enlèvements de chrétiens, les tortures sont pratiqués assez couramment dans les régions musulmanes', ibid., p. 37; 'Les familles chassées, sinon exterminées ... Un grand nombre de concierges et d'ouvriers de la construction, employés dans les quartiers chrétiens y trouvent la mort. Ces derniers sont généralement de nationalité syrienne ...' ibid., p. 26.

⁵ In an interview with the author in 1979 Assem Kanzo, chairman of the pro-Syrian Ba`ath Party, stated: 'My wife and I spent weeks rescuing kidnapped people — I think we must have saved four to five-hundred. We issued Ba`ath Party membership cards to thousands of Christians in west Beirut to save them. Sometimes even that didn't help them. A genuine Maronite Ba`athist was murdered at the Museum; the murderers simply couldn't believe it was true. That's civil war.'

⁶ The massacrers did not discriminate by age or gender: '... les viols et massacres ne les épargnent pas lors des attaques victorieuses contre un village, un camp ou un quartier.' Selim Accaoui and Magida Salman, *Comprendre le Liban*, p. 68.

were driven out by similar methods: extremist Shi`i groups occupied houses and apartments, blew up shops, murdered a few and kidnapped a few. In these instances, forms of terror were 'economical'. In the Chouf and Aley regions they were anything but. The Lebanese Forces utterly misjudged the ferocity of the Druze reaction to what the Druze saw as a threat to their survival. After the quick defeat of the Lebanese Forces, most Christians in the region fled. What followed was new: the — mostly elderly — Christians who had remained were massacred. Massacre was no longer only a means to an end, but one of revenge too.

With increasing regional homogeneity, murder by confessional affiliation declined. Kidnapping became the means to political ends. For years it was extremely hazardous for Christians to use the road to Beirut airport. This considerably complicated travel, for the sea-route to Cyprus is time-consuming and expensive. Vehicles taking people from east Beirut to the American University or the University Clinic were attacked by pro-Iranian groups that wanted to force the closure of these symbols of American presence. The spate of foreign hostage-taking from 1984 onwards had the same objective, but included every western presence. These hostages received far greater attention in the western media that the far larger number of kidnapped Lebanese. Like shelling, hostage-taking was based on the principle of reciprocity. The militia of the hostage's community, or even the hostage's family, kidnapped someone in turn to offer in exchange. There have been many exchanges. But many people are still missing, probably victims of reciprocal murder.

Kidnapping and murder threatened primarily those who entered or remained in the territory of the other confession. However, homogeneity did not mean danger for 'us' from shelling by 'them'. A lull in the fighting along the main fronts in Lebanon was almost inevitably followed by conflicts within the different camps.[7] These were often more bitter than those across the major divides. Among the Christians the struggles between the Kata'ib and Marada and then between the Kata'ib and the Tiger militia of the NLP were exceptionally bloody. After the different militias had been whipped into the Lebanese Forces there was a period of relative calm, until the short but deadly clashes between Geagea's and Hobeika's supporters over the militia agreement of Damascus.

---

[7] Cf. Samir Khalaf, 'On Entrapment and Escalation of Violence', *American Arab Affairs*, 24 (1988), p. 15: 'Lately, in fact, the conflict has been fractured even further as inter-communal rivalries degenerated into intra-confessional hostilities. The ecology of violence ... is now assuming more intensive forms as street and quarter in-fighting displaces and/or compounds the earlier communal violence. Hence, much of the former characterization of the initial stages of civil unrest — i.e., "Christian versus Muslim", "right versus left" — is outmoded now. They clearly do not help in accounting for the upsurge in the level of hostility between Sunnis and Shi`is, Druze and Shi`is, Kurds and Shi`is, Palestinians and Shi`is, Maronites and Armenians or between Maronites and Maronites. Indeed, casualties of intra-confessional violence during the past two years now outnumber those generated by inter-sectarian or inter-religious hostility.'

Armed conflicts among west Beirut militias and Muslim forces have been much more frequent. Prior to 1982 there were innumerable clashes among ostensibly allied militias, often unconnected with politics. Disputes over 'protection money' from certain firms or streets, but also road accidents or personal quarrels, degenerated into street-fighting with heavy weapons because all sides possessed them.[8] The PLO, especially Fatah's military police, frequently intervened to restore order, though sometimes the Palestinians themselves were involved in these incidents. With the departure of the PLO their restraining hand went too, and a contest for ascendancy among the Muslim militias as well as militias of the left-wing parties erupted in 1984. Together the Druze and the Shi`is knocked out the Mourabitoun; then the Druze and the Left, with the remnants of defeated Muslim militias, took on Amal. The Syrians intervened to save Amal from defeat, whereupon Amal tried to assert itself against the Palestinians and Hezbollah. The cumulative damage to west Beirut in these conflicts was probably as great as that during the Israeli invasion.

The daily horrors were worst for civilians in areas where one side did not have the upper hand and zones of influence were not clear. It was not the fighting alone, but the sense of being at the mercy of several parties. Flats would be requisitioned by militia commanders because of their 'strategic value', or as accommodation for their men or simply because they liked them. People's cars would be stolen or they themselves robbed, and they would not know whom to turn to for help. And then the inducements, at gun point, to make a contribution to the respective 'good cause'. At different phases in the war ordinary crime flourished in political uncertainty. In the first two years of the war, looting — with scant regard for the victims' religion — cost various militias potential victories. The fighting in the souk and banking district precipitated what is probably the greatest redistribution of wealth in modern Lebanese history. Inevitably, subsequent forays were less rewarding: Lebanese citizens, irrespective of religion, had learnt their lesson; those with any wealth got it out of the country or paid protection money.

[8] 'A Beyrouth-Ouest ... au cours des dernières années (1984–1986), le contrôle des petits chefs était précaire et le niveau de pressuration des territoires urbains avait atteint des degrés très élevés. A l'intérieur de chaque Mouvement, il y avait compétition interne, rivalité et parfois même affrontement entre les clients des divers "hommes forts" du Mouvement. ...
'La prolifération des "Bureaux armés" à Beyrouth-Ouest ... a été une des manifestations les plus visibles du quadrillage de la ville par les diverses milices. En 1986, plus de 120 de ces "Bureaux" se partageaient ou se disputaient le contrôle de divers quartiers. ... La plupart des affrontements armés mineurs ou majeurs qui ont déchiré la ville au cours des dernières années ont été déclenchés à partir d'un conflit sur l'ouverture d'un nouveau "Bureau" ou sur les zones d'influence respectives de "Bureaux" parfois très proches les uns des autres.' Salim Nasr, 'Beyrouth: Remarques sur les acteurs d'un drame urbain', in Salim Nasr and Theodor Hanf (eds.), *Urban Crisis and Social Movements: Arab and European Perspectives* (Beirut, 1987), pp. 144f.

But the latter solution was not dependable where no one militia was in complete control, that is, above all in west Beirut. Between 1979 and 1982 and again from 1984 the rate of non-political crime was much lower in areas controlled by the Christian militia — a new form of inequality.

Of course, it is impossible to draw a clear distinction between political and 'ordinary' crime. After the outbreak of war, 'dissidents' in any camp were intimidated by attacks on property or person. In many ostensibly political kidnappings, especially in west Beirut, ransom was demanded, and it was impossible to say whether the reason was political or not.[9]

Finally, there was not a great difference between soldiers of regular armies and militiamen in their attitudes towards private property. Syrian units stationed in Lebanon has serious problems with discipline on being transferred back to Syria, not least because of the drop in soldiers' de facto incomes. All returning Israeli soldiers had to pass through the strict customs control of their own army on crossing the border.

In summary, terror in everyday life came in many guises: danger to life and limb, or 'only' to property, sometimes from foreigners and sometimes from Lebanese, the threats of 'the others' as well as those of 'one's own'. When one side started shelling, the targets hoped 'our boys' would return the fire — for, people came to expect that only an equilibrium of terror-bombing could put an end to it. Even civilians who abominate murder and kidnapping found it necessary to excuse that of their own side on the ground that only retaliation could make the other side think twice. The same applied to massacres and expulsions. The greater the terror, the more strongly people identified with 'my militia, right or wrong'.

If the main fronts were quiet, the militias on each side started squabbling among themselves, and civilians within the respective camps gradually lost patience with the innumerable checkpoints and traffic controls, with the levies and tolls and with the arrogance of armed men — until the next shelling or the next car-bomb.

---

[9] There was less political and non-political crime in areas controlled by the Lebanese Forces than in other parts of the country. Figures published by the Republic of Lebanon Internal Security Forces for 1981 give the following comparisons between areas under control of the Lebanese Forces and of other forces respectively: 35:417 murders, 15:323 attempted murders, 34:430 thefts, 8:356 armed robberies, 6:33 kidnappings, 2:22 cases of frauds and embezzlement, 3:89 drug offences, 51:568 cases involving terrorism and explosives, 10:80 cases of assault against policemen and soldiers, 2:206 armed clashes and 2:211 car thefts. For details see Lewis W. Snider, 'The Lebanese Forces: Wartime origins and political significance', in Edward E. Azar et al., *The Emergence of a New Lebanon: Fantasy or reality?* (New York, 1984), pp. 142ff.

## From ethnic mobilization to ethnic domination

Before the war only the Palestinian organizations had professional guerrillas in any large numbers. All each of the different Lebanese factions had was a small group of cadres with basic military training. Even the long-standing 'militias' of the parties were essentially volunteers who attended weekend and holiday paramilitary courses. Fatah and Lebanese army officers, who had been training militias of one or other side since 1973, tended to look down on these recruits as highly motivated boy scouts, able to hit a target but incapable of operating in units. Above all, the militias lacked the equivalent of non-commissioned officers. The militias of the National Movement remedied this with Palestinian cadres, those of the Christian parties with special courses run mainly by the Tanzim.

On the outbreak of war all sides immediately embarked on an intensive mobilization of the religious communities from which they drew most of their support. The Christians made no secret of this. Initially, leaders of the left-wing parties had inhibitions: many were themselves Christians and convinced opponents of 'confessional' mobilization. But they overcame their secular scruples on realizing that appeals to class solidarity won them few Christian recruits, whereas appeals to religious solidarity won them many Muslims.[10]

But appeals were not nearly as effective as the solidarity that appeared almost overnight among anxious neighbours in the suburbs. These residents were often members of the same extended families and village communities — and thus usually of the same denomination. A family would man a barricade, a 'village' assumed responsibility for a street, 'the' Shi`is or 'the' Maronites for whole quarters. The upper middle class lived in 'mixed' residential areas. They resisted initial attempts at mobilization, until some months later the first militiamen arrived, bent on violently 'homogenizing' them. A pervading sense of threat and, in consequence, general mobilization of entire religious communities only became widespread with the 'identity-card murders' and random shelling of whole districts.

This proceeded more slowly among Muslims than Christians. Many Sunnis felt that the Palestinians adequately represented their interests in the war — the 'Army of Islam', in the words of the Mufti of the Lebanese Republic — and were, in any case, superior to other forces. Although Shi`is provided most of the fighters

---

[10] Selim Accaoui and Magida Salman, *Comprendre le Liban*, provide a left-wing critique of the progressive group: '... la connotation progressiste a été trop souvent contradictoire aux pratiques militaires et politiques de ce camp ...' (p. 14); the combatants lack political awareness (p. 56), are increasingly depoliticized (p. 38), have failed to involve the people in the struggle (loc. cit.), and, above all, resort to confessionalist practices (p. 41); nor have the parties of the Left ventured to check theft and looting, for 'ils ont besoin de combattants, voleurs ou pas' (p. 31).

in the left-wing parties, Imam Musa Sadr kept them neutral as a religious faction. Only when the Palestinians organizations wanted to make the war 'appear more than an internal Lebanese affair' did the Sunnis start turning the Mourabitoun into an effective fighting force.[11] Widespread mobilization of the Shi'is took place only at the end of the 1970s as they began to fall out with the Palestinians. The Sunnis in Tripoli mobilized only from 1981 in opposition to Syrian occupation forces and their Lebanese Alawite allies. The Druze were the last to mobilize fully, after the Lebanese Forces entered the Chouf in 1982.

Already in 1975 the Christians, especially the Maronites, felt they faced a deadly threat. They had no 'Army of Christendom' to fight for them; they had to defend themselves. In the first two war years, Christian civilians from all classes were active to a remarkable extent. Engineers turned lorries into primitive tanks and constructed equally primitive mortars from what they had to hand. Ladies of rank and fashion looked after the fighters and tended the wounded. To the astonishment of the American ambassador, Lebanese studying abroad returned in droves to fight and novices in the monasteries took up weapons. Civil servants, white-collar workers and even businessmen did duty after work in evening and night shifts along the fronts. In the autumn of 1976, when the war seemed over, the Christians started demobilizing. Professionals and businessmen returned to their offices, and many, after waiting in vain for the economy to pick up, sought new ones abroad. The students started studying again. The leader of the Tanzim, a surgeon, returned to healing people.

Upon the recrudescence in early 1977 only young people were prepared to make a career of militia service. At the outbreak of war they were twelve- to seventeen-year-olds. Two years later they found it difficult to readjust to the classroom. Many came from urban lower strata with few prospects of success in civilian life. Most of the rural youths had fled or been driven from their homes with their families, from the Christian north, the Bekaa, the Chouf or Damour. They had even fewer prospects, and their expulsion gave them an added motivation: to fight to regain their homes.[12] Henceforth the militias were garrisoned and trained systematically. Recruits also included former soldiers of the Lebanese

---

[11] The Palestinians remained sceptical about the prowess of their militia allies. In an interview with the author in 1980, Hassan Dudin of the PLO Information Service expressed the Palestinian view: 'Who counts in this country? The Kata'ib over there, we here, and Jumblatt too, but only because he's got a tribe behind him. The others count nothing. They depend on the Syrians or on us. Take these so-called Nasserites. Now there are six groups of them. They've got less than a thousand men, including the Mourabitoun. They get their commands by telephone — when the telephones are working. We leave them in charge of city districts, so long as they don't make a nuisance of themselves'.

[12] 'The exiles form the hard core of the Lebanese Forces. They don't think much of partitioning the country; they'd rather take revenge on those that drove them out of their villages'. Author's interview with a Maronite clergyman, 1981.

army and some of the officers who had resigned their commissions in 1976. Training courses in Israel started in 1978. The hard core of 'dad's army' of 1975–76 was gradually knocked into shape. This development towards a regular force was accelerated by Bashir Gemayel's ruthless unification of the separate militias in the Lebanese Forces.

Militias need independent sources of revenue. One is taxation.[13] All businesses and house-owners had to pay a direct levy. 'Indirect taxes' included a sales tax on restaurants — shown on every bill — and filling stations. Custom duties were more lucrative; the Lebanese Forces — instead of the Lebanese state — long ran a section of Beirut harbour and a number of illegal ports. The Forces placed the administration of their funds in the hands of professional bankers.

These revenues covered not only the militiamen's pay, uniforms and weapons — the 1975 recruits had fought in jeans and gym shoes with guns most had bought themselves — but also the military and political administrations. At one time the Lebanese Forces maintained their own military intelligence and separate military and civilian police forces, press and information and social-welfare departments, radio and television stations and offices in several western capitals. This administrative machinery offered a considerable number of talented young intellectuals not only the attraction of radical action — the 'complete liberation of Lebanon' by a 'resistance movement' — but equally attractive 'career' prospects no longer available in the public or private sectors.

By 1981 the Lebanese Forces had attained what the PLO ran in another part of Lebanon: a state within the state. They went even one step further than either the PLO or the Lebanese state: they introduced conscription. Within five years the voluntary mobilization of 1976 had been replaced by organized, compulsory military service.

Until 1982 the organization of the various Muslim militias could not compare with that of the Lebanese Forces. With time they too were becoming forces of full-time militiamen of similar age and social background. However, their fighters did not so much live in barracks as congregate in so-called shops, military offices in different districts. They also ran political offices staffed with articulate intellectuals, radio stations and newspapers. But as each had fewer supporters than the Lebanese Forces, their institutions and organs were far less professional. They too derived their income from levies, illegal ports and, above all, foreign patrons, not least Libya, though the flow of funds was less regular because less organized or dependent on the good will of the donor. They remained very dependent upon the

---

[13] From the perspective of the Lebanese Left: 'Cette politique ... contribue à rapprocher la petite bourgeoisie chrétienne des partis d'extrême-droite qui semblent ainsi "s'attaquer aux riches".' Selim Accaoui and Magida Salman, op. cit., pp. 31f.

PLO for their weapons and military training as well as finance. And the PLO had little interest in fostering militias that were too strong or too autonomous. Their greatest weakness, though, was fragmentation. Competition for influence caused incessant dissension and strife. The projected joint civil administration in west Beirut foundered on discord and mutual suspicion.

The situation changed when the Shi`is and Druze — as the Christians before them — felt their existence threatened and resorted to mass mobilization. In 1979 and 1982/83 extensive recruitment enabled the two communities, like the Christians in 1975/76, to withstand the respective challenges to them. Both began to build up full-time militias only after considerable military success had not put an end to conflict. By 1985, at the latest, Amal as well as the PSP were strong militias with their own political organizations rather than parties or mass movements of their respective communities.

The Lebanese Forces, Amal and the PSP became very similar in appearance and behaviour. All three militias controlled large parts of the country they had more or less 'homogenized', had 'their' ports and, thus, an independent source of revenue, and established some form of civil administration, or took control of state facilities in their regions. Most of the old-school civilian politicians lost their influence. The Lebanese Forces reduced the Kata'ib to their tool. Amal put such pressure on the Shi`i zu'ama that some of the most prominent sought refuge in the Christian heartland. Walid Jumblatt, the Druze nobleman, was one of two Lebanese politicians — Suleiman Franjieh was the other — who mastered the art of combining traditional legitimacy with militia command; but even he could not halt the reduction of the PSP to an appendage of the militia.

Yet, none of these militias rested easy in its ascendancy. In the Christian region, the Lebanese Forces shared power with the Christian part of the army, which continued to represent the Lebanese state in that region. Amal was — and is — caught up in a vicious rivalry with Hezbollah, and after Israel's withdrawal Arafat's PLO rebuilt its base in the south. The PSP militia did not face any immediate challenge; but after the expulsion of the Christians the region was almost too large for the small Druze community to defend by itself. Jumblatt's search for alliances with the Sunnis and the PLO, and even Christians willing to return to the Chouf, was not guided by altruism.

The fact that none of the three major militias could be absolutely confidant of their control over their 'cantons' induced their leaders to pay particular attention to the interests of their officers and ranks.

Jumblatt's and Berri's influence has civilian roots, though for different reasons. Apart from them, the political leaders of the militias, even Geagea, have few prospects in a non-military political system in Lebanon. Members of the militias' political sections and staff officers have no chance of being elected, or of otherwise acquiring administrative positions of comparable influence in a civilian government. Their power, their prestige — and their income — depend on the existence of the militias. In this respect they can be compared with the mercenary leaders of the Thirty Years' War.[14] The same holds for the mercenaries themselves — the professional militiamen. As soldiers, they received respectable pay and had numerous other 'perquisites'. The only trade they learnt was the trade of war — and that not very well. Peace could bring dislocation, possibly a social abyss. Mercenary leaders and mercenaries have a profound interest in mercenary rule. And mercenary rule requires the perpetuation of war.[15] The war brought forth the militias; it was in their interest to prolong it.

## Militias and armies in an uneasy stalemate

The longer the war continued, the greater the efforts of the large militias to emulate the organizational structures, weaponry and discipline of regular armies. Conversely, the longer regular armies were — and are — stationed in Lebanon the more closely they seemed to resemble militias.

This convergence was a result not only of mutual imitation, but also of the peculiar conditions of this war. In conventional warfare military decisions depend, as a rule, on mobile warfare in open country. One has to defeat the enemy forces as well as occupy and secure territory. The closest the war in Lebanon came to this kind of warfare was the confrontation between the Israeli and Syrian armies in 1982. When the Israelis occupied southern Lebanon they initially bypassed cities, towns and Palestinian camps, storming them later. The Syrians, once their air force had been shot down, withdrew to positions from which they could best repulse an Israeli advance on Syria.

Earlier, on a much smaller scale, the Palestinians had advanced in a pincer movement against the Christian heartland during the 'Mountain War' in the

[14] The analogy derives from Arnold Hottinger, Dreissigjähriger Krieg der Araber?, *Neue Zürcher Zeitung*, 24 November 1987: 'The longer the current Middle Eastern wars go on, the more they seem to assume certain features reminiscent of the Thirty Years' War in Europe. Lebanon, for example, is ruled by armed bands. They make policy, they keep the war going, because they need it to survive as bands. This reminds one of Wallenstein's doctrine of war to keep war alive.'

[15] 'Those who dominate the existing internal war system have a stake in its perpetuation, not its replacement.' Augustus Richard Norton, 'Waiting for the Nadir', *American Arab Affairs*, 24 (1988)1, p. 22. Salim Nasr, 'A New Approach to the Conflict: The social dynamics of an internal war', ibid, p. 20, identifies as the pillars of the war society 'the warlords and the war profiteers; the managers, ideologues and staff of the newly erected local administrations, regional university campuses, ... political and admnistrative apparatus ...; ... intermediaries that emerged to deal with and live on the segmentation of the Lebanese market; the mobile class of full-time and part-time fighters ...; and, most tragically, the large mass of displaced populations generated by the violent drive of the different factions to constitute "homogeneous" territories.'

spring of 1976. But it was a half-hearted attempt and soon got bogged down. These are the only two instances of 'classic' warfare in a decade and a half of fighting.

This was partly due to the geography of the country. Apart from the Bekaa, it does not lend itself to rapid advances. 'Tanks can't climb like goats' a Lebanese general explained the drawbacks of motorized units. A local defence force armed with anti-tank rockets that knows every inch of the terrain is an enormous headache for superior enemy forces advancing into the hills. The mountains in Lebanon are not only a last defensive position, like the redoubt the Swiss army would have withdrawn into had the Germans attacked the country in the Second World War. For both the Maronites and the Druze the mountains are important settlement areas. So long as they have not been occupied, these communities feel free, even if the rest of the country has been overrun. The same applies to the cities, especially Beirut, where half the country's population live. Cities are always major obstacles for conventional invading armies, and Beirut more than most. The city grew haphazardly, each successive quarter a maze in itself; straight, broad streets were the exception. Only in the 1960s did the first through-roads and city motorways appear, the few thoroughfares that afford tanks the necessary range, visibility and manoeuvrability. Most buildings are of solid concrete. Hence, conditions in the Beirut cityscape resemble those of the mountains in many ways. Appropriately armed, a small number of defenders can easily hold up a far more numerous attacking force — all the more so when the attackers are strangers to the city, the defenders thoroughly acquainted with it, able to strike and melt away, ambush the enemy or suddenly appear behind him.

The modalities of mountain and city warfare favour the defenders, even when they are vastly inferior in numbers and equipment, provided that they are determined to resist even at the cost of considerable destruction and civilian casualties — which the Lebanese and Palestinian guerrillas always were. All of them were convinced that, in their respective regions and respective city districts, they were fighting for the survival of their communities. The fate of the inhabitants, as one isolated 'pocket of people' after another was 'mopped up', strengthened this conviction. When attacked they fought with the courage born of despair. As attackers they proved to be far less motivated and capable, apart from operations against barely defensible 'pockets'. For, most militiamen had at best a very vague knowledge of the mountains and valleys, twisting streets and hidden corners of enemy territory. They were as discreet in taking the offensive as they were valiant on the defensive. Even outside of Beirut the militias rarely resorted to mobile warfare: in the Chouf in 1982/83 and in the hinterland of Sidon in 1985. In both cases the militias fighting on their home ground won: the Druze and the Sidon Sunnite–Palestinian alliance respectively. The only instance of mobile warfare in Beirut itself was the battle for the hotel district in 1975 and 1976, a terrain both sides knew. The Kata'ib were at a disadvantage from the start: they held a narrow strip along the sea front, exposed to attacks from higher parts of the city and hazardous to supply or relieve. Yet, a few dozen militiamen were able to hold part of the hotel district for months, until well-equipped units of the dissident Lebanese Arab Army reinforced their opponents. After that, the war in Beirut became a 'sitting war' — shooting and shelling across the durable 'green line', not even the odd commando raid across the front. Hobeika's offensive across the green line in the summer of 1985 was not an attack against the 'other' side, but an attempt by a minority fraction in the Lebanese Forces to return to their 'own' territory and reassert themselves.

The heaviest street-fighting took place not between the two major blocks but among factions within each block. The Kata'ib versus the Tigers, Amal versus the PSP, Amal versus Hezbollah; in these conflicts there were neither fronts nor holds barred between fighters who knew the terrain: internecine clashes, and exceptionally bloody.

In a nutshell: guerrillas, irrespective of militia, were superb defenders of their own, but poor invaders of others' territory.[16] After the fronts were established, the enclaves overrun and the respective minorities expelled, there was a military stalemate between the Lebanese adversaries.

The militias also proved remarkably good at resisting regular army troops.[17] Both the Syrian and the Israeli armies had to learn by experience that military victory in Lebanon can be very costly.

The Syrians had their first lesson in 1976 when they attempted to occupy Sidon. The Palestinian defenders wiped out almost an entire Syrian battalion. In 1978 the Syrians tried to take Ashrafieh from the Christians, and again failed. The tanks they sent in were quickly driven back; in street-fighting even Syrian

---

[16] 'Both sides are able defend their areas, but can't conquer anything. At some points along the front they had not even crossed a narrow street or taken one block of flats after months of fighting. It was and is a war with fixed positions. The Galerie Semaan is a typical example. The Libyans invested enormous sums to achieve a breakthrough to Tel al-Za`tar. In vain. And only a small number of men were defending it. Certainly, they were very brave. But they weren't supermen. From begining to end both sides held their positions.' Fouad Chemali, former commander of the Tanzim, in an interview with the author, 1979.

[17] 'It is virtually useless to deploy guerrillas in open terrain, where they lack the semblance of protection of trenches, buildings or makeshift bunkers. But in built-up areas, where closely packed buildings guarantee a certain anonymity and security against a) observation and identification and b) enemy fire, guerrilla troops can operate effectively. They are even able to resist regular troops ..., as the presence of civilians prevents means of mass destruction being used against them. The Syrian and Lebanese armies have had to learn, as before them the Americans in Hué and Saigon, the Russians in Berlin and the Israelis in Suez, that short of razing whole districts to the ground, or high-casualty house-to-house fighting, it is impossible to neutralize small nests of guerrillas.' David Th. Schiller, 'Entstehung und Verlauf des libanesischen Bürgerkriegs', op. cit., p. 206.

troops stationed in the quarter were put on the defensive. In 1981 all Syrian assaults — tank and infantry — on the isolated town of Zahle failed to break through the ring of defence.

In 1982 the Israeli army broke Palestinian resistance in the camps in the south only with greatest difficulty. Although they besieged Beirut and gradually tightened their ring, they hesitated to storm the camps and the centre of west Beirut; attempts to drive a wedge between the two from Beirut Museum were soon abandoned.

Ultimately, both armies could have attained their objectives, had they thrown in all their resources. They did not do so because they were not prepared to pay the price required in lives. The cost in casualties of house-to-house fighting is always high. Facing cornered, desperate militias, the invading armies were soon made to realize that in Lebanon it would be exorbitant.

Like the militias before them, the regular armies quickly abandoned attempts to gain ground and resorted to random shelling. The Syrians favoured saturation shelling of one grid square after another; the Israelis threw in occasional air-attacks for good measure. The Syrians were reticent to deploy their air force against the Christian militias, because Israel had declared the airspace to be within its 'red line', and the Syrians did not wish to risk provocation.

Israel ultimately achieved the withdrawal of the PLO from Beirut. The fact that most Lebanese in west Beirut had ceased to show much solidarity with the Palestinians probably helped. As important, though, was the perception that, by withdrawing, the Palestinians had lost a battle, but not the war.

The Syrian army, however, was unable to force the Christian militias to capitulate, either in 1978 or in 1981, above all because the populace overwhelmingly identified themselves with the militias out of the elementary fear that capitulation would mean the end of Christian Lebanon.

The tactics of siege and shell warfare did not bring Syria any success, and Israel only for a short time. Bombardments seldom weaken the enemy and may strengthen civilian resolve. Moreover, both the Syrian and Israeli commands discovered that their soldiers soon lost enthusiasm for this sort of war. Israeli officers protested or resigned because they disapproved of a war against civilians. The Syrian army, too, had problems with discipline: soldiers had little motivation to risk their own lives fighting against Palestinians and Lebanese Christians. Furthermore, all regular armies that have operated in Lebanon since 1975 have had to learn that they are helpless against ambushes and suicide attacks. This form of fighting forced the Americans, French, English and Italians, and, ultimately, the Israelis to withdraw. The Syrian leadership is less sensitive to public opinion and can, therefore, afford greater losses in unconventional warfare.

Yet from 1988 onwards it too showed greater concern for the safety of its troops in west Beirut by regrouping them in bases where practicable.

Despite superiority in numbers, weaponry and discipline, none of the regular armies crushed an opposing militia in all the years of war.

It seems that Syria took a decision in the early 1980s not to use its army to enforce its will.[18] This army has left fighting in Lebanon to its allied militias. Instead, it resorted to attrition shelling, initially of pro-Arafat Palestinian, and then, repeatedly, of Christian areas — in the hope that human casualties and destruction of property would weaken their adversaries' resolve.

The violence since 1975 brought none of the belligerents victory, at best limited, and possibly temporary, success. But it took a heavy toll of lives, cost tens of thousands house and home, caused others to emigrate, and impoverished the majority of Lebanese. Khalil Abu Rjaily and Boutros Labaki have done a detailed, meticulous and as yet unpublished analysis of the costs of violence for the period 1975 — 1987.[19] Much in the following four sections is based on their work.

## The toll of lives

From the beginning of 1975 to the end of October 1987 casualties of the war in Lebanon amounted to 62,000 dead and 83,000 injured. Estimates of the number of missing persons, now almost certainly dead, range between 2,000 and 17,500.[20] In terms of the population of the United Kingdom, this would be roughly one and a half million dead and two million injured.

The civilian population suffered most, accounting for about 75 per cent of all deaths and 86 per cent of the injured. About 15 per cent of the dead were militia-

---

[18] A Lebanese general assessed the situation as follows: 'It is unthinkable to take Ashrafieh in house-to-house fighting, it can't be done. You'd need a three-month land and sea blockade, and probably heavy aerial bombing, to force it to capitulate. An infantry assault? Regular troops haven't a hope against militiamen fighting in their own backyards.' Interview with the author, 1981.

An Israeli officer gave the following estimate of relative strengths: 'If the Syrians are really serious and throw in all they've got they can roll up the Christian areas in twenty-four hours. But for every ten Syrian soldiers that go in, only five come home. It'll cost the Syrians a full division. They'll win, but at what price?' Interview with the author, 1985.

A high-ranking Palestinian officer takes a similar view: 'Ashrafieh can't be taken — it'd be a disaster for any regular army, or it would have to be bombed flat first.' Interview with the author, 1981.

[19] Khalyl Abou Rjaily and Boutros Labaki, 'Bilan de treize ans de guerres au Liban: Les pertes', provisional draft, Beirut 1987. The author is extremely grateful to both for permission to study and quote from their manuscript.

[20] Press reports as well as Lebanese and Palestinian politicians mention much higher figures. Khalyl Abou Rjaily and Boutros Labaki base their figures on information from the Forces de Sécurité Intérieure, the Lebanese army, the Sûreté Générale, and the Lebanese Red Cross as well as interviews with spokesmen for professional associations, parties and militias.

men and 10 per cent regular army soldiers. The most accurate figures are those for army casualties:[21]

**Table 5.1**

|  | dead | wounded |
|---|---|---|
| Lebanese army incl. paramilitary police | 2,064 | 2,428 |
| Syrian army | 2,500 | 2,500 |
| Israeli army | 673 | 3,890 |
| Multinational forces | 306 | no figures |
| UNIFIL and UN observers | 155 | no figures |
| Total | 5,698 | 8,818 |

In relative terms, the American and French contingents of the multilateral peace force have suffered the highest casualties, followed by the Lebanese army, of which about 7 per cent fell.

Figures for militia casualties are less accurate because of structural reorganization — some disbanded, others merged, and yet others emerged in the course of the war — and the difficulty of distinguishing between militiamen and civilians who take up arms in certain circumstances. Figures for casualties of the Lebanese Forces and their constituent groups are fairly reliable: 3,061 dead, 855 wounded, half of them in the first two years of war.[22] As many as 880 guerrillas in Palestinian organizations are said to have died in the Israeli invasions of 1978 and 1982; 507 fell in Tripoli in 1985 in fighting against Syrian troops and their Palestinian and Lebanese allies.[23] Losses among Lebanese and Palestinian militias total about 10,000 dead. The course of the war is reflected in the annual casualty figures.

Greatest losses were suffered during the Israeli invasion of 1982, in the war between the Lebanese Front and the Palestinians and their allies in the first two war years, followed by the Chouf War in 1983 and the 1985 fighting in the vicinity of Sidon, in Tripoli and over the camps in west Beirut. Even in 'peaceful' 1977, a year of peace hopes, the conflict cost a few hundred people their lives. The level of fighting may have fluctuated, but there was always fighting somewhere.

There are few substantiated figures on how many people died by what sort of violence. A rough classification for 1986 shows that one-quarter of all violent deaths occurred in the 'Camps War' between Shi`is and Palestinians, another

---

[21] Khalyl Abou Rjaily and Boutros Labaki, op. cit., chapter 1, p. 11.
[22] Ibid., p. 20.
[23] Ibid., p. 19.

quarter in clashes between — theoretically allied — militias within the two confessional blocks, (only) 15 per cent in confrontations along the 'classic fronts' and 2 per cent in Israeli air-raids; murders also accounted for 2 per cent and car bombings no less than 7 per cent; in 23 per cent of all cases of death by violence the cause could not be unequivocally established.[24] Thus, almost one-third were victims of various forms of violence not directly related to a particular conflict. Rjaily and Labaki regard this range of violence as typical for the years from 1984 to 1987.

Table 5.2 War casualties, civilians and militiamen 1975–1987[25]

| Year | Dead | Wounded |
| --- | --- | --- |
| 1975 | 3,799 | 1,995 |
| 1976 | 14,714 | 13,209 |
| 1977 | 676 | 623 |
| 1978 | 2,093 | 2,164 |
| 1979 | 1,327 | 854 |
| 1980 | 1,578 | 1,054 |
| 1981 | 2,162 | 3,902 |
| 1982 | 17,000 | 30,000 |
| 1983 | 3,632 | 3,704 |
| 1984 | 2,161 | 2,614 |
| 1985 | 3,693 | 4,718 |
| 1986 | 2,668 | 7,237 |
| 1987 | 1,292 | 2,715 |
| Total | 56,795 | 74,789 |

Murder was common throughout the war, at least 500 a year since 1978. In the first two years of the war the majority were 'identity-card murders'. Later murder was used to intimidate certain target groups: politically motivated murders include those of sixty-one journalists and publicists and no less than 116 diplomats[26]. Few foreigners were taken hostage prior to 1984. This changed with the upsurge of pro-Iranian and Iranian-sponsored groups. About fifty foreigners in all were

[24] Ibid., p. 29.
[25] Ibid, p. 27.
[26] Including seventy Iraqis killed in a bomb attack on the Iraqi embassy, thirty Americans and four Frenchmen, including the ambassador.

kidnapped.[27] The number of kidnapped and missing Lebanese runs into thousands. The list of collective massacres is also long. It is not known how many Palestinians in Sabra and Chatila were murdered by Christian militias in 1982 and Shi`i in 1985; estimates range from 800 to 2,000 in both cases. More accurate figures for inner-Lebanese massacres are based on interviews with refugees:[28]

**Table 5.3** Civilians killed in collective massacres

| Year | In Christian villages | In Muslim villages | Total |
|---|---|---|---|
| 1975 | 123 | 15 | 138 |
| 1976 | 953 | 63 | 1016 |
| 1977 | 221 | 65 | 286 |
| 1978 | 51 | – | 51 |
| 1979 | 12 | – | 12 |
| 1980 | 11 | – | 11 |
| 1981 | 30 | – | 30 |
| 1982 | 91 | – | 91 |
| 1983 | 1,155 | 160 | 1315 |
| 1984 | 154 | – | 154 |
| 1985 | 121 | – | 121 |
| 1986 | 50 | 526 | 576 |
| Total | 2,972 | 829 | 3,801 |

Almost four-fifths of the victims of massacres were inhabitants of Christian villages, the 'pockets of allogeneous population' in predominantly Muslim or confessionally mixed regions. The massacres were seldom spontaneous; they were usually perpetrated to provoke the departure of the respective minorities.

## Flight and expulsion

The war made of the Lebanese a people of refugees and expellees in their own country. 700,000 people had to flee, many of them several times, and were always

---

[27] These included twenty Americans, nine Frenchmen, four Britons and Russians, and one or two Saudi Arabian, Egyptian, Iranian, Syrian, German, Italian, Swiss and Canadian nationals.
[28] Khalyl Abou Rjaily and Boutros Labaki, op. cit., chapter 1, p. 32.

able to return to their home areas. Most of the 790,000 who were driven out have still not been able to return.

In several parts of the country this has wrought marked changes in the pre-war composition of the population by denomination.

There have been radical changes in the southern section of the Lebanon Mountains, i.e., the Upper Metn, the Aley region and the Chouf. In 1975 the Christians comprised a good half of the population, a decade later about 1 per cent. The Christians were expelled from the coastal strip in the first two years of the war. The first victims were the inhabitants of the village of Ain Assad in Iklim al-Kharroub; after Palestinians occupied it, Christians in numerous other villages in the region began to leave. The massacre of Damour took place in early 1976, signalling the end of Christian settlement in the entire coastal region along the Chouf. In the early war years most of the able-bodied Christian population in the Chouf proper (about 100,000 people) left the region. Many returned after Syrian troops had marched in. In the aftermath of Kamal Jumblatt's murder in 1977, Christians were murdered in a number of Chouf villages, precipitating the flight of a further 25,000. But the catastrophe came in 1983, when the Lebanese Forces entered the Chouf, thereby provoking the calamitous war of 1983. About 164,000 Christians fled; many of those that stayed were killed. Since 1986 Walid Jumblatt has repeatedly invited the Christians of the Chouf and the Aley region to return, most emphatically in January 1989. Few have accepted: the threat to life and limb during the events of 1983 is still too fresh in peoples' memory. For the time being, the Chouf remains a 'Druze canton' with a small Sunni minority in the Lower Chouf.[29]

The changes in the Bekaa are scarcely less radical. Before the war 40 per cent of the inhabitants were Christian. Zahle was the largest city with a Christian majority; eighty-five Christian towns and villages were scattered over the region from the far north to the far south. From the earliest stages of the war in 1975 these virtually indefensible and often unarmed villages were favoured 'whipping boys' of Palestinian and left-wing Lebanese organizations unable to exact direct retribution from Christian militias in the Christian heartland. Hoch Omara, a village near Zahle, was devastated, the Christian inhabitants of Taalabaya expelled. Murders and requisitions provoked flight and migration from other villages. As in the Chouf, many Christians returned in the wake of Syrian troops. However, after the outbreak of hostilities between Christian militias and Syrian troops in 1978, the Syrian army frequently turned a blind eye to the lot of the Christians in the Bekaa. The Syrians stood by during the massacre in Qaa in 1978; they may well have instigated it. Again the Christian villages of the

[29] In 1985 about 25 000 Sunnis in the coastal strip along the Chouf fled to Beirut.

northern and central Bekaa emptied. The Israeli withdrawal from the southern Bekaa in 1984, was followed by an exodus of Christians defenseless against assault, murder and requisitioning of houses.

About 150,000 Christians left their towns and villages in the Bekaa; about 40,000 sought refuge in Zahle, most chose the Christian heartland. Conversely, the Bekaa became a haven of refuge for tens of thousands of Shi`is that fled the contested southern suburbs of Beirut in 1976, 1982 and from 1984; most of them were people from the Bekaa who chose to return to their origins. In 1982 many Palestinians in Beirut sought the relative security of the Bekaa; the formerly Christian villages of Taalabaya and Sadnayel are today predominantly Palestinian. Kurds were among the first to flee to the Bekaa when fighting early in the war turned their residential districts in the centre of Beirut into a battlefield. On balance, the influx of Shi`is, Palestinians and Kurds is probably greater than the flight of Christians. The northern Bekaa, in particular, has become a largely homogeneous Shi`ite 'canton'.

Expulsion and flight in northern Lebanon has been largely contained within the region, reflected in exchanges of population. In the autumn of 1975 Christians were driven out of the Akkar and Muslims out of the districts of Koura and Batroun. In 1978 fighting between the Christian Kata'ib and Marada militias led to the flight of about 25,000 Kata'ib supporters to areas under Kata'ib control, while an unknown, probable equivalent, number of Franjieh's supporters in east Beirut, the Metn and the Kisrawan returned to the Christian north. The struggle for the control of Tripoli between Syrian-sponsored militias and Syrian troops, on the one hand, and Palestinians and Sunni fundamentalists, on the other hand, caused up to 100,000 civilians to leave the city intermittently between 1980 and 1985; they always returned.

The population forced to flee most often is that of southern Lebanon. Pre-war Palestinian–Israeli confrontations caused about 25,000 Shi`is to flee their villages between 1969 and 1975. The Israeli invasion of 1978 caused a wave of between 150,000 and 200,000 refugees. The Israeli siege of west Beirut induced a similar number of inhabitants in the Shi`ite suburbs of Beirut to flee back to the south. There are no reliable figures for refugees from the fighting between Shi`is and Palestinians in Beirut in 1984 and their simmering warfare since 1985, nor for the Shi`i in-fighting. Whenever heavy fighting flares up in Beirut or the south, waves of civilians seek refuge in the relatively calmer of the two areas.

About one-quarter of the pre-war population in southern Lebanon was Christian. They lived mainly in the hills east of Sidon, in the Jezzine, in the Zahrani region and in the vicinity of Marjayoun in the extreme south. In October 1976 the dissident Lebanese Arab Army attacked the village of Aichieh and expelled its inhabitants. Christian militias retaliated by doing the same to the Muslim village of Khiam. Although both Christians and Muslims were leaving the south, the causes lay in the fighting and the miserable economic situation; for a long time, apart from the incidents mentioned, neither side practised systematic expulsion. This changed in 1985. Militiamen of the Lebanese Forces had entered the south after the Israeli invasion in 1982. In 1985 they shelled Sidon and the neighbouring Palestinian camps. What followed was, for the Christians, a repetition of the Chouf catastrophe two years previously. 86,000 fled into the Jezzine, controlled by General Lahad's South Lebanese Army, and the Israeli 'security zone'; most of them later made their way to the Christian heartland.

From 1975 onwards waves of refugees frequently flooded into Beirut. The capital was also the scene of nasty internal expulsions.[30] As early as April 1975 about 40 000 inhabitants were forced to leave the Christian 'pockets' in the southwestern suburbs — like the old Christian villages of Haret Hreik, Bourj al-Barajneh and Chiyah, around which predominantly Muslim suburbs and Palestinian camps had subsequently spread. A further 35,000 Christians fled from the heart of west Beirut to the east sector, most of them during the wave of 'identity-paper murders'. The same fear drove numerous Muslims from the east to the west, especially after 'Black Saturday' in December 1975. In the summer of 1976, as the Christian militias were storming the east Beirut Palestinian camps, the Shi`i populace was forced to leave the eastern suburb of Nabaa. The total number of Muslims who left east Beirut because of fear or coercion is thought to lie between 115,000 and 120,000. 15,000 Christians were also driven out of east Beirut, members of the parties of the Left or the National Movement and, therefore, regarded as suspect by the Christian militias in local control. By the end of 1976 there was hardly a Muslim left in the eastern sector of the city.

By contrast, many Christians remained in the western sector, above all in the old Christian residential areas in the city centre and in the traditionally mixed quarters of Hamra and Ras Beirut. From 1977 to 1982 they were left more or less in peace. During the presence of the multilateral peace force in 1982 and 1983 some former Christian residents even returned to west Beirut. The situation changed with the Shi`i uprising in the autumn of 1983. On September 23rd Amal expelled the inhabitants of the village Mreij, the last pocket of Christians in the southwestern suburbs. After the east-west divide was re-established in February 1984, radical Shi`i organizations launched on a series of individual murders, kidnappings and attacks on Christian businesses, institutions and churches with the object of ending the Christian presence in west Beirut. Many Sunnis suffered too. Although the Druze militias, the SSNP and the Communists tried to combat

---

[30] Cf. Ali Faour, 'The Displacement Crisis and Forced Migration in Beirut in 1984', Salim Nasr and Theodor Hanf (eds.), *Urban Crisis*, pp. 165–198.

these practices, the Christians could feel safe only in their strongholds; from 1984 about 50,000 Christians were intimidated into leaving the western sector.

Muslims, too, left west Beirut, where, from 1984 on, one armed clash after another drove about 100,000 residents into the Bekaa and the south. Over one-third of the Lebanese population had to flee at least once because of the war and related incidents, and could return.

Table 5.4 Temporary refugees[31]

| Year | Cause | No. of refugees |
|---|---|---|
| 1975/76 | Fighting in Beirut and suburbs, in Northern Lebanon, the Bekaa, in the mountains and in Southern Lebanon | 450,000 |
| 1978 | Israeli invasion | 150,000 |
| 1981 | Syrian shelling of east Beirut | 150,000 |
| 1982 | Israeli invasion and siege of west Beirut (flight to the Bekaa, Northern Lebanon and east Beirut) | 200,000 |
| 1984 | War over the Lebanese–Israeli treaty: | |
| | flight from east Beirut to its hinterland | 40,000 |
| | flight from west Beirut to the south and the Bekaa | 150,000 |
| 1983–1985 | Fighting in Tripoli | 100,000 |
| 1985–1987 | Fighting beween Amal and the PLO, and between Amal and the PSP | 60,000 |
| | flight from the southern suburbs and west Beirut | 60,000 |
| Total: | | 1,460,000 |

And over one-third was expelled or fled with little prospect of an early return — 80 per cent of these were Lebanese Christians. Before the war, there were Christians in most parts of the country. Now there are hardly any Christians at all in the Chouf, most of the Bekaa, most of the south and most quarters of west Beirut. Conversely, there are no Muslims left in east Beirut and, with the exception of Jbeil, the Christian heartland. Today, areas are more sharply defined by confession than before the war. The Shi`i community have suffered most from forced migration. Almost a quarter of a million Shi`is fled at least once from southern Lebanon to Beirut or from Beirut to southern Lebanon or the Bekaa. The Christians have suffered most from expulsions. Over 600,000 were driven out of

---

[31] Khalyl Abou Rjaily and Boutros Labaki, op. cit., chapter 2, p. 33, table 2.6.

different parts of the country and forced to take refuge in east Beirut or its hinterland.

**Table 5.5** Population movements by region and religion 1975–1986[32]

| Region | Christians | No. | Muslims | No. |
|---|---|---|---|---|
| Beirut and suburbs | Out of the southern suburbs and west Beirut 1975–1986 | 125,000 | Out of east Beirut and the eastern suburbs 1975–1976 | 115,000 |
| Mount Lebanon | Out of the Chouf, Aley, the Upper Metn and Iklim al-Kharroub 1975–1986 | 240,000 | Out of Laqlouq (Jbeil) 1976 | 500 |
| Northern Lebanon | Out of Akkar, Zghorta, Beshara, Batroun and Koura 1975–1986 | 30,000 | Out of Batroun and Koura | 2,000 |
| Southern Lebanon | Out of the hinterland of Sidon, Jezzine, Nabatieh and Tyre 1975–1986 | 125,000 | Out of the border strip, Jezzine and Nabatieh district | 40,000 |
| Bekaa | Out of Baalbek, Hermel, West Bekaa and Rashaya 1975–1986 | 110,000 | – | |
| Total | | 630,000 | | 157,500 |

## Migrant workers and emigrants

Nearly one-quarter of all Lebanese were abroad at some point during the war. As always, as soon as there was some promise of peace, many returned. However, those who have created new livelihoods abroad will need more convincing. Net

[32] Ibid., chapter 2, p. 34, table 2.7.

annual emigration figures[33] since 1975 show a close correlation between migration and the intensity of fighting:

Table 5.6  Annual net migration

| Year | | | net migration |
|---|---|---|---:|
| 1975 | | | 400,000 |
| 1976 | | | −297,000 |
| 1977 | | | 38,000 |
| 1978 | | | 76,000 |
| 1979 | | | 49,000 |
| 1980 | } | | |
| 1981 | } | total | 132,000 |
| 1982 | } | | |
| 1983 | } | | |
| 1984 | | | 61,605 |
| 1985 | | | 70,201 |
| 1986 | | | 73,907 |
| 1987 | (six months) | | 33,541 |
| Total | | | 637,254 |

In the first year of the war 15 per cent of the population left the country;[34] in 1976 three-quarters of them returned in the belief that the war was over. As neither peace nor economic recovery materialized, emigration resumed in 1977 and doubled in the following year, after the Israeli invasion of the south and clashes between the Syrian forces and the Lebanese Front. It dropped in the relative calm of 1979, only to rise subsequently. The total for the years 1980 to 1983 conceals significant fluctuations: after considerable remigration in 1982, a year in which it seemed the war might end, migration rose again in 1983 when these hopes were dashed. All subsequent years have been marked by heavy fighting, compounded by inflation and the collapse of the currency.

---

[33] Ibid., chapter 3, p. 17. Cf. also Riad Tabbarah, 'Le développement arabe et les ressources humaines libanaises', Université Libanaise, Institut des Science Sociales (ed.), *La politique de la population au Liban*, Beirut 1982; Boutros Labaki, 'L'économie politique de la crise libanaise. Impact et enjeux', Université St Joseph, Faculté des Lettres et des Sciences Humaines, Beirut 1988 (mimeograph).

[34] The figures in the rest of this section are taken from Khalyl Abou Rjaily and Boutros Labaki, op. cit., chapter 3.

In 1982 nearly 60 per cent of Lebanese migrants were working in Arab states, 33.5 per cent in Saudi Arabia alone and 8.3 per cent in Kuwait. In the same year 12 per cent were in Europe, 7 per cent each in North and South America and just under 6 per cent in the USA. The proportion in the Gulf states has probably increased since then.

Most of the migrants were skilled workers. Almost one-third of the economically active migrants were trained industrial workers, another third construction workers and one-fifth in the hotel industry. Engineers, architects, doctors and people in financial services were heavily overrepresented. Many firms transferred most of their activities abroad — and sent their trained staff too. Since 1975, sixteen Lebanese insurance companies have founded forty-three branches in the Arab world, Greece and Cyprus; twenty-three Lebanese banks have opened seventy-four branches abroad, most of them in the Arab states but some in Europe and the USA. The banks generally followed commercial firms, which retained an office in Lebanon but moved most of their operations abroad.

Therefore, it was not only a matter of individual Lebanese in war-hit sectors — manufacturing, construction and tourism — seeking work abroad because they could not find any at home, but of whole branches, with personnel, following transferred business.

The migrants' social profiles varied by target country. Young, unmarried men, two-fifths of them university graduates, preferred the Arab states. Emigrants to the United States tended to be families, usually with a relatively low educational background — only 9 per cent held a university degree; nearly 30 per cent were Armenian. Australia and Canada attracted numerous small and medium-sized businessmen with some capital. Scientists and intellectuals preferred France. There was a significant increase in emigration to West Africa. In 1970 the region had 74,000 Lebanese residents, in 1985 147,000, 60,000 in the Ivory Coast alone. Whereas most of the Lebanese in Africa pre-war were merchants, many of the recent immigrants went into the construction industry and road-building. The proportion of migrant workers was highest among the Lebanese in the Arab states, that of permanent emigrants among those living in the United States.

This enormous migration has had far-reaching consequences for Lebanon. Although births continued to outnumber deaths, the number of Lebanese in Lebanon in 1985 was much the same as in 1975. In spite of the dismal economic situation, there was a shortage of skilled labour, partly alleviated by migrants — notwithstanding the war — from Syria, Egypt and, increasingly, Asian countries. The economic effects cut both ways. On the one hand, remittances from Lebanese abroad enabled large numbers of Lebanese at home to survive, especially as prospects of employment worsen. They also improved the balance-of-payments. On the other hand, the macroeconomic effects were predominantly negative. The loss of skills reduced productive capacity, while remittances from abroad raised demand and, hence, imports of consumer goods, with consequent worsening of the trade deficit, inflation and the exchange rate.

In brief: Migration 'may have advantages for the individual in the short run; for society as a whole and in the long run it is, all things considered, a disadvantage'.[35]

## The war economy[36]

On the eve of the war the services sector accounted for 70 per cent of the gross national product. Domestic demand was only a minor part of the commercial, banking and tourist industries, which catered to the needs of the entire region. The rapidly growing manufacturing sector was also tuned to the needs of the Arab world, and the Gulf states in particular. The motor of impressive growth and spreading prosperity in times of peace was endangered by the political instability from 1967 onwards, and proved particularly vulnerable in wartime.

Yet, the Lebanese economy showed extraordinary flexibility even under conditions of war. Wherever possible, damage was repaired and houses rebuilt after each round of fighting. Commercial and financial companies and businessmen would transfer their operations abroad, only to return to Beirut after each ceasefire. New factories were built at a greater distance from the fronts. Banks and the catering trade, formerly concentrated in the centre of Beirut, opened branches or new premises in what had previously been purely residential areas. Food markets, wholesale businesses and shopping centres were also decentralized. Provincial towns became new business centres. The Lebanese quickly mastered the art of business in war. Nonetheless, the economic consequences of the war were disastrous. By 1976 the losses in fixed capital due to the war were put at about US$ 2,500,000 000. According to the figures of the Lebanese Confederation of Trade Unions, after the Israeli invasion of 1982 they had virtually doubled:

---

[35] Ibid., chapter 3, p. 145.
[36] This section is based largely on Khalyl Abou Rjaily and Boutros Labaki, op. cit., chapter 5.

**Table 5.7** Capital losses 1975–1982[37]

| Sector | Losses in LL billions | Nature of losses |
| --- | --- | --- |
| Housing | 3.6 | 11,200 dwellings destroyed |
| Tourism | 1.2 | 65 hotels destroyed (40 in 1975/6, 25 in 1982) |
| Trade and services | 9.3 | ca. 13,400 shops and service enterprises destroyed |
| Manufacturing | 1.5 | 300 factories destroyed or damaged |
| Agriculture | 1.0 | destruction of irrigation systems, wells, plantations and equipment (FAO estimates) |
| Public buildings and infrastructure | 4.0 | roads, ports, docks, airports, telephone, electricity and water services, schools and hospitals |
| Moveable goods and private property | 2.0 | raw materials, finished goods, other wares of businesses, goods in private homes, cars |
| Total: | 22.6 | |

At the then exchange rate, capital losses amounted to US$ 4,780,000,000. The value of output lost was far higher, as the decline in gross national product indicates:

---

[37] Ibid., chapter 5, p. 32, table 18.

Table 5.8

| Year | GDP (1974 LL billions)[38] |
|---|---|
| 1974 | 8.1 |
| 1975 | 7.5 |
| 1976 | 4.3 |
| 1977 | 6.0 |
| 1978 | 6.1 |
| 1979 | 6.3 |
| 1980 | 6.7 |
| 1981 | 6.6 |
| 1982 | 6.0 |
| 1983 | 5.6 |
| 1984 | 5.6 |
| 1985 | 5.0 |
| 1986 | 3.8 |

Taking 1974 as base year, the cumulative losses in GNP through 1986 total LL 27,700,000,000, or (1974) US$ 11,600,000,000. Assuming pre-war rates of growth, i.e., including potential output, the loss amounts to US$ 75,000,000,000.

The first sharp drop in output came in 1976. It then recovered to roughly three-quarters of the pre-war level, which it maintained until 1982, after which it declined to less than half the 1974 figure in 1986. In the circumstances, and with the exception of 1976, the economy proved remarkably resilient during the first seven years of war. Then came the crisis. Markets for Lebanese products and labour in the Gulf states shrank as they restrained spending to cope with the cumulative effects of the international recession and financial commitments to Iraq in its war with Iran. From 1982, some Arab states boycotted Lebanese products because of the Israeli occupation. The resurgence of fighting and the decision of western states in early 1984 to withdraw their troops dashed hopes of imminent peace and, hence, early prospects of rebuilding the country.

The balance of trade and the balance of payments reflect the decline in output. The Lebanese balance of trade is traditionally in deficit. In 1974 exports covered 41 per cent of imports. This pattern continued, with minor fluctuations, until 1982. In 1983 and 1984 it fell to 17.4 and 16.2 per cent respectively, rising slightly to 21.3 per cent in 1985. By contrast, with the exception of 1976, the

[38] Ibid., chapter 5, p. 34, table 19.

balance of payments remained in surplus until 1982, when the downward trend began.[39]

Until 1982 the visible deficit was more than covered by migrants' remittances, estimated to have run at US$ 150 millions per month, and foreign subsidies for the warring parties. US$ 80 millions per month are thought to have flowed into the 'war chest' of the PLO alone. When the PLO were expelled from Beirut in 1982 their 'war chest' went too.[40] At the same time, the Gulf states were sliding into recession, which reduced Lebanese exports to as well as migrants' remittances.

Table 5.9

| Year | Balance of payments surplus/deficit (LL billions) | |
|---|---|---|
| 1974 | + | 1,493 |
| 1975 | + | 350 |
| 1976 | − | 239 |
| 1977 | + | 2,404 |
| 1978 | + | 541 |
| 1979 | + | 1,270 |
| 1980 | + | 1,717 |
| 1981 | + | 2,707 |
| 1982 | + | 964 |
| 1983 | − | 5,121 |
| 1984 | − | 12,028 |
| 1985 | + | 6,896 |
| 1986 | − | 22,527 |

The most serious cause of the crisis was a dramatic rise in the budget deficit from 1982 onwards. Pre-war budgetary policy had been very conservative; the state should live within its means. The 1974 fiscal year ended with a surplus of 4 per cent.

The budget went into deficit with the outbreak of war. The state continued to pay civil servants' salaries and, during lulls in the fighting, build roads; in 1977 in started re-equipping the Lebanese army with modern weaponry. But revenues

---

[39] Ibid., chapter 5, p. 39, table 21.
[40] Prior to the PLO's departure, the Arab Bank in Beirut is said to have transferred US$ 800,000,000 to PLO accounts in other countries. Cf. John Bulloch, *Final Conflict*, op. cit., p. 216.

sank. Falling output and rising emigration reduced income-tax revenues. In wide areas of the country people stopped paying for water, electricity and telephone. Above all, revenues from customs duties, previously the major source of public income, declined considerably. All the warring parties ran their own ports and used the revenues to finance their organizations and militias. The national debt grew rapidly:[41]

**Table 5.10**

| Year | Budget deficit (%) |
|------|-------------------|
| 1975 | 21.8 |
| 1976 | 76.3 |
| 1977 | 28.2 |
| 1978 | 27.6 |
| 1979 | 35.8 |
| 1980 | 38.1 |
| 1981 | 37.6 |
| 1982 | 63.5 |
| 1983 | 53.1 |
| 1984 | 78.5 |
| 1985 | 75.4 |
| 1986 | 81.1 |

State authority first broke down seriously in 1976, as reflected in much reduced tax revenues. The deficits were comparatively moderate from 1977 to 1981. The events of 1982 brought the next breakdown. In 1983 the government succeeded in closing the militias' ports for a few months, improving customs revenues and reducing the deficit. By March 1984 the state was weaker than ever, and the deficit out of control.

To finance the deficit the government borrowed from private banks and, increasingly, from the central bank. In 1982 the latter funded 12 per cent of public sector borrowing, in 1986 it was 45 per cent. As it became more difficult to raise credit, the government turned to printing money. The result was inevitable: inflation soared and the currency collapsed.[42]

---

[41] Compiled from the data in Khalyl Abou Rjaily and Boutros Labaki, op. cit., chapter 5, p. 42, table 22.

[42] Following table compiled from figures published by the Banque du Liban, *Bulletin Mensuel*, and the CGTL, Beirut, quoted from Khalyl Abou Rjaily and Boutros Labaki, op. cit., chapter 5, p. 52.

## Table 5.11

| Year | Retail price inflation (%) | LL to the US$ |
| --- | --- | --- |
| 1980 | 23.7 | 3.43 |
| 1983 | 9.8 | 4.52 |
| 1984 | 25.8 | 6.51 |
| 1985 | 69.7 | 16.00 |
| 1986 | 162.0 | 35.00 |
| 1987 | 620.0 | 520.00 |

With the economic crisis came a dramatic fall in the living standards of broad sections of the Lebanese population, as changes in per capita income reveal:[43]

## Table 5.12

| Year | Income per head (US$) |
| --- | --- |
| 1974 | 1,869 |
| 1982 | 2,917 |
| 1983 | 1,917 |
| 1984 | 1,593 |
| 1985 | 979 |

The damage to the economy was reasonably contained; indeed, average income rose until 1982, after which it fell drastically, and was only half its pre-war level in 1985. Salaried employees were hit hardest. Despite regular increases, salaries did not kept pace with inflation.

By 1986 the buying power of the minimum wage had fallen by 40 per cent, that of the average income of salaries employees by 60 per cent. At the end of 1986 the buying power of the statutory minimum wage was 13 per cent of its 1974 level. The minimum wage in 1974 was 70 per cent of average per capita income, at the end of 1986 only 20 per cent. These figures are indicative of widening income disparities since the outbreak of war. Hardest hit were the wage-earning middle classes. Furthermore, unemployment rose from a pre-war rate of 5.5 per cent to 15.2 per cent in 1985, and was much higher among refugees.

[43] Khalyl Abou Rjaily and Boutros Labaki, op. cit., chapter 5, p. 51, table 25.

**Table 5.13** Loss of purchasing power of wages and salaries 1974–1986[44]

| Year* | Legal minimum wage (%) | Average salary (%) |
|---|---|---|
| 1975 | 5.5 | 7.1 |
| 1977 | 11.3 | 17.5 |
| 1978 | 18.9 | 24.5 |
| 1979 | 17.3 | 27.2 |
| 1980 | 13.9 | 26.0 |
| 1981 | 14.5 | 28.5 |
| 1982 | 16.6 | 30.0 |
| 1983 | 8.6 | 27.9 |
| 1984 | 13.6 | 33.7 |
| 1985 | 35.9 | 51.0 |
| 1986 | 38.0 | 60.0 |
| 1986 (December) | 48.0 | 76.0 |

* Base year 1974

The war in Lebanon has not been the great leveller anticipated by some of its initial protagonists. It has impoverished most Lebanese, and some very much more than others. It is still difficult to predict its long-term effects. For, reconstruction, too, will be difficult. The country needs the skills of those who have left to work elsewhere; it is impossible to say how many might return. Then there is the question of capital: so far, no country has declared its willingness to initiate or fund the sort of Marshall Plan that would be required — hardly any of the Arab states have kept their previous promises of aid. The struggle to regain lost markets will be arduous. Petrodollars now lie in other banks. The Gulf states are developing their own industries. The agricultural sector will take time to recover: most of the irrigation systems in the Bekaa have been destroyed, the people who maintained them driven out; it will take years to re-establish the interrupted rotation cycles of export crops on a profitable basis. Much of the land farmed in 1973 lies fallow, and in many former orchards and tobacco and wheat fields hashish now flourishes.

[44] Ibid., chapter 5, p. 56, table 28.

But the short-term concerns of many Lebanese are more immediate. In the late 1980s hunger reappeared in Lebanon, for the first time since the First World War: not relative, but absolute deprivation.

## Life in war

Quite apart from economic decline, the war affected everyday life. Fear became a habit, barely veiled in nonchalance. People could not be sure as they left for work, school or the shops that they would return, but most continued to go their way as though the danger had passed. They took precautions: shorter distances wherever possible: jobs, shops and markets, business contacts and schools closer to home; television and video-recorders instead of the cinema; family instead of friends. People avoided going out in the evening or, if they had to, made arrangements to overnight if necessary.

The customary kindness in social intercourse suffered too. Rudeness became commoner, an ill-concealed nervousness. Political jokes were no less popular than before, but more caustic. Rumour, too, gained a new role; for, the press might be as varied and informative as ever, but carried little interpretation and comment. And then there was the next 'date' — an Arab or other summit meeting, the arrival of an envoy, elections in Israel, some autocrat's demise, a deadline or peace talks. These dates were the small change of hope, each a possible pointer to Lebanon's destiny.

In the early days of the war the Lebanese made a show of ignoring it. Money flowed: lavish parties, jam-packed department stores, the beaches a sea of extravagantly fashionable scantiness. Western journalists moralized over such recklessness, and oversaw the element of valour in it. To act in the constant presence of war as though it did not exist was a very civil and civilized form of protest and resistance to a war virtually nobody wanted or approved of. As countless wars have taught, it was also a very normal reaction to living cheek by jowl with death.

Inflation and the collapse of the currency curbed sumptuous entertainment. Most people lacked the means for extravagant hospitality. Only a minority could afford prodigality. The old moneyed classes had the breeding to flaunt their remaining wealth less openly; the Casino du Liban and the Summerland catered to the nouveaux riches — often war-profiteers — of east and west Beirut. As long as 'ordinary people' could afford to celebrate whenever the occasion called for it, Mediterranean live-and-let-live restrained envy of those that splurged to find themselves splashed across the social columns of the next day's newspapers. As impoverishment spread, ostentation aroused social indignation. The reaction to the indecency of the parvenus and boors, 'a world of graceless hedonists,'[45] was warranted, but just as graceless. In areas dominated by Hezbollah social envy wore a pious face. Beauty had to be veiled. Alcohol, to which many Muslim Lebanese were not averse, was no longer an acceptable means of keeping one's spirits up under soul-destroying conditions. It took a Muslim girl courage to wear elegant western clothes; a glass of whisky was a profession of faith in secular principles — both rare attributes.

The difficulties of daily life cut across class and creed: power-cuts, water rationing and poor telephone service.

Schooling was a constant problem for parents. State schools were badly equipped after years of neglect, with little hope of improvement; many teachers could not survive on their salaries and neglected their duties to moonlight. Private schools were in better shape, but had become so expensive many could not afford to sent their children to them. Between 1975 and 1990 there was not a year in which most schools did not close because of fighting or shelling. Up to 1988, in two war years one month of schooling was lost, in seven two, in two three and in two others six and seven months respectively. To ensure that the pupils 'covered' important syllabi, subjects regarded as less important — sport, art, history and geography — were skipped. The pressures on all pupils increased; few had the time or the opportunity to play. A number of new universities opened during the war. The Lebanese University split; some denominations opened their own universities. Both the student body and the teaching staff became more homogeneous, which impaired the quality of education. Lecturers of different denominations who proposed to run a joint course on a topic that might have even the remotest political connotations, found it expedient to do so on Cyprus.

All citizens of Lebanon — not just professors — found it easier to travel from any part of the country to Cyprus than from one Lebanon to another. Many Lebanese tried never to pass from the control of one militia to another; internal checkpoints were bothersome enough. The respective Lebanese worlds of the Lebanese have shrunk. Young men in Zahle may have visited Paris but never Baalbek, their contemporaries in Sidon perhaps Cairo or Abidjan but not Jounieh. Regardless of the wishes of the people, Lebanon became a country of small and mutually exclusive ghettos; it will take time to reopen them in people's minds.

Before the war Martyrs Square was the centre of Beirut. Here all routes of the collective taxis, the main form of transport, converged. Behind it lay the banking district and the souk. During the war, the taxi routes led to separate 'stations' in either sector of the city. The banks and bazaars moved to the suburbs. Bushes and

---

[45] Samir Khalaf, *Lebanon's Predicament*, op. cit., p. 241.

trees edged the 'green line' — nature staking its claim.[46] The city centre was devastated, the residences of old merchant families crumbling piles of dressed stone, arcades and lancets between the skeletal sentinels of holed and gutted concrete. From the mountains above Beirut one looked down at night on the lights of the eastern and western sectors, and between them the triangle of darkness where the heart of old Beirut lay buried.

In both sectors of the city daily life went on, and each had its night-life, but they had visibly turned their backs on each other.

## The equilibrium of terror

The forms, costs and consequences of war were closely linked. Pre-war paramilitary groups were little more than party toughs. In the first round of fighting the conflicting factions and the communities mobilized en masse. But when this ended in stalemate, a division of labour gradually spawned properly organized, full-time militias. In time they grew strong enough to frustrate the objectives of regular foreign armies that intervened in Lebanon. The end was always to force a particular adversary to make concessions; the means, though, were seldom regular campaigns or occupation of territory, but rather the infliction of damage. The end was seldom achieved; the damage was always enormous. The Lebanese become a people of refugees and 'displaced persons', and, to a degree unparalleled in their history, a people of migrant workers and emigrants. The economy was ruined, the Lebanese impoverished. The conditions of daily life, even in the absence of fighting, were enervating and degrading.

Domination by the militias was rule by mercenaries. The damage they caused, ably assisted by foreign armies, entrenched their dominance. There was no lack of recruits among refugees and unemployed that either wanted to win back their homes or had no alternative prospects. Migration depleted the country of those citizens that, as a rule, constitute the social background of any middle-class society: people with skills and qualifications. Their absence, in turn, weakened the moderates in every faction as well as those aloof from the fighting.

The militias assumed some of the state's functions, above all the collection of revenues due to the state, forcing the state to resort to inflationary policies. None of the militias would willingly forgo any authority or revenues in the interests of

---

[46] 'La végétation s'empare d'ailleurs de ce paysage de pierre: Quiconque a pénétré le centre de Beyrouth au cours des périodes de trêves qui ont ponctué la guerre libanaise, n'a pu qu'être frappé par l'étrange spectacle du construit et du 'non-construit' qui s'amalgament, du minéral et du végétal qui s'interpénètrent, jeu fascinant de la vie et de la mort, comme dans ces cités perdues, enfouies dans la jungle, ou ces temples angkoriens, témoins oubliés d'une civilisation passée.' Jad Tabet, 'Images de Beyrouth', in Salim Nasr and Theodor Hanf, *Urban Crisis*, p. 132.

the state; for, the state's gain would be their loss, an unappealing prospect for both leaders and rank and file. The economic crisis strengthened their position and continuing tension legitimized it in the eyes of their respective communities, despite the fact that the great majority in each had long since tired of war.

The militia leaders themselves, without exception, were utterly convinced they were acting in the best interests of their respective communities. That their own interests and their convictions coincided strengthened the latter. The pillar of pre-war Lebanon was the conviction of the fathers of the National Pact that no single community could dominate and that, therefore, the only solution was to exercise power jointly. After years of war the militia leaders, too, had to realize that no single community or its militia could win or dominate. However, each preferred full power in one part of Lebanon to a share of power in Lebanon as a whole. Hence the development from fighting between the communities to fighting within the communities was consistent. Instead of sharing power they were partitioning the country.

There was always the danger in pre-war Lebanon of political leaders seeking foreign support for domestic ends. In war-torn Lebanon this danger was incomparably greater, because each militia was far weaker than the old state — itself hardly a byword for strength. War and economic crisis produced an equilibrium of terror, expressed in the stalemate between the militias. As long as there were militias open to manipulation by foreign powers, there was the danger that these powers would again be tempted to regulate their own conflicts on Lebanese soil, would once more seek victory through violence.

# 6

# Foxes and Lions
## Politicians' and Militia Leaders' Perceptions of the Conflict

A mere handful of citizens, so long as they are willing to use violence, can force their will upon public officials who are not inclined to meet violence with equal violence ... To prevent or resist violence, the governing class resorts to 'diplomacy', fraud, corruption — governmental authority passes, in a word, from the lions to the foxes. The governing class bows its head under the threat of violence, but it surrenders only in appearances, trying to turn the flank of the obstacle it cannot demolish in frontal attack ... [The foxes possess] precisely, the artistry and resourcefulness required for evolving ingenious expedients as substitutes for open resistance, while the residues of group-persistence stimulate open resistance, since a strong sentiment of group-persistence cures the spine of all tendencies to curvature ... The potency of an ideal as a pilot to victory is observable in both civil and international strife. People who lose the habit of applying force, who acquire the habit of considering policy from a commercial standpoint and of judging it only in terms of profit and loss, can readily be induced to purchase peace; and it may well be that such a transaction taken by itself is a good one, for war might have cost more money than the price of peace. Yet experience shows that in the long run ... such practice leads a country to ruin.

Vilfredo Pareto

> We Swedes are fighting for a righteous cause
> With righteous swords and with our conscience clear.
> Conditions now, it seems, are in our favour,
> We must seize every opportunity,
> Take every chance that offers, without scruple;
>
> Friedrich Schiller, Wallenstein

It is easy to recognize in Pareto's foxes Lebanon's traditional politicians. Schiller's description of warlords in the Thirty Years' War does equally well for the Lebanese lions. And indeed, the foxes, despite zealous pursuit, have not succeeded in buying sovereign peace. 'Pareto's theory is disinterested, and sounds cynical. It proceeds ... from the premise that thinking reason obeys a stronger spiritual power. It is not for nothing that agents are present in the guise of animals, and not for nothing that he is more sympathetic towards the lions than the foxes. This element encapsulates the cognitive value and limits of his theory.'[1] He puts his finger on the foxes' weakness, and idealizes the lions. History is full of lions that 'transposed humanity to a distant future and made of it an object of faith, all the while resorting to relentless violence.'[2] As will be seen, all lions in the war in Lebanon are adequately equipped with 'righteous swords' and 'clear consciences'. Yet in Lebanon the proof of Pareto's force of the ideal has not been in the winning. Neither has any lion been able to impose his will on all others, nor is it certain that in the end the foxes will have lost. But each in his own way has brought the Lebanese people to the brink of ruin.

The next section will examine views of the leading players: their assessment of the causes of the conflict, of themselves and of each other as well as, finally, their visions of the country's future.[3]

## Perceptions of problems in pre-war Lebanon

In 1961 it was only three years since the first Lebanese civil war. President Chehab's administrative and economic reforms were starting to take effect. The agreement between Chehab and Nasser had ended controversy over foreign policy. But the question of Lebanese identity had lost none of its explosive potential. Statements of a number of politicians at this time reveal elements of different

---

[1] Arnold Bergstraesser, *Die Macht als Mythos und als Wirklichkeit* (Freiburg, 1965), p. 132.
[2] Ibid.
[3] The quotations in this chapter are extracts from interviews with the author. Anonymity respects the wish of the respondent.

ideological stances that would underlie the future armed conflict, as well as different views on dealing with the conflict of identity.

Rashid Karami, President Chehab's first Prime Minister, put his view firmly, yet with tolerance and an understanding of the need for common ground.

> Lebanon is an Arab country with all the characteristics of Arab countries. However, that does not prevent it from absorbing what has been useful to other countries, turning it to its own use without losing its Arabness. Of course, all religions have one and the same origin, manely God. In principle all are equal. If every one of us lived by the teachings of his religion, we would be happy and united. What makes us afraid is people who exploit religion for other purposes. The weakness of our state makes group fanaticism possible. A strong regime must implement healthy, logical and moderate policies to hinder the fanatics from doing what they want ... This state is there for every citizen, not for one party or another. Therefore, what we need at the moment is a government prepared to exercise authority. A people with a common country must have something in common.

The fear of a repetition of the events of 1958 is manifest, as is the conviction that the authority of the state must assert common interests against divisive claims. This conviction is shared, albeit more soberly and sceptically, by another Chehabist, the then Minister of Justice, Fouad Boutros.

> The problem of two nationalisms, Arab and Lebanese, is insoluble in the short term. It is questionable whether a strict Muslim can accept secularism at all. This may be possible in other Arab states; Arabism sometimes does take secular forms. However, here in Lebanon the confessional divisions will probably last longer than in other Arab states. One should not forget that there are considerable economic differences between the two camps. Even if one makes an effort to raise Muslim living standards, one should not delude oneself that this will reduce fanaticism quickly. Quite the contrary. I think economic progress will make Arab nationalism more powerful and more violent. Nevertheless, I am convinced that the only sensible policy for Lebanon is to raise the living standards of all, and in particular those of the deprived Muslim part of the population. Despite the risks, it is the only chance the country has of surviving as an independent state. For this reason, the studies of Father Lebret and the IRFED will no doubt be useful. Not that I think they will lead to major change, let alone directly influence the political situation. Father Lebret's programme deals primarily with rural areas; Lebanon's political problem is urban. Arab nationalism is strongest in

Beirut, Tripoli and Sidon ... That may sound pessimistic — I think it is a realistic assessment of the situation. We must look at things as they are and act accordingly. The chance for our country lies in steady and realistic policies. One must avoid aggravating the existing divisions.

Both Karami and Boutros saw 'fanaticism' as the problem, and a more powerful state pursuing social and economic development as the best means of crisis management. The following quarter of a century has proved Boutros's prediction: reducing existing inequalities aggravated the ideological tensions, particularly in the cities. These tensions are explicit in the way representatives of populist parties saw the country. Adnan Hakim, head of the Najjadé, explained:

There is no such thing as a Lebanese culture. That is an invention of the French and people influenced by them. Lebanon is an integral part of the Arab world. The only peculiar thing about its character is that it is more strongly influenced by imperialism than other countries. It is the task of the Najjadé to change this.

The goal of his party is 'to fight to stop Lebanon being cut off from the Arab area and from its roots'. It has a sharp foe image: 'If we did not have the religious minorities, which are exploited by political and foreign missionary tendencies, [Lebanon] would not be facing a battle of annihilation.' The Kata'ib formulates the alternative position of an independent Lebanese culture:

One must think of Lebanese culture in the same way as one speaks of separate French, German or Italian cultures, cultures that want to exist free of external coercion. Of course our culture cannot be indifferent to what happens in the Arab world; that would be ahistorical and unrealistic ...; we find the expression 'land of cultural integration' a happy choice.

But even in 1961 the identity debate was not only academic. Two statements made that year reveal the extent to which the rival concepts of Arab and Lebanese nationalism were, in the final instance, already codes for the religious communities and their claims to power.[4] Omar Farroukh, a teacher of philosophy at the Sunni Makassed Schools, was also an influential author who had no inhibitions about expressing his opinions on any political matters:

Islam is essentially the religion of Arab nationalism. Personally, I believe that the two, Islam and Arab nationalism, are identical. In politics Islam is

---

[4] See Chapter 2, pp. 131–3.

defined as a major component of Arabism. But that's just a concession on the part of politicians; in reality the two have to be identical, and they are identical ... Look, the question is always asked: What role does Islam play in Lebanon? Is it only a religion? No, far more than a religion; it has a lot to do with our culture. What does one mean by Mediterranean culture? What does the slogan 'Graeco-Latin origins' mean? That's all tied up with Christianity. That's utterly foreign to us ... Of course, one has to make concessions in day-to-day politics. Everyone should have the same rights, for all who recognize one fatherland are equal in it. Lebanon is now supposed to be independent. But our goal is unity, even if this is at the moment politically impractical.

Concerning the Christians in Lebanon, Farroukh stated:

If the Christians call themselves Arabs and also act as Arabs they are our equals. But they must behave as a minority in the democratic sense, as, say, the Protestants in France behave as a minority. In England a member of the Catholic minority cannot become king ... In religious terms all are equal. But in politics the majority rules.

In reply to the author's question, whether politicians, like Raymond Eddé, were right to believe that in a Pan-Arab state Christians would be second-class citizens, Farroukh replied: 'Once Arabism is ascendant in Lebanon, there won't be any place at all — neither first-class, nor second-class, nor third-class — for people like Raymond Eddé, who can't speak Arabic and don't want to be Arabs.' Eddé's opinion on identity was pragmatic and liberal:

Of course Arabic should have preference. I went to a Jesuit school where we had only one hour of Arabic a week; that was wrong. But for economic reasons it is necessary for Lebanese to have a command of several languages. Lebanon should be open to all currents of thought. I disapprove on principle of any form of intellectual prescript.

He mounted a spirited defence of his right to be 'Lebanese first':

My view of Arabism? Most Arabs do not distinguish between Arabism and Islamism. For these, a Christian Arab remains a second-class Arab. Do you think we find that pleasant? I have no desire to be a second-class Arab. My name is Eddé, a Phoenician name. I am the deputy for Byblos. Do you really believe that Pan-Arabism would become me?

The views of the Najjadé and the Kata'ib, of Farroukh and Eddé, reflect in all clarity the differences in opinion on the cultural, religious and political character of Lebanon. The fathers of the National Pact had hoped to bridge these differences, and the Chehabists tried to diminish them through social equalization. Yet they have proved virulent enough to withstand all countermeasures. By 1961, a further potential for conflict was already recognizable, although its force only became apparent very much later: the claim of the Shi`i community to greater involvement in the political system.

The Shi`i deputy Mohsin Slim pointed out that the urbanization of his community was already far advanced: 'Adnan Hakim's voters are mostly Shi`is. Shi`is now constitute 60 per cent of the population of Basta. In Beirut what is called the 'street' is now Shi`i.' He observed a dearth of effective political leadership among the Sunnis: 'This is the reason why Kamal Jumblatt's position among the Sunnis is so strong. Many Sunnis see him as their boss because they're disappointed in their own leaders.' The truth in this analysis became clear a year later.[5] However, Mohsin Slim did not think much of Sunnis leading Shi`is, or a Druze leading Sunnis; he gave notice of Shi`i aspirations to leadership:

> In the future, young, dynamic and better-educated people will replace the old, largely feudal elites in each community. In the long term I see prospects of decisive changes in the fundamentals of Lebanese politics. This would involve changing the National Pact so that it reflects the true numerical proportionality of the communities. In concrete terms: the Sunnis must make way for the Shi`is, who would then fill the premiership. As the Shi`is have fewer ties with neighbouring Arab countries than the Sunnis, a truly Lebanese policy would be a possibility.

A decade later, in 1971, Shi`i demands were an important issue in domestic Lebanese politics. Their spokesman was Imam Musa Sadr. In an interview he emphasized, above all, practical methods of removing the current discrimination against his community: greater state investment in the infrastructure of the south and the Bekaa, subsidies for the tobacco industry, more schools and more scholarships for Shi`is to the American University and St Joseph's University. He had a subtle understanding of the Lebanese political system:

> Personally, I think the Lebanese confessional system is out of date and should be abolished. Nevertheless, it has many advantages for the individual communities in the present situation ... Basically, it's a bad thing, but, if

---

[5] See Chapter 3, pp. 128.

applied fairly, has its uses. Our community has long been at a disadvantage, partly for historical reasons and partly as a result of deliberate policies. We won't tolerate the latter in the future. We want a share in the economy, the culture and the political power of this country in accordance with our strength.

Sadr expressed himself much as the fathers of the constitution and the National Pact had done. They may have created the system of proportionality and quotas as a provisional measure, but had lived with this interim solution for a long time. Sadr did not want to abolish the quotas but to amend them, so as to obtain a larger quota for his community. He also strove to renew the political cadres in this community. As one of his associates said: 'These feudalists are at best good administrators, but not reformers. Until the Shi`is get rid of them the community won't make any progress. We're not against the system of 1943, but we want changes in the way it functions, and above all, fairness and a change of faces.'

Besides the rise of the Shi`is, the other significant development of the early 1970s was the end of Chehabism. Opponents of Chehabism interpreted this as an end to the army's involvement in politics, whereas adherents saw it as an end to reformist policies. Raymond Eddé's view is typical of the former:

> Lebanon can only be governed by parliament; that is my deepest conviction. That is why I stood against Chehab in 1958, despite the Sixth Fleet off our coast. There simply had to be one civilian candidate to prevent the military winning on the first ballot. All my fears have been confirmed. Like any military man, Chehab is essentially contemptuous of democracy. When I served as a minister under him I observed in detail how the military tried to take charge of everything, most brazenly in the ministry of internal affairs. The more intelligent among them at least wanted to maintain the façade of civilian authority; they specialized in manipulating elections. Under Helou they became more and more impertinent. They were determined to elect as his successor a front man. The Republic was barely saved, by just one vote ... Helou was unbelievably weak; he did not dare to curb the power of the military. Since 1966 I have introduced bills, for instance to remove the press from military jurisdiction. Like Briand, I believe that military justice is as much justice as military music is music. But Helou talked a lot and did little. In the presence of the military he always snapped to attention. He always addressed General Boustani, that thief, as 'Mon Général; Helou never dared give him orders. We have had enough of these tin hats ... Now we have a little more freedom. A week after he took office, Premier Salam gave orders to break into the rooms reserved for the military in the ministry of posts and

telegraphs and the general post office. There they were all sitting, with their tape recorders and headphones, the great tappers. Now they are on the dole, just like their chiefs in the Deuxième Bureau. Chehab was dismayed at the victory of the politics he disdained. That was my victory.

Even supporters and leading members of the Chehabist system, for example Fouad Boutros, often felt that the political operations of Military Intelligence went too far. But they were unanimous in regretting the end of the era of social reform. As Mohsin Slim put it:

> What we are seeing now is the return and revenge of political feudalism. Suleiman Franjieh is an extremely nice person, but not a great intellect. He has chosen assistants of the same cast and surrounded himself with sons of old families. In doing so he is paralysing Lebanon — for these families have not the slightest interest in progress in Lebanon. Certainly, there's still lots of talk about reform — a real battle of reformist words — but nothing's being done.

Kamal Jumblatt, as a minister, for a long time one of the pillars of Chehabism, helped bring about its end. Asked for his reasons, he replied with a fundamental criticism:

> Chehab wanted more equality in Lebanese society. That is the very reason why Chehabism was not seriously practised in later years, although people continued to profess it, with a certain degree of hypocrisy. Post-Chehabism offered nothing serious — a void one had the audacity to call Chehabism. But even the shadows of Chehabism were too much for some people, for political frauds, on the one hand — I mean Chamoun — and, on the other hand, for those who were afraid — I mean Gemayel. Finally, all young people were also against the regime, but for the opposite reason, because of its immobility. I opposed it because of the undemocratic practices of the Deuxième Bureau.
> 
> But Chehabism in its original form was fundamentally flawed. Fouad Chehab never tried to gain support for what he actually wanted. He never understood how to stir the country's awareness. He wanted a form of socialism without socialists and without the Left. That was absurd. All other mistakes can be traced to this. He relied too heavily on the Deuxième Bureau. He left too many people in office who had served under all previous presidents. He worked with tin hats and lackeys. He never succeeded in implementing his economic and social reforms. He wanted to scramble the eggs without breaking them. In the final analysis he was timid.

> A pity: He was a valuable man. Unfortunately, he did not trust the people. He was afraid of his own instincts. When he saw the *fromagistes* in the Place de l'Etoile[6] he would have liked to send in tanks. But he had taken the oath to the constitution, and respected it to the letter, and refused to use his powers to the full. Perhaps he was too Christian, both in mind and heart, doctrinaire and clerical at the same time, a man of the calibre of a General Pétain. Better: he wasn't really a president but an emir in the guise of a general.

This description of Chehab may or may not be accurate. But it is very instructive about Kamal Jumblatt's views on a man whose policies fundamentally altered Lebanon and, hence, about Jumblatt's view of himself. Taken positively, his criticism of Chehab is tantamount to a political programme.

The demise of Chehabism stimulated and encouraged the Lebanese Left, for two reasons. Firstly, the Chehabist state had kept them firmly under control. Secondly, its reformism had robbed more radical leftist demands for social change of their credibility. The return of the old-school politicians gave such demands new credence. Characteristic of the Left's view is the analysis by Inam Raad, president of the SSNP:

> The general reaction against the rule of the Deuxième Bureau helped us. These people formed a new sort of class. Chehabism was a specific compromise between progress and reaction that was possible given the Lebanese status quo. Its aim was greater social security, but not fundamental change. Its object was not the creation of a secular state, but to ensure that all communities got their share of the cake — to make *fromagistes* of all of them.
>
> The fog is clearing now. There's a lot of new thinking about Lebanon. People are questioning the existing political system. One sees that the poor are growing poorer and the rich richer. Inflation is hurting the poorer half of the population badly. There is a growing feeling that the Lebanese system is incapable of fulfilling its duty.
>
> Parliamentarism is discredited. There is no confidence in the regime. The deputies are called the 'ninety-nine thieves', and not only by students but by every taxi-driver. People view the country as a federation of sect-leaders, as an oligarchy. There is rising revolutionary discontent. The politicians live in different world from the people, in particular from youth. Their world is one of compromises, tricks, changes of government and intrigues. They don't

---

6 That is, in front of the parliament building.

understand what is really taking place in the economy and society. The most intelligent of the old school of politicians is Raymond Eddé. He is at least aware of what is happening. He regards it as a calamity — but we regard this development as quite normal.

In interviews in 1971 the old school of politicians were confident of coping with the difficulties. On the problems qualified school-leavers and university graduates had finding jobs, Rashid Karami said:

> Given the nature of our economy, certain problems in the labour market are unavoidable. Because we don't have any natural resources, our only option is a market economy as free and open as possible. There are still a lot of jobs waiting to be filled in the services sector, the backbone of our economy. Lebanon can become the hospital, the recreation and research centre of the entire Near East. There are many additional employment opportunities for our youth, above all the academic youth.
>
> We should also provide greater incentives for foreign capital to build up new industries in Lebanon. Our experience with foreign investment has so far been very good. We must be very careful that our fiscal policies do not cause a flight of capital.

In other words, there should not be too many social policies that would necessitate higher taxes and stringent tax collection. Regarding political structures, Karami thought limited reforms desirable and possible:

> Every political system is as good or bad as the basic structures of a people allow. The Lebanese system mirrors Lebanese society. Certain modifications are, I think, necessary, and constitutionally possible. I do not see any problem in this respect. On the whole, our system functions very well. So far, it has been able to react appropriately to all challenges. The only thing I should like to see is certain adjustments to safeguard our equilibrium.

Rashid Karami, like most establishment politicians, felt the Lebanese Left was insignificant: 'The Left shout a lot. But in elections none of them can even get elected village mayor.' Even Omar Farroukh felt that the Left did not represent a serious ideological challenge:

> Granted, the Left have won influence, but there has also been an upsurge in religious interest ... Marxism hasn't a chance among the country's Muslim intelligentsia. Marx is a great name, but only his name is known. We have nothing to gain or learn from Marxism. Marxian economic principles are

already contained in the chapters on economics in Ibn Khaldun's writings. Arab reception of Marx — what can that lead to? Quite apart from the fact that the translations are appalling. It would be more worthwhile reciting the prologue to Faust ... I have always believed that Muslim Communists see party membership as some type of shirt one changes at one's discretion. Here, Communism does not mean that one is for Moscow but that one is against Washington — it is a symbol of anti-imperialism.

Pierre Gemayel saw the matter differently:

> As in many other countries, certain groups among us stir up unrest. The struggle between Communism and the non-Communist world, especially between the two superpowers, is taking place in Lebanon, the entire Orient, and many other parts of the world. Communism stokes unrest wherever it can. Better education, jobs, social justice — who is against them? I am head of a party that has been fighting for sound social policies and social justice for decades.

He too did not think there was a serious crisis: 'It is true that we have unemployment problems — but they are no greater than in other countries, if anything less. Emigration has disadvantages, but also advantages. Lebanon has always been a country of emigration; half the population lives abroad. One should not exaggerate the problem.' Almost all the politicians interviewed anticipated 'business as usual' in domestic politics. To varying degrees they saw what they called the 'alien question' as a cause for concern:

> The demographic development of the alien population in the country is ominous. At least 300,000 Palestinians and 400,000 Syrians now live here. To these must be added numerous Kurds, refugees and migrant workers from other areas in the region. All in all, there must be about one million aliens in the country. How shall we ever get these people out of the country? The only hope I see is in a just solution to the Palestine question. Otherwise, the future for this country is very bleak.

Even this opinion of a leading Maronite treats the presence of the Palestinians only as a threat to the equilibrium of the country in the long term, and not as an immediate military danger, despite the events of 1969:

> It is absurd to spend about one-third of our budget on defence. It is perfectly plain that the defence of our country is a diplomatic, not a military problem. If Israel attacks, we shall respond — as Belgium did in 1939. We can never

withstand an Israeli invasion, whether we have an army of 5,000 or 50,000 men. But 5,000 professionally trained soldiers can cope with internal problems. We desperately need the money being poured into the army for economic development.

Rashid Karami felt the 'aliens' not only constituted no military threat, but no threat at all: 'Lebanon has always practised an open-door policy. Arabs are 'part of the family here. Lebanon benefits from their presence: they provide labour we need but do not have. I do not believe that aliens in Lebanon present a danger. We are a sovereign state and in a position to do what is necessary.' The Lebanese Left took quite a different view: 'The emergence of the Palestinian liberation Movement and their strong presence in the country has certain consequences, namely their alliance with a section of the Lebanese population. The resistance protects us against the state oppression that was everywhere before but today seems impossible.'

By 1971 the Left felt they were riding the crest of a wave. As Inam Raad put it: 'Wherever possible we prefer to avoid armed clashes. We believe that the real struggle is ideological — and we believe we can win it.' His statement reveals that he did not exclude armed clashes. Kamal Jumblatt, for his part, saw his prospects improving:

> Helou's presidency was six precious years wasted. Most of our politicians have lost all touch with reality. Policies of regional and social development have never been seriously pursued. A sober analysis of our economic and employment situation shows that industrialization alone can save us. The state must take action to avert an explosion. The lack of state intervention, the lack of serious social and economic policies, will very soon throw the country into a very serious crisis.
>
> Most members of the political class live only in the present, if not in the past. They have no vision of the future. Time is on our side. The industrial workforce is growing. In twenty years it will be impossible to govern against them. What I find encouraging is the growing support we have among a section of the Christian clergy. Today the Christian Left is a body to be reckoned with. Unfortunately, the Muslim clergy has nothing similar; progressive ulema are rare 'birds' in the Lebanese sky. But socialist ideas are spreading. Had we a different electoral system, there would be at least thirty socialist deputies in parliament.

The time when one could take very small steps is passed. We need a secular state and a start to socialism. I wonder whether it is not already too late for a policy of gradual reform. Social strains will worsen, and those responsible will remain incapable of treating the causes. Asked whether he thought peaceful change was possible under these circumstances, Kamal Jumblatt hesitated and then replied with a wry smile: 'I don't know.' Four years later everyone knew. The Chehabist experiment of giving the state a lion-like aspect, in Pareto's sense, failed in the late 1960s. Victory for the foxes came in 1970. They were convinced they could continue to buy peace, at the very time the lions were beginning to bare their fangs. In 1975, various prides of lion began to tear one another apart.

## Perceptions of the causes of war

Only one of the leading players in the armed conflict in Lebanon claimed with pride to have unleashed what he regarded as a revolution, but which turned out to be a many-sided war: Kamal Jumblatt. Regrettably, the author of this study was unable to interview him after the outbreak of hostilities: Jumblatt was assassinated on March 16th, 1977. Matthias Claudius puts the replies of the politicians and militia commanders interviewed in a nutshell: 'Tis war, so help us, and I want only not to bear the guilt.' The assignment of guilt is extremely complex and, as might be expected, views diverge considerably.

The traditional Lebanese politicians do not, as a rule, deny that domestic problems enabled war in the first place and facilitated its outbreak, but generally give greater weight to non-Lebanese factors. Typical of this view is the statement of Takieddine Solh, a former prime minister:

> Internal factors are, on the one hand, the Christians' feeling of fear and, on the other hand, the Muslims' feeling of inequality. The existence of these feelings in Lebanon helped to turn Lebanon into a field for others' battles.
>
> On the whole, we lived together well in Lebanon. Granted, there was a lot that was not in order. We had social problems, like other countries. Our civil service was certainly not in a position to carry out all their duties; nor is it any secret that there was corruption. But social tensions and corruption cannot explain the conflict. They were exploited. But our qualities were exploited as well: our freedom, our prosperity and our progress. Anyone could enter Lebanon. Our economy attracted a lot of labour from neighbouring countries. Many intellectuals came because they were not allowed to write or speak at home. Lebanon had to pay for its mistakes as well as for its qualities.
>
> The Palestinian factor was very important. In 1948, 6,000 refugees were living here; at the outbreak of war there were between 400,000 and 600,000 — nobody knows exactly how many, probably in the region of half a million. Their numbers increased dramatically after the massacres in

Amman in 1970. At that time they left Jordan for the nicest and freest country, for Lebanon. This freedom annoyed many governments — because here people could say and write things about these countries that they couldn't within their borders. In the case of the Palestinians, however, it was not only a matter of their numbers and the freedom they enjoyed here, but of the complete qualitative change within the Palestinian people. A qualitative revolution had taken place within the refugee camps. Previously they had been poor and badly paid. Two gendarmes were enough to control 15,000 to 20,000 of them. Fear bred subservience. Now, however, the Palestinians have recovered their personality. They have become proud and free, but they have also armed themselves. Aliens — worse: armed aliens who allow themselves certain liberties, and go beyond accepted limits — aliens who show no respect for the law must come into conflict with the inhabitants of the country. Of course the Palestinians are our brothers, but even among brothers such behaviour causes conflicts.

What was the ultimate cause of the conflict, the problems among the Lebanese themselves, or between the Palestinians and the Lebanese? I am convinced that the Lebanese would have been able to solve their own problems without resorting to arms. There would have been the normal economic or political conflicts, but they would never had led to war. No, in the absence of the Palestinians this war would never have started. However, the domestic Lebanese problems created an climate favourable to the outbreak of war.

In Solh's opinion, the Christian sense of fear was rooted in demographic considerations: 'The reason is the fact that Muslims produce more children, and they do this because the Muslim parts of the country are the underdeveloped regions, and throughout the world such regions produce more children. The demographic ratio would have shifted even without the Palestinians. Everyone here feared a new census. We preferred to overlook and forget demographic realities.' That is, according to Solh, until social inequalities between the communities caused the Muslims to reconsider:

> Christian society is more advanced than Muslim in almost all spheres, even though the Muslims have been catching up. This is chiefly because the Muslims took far longer than the Christians to open themselves to western civilization ... When some Muslims now accuse the Christians of enriching themselves at the expense of Muslims and exploiting them, that is false. The Christians gained their lead in the time of the Turks, through their own work and efforts. To my mind, the Christians made a mistake later. After independence they neglected to develop the Muslim regions. President

Chehab realized this and tried to institute development policies for Muslim regions. He knew that social inequalities could imperil Lebanon.

Another prominent Sunni, Mohammed Shukair, stressed that it was the weakness of the Lebanese state that had enabled foreign intervention, and held both Christians and Muslims responsible:

> The Christians wanted to retain all positions of power, regardless: the presidency, the army command, military intelligence, etc. They did nothing to dispel Muslims' feelings that they were second-class citizens, rightly or wrongly. The Christians neglected to win over the Muslims to Lebanon's cause. ... The Muslims, on the other hand, neglected to let the Christians feel they were not a minority, that they were recognized and their lives secure, and that, in all events, they would not be overruled by a majority. So Lebanon remained a weak state. And because it was weak, it served any outside interest as an arena. Switzerland is also affected by outside influences. Why do they have so little effect? Because the Swiss are united and therefore strong.

Another influential Sunni regarded Palestinian policies as the most important cause of the war: 'After the events in Jordan in 1970 the Palestinians believed they had learnt a lesson: they involved themselves in Lebanese politics. It seemed sensible to them to support ideological parties so as to use them as a protective shield. These parties, in turn, were extremely interested in Palestinian support; they became totally dependent on them.' He too stressed that the Lebanese were partly to blame:

> The Muslim bourgeoisie, stupid as they are, continued playing their old confessional games, while the Palestinians were undermining their standing among the Muslim masses. But the Christians were just as shortsighted. How could they ruin the Chehabist reform policies, the appropriate way to put Lebanon to rights? Chehabism certainly did have its dark side, above all the constant manipulation by military intelligence. However, it was not only the Deuxième Bureau that was smashed, but Chehabism in its entirety. And it was replaced not by the liberalism of a Raymond Eddé but by the feudalism of a Suleiman Franjieh ... Granted, it was right to resist the drift towards a police state. But not to help a real gangster to power. What we needed was a liberally- and socially-minded regime. Sarkis was elected six years later: they called the doctor after the patient had died.

Shi'i politicians emphasize Palestinian responsibility for the war. In the opinion of Adel Usayran, long-serving speaker of the Chamber of Deputies, Israel was the cause of the problems in general, but the Palestinians were the cause of the war in Lebanon in particular. 'They believed they could turn Lebanon into their own state, dominate and govern it. Their objective in turning Lebanon into their own state was to use it to regain Palestine. That was their dream. For us it was a nightmare.'

For a former minister, Ibrahim Cheito, the causes of the war were exclusively external: 'We had many domestic crises in the past — but nothing like what has happened in recent years. The Lebanese didn't light the fire that is still burning in Lebanon. Left to themselves, the Lebanese would have been reconciled long ago.'

The analyses of the Christian notables differ little from those of their Muslim colleagues. In the words of a Maronite deputy: 'The war was not caused by internal factors. There are internal conflicts. The Muslims speak of Maronite privileges — but that was not a cause for war. There is social injustice — but it has never been extreme enough to cause an explosion. The failings of the social and political system cannot explain what has happened.'

The Greek Catholic former minister, Henri Pharaon, one of the architects of the National Pact, was aware that the Christians had made some grave mistakes:

> Unfortunately, the Maronites failed to adopt wise policies that would have given the Muslims a greater interest in an independent Lebanon. Terrible, how they grabbed everything for themselves, not only the presidency and the army command, but also the supreme court, the audit office, the chairmanship of this and that institution, though they were not remotely involved with the security of the Christians. Had they given some of the positions to the Shi'is, things would be quite different.

Yet:

> In spite of all mistakes — not only those of the Maronites — the causes of the war are predominantly non-domestic. Our formula could deal with Lebanese problems — but we could not cope with the Palestine question. Suddenly we were faced with a huge foreign population in the country that had been expelled from its country by people who, in turn, had been victims of Nazi Germany. This would have created problems for any country — even countries larger and more powerful than Lebanon.

The deputy Fouad Tehini, a member of Jumblatt's parliamentary faction, regarded the presence of armed Palestinians as an important cause of the crisis.

Unemployment swelled the ranks of the militias, and disunity had attenuated the state. But the crucial cause of the war was:

> The Americans' intention to end the Middle Eastern conflict by any means whatsoever. It served their purpose to uphold and freeze the *de facto* Palestinian occupation of part of Lebanon. They saw permanent Palestinian settlement in Lebanon as a card in the Middle Eastern poker game: Israel keeps the south, Syria the Bekaa — and between Beirut and Sidon there's plenty of space for Palestinians. I'm convinced they're still thinking along these lines.

Musa de Freije, deputy for the Latin minority, suspects as much: 'The cause of the war is without doubt the Kissinger Plan: the settlement of Palestinians in Lebanon. This plan is the scandal of the century. The Americans first wronged the Palestinians in 1948, and now they're doing the same to the Lebanese.' Leading Lebanese politicians were also convinced that such a plan existed. The first to mention it was Raymond Eddé:

> To my mind, Henry Kissinger must take the blame for Lebanon's fate. I have absolutely no doubt: after Chile and Cambodia, Lebanon is Kissinger's third victim ... In Moscow I once met an American journalist who was neither particularly intelligent nor had ever been to Lebanon. I was all the more surprised when he told me — in great detail — of a plan he had heard to settle the Palestine question. He mentioned the analogy of Cyprus. Lebanon was to be partitioned along the Damascus highway, as in 1842. There would be a small Christian and a Muslim Lebanon; the Palestinians would be settled in the latter. I am not in a position to mention the journalist's name. At any rate, everything I have learnt since completely fits the thrust of this plan.

Former president Franjieh is even convinced that:

> The American Plan consists of arranging for all Christian Lebanese to emigrate and Palestinians to replace them. What proof do I have? An American envoy approached me and offered American ships for the evacuation of the Christians. The necessary transport capacity could be available within forty-eight hours. This envoy came to me three times in the space of a month — twice to ask me how long we could continue to resist. Fortunately for us, the plan came to nothing.

Saeb Salam, the former prime minister, spoke of an international conspiracy in a somewhat different context.

> I do not wish to excuse us. Our democracy was extraordinarily free, indeed, almost chaotic. It had many weaknesses, a great many. But what followed was not our fault but the consequence of an international conspiracy. Certain Arab countries wanted to settle their power struggles. And Israel sought out the weakest link in the Arab chain for its attacks, and that was us. The immediate reason for the war was the Palestinian presence in our country. It gave Israel the pretext to attack us. Without Israel and without the USA's shortsighted support for Israel it would never have reached this stage.

Fouad Boutros, for many years foreign minister under President Sarkis, is sceptical about such explanations:

> I do not believe the innumerable conspiracy theories. They are all too complicated to be true. National and international conditions are so complicated as it is, who can anticipate developments six months in advance, let alone plan them? The major powers act in accordance with their shifting interests. And the Lebanese debacle suits the interests of many powers. Put yourself in the shoes of the Americans. If one sees the possibility of solving the Middle East problem at the expense of the Lebanese, why should one, as an American, not make the attempt if the Lebanese themselves abet it? All politics has a streak of cynicism. Who cares about the Lebanese if there is the chance of settling at their expense something regarded as more important than Lebanon? Whether the respective calculations are correct or not is another matter. For instance, few expected that the Christians would, driven by fear, put up such desperate resistance. And if the calculations prove wrong the reaction is to reassess the situation, not to change one's interests.

A Greek Catholic notable stressed the inability of the Lebanese system to cope with external challenges:

> Lebanon always enjoyed peace and moderate prosperity in the absence of heavy outside pressure. Peaceful coexistence between the communities was never an easy matter, but was only endangered when foreign powers exploited Lebanese pluralism in order to divide and rule. When none of these powers predominated, Lebanon faced difficult times — as now. When hostile powers sought allies among the various communities in the country, to support them and use them as supports, Lebanon always threatened to

break apart. Today rival powers again have an interest in destroying our peaceful coexistence.

Because most Lebanese — Christians and Muslims — desire peaceful coexistence, they have grown accustomed to ignoring unpleasant and difficult questions whenever possible. Lebanese think one thing, say another and do yet another in the interests of coexistence. Lebanese politics used to be like a solid middle-class marriage: 'deception within bounds'. And like a solid middle-class marriage, Lebanese coexistence proved a great survivor — so long as outside pressure was not too heavy.

The explanations of the causes of the war given by the traditional political class reveal the qualities and weaknesses of these foxes. The foxes are too intelligent to present monocausal explanations. They present themselves as moderate, self-critical and open about socio-political omissions, albeit with understatement. There are no fundamental differences between the analyses of Muslim and Christian notables. The rules of the game are respected. Even when blame is apportioned one-sidedly, it is done so in moderation and in words of tolerance and understanding — as in a solid middle-class marriage. Even the attraction of conspiracy theories is functional in terms of the traditional system of conflict regulation: the further away the blame for the war can be shifted, the easier it is to compromise anew.

The language and the contents of statements by representatives of the fighting organizations and movements differ enormously from the above. The spokesman for the Mourabitoun, Ziad el-Hafez, spoke of the 'many causes of the Lebanese war', but in fact put the blame chiefly on the 'isolationists', i.e., the militant Christian organizations:

> The isolationists want to sever the ties between Lebanon and the Arab world. They only see the Arab world as a market and the Arabs as casino-goers. They want a Lebanon that is a homeland for Maronites. We regard them as fascists who collaborate with Israel. They don't want to partition Lebanon, they just want to dominate it. They speak of partition only to blackmail others ... The extremists among them think in terms of a population exchange: drive out Muslims, bring in Christian emigrants from other Arab countries. What most of them want may be less radical, but nevertheless a real danger: by driving out Muslims they have created their own enclave as a power base to dominate all Lebanon. The gulf between them and us is deepest over the question of identity. We are Arabs, they don't want to be Arabs. It's hard to imagine a compromise ... In any case, we want to prevent the victory of the isolationists, and we want to conquer them.

The Sunni Deputy-Mufti, later assassinated, was hardly less militant: 'The causes of the war were: first, the attempt of the Maronites to isolate Lebanon from its Arab environment; second, their intention to destroy the Palestinian movement — the Maronites still believe that the Palestinians are the army of the Muslims and perhaps they are not so wrong ...; third, the preservation of Maronite privileges at all costs.'

Amal's leaders saw other causes. The former chairman and later Speaker of the Chamber of Deputies, Hussein Husseini, apportioned the blame severally:

> In 1975 the left-wing parties wanted to do political business with the Palestinians' military power. The Palestinians let themselves be dragged in. But the Maronites are also to blame; after all, they signed the Cairo Agreement. Once the fighting had started, all of them were to blame for its continuance. Horrible things have happened. People of the National Movement, Palestinians and the militias of the Lebanese Front have committed identity-card murders. Amal has always refused to have anything to do with these things.

Husseini's successor, Nabih Berri, accused the Palestinians of 'having created a state within the state and fought harder to control Lebanese territory than to liberate their own country'. But blame for the war must also be shared by those 'who clung to confessional privileges and stopped Lebanon developing into a true democracy — a democracy like everywhere else in the world, where the majority decides'. One of his associates was very bitter about the Palestinians:

> Today no one is more disappointed with the Palestinians than the Shi`is. The Deuxième Bureau first acted against the Fedayeen in 1964. At that time we demonstrated for them against our own army. The people we defended then are now against us; for years they oppressed us and killed many of us. As people we can't understand that at all. The Palestinian soul is twisted — that is the worst thing Israel has done to them. The Palestinians only respect and honour power. They beat those who embrace them. If you beat them, they embrace you. They want substitute enemies more than a substitute fatherland. They found them first in the Christians and now they have us. This is what has made the Shi`is so bitter. Today we are far more anti-Palestinian than the Christians were before.

The SSNP saw the Lebanese war primarily as part of the Israel's overall war against the Arabs. As Inam Raad explained:

> Israel wants to divide the entire region into ethno-religious states — then Israel would not be an exception and a foreign body. Israel wants to prevent

the emergence of a united nation to its east, and to do this it is far easier to utilize the social boundaries of confessionalism than the artificial state boundaries of the mandate powers. That is the pax Israelica. What has happened in Lebanon is a consequence of this Israeli policy. The concept of the isolationist wing of political Maronitism is the local component of this Israeli policy. The war started with the run-up to Camp David; once peace had been made with Egypt, peace was to be forced on Lebanon.

By contrast, the two Communist parties argue for predominantly domestic causes of the war. Albert Farhat, member of the central committee of the Lebanese Communist Party explained:

> We believe that the social and economic crisis motivated the Lebanese financial oligarchy to choose fascism as a solution to the crisis ... In the past this financial oligarchy was able to stay in power with the support of an equilibrium that has since collapsed. It was based on the subjection of the petty bourgeoisie and the middle class by the oligarchy — an ideological and political subjection ... The working masses had lost patience before the war. Farmers, teachers and students, workers and civil servants participated in the social struggle, above all the Lebanese working class. The oligarchy saw a great danger in this ... At the level of the masses, the members of the different religious communities were drawing closer together, the confessional distinctions were beginning to disappear at this level ... In Lebanon the oligarchy has always used confessionalism to divide the workers. The Lebanese CP does not agree with the concept of the 'class-community'. Class privileges do exist, which have a confessional character. But there are clear social distinctions within the communities. The Christian masses in the mountains in particular certainly belong to the poorer strata; it was impossible to overlook their impoverishment as a result of the breakthrough of modern capitalism in the agricultural sector. The social struggle helped us to unite the Lebanese masses of all communities. The Lebanese bourgeoisie as a class was not in a position to create genuine parties. They had delegated political power to political feudalism. The oligarchy had complete control over the bourgeoisie. Because the oligarchy was not interested in developing the national economy — they were happy with their lucrative role as intermediaries of international capitalism — it was impossible to institute reforms and social change. Hence, faced with the threat of the masses, the financial oligarchy turned to fascism.

However, the CP also recognized international factors that contributed to the war:

There was an American plan to settle the Middle East problem. To achieve it, it was necessary to break the Palestinian resistance, whose last bastion was in Lebanon. Only in Lebanon did the resistance movement have freedom of political expression, free of the pressure of an Arab regime ... The imperialists, both the Zionists and the Lebanese reactionaries, wished to transform Lebanon into a Zionist type of state and to weaken Syria through Lebanon, so as to include it in the Camp David settlement.

In contrast to the CP, the Organization for Communist Action in Lebanon (OCAL) saw a closer relationship between economic and confessional discrimination. Fawaz Traboulsi regarded 'fascism in Lebanon as a means of preserving confessional privileges':

In respect of education, access to the civil service and political representation Muslims, like non-Maronite Christians, are at a disadvantage. The confessional system itself was a source of conflict. But Lebanon was modernizing rapidly. 'Primitive capitalism' was creating dramatic problems, and confessionalism blocked any possible solution. The country was on the verge of a democratic revolution; the Left was growing fast. On the other hand, Lebanese fascism was developing rapidly. A large number of people with petty privileges were in trouble because of the economic crisis. It was easy to distract their attention from the real causes of the crisis. Fascism made ideological use of the historical links between Islam and underdevelopment and between Christians — especially Maronites — and capitalism. The fascists took up arms.

In their struggle against fascism as it understood it, the OCAL were 'encouraged by the presence of the Palestinians. The Palestinian resistance movement became the catalyst of the crisis. The question of what attitude to adopt towards it accelerated the outburst of inner contradictions and tensions.' The differences and contradictions between what broadly allied organizations see as the causes of the war are astonishing. With little in common beyond the conviction of having been attacked, they could have been fighting different wars.

Very different groups and factions among the militant Lebanese Christians also felt they had been attacked. The commander of the Guardians of the Cedar, Abu Arz, the *nom de guerre* of Major Etienne Saqr, put his view as follows:

We fought against Palestinians and Syrians. Where? In Palestine or in Damascus? We fought here, we defended our wives and children, our houses and districts. In 1975, Palestinians accounted for one-sixth of the country's population. If there were 11 million Algerians in France, and if these

Algerians occupied parts of the country and erected road-blocks, if they arrested or abducted Frenchmen, if they created a state within the state, what would the French do then?

Antoine Moarbes, of Kata'ib's politburo, also saw the Lebanese in general and the Christians in particular as victims:

> What we are dealing with is an attempt by a foreign group to seize power in our country. This country has never done anything to anyone; again and again it has welcomed refugees and persecuted. Now refugees are trying to take control of the country and plunge Lebanon into war. The Lebanese state was too weak to resist, so we have to do it.

Another member of the politburo felt:

> The Palestinians are the real cause of the war. Since 1969 they have tried to establish the type of regime they want under their influence. The state could not deal with this because Muslim leaders did not dare undertake anything against the Palestinians. They lost their influence over the Sunni 'street' and then raised more radical demands to try to regain support. And look there, none of the Lebanese Muslims, established notables and new militia commanders, had anything to say. The Palestinians controlled everything.

Many Christian leaders also felt that, apart from the Palestinians, Syria was responsible for the outbreak of war:

> Syria has systematically fuelled the crisis in Lebanon. What took place in Akkar, in the Bekaa, in Jezzine, was all fomented by Syria to provoke pleas for help. Syria is brilliant at bluffing the outside world and presenting itself as the guardian of order. It has bluffed the Western states and even, for a short time, the Lebanese Christians. Initially we were deceived — the Palestinians grasped the fact much earlier that for Syria they were just a negotiable position in future peace negotiations. Syria wants to be a political force in Lebanon, wants to dominate both the Palestinians and the Lebanese.

Ibrahim Najjar, also of Kata'ib's politburo, came to a similar conclusion:

> There is any number of interpretations of the causes of the war: Christians against Muslims, rich against poor, Christians against Palestinians, Israeli collaborators against true Arabs, Palestinians against Shi`is, Syrians against Sunnis. Each of them contains a grain of truth. And all have only one common denominator: they all fit the Syrian concept of 'divide and rule'.

> One thing is evident: each time the situation quietens down, Syria fans the flames again.

But Najjar also put part of the blame on the Lebanese:

> Syrian policies were facilitated by the utter lack of any [Lebanese] social policy and clear social perspectives. The social question did not cause the war, but without the social question there never would have been a war. If you have a lot of unemployed, and then give each 500 US dollars and a Kalashnikov, you get war.
>
> But the Syrian factor triggered off the war: in 1975 all the Palestinians entered Lebanon, from the Saiqa to the PLA. Whence did they come? Which frontier did they cross? Where did the weapons come from?

One of the 'four wise men' of the Lebanese Front, Charles Malek, a philosophy professor and former foreign minister, felt that external factors alone caused the war:

> The three most important causes are: first, the presence of armed Palestinians — without them there would not have been a war; second, Syria's ambitions, and the collaboration between Syria and the Palestinians; third, the intention of certain Arab states, especially Libya, to destroy Lebanon.
>
> What motivated the Palestinians? Fear of a repetition of the events in Jordan might have played a role, but this fear is — consciously or unconsciously — a way of saving face. The crucial factor is another. I am convinced that not one Palestinian leader still seriously believes that they will ever return to Palestine. Rather, they now believe that Lebanon will make a suitable Palestinian country. In short: they want to take over this country. What do the Palestinians want? Do they want a secular and democratic state? They have no notion of a secular state; they only know that this demand sounds good to Western ears. Have they read the Old Testament; do they know what Jerusalem means to the Jews, what power this millennial dream has exercised? No, for otherwise they would not be spouting this nonsense about a secular state. Does any other Arab state want the Palestinians? No. They either keep them under strict surveillance or throw them out. Only stupid Lebanon allowed itself to be overwhelmed by the Palestinians.
>
> It is quite simple. Half a million people have entered this country. They are armed to the teeth. They are swimming in money provided by the terrified oil states. They know they have nowhere else to go. What is the conclusion? Does it really require great effort and western rationality to draw it?

The conclusion is: 'The Palestinians want to turn this country into their own.'

Another leading member of the Lebanese Front, the head of the Order of Maronite Monks, Boulos Naaman, saw in the Palestinians and Syrians only the current manifestation of a far more fundamental threat to the Christians:

> The Islamic claim to ascendancy is the underlying cause of the Lebanese crisis. This claim is repeated whenever an opportunity of fulfilling it presents itself. The National Pact of 1943 collapsed for this reason. Islam is a system with totalitarian demands on all aspects of society, as Iran has demonstrated to a global public for the first time. If there is any provision for people of a different faith, then it is only in a subordinate position. Islam is not backward compared to Christianity, as many believe. It is simply different; its character prevents it changing. An Islam that accepted a secular society would no longer be Islam.

The former leader of Tanzim, Fouad Chemali, went beyond purely political or ideological interpretations of the causes of the war:

> It does not help much accusing the Palestinians, the Syrians, the Left, Islam. They are to blame for the war. But the existence of poverty in Lebanon, which made the war possible — that is primarily our responsibility. Let us not deceive ourselves: the social basis for war existed in Lebanon. Social problems did not lead to war. But deficiencies in social policies had left Lebanon extremely weak, and fertile ground for subversion. Our enemies have exploited poverty and confessionalism. But we allowed them to find something to exploit. Poverty is prevalent in the peripheral areas of Lebanon, among both Christians and Muslims. Our political leaders and our bishops are reluctant to admit it. For should they admit it, they would lay themselves open to criticism. What distinguishes the village of Qaa from the neighbouring villages, and Deir al-Ahmar from Hermel? Perhaps a few more Christians can speak French, perhaps they are economically a little better off. But none of these villages can market their goods properly, and therefore they have remained poor.

Bashir Gemayel also saw the social question as more than a cause of war:

> Yes, there were enormous social and economic problems. For years they were criminally neglected. Perhaps better social policies might have prevented war: I don't know. On the one hand, it would not have been so

easy for the Palestinians to find Lebanese cannon-fodder. On the other hand, they had enough of their own. They also caused a war in Jordan, though there was no talk of social problems in Jordan. Here the poor have been fighting against the poor, not the poor against the rich; the rich are sitting on the Côte d'Azur. But those who have fought for Lebanon will never again tolerate policies, or better: a lack of policies, that neglect the mass of the population, regardless of community.

All in all, the differences in the statements of the various militant Christian representatives are minor: all feel they are victims of Palestinian and Syrian threat and aggression, and that the West does not understand them. They differ in the importance they attach to the social question. Even those who stress its significance do not see in it the major cause of war, but a lost opportunity to reduce the likelihood of war. What did the leaders of the Palestinians regard as the causes of war? Abu Iyad (Salah Khalaf), Arafat's deputy for PLO policies in Lebanon, had no doubts:

> We did not attack, we were attacked. We were targets. We had no choice, we had to defend ourselves ... The Israelis believed they had found a wonder drug to fight us. As long as we have to fight in Lebanon we can't concentrate on Israel.
>
> It was easy for them to manipulate things. There have always been conflicts in Lebanon. We Palestinians have been here only since 1969; there were conflicts before then: in 1860 the Maronites fought against the Druze, and in 1958 there was civil war — we had nothing to do with any of that.
>
> In 1975 the domestic situation in Lebanon was explosive. The Lebanese formula of 1943, confessionalism, aggravated the conflicts. The Christians were anti-Arab, and the Muslims pro-Arab. There were also social conflicts. There were rich Sunnis and rich Maronites, very few rich Shi`is. Most Shi`is are poor and underprivileged — like most of the working class in all communities. Then there were international factors: the signatories of the Sinai Agreement had an interest in our involvement in a conflict here.
>
> In reality, one section of the Lebanese made war on us. One side started the war. For us Palestinians it was a defensive war in which our existence was at stake. But we were not alone. The poor masses of Lebanon helped us, as did the progressive parties ... The poor were led by Kamal Jumblatt.
>
> The war revealed a lot of things that were hidden before. The sordid nature of confessionalism was revealed, and the social tensions.

Mahmoud Labadi, official spokesman for the PLO until the Abu Musa faction broke away, elaborated:

> Four or five families started the war. A strange war: the rich attacked the poor. To mobilize enough people they used religion. They wanted to imitate the Jordanians, and throw the Palestinians out of the country. They did not reckon with the impoverished masses joining us.
>
> We were very restrained until December 1975. We let the Lebanese do our fighting for us. That was our tactic. We knew very well that we were the rightists' real target, but we wanted it to look like an internal Lebanese war for as long as possible. We only intervened directly when our camps were attacked ... The Lebanese Right embarked on a 'game of nations', and bit off more than they could chew.

A PLO diplomat underlined the importance of the fear factor:

> We were afraid — especially after the clashes with the Lebanese Army, when even the air force attacked our camps — that they were preparing the same fate for us in Lebanon as in Jordan. Pierre Gemayel was continuously making speeches that could be interpreted in this way. This fear was very real. 'Lebanization' after 'Jordanization' could have finished the resistance movement for years. We could not let that happen.
>
> From the start I saw this conflict as bad for both sides. The Palestinians were not interested in fighting a war in Lebanon. And the Lebanese Christians, what could they gain? Consciously or unconsciously, they have turned themselves into tools of the Israelis.

But he did not blame the war only on the Christian parties: 'From the start Syria has played a very dubious role. Saiqa has provoked both sides; it is largely responsible that the fighting is between the confessions.' Issam Sartawi, Arafat's adviser until he was murdered, thought the war was a result of two distinct conflicts that coincided, but could easily have erupted separately:

> [It was] an internal Lebanese and a Lebanese-Palestinian confrontation. Before the war, Lebanon had an anachronistic political system: theocracy and feudalism mingled in the cloak of European democracy. This polity was already endangered in itself, even without the presence of Palestinians. The Lebanese establishment had long sought to use 'outside threats' to conceal internal Lebanese contradictions and stabilize the situation. However, to acute observers, it was only a question of time before Lebanon blew up of its own accord. The Maronites' monopoly of power was one factor, social injustice another. The Palestinian presence simply caused these contradictions to emerge earlier than they otherwise would have.

As far as the Palestinians were concerned, they had no alternative to Lebanon:

> Jordan was naturally our first choice. Demography and geography spoke for it: the majority of the population are Palestinians, and its border with Israel is the longest between an Arab territory and Israel. Contacts with the West Bank were very close. We were able to develop rapidly because the Jordanian Army of 1967 had been thoroughly defeated. But then we lost the war with the Jordanians, politically and militarily. There's no question about that. After that, Lebanon was our only option for an independent base. Syria under its pseudo-progressive regime would never have allowed us to achieve what we did in Lebanon. Our view is that we have the right to run an independent base in any Arab country, and to use it for our struggle against Israel. We claimed this right where we had the opportunity: in Lebanon.
>
> We didn't want the war in Lebanon. Basically, in 1975 we wanted no more than we'd already achieved there. That we got involved in a war there was due to factors beyond Lebanon ... Basically, the Syrians don't want the Palestinians to be politically independent. And they haven't given up hope of turning the Palestinians into their political instrument. Nor have they given up hope of establishing permanent influence in Lebanon. Incidentally, from their point of view they'd be mad not to try, for basically they don't want an independent Palestine or an independent Lebanon.
>
> The Israelis wanted something different in Lebanon. In the 1950s Abba Eban developed a concept for Israel's future within the general context of the Near East. It was a typical intellectual solution — one can read it in his collected speeches. His idea was to give Israel an equal place in the region by Balkanizing the region along religious lines. Lebanon was the best laboratory for this concept.

Hassan Dudin, member of the PLO's Press and Information Section, placed even greater emphasis on Syrian policy as a crucial cause of war:

> Only one thing really counts: the Syrians wanted to intervene here and they did everything they could to bring about intervention. As early as 1975, Saiqa were isolating and shooting up Christian villages in the north of the Bekaa, until they turned to Assad with pleas for help against 'the Palestinians'. When there was a lull along the Beirut fronts, Saiqa fired on us and the Phalangists, and sometimes on both at the same time. The Syrians want to control us, and the Lebanese too — and to do that they needed the war.

A representative of the Iraqi-sponsored Arab Liberation Front expressed the same conviction in more guarded terms: 'Foreign powers with specific interests in the region as a whole have undoubtedly exploited and aggravated the confessional and social divisions in Lebanon. Above all, the Palestinian movement has been used for purposes that are not their own, and run counter to their true interests.'

The Analysis of the Popular Front for the Liberation of Palestine of the causes of the war was similar to that of the Lebanese CP and OCAL: 'The Palestinian presence in Lebanon is not at all the factor which caused the Lebanese explosion. Our position in the Lebanese war is simply a consequence of the alliance with the Lebanese National Movement and our contribution within the Arab liberation movement in the first place.' Instead, it saw the Lebanese crisis as a cumulative consequence of developments since the time of the mandate: 'Constitutionally entrenched confessionalism strengthened feudal interests and the traditional political elite and enabled them to exploit the country. This led to the emergence of a capitalist class that can't be defined in confessional terms at all. Lebanese monopoly capitalism is a part of imperialistic capitalism. The comprador bourgeoisie ruled the country.'

One-sided concentration on the service sector made it easier for this class to dominate, but also generated its crisis: because of its dependence the capitalistic system in Lebanon was hit particularly hard by the worldwide crisis of capitalism:

> The regime could no longer count on the loyalty of the masses. This was made particularly clear by the frequent use of the army in social conflicts, whereas this same army was not prepared to defend the country against external attacks ...
>
> The masses in Lebanon, however, saw the Palestinians as allies. When the Palestinians were attacked, the mass of the people supported the Palestinian resistance movement, especially in the great revolt in April 1975. For the first time the Palestinian resistance movement gave the Lebanese masses the chance to support patriotic parties fighting for social and economic reforms ... We believe our relationship with Lebanon is based on the existence of a vital community of destiny, a common bond against the enemy. Lebanon is the base we can attack the enemy from. It was the Lebanese masses who forced the ruling class to sign the Cairo Agreement. From 1969 to 1973 the ruling class tried to crush the Palestinian resistance ... When the army was unable to carry out its task ... the ruling class began to look for support among the reactionary reserve of fascist confessionalists.

But it also identified external reasons for the war:

> The Arab reactionaries made efforts to control the region in the interests of international imperialism. The Arab reactionaries demanded that the

Lebanese reactionaries eliminate the revolutionary movement in the country. Lebanon was chosen for this experiment because the Palestinian resistance, the vanguard of the whole Arab revolution, had its centre here; a secondary objective was to destroy the Lebanese National Movement. It was part of the attempt to find a political solution for the Palestine problem. Imperialism believed it could not achieve the political solution it wanted on its own conditions without first destroying the Palestinian resistance movement and ensuring the victory of the reactionaries.

The Democratic Front emphasized other points:

> The internal tensions in Lebanon were not insignificant. Progressive forces were attracting support not least from Christians: almost all the leaders of the National Movement — with the exception of the Mourabitoun — were Christian. A class consciousness was starting to emerge ... Even without the Palestinians, Lebanon would sooner or later have collapsed under its own contradictions. To preserve their privileges the conservatives unleashed the civil war. But for a country as small as Lebanon external factors were decisive for the outbreak of war. The USA and Israel tried to weaken and annihilate the PLO, to place Syria in a difficult position and to support Sadat. The Lebanon war was started as a sort of red herring that would make the Israeli-Egyptian rapprochement easier. The Lebanon conflict was to keep the PLO and the Arab countries in suspense, while Sadat pursued his objectives in peace. The aims of the Lebanese conservatives coincided with those of the Americans and Israelis: smash the Palestinian resistance and help Sadat.

The perceptions of all organizations, parties and movements that have been party to the armed conflict differ considerably from the perceptions of civilian Lebanese politicians of the old school. The attempt to justify their actions is far more pronounced. All have fought, yet, as they see it, only in reaction to others' aggression: the lions choose to present themselves as tame animals that flex their muscles only when forced to do so. All the foxes avoid ascribing to Syria any role in the outbreak of war: they know that their only future role lies in a mutually acceptable, negotiated peace agreement, and that such a regulation is virtually inconceivable without Syria's consent — it would be rash to brand someone an arsonist who may be needed as a fireman later. And not only the foxes: this topic is too hot even for the smaller lions; Syria is, after all, a much bigger lion. Only the representatives of Fatah and of the militant Christian organizations hold Syria co-responsible for the outbreak or prolongation of the war: they are in open conflict with Syria anyway. They blame each another for the war, yet agree that not only were they the principal resistance to Syrian hegemonic aspirations, but also the objects of these aspirations. Only the small organizations of the Lebanese and Palestinian Left genuinely believe that social conflicts were the prime cause of war; most other parties treat the social question as a factor that enabled, even facilitated, but did not cause the war.

The spokesman for Amal — a leading belligerent since the early 1980s, but free of any blame for the outbreak of war — puts the blame on all the others: the parties of the Left, the Palestinians and the Maronites, but not, of course, the Syrian allies. In short: even lions practise the art of foxes when bigger lions are about.

It is striking that, without exception, civilian politicians and representatives of the belligerents placed responsibility for the war only on groups, organizations, communities or states, and never mentioned a single person — with one exception: Henry Kissinger, whose name is synonymous with the theory of a 'plot' against Lebanon. This probably has little to do with the tendency of modern historiography to prefer socio-historical explanations to the role of individuals: in the Levant the perception of politics is, as a rule, eminently personalized. The lack of personal accusations should rather be taken as a reflection of the fact that most of the respondents were very much aware of an individual's limited scope to affect the course of complex events — as a way of concealing embarrassment at having to concede the limits to personal influence and personal power.

Informed and influential respondents only indirectly involved in decision-making of various conflicting parties mention the role of personality more often, though most prefer to remain anonymous themselves. Only one name is mentioned in these explanations: Kamal Jumblatt, probably the most influential of all individuals directly involved in the events leading to war, and also the most difficult to understand. Friends and enemies alike recognize his standing, and his responsibility.

An adviser to one of the parties of the Left expressed his admiration for Jumblatt, before continuing:

> Jumblatt wanted total victory. Partial victories were not enough. He believed in his 'star', thought his historic hour had come and was determined not to let it pass. He was not prepared to accept that a cataclysm at a specific time was improbable in Lebanon because of its complicated social fabric. He failed to understand that Baabda was not the Bastille or the Winter Palace. This mistake cost a lot of people their lives, and set back the cause of progress in Lebanon.

A close friend and adviser to a former prime minister did not mince his words:

> The real culprit for the war is Kamal Jumblatt. He was the legend of a mislead generation, but he was a criminal. His driving ambition was to be the ruling Emir of Lebanon. 1976 made this utterly clear. To realize his ambition he would stoop to any means, any trick, any lie. He lured the Palestinians into their greatest mistakes.

A well-informed political writer and adviser to moderate deputies appraised the later Jumblatt:

> In the last two years of his life Jumblatt became a terrible fanatic. His views about Christians became more and more extreme. He talked of killing and death with an ease that bore no relation to his military power, but deeply influenced the Palestinians and the Lebanese Left. He openly stated that one-third of the Christians would be killed, one-third forced to emigrate and one-third subjugated — and that was not the worst of his views. No wonder his opponents resisted desperately.
> Jumblatt underestimated the Christians — he above all — and this influenced his allies. He was ignorant of working life: the markets, the workshops and the factories. He believed that a general strike for a few days would ruin the Christians, and that would bring them to their knees. He never imagined that to survive the Christians would hurl bombs into the bazaars, destroy factories and blow up banks. He talked like a murderer and was then surprised at the resistance against him.

A notable in his own party interpreted his personality:

> The development of Jumblatt's personality is a tragedy, and lead to a far worse political tragedy. Jumblatt was a very gifted, astute, well-read and educated man, but unstable, full of complexes and conflicting traits. He lost his father young and was brought up by a dominating mother of great beauty and intellect; she was known as 'the only man among the Druze'. His spiritual influences were extremely varied: Lebanese and French Catholicism, Indian mysticism and traditional Druze beliefs. His marriage was a failure; his wife, a self-assured noblewoman of the Arslan clan, made no secret of her contempt for him. To compensate he craved to be admired by others as intelligent and powerful. He was always trying to impress in conversation. His hunger for power grew from year to year. It was striking how the concept of blood fascinated him in his last years. On the one hand, he had a morbid fear of blood; he could not watch a chicken being slaughtered. On the other hand, his language became more and more bloodthirsty: 'I'll wade in blood; this country needs a bloodbath to purge it; what does killing people

matter?' This mixture of mysticism and hunger for power grew into megalomania. He compared himself to pharaohs, identifying himself with Echnaton. There were bizarre scenes during tours of museums in Egypt ...

Haughty disdain coloured his political dealings. He regarded Maronites as ungrateful and recalcitrant former serfs not really worthy of a nobleman's company. In small circles he ridiculed the Muslim and the Christian religions. He termed Hafez el-Assad a tenant farmer and political parvenu. He boasted he could have Assad killed whenever he wished. Someone else was quicker.

Even in his lifetime portrayals of Jumblatt's character were many and varied. His contemporaries — be it in admiration or hatred — attribute to him alone among the Lebanese enough greatness or wickedness signally to influence the course of Lebanon's history.

## Digression: Views of Lebanese 'doves'

The political world of pre-war Lebanon was peopled not only with lions and foxes. There was a free press of the first order, open-minded men of religion, socially committed scientists and young, competent politicians who belonged to neither of Pareto's species. This type of person cannot be compared to lesser or more dangerous carnivores; rather, to stay in the animal kingdom, they should be compared to doves. Their number is far greater than that of openly political or military players, and, accordingly, their variety of opinions is also greater. They are not attached to political parties or organizations; they belong to different communities and hold socio-political views that, by the criteria of homogeneous political cultures, may be broadly termed liberal or social-democratic. As the discussion of attitudes among ordinary Lebanese will show below, this class of opinion is not the preserve of minorities. The following is a selection of particularly articulate examples of what this body of opinion sees as the causes of the war.[7] A leading Lebanese publicist, who wishes to remain anonymous:

> What Lebanese politician could have an interest in an honest explanation of the causes of the war? Chamoun perhaps? Or Walid Jumblatt — does he want to know the truth about his father? No one dare speak openly.
>
> The origins of the war are easy to understand: the Palestinians fought in Lebanon to gain international recognition. They took a country hostage. Granted, Lebanon was a problem all on its own. There was the identity

---

[7] These examples are not statistically representative; the intention is to convey some idea of the range of opinion among the Lebanese 'doves'.

question, which the Lebanese could never agree about. If the outside world should ever leave Lebanon in peace again, this question will resurface immediately. The fundamental antithesis was present at the founding of the state. The Christians regarded the cedar as a cross, the Muslims too. Here 'Arab' means Muslim, and 'Lebanese' means Christian. But the Lebanese problem did not cause the war. We have lived with this problem for a long time, and will have to live with it for a long time to come — like Belgium, Canada or Yugoslavia.

The Palestinians were not a problem before 1967: they were unarmed. But the Palestinians as an army upset everything. The Kata'ib was also armed before the war, OK. The Kata'ib is a party for Christian self-defence. In Lebanon people have always kept arms, if only to kill their cousin. But everybody knew that they could not defeat and destroy the others. It was a mutual deterrence, and it functioned.

The armed Palestinian element changed that. Jumblatt wanted to take power with the help of the Palestinians, as did the Lebanese Left. But the Palestinians did not want power but Lebanon as a hostage to bargain for their own state — not here but in Palestine. And for that they had to try to exercise pressure somewhere. They were also afraid that Israel and the Christian parties would start a crusade to annihilate them. The hostage-taker and the hostage were both afraid. That's how the war started.

A leading representative of the Greek Orthodox church made subtle distinctions:

It is correct, on the one hand, that the Lebanese Left tried to use the Palestinians for their own purposes. They miscalculated because political Christianity was far stronger than anyone had believed. Yet, on the other hand, one may not overlook the fact that some of the Palestinians were tempted to take power *de facto* in Lebanon, as they had been tempted in Jordan.

This produced an ideological and political dichotomy in Palestinian policies. On the one hand, there was the association with the Left — a Left largely forged by Arab Christians. On the other hand, there was the desire for power in Lebanon, which led to an alliance with political Islam, and, above all, the attempt to gain mass support through confessionalization. The result was the Palestinians' remarkable alliance with both the secular Left and political Islam. It was never clear whether the Palestinians were in fact the army of the Left or the army of Islam. The Left believed the revolution was about to break out. The Muslims felt they were about to gain power: the Sunni Mufti made statements to this effect, and even Musa Sadr thought initially that this was an auspicious moment to shift the balance of power in his favour.

The sociologist Salim Nasr analysed the relationship between social tensions and confessional tensions:

My view on the effects of social tensions on politics? I think the crisis in rural Lebanon is more significant than the disappointing level of industrialization. The 'belt of misery' round Beirut was not quite so miserable. In 1974, there were enough jobs in the city. Workers had no trouble finding new jobs. Wages were rising. Hence, it is not surprising that Sunni workers hardly took part in the fighting. The crisis in the rural areas was far more acute. There were obvious social motivations to the fighting in, say, the Bekaa. Zahle had become a city of large landowners, traders and banks, a centre that exploited the surrounding rural areas. Of course, confessional differences aggravated social distinctions. Sidon had the same economic function in the south as Zahle in the Bekaa. Yet nothing happened there: both city and hinterland are predominantly Muslim ... Social tensions culminated in open conflict where they coincided with tensions between communities ...

The social log-jam was the work of the entire bourgeoisie. The traditional Muslim landowners were as instrumental in this as the Christian business elite. The crucial factor was the perception of the Muslims: the state let the landowners, capitalists and monopolists do what they liked; the state was dominated by Christians; ergo, the Christians should be fought.

Clashes of interests were different in the urban sphere, but the result was the same. Between the upwardly mobile Muslim and the Maronite middle classes competition was growing keener: for jobs in the civil service, posts in the army, state investment at regional and local levels. The Maronites' social advancement had been achieved largely through the civil service; Sunnis and Shi`is were following them. Of course, the real wealth of the Christian bourgeoisie did not come from the public sector: Greek Orthodox and Greek Catholics took little interest in it. But in the middle of the recession, as the number of jobs was shrinking, the Muslim and Maronite middle strata happened to be competing for them.

Hence the demands of the Muslim middle strata concentrated on changing the quotas: they wanted a bigger slice of the cake. Their spokesmen were less the traditional politicians than people like Chafiq Wazzan, as well as the Higher Islamic Council, rising elites that forced politicians of the old school in their turn to make tougher demands.

In the eyes of the social scientist Riad Tabbara, pre-war Lebanon, with all its social and confessional strains, was not on the path towards civil war. Quite the contrary:

> Lebanon was a societal experiment. Of course it had its weaknesses — but the experiment was proving successful. Social integration was taking place. This success was not the outcome of a plan or purposeful political will. Rather, the driving force behind social integration was economic development. It was precisely 'Manchester capitalism', the cause of social tension, that tended to foster the integration of the communities. Building speculation hit Beirut like a whirlwind. Historically, Beirut was a Muslim city, most of the property and buildings belonged to Muslims, and thus Muslims profited most from the boom. Rising property prices created crowds of Muslim millionaires, and in their children's generation crowds of Muslim academics. The development among the Christians moved in the opposite direction. The people from the countryside lost during the boom, and the Maronites came mostly from the countryside. A new phenomenon appeared: poor Christians. The Shi`is were in the worst situation. They were Muslims and, therefore, historically at a disadvantage; they were rural and, therefore, did not benefit from the boom. The social consequences of economic change were enormous. *De facto* the Muslims accepted the secular society. Until 1970 marriages between Christians and Muslims were extremely rare. Then their number rose rapidly. Granted, for the country as a whole, mixed marriages were still a statistically marginal phenomenon. But in urban society, especially among the upper middle class and the intelligentsia, they were common. This new society shared the same habits, the same interests and the same tastes. Mixed marriages — in both directions, I may add — were a natural consequence. Change was already coming.
>
> And then outside influences brought war. This war could have happened in any country in Lebanon's strategic position. Weapons worth three times the gross national product were brought into the country. If someone gives me three times the value of the USA's gross national product, I'll give that country the nicest civil war you can imagine.

Of all the analyses of the war's causes in all the interviews with members of Lebanese elites, a Muslim reformist — who has withdrawn from politics for the time being — presented the acutest and bitterest. It deserves to be given at length:

There are three principal causes of the war: firstly, the Palestinians' armed presence; secondly, Arab unwillingness to oppose Israel realistically and effectively; and thirdly, Syria's determination to dominate Lebanon.

I wish to stress one point: the much-quoted social factor played only a secondary role. Once the shooting had started, some people also shot for social reasons; but no one would have shot because of social inequality alone. What we have here is not class struggle, is not the overthrow of a regime; this is the destruction of an entire society. Israel naturally plays an important role too, but not a causal one. Israel is profiting from the golden opportunity offered it. Israel's contribution to the war is not so much a cause as an epiphenomenon.

Then there are the conspiracy theories ... It is pitiful how many people seek to shirk their own responsibilities by searching for the 'invisible hand'. These are explanations for primitive societies, below the dignity of a region with seven thousand years of history. Anyway, they are of no help.

But to the main cause: the Palestinians have been chased out of all Arab countries. Lebanon was their last refuge, a liberal country open to all opinions and migrations. In the past decades the Arabs and the Palestinians attacked Israel several times. Each time they failed, and each time they sought to explain it away by external factors. In 1948, they fought a form of Bedouin war, and lost. They maintained that they had not been beaten by Israel, but by England, the USA and even the USSR, who had all helped Israel. In 1956, the great slogan was 'the threefold aggression'. It existed all right, but one deliberately overlooked the fact that Israel marched to within ten kilometres of the Suez Canal all by itself. In 1967: Nasser could not imagine Israeli planes attacking from the west; he blamed the Americans. Since 1967, the Palestinians have been trying their own hand at revolution, citing the example of the Algerian FLN. They have learnt their Algerian lessons badly. They have not made any progress. They have stuck to the methods used in 1967: put a bomb in a dustbin and wait for chance victims ... Like the Arab states, the Palestinians have also looked for excuses for their failures. Who is their scapegoat? The reactionary Arab regimes who will not run the risk of fighting. These reactionary regimes, Saudi Arabia and the Gulf States, finance the Palestinians — so that they will not cause them any trouble. Yet they must let themselves be reviled.

The Palestinians tried to get their way in Jordan and Lebanon. Jordan had a king and an army that successfully resisted. Syria did not allow the Palestinians fleeing Jordan to stay in, let alone operate from, Syria. Why did Lebanon accept the Palestinians? Christians and Muslims supported the Palestinian cause. The Christians, one must give them credit, were the first to see the dangers in the presence of armed Palestinians; the Muslim leaders did not, or did not want to see them. They got the OK for commando raids against Israel from Lebanese territory, but no one had considered the consequences.

The Palestinians were consistent. They tried to weaken the Lebanese Army because it might obstruct them. They started undercover operations in the army, financed with petrodollars. At the same time, they built up Lebanese militias to support them, again with petrodollars. Qaddafi was a great help: he financed the Mourabitoun and paid many others. The Muslim politicians objected to none of this, least of all Rashid Karami. Later, most Muslims, Sunnis and Shi'is alike, regretted what had happened. The Muslim leaders had failed in their duty. They did not lead; they followed what they took to be the masses. Matters took a different turn among the Christians. They, too, had no sympathy for Israel. On the contrary: the Syrian and Lebanese Christians were traditionally the strongest opponents and intellectual critics of Zionism ... But they also grasped the possible consequences of inefficient Palestinian operations from Lebanese territory and tried to stop them.

Why did the Arabs in general and the Palestinians in particular act as they did? Personally, I see the explanation for their behaviour in the discrepancy between their glorious past and their sorry present, between pretensions and reality.

One must study Lebanon's Muslim political elites to grasp their lack of ability. Who is there? There are the large landowners: Hamade, Assad, Khalil, Ali, Skaff. They represent their own interests. There are the urban leaders like Salam and Karami. They represent the devout petty bourgeoisie, essentially apolitical people whose behaviour is based on their religious beliefs. What do these political leaders think? The best guide to their thoughts is their stock phrases and sayings, which are simultaneously the maxims by which they act: 'Half a loaf is better than no bread'; 'How? Time will tell'; 'Things must get worse before they get better'; 'Inshallah' (if Allah wills it); 'If time is on your side everything will turn out right'; 'Let's meet again another day; a new day is better than an old'; 'Let's meet again later — better evil at night than haste in the morning'. These maxims are products of a religion incapable of change. God disposes, and why should we venture to propose better? It all boils down to 'maktub', i.e., it is written, everything is predestined. Therefore one needn't do anything really.

These leaders were not in a position to educate the masses. They were powerless when a man with charisma like Nasser electrified and manipulated the masses. The old political caste in Lebanon could exist as long as life was simple, as long as there weren't any serious difficulties. They were not equal to an existential crisis for the country. For thirty years they were able to avoid the worst — though there was a minor civil war after just fifteen years — but what are thirty years in the life of a nation? The political elite failed.

Then there was this thing called the Lebanese Left. What might that be? The Communist Party was founded in 1924. It has never had a seat in the cabinet, never had a deputy, never had a single village mayor, not even in southern Lebanon, where it ostensibly has such strong support. Then there is the Baath, a form of Arab nationalism that formed a tactical alliance with the CP.

The Left — that is Kamal Jumblatt's invention. Jumblatt had a complex about the Maronites. He wanted to be president. He exploited the complexes of the 'Left', the complexes of people who had coveted the mantle of power for decades and not even touched its hem. Now, after forty or fifty years, they suddenly found the Palestinian resistance movement on their side. The Palestinians could act as a counterweight to the Lebanese Army, the army that for the 'Left' embodied feudal and capitalist interests, and that had for years wiped the floor with left-wing demonstrators. Now they discovered 20,000 to 30,000 armed men together with whom they could do something about the army.

Finally, there is the Syrian version of Arab nationalism: lots of talk to little effect. This nationalism holds that all Arabs belong to one and the same country. Foreigners divided the nation and created artificial states ... The Palestinians are strongly influenced by this nationalism. They regard all Arab countries as their country. They regard it as their natural right to use any Arab territory against Israel. They felt at home in Lebanon, in one part of their great fatherland, a part that naturally had to serve the reconquest of Palestine.

There is an enormous gulf between the claims and the reality of the Palestinian resistance movement. Only distant Arab states still show any enthusiasm for them. In the confrontation states themselves matters are very different. Syria and Jordan have not granted the Palestinians any freedom of movement, Egypt threw them out.

Let's call a spade a spade: the Palestinian resistance was a sham resistance. It was strong only in their propaganda, lousy and ineffectual in the field. Incompetence and unwillingness to fight their real enemy caused them to seek a substitute enemy they thought they could handle more easily: the Maronites.

Syria also played an important role. We can observe the same phenomenon among the Syrians. The Syrians see themselves in the historic role of Saladin. But they could not and cannot chase away the Israelis either. Hence, they also seek substitute enemies easier to beat. Assad was the great coward of 1967. As head of the air force, he announced the fall of Quneitra long before Quneitra was actually taken. Now he is attempting to play the hero in Lebanon.

Syria's current policy towards Lebanon goes back to the beginning of the century, and has not changed since. The Syrians want to subjugate and rule Lebanon. Since the break-up of the Syrian-Lebanese economic union in 1950 the Syrian bourgeoisie has coveted at least Lebanon's economic role: its entrepôt, its tourism, its banking, its ports and airport. Whenever I look at the destruction that was Beirut I think of the deep-seated Syrian rancour.

In 1971, there were clashes between farmers and feudal landlords in Akkar. Sheikh Azzam, a Druze, the administrator of northern Lebanon accused the Syrians of having caused the unrest. At that time I really did believe that it was a bit of class struggle; today I know that Azzam was right. In 1975, he was murdered by unknown assailants in Tripoli. A spy ring operating from the ministry of posts and telegraphs was cracked in 1972; it was spying mainly on the foreign ministry. The agents were Syrian. Whether out of weakness or embarrassment, the file was closed without much to-do. In 1972, Khaddam encouraged Lebanon to act against the Palestinians. He called on the Lebanese Army to re-establish control over Lebanese territory. Were the Syrians even then trying to provoke a war? After 1975, the Syrians pursued a policy of confessionalizing the war, though they were not the only ones. Initially the Christians in the Bekaa did not take part in the war. The Syrians played a very dirty role. They incited massacres in several Greek Catholic villages. Musa Sadr was still on a hunger strike. He had to break it to intervene in the Bekaa. Sadr wanted to arrange a cease-fire, followed by negotiations. That did not suit the Syrians; their agents are responsible for the massacres.

Syria's objective is the greatest possible influence in Lebanon. But fortunately for us, it has not gone about it very well. The Syrians thought they could rake up Lebanon like a leaf that has fallen in autumn. They did not foresee Lebanon's powers of resistance, both active and passive. The Sunnis long for the old Lebanon, the Shi`is want an independent fatherland. They do not dare speak out. They are afraid of the terror, and this terror is very real. A hero is he who thinks aloud. If the Lebanese have so far failed in their attempts to reach an understanding among themselves, this is largely Syria's doing. This does not make Syria's objectives any more acceptable.

Compared with the perceptions of the Lebanese notables and the leaders of the conflicting parties, these views of the country's modern elites are disillusioned and unsparing about foreign parties and domestic weaknesses. Their intention is to explain, not to justify. The majority are in no doubt that regional conflicts were the prime cause of war. But they are also aware of the potential for conflict that existed within the country, because of differences between classes and communities, and their linkage. The traditional political leaders, and those of the belligerent parties, are harshly criticized. Both are held responsible for obstructing, interrupting and reversing economic development and social integration. The doves are bitter about the impotence and foreign domination in Lebanon, yet are still confident that Lebanese society is undaunted.

They no longer, do not or do not yet belong to the country's power elite. But this digression on their perceptions illustrates that in Lebanon there are also more modern and more moderate alternatives to foxes and lions respectively.

## 'We' and 'they'

In a complex conflict like the war in Lebanon, with frequent changes of alliance, friend and foe images are equally complex. Nevertheless, examined over the entire period of the war, they remain considerably stable. Their intensity may fluctuate, but not the basic pattern. The following selection of political and military elites' self-perceptions and perceptions of others will concentrate on these constants.

A former prime minister is 'satisfied ... with Sunni attitudes during the war. They have behaved very wisely, more than wisely. It is, I think, a strength not to take up arms, even when threatened. One day one will be able to find the others again without blood on one's hands. War breeds hatred. The Sunnis don't hate anybody.' Another Sunni politician is more critical:

> The traditional Sunni leaders have lost a lot of influence. We ourselves are to blame, I regret to say. When the conflict started we remained aloof, wanted to wait and see who would win, wanted to profit from the situation. The reason for this lies deeper and further back in the past. The Sunni leaders lost their local leadership position in Nasser's time. Why? They wanted to please the mob, whatever the cost. For that reason, they became Nasser's local representatives, his underlings, his satellites. Upon which many people chose to turn directly to the sun and not the moon. The leaders paled as the moon pales at dawn.

Nonetheless, this politician believes that these leaders are still more representative of the majority of the Sunnis than the militia bosses in this or any other community: ' Politically, the warlords mean nothing to the Sunnis. Even at the peak of his popularity, Qulaylat had the backing of perhaps 1 per cent. The warlords only represent something by force of arms. In free elections the old *zu`ama'* would, in spite of everything, certainly get the support of over half the Sunnis.' Saeb Salam expressed his opinion of the Mourabitoun and other militias more drastically:

> These 'shops' [militia meeting places] are a nuisance, but in the long run politically irrelevant. The Mourabitoun's only aim was to get a lot of money; as it happens, they were pretty successful. It's a gang of thieves and murderers without any ideology whatsoever. They would never have existed if the Palestinians hadn't found it a useful organization at times. Abu Ammar [Arafat's nom de guerre] paid them himself and kept them on a rein — though one usually not tight enough.

His opinion of the Christian militias was similar: 'Those on the other side were gangsters too, only better organized.' A Sunni deputy also thought the communities religious leaders had no political clout:

> They have practically no influence. Sunnis don't have clergy, priests, intermediaries between God and man. In the last few years they have made the Mufti and his deputy seem important, but only as a counterweight to the strong position of the Maronite Patriarch. But that doesn't mean much. It isn't so easy to turn a clerk or civil servant into a Patriarch; the Mufti can't excommunicate anyone. Take the Christians: Chamoun was perhaps the only person who could afford to attack the Patriarch, but when the Mufti says something every Sunni politician attacks him if he doesn't like it.

Saeb Salam did not have a high opinion of the Left, and protested against the label 'left-wing Muslims':

> Without the Palestinians the local Left wouldn't have had a chance. The Lebanese Muslims aren't leftists, they're against the Left and strongly anti-Communist. Take Kamal Jumblatt and his so-called Progressive Socialist Party: its name could not be more wrong. Jumblatt was a man from the Chouf, leader of a Druze clan. His party is the Druze and a few infiltrated Communists, that's all. Not even Kamal himself was a socialist. Once when we were returning together from Nasser's Cairo he said to me: 'Saeb, I don't think this society is anything for our country'. And now his son is party leader — really good socialists, socialists with hereditary succession. Incidentally, the Palestinians aren't really Leftists either. They sometimes speak left because their loudest supporters are the European Left.

Another Sunni notable spoke about the Palestinians with great bitterness:

> They never wanted an independent Lebanese Islam alongside them. They liked to work with people like Sobhi Saleh, who was paid by Libya, or the Mourabitoun, who were one hundred per cent dependent on Fatah and whose political line was a simplistic Arab nationalism. Incidentally, the worst agitators were a few Christian intellectuals who enjoyed keeping Muslim fanaticism on the boil. The Palestinians are mostly to blame that political Sunnism in Lebanon is now almost irrelevant.

Mohammed Shukair summed up with resignation:

> Today most Sunnis are convinced Lebanese. But they dare not admit it. They are afraid. Granted, this fear is justified — but it wasn't at the start of the war. I'm sure history will pass a harsh judgment on the Muslim leaders of Lebanon. They were clever, but cowards — great cowards. The leaders on the other side had courage, but they weren't wise, unfortunately. Thus, Lebanon wasn't able to benefit from the wisdom of the one or the courage of the other.

Another Sunni notable described the ambivalent feelings of his community:

> We'd have been pleased if Palestinians or Syrians had engineered a change of power in Lebanon. For some time now many Sunnis, both old families and ordinary people, have been asking whether this goal is really worth the heavy sacrifices. One can't deny that a lot of Muslims long for the Lebanon of pre-war days. It wasn't what we wanted, but it was a lot better than what we've got now. Muslim emotions run hot and cold; in the morning they are cross with the Syrians or the militias, in the evening shells from Ashrafieh revive their solidarity.

Moderate Christian politicians take a similar view: 'The silent majority of ordinary Muslims are fed up with the Syrians as well as the militias. But they have no way of expressing themselves. As long as the Christian militias continue to articulate themselves in confessionalist terms, they will continue to drive the Muslim masses into the arms of their extremists or the Syrians.' The former foreign minister, Fouad Boutros, was terse in his assessment of the role of the Muslim notables: 'Certain former political forces no longer exist. Lebanese political Islam is dead, above all the Sunni version. It abdicated in favour of the extremists years ago. It kept out of the war — and bore false witness.' He also saw the position of moderate Christian politicians endangered:

The effects of the war are alarming. There is widespread bitterness, fanaticism and intransigence. Three attempts have been made on my life — because I am a moderate. There is a tendency on all sides to interpret moderation as betrayal. There are still enough moderates on all sides, probably a majority. But they feel intimidated, and with good reason: their lives are at risk. Pure terror prevents them from speaking their mind.

A Maronite deputy criticized the Christian militias, though he could understand their position:

My opinion of their leaders is no better than my opinion of leaders of the other side. They don't have any clear political concepts: simplistic anti-Communism, a few vague ideas on federalism, and nothing else. At least Pierre Gemayel was clever enough to speak of love as his militias murdered. All in all, the Christian militias have been more ruthless and have killed more people, above all in Tel al-Za`tar. Many people living near the camp avenged their earlier maltreatment at the hands of the Palestinians: no man on the losing side survived. Yes, the Christians were more ruthless, but with good reason: they were fighting for their survival. The Druze outdid them later in the Chouf, for the same reason. People who fear for their existence will stop at almost nothing.

Another Christian deputy concedes that without their militias the Christians would have been lost in 1975 and 1976, but feels that since then they have done more harm than good:

The first catastrophe they must take the blame for is the feud with the Christian north. This caused bad blood between Maronites, and the oldest Christian parts of the country have been occupied: Syrian tanks stand parked under the cedars. The Chouf is the second catastrophe; it has thrown us back more than a century. What they then did in the hinterland of Sidon wasn't only criminal, it was criminally stupid. God protect the Lebanese Christians against Islam and the Syrians, and above all against the great strategists in their own militias!

Muslim and Christian politicians speak of one another in terms of, at best, qualified respect. Each side apportions greater responsibility to the other, but seldom levels fundamental accusations. Criticism generally revolves around blunders in crisis management on both sides. By contrast, they all speak of the commanders of all warring parties with contempt and barely suppressed anger.

They reproach the foxes with not having prevented the destruction of the country; and they accuse the lions of having destroyed it.

In contradistinction, the leaders and spokesmen of the warring parties take great trouble both to present themselves favourably and, at the same time, to disparage and demonize their respective adversaries. The Mourabitoun presented their own political philosophy as the identity between Arabism and Islam:

> We do not see any contradiction between the two. We are trying to return to our cultural roots. The ordinary Muslim has suffered a culture shock. His first reaction is frustration, the second a return to religion. He builds himself a shell to survive. Even if he doesn't know it, he is rejecting the TV and Coca-Cola culture. Arab nationalism helps him defend himself against political imperialism. Islam helps him against cultural alienation.

They regarded the Lebanese Front as their main adversary:

> For us they are fascists collaborating with Israel ... Christian leaders systematically play on Christian fears to keep them mobilized. There is no reason for this since the Muslims are basically tolerant. The Muslim presence in Spain was completely eradicated. We could have eliminated the Christian presence in the Arab world long ago — but oriental Christianity still exists.

The Mourabitoun were critical of their allies: 'Unfortunately, the Palestinians sometimes behave like "Big Brother". They tell us nothing and present us with one fait accompli after another.' They dissociated themselves from the Lebanese Left:

> Western-style class analyses don't help Lebanon much. For instance, we don't have a large working class. The Communists in Lebanon have never had much support outside student circles. Only when the CP started supporting nationalism it at least got accepted. Our struggle is not a class struggle, it's a national struggle. We've got no time for ideological café debates — the enemy doesn't classify us ideologically but nationally. The real Left in this country isn't Marxist, it's nationalist.

They were scathing about the progressive Christian intelligentsia: 'They let themselves be influenced and taken in by their social milieu. The intelligentsia of the Café Trottoir denied their background and origins. Progressive ideals were nice, provided they didn't disturb their private comfort. Afterwards they joined the "Resistance" in St. Germain des Prés and on the Champs Elysées.' The characterization and assessment of the traditional Muslim politicians were similar:

The role of the Sunni *zu`ama'* is over. We know they are to blame that the Muslims are still in such a bad position in the country. They didn't even realize there was going to be a war. The young people are absolutely against them — and half the population is under twenty. The *zu`ama'* don't understand how to mobilize the masses. They are symbols of corruption and political senility.

The Amal leaders use much more moderate language: 'Our movement is there for all deprived people. For the small communities, the Orthodox, the Catholics, the Druze, but also the poor Maronites — there are a lot of Maronites who are just as poor or even poorer that the Shi`is. We are there for all people who have been disadvantaged by the system of 1943.' They dissociate themselves from the Shi`i notables, but their criticism is mild:

> During the mandate the French did not create institutions; instead, they negotiated with individuals who served as intermediaries between them and the people. These then became the old political elite. The mandate period led to a Maronite-Sunni ascendancy that was not at all in keeping with Lebanese tradition. The Shi`i leaders' only role was to guarantee the stability of the regime. The Shi`i parts of the country were neglected. The people noticed this. They know that the traditional leaders did nothing for them. When the war started no one was prepared to carry arms for these leaders. The Shi`a tradition is one of permanent revolution. Under Ottoman rule we were treated as a sect. Nonetheless, the Shi`a has remained a revolutionary movement in Islam. The movement of the Imam Musa Sadr is in this tradition.

A clear distinction is drawn between the Christian parties and militias, on the one hand, and the Maronites as a body, on the other:

> The political uniformity of the Maronites is frequently overestimated. It is questionable whether more than 20 per cent of the Maronites back the Lebanese Front and their militias. There are other Christian leaders with strong backing who are also accepted by Muslims: e.g., Raymond Eddé, Suleiman Franjieh, Jean Aziz and Michel Khoury. Parties like the Kata'ib and the NLP do not have deep roots, they are very shallow. If the electoral law were changed, the old Maronite two-party system, the National Bloc and the Destour would probably re-emerge. The Kata'ib have very cleverly exploited the war to their advantage. They invented bogeymen and used figments of the imagination to frighten the Christians. Fear and terror brought them adherents. Notwithstanding this regrettable development we

have not forgotten the Maronites' historic achievement. Under Ottoman rule they were the first to seek liberation. Only under the French mandate, when power was played into their hands, did they change completely. But we shall never forget their earlier struggle ... As soon as the situation calms down, the Maronites will realize where their true interests lie. The leadership that has emerged during the war is a leadership for a time of struggle — nothing more and nothing less. But the other leaders know that a 'Christian Israel' would never be recognized by the Arabs and would only be detrimental to the Christians. Kisrawan and the Metn — that is not much; previously the Maronites held influence throughout Lebanon. The Christian warlords are leading the Maronites in the wrong direction. They have not yet understood the workings of modern international politics. Either, as in 1860 and 1920, they still look to France as their protector — which can no longer fulfil that role — or they are casting about for a substitute for France. Yet they have no need of protection. They themselves are Arabs ... Economically, everything speaks in favour of an active Maronite commitment to the Arab world. The Arabs have the money, the Europeans the know-how. Together, Arabs and Europeans could be a third power in international politics. And the Maronites could be our ambassadors in Europe, our bridge to the West.

The head of the PSP militia, Walid Jumblatt, thought it hardly likely that the ambitious political blueprints of the pre-war period could be realized:

Our party has a good programme with lots of ideas that can really appeal to people: Arabism, socialism, secularism. But just look at the situation throughout the Middle East. Arabism? The Arabs are more divided than ever. Each wants a different Arabism. Socialism? Many states talk about it, but almost all pamper their middle class, the businessmen and industrialists, so that capital doesn't leave the country via various channels. In Lebanon it would be good if the existing social legislation was properly applied, not to mention the tax laws. A bit more social welfare would be a great improvement. Secularism? From Israel to Iran the fundamentalists have the wind in their sails, and in this country one wonders who has been worse infected, the Christians or the Shi`is. None of this means the basic ideas in our programme are wrong. But one shouldn't have any illusions about their being realized soon.

Asked about his motivations for assuming his father's duties and functions, he replied:

> I didn't seek this role, and, in any case, never believed I should have to take it over so soon. But I regard it as an honour to be able to do so. The Druze are a small, proud people. I find it rewarding to do everything I can so that they can live as they want, and keep their pride. They have shown that they are prepared to fight for this — and they don't fight badly. I like working together with the Left in the National Movement. There aren't many of them, but at present they are among the few who are not religious fanatics and who want a modern state.

He had nothing but contempt for the militant Christian leaders: 'It's simply not worth discussing Bashir and his epigones. Amin Gemayel is an insignificant, but pretentious, man who played the moderate for a time in order to become president. All of them have done immense harm to the country — and, in the long run, most of all to their own people.' He hoped that in the medium term new Maronite leaders would emerge:

> Perhaps Samir Franjieh can play an important role some day. He long ago discarded the wild, left-wing ideas of his youth. He has matured. He is intelligent and understands the problems of Lebanon as a whole. Chamoun's sons have also become very much more reasonable. They've seen what the Phalangists are capable of and what their crazy ideas lead to.

On the foreign forces in the Lebanon conflict he chose his words very carefully:

> Here in the Chouf we are surrounded by all sorts of forces. At times they need me, at times I need them. I needn't mention the reasons. One thing is striking. For decades many Lebanese demanded union with Syria. Now Syria is in Lebanon, and not one political leader of importance has suggested union. It's hardly surprising the Maronites haven't. But that no important Sunni or Shi`i has, either; that I find very striking indeed.

Inam Raad thought the events of the preceding years had proved just how necessary and realistic the objectives of the SSNP were:

> We continue to regard Lebanon as part of Syria, as an integral part of the Arab East. There is no geographic or geopolitical justification for Lebanon's separate existence. Economically, Lebanon has always suffered because of its independence. Two and a half million Lebanese live in the country, three million have had to emigrate. Isn't that the best proof that Lebanon is really part of a larger country? There is only one reason for its existence, to give minorities a state. We don't believe in a state of minorities. We have a

radical alternative: a secular and democratic state. Of course the fears of the various confessional communities have increased in the course of the war. On the other hand, a lot of people realize that the blood-letting goes on in the name of confessionalism, which makes our insistence on a secular state more and more plausible.

The leaders of the SSNP regarded 'isolationism' as their chief enemy:

> The isolationists talk about the everlasting independence of Lebanon, about its separate identity. One section of them, the same section that previously wanted to retain the French mandate, now seeks Israeli protection. They never look towards the hinterland, only towards the coast. They overlook the fact that we can have a healthy, productive economy only if we are part of the Arab world.

However, they wanted to make it clear that they distinguished between 'isolationists', on the one hand, and Christians, even Maronites, on the other:

> By attacking 'the Maronites' at the beginning of the war, the Left and the Palestinians made a disastrous mistake. The isolationists form only a part of political Maronitism. We may be worlds apart from people like Eddé, Aziz and Franjieh, but they have never collaborated with Israel. Our struggle must essentially be only against those who are Israel's allies. The Maronites are an important part of our tradition and our nation. Their history began with defending the Syrian heritage against Byzantium. Last century they were the avant-garde of the Arab renaissance, which was directed against Ottoman rule. Thus, Maronites have opposed both alien Christian and Muslim domination at crucial stages in our history. It is an important task to win the Maronites for our national task. I say that in spite of the fact that the SSNP has suffered particularly heavily in the war. Some of our roots were in the Christian part of the country, and hundreds of our members were the first to be liquidated by the troops of the isolationists.

The SSNP drew a sharp distinction between itself and the other parties of the Left:

> The analyses of the left-wing parties have concentrated on social issues. This is where our differences of opinion are greatest. Not that we want to play down the social problems — they are important. But we see them in the context of the problem of national identity. The Communist parties have had to revise their way of looking at Lebanese problems. At first they only talked

about class struggle; now they put the national issue in the foreground, although class aspects naturally play a role for them.

The Sunni and Shi`i notables might not have wanted any armed struggle. But: 'In peacetime they count, in war they don't. In the course of the war the pro-Syrian Baath Party has faced very different opponents. In their own view they have been consistent:

> Our party is closely allied with Syria. What we want is the unity of the country. But we are against confessionalism, the disease of this century, and against a future Lebanon based on a confessional balance between Christians and Muslims: if that happens we'll have the same story all over again in ten years time. The Baath is the only party that hasn't killed anyone, not at roadblocks or anywhere else.

How does it view its adversaries?

> In 1976 we were involved in heavy fighting with the National Movement and a section of the Palestinians. Our houses and offices were burnt out, our organization was smashed. We had to flee to Damascus. For a year our newspaper couldn't be published. Forty-two party members were murdered by the National Movement. But we returned. Since then our chief enemies are the Lebanese Front and their militias. They are working against the security of Syria and Lebanon, in Israel's interests. Who is for them is against Syria. The new link between them and Iraq serves only one purpose, namely to make difficulties for Syria, but without Syria nothing will work for a long time to come.

The confessionalization of the war caused enormous internal problems for the Organization of Communist Action in Lebanon. Fawaz Traboulsi explained:

> Our organization never equated community with class — not us. However, we try to analyse the relationship between the two more precisely. We think this is particularly important because one part of the Left regards confession and confessionalism as pure ideology. We want to separate the class struggle from the conflict between the religious communities. The fascists have made a great effort to spread the ideology that Maronites and capitalists are the same, although the Maronites suffer most under the capitalists. That was the attempt by Lebanese fascism to combine the economic privileges of the bourgeoisie with the political privileges of the Maronites. We want to end this confusion.

The war has created a paradoxical situation. The religious communities are more anachronistic than ever; on the other hand, because of the war confessional feelings have become very strong again. The suffering caused by the war has regenerated confessionalism. The old system has been regenerated; previously it was emigration that reduced the element of protest, nowadays it is war emigration. The surplus of labour that could lead to revolution disappears through migration.

All matters relating to changes in the economic system have to be postponed for a while; the immediate issue is to maintain the unity of the country. The problem of minorities becomes more and more pressing, in Lebanon and the entire Orient. Twenty-five years of so-called modernization — here that means simply wishing away the minorities — what's the result? Only accepting and affirming diversity and cultural and religious particularisms can bring unity. Arab unity has failed, because this truth was overlooked, and attempts to create unity were only based on the so-called majority. But in the Orient there are a whole number of minorities. Arabism must be democratic and secular, otherwise there cannot be any Arabism. But every setback is exploited by imperialism.

Initially, OCAL saw their chief adversaries in the bourgeoisie: 'The Muslim bourgeoisie — Saeb Salam is a typical example — joined up with the Christian bourgeoisie. It was the first to lead the armed class struggle from above. Only when Saeb Salam failed did the army and then the Kata'ib intervene.' Since then the Kata'ib and the Lebanese Forces have been their chief opponents:

In the years preceding the war a section of the Maronites participated in the social struggle and became more radical. Precisely this was an important reason for the fascist project. The Kata'ib pretended to be 'social'. Their social component was deceptive, though. Whenever it came down to real economic change or far-reaching social concessions they were always on the side of the employers and the bosses. In historical terms, they became the armed gangsters of the bourgeoisie. Incidentally, they don't have the unanimous support of the Christians by any means. Today the Kata'ib controls areas where they don't have a majority. They are strong in the Metn, in parts of Kisrawan and in East Beirut. But they are fairly weak in Jbeil, Batroun and the north. The majority of the Christian deputies are also against them. Our strategy is cooperation with all non-fascist forces among the Christians.

After the first two years of war OCAL lost numerous adherents. A former member explained why:

Today most left-wing intellectuals are completely disoriented and don't know where they stand politically. They aren't prepared to accept the positions of one or other side, and they are unable to define their own position in the growing polarization. Their attitudes fluctuate between cynicism and gloom. Very few still believe in the Utopia of a secular centralized state — and most of them are abroad.

In the 1970s we put incredible energy into discussing, formulating and writing. The newspaper *al-Huriyya* became a platform for fascinating opinions. We were terribly enthusiastic about the concept of mass organization, working with the basis. But we never really defined 'the masses', or even reflected on it. 'The masses' — those were the poor, the Muslims, the Palestinians, the 'street', etc. We got passionately involved in organizational work in the Beirut suburbs. That was incredibly satisfying. Overnight every intellectual became a 'caïd de quartier'. We enjoyed all the pleasures of a '*za`im*' — naturally the ordinary people were very happy to have 'intellectuals' taking an interest in them — and at the same time tended our progressive consciousness. But what we overlooked, consciously or unconsciously, was that the fundamental motivation of the basis we were working with was confession. Most of them were Shi`i migrants or refugees who did not have a traditional *za`im* they could turn to in their new surroundings, and therefore accepted us. Many of my former comrades still won't accept the truth and carry on deceiving themselves. Others turned without qualms to a superficial left-wing neo-confessionalism. A particularly sinister example of intellectual dishonesty is the 'theory' of the 'community as class'. Those who thought it out knew exactly what they were doing. They applied the concept of 'tactics' to the analysis itself. That way one ultimately reaches the banal conclusion that the end justifies the means. 'Community as class' provides a free ticket for one's conscience to run amok in confessionalism. Through this sort of behaviour the Left has utterly discredited itself in this country. The years when we were dependent on the Palestinians organizations strengthened this tendency. Pragmatic cynicism was already far more normal among them. Whatever the reasons, they welcomed anyone who helped them — and regarded him as a useful idiot. The result? The social revolution did not happen in the wrong place at the wrong time — it didn't happen at all.

Perceptions such as these make it easier to understand why a number of cadres in left-wing parties and organizations chose migration, within Lebanon or abroad, and others joined militant Christian organizations. These organizations never developed a uniform self-perception and common political objectives. Differences over goals and what type of political order they want run right through all of them:

> Some people on our side basically want to partition the country, or to reconquer all Lebanon. They think simplistically: if the whole of Lebanon can't be the way we want it, then we'd rather have just a piece of the country. Young militia commanders, above all, simply don't believe in coexistence with the Muslims. Then there are others who want a federation where the central government is as weak as possible. All the communities could then live as they like, but there wouldn't be partition, which is economically crazy. Others again are convinced that there can be no solution without the Syrians, and that we should try for it by reaching agreement with them, whereas the supporters of partition tend to look to Israel, though they don't really trust them. There are supporters of a secular centralized state, and quite a number think it best to return to the National Pact with, at most, a few extra 'guarantees' for the Christians. Thus, concepts and ambitions diverge considerably.

That was the view of one of Camille Chamoun's leading associates. But what do the militant Christians have in common? 'They are united only in their determination not to be beaten by anyone. And their determination will take some beating.' This determination for self-preservation is rooted primarily in a feeling that they are threatened by 'Islam', and the fear of being subordinated to it. How do militant Christians see 'Islam'?

> Islam, that's not a religion first of all. It's an empire founded on a religious ideology, an empire with totalitarian claims. Muslims have it hammered into them from childhood that the Islamic nation is the best that God ever created, a religion destined to rule, and superior to all other religions. The similarities to racism can't be denied. Everything that's not Islamic is seen as inferior: one only gives to Caesar what is Caesar's if Caesar is Muslim. In the world there is only the 'land of Islam', where peace reigns, and the 'land of war', where they fight until Islam wins. If the Muslims are strong enough they have a duty to try and take power. Therefore there can only be ceasefires with non-Muslims — when the Muslims aren't strong enough — but no permanent peace.
>
> It was never Muslim policy to convert, only to subdue others: they wanted to live on the tribute of the unbelieving subjects. Under the Umayyad dynasty, Syria was only about 20 per cent Muslim. The majority were 'converted' only later, through poll-taxes and discrimination: people who

wanted to avoid these became Muslim. The status of the 'dhimma', of 'wardship' for conquered non-believers, that is more or less what Hitler was planning for the conquered Slav peoples.

Because Islam as a religion became so inflexible, it could not keep up economically, culturally and politically. The revolt against Western civilization that you witness among so many Muslims is explained by the gulf between their claim to superiority and their actual inferiority. The Muslims have never been able to modernize. The Jews did, and that saved their religion and culture. The Japanese did, the Muslims didn't. The Christians in the Orient never had this problem because their religion and cultural traditions linked them to the West, where the drive for modernity originated.

Even in Lebanon it was impossible to overcome these differences, although one liked to hope so for a long time. The war has shown this. Today a federation can perhaps solve the problems of coexistence: everybody can stay what he is where he is and keep his culture and religion.

But the Christians have to build up a position of strength and keep it, so that they can resist the permanent threat of subjugation.

The Greek Orthodox who gave this explanation was active in the Lebanese Left for many years before the war. Today he has a high reputation as a political thinker in militant Christian circles. His views are shared by a member of the Kata'ib central committee:

In most other Arab states Christians try to escape the problem by becoming active in secular ideological movements, in particular Arab nationalism. They want a modern Arab nation. But the secularism they demand is rejected by Islam. The Lebanese Christians were probably well advised to dissociate themselves from Arab nationalism at an early stage. The Christians in the other countries, so we believe today, cling to a wild hope. What has happened to Arab nationalism will be repeated in the socialist ideologies in the Orient. The only real socialists have a Christian background. The demographic development of oriental Christendom is probably more important than the opinions of thinkers and ideologists. The number of Christians is declining, mainly because of emigration. Previously the Syrian Gezira was 90 per cent Christian, now it is only 40 per cent. Many Iraqi Christians and even whole orders have started buying property in Kisrawan and settling there. Fundamental Islam is speeding up a development that had already begun before its reawakening. Even in a country like Turkey, which, officially, is completely secular, political Islam has raised its head. Even the

Turkish Communist Party speaks of Islam with respect. Secularization seems only to have touched the surface.

The Lebanese Christians must take all these lessons to heart. The constitutions of the Arab countries are deceptive; constitutional reality is continued Islamic rule. We must not become victims of illusion. We cannot expect any help from the West. If the Christians in Lebanon want to live in freedom, they can rely only on themselves.

Former president Chamoun saw the concrete political danger to the Christians in, above all: 'the outward orientation of the Lebanese Muslims. Immediately after independence they looked towards Syria, then towards Nasser, whose policies they followed blindly at each turn. The Lebanese Muslims are 'right' or 'left', depending on which way the Arab wind is blowing. Today the danger lies in their subservience towards Syrian policies.'

Former president Charles Helou expressed the same in metaphor: 'The Lebanese Muslims are like La Fontaine's tame geese. They are happy. But when they see the flight of the wild geese they grow restless.' Chamoun, and many other Christian leaders, did not think much of the Muslims' political influence:

> They are of little account, no significance, or just as much as the Syrians permit. None of them has any say. It is said they pine for the good old times. That may be true. But why do they not say so themselves, loudly and clearly? Instead of mumbling in their salons, where they cultivate their nostalgia. They do not say anything and they cannot do anything. They are afraid — and honestly, I cannot blame them.

Fouad Chemali, former head of the Tanzim, put it more mildly: 'There is no Islam in Lebanon, only Muslims. Many of them repudiated the fanaticism of neighbouring countries long ago; they have been Lebanonized. Especially among the Sunnis there is a reawakening of Lebanese patriotism such as never before.' The main issue for Samir Geagea, head of the Lebanese Forces, was the long-term security of the Christians:

> I am convinced that nowadays most Muslims want to live in peace with us. But what was the situation in 1975? It doesn't matter what the majority of the Muslims think: who gives us the guarantee that their militias won't start shelling our regions tomorrow if the Syrians order them to? We can't afford a political system that allows a bloody conflict every fifteen or twenty years first, before we re-establish coexistence.

The militant Christian leaders do not attach much importance to the parties and organizations of the Left:

> They played a role once, when they convinced the Palestinians before 1975 that the Lebanese state was rotten and the Christians weak; one hefty shove and they'd all capitulate. They've thought of nothing new since then. They're still shattered by the failure of their predictions and the phenomenon of confessionalism, especially as the Shi`i version of this has turned on them. Many of the formerly left-wing Christians have pulled out. One of my cousins was a Communist. He left the CP in 1975, highly irritated that party meetings and mass rallies opened with leftist slogans, but closed with quotations from the Qur'an. The quotations from the Qur'an have finished too, since the people who wanted to hear them don't come any more, and the mass rallies of the Left don't take place any more.
>
> What counts today on the other side of the country are the Shi`is and Druze — and they only so long as they have Syrian backing.

Interviewed representatives of Palestinian organizations revealed a range of perceptions of adversaries and allies as broad as that among the Lebanese. Most Palestinian respondents emphasized the point that essentially they had nothing to do with the conflict between the religious communities in Lebanon because confessionalism was alien to them:

> Religion is not a problem at all for us Palestinians. About 20 per cent of us are Christians, perhaps more, we're not really interested. Whether we believe or not, whether Muslim or Christian, at any rate we belong to a civilization that is Arab and Islamic, and we are first and foremost Palestinians. If a particular group here in Lebanon has turned against us, we're not responsible, that's their problem.

Notwithstanding this basic position, leading Palestinians regarded the Maronites as their chief opponents. Mahmoud Labadi, former PLO spokesman:

> The Maronites? Who's interested in them? Soon nobody'll even mention them. French names don't make Europeans. Those who want to be Europeans will emigrate — lots have already gone. There are only 400,000 Maronites at the most left in the East. They mean nothing to the USA, perhaps a toy in the jacket pocket. They'll never play a leading role again, not in the Middle East as a whole nor in Lebanon. They lose and they leave the country. History will march over them. Who still bothers about the Maronites? Nobody, not even themselves. Even in Ashrafieh only 20 per

cent of the population supports them. There are more Christians here in the West than over there. The Lebanese bit off more than they could chew. And they think they are the most intelligent people in the Middle East. They believe they're descended from the Phoenicians and the cleverest people in the world. They weren't very clever, after all. They've become the toys of Israel, pawns, and Israel won't ever let them do anything except what it wants.

Realpolitik marked leading Palestinians' view of their relations with the Lebanese Muslims:

> Of course, we realize the Sunnis are no longer very enthusiastic about us — if they ever were. But we cannot allow ourselves to let them plot against us. We can't permit them to act independently of us and make peace with the Lebanese Front on their own, or to do some big deal with Syria. We would prevent that, as we forced Saiqa to stop plotting against us. We have had to accept some coordination with Syria, but we'd fight with all we've got to prevent complete domination by Syria.

Issam Sartawi commented on Palestinian-Shi`i relations as follows:

> The Shi`is have always been the social victims of underdevelopment in the south. This underdevelopment existed because Israel did not want any development in the south. This all got much worse when the south was turned into a typical battlefield. Anti-Palestinian resentment, which undoubtedly exists among the Shi`is, is quite normal. After all, they are suffering because of our presence in the south.
>
> For simple people, politics is what makes their lives easier or more difficult. What the Shi`is have had to endure would have tried the patience of saints. They were evicted from their villages, returned, and were evicted again. No one who has seen Tyre — a proper ghost-town — or the destruction in Nabatieh can be surprised at this resentment.
>
> But regardless of what their emotional state may be, the Shi`is have no choice but to collaborate with us. It is also obvious that for the foreseeable future — as long as the war continues — the Shi`is' lot as such can hardly improve. What is the sense in a front that doesn't fight?

The Popular Front and the Democratic Front had close relations with the Lebanese Left based on ideological similarities; there was little difference between their perceptions of adversaries and allies and those of the Lebanese organizations. Fatah, on the other hand, took an instrumental view of the Left, blaming them — Palestinian and Lebanese — for falsely assessing the situation: 'The assessment of the situation in Lebanon was wrong in many respects. Primitive class analysis is not enough for a proper understanding of this country. We underestimated the cohesion of the religious communities as identity groups.' Another Fatah spokesman was more emphatic:

> What rubbish — where is the class struggle in Lebanon? Our own ideological eggheads infuriate me sometimes. One of them was a Marxist in Heidelberg for years; now he shouts 'Allah Akbar' as a pan-Islamic fundamentalist, and the man was born a Christian on top of it. How can one take that seriously? Take the case of a member of the CP central committee who was shot and buried. A sheikh quoted what-have-you from the Qur'an about the evil unbelievers — and there they were burying an unbeliever. Or was he perhaps not an unbeliever? Leftists and ideologists in this part of the world, that's a chapter in itself. As far as the left-wing militias are concerned, they are one hundred per cent dependent on us — weapons, training, supplies. They're not very important, anyway. In the meantime OCAL follows the same line as the pro-Moscow CP. Why do they remain separate organizations? That's Lebanon. Do you know what the best thing for this state would be? Raymond Eddé as president and Yassir Arafat as prime minister — then there would be peace and order, and everything would function.

The perceptions of leaders and spokesmen across the entire spectrum of belligerent parties are similar in many points. Generally, self-presentation is brief: the respondents assume they are well-known, and feel so secure in their respective organizational identities that it seldom occurs to them to reflect. Within this general pattern though, the smaller the organization, the greater the effort at self-presentation and at justification of the ideology. Principal opponents are harshly criticized, frequently in a tone of contemptuous dismissal, as though they were utterly inferior. Allies are often spoken of disparagingly; their intentions are good, but they cannot really be taken seriously. There is frequent speculation that the opponent's organization is not truly representative of the community concerned: potential allies on the opposing side are constantly sought. The surmise that the militant parties might not be representative is probably realistic, and applies to all sides. By groping for non- or less militant partners among opponents, all the militant factions implicitly admit that none of them seriously believes in conclusive victory.

Other remarks indicate that each of the belligerents is quite satisfied not to be beaten or, possibly, annihilated: survival and a bit of territory, no matter how small, is in itself victory. This is explicit in the unfailing ability of each side to register opponents' miscalculations, in the knowledge that the Damocles' sword over its own head will thereby hang that much longer. A few characteristic statements may serve to substantiate this. Issam Sartawi saw:

> In retrospect, a number of miscalculations on the part of the political actors. As far as the Lebanese leaders are concerned, the Christian as well as the Muslim political elite basically supported the Kata'ib in their attempt to throw the Palestinians out of the country. The result: the Christians now control only a small area; the Muslim reactionary forces still exist, but their political influence has been completely neutralized ...
>
> Even today I don't understand how this miscalculation was possible. By 1974, we were a powerful military force in the country; at any rate, the Lebanese institutions were already too weak to control us.
>
> 'What could not be totally excluded at the time was an attempt by the Palestinians to extend their sphere of influence. I could not imagine that the Lebanese themselves were mad enough to attack us. They set fire to their own house. Yet, at that time we wanted neither greater influence nor more territory than we already had.
>
> Ultimately, the explanation lies in the fact that the Lebanese leaders, Christian and Muslim, are neither rational nor logical. One simply cannot overlook the fact: these people are irrational, they couldn't care two hoots about the country and its people.

Fouad Chemali elucidated the perceptions of the other side:

> The Palestinians were extraordinarily confident of victory. In private conversations they often told us: 'We know you Maronites. You're used to the good life and prosperity. You're no longer prepared to fight. When we feel like blowing, you'll vanish overnight.' Above all Palestinians who arrived from Jordan in 1970 held this attitude. Well, we weren't so sure.
>
> When war broke out in 1975, everybody got a huge surprise. The Christians discovered they could fight. The crucial factor was the will to survive, not somewhere abroad but here, and not as individuals but as a community. The people who conceived the entire assault on us also believed these shopkeepers would just turn and run. They deluded themselves.

Michel Abu Jaude, editor-in-chief of *an-Nahar*, gave his opinion of the opposing sides at the outbreak of war:

> An unusual degree of mutual ignorance in all groups has negatively influenced developments in Lebanon. The Maronites don't know the

Palestinians. Sarkis and Boutros, for example, don't have the slightest notion about the Palestinians, not to mention the Gemayels — not even Eddé and Tuéni. The Palestinians didn't know the Maronites: the Institute of Palestine Studies opened a Lebanon section only in May 1975. They were almost deliberately indifferent to Lebanon; nor do they want to see Palestinian reality. Finally, the Israelis and Palestinians don't know each other either. Each ignores the other, and makes the unknown other out to be a devil. This was a cause of terrible mistakes.

One could produce numerous other examples. Misperceptions were not limited to the outbreak of war, but recurred in the course of the war. Lebanese miscalculated each other. In 1976 Jumblatt believed he could conquer the Maronites; in 1983 the Lebanese Forces believed they could conquer the Druze. Nor were the foreign forces immune: Syrians underestimated the Palestinian as well as the Christian will to resist, Israelis underestimated the Shi`i'.

The respective assailants have persistently miscalculated. Their underestimation of their opponents may be explained in part by the ignorance Abu Jaude put his finger on. What was underestimated above all, though, was the desperate determination to resist at all costs on the part of those who felt — rightly or wrongly — that they were under attack. Only assaults based on miscalculation are, to use Sartawi's word, irrational; resistance is not. Every group under assault knows that defeat will spell their end, at least as a group. The study has revealed that most parties to the conflict feel they are under attack. The bitterness and prolongation of the war in Lebanon might well, in the final analysis, be best explained by this perception.

## Compromise or victory?

What did Lebanese politicians and the leaders of the belligerent parties think would be the likely result of the war? In the replies to this question the respondent's view on what is probable is virtually inseparable from what he would like. The normative element dominates throughout; some interviewees refused to admit the distinction.

Nor need this harm the prospects of conflict regulation. The strength of norms, especially the norms of the actors concerned, may say more about such prospects than any detached analysis of facts: in conflicts the factual strength of normative views is itself a reality.

Among Lebanese politicians, the hope of a return to compromise, and the certainty that compromise is possible, clearly predominated. A Sunni *za`im* postulated:

A compromise must be found, for there is no other solution. The Lebanon to come will be one in which the strong don't devour the weak. It won't be a Lebanon that believes 'its weakness is its strength', but a Lebanon of strength. We need a strong army to overcome the dismemberment of the country. The Lebanese have had their fill of war; they'll know how to reach an understanding.

A former premier explained why he believed in a new compromise:

Why of all countries in the Arab East could democracy hold its own only in this small country? This freedom is a consequence of communal diversity alone. Freedom would be imperilled in a purely Christian or purely Muslim Lebanon. No community has an overwhelming majority in Lebanon as a whole; they balance each other. One cannot live in this country without learning to respect others. The essence of democracy lies not only in the minority respecting the majority, but also in the majority respecting the minority.

On balance, the Sunnis have stuck to their pre-1975 positions. They don't accept the inequality in the country, they want equality. But they are not against the Christians, they want to coexist with them. There won't be a second Cyprus in Lebanon. I am very confident that we will reach a good solution soon.

The Lebanese showed what they really feel years ago, when the army marched into certain areas: the people danced in the streets. And you could see it when Gemayel and Karami entered liberated Sidon. Despite the external threat, I have a faith in the future of Lebanon. This country will recover, and it will be a better country than before.

A Shi`i minister: 'Compromise is necessary. However, the Pact of 1943 is antiquated. We must build a state like Switzerland. This also means that decentralization is quite conceivable. The only thing that's out of the question is partition.'

A Sunni notable:

The National Pact has often been prematurely declared dead. The reason is frequently ignorance, or the desire for revenge. Revenge on the part of those who believe that Emile Eddé was right in 1943, or the revenge of those who don't want a Lebanon. But in most cases it's ignorance.

'What was the Pact of 1943? It was a compromise on all issues that were important at the time; it suited the situation in 1943 perfectly. What do we need today? In principle the same. We need a compromise, a formula for unity and collaboration. I'm optimistic that it'll come.

A former Shi`i minister:

> The Lebanese are basically conservative. Many of the old leaders will return, and there will be a new pact similar to that of 1943. Similar, but more precise and more detailed. The country's social problems were forgotten in the Pact of 1943. Most Lebanese want the old Lebanon again, with all its failings, if needs be. But there is no reason why we should repeat the same mistakes.

What do Muslim notables see as obstacles in the path to a new compromise? A Sunni politician mentioned the Muslim population growth, which could seriously endanger the population balance in the long run. But he does not think the problem insurmountable: 'Educated Muslims don't have larger families than Christians; only the lower classes do. If everyone got the same education the growth of the Muslim population would also slow down.'

A former Shi`i minister regards the militias as a grave problem; yet:

> Some young people have indeed become fighters. But most of them, specially the Muslims, join the militias purely for financial reasons. A place can be found for many of them in the army. The others need jobs — and they'll come with peace.
>
> Many countries operate on the principle that power goes to the highest bidder. But that's not true of Lebanon; here there's a sort of democratic ingratitude. In 1945, the English voted Churchill out after he'd won the war. We won't have any trouble not voting for non-winners. In the war of 1958 the Christians all rallied to the Kata'ib; but after 1958 they didn't dream of giving them power in peacetime.

A Sunni politician feels that there can't be peace in Lebanon without a solution to the Palestine question. As long as it persists, Lebanon will be harassed by foreign forces using it as a tub to thump out their opinions on Palestine. He feels the only feasible solution is the creation of a Palestinian state:

> Once the Palestinians have their own state, no matter how small, they'll be preoccupied with themselves rather than with revolution throughout the region. What they need is a passport, respect, a homeland, even if they can't all go back. They'll get used to the fact that part of their country has been lost forever. Yugoslavia gave up Trieste, Germany gave up Alsace; the Palestinians will give up part of Palestine. Then Lebanon can also get some peace.

Christian politicians not associated with militant groups share the views of their Muslim colleagues. Former President Franjieh believes the Pact of 1943 should be modified: 'The same number of Christian and Muslim deputies and no confessional quotas below the level of departmental secretaries: there'd be a large majority for that.'

Henri Pharaon, one of the fathers of the National Pact, thinks 'the formula of 1943, perhaps with modifications' is the only practicable way of ending the war; anything else is unrealistic:

> Of course, some Christian extremists would prefer partition; but they know they won't get their way. The threat of partition, therefore, is little more than an opening move towards possible negotiations. Complete secularization? That is a stupid, a crazy idea. How could complete secularization be implemented after a war like this? What do you do with the diversity of communal laws of marriage and inheritance? The personal statute is to us what the canton is to Switzerland. When all is said and done, no one wants to dispense with it, least of all the Muslims.
>
> And political secularization alone is unacceptable to the Christians. They know too well what a deplorable situation the millions of Copts in Egypt are in. They'll never tolerate that. Something is anathema to each side — and that keeps the balance. And because that's so, the only way is to return to compromise.

A very influential high-ranking civil servant, a Maronite, draws the same conclusion: 'This country's *raison d'être* is the plurality of its communities. The principles of the Pact of 1943 are still the best solution for coexistence; there's simply no other choice. It may be sensible to make a few minor changes, but there is no real alternative.' On the other hand, Manuel Younes, a Maronite deputy frequently mentioned as a future president, proposes a fundamental revision of the system of government, though this too on the basis of the Pact of 1943:

> The Muslims' main objection to the present system concerns its heart: the presidency. This is the crux of the matter. Whenever a Lebanese Muslim has a problem, no matter what it is, he blames it on the so-called privileges; what he means, though, is this office. The Christians, in reply, maintain that the presidency is not a privilege but a guarantee.
>
> In reality it is neither a privilege nor a guarantee. It is not a privilege, because the president can only take decisions in conjunction with the prime minister. It is not a guarantee, because the president is often a compromise

candidate and, accordingly, cannot safeguard Christian interests as resolutely as the prime minister can those of the Muslims.

A new constitutional formula ought to abolish what the Muslims regard as privilege. But it also has to give the Christians some guarantee against majority decisions contrary to their vital interests.

My proposal is to replace the offices of president and prime minister by a presidential council, in which the largest communities, Christians and Muslims, would have equal representation. The presidential council would be a collegial institution, similar to the Swiss Federal Council, but with far wider powers. A strong central authority is part of oriental tradition. The chairmanship of the council would rotate. Unlike Switzerland, the chairman would not be state president, but only executive chairman of the collegial body; the body as a whole would exercise presidential authority.

I envisage a bicameral parliament: a chamber of deputies without quotas or group representation, and a senate whose composition would reflect the communal structure of the country.

This would put an end to the presidential 'privilege', and give Christians guarantees and security in the form of two institutions that did not function on the principle of majorities and would, therefore, not be influenced by constant speculation about demographic shifts.

Like their Muslim colleagues, many Christian politicians also believe that a Lebanese compromise is possible only when settlement of the Palestine question removes the international pressure the country has been subjected to for the past twenty years. In the opinion of a Maronite politician:

The Palestinian problem will be a simple matter once there is a Palestinian state. Things will work out like 1932 in Lebanon. Then the overseas Lebanese got nationality, a passport and the right to settle here — and stayed where they were.

It's obvious that not all the Palestinians want to go to Palestine. Lots of them want to live elsewhere, but with a Palestinian passport. When the Palestinian problem is solved, many Palestinians can become Lebanese, why not? The problem of equilibrium? We could agree to bring in just as many Christians from Arab countries, then we'd have equilibrium again. The question of equilibrium is something we Lebanese can settle ourselves, provided that the Syrians, Israelis, Palestinians, Iraqis and Americans stop trying to force through their solution to the Palestine problem right here.

The picture is clear: the civilian politicians want a compromise, a return to the Pact, in its original or a modified form. Demands are expressed, though nothing too specific; details are negotiable. The statements indicate that the scope for negotiation is considerable: one Muslim could live with the old Lebanon, even 'with all its failings, if need be'; one Christian — by no means the only one — proposes a new formula that meets most Muslim reservations about the old division of powers.

This reflects the notables' political qualities: tolerance, belief in coexistence, forceful pursuit of the interests of their respective communities, coupled with a willingness to make concessions in the interest of compromise. Their major weakness is less explicit, deduced from what has not been said, or from between the lines. How can the country extricate itself from a conflict that involves more than Lebanon, and is being fought out on its territory? Their strength is their ability soberly to assess the strength and play of domestic political forces, and to draw rational conclusions from it. Their limits lie in their discretion in all matters pertaining to foreign policy. Christian and Muslim politicians alike speak of a future Palestinian state resolving the cause of the regional conflict. But none will openly consider whether Syria or Israel, or both, might be pursuing objectives in Lebanon that go beyond the Palestinian question. Their fears on this point are rational too. They know only too well that unequivocal opinions on international or regional issues are likely to harm them and achieve little. They talk only about issues they can partially influence — the compromise between Lebanese — and, for the rest, wait for better times. Should such times dawn, the old political elite could very well have a role again, and for this eventuality they are prepared.

The leaders of the militant factions hold very different opinions on the possibilities of ending the conflict. They have fought and let others fight, and need to prove to their adherents that the fight has been worthwhile; if not victory, then at least obvious improvements on the status quo ante bellum. The Mourabitoun spoke of victory: 'Lebanon's existence is itself a mistake. It's a product of colonial rule, created to allow the Christians to dominate. The Muslim leaders made the Pact of 1943 because there was nothing else to do then. Today the balance of power has changed, and you have to draw the consequences.' The Deputy-Mufti, Sobhi Saleh, was more explicit: 'Now that the war has started it will have to have consequences. Today we say: Lebanon must be purely Arab, no ifs and buts; Maronite privileges and political confessionalism must be abolished. The war will change the face of the country, otherwise we will carry on fighting. Either there is radical change, or the war goes on.' The Mourabitoun no longer exists, and Sobhi Saleh was murdered. The larger parties and militias were far more guarded. Walid Jumblatt, leader of the PSP, does not believe that all the demands of his party and the National Movement will be fulfilled:

> For years we have been fighting for our existence, which was under threat. We have a programme we think is right. However, it is doubtful all of it will be accepted.
>
> The Sunnis are incapable of understanding the concept of complete secularization. All the nationalisms and ideologies in the region have been developed by members of the minorities: Aflak is Christian, Saadeh was Christian, my father was Druze. All the Sunnis produced were Muhammad Abduh and al-Afghani, and they weren't Arab nationalists, but Islamic fundamentalists. Arab unity has failed — a pity!
>
> Eventually, there will have to be a compromise in Lebanon, and the Maronites will be part of it. However, I hope the compromise will be more inspiring than that of 1943. High offices of state can no longer be tied to certain confessions, I'll fight to ensure that. Things would be easier if the reasonable people among the Maronites get their way against the militarists. There are also a lot of people among the Christians who want a state that's at least a little bit more modern.
>
> However, I don't think a spectacular reconciliation is probable in the foreseeable future. We still don't have the right conditions, especially the agreement of the Syrians. This agreement isn't there. The Syrians want a price for it, and not all the relevant forces are prepared to pay them a high price.

Nabih Berri, Amal chairman, elucidated the priorities of his movement as follows:

> The most important thing is that the war stops. Then we can talk about political reforms, and we have to talk about them. But after all that's happened we can't return to the system that couldn't save us from this war. What most Lebanese want and what the country needs is normal democracy, majority democracy. There should be equal rights for everybody, and all posts should be filled by the best people, regardless of religious affiliation. We won't be satisfied with less. We can talk about transitional periods, but the goal must be clear: democracy without any restrictions, special rights or complications.
>
> The people who keep talking about guarantees should consider that the best guarantee is a genuine democracy — and this is the democracy we propose.

Assem Kanzo, chairman of the pro-Syrian Baath Party, would like the electoral law to be changed:

Democratic elections in Lebanon: that is the best thing we can do. We have tried violence and breaking the law, and what was the result? We must use democratic means. But we're against this voting system where minority votes count for nothing. I'm for a pure proportional voting system — it would give the parties a better chance. In the present system the traditional leaders dominate. A Faisal Arslan got elected just because he's called Arslan. In Baalbek there's a clan that's always got 2,500 votes to sell. When its chief dies the son can sell 2,500 votes. To get 2,500 votes I have to work ten years. But with a new voting law and Syria's greater influence enough progressive people would get into parliament to create a modern Lebanon.'

What Berri and Kanzo see as normal democracy, namely majority rule, the leaders of the militant Christian organizations — and the Christian notables — see as a threat: the threat of being condemned to permanent minority status. What the pro-Syrian organizations regard as a salutary Syrian influence horrifies them even more.

A senior judge, influential adviser to Christian politicians, expounded on these misgivings:

Assuming we get rid of our foreign factors of conflict, we would be sitting with the Lebanese Muslims. Of course a lot of them are modern democrats. But most of them are simple Muslims who will, presumably, remain Muslims, religiously and politically. It would be unreasonable to expect them to stop being Muslims. And as Muslims they accept the community of the believers and the duty to create a Muslim state whenever possible. That means they will always try to do so.

For the moment, our Sunni friends are undoubtedly convinced that this is impossible. Moreover, they are so sick of their Palestinian and Syrian brothers that they long for the old Lebanon and are thoroughly Lebanese — for the moment. The Shi`is, on the other hand, simply count on time and demographic developments: 'One day Lebanon will be ours and part of the Islamic world.' Majority-vote democracy is for them the easiest way to an Islamic state.

The Palestinians to start with, and subsequently the Syrians, must take the credit for making Lebanese of Muslims, at least for the time being. For how long? One thing we do know: there will be no Islamic state only as long as we remain strong. We are determined to keep our militias, be they open or clandestine. We won't let ourselves be caught unprepared again, as in 1958 and 1975 when the Muslims cast their veto against deploying the army. The Lebanese Christians have survived 1840, 1860, 1958 and, so far, this war. But at what cost? Does this have to be repeated every few decades? Will we always have to pay such a price so that the survivors can live in peace for a few years? Can we answer to our children for that?

What is the difference between Lebanon and other multi-communal states? When someone in this region cries 'Allah Akbar', then Muslims are Muslims only and no longer Lebanese. Our country is not a country in Oceania; it has neighbours. When a new Nasser appears next door, or a new charismatic Lebanese leader, it will start all over again.

That is why the thought of a separate state is so tempting. No one dares to think it through to the end. The consequences are appalling: more war, 'an exchange of population' — what a euphemism. But sometimes I think all of this might also happen, without our wanting it. And sometimes I hazard the thought that the price is perhaps not too high if it brings peace in the end, and we are left to ourselves.

Few in the inner circles of the Christian organizations think over the consequences of partition thoroughly, as a rule only the advisers, not the decision-makers. The main argument is the following:

> Let's not kid ourselves: the Muslims have never accepted equal treatment for minorities. There are any number of slogans against the alleged privileges of minorities, but the message is the same: the minorities should accept the traditional Islamic rules of domination and discrimination. Why not a separate state? When everybody thinks it normal for Khomeini to create an Islamic republic, why not a Jewish or a Christian republic?

One of the most influential intellectuals in the Lebanese Front stated with regret:

> The creation of Greater Lebanon was a mistake ... We mistakenly believed that progress would turn the Muslims into good Lebanese. We simply could not imagine that Islam was so immutable ... Now — unfortunately — partition is almost impossible. I'm in favour of a federal solution. If we have a federal state we can take in two million Christians from Syria, Iraq and Jordan. The Christians' position in these countries will worsen rapidly in the future ... I am optimistic. Demographic developments will change everything here. The present Syrian state will disintegrate; Alawite, Druze and Sunni states will emerge.

This 'strategist' also thinks 'population shifts' are possible:

Then perhaps the Lebanese Druze will leave Lebanon, as has happened before in history. When two Druze clans fight, the loser flees to the Jebel Druze. History has shown that it is very easy to get the Druze to leave. It's more difficult with the Shi`is, because there's no common border with Iraq. But it's not impossible. The Sunnis are less of a problem.

Another thinks along the same lines:

If it's a question of majorities, well, we'll just have to be the majority. We'll start a massive programme to bring back the emigrants. Once we have peace and democracy here, they'll come. And then, when they threaten us with majorities: we know that new majorities were made in a few days in Damour and the Chouf. If we have to, we can do it too.

However, he does not believe the present Christian politicians will accept such a policy:

We'll never build a new Lebanon with the old leaders and the old political mentality, but we can with the young. Moses let his people wander in the desert for forty years until all those who knew slavery had died. We can't build a new state with people from the mandate period, who are used to doing politics and business in the old republic. That's one lesson we've learnt.

These views on Lebanon's future hardly influence the practical politics of the militant Christian organizations. But they speak volumes about the disappointment, fears and despair the war has generated in sections of the Christian command, and especially about their determination to use all means to defend the independent existence of the Christian communities. An official spokesman of the Lebanese Forces commented:

Considerations about other oriental Christians immigrating are a creative Utopia, talk about driving out the Muslims only an — utterly unacceptable — expression of people prepared to fight to the end. Responsible political and military people don't share these views. We've not got a Masada complex; we don't want to be finished off, we want to save ourselves. In spite of everything that's happened in Lebanon, we don't question the principle of coexistence — and not because we've got no choice, but because coexistence is what we desire.

But opinions on the form this future coexistence should take diverge across the board of militant Christian leaders, irrespective of organization or political leanings. And the debate is more intense and far more controversial than among their Muslim counterparts. Bashir Gemayel favoured different concepts at different times. In one interview he declared: 'We want one single, entirely secularized and modern Lebanon on the territory of the whole republic.' One of his associates explained the reasons for this option:

> In a completely secular state the issue of majorities would be irrelevant. However, it must be a radically secularized, modern state. We've got nothing against a Muslim president if the state is secular and the president a loyal Lebanese. But we won't be satisfied with any more half-solutions. We're sick and tired of people always wanting to change the status quo and of always linking new conditions and demands to national identity. It's out of the question fighting for years just to return to the old Pact. The other side always wanted to change the Pact and always came back to it with apologies when they couldn't get their way. We're not playing that game any more, too much blood has flowed. Now we want a stable and permanent solution.

In another interview Bashir Gemayel took another tack:

> But above all, we want a federal state organized so that if there's a new war we won't be driven into the sea. In one part of the state the Christians will form the majority of the population, in another the Muslims. Beirut can be the federal capital. Education — to preserve our cultural existence — as well as defence, belong in the hands of the individual states. Why must the army also be federal? We want an army that is really motivated to fight in the case of danger ... Only when the army is also decentralized can the populations of all regions feel secure.

The aim of both concepts is security for the Christians. Either the state must be so constituted that the Christians need have no fear of majority domination and, hence, of attempts to establish an Islamic state, or they should be secure from both these threats in at least one part of the country's territory. How this security can best be achieved depends, in the opinion of various militant Christian leaders, on circumstances and political purposes.

As Professor Ibrahim Najjar, a member of the Kata'ib central committee, pointed out:

> One has to admit that our political concept was often not very clear. Since the war started we have only reacted; also we have frequently overreacted for fear of being completely eliminated. Sometimes we were really in a predicament when our men asked what we were fighting for — over and

above simple survival. Partition was an attractive answer, maybe because it is easy to understand — but in terms of our convictions the wrong answer.

He also favours a decentralized federal state, but adds: 'It is not appropriate at the moment to define exactly what a new system would look like. We have a state of emergency, and in states of emergency one should never take a definite position. The most decided champions of a federal regulation were the former president, Chamoun, and the National Liberal Party:

> In my fifty years in politics I have seen what contrasts and strains there are in this country. We have to channel and regulate them — and that is only possible in a decentralized federal state. Other nations have successfully regulated coexistence between different groups in this way, for instance Switzerland and Yugoslavia. Switzerland preserved its unity in the Second World War despite centrifugal forces. We could do so too. We need a federal state in which the provinces are as autonomous as Swiss cantons. There is no other way if we wish to preserve the unity of the country — unless one settles for a loose confederation of two states without further ado. We would prefer a federal state. I see no other alternative.

If the Muslim Lebanese were prepared to accept a decentralized federal state, some of the militant Christian politicians would be prepared to relinquish the Christians' claim to the presidency. Charles Malek: 'The plan Manuel Younes worked out seems thoroughly acceptable to me, provided that decentralization is an unequivocal guarantee of our security. The collective body he proposes for the executive — in which large and small communities would have the same rights — has the virtue of considerably downgrading the demographic question.' A Maronite member of the Kata'ib leadership thinks:

> A new compromise is possible, if the Muslims renounce the centralized state and the Christians the presidency in favour of a collective executive.
> Personally, I prefer centralized government in small countries like ours. But I've given up hope that the Muslims will ever accept full secularization — and a centralized state without full secularization means turning the Christians into 'dhimmis'. Therefore: either 'a republic, one and inviolate' with complete separation of church and state, civil law for marriage and inheritance, complete freedom of religion — and the freedom to have no religion — or no centralized state.
> Then, we'd prefer cantons like those in Switzerland with complete autonomy in cultural matters and partial autonomy in matters of defence, and over both a federal council like Manual Younes has proposed with a representa-

tive from each of the Sunni, Shi`i, Druze, Maronite, Orthodox and Catholic communities. I think this proposal is the best. The role of the smaller communities would be strengthened, the direct Maronite-Sunni dualism replaced by diversity. Communities would count, not heads or noses. But this new executive could exist only on condition that the guarantee the presidency has given us up to now is replaced by the guarantee of wide autonomy for the cantons.

Samir Geagea, commander of the Lebanese Forces, put his views bluntly:

All I'm interested in is the Christians' security. If it was possible I'd like to lead my people to a country where they were safe. But this possibility doesn't exist. We've only got this country, and we've got to make sure we have security here. The 1943 system doesn't give it, it's broken down two times. Here majority-rule democracy means Islam rules. We've refused to accept this for a thousand years and we won't accept it now.

We're ready to coexist with the Muslims. But we want forms of coexistence where we can't be blackmailed. We want serious security guarantees — that means territory.

If the other side keeps up its demands the war will go on for a long time.

Geagea's view of Syria's role is equally forthright: 'The other side makes demands because they've got Syria behind them, and probably because Syria wants them to make these demands. But we also won't capitulate to Syria. That is why the war will go on for a long time.' Most of the political respondents reveal a mixture of hopes and fears, for their respective groups as well as for the country as a whole. Fears predominate. Shortly before his death, Charles Malek spoke about his greatest worry:

Will there still be free Christians in this country in the future? All threats point in the same direction: to reduce our status to that of Christians in Syria, Iraq or Egypt, or even lower. Christianity has all but disappeared in many countries in the Orient. In 1920 there were still four million Christians in Turkey. One million lived in Constantinople, Smyrna was a Christian city, there was a large Christian community in Alexandretta. Today, Turkey is a country with practically no Christians; the last Syrian Orthodox are emigrating to Western Europe. Christian communities have been compelled to leave, driven out, forced to emigrate. What will historians in Freiburg and Tübingen say in fifty years' time? Much the same, I fear, as about the Christians in Turkey today. I fear we are living through the last days of the last free Christian community in the Orient.

Muslim politicians also fear for their freedom. A Sunni notable wonders:

> What will Lebanon's fate be? What ties me to this country is the idea of liberty, that liberty that no longer exists in other Arab states. Until 1975 we were the land of liberty. This liberty no longer exists, neither among the Christians nor among the Muslims. A partitioned Lebanon would go the way of the Arab dictatorships, even its Christian part. As a Sunni Muslim I want to be Lebanese, not because I would adopt political Maronitism — how could I? — but because only Lebanon, Christian and Muslim, can be the land of liberty I would like to live in. At present I work in Paris, Riyadh and Beirut. In Paris I'm among strangers, in Riyadh among Bedouins, in Beirut — unfortunately — among bandits.

In summary: most Lebanese politicians believe the pre-war system can be restored; the political and military leaders of the belligerent parties reject this system. The political creed of the 'foxes' was and is compromise. The militia commanders see no basis for compromise. In essence, the political choice is between 'political secularization', i.e., majority-vote democracy without societal secularization, and either complete secularization or a strongly decentralized federal state. None of the 'lions' any longer speaks of military victory, but each is still determined to prevent the others realizing their political objectives. The prolongation of the conflict between them is not a consequence of misperceptions, but of a clash of objectives that are in each case correctly perceived but irreconcilable.

# 7

## Coexistence in War
## Attitudes and Opinions of Economically Active Lebanese 1981–1987

> 'An opinion poll today, would probably show that more than half the people don't like any politician.'
>
> Walid Jumblatt, 1979

> 'Now both of us ... are afraid, on this side and on the other side. But if a referendum were held today — without armed intimidation, of course — ninety per cent on each side would favour cooperation. The ordinary people on both sides have had enough of the leaders who led them into this disaster. Deep down the Lebanese people feel they belong together and can get on well together.'
>
> Saeb Salam, 1979

The 1972 elections were to be the last for twenty years. The spiral of violence began three years later. Regardless of outsiders' actions, Lebanese have murdered, injured, tortured, robbed and displaced other Lebanese. After this, is it possible for the Lebanese to live together, and if so, how?

These questions are not new. But they were never so important as during the years of war. Yet many ordinary Lebanese can still not express their opinions through the channels of a properly functioning parliamentary democracy. The term of the Lebanese parliament elected in 1972 was extended constitutionally several times, as it was impossible to hold even bye-elections for seats that became vacant, let alone national elections. Parliament was hardly in any position to influence the destiny of the country. No one could say whether the deputies elected in 1972 still represented the opinions of the voters, or if the self-appointed militia leaders and commanders, who, after 1975, claimed to speak and act in the name of the Lebanese people or its constituent communities, ever did so.

Empirical social research is not a substitute for free elections. However, in the absence of elections it can establish what people's preferences might be if ballots counted more than bullets. It can provide insights into the nature of the conflict, and thereby help to assess possibilities of peaceful conflict regulation. Are conceptions of a future Lebanon so contrary as to be irreconcilable, or is there room for compromise, as so often in the past? What kinds of compromise can provide a basis for coexistence, and remove the threat of violence?

The force of arms, the belligerent diligence of small, determined groups and the might of non-Lebanese powers may be more important than the thoughts and wishes of Lebanese citizens. But what these citizens think and wish cannot be totally irrelevant to what those who decide on open warfare, intermittent strife and peace are able to do in the medium and long term. A few citizens may be able to prolong war, especially civil war, for a long time, but not without the acquiescence of many. Hence, it is worth knowing how many this 'many' actually are. However, there can be no lasting peace unless a large majority of the citizens want it, and are reasonably agreed on what it entails.

In general, empirical social research can determine attitudes, opinions and basic political orientations fairly reliably. Is it able to do so under the particular conditions of more or less intensive warfare? Experience with surveys conducted in areas of tension below the threshold of armed conflict speaks in favour.[1] From September to December 1981, the author and Salim Nasr conducted a trial run in Lebanon. This was a relatively quiet period, although raids, armed clashes, shelling and artillery duels within or between the various militia zones in the country occurred almost daily. These circumstances did not impair the quality of the material. On the contrary, almost all respondents were very cooperative and open,

---

[1] For instance, in South Africa it proved extraordinarily difficult to conduct opinion polls among the black population before the Soweto uprising of 1976; the respondents were — understandably — mistrustful and afraid. However, once the uprising had started, the climate changed completely. There was a marked decline in fear, and the respondents answered clearly and without ambiguity; 77 per cent expressed their satisfaction at being able to give their opinion on matters they considered vital. See Theodor Hanf, Heribert Weiland and Gerda Vierdag, *South Africa: The prospects of peaceful change* (London, Cape Town and Bloomington, 1981), pp. 67–8.

and many extremely grateful to be able to speak their mind in such a situation. By comparison with surveys in peaceful countries, the refusal quota of under 2 per cent was exceptionally low, which speaks for itself.[2] The crucial factor was the interviewers: a dozen committed and dependable young social scientists from different denominational communities and regions with experience in interviewing. The sample for this pilot survey consisted of unionized employees; the control groups were non-unionized employees and self-employed.

After the success of this trial run, three further surveys were conducted in 1984, 1986 and 1987. These included all economically active persons, not just union members. Besides socio-structural data, questions dealt with psycho-social attitudes, attitudes to occupation and working conditions, perceptions of Lebanese society, religion and denominational communities, the political system, political orientation and preference, the relationship between religion and politics and, finally, the fundamental questions of coexistence in Lebanon: whether and how it was possible.[3] This broad approach was chosen because earlier studies on political opinions and attitudes, in Lebanon as well as in other societies in crisis, had revealed a close, and analytically fruitful, relationship between different clusters of attitudes.[4] A standardized, structured questionnaire was used. Most items were affirmative statements requiring a Yes/No response, and, as controls, there were negative statements elsewhere in the questionnaire. The interviewers recorded the verbal responses. On average, it took an hour to cover the wide range of topics.[5]

Why was the survey repeated? Topical political and economic events always influence attitudes and opinions. Repetition under different circumstances reveals with some certainty which attitudes should be treated as momentary and which as more permanent. The series of surveys in this book record the attitudes of Lebanese under extremely varied political and economic conditions:

---

[2] Theodor Hanf and Salim Nasr, *Urban Crisis and Social Movements: Arab and European perspectives* (Beirut, 1987), Chapter 2.

[3] The complete questionnaire is included in the Appendix.

[4] For example, the South Africa study cited in n. 1 above. On Lebanon, see Theodor Hanf, Le comportement politique des étudiants libanais, *Travaux et Jours* 46 (1973); Halim Barakat, *Lebanon in Strife: Student preludes to the civil war. Modern Middle East Series No. 2* (Austin and London, 1977) and 'Social and political integration in Lebanon: A case of social mosaic', Middle East Journal, 27 (1973), pp. 301–18; Iliya F. Harik, 'The economic and social factors in the Lebanese crisis', *Journal of Arab Affairs* 1/1 (1982).

[5] The questionnaire was constructed by the author and Salim Nasr. Nasr was also responsible for the random samples and overall monitoring of the interviews. Nasr and the author evaluated the 1981 survey together; see n. 2 above. The author alone is responsible for the evaluation of the later surveys. The author had already used some of the items in earlier inter-cultural surveys.

- The last quarter of 1981 was a period of relatively low-level warfare and of relative 'equilibrium of (regional and internal Lebanese) terror'; economically it was a period of recovery.
- Early 1984 was a period of extreme tension. The Israeli invasion had shattered any illusions of governmental and economic reconstruction. The Chouf War had ended in the expulsion of tens of thousands of Christians. On February 7th, 1984, the Lebanese Army disintegrated; Shi`i and Druze militias took control of West Beirut — a phase of 'genuine' civil war. Confidence in the Lebanese economy was badly shaken.
- The summer of 1986 was also a period of acute crisis. The Damascus Agreement between the three most powerful militias had collapsed after the violent change in command of the Lebanese Forces and rejection by President Gemayel. Heavy fighting seemed imminent. As a result of the economic crisis and the collapse of the Lebanese currency, poverty was becoming widespread.
- The mood in autumn 1987 was one of pervasive hopelessness: it was relatively quiet — a little fighting within the opposing camps, fighting between Shi`is and Palestinians, growing confrontation in the south — and economic misery was worsening.

Thus, the surveys cover periods of relative quiet and heavy fighting, periods in which the one side and then the other side were anticipating victory, periods of relative prosperity and of rapid economic decline. Attitudes and opinions that remain stable through all these phases may be accepted as deeply rooted and lasting.

The following analysis is based primarily on the data of the 1987 survey. It was the last and had the largest sample (N = 2003), which allows a more detailed breakdown by age, education, occupation, religion and region. In each section detailed analysis is preceded by a comparison over time; by distinguishing stable from changing attitudes it will be possible to establish 'hard core' social and political opinion in Lebanon.

## The comparability of the surveys

Are representative surveys at all possible in a country that held its last census in 1932, and in which the question of the numerical strength of the religious communities is at the root of political conflict? Lebanon is a country of paradoxes. For political reasons, politicians and civil servants have refused to allow a census, but, for economic reasons, have always kept detailed statistics on the economically active population.[6] A number of separate surveys carried out since the outbreak of war allow approximate estimates for adjustments to the statistics for 1972. Although there are no figures for the whole population by religious community, there are approximate distributions of the economically active population by gender, age and economic sector as well as by region, though the latter is distorted by flight, displacement and expulsion.

Accordingly, it was decided not to attempt representative surveys of the population or electorate as a whole. Instead, quota samples of the economically active population were constructed on the basis of known characteristics. This has drawbacks for an analysis of political attitudes: it excludes the oldest age groups and housewives, groups which tend to be conservative in most societies. But it also has advantages: as a rule, the economically active population is also the most active socially and politically. Samples were constructed by economic sector and region, and subsequently broken down by gender and age group; all characteristics were run in combination. The 1981 survey is comparable only with qualifications because of the different initial breakdown: unionized workers, non-unionized workers and self-employed (N = 350, 50, 100). Only then was each sample broken down by the other characteristics. The distribution of respondents by economic sector in the four questionnaires is as follows:

Table 7.1

| Economic sector | 1981 | 1984 | 1986 | 1987 |
|---|---|---|---|---|
| (Agriculture) | (1) | (7) | (9) | (8) |
| Manufacturing, construction | 25 | 24 | 20 | 20 |
| Commerce, transport | 22 | 26 | 28 | 22 |
| Banking, insurance | 8 | 6 | 5 | 8 |
| Other private-sector services | 19 | 13 | 20 | 18 |
| State, education | 25 | 25 | 18 | 24 |
| N = | 500 | 783 | 480 | 2003 |

Figures in %

---

[6] République Libanaise, Ministère du Plan, Direction Centrale de la Statisque, *L'enquête par sondage sur la population active au Liban*, Vols. 1 and 2 (Beirut, 1972).

Agriculture has lower than average representation in the 1981 survey because of low trade-union membership. Apart from it, there are no statistically significant differences by economic sector between the samples. But there are by region:

**Table 7.2**

| Regions | (1981) | 1984 | 1986 | 1987 |
|---|---|---|---|---|
| East Beirut, Metn, Kisrawan, Jbeil | (26) | 26 | 32 | 29 |
| West Beirut & suburbs | (38) | 34 | 32 | 30 |
| Chouf | (20) | 3 | 6 | 5 |
| Tripoli, Sidon | (4) | 12 | 5 | 9 |
| Southern Lebanon | (–) | 9 | 8 | 8 |
| Northern Lebanon | (7) | 10 | 8 | 9 |
| Bekaa | (5) | 6 | 9 | 10 |

Figures in %

The 1981 sample differs from the others because the level of unionization varies greatly by region; for instance, it is well above average in the Chouf. Population movements since 1984,[7] in particular the expulsion of Christians from the Chouf and the hinterland of Sidon as well as the remigration of Shi`is to the Bekaa, have been taken into account. Because of these deviations, the analysis of the factor 'region' is based solely on the data of the 1987 survey. There are no significant deviations by gender; females consistently constitute one-fifth of the working population. For the factor age, the 1981 survey differs from the others because the youngest age group has lower than average representation in the trade unions; there are no significant deviations between the later three surveys.

Because of hyper-inflation, absolute values for the distribution of income have been meaningless since 1984. So, for each of the samples we have divided the absolute levels of income into four income groups, which are then compared. There are no significant deviations by education between the samples, although no quotas had been prescribed.

---

[7] See Salim Nasr, 'Redrawing the social geography of Lebanon', Research Report, Fletcher School of Diplomacy, Tufts University, Cambridge, Mass., 1988.

## Table 7.3

| Age group | (1981) | 1984 | 1986 | 1987 |
|---|---|---|---|---|
| 15–20 years | (6) | 10 | 10 | 10 |
| 21–35 years | (60) | 62 | 62 | 58 |
| 36–45 years | (22) | 19 | 18 | 19 |
| 46 years and older | (12) | 8 | 10 | 13 |

Figures in %

## Table 7.4

| Educational level | 1981 | 1984 | 1986 | 1987 |
|---|---|---|---|---|
| Primary schooling and less | 26 | 29 | 24 | 27 |
| Technical, vocational schooling | 24 | 20 | 23 | 24 |
| Secondary schooling and further education | 50 | 51 | 53 | 49 |

Figures in %

The factor religious community was not prestructured either. The 1981 results differ markedly from the later three, between which deviations are insignificant.

## Table 7.5

| Religious community | (1981) | 1984 | 1986 | 1987 |
|---|---|---|---|---|
| Sunni | (18) | 22 | 16 | 21 |
| Shi`i | (26) | 26 | 27 | 27 |
| Druze | (4) | 5 | 6 | 4 |
| Maronite | (38) | 24 | 29 | 25 |
| Greek Orthodox and Greek Catholic | (12) | 18 | 17 | 19 |
| Armenian and other Christian | (2) | 5 | 5 | 4 |

Figures in %

In summary: the samples of 1984, 1986 and 1987 are fully comparable for the factors economic sector, gender and age; for the factor region they have been adapted to the changed conditions and vary accordingly. Although the target group of the 1981 survey was different, it results are, with appropriate qualifications, comparable.

The distributions by education and religious affiliation may be taken as controls of the comparability of the questionnaires as there were no prescribed quotas for these factors. Education is comparable in all four surveys, religious affiliation in the last three. The data for both variables are consistent enough to warrant the use of all four surveys for an approximate trend analysis.

## The 1987 survey

As the 1987 survey is the most recent and most comprehensive, it will be used for the detailed analysis. Seventy-nine per cent of the respondents are male, 21 per cent female. Economically active women are considerably younger than men. Four-fifths of them are under thirty-six, compared with two-thirds of the men. Fewer are married, and more than half of them do not have any children. Although their standard of education is above average — two-thirds are secondary school or university graduates, compared with 42 per cent of the men — their frequency in the lowest income groups is twice that of men, but in the highest income groups only one-third. Their numbers are high in education, banking and other services. Geographically, they have higher than average representation in East Beirut, the Metn, Kisrawan and Jbeil. Sixty-one per cent of all working women are Christian — mainly Maronite and Greek Catholic — as against 45 per cent of all working men: Lebanese working society is predominantly male, especially the Muslim part. The distribution of respondents by age is as follows:

**Table 7.6**

|  | % |
| --- | --- |
| 15–20 years | 10 |
| 21–25 years | 16 |
| 26–35 years | 42 |
| 36–45 years | 19 |
| 46 years and older | 13 |

Forty-two per cent are single, 46 per cent have no children, 24 per cent have between one and three children, and 30 per cent four and more.

People tend to marry late in Lebanon, primarily for economic reasons. Thirty-five per cent of respondents up to the age of thirty-five are in the lowest income groups. People marry only when they are in a position to support a family. Most single people are active in the service sector or manufacturing, in occupations with the lowest wages and salaries. Farmers tend to have the most children: two-thirds have four or more.

Lebanese demographic developments seem to be in transition. Large families are a phenomenon of the agricultural population, but even here they are now less common. The residual influence of the agricultural milieu is reflected in urban demographic trends: recent migrants from the rural areas of southern, northern and eastern Lebanon are more likely than others to have large families.

Young people from all parts of the country are streaming to Beirut. Over half the respondents under twenty-five years of age come from peripheral areas of the country. Today, the portion of young people is higher in heavily urbanized areas than in other parts of the country.

**Table 7.7**

| Area | 15–25-year-olds (%) |
| --- | --- |
| East Beirut and suburbs | 28 |
| West Beirut and suburbs | 28 |
| Metn | 27 |
| Kisrawan, Jbeil | 29 |
| Chouf, Aley | 24 |
| Tripoli, Sidon | 22 |
| Southern Lebanon | 21 |
| Northern Lebanon[8] | 29 |
| Bekaa | 22 |

The respondents were divided into four income groups of approximately equal size: less than 6,000 Lebanese pounds (LL) a month, LL6,000–8,000, LL8,000–

---

[8] The figure for northern Lebanon probably reflects the political situation. The enmity between the Christian militias then controlling the Koura and Zghorta regions and East Beirut respectively discouraged migration, and northern Christians did not migrate to West Beirut.

10,000, and more than LL10,000 (1987 incomes).[9] Twelve per cent have a second source of income; just under half own a house or land.

Large landowners, industrialists and professionals people have higher than average representation in the highest income group: half of the respondents are in these occupations; civil servants, white-collar workers, artisans and farmers are in the middle groups; and clerical workers, teachers, industrial workers, manual workers and employees of small service firms are in the lowest income group.[10]

Incomes that are higher than average are most common in East Beirut, the Metn and the Chouf, whereas the lower income groups have higher than average representation in southern Lebanon and West Beirut. This undoubtedly reflects the security situation in the different regions: in 1987 the economic situation in relatively quiet areas was far better than in war-torn regions. By completed level of education the 1987 sample is as follows:

**Table 7.8**

|  | % |
|---|---|
| no formal qualification | 14 |
| primary school | 13 |
| technical school (brevet)[11] | 24 |
| secondary school | 30 |
| university | 19 |

Although education is not compulsory in Lebanon, it is a highly educated society. This is especially true of its working population, of whom over half have completed secondary school and one-fifth university — figures comparable with western industrial societies.[12] On the other hand, a not inconsiderable number of Lebanese have little formal schooling. The causes lie in educational policies prior

---

[9] Eleven per cent of respondents left this question unanswered. Most of them were people with seasonal or irregular incomes, either in agriculture — large landowners, farmers and agricultural labourers — or self-employed professionals.

[10] By sector, earnings are highest in commerce (over 50 per cent in the highest income group) and in banking and insurance (38 per cent).

[11] The brevet, which is roughly comparable to a trade-school certificate or vocational training at secondary-school level.

[12] The comparison holds not only for quantity but also for quality. The requirements for the Lebanese baccalaureate are equivalent to those for the French, with the exception of foreign languages, for which Lebanese requirements are very much higher. Since the 1960s the standard of vocational training has compared with the best anywhere.

to and since independence. The Ottomans left schooling to the religious communities, a responsibility taken most seriously by the Christian Churches in Mount Lebanon. The French mandate authorities introduced state education to remedy regional disparities; in the peripheral territories under direct Ottoman administration up to 1920 there were hardly any schools at all. During Fouad Chehab's presidency (1958–1964) a policy of regional development was energetically pursued, without going as far as compulsory education. In a predominantly service-based economy that rewarded educational qualifications greater hopes were placed in the pull effect of economic gain than the push effect of compulsory schooling.[13]

The distribution of education by age reflects the consequences. Seventy-two per cent of the respondents without any certificate of schooling are over thirty-five, that is, were of school-going age before the Chehab era; only 4 per cent are younger than twenty-five. The educational level of young people is higher than average.[14] The proportion with secondary school certificates is approaching 60 per cent, and every fourth person in the 26–35 age group has a university degree.

The bulk of respondents without any formal qualifications are farmers and agricultural and manual workers, people in occupations which place little importance on certificates. As one might expect, there is a high proportion of highly educated persons among professional people, civil servants, teachers and employees in banking and insurance.

Although the expansion in education has reduced regional disparities over the past quarter of a century, it has not eliminated them. In Beirut the poorly educated are found mainly in Chiyah and Jnah-Ouzai, Shi`i suburbs housing many migrants from the south and east of the country. Outside Beirut, the poorly educated are also found predominantly in Shi`i regions — Baalbek-Hermel, Jezzine and the extreme south, Nabatieh — as well as in the Chouf: the historic lag persists.

'Mount Lebanon' still retains its historic lead at university level. In East Beirut, its suburbs and the Christian regions of central and northern Lebanon — the Metn, Kisrawan, Jbeil, Koura and Zghorta — as well as Tripoli, the number of university graduates is higher than average, and in the Metn over twice the national average. The effects of the 1960s policy of compensatory education are most pronounced in secondary school education. Hence, it is probably only a question of time before regional equilibrium is established at university level as well. The relationship between education and income is complex:

---

[13] See Theodor Hanf, *Erziehungswesen in Gesellschaft und Politik des Libanon* (Düsseldorf, 1969).
[14] Of the 21 to 25 age-group, 38 per cent are secondary school and 19 per cent university graduates. As many working Lebanese are enrolled at university, this figure is likely to rise.

**Table 7.9** Education by area

| Area | none | primary school | brevet | secondary school | university |
|---|---|---|---|---|---|
| Beirut: | | | | | |
| Ras Beirut | 9 | | 27 | 38 | 16 |
| Mseitbeh, Mazraa | 18 | 9 | 26 | 30 | 17 |
| Basta | 12 | 16 | 23 | 38 | 12 |
| Tarik al-Jadideh | 17 | 12 | 31 | 32 | 7 |
| Ashrafieh | 13 | 11 | 27 | 28 | 22 |
| Eastern suburbs | 11 | 12 | 30 | 25 | 22 |
| Chiyah | 21 | 21 | 20 | 30 | 9 |
| Haret Hreik | 15 | 12 | 22 | 37 | 15 |
| Bourj al-Barajneh | 14 | 18 | 25 | 32 | 12 |
| Jnah, Ouzai | 21 | 14 | 32 | 29 | 5 |
| Beirut overall | 14 | 13 | 27 | 31 | 15 |
| Other regions: | | | | | |
| Metn | 7 | 4 | 13 | 35 | 41 |
| Kisrawan | 8 | 8 | 16 | 36 | 31 |
| Jbeil | 7 | 14 | 26 | 19 | 34 |
| Chouf, Aley | 20 | 20 | 22 | 21 | 16 |
| Sidon | 17 | 7 | 21 | 42 | 14 |
| Nabatieh | 20 | 19 | 25 | 20 | 16 |
| Jezzine | 24 | 9 | 15 | 42 | 11 |
| Central & western Bekaa | 15 | 17 | 34 | 27 | 8 |
| Baalbek, Hermel | 25 | 21 | 25 | 18 | 12 |
| Tripoli | 9 | 12 | 26 | 24 | 30 |
| Koura, Zhgorta | 8 | 7 | 18 | 33 | 34 |
| Akkar | 8 | 19 | 30 | 30 | 12 |
| Other regions overall | 14 | 13 | 22 | 29 | 22 |
| RESPONDENTS OVERALL | 14 | 13 | 24 | 30 | 19 |

Figures in %

## Table 7.10

| Education | Income groups | | | |
| --- | --- | --- | --- | --- |
|  | 1 (lowest) | 2 | 3 | 4 (highest) |
| No formal qualification | 17 | 31 | 33 | 19 |
| Primary-school certificate | 25 | 20 | 26 | 29 |
| Brevet | 38 | 19 | 20 | 23 |
| Secondary-school certificate | 29 | 35 | 17 | 19 |
| University degree | 19 | 27 | 17 | 37 |
| All respondents | 27 | 27 | 21 | 25 |

Figures in %

In Lebanon a lack of formal education does not imply a low income. The number of respondents in this category may be below average in the highest income category, but this is also the case in the lowest. On the other hand, they have higher than average representation in the middle income groups. The majority of them are farmers and manual workers who make a decent living and are therefore fairly immune to the 'pull' of the educational system.

The number of people with only primary-school education is higher than average in the upper income groups. In Lebanon many occupations, especially in commerce, reward resourcefulness, versatility, an outgoing personality and experience — qualities and attributes seldom taught at school or university — more generously than educational qualifications. Formal education need not bring exceptional material advantages. The more or less average proportions of people with a brevet in the upper two income groups is evidence of the potential of this education. On the other hand, the proportion of such people in the lowest income group is well above average. This is largely explained by the fact that certain occupations that offered employment opportunities for this group have been hardest hit by the war: manufacturing, on the one hand, and tourism, on the other.[15] As will be seen below, brevet-holders are particularly interested in a peaceful solution to the conflict, as this markedly improves their job prospects.

---

[15] Lebanese vocational and trade schools were attuned to the needs of those industries that were expanding strongly in the first half of the 1970s. In the same period the schools of hotel management expanded rapidly. They ran their own chain of restaurants and hotels and their graduates were sought after on account of their practical experience. Manufacturing industries were badly hit by the war, and tourism virtually ceased.

The most critical level of education from the economic point of view is the secondary school certificate. Secondary school graduates have lower than average representation in the upper two income groups and higher than average representation in the second lowest. In the early 1970s, even before the outbreak of war, the supply of secondary school graduates on the Lebanese labour market was considerably greater than demand. The market value of the secondary school certificate has declined in step with the economy since 1984. Since the late 1960s, the country's secondary school system has closed the educational gap between the regions, but this, in turn, has not automatically reduced the income gap. Today, discontented secondary school graduates are a strongly politicized, articulate group for whom radical policies have a higher than average appeal.

Nor does a university degree guarantee a good income. Almost one-fifth of all university graduates fall into the lowest income group. Notwithstanding this, investment in university education makes economic sense: the proportion of university graduates in the highest income group is well above average. They have access to the lucrative professions, to top positions in banking and insurance and in the civil service. In contrast to the secondary school certificate, the university degree remains a reliable indicator of relative prosperity, although by no means the only one. The respondents divide by occupation as follows:

**Table 7.11**

|  | % |
| --- | --- |
| large landowners, industrialists | 6 |
| self-employed professionals | 13 |
| civil servants, white-collar workers | 35 |
| artisans | 13 |
| farmers | 3 |
| industrial workers | 13 |
| service sector | 12 |
| agricultural labourers | 5 |

And they work in the following economic sectors:

## Table 7.12

|  | % |
|---|---|
| state and para-statal enterprises | 13 |
| agriculture | 8 |
| manufacturing industry | 14 |
| building and construction | 6 |
| commerce and trade | 14 |
| banking and insurance | 8 |
| transport | 8 |
| education | 11 |
| other service industries | 18 |

The number of professionals is higher than average, particularly in the Metn, and lower than average in West Beirut, almost certainly a consequence of war-induced migration. Manual workers are less common in West Beirut and southern Lebanon, also independent farmers in southern Lebanon, and agricultural workers in the Chouf and in the Bekaa, the last bastions of the traditional large landowners.

The war has caused Lebanese industry to decentralize. This process in reflected in the distribution of industrial workers by region. They constitute a higher than average proportion of the economically active population in the Shi`i suburbs of West Beirut and the Maronite suburbs of East Beirut as well as in Jbeil and Kisrawan, areas of the less endangered Christian enclave to which a number of manufacturers from the heavily contested peripheral zones of Beirut have moved.

The next table shows occupational mobility between generations, which illustrates the dramatic structural change that has taken place in the economy.

Only the proportion of large landowners and industrialists has remained constant. In one generation, professionals have risen from 5 to 13 per cent and civil servants and white-collar workers from 15 to 35 per cent. The proportion of manual workers has halved, that of farmers fallen 18 to 3 per cent. The proportion of industrial workers has declined slightly, almost certainly an effect of the war, while that of the service sector has doubled from 6 to 12 per cent. Agricultural labourers, a generation ago still 10 per cent, now constitute only 5 per cent. In short: the decline of the working force in agricultural employment is comparable with that in Germany and France; the proportion in manufacturing industry has remained stable, while employment in both the public and private service sectors has expanded tremendously.

Table 7.13 Occupational mobility between the generations

| Father's occupation: | large landowner, industrialist | self-employed | civil servant, white-collar worker | artisan | farmer | blue-collar worker | tertiary sector | farmworker | occupation: all respondents |
|---|---|---|---|---|---|---|---|---|---|
| Respondent's occupation: | | | | | | | | | |
| large landowner industrialist | 30 | 12 | 12 | 33 | 9 | 1 | 2 | 1 | 6 |
| self-employed | 12 | 14 | 23 | 23 | 10 | 10 | 4 | 4 | 13 |
| civil servant, white-collar worker | 6 | 5 | 21 | 25 | 14 | 15 | 8 | 6 | 35 |
| artisan | 3 | 3 | 4 | 28 | 29 | 18 | 8 | 7 | 13 |
| farmer | 2 | – | 4 | 15 | 40 | 10 | – | 29 | 3 |
| blue-collar worker | 2 | 3 | 7 | 24 | 22 | 18 | 8 | 16 | 13 |
| tertiary sector | 2 | 1 | 12 | 29 | 16 | 26 | 4 | 10 | 12 |
| farmworker | – | – | 2 | 15 | 26 | 5 | 3 | 49 | 5 |
| Father's occupation: all | 6 | 5 | 15 | 25 | 18 | 15 | 6 | 10 | 100 |

Figures in %

Attitudes and Opinions of Economically Active Lebanese 451

**Table 7.14** Place of birth and current area of domicile

| Current domicile: | East Beirut & suburbs | West Beirut & suburbs | Metn | Kisrawan, Jbeil | Chouf, Aley | Tripoli, Sidon | Southern Lebanon | Northern Lebanon | Bekaa | Place of birth: all |
|---|---|---|---|---|---|---|---|---|---|---|
| Place of birth: | | | | | | | | | | |
| East Beirut and suburbs | <u>75</u> | 4 | 5 | 5 | 1 | – | – | 1 | 8 | 9 |
| West Beirut and suburbs | 6 | <u>86</u> | 4 | – | 1 | 1 | – | – | 2 | 12 |
| Metn | 20 | 8 | <u>57</u> | 5 | 1 | – | – | – | 9 | 6 |
| Kisrawan, Jbeil | 3 | 4 | 6 | <u>82</u> | – | 1 | – | 1 | 3 | 7 |
| Chouf, Aley | 11 | 26 | 5 | 3 | <u>52</u> | 1 | 1 | – | 1 | 9 |
| Tripoli, Sidon | 2 | 13 | 1 | 1 | – | <u>80</u> | 1 | 1 | 1 | 8 |
| Southern Lebanon | 1 | 56 | 1 | – | – | 1 | <u>41</u> | – | – | 18 |
| Northern Lebanon | 12 | 5 | 2 | 5 | – | 10 | – | <u>65</u> | 1 | 14 |
| Bekaa | 17 | 23 | 3 | 1 | – | – | – | – | <u>56</u> | 16 |
| Place of residence: all | 15 | 30 | 6 | 8 | 5 | 9 | 8 | 9 | 10 | 100 |

Figures in %

Lebanese society is characterized not only by high social and occupational mobility but also by considerable geographic mobility. Only part of this has been voluntary or economically motivated. Much is accounted for by war-induced displacement. By comparing the respondents' places of birth and residence one can discern outlines of the pattern of migration.[16]

The majority of respondents live in the region in which they were born. However, only 41 per cent of the southern Lebanese still do, and only 52 per cent in the Chouf-Aley region. Emigration has been strongest from southern Lebanon. Fifty-six per cent of the respondents born there now live in West Beirut, either attracted by the economic opportunities available in the capital, or repelled by the poverty of their home region, or escaping from the fighting that has ravaged this part of the country since 1969. The pattern of emigration from the Chouf and Aley is similar. Most of the 25 per cent from this region living in West Beirut will have sought better living conditions and job opportunities, while most of the 19 per cent living in East Beirut, the Metn, Kisrawan and Jbeil are probably refugees from the 1983 and 1984 wars in the Chouf.

Of the respondents born in the Bekaa, one-fifth now live in East Beirut and its hinterland and one-fifth in West Beirut. The former are exclusively Christians, for whom survival in the Bekaa was difficult after 1975 and precarious after 1983; the latter are predominantly Shi`is who have settled in the southern suburbs of the capital.

Eight per cent of those born in East Beirut and 9 per cent in the Metn today live in the Bekaa, for the most part probably Shi`is driven out of the Nabaa and Karantina districts and the Palestinian camps of Jisr al-Pasha and Tel al-Za`tar in 1976. A further 4 per cent from East Beirut and 8 per cent from the Metn now live in West Beirut, and 10 per cent from West Beirut in East Beirut and the Metn — victims of the 'homogenization' of the two halves of the capital.

Migratory movements that might be classified as 'normal' are of secondary importance in numerical terms, such the exchange between East Beirut and its Christian hinterland or between northern Lebanon and Tripoli. The great streams of internal Lebanese migration have been made up, on the one hand, of the exodus from peripheral rural areas to Greater Beirut — in the pre-war period chiefly economic, since then also war-motivated, particularly from the south — and, on the other, by the flight or expulsion of the respective minorities from areas in which religious communities coexisted before the war.

---

[16] Of course, the sample is too small to draw statistically relevant demographic conclusions; it cannot do duty for a census. However, it can illustrate the nature and approximate magnitude of the internal migration.

For whatever reason, in 1987, 35 per cent of all respondents no longer lived in the region in which they were born. This is a greater redistribution of population than in post-war Germany. A comparison between respondents' place of residence and confession gives some indication of the trend towards homogeneity.[17]

Table 7.15 Religious community by area

| Area | Sunnis | Shi'is | Druze | Maronites | Greek Orth. | Greek Cath. | Armenians |
|---|---|---|---|---|---|---|---|
| Beirut: | | | | | | | |
| Ras Beirut | 41 | 13 | 14 | 8 | 6 | 6 | 13 |
| Mseitbeh, Mazraa | 27 | 27 | 24 | 5 | 9 | 3 | 5 |
| Basta | 46 | 41 | 6 | – | – | 1 | 5 |
| Tarik al-Jadideh | 42 | 41 | 12 | 1 | – | – | 4 |
| Ashrafieh | – | 1 | – | 26 | 55 | 11 | 7 |
| Eastern suburbs | – | – | – | 70 | 8 | 17 | 5 |
| Chiyah | 7 | 87 | 6 | – | – | – | – |
| Haret Hreik | 7 | 88 | 6 | – | – | – | – |
| Bourj al-Barajneh | 4 | 92 | 4 | – | – | – | – |
| Jnah, Ouzai | 6 | 91 | 3 | – | – | – | – |
| Beirut overall | 16 | 40 | 6 | 17 | 11 | 5 | 4 |
| Other regions: | | | | | | | |
| Metn | – | – | – | 33 | 21 | 24 | 22 |
| Kisrawan | – | – | – | 99 | – | 1 | – |
| Jbeil | 16 | 11 | – | 73 | – | – | – |
| Chouf, Aley | 55 | 5 | 19 | 4 | 8 | 9 | – |
| Sidon | 74 | 6 | 1 | 4 | 1 | 13 | – |
| Nabatieh | – | 81 | – | 7 | – | 12 | – |
| Jezzine | 14 | 2 | – | 31 | 29 | 24 | – |

[17] The sample is inadequate for establishing demographic trends. Although it is not prestructured by religious affiliation — this is an incidental result of the selected quotas — the sample is a useful illustration of the regional composition of the population by religious community. On this point see also Khalyl Abou Rjaily and Boutros Labaki, *Les paroisses déplacées des églises du Liban* (Paris and Beirut, 1987).

| | | | | | | | |
|---|---|---|---|---|---|---|---|
| Central & western Bekaa, Zahle | 10 | 16 | 3 | 33 | 2 | 25 | 12 |
| Baalbek, Hermel | 13 | 72 | – | 6 | – | 9 | – |
| Tripoli | 72 | 1 | – | 13 | 14 | – | – |
| Koura, Zghorta | 4 | – | 1 | 62 | 32 | – | 1 |
| Akkar | 73 | – | – | 13 | 13 | – | – |
| Other regions overall | 25 | 15 | 2 | 32 | 10 | 11 | 4 |
| All respondents | 21 | 27 | 4 | 25 | 11 | 8 | 4 |

Figures in %

Communal 'de-mixing' has been strongest in the capital. In what was once the most multi-confessional and cosmopolitan area of the city — Ras Beirut in the western half, seat of the American University of Beirut — one-third of the respondents were Christian, in Mseitbeh and Mazraa one-fifth. In the southern suburbs of West Beirut the interviewers did not meet a single Christian, in Ashrafieh and the suburbs of East Beirut not a single Muslim.

On the basis of the sample it appears that the Sunnis are now in the minority in their previous stronghold of West Beirut. Only in the heart of the old city — Basta, Sokak al-Blad and Bourj Abu Haidar — did they constitute almost half the respondents. In Mseitbeh, Mazraa and Tarik al-Jadideh the numbers of Sunnis and Shi`is were about equal. The southern suburbs are 90 per cent Shi`i. Ashrafieh has apparently retained its predominantly Greek Orthodox character, while the suburbs are predominantly Maronite. Outside Beirut the homogenization appears to have been less radical.

The pre-war population of the Metn and Kisrawan was already almost exclusively Christian. Whereas Kisrawan is a Maronite bastion, the Metn has a broad cross-section of the Christian communities: about one-third Maronite, almost one-quarter Greek Catholic and one-fifth each Armenian and Greek Orthodox. Jbeil is the only region once controlled by Christian militias that still has a substantial Muslim minority. As might be expected after the events of 1983 and 1984, hardly any Maronites live in the Chouf, Aley and the upper Metn.

Table 7.16 Religious communities by occupation

| Religious community | large landowner, industrialist | self-employed | civil servant, white-collar worker | artisan | farmer | blue-collar worker | tertiary sector | farm worker |
|---|---|---|---|---|---|---|---|---|
| Sunni | 7 | 11 | 36 | 12 | 3 | 10 | 15 | 5 |
| Shi'i | 5 | 8 | 27 | 19 | 2 | 18 | 14 | 6 |
| Druze | 3 | 9 | 47 | 12 | 1 | 10 | 16 | 3 |
| Maronite | 8 | 15 | 39 | 7 | 3 | 14 | 10 | 5 |
| Greek Orthodox | 7 | 18 | 42 | 8 | 3 | 8 | 11 | 4 |
| Greek Catholic | 4 | 18 | 38 | 10 | 4 | 11 | 9 | 6 |
| Armenian | 10 | 17 | 33 | 21 | 1 | 11 | 7 | – |
| ALL RESPONDENTS | 6 | 13 | 35 | 13 | 3 | 13 | 12 | 5 |

Figures in %

The composition of the remaining regions as reflected in the samples is much as would be expected: Sunni majorities in Tripoli, Sidon and Akkar, Shi`i majorities in Nabatieh, Tyre and Zahrani as well as Baalbek-Hermel, and a Christian majority in Jezzine and Koura-Zghorta.

In summary, it may be said that the composition of the population by religious community has remained far more stable in the regions outside the capital and, in particular, its western and eastern suburbs. How do the communities differ by other social indicators? Although there are no significant distinctions by age structure, there are by marital status. Only 36 per cent of the Muslim, but 49 per cent of the Christian respondents, were single. This may also account in part for the differences in the average number of children[18] by denomination.

**Table 7.17** Religious communities, area and number of children

| Religious community | Out of Beirut | Area in Beirut | total |
|---|---|---|---|
| Sunnis | 4.3 | 4.0 | 4.2 |
| Shi`is | 5.3 | 4.6 | 4.9 |
| Druze | 3.8 | 4.0 | 3.9 |
| Maronites | 3.3 | 3.1 | 3.2 |
| Greek Orthodox | 3.6 | 3.3 | 3.4 |
| Greek Catholics | 3.5 | 3.4 | 3.5 |
| Armenians | 2.8 | 3.5 | 3.0 |

Muslims have on average 4.5 children, Christians 3.3. The distribution of communities by occupation is as follows: Large landowners and industrialists are fairly evenly distributed among the different denominations. Among professional people, the number of Greek Orthodox, Greek Catholics and Armenians is higher than average. Among civil servants and white-collar jobs the Druze have higher than average representation and the Shi`is lower. About one-fifth of the Shi`is and Armenians are manual workers, against an overall average of 13 per cent. The proportion of Shi`is among industrial workers is comparatively high. The distribution by income groups is just as differentiated:

The number of Shi`is is higher than average in the two lower income groups. However, in the lowest group there are, relatively speaking, just about as many

---

[18] Because the female composition of the sample is atypical of the population as a whole, this figure is based on the number of children per married male.

Maronites as Shi`is, and Greek Catholics[19] and Armenians have a higher percentage than either. Armenians also lead in the highest income group, followed by the Greek Orthodox. The numbers of Druze and Sunnis[20] are higher than average in the second highest income group. Combining these results of the two broad confessions — a problematic proceeding in view of the specific social profiles of the individual communities — gives the following distribution:

Table 7.18 Religious communities by income groups

| Religious community | Income groups | | | |
|---|---|---|---|---|
| | 1 (lowest) | 2 | 3 | 4 (highest) |
| Sunnis | 21 | 27 | 27 | 24 |
| Shi`is | 30 | 33 | 20 | 17 |
| Druze | 19 | 28 | 29 | 24 |
| Maronites | 29 | 24 | 19 | 29 |
| Greek Orthodox | 26 | 20 | 20 | 34 |
| Greek Catholics | 31 | 31 | 16 | 22 |
| Armenians | 32 | 20 | 13 | 35 |
| All respondents | 27 | 27 | 21 | 25 |

Figures in %

Overall, the topos of 'wealthy Christians' and 'poor Muslims' is not substantiated by empirical findings. There are fewer Shi`is than average in the highest income group, yet in the lowest, which can be justly termed poor, their percentage is much the same as that for Greek Catholics, Armenians and Maronites. Moreover, each community is stratified by income, has its rich, its middle strata and its poor. As for differences in education between the communities:

---

[19] The war in the Bekaa and the hinterland of Sidon has considerably affected Greek Catholics, traditionally a relatively prosperous community. An exceptionally high percentage of them are now refugees.

[20] In the 1981 survey Sunnis were by far the strongest group in the two upper income groups. At this time, as pre-war, there was a boom in property prices and rents in Beirut and Tripoli, and Sunnis owned large tracts of property in both cities. Since 1984 inflation has reduced real income from these sources.

**Table 7.19** Muslims and Christians by income groups

|  | Income group | | | |
|---|---|---|---|---|
|  | 1 (lowest) | 2 | 3 | 4 (highest) |
| Muslims | 25 | 30 | 24 | 21 |
| Christians | 29 | 24 | 18 | 29 |
| ALL RESPONDENTS | 27 | 27 | 21 | 25 |

Figures in %

**Table 7.20** Religious communities by education

| Religious community | no formal qualification | primary school | brevet | secondary school | university |
|---|---|---|---|---|---|
| Sunnis | 15 | 14 | 25 | 31 | 15 |
| Shi`is | 22 | 19 | 25 | 27 | 7 |
| Druze | 17 | 9 | 20 | 34 | 20 |
| Maronites | 9 | 10 | 22 | 29 | 30 |
| Greek Orthodox | 8 | 7 | 19 | 37 | 29 |
| Greek Catholic | 12 | 11 | 28 | 27 | 22 |
| Armenians | 3 | 15 | 27 | 38 | 16 |
| ALL RESPONDENTS | 14 | 13 | 24 | 30 | 19 |

Figures in %

In the two lowest educational strata the number of Shi`is is greater than average and among university graduates far below average. Maronites and Greek Orthodox are highly represented among university graduates. The rapid growth in the number of Shi`i university students in the past two decades is not yet reflected in the working population as a whole.

Although, as shown, there is no simple linear relationship between education and income, the confessional imbalance in education is probably an important reason why so many Shi`is feel relatively deprived. Upwardly mobile groups trying to catch up with the rest of society — be they strata or classes, communities or both simultaneously — often regard the civil service as a suitable vehicle. So do the Shi`is. And all states have certain formal educational requirements for employment in the civil service. So does Lebanon. And for senior positions the qualification is university education. It may be true — indeed, on the evidence of the discrepancy between education and income, it is probably true — that the opportunities of advancement via formal education are illusory in times of rapidly expanding education. The more degrees there are, the less advancement each can buy — and the more rewarding alternative channels become. But if education is a prerequisite, then as long as disparities exist in the opportunities of education, they will be perceived as barriers to advancement.

In no community is the quantitative difference between secondary school and university graduates — and therefore the discontent among the former — so great as among the Shi`is. The disparities in income between the communities may give objective credence to the sense of deprivation; but it is the disparities in education that give rise to this feeling in the first place. Whether deprivation exists or not, or whether it is regarded as excessive or not, barely influences its political effect: the very nature of relative deprivation lies in perception. How widespread it is in Lebanon, especially among the Shi`is will be considered below.

Sampled social data seldom make for exciting reading. Yet, in this case certain outlines of the basic state of Lebanese society are already apparent and deserve attention. The respondents' working world is fundamentally different to their parents'; many of them do not live where they were born: the experience of enormous changes in economic structures and their own immediate environment is part of their background.

The respondents' classification by income and education reveals a horizontally stratified and communally differentiated society. Although all communities are stratified, the Shi`i community — contrary to the Muslims as a whole — is relatively disadvantaged in terms of both education and income. To what extent the basic social data can explain attitudes and opinions will be examined in the following sections.

## Psycho-social attitudes

Political attitudes and opinions are not formed solely by 'objective' socio-structural factors such as age, background, income and education. Deeply-rooted personality traits also influence attitudes to life and social environment: caution or openness to change, fear of the future or the lack of it, mistrust or trust in people with whom one lives and works, and above all the sense of passively accepting or actively shaping one's own destiny and the fortunes of others.

A study of political attitudes can treat of personality factors only in broad outlines. The attitude markers discussed in this section have been selected for their proven political relevance. Social conservatism is frequently measured by the reactions to two statements: 'Before you start something, you should know whether it will work or not.' 'When you start changing things, they usually get worse.' In many societies people tend either to agree or disagree with both statements; in Lebanon such coincidence is limited.

The first statement expresses a fundamentally cautious approach to unknown matters. Agreement in the four surveys varied between 71 and 74 per cent. The second statement expresses a sceptical attitude towards change. Only a stable minority of about one-third shared this view. For a majority, 'change' is obviously a positive concept, which many respondents can reconcile with conservative caution.

Who are the cautious conservatives? They are more common among older than younger people.[21] Their numbers vary in inverse proportion to the level of education: among university graduates only 64 per cent agreed. Cautious conservatives are more comon than average — between 86 and 90 per cent — among the inhabitants of the south-eastern, Shi`i suburbs of Beirut as well as among the inhabitants of the Nabatieh, Sidon and Jezzine regions, that is, in those regions afflicted by war and unrest in the year of the survey. Respondents in relatively peaceful areas were less cautious: between 51 and 62 per cent in Baalbek and Hermel, Tripoli, the Chouf and Kisrawan. It is fairly probable that in Lebanese conditions caution is a personality characteristic influenced not only by age and education but also by the prevailing security.[22] In short: acute warfare produces caution — not a surprising finding, perhaps, but politically not irrelevant.

Openness to change can also be interpreted politically. The differences by age, income and education are small, but by region they are huge. People in Ashrafieh, the Christian suburbs of East Beirut and Jezzine are least open to change, those in the Shi`i suburbs and in some areas of the old city of West Beirut most open. The picture by religious affiliation is even clearer: 83 per cent of the Druze favour change, 69 per cent of the Shi`is, 64 per cent of the Maronites, and only 62 per cent of the Greek Orthodox and Greek Catholics. Druze and Shi`is are also those communities whose political leaders demand social and political reforms.

An individual's view of his social environment and his attitude to it is determined not least by trust or mistrust in the people around him. Whom do you trust?

---

[21] As all results reported are statistically significant at at least the 5 per cent level, the statistical significance between variables in each individual relationship is not given.

[22] This surmise confirms the results of the earlier surveys: cautious conservatism tends to be stronger in areas of fighting. For example, in 1981 agreement was strongest by far in West Beirut, then racked by incessant militia warfare, whereas the inhabitants of East Beirut and the Metn were the least conservative.

Most respondents feel their world within their immediate circle of family and friends is intact. But it is not impervious to politics.

In 1987 Maronites trusted friends less than in earlier years: the previous year's conflicts within the community had left their mark. Only a minority of Lebanese trust their neighbours. Older people find greater security in their neighbourhood than do younger people. Mistrust increases with the level of education. Only 10 per cent of secondary school and university graduates trust their neighbours. By religious community, Sunnis and Shi`is are more accepting of the trustworthiness of their neighbours than members of the Christian communities.

Table 7.21

|  | % |
|---|---|
| Close relatives | 67 |
| Friends | 59 |
| Colleagues | 20 |
| Neighbours | 15 |
| Employers | 10 |
| Nobody | 26 |

Mistrust predominates in the working environment. Only 20 per cent trust their colleagues and 10 per cent their employers. Good employer-employee relations are most common in Tripoli, the Chouf and northern Lebanon, that is, areas with relatively traditional societies. Of all communities, the Shi`is trust their employers least; few are members of the same community and many pay wages that do little to promote healthy relations with their workers. On the whole, economically active Lebanese trust their immediate family and, if there is no political discord between them, their friends; otherwise they trust nobody. Few find security in their neighbourhood, not surprising in view of the massive movements of population.

Yet even the apparent potential for trust must be qualified. In three of the four surveys one-fifth of all respondents said they trusted nobody: 19 per cent in 1981, 18 per cent in 1984, only 4 per cent in 1986, but 26 per cent in 1987, a significant rise in general mistrust. Such widespread mistrust is remarkable in a society characterized by personal contacts rather than anonymous, functional relationships. Although seldom alone, people do not necessarily feel secure.[23]

Like the questions on conservatism, that on fear of the future mirrors not only personality characteristics or the general state of society, but politically determined fears as well. 'When I think about the future, I feel uncertain and afraid.'

In all four surveys, about 60 per cent answered Yes. Fears of the future decrease with income and education.[24] An important determinant of fear is undoubtedly the individual's economic situation, either actual, or if not yet working, what is thought possible. There is a direct relationship between fear of the future and the current politico-military situation. Fear is higher than average in the Shi`i suburbs of West Beirut, and lower in the West Beirut city centre and East Beirut.[25]

As for other areas, almost all respondents in Sidon and Nabatieh expressed fear, but only a minority in Baalbek, Hermel, Kisrawan and, above all, the Chouf. The picture becomes clearer if one classifies the districts of Beirut and the other regions of the country by military zones:

Table 7.22

|  | fear of the future (%) |
|---|---|
| areas controlled by Shi`i militias | 84 |
| areas controlled by Christians militias (FL) | 61 |
| areas controlled by the Syrian army with predominantly Muslim population | 58 |
| areas controlled by the Syrian army with predominantly Christian population[26] | 56 |
| areas controlled by the Druze militia | 38 |

From this table it is clear that fear of the future is primarily fear of imminent or current warfare. In 1987, there were recurrent hostilities between Amal and Palestinian guerrillas in the Shi`i suburbs of Beirut, while in the Shi`i south, anti-Israeli commando raids alternated with Israeli reprisals. In areas controlled by

---

[23] For similar findings among Lebanese students, see Hanf, 'Le comportement politique des étudiants libanais'.

[24] Percentages by income: 69, 66, 56, and 45 per cent; by education: 68, 63, 60, 62 and 53 per cent.

[25] Percentages: Bourj al-Barajneh 70; Haret Hreik 69; Mseitbeh and Basta each 39; Ashrafieh 43, eastern suburbs 47.

[26] Koura, Zghorta and Zahle.

Christian militias the relative quiet in the Christian heartland north of Beirut, especially in Kisrawan, contrasted starkly with the high level of fear — 90 per cent — in disputed Jezzine held by the Lahad militia. There is less fear where Syrian troops are stationed, though figures fluctuate between the northern Bekaa, where they are in firm control, and West Beirut, where the Syrian presence is anything but unchallenged. Finally, the military situation in the Chouf is unequivocal: only one militia has the say.

'People like me can't do anything to improve people's lives.' Reactions to this statement give a rough idea of individuals' views of their own possibilities of social action. Agreement has risen from 66 per cent in 1981, through 67 per cent in 1984 and 72 per cent in 1986, to 80 per cent in 1987. The picture is one of social impotence and helplessness. As with fear of the future, the sense of powerlessness declines significantly with rising income[27] and education[28].

Once again, area of residence or zone of military control are far more important than other factors. The sense of impotence is all-pervading in the Shi`i suburbs: there was hardly a respondent in Chiyah, Jnah, Ouzai, Haret Hreik and Bourj al-Barajneh who did not admit to it. Yet in the heart of West Beirut — Mseitbeh, Basta and Tarik al-Jadideh — where there is less fear than in the suburbs, it is also widespread. In clear contrast to these are the Christian suburbs with 75 per cent, and especially Ashrafieh with 58 per cent.

The contrasts between the regions are similar. In Jezzine, Baalbek-Hermel and Sidon people feel utterly helpless, but less so in the Chouf, the Metn, Jbeil and Kisrawan, where about two-thirds of the respondents agreed with the statement.

Thus, impotence is felt chiefly in areas of fighting and areas under foreign occupation, and under Israeli occupation far more than Syrian. This sense is least in homogeneous areas under the control of Druze or Christian militias, but even here more than half the respondents see no chance of influencing events themselves.

On the whole, psycho-social attitudes are decisively shaped by external conditions, above all the acute threat of warfare and insecurity. Hence, it would be wrong to interpret them primarily as personality traits.

Influenced by these external conditions, almost three-quarters of Lebanese are conservatively cautious, but two-thirds are open to change: the circumstances in general are so bad that change can hardly bring worse. People trust only their immediate families and circles of friends. Those living in regions of acute crisis — the majority — are afraid of the future and feel powerless.

---

[27] 85, 85, 81 and 69 per cent.
[28] 91, 88, 79, 81 and 70 per cent.

## Economic ethos and job satisfaction

The following question explored propensities to invest and consume: 'Imagine you won some money in the national lottery. What is the first thing you would do with it?' Few respondents plump for consumption. Most would start their own business. Of those who would like to make themselves independent, a higher than average portion are found among the lower-income groups and the Shi`is. Investments in property, in the first half of the 1980s the most secure and profitable form of investment in Lebanon, had fallen to third place in 1987. This option was most popular among Maronites; in the overpopulated Christian enclave the values of property and land are higher than elsewhere in the country.

**Table 7.23**

|  | 1981 | 1984 | 1986 | 1987 |
|---|---|---|---|---|
| buy a house or property | 37 | 33 | 26 | 19 |
| buy a car or new furniture | 5 | 3 | 3 | 4 |
| start my own business | 42 | 46 | 57 | 51 |
| put the money in a sound investment with the bank | 16 | 17 | 14 | 26 |

Figures in %

The increased popularity of bank investments is remarkable. Since the onset of hyper-inflation in 1984 investments in foreign currency have proved the best means of preserving the real value of savings. The image of a society in an orgy of consumption, beloved of certain international media, is atypical of the majority of the population. This majority dreams of winning the lottery not to eat, drink and be merry, but to start their own business. And most of the remainder would soberly and rationally protect their windfall; the preference for bank investments to property simply reflects the economic situation in the country.

This sober and rational streak in economic and business matters is dominant in replies to a question on factors making for success: 'In your opinion, which of the following factors counts most for success in life?'[29]

---

[29] Deviations between the four surveys were insignificant.

**Table 7.24**

|  | % |
|---|---|
| Own efforts | 21 |
| Experience | 21 |
| Education and training | 16 |
| Connections | 16 |
| Luck | 14 |
| Astuteness | 7 |
| Inheritance | 5 |

Inheritance counts least, a clear indication that few Lebanese perceive their society as status-oriented. Achievement-oriented factors, like one's own efforts and experience, are most often mentioned, followed by education and connections. Given the strength of patronage in the Lebanese economy and society, only 16 per cent for connections ('wasta') is astonishing. Astuteness is an inadequate translation for 'combines', that is, complicated, intelligent and profitable business deals. Lebanese businessmen enjoy a reputation as past masters in such affairs. Yet, the fact that only 7 per cent marked this choice illustrates the importance of achievement-oriented factors. Finally, the fact that luck was chosen by only 14 per cent refutes the widespread stereotype of 'Oriental fatalism'. Economically active Lebanese prefer to believe — to use another stereotype — that 'life is what you make of it'. All in all, the replies reveal almost idealist perceptions of opportunities for success and betterment in an open, meritocracy.

The Lebanese economy has been in spectacular decline since 1984. How has this affected attitudes to work and occupation? The first step was to examine attitudes to economic risk-taking.

'One man says: "I'd rather work hard, build up my own business and take risks to get ahead and make a lot of money." Another says: "I'd rather have a safe job with a regular income so that I don't have to think about the future." Do you agree with the first or the second man?' The choice of the Lebanese respondents is unequivocal: agreement with the first man rose from two-thirds in 1981 to almost three-quarters in 1987. Is this a manifestation of the legendary Lebanese business spirit, perhaps even stimulated by current difficulties? The level of agreement cautions against such an interpretation. Even granting that the Lebanese are an exceptionally enterprising people, it is scarcely credible that under normal circumstances only 27 per cent would prefer a guaranteed, regular income. So, how can one plausibly explain this finding?

Risk-takers are found in all income groups and at all levels of education. That 80 per cent of those engaged in commerce opt for risk is hardly surprising — they live with it. But industrial workers also prefer risk to regular wages. Perhaps the fact that 80 per cent of the Shi`is choose this option as against an under average 68 per cent of the Maronites provides the key. The replies are probably not so much reflective of basic dispositions as symptomatic of Lebanon's deep economic crisis.

A comparison of risk-taking by Beirut district and by region supports this surmise. The respondents most willing to take risks live in the Shi`i suburbs as well as in Ras Beirut; almost all agree with the first statement. Far fewer do in Basta and Mseitbeh, Ashrafieh and the eastern suburbs. Four-fifths of the respondents in Jezzine, Sidon and Nabatieh are willing to take risks.

In areas controlled by the Druze militia, the Syrian Army and the Christian militias — all relatively quiet in 1987 — between 60 and 70 per cent were venturesome, but, by contrast, over 80 per cent in areas controlled by Shi`i militias and in the extreme south of the country. In short: risk appears attractive in areas of acute crisis, where regular salaries are hard to come by anyway.

Finally, the majority of those in favour of risk-taking have a higher than average sense of impotence and fear about the future. Their choice reflects the crisis syndrome. This finding is confirmed by the replies to another statement: 'I don't want to work for someone else all my life; some day I want to be my own boss.' Once again, three-quarters agreed. Socio-structural factors explain some of the differences. The desire for independence is inversely proportional to salary and educational levels.

**Table 7.25**

| | Agreement(%) |
|---|---|
| 'It's a pity, but I don't have any prospects in my job.' | 47 |
| 'On the whole I'm satisfied with my boss.' | 47 |
| 'Of course, everyone would like to earn more, but I'm satisfied with my salary.' | 24 |
| 'If I could, I'd like to have a different occupation.' | 70 |
| 'If I could, I'd like to work in the Gulf.' | 52 |

Yet again, the differences by community and region were greater. Eighty-three per cent of the Shi`is agreed, 74 per cent of the Maronites and 69 per cent of the Greek Orthodox. In the Shi`i suburbs of Beirut over 90 per cent want to set up on their own, but in East Beirut and its suburbs only 60 per cent; in the unsettled regions of Jezzine, Sidon and Nabatieh over 80 per cent, but in the calm regions of Kisrawan and the Chouf only 59 and 44 per cent respectively. Once again, the majority of those who would like an independent existence have higher than average fears of the future and sense of powerlessness.

Lastly, reactions to statements concerning job satisfaction reveal the extent of the crisis among working Lebanese.

The fact that half the respondents do not see any prospects in their present jobs and are dissatisfied with their bosses is in itself not exceptional; but that only one-quarter are happy with their salary, 70 per cent would like to find another job and half are prepared to work as migrants in the Gulf States is alarming.

In the previous surveys, attitudes to job prospects and employers were similar. But between 1981 and 1986 about half the respondents thought they were reasonably paid. The desire to change jobs has risen from 60 to 70 per cent, and to work in the Persian Gulf from 38 per cent in 1984 to 52 per cent. The collapse of the currency and the rising cost of living have caused job dissatisfaction to rise to previously unknown levels. The statements on job satisfaction and dissatisfaction are closely connected, which makes it possible to draw up a scale of 'job satisfaction'.[30] The distribution for the sample as a whole is as follows:

**Table 7.26** Income and job satisfaction

|  |  |  |  |  | % |
|---|---|---|---|---|---|
| satisfied | 15 | 19 | 27 | 53 | 28 |
| fairly satisfied | 21 | 17 | 20 | 23 | 21 |
| dissatisfied | 31 | 28 | 31 | 17 | 27 |
| very dissatisfied | 33 | 36 | 22 | 7 | 24 |

Figures in %

A good quarter of the respondents are satisfied with their work and occupation, another fifth somewhat less so. Half of all respondents are either dissatisfied or very dissatisfied. Dissatisfaction is prevalent above all among the young, the less educated and the less well paid.

---

[30] A point was awarded for each statement agreed with. The totals were classified in four categories. Reliability coefficient alpha = .63.

**Table 7.27** Income and job satisfaction

| job satisfaction | Income group | | | | all respondents |
| --- | --- | --- | --- | --- | --- |
| | 1 (lowest) | 2 | 3 | 4 (highest) | |
| satisfied | 15 | 19 | 27 | 53 | 28 |
| fairly satisfied | 21 | 17 | 20 | 23 | 21 |
| dissatisfied | 31 | 28 | 31 | 17 | 27 |
| very dissatisfied | 33 | 36 | 22 | 7 | 24 |

Figures in %

The relationship between income and satisfaction is not completely linear. There are more 'very dissatisfied' people in the second lowest income group than in the lowest; and even in the second highest income group just about as many respondents are 'dissatisfied' and 'fairly satisfied' as in the lowest income group. This may well be a manifestation of the relative deprivation of the middle classes, whose relative prosperity has been jeopardized by inflation.

A comparison by occupational groups confirms this surmise. The proportion of 'very dissatisfied' and 'dissatisfied' employees is higher than average not only in the service sector (62 per cent) and manufacturing (57 per cent), but also among manual workers (65 per cent) and civil servants (56 per cent). Job satisfaction is greatest in commerce (46 per cent) and banking and insurance (40 per cent).

**Table 7.28** Education and job satisfaction

| Job satisfaction | no formal qualif. | primary school | brevet | secondary school | university | all respondents |
| --- | --- | --- | --- | --- | --- | --- |
| satisfied | 21 | 26 | 24 | 25 | 45 | 28 |
| fairly satisfied | 20 | 25 | 22 | 19 | 21 | 21 |
| dissatisfied | 31 | 25 | 27 | 30 | 20 | 27 |
| very dissatisfied | 28 | 24 | 27 | 26 | 14 | 24 |

Figures in %

*Attitudes and Opinions of Economically Active Lebanese*

The relationship between education and satisfaction also exhibits interesting deviations from the one-sided hypothesis of 'the better the education, the lower the dissatisfaction'.

Table 7.29 Job satisfaction by area

| area | satisfied | fairly satisfied | dissatisfied | very dissatisfied |
|---|---|---|---|---|
| Beirut: | | | | |
| Ras Beirut, Mseitbeh | 6 | 7 | 45 | 42 |
| Mazraa | 47 | 24 | 21 | 8 |
| Basta | 41 | 26 | 26 | 8 |
| Tarik al-Jadideh | 6 | 9 | 38 | 47 |
| Ashrafieh | 44 | 30 | 19 | 7 |
| Eastern suburbs | 39 | 29 | 23 | 9 |
| Chiyah | 6 | 12 | 18 | 64 |
| Haret Hreik | 12 | 4 | 28 | 56 |
| Bourj al-Barajneh | 8 | 11 | 29 | 52 |
| Jnah, Ouzai | 2 | 8 | 36 | 54 |
| All Beirut | 25 | 18 | 27 | 30 |
| Other regions: | | | | |
| Metn | 50 | 29 | 13 | 8 |
| Kisrawan | 44 | 33 | 18 | 5 |
| Jbeil | 23 | 29 | 34 | 14 |
| Chouf, Aley | 55 | 24 | 21 | – |
| Sidon | 7 | 14 | 40 | 39 |
| Nabatieh | 10 | 19 | 31 | 40 |
| Jezzine | 12 | 7 | 31 | 50 |
| central & western Bekaa, Zahle | 32 | 14 | 32 | 22 |
| Baalbek-Hermel | 42 | 28 | 23 | 6 |
| Tripoli | 39 | 29 | 24 | 8 |
| Koura, Zghorta | 32 | 26 | 32 | 10 |
| Akkar | 8 | 20 | 24 | 48 |
| All other regions | 31 | 23 | 27 | 19 |
| ALL RESPONDENTS | 28 | 21 | 27 | 24 |

Figures in %

Strong dissatisfaction and dissatisfaction are indeed commonest among people with little formal schooling, and university graduates comprise by far the largest group of satisfied respondents. But there are substantial groups in both extremes at all levels of education. The level of dissatisfaction among technical and secondary school graduates is higher than average. The latter especially are not paid very well and have few job prospects. This finding confirms the hypothesis of relative deprivation.

The geographic distribution of dissatisfaction is equally interesting. It is more frequent in Beirut than in other parts of the country, and in the capital is concentrated in certain districts: every Shi`i suburb as well as Ras Beirut and Tarik al-Jadideh. Satisfied people are far more common in East Beirut and its suburbs and in the districts of old West Beirut, Mseitbeh and Basta. The contrasts between the regions are just as strong. Most respondents in Sidon, Nabatieh, Jezzine and the central and western Bekaa as well as in Akkar in the extreme north of the country are dissatisfied.

At first sight, differences in security may seem to offer an explanation. The southern suburbs of Beirut and the entire south were the most disturbed regions at the time of the survey. However, a closer analysis shows that this explanation is inadequate. Within West Beirut the threat of danger was no greater in Ras Beirut and Tarik al-Jadideh than in Basta and Mseitbeh, in Akkar no greater than in Koura and Tripoli; yet dissatisfaction among the inhabitants of these urban districts and regions varied considerably. It is also obvious that the regional differences go hand in hand with religion.

How does job satisfaction differ by religious community?

**Table 7.30** Religious communities and job satisfaction

| Job satisfation | Sunnis | Shi`is | (Druze) | Maron-ites | Greek Ortho. | Greek Catholic | Armenians |
|---|---|---|---|---|---|---|---|
| Satisfied | 24 | 17 | 28 | 37 | 40 | 31 | 36 |
| Not very satisfied | 18 | 13 | 19 | 28 | 21 | 25 | 37 |
| Dissatisfied | 30 | 29 | 27 | 24 | 27 | 25 | 13 |
| Very dissatisfied | 28 | 41 | 26 | 11 | 12 | 20 | 14 |

Figures in %

**Table 7.31** Religious communities, income and job satisfaction

| Religious communities | income group 1 (lowest) | very dissatisfied | income group 2 | dissatisfied | income group 3 | not very satisfied | income group 4 (highest) | satisfied |
|---|---|---|---|---|---|---|---|---|
| Sunnis | 21 | 28 | 27 | 31 | 27 | 18 | 24 | 24 |
| Shi'is | 30 | 44 | 33 | 29 | 20 | 12 | 17 | 15 |
| Druze | 19 | 27 | 28 | 27 | 29 | 20 | 24 | 27 |
| Maronites | 29 | 11 | 24 | 24 | 19 | 28 | 29 | 37 |
| Greek Catholics | 26 | 12 | 20 | 25 | 20 | 22 | 34 | 41 |
| Greek Orthodox | 31 | 21 | 31 | 26 | 16 | 21 | 22 | 31 |
| Armenian | 32 | 15 | 20 | 13 | 13 | 39 | 35 | 33 |
| All respondents | 27 | 24 | 27 | 27 | 21 | 21 | 25 | 28 |

Figures in %

Fifty-one per cent of the entire sample are dissatisfied or very dissatisfied. However, 70 per cent of the Shi`is are, 58 per cent of the Sunnis and 53 per cent of the Druze. All Christian communities are below average: Greek Catholic 45 per cent, Greek Orthodox 39 per cent, Maronites 35 per cent and Armenians 27 per cent. Thus, dissatisfaction is in general a Muslim, and in particular a Shi`i phenomenon. Is there a direct relationship between this and communal income differentials examined above? The following table compares income groups with the four categories of satisfaction by community.

On the whole, there is a close approximation between the four income groups and the four categories of satisfaction. However, there are considerable differences between the communities' respective representation within an income group, on the one hand, and their representation in the corresponding category of satisfaction, on the other.

Among the Druze, Sunnis and, above all, Shi`is the percentages of very dissatisfied are very much greater than their respective shares in the lowest income group might suggest. For all three communities the reverse relationship holds between the category 'fairly satisfied' and the second highest income group, again contrary to expectation. Although the Druze proportions coincide for the category 'satisfied', the Sunnis and Shi`is still lie below the average.

The figures for the Christian communities are broadly the reverse. Their shares of very dissatisfied, especially those of the Maronites and Armenian, lie far below what one might expect from their shares of the lowest income strata. And their percentages of satisfied and fairly satisfied lie well above their respective representation among the upper income strata.

Therefore, income differentials alone cannot explain the communities' different levels of dissatisfaction. Differences in educational levels between the communities may throw some light on their relative satisfaction and dissatisfaction. These findings do present a different picture. There is a very high coincidence (relative to the respective average) between the three Muslim communities' shares of least educated and least satisfied. The percentage of very dissatisfied Maronites is far lower than the corresponding figure for least educated Maronites might suggest: even with little education they are more satisfied than others. Among the smaller Christian communities high job dissatisfaction tallies with low education. In all communities the portion of dissatisfied people is greater than the portion of brevet-holders, except for the Greek Catholics, Maronites and, above all, the Armenians. The same holds for the relationship between 'fairly satisfied' and secondary school education in all communities. The percentage of satisfied members is consistently similar to the corresponding percentage of university graduates in all communities with the exception, once again, of the Armenians.

Attitudes and Opinions of Economically Active Lebanese 473

Table 7.32 Religious communities, education and job satisfaction

| Religious communities | no formal & primary school | very dissatisfied | brevet | dissatisfied | secondary school | not very satisfied | university | satisfied |
|---|---|---|---|---|---|---|---|---|
| Sunnis | 29 | 28 | 25 | 30 | 31 | 18 | 15 | 24 |
| Shi`is | 41 | 42 | 25 | 30 | 27 | 13 | 7 | 16 |
| Druze | 25 | 25 | 20 | 28 | 34 | 19 | 20 | 28 |
| Maronites | 19 | 11 | 22 | 24 | 29 | 28 | 30 | 37 |
| Greek Catholics | 15 | 12 | 19 | 27 | 37 | 21 | 29 | 40 |
| Greek Orthodox | 23 | 20 | 28 | 24 | 27 | 25 | 22 | 32 |
| Armenian | 18 | 15 | 27 | 12 | 38 | 37 | 16 | 36 |
| All respondents | 27 | 24 | 24 | 27 | 30 | 21 | 19 | 28 |

Figures in %

However, in the three Muslim communities 'satisfied' and 'fairly satisfied' together are lower than 'secondary school' and 'university' education together, whereas among the Christian communities, with the single exception of the Greek Orthodox, basically satisfied people are relatively more numerous than well-educated people. In short: Christians with less education are less dissatisfied than Muslims, and those with better education are more satisfied.

Are there differences between the discrepancies in income and dissatisfaction, on the one hand, and in education and dissatisfaction, on the other? If one conflates each community's shares of the two lower income and educational strata, on the one hand, and the categories 'very dissatisfied' and 'dissatisfied', on the other, they can be presented in the form of comparable indices.

**Table 7.33** Religious community by income and job dissatisfaction and by education and job dissatisfaction

| religious community | dissatisfaction and income[*] | dissatisfaction and education[*] |
|---|---|---|
| Sunnis | +14 | + 4 |
| Shi`is | +13 | + 6 |
| Druze | +10 | + 8 |
| Maronites | −15 | − 7 |
| Greek Orthodox | − 6 | + 5 |
| Greek Catholic | −12 | − 7 |
| Armenians | −21 | −18 |

[*] Deviations from overall averages of the respective categories

Even in terms of educational levels, dissatisfaction differentials between the Muslim and Christian communities are still considerable. But they are far narrower than those in terms of income.

However, even differences in education cannot adequately explain the varying levels of dissatisfaction between the communities. It is conceivable that politically symbolic feelings of deprivation play a role, for instance, that the Muslims believe that they do not enjoy the social and political standing they are entitled to, whereas the Christians — notwithstanding their incomes and education — are happier with life in Lebanon. The extraordinarily high level of satisfaction among the Armenians may mean that this community is quite simply happy to have found a new homeland in Lebanon after persecution elsewhere. However, this possibility must remain hypothetical as the surveys did not collect data on politico–symbolic deprivation. At any rate, the discrepancies in the levels of dissatisfaction between the communities, despite comparable levels of income and education, are a classic syndrome of relative deprivation.

In summary, attitudes towards work and occupation further illuminate and substantiate the situation of crisis obtaining in Lebanon. Basic attitudes like a willingness to save and invest and individual enterprise are characteristic of achievement-oriented societies. At the same time, however, the social acceptability of risk-taking and the preference for self-employment, both closely linked to fears of the future and a sense of powerlessness, are indicative of an almost abnormal mobility of labour, even allowing for the traditional mobility and flexibility of Lebanese economic life.

The economic depression has left its mark: since 1981 there has been a striking increase in dissatisfaction with salaries and jobs as well as in the readiness to become migrant workers. There is open and general dissatisfaction with working conditions and jobs. The enormous variations in dissatisfaction between regions and communities cannot be explained by the effects of war alone. The greater level of dissatisfaction among the Muslim communities is only partly explained by income and educational differentials. This is ground for the surmise that a social crisis has long existed in the perception of the Muslim community, a crisis — to go by the comparative lack of dissatisfaction among even lower paid and less educated Christians — that is less obvious to the Christian community. Regardless of what may or may not have been objective or only one or the other's perception, the data reveal that there is a deep social crisis — which, if not a cause, is then a consequence of the war and its economic effects.

## Economy and society

The attitudes to work and occupation manifest a crisis in society. Has this affected the views economically active Lebanese have of the economy and society?

**Table 7.34**

|  | Agreement (%) |
|---|---|
| *'Compared to how my parents lived, I think I'm much better off.'* | 71 |
| *'I fear my children won't have it as good as me.'* | 66 |

The dominant perception is one of marked improvement on the parents' generation, but the fear that the children will be worse off is almost as strong. There are clear differences by region and community.

Agreement was lower than average in East Beirut (65 per cent) and the Metn (49 per cent), higher than average in West Beirut (77 per cent), in southern Lebanon (76 per cent) and, above all, in the Chouf (85 per cent). Fewer Greek Orthodox, Armenians, Maronites (all 67 per cent) and Greek Catholics (61 per cent) thought they were better off than their parents, while Sunnis (81 per cent) expressed this view most often.

Compared with the parents' generation, there has obviously been a trend towards greater social equality: regions and communities that were better off in the previous generation see less progress, those that were worse off see more.

Fears that the next generation's prospects are worse found a majority among all respondents and also among all strata, in all regions and all communities, though with variations. Higher-income strata, landowners, professionals and people in trade and commerce, banking and state employment are less concerned about their children's prospects. Fears are greatest among farmers (87 per cent). There was higher than average agreement among Greek Catholics, Armenians and Sunnis, and least agreement among the Druze (53 per cent).

A comparison by region reveals the influence of security considerations on fears for the children's future.

They are highest in the areas under control of the Shi`i militias (77 per cent), in the insecure areas of Sidon (82 per cent), Jezzine and the extreme south (81 per cent) lowest in areas of least disturbance at the time of the survey: Baalbek and Hermel (47 per cent) and the region controlled by the Druze militia (53 per cent). Perceptions of one's own position relative to that of one's parents and that of one's children are closely linked to psycho-social attitudes and attitudes towards occupation and working conditions. Those who think they are not better off than their parents, and that their children will not be better off either, are, on average, more likely to be afraid of the future, feel powerless, take desperate risks and be dissatisfied with occupation and working conditions.

How do the respondents perceive the social distinctions in Lebanese society and the distribution of wealth and economic power? Some highly significant changes in replies between 1981 and 1987 are further evidence of the deep social crisis in Lebanon. In 1981, already 90 per cent of the respondents did not regard the war as the great equalizer, in 1987 hardly anyone did; rather, it is held responsible for the widening social distinctions. There is virtual unanimity that the 'rich minority', a Lebanese topos since the appearance of the Lebret Report,[31] are a crowd of exploiters.

Table 7.35

|  | Agreement (%) | | | |
| --- | --- | --- | --- | --- |
|  | 1981 | 1984 | 1986 | 1987 |
| 'The differences between the social groups have widened since 1975.' | 90 | 91 | 94 | 96 |
| 'In Lebanon a rich minority is buying up everything and the large majority is losing out.' | 87 | 92 | 94 | 95 |
| 'In Lebanon the majority of people are middle-class, and there are only a few rich people and not very many poor people.' | 68 | 54 | 46 | 17 |
| 'It doesn't matter what the workers do, they can never win against the bosses.' | 25 | 37 | 40 | 52 |
| 'Even ordinary people can get ahead if they help one another and act together.' | 97 | 96 | 97 | 79 |
| 'When I see the people from the wealthy parts of town I think to myself that's how I want to live, and I have a right to live like that.' | 66 | 67 | 63 | 72 |

The image of Lebanon as a 'middle-class society' has been shattered since 1986. A majority still shared this view in 1981 and 1984; in 1987 they had shrunk to just 17 per cent. One-quarter of those over forty-five, of the highest income group and of the most educated hold this view, as do just under half the respondents in the Metn, in Tripoli and Jbeil. There are clear distinctions by community: 33 per cent of the Maronites and roughly one-fifth of the other Christian communities continue to believe that the majority of Lebanese have a middle-class standard of living, but only 13 per cent of the Sunnis, and just 5 per cent of the Shi`is. Those in agreement are, on average, less open to change, more satisfied with their occupation and working conditions, more achievement-oriented and do not feel powerless. The image of a middle-class society, a few years ago the perception of the majority, now appears to be the wishful thinking of a self-assured minority.

[31] IRFED, Le Liban face à son développement (Beirut, 1963).

In 1981 one-quarter thought employers had too much power, in 1987 over half did. The 1981 sample consisted largely of trade unionists, who would not have been trade unionists if they thought the statement correct. But the rise from 37 per cent in 1984, through 40 per cent in 1986, to 52 per cent in 1987 reveals that the working population as a whole feels that their position vis-à-vis their employers has continually weakened; this is almost certainly a consequence of the economic crisis and mounting unemployment.

The belief that ordinary people can help each other get ahead is still strong (80 per cent), but considerably weaker than in 1986, a symptom of growing resignation. There are remarkable differences between the districts of Beirut and the regions. The belief in mutual aid is higher than average in Ashrafieh and the Christian suburbs as well as in the old districts of West Beirut, Mseitbeh and Basta. It is far lower in the Shi`i suburbs of Bourj al-Barajneh (56 per cent), Chiyah (60 per cent) and Haret Hreik (66 per cent). In Tripoli, Akkar, the Chouf, the Metn and Jbeil agreement is higher than average, in Sidon well below (46 per cent). The replies to this statement may well reflect the social cohesion in urban districts and regions. Respondents in areas of homogeneous, long-settled population tended to answer Yes, those in areas that have suffered great upheaval and fluctuations in population tend to answer No. This assumption is supported by the fact that Druze and Maronites believed most strongly in mutual support, Shi`is and Greek Catholics least strongly — the latter are the communities most affected by forced migration in recent years.

In view of the economic and social crisis, it is not surprising that social envy of 'people in the wealthy part of town' is increasing. Social envy is higher than average among the youthful, low-income groups, the less-educated and people who do not own their own home or land. In Beirut the lowest levels of social envy are in Ashrafieh and the eastern suburbs, on the one hand, and Mseitbeh and Basta, on the other; out of Beirut the lowest levels are found in Kisrawan, the Chouf, Tripoli and Koura. It is especially pronounced in the Shi`i suburbs of Beirut and Ras Beirut, and, out of Beirut, in Jezzine. The reactions by community are further evidence of the phenomenon of relative deprivation: social envy is greatest among the Shi`is (84 per cent) and the Greek Catholics (73 per cent).

There is a higher than average correlation between social envy and fear of the future, powerlessness and dissatisfaction with occupation and working conditions, another facet of the same phenomenon.

What do the respondents want and expect for the Lebanese economy? The level of agreement with the following statements has hardly fluctuated. The need to remain an economic entity finds least support in the Chouf, the Bekaa, Kisrawan and Jbeil, that is, in regions in which some degree of autarchy is already practised. Support for a single economic entity is higher than average among Beirutis and in

Jezzine, Sidon and Nabatieh, regions either marginalized or badly affected by economic disruption and segregation.

Table 7.36

|  | Agreement (%) |
|---|---|
| 'Whatever the political solution is, Lebanon must remain a single economic entity.' | 89 |
| 'The services that Lebanon provides for the region are unique. Despite the crisis, Lebanon has consolidated its position. | 86 |

The differences by community are also revealing. The desire for a single economy is shared by only 75 per cent of the Druze and 83 per cent of the Maronites, two communities with their own de facto cantons. The desire for unity is higher than average among Greek Orthodox, Sunnis and Shi`is. Neither the Sunnis nor the Greek Orthodox control any territory, and the Shi`is are spread around the Bekaa, West Beirut and southern Lebanon; for these communities, economic partition would be tantamount to partition of their own communities. However, notwithstanding all relative distinctions, even in that community most tempted by territorial autarchy, the Druze, a three-quarters majority favours unity.

Agreement with the statement that Lebanon's regional position has been consolidated and Lebanon is irreplaceable can scarcely be interpreted as anything but an expression of hope. University graduates and members of all Christian communities tend to be more sceptical. Agreement is also slightly lower in regions under Syrian control, where people are daily confronted with the reality that Lebanon's role has not been consolidated. Agreement was greatest in precisely those regions in which the situation was most desperate at the time of the survey, namely the Shi`i suburbs of Beirut. Of all communities, the Shi`is believe most strongly that Lebanon is unique: they have no hope but Lebanon, but they still have hope.

The perceptions of the economy and society confirm and supplement what was revealed by attitudes to occupation and working conditions: a social crisis of enormous dimensions. Although the majority of respondents believe they are better off than their parents, they fear their children will be less well off than themselves. They believe social cleavages have deepened, and that a small minority are piling up wealth at the expense of the others. The view of Lebanon as a middle-class society, a majority view in 1981, is shattered, now held by a minority of only 17 per cent. Employers are regarded as more powerful than ever, fewer people believe in progress through mutual support and social envy has spread.

All that is left is hope — the hope the economic unity of the country can be re-established and the role of Lebanon as the hub of the entire Arab East may be preserved. This hope is strongest among those who are most dissatisfied, are afraid of the future and feel themselves powerless.

## Religion, family and community

As the data so far have shown, each of the Lebanese religious communities is distinct in terms of social profile, psycho-social state, attitudes to work and occupation and views of the economy and society. But these data tell us nothing about that peculiar quality that makes each community unique. How religious are the religious communities, and to what extent are they just communities? How strong are family ties, on the one hand, and bonds with the community, on the other, and what is the relationship between the two? Finally, How are differences between the communities, on the one hand, and between strata and classes, on the other, perceived and assessed?

**Table 7.37**

|  | Agreement (%) |
|---|---|
| *'I believe in a life after death, in which the righteous will be rewarded and the wicked will be punished.'* | 71 |
| *'I try to live by the teachings of my religion.'* | 75 |
| *'I often visit a place of worship.'* | 38 |
| *'I can be happy and enjoy life even if I don't believe in God.'* | 11 |

Even cautious interpretation and allowance for 'socially desired' responses cannot disguise the fact that the economically active Lebanese population interviewed is strongly influenced by religion. West European clergy can only dream of such figures. For the time being, one cannot speak of secular beliefs in

Lebanon. Factor analysis confirms that responses on religiousness are closely related; hence, they have been scaled:[32]

**Table 7.38**

|  | % |
|---|---|
| very religious | 26 |
| religious | 39 |
| not very religious | 22 |
| not religious | 13 |

Sixty-five per cent of all respondents are religious or very religious. Only one-eighth of the respondents are secularized, and in recent years their numbers have fallen significantly, as shown by agreement with the statement: 'I can be happy and enjoy life without believing in God' in the four surveys since 1981 where the figures were 20, 22, 15 and 11 per cent respectively.

Who is religious and who less so? There are no differences by gender, but by age. Fifty-three per cent of the 20–25 age group are not very or not religious, a considerable deviation from the average of 35 per cent for these two categories. Education is an important factor in secularization.

**Table 7.39** Education and religiousness

|  | no formal qualification | primary school | brevet | secondary school | university | all respondents |
|---|---|---|---|---|---|---|
| very religious | 52 | 28 | 20 | 22 | 17 | 26 |
| religious | 34 | 46 | 40 | 39 | 38 | 39 |
| not very religious | 10 | 19 | 26 | 24 | 24 | 22 |
| not religious | 4 | 7 | 14 | 15 | 21 | 13 |

Figures in %

---

[32] The scale is based on six items; two items will be considered below. One point was awarded for each statement agreed with. The scale values between 0 and 6 were conflated into four categories; reliability coefficient alpha = .77.

The number of university graduates is lower than average among the very religious and higher than average among the non-religious. But even in this group only one-fifth are not religious, whereas 55 per cent of them are religious or very religious.

Geographically, bastions of religion are Basta in West Beirut, the suburbs of East Beirut, and, out of Beirut, Tripoli and Sidon, Jezzine, Kisrawan and Jbeil, all with 80 per cent religious and very religious. The distribution by community is as follows:[33]

Table 7.40 Religious communities and religiousness

|  | Sunnis | Shi`is | (Druze) | Maronites | Greek Orthodox | Greek Catholics | Armenians |
|---|---|---|---|---|---|---|---|
| Very religious | 26 | 32 | (6) | 26 | 18 | 21 | 23 |
| Religious | 42 | 33 | (26) | 43 | 43 | 40 | 41 |
| Not very religious | 20 | 21 | (32) | 20 | 25 | 27 | 30 |
| Not religious | 12 | 15 | (36) | 11 | 14 | 12 | 6 |

Figures in %

The Sunni and Maronite profiles are almost identical. The Shi`is have the highest percentage of very religious; but if one conflates the two upper and two lower categories respectively, the Shi`i distribution coincides with the overall average. Greek Catholics and Greek Orthodox are somewhat more numerous among the not very and non-religious. But, in general, there are few differences in the degree of religiousness between the communities.

The point to note is that, in terms of the criterion 'religiousness', the communities are in the eyes of two-thirds of their members religious communities. All four surveys confirm this, and as the small group of secularized Lebanese has shrunk, it is unlikely that this will change for some time.

---

[33] A note on interpretation: Druze ratings on the scale of 'religiousness' must be treated with caution. The Druze do not have places of worship in the narrow sense; attendance at religious gatherings is restricted to the 'initiated', who alone know all the Druze 'religious teachings'. But this does not imply that the Druze are irreligious. Eighty-one per cent of them believe in life after death — the highest percentage of all communities — and only 3 per cent can conceive of happiness without God.

Strong family loyalties are occasionally thought to clash with communal loyalties, but occasionally also to provide the social foundations of the latter. Some authors regard family solidarity as a more traditional form of group solidarity, and communal solidarity as a more modern form.[34] Family loyalties were measured by the reactions to the following statements:

**Table 7.41**

|  | Agreement (%) |
|---|---|
| *'Stand by your brother, be he oppressor or oppressed.'*[35] | 45 |
| *'If my family disagrees with the strongest political tendency in my community, I'll side with my family.'* | 50 |

The following statements established individuals' communal identification.

|  | |
|---|---|
| *'It doesn't matter if they are rich or poor, I feel close to all members of my community.'* | 58 |
| *'It is good if there are no conflicts between the sons of the same community.'* | 91 |
| *'One man says: "It is not so important if my daughter marries a man from another religion, as long as she loves him." Another man says: "Marriages between people of different religions are not good and are often unhappy. I don't want my daughter to marry someone from a different religion."'* Agreement with the first man: | 40 |
| *'I prefer neighbours who have the same background as myself.'* | 55 |
| *'If my colleagues are honest and cooperative, I don't mind what group they belong to.'* | 90 |

---

[34] See Fuad I. Khuri, *From Village to Suburb* (Chicago and London, 1975), pp. 201f.
[35] A Lebanese proverb.

Family loyalties are strong, and have grown stronger in recent years. In 1981 and 1984 respectively only one-quarter accepted the principle of 'my brother, right or wrong'; by 1986 one-third did, and in 1987 almost half. Half are also prepared to take the side of their family if the family disagrees with the opinion of the majority of the community. However, such a situation is extremely unwelcome, as the extraordinarily general desire to avoid conflicts within the community shows. Here, too, agreement has risen significantly from 69 per cent in 1981 to 91 per cent in 1987. In other words: identification with both the family and the community has strengthened. And in the event of conflict between the two, opinion is equally divided.

Among which groups are family and communal loyalties respectively stronger or weaker? The strength of family ties increases with age and decreases with education. They are stronger in Beirut (52 per cent) than in the regions (41 per cent). In agreement with earlier findings, they are strongest in suburbs where families have lived for generations, especially in Basta (83 per cent), and lower in those with large fluctuations in the population, for instance, Ras Beirut (23 per cent). Outside Beirut bonds of kinship are strongest in the Chouf.

There are considerable differences by religious community. Fifty-eight per cent of the Shi`is and 53 per cent of the Sunnis are prepared to stand by their brother through thick and thin, but only 39 per cent of the Maronites and 26 per cent of the Greek Catholics. In the event of conflict between the family and the majority opinion in the community, only 42 per cent of the Shi`is would side with the family, but 63 per cent of the Greek Orthodox, 56 per cent of the Greek Catholics and the Armenians and 54 per cent of the Druze would do so.

Thus, family loyalty is particularly pronounced among 'the ordinary people' with low incomes and little education. By contrast, family loyalty even to the extent of conflict with the community is a privilege of a self-assured, relatively prosperous minority. Those who chose the family without reservation show higher than average openness to change, are less afraid of the future and tend to be satisfied with their occupations.

Fifty-eight per cent of all respondents have a strong sense of community, irrespective of the material well-being of their fellow-religionists. There are considerable disparities by urban districts and regions. Like family ties, communal ties are stronger in the capital (62 per cent) than in the provinces (40 per cent). But whereas both ties are equally strong in the provinces, in Beirut identification with the community is stronger than with the family (62 to 52 per cent).

But the urban milieu alone does not automatically foster communal loyalty, as the differences both between districts in Beirut and between regions testify. A sense of community is stronger is the old districts of Mseitbeh (79 per cent) and Basta (83 per cent) in West Beirut and Ashrafieh (76 per cent) in East Beirut than in the new suburbs: in Haret Hreik only 40 per cent and in Jnah just 35 per cent professed such a sense. The lowest figures were for Ras Beirut (31 per cent) and Tarik al-Jadideh (19 per cent).[36] Outside Beirut communal bonds are particularly strong in the Chouf (87 per cent) and Kisrawan (83 per cent).

There are also differences between the communities. The Armenians are most conscious of being a community (64 per cent), followed by the Maronites and Druze (63 and 61 per cent respectively). A little over half the Shi`is are (53 per cent).[37] These are the communities with the longest histories of ethnic identity, that are most aware of their uniqueness, and proud of it.

Almost all respondents (91 per cent) wish to avoid conflicts within their community, that is, one third more than those who profess a sense of community. In other words, some form of identification with the community, even if weaker, exists well beyond the latter circle. Which people do not disapprove of such conflicts? They tend to be university graduates and professional people — people able to view their community with detachment — and live in the Koura and Zghorta, the Metn, Jbeil and Akkar, all regions that have experienced intra-communal conflict. Maronites especially are expressly prepared to tolerate conflict among themselves. By contrast, only 5 per cent of the Shi`is are, evidence that strengthens the doubts about figures for their sense of community.[38] Finally, the Druze are unanimous in their disapproval of internal conflicts.

The touchstone of a group's will to preserve itself as a group, or conversely, of potential social integration, is its acceptance of inter-group marriage. Under Islamic law a Muslim man may marry a Christian or Jewess, but a Muslim woman may not marry a Christian or a Jew. Therefore, the question of whether a man is willing to allow his daughter to marry a man of another religion is, for Muslims, hypothetical.[39]

---

[36] These two districts are probably sui generis: as will be discussed below, disapproval of close identification with a community probably has political and ideological grounds.

[37] This finding must be qualified. The formulation 'be they rich or poor' may have encouraged many a Shi`i to respond negatively. In their long fight against the wealthy *zu`ama'* of their own community the leaders of the successful Shi`i political movements presented their cause as that of the poor and oppressed. The low level of agreement in the highly politicized Shi`i suburbs of Beirut supports this surmise. Compare also the high level of social envy among the Shi`is of the capital.

[38] See preceding note.

[39] Of course, this topic highlights, as no other, the classic question of discrepancies between words and deeds. It is one thing to declare in favour of mixed marriage during an interview, and quite another thing to practise one's convictions. Notwithstanding this, a comparison of the replies of respondents from different social categories allows at least an exploration of the awareness of the problems of segregation and integration.

It should be pointed out that the question of mixed marriages is also taboo for Oriental Christians, chiefly in reaction to the Muslim 'one-way street', though unlike the latter, sanction lies not so much in canon law, which grants dispensation, as in social pressure.

Still, 40 per cent professed their readiness, and among female respondents the figure was 51 per cent, one of the few instances of significant divergence between the attitudes of men and women in the survey.[40] Agreement was greater among younger and single people and well above average among the educated — 55 per cent among university graduates.

There is a bare majority in favour in two districts of Beirut: in Ras Beirut and the Christian suburbs; rejection is strongest in Chiyah (22 per cent). Outside Beirut there was a majority — and a surprisingly high one — in only one region: the Metn (63 per cent). The figures for Jezzine, the Chouf, Sidon, Baalbek and Tripoli were all under 30 per cent.

There are large differences by community: 66 per cent of the Armenians accept mixed marriage, 48 per cent of the Greek Catholics and 47 per cent of the Maronites, 37 per cent of the Sunnis and 32 per cent of the Shi`is.

From these results one may gauge how advisable caution is in interpreting professions of communal solidarity. Although strong among Armenians and Maronites, it has not prevented half or more of the members of these communities from accepting the idea of mixed marriage. Conversely, only half the Shi`is professed a strong sense of community, yet more than two-thirds reject mixed marriage.

The profile of those who accept mixed marriage is that of self-assured people: generally not conservative and open to change, they do not feel powerless and are relatively satisfied with their occupations and jobs.

It is far more difficult to interpret these results than those of any previous topic, even if one takes them at face value. Lebanese Christians will be inclined to stress the effective rejection of social integration by the majority of Muslims. On the other hand, liberal Muslims will point out that agreement by one-third of the Muslims with a statement — even if hypothetical — that diametrically contradicts Islamic law is in itself a striking expression of the desire for coexistence. Both arguments are probably right. But within our context, the important point is the usefulness of a prohibition on mixed marriages as a means to preserving group-consciousness: it is far greater in the Muslim than in the Christian community.

In 1981, 49 per cent of the respondents preferred to have neighbours from the same community, in 1987, the figure was 55 per cent. This reflects the effects of the fighting and expulsions. There are only minor differences by the usual social factors; only university graduates (46 per cent) have somewhat fewer reservations about neighbours with a different background. Homogeneous neighbourhoods are particularly favoured in East Beirut and Kisrawan, where numerous refugees and

---

[40] It should be recalled that the respondents are economically active women and therefore not representative of Lebanese women as a whole.

expellees from previously mixed areas have settled. There is also widespread agreement in Sidon, Nabatieh, Baalbek and the Chouf, all regions that have become homogeneous by driving out minorities. The victors obviously enjoy the new state. Put another way, de facto cantons are approved of where they already exist. The astonishing figures are those for the southern suburbs of Haret Hreik and Bourj al-Barajneh, where only a minority of 37 per cent voted for neighbours from the same community. Since the expulsion of the old Maronite minorities of Haret Hreik and Bourj al-Barajneh in 1975 and 1983 respectively, both have been exclusively Shi`i residential areas. Do the results imply that a majority of the Shi`is disapprove of the actions of some militias, or do they reflect a symptom of the nostalgia for the better times of coexistence? It is impossible to decide from the present data.

The preference for neighbours from the same community is not only a consequence of war experiences. It correlates closely with a professed sense of community and the rejection of mixed marriages. The rejection of mixed marriages and, increasingly, the desire for geographic segregation represent the hard core of community consciousness.

In contrast to the above, acceptance of colleagues at work from other communities hovered around 90 per cent between 1981 and 1987.[41] Who rejects such colleagues? In the main, Shi`is (19 per cent) — compared to 1 per cent of the Druze and 5 per cent of the Maronites — in particular Shi`is in Beirut: in Chiyah a full quarter and in Haret Hreik as many as 28 per cent. Only 6 per cent of the inhabitants of Ras Beirut and the Christian suburbs do. Out of the capital there is little intolerance towards colleagues: only 7 per cent disapproval.

How does communal identification compare with economic group interests, or, to put it simply, 'confession' versus 'class'?

Two statements were used to examine this question. These statements are formulations of classic arguments long the preserve of the Lebanese Left and adopted by the Shi`i movement at the beginning of the 1970s. For the latter, however, 'poor' and 'Shi`i community' are synonymous. A clear majority of respondents agreed with the first statement, a small majority with the second. Who agreed and who disagreed? Agreement with the first statement decreases with rising income.[42] In the lower two income groups two-thirds agree, in the second highest 58 per cent, and even in the highest group half. By education, agreement was greatest among the least educated (70 per cent); 62 per cent of secondary school graduates agreed, and 53 per cent of university graduates.

---

[41] Acceptance was facilitated by the qualification 'if they are honest and cooperative'.

[42] Only replies to this statement are analysed. Although fewer agreed with the second statement, the pattern is similar.

**Table 7.42**

|  | Agreement (%) |
|---|---|
| *'Of course there are political and religious differences in this country. But the differences between rich and poor are more important.'* | 59 |
| *'People who try to exploit differences between the communities in politics do this to hide the real differences between rich and poor.'* | 52 |

The differences by region and community are greater. Respondents in Beirut answered Yes (67 per cent) more often than those in other regions. There is very strong agreement in the bastions of the Lebanese Left,[43] Ras Beirut, Tarik al-Jadideh and Akkar, on the one hand, and in the Shi`i suburbs as well as in Sidon, Nabatieh and Jezzine, on the other. There was lower than average agreement not only in the Christian districts and regions, but also in the old heart of West Beirut, in the Chouf and Tripoli. By community, Shi`i agreement is well above average (79 per cent), Sunni, Druze and Greek Orthodox average, Maronite, Greek Catholic and Armenian below average.

A comparison with attitudes examined above reveals all the syndromes of relative deprivation: agreement correlates with being conservative and cautious, fear of the future, a sense of impotence and dissatisfaction with occupation and working conditions. But it must be pointed out that support for the 'class thesis' of domestic Lebanese conflict has decreased from 66 per cent in 1981 to 59 per cent in 1987.

This said, class remains the dominant perception of the conflict, as underlined by the fact that half the respondents in the highest income group and — which, as shown, is not the same — half the Christians answered in the affirmative. Above all, it is the common opinion of all those feeling the consequences of war, regardless of communal affiliation. This finding is especially telling in that it highlights a potentially explosive situation: the Shi`is draw no clear distinction between their communal deprivation and their economic impoverishment. To them, 'community' and 'class' are more or less identical.

The relationships between religiousness, family loyalty, communal identity and the socio-economic view of the war in Lebanon can be summarized as follows.

---

[43] To be discussed in detail below.

The respondents, apart from a minority of 13 per cent, are religious. The level of religiousness is similar in all communities, though the proportion of Shi`is is high in the category 'very religious'.

Religiousness is closely linked strong family loyalties. Half the respondents have strong family ties, Shi`is a higher than average 58 per cent.

An explicit sense of community, of cohesion, irrespective of material wealth, is most pronounced among the communities with the strongest traditions — Armenians, Druze and Maronites — less so among the Shi`is. Family and communal loyalties correlate closely. In the hypothetical event of conflict between the family and most of the community, half the respondents would stand by their family. Ninety per cent of all respondents disapprove of conflicts within the community. Forty per cent of the sample express acceptance of mixed marriages, including 37 per cent of the Sunnis and 32 per cent of the Shi`is. Ninety per cent of all respondents accept colleagues at work from other communities, including 80 per cent of the Shi`is, and 75 per cent of the Shi`is in the Beirut suburbs. The Shi`is' explicit sense of community is lower than average. This goes hand in hand with a higher than average dislike of conflict in the community, higher than average support for the community against the family, higher than average rejection of mixed marriages and higher than average unwillingness to work with colleagues from other communities. In short: by all criteria with the exception of an explicit sense of community embracing all, both rich and poor, the Shi`is exhibit the strongest cohesion and the greatest social distance from others.

The majority of respondents regard the conflict between rich and poor as more important than that between the communities. This is true of all categories of respondents. This perception of the conflict is most pronounced among non-religious people, on the one hand, and Shi`is, on the other. However, people who are non-religious are simultaneously not family-oriented, have a weak sense of community, express an acceptance of mixed marriages far higher than average and accept neighbours and colleagues from other communities. The 79 per cent of the Shi`is — a far higher figure than in any other community — who share with non-religious people a view of the conflict as one between rich and poor differ radically from them in terms of all other criteria. Without putting too fine a point on it, four-fifths of the Shi`is express their sense of community as a type of 'religious class consciousness'.

The concept of the 'classe communauté' — developed by a pre-war Lebanese left-wing splinter group — has been realized in the self-perception of the majority of Shi`is: a classic case of a self-fulfilling prophecy. What is objective reality in terms of hard economic facts has become even more concrete in the consciousness of the subjects: the crux of Lebanon's social problem is its Shi`i problem. In acute political crises, however, the software of perception is usually more telling than economic hardware.

## The political system

How did economically active Lebanese perceive the distribution of political power and influence in their state in a time of crisis? What were their opinions on the two most important types of political leader in Lebanon, the traditional za`im — the political broker who represents the interests of his regional or communal groups of clients — and the new party and militia leader? Did they think it necessary to hold and express clear political options, or did they think political continence more sensible? Finally, did they think the internal conflicts would worsen or that a return to the Lebanese equilibrium of the pre-war period was possible?

It is necessary to know the broad outlines of respondents' views of their political system before turning to their political orientations, and their opinions and attitudes on contentious questions.

'In your opinion, which of the following groups has the greatest influence in Lebanon?'

**Table 7.43**

|  | pre-1975[44] | 1981 | 1984 | 1986 | 1987 |
|---|---|---|---|---|---|
| Large landowners | 7 | 4 | 7 | 2 | 2 |
| Religious leaders | 11 | 7 | 10 | 12 | 3 |
| Bankers | 2 | 5 | 5 | – | 8 |
| Zu`ama' | 57 | 6 | 17 | 18 | 38 |
| Merchants | 3 | 13 | 16 | 17 | 14 |
| Party leaders | 4 | 54 | 38 | 41 | 30 |
| Industrialists | 2 | 4 | 1 | – | 1 |
| Ministers | 9 | 1 | – | 3 | 1 |
| Military officers | 4 | 5 | 6 | 6 | 3 |

Figures in %

The respondents' perceptions mirror the changes in the power structures. The greatest changes are in the assessment of the party leaders, on the one hand, and

[44] Estimates from the 1981 survey.

the traditional politicians, on the other. The party leaders hardly counted in prewar Lebanon. In 1981 they were triumphant, named by 54 per cent of the respondents. At that time power, in the respondents' eyes, came out of the barrel of a gun; those with guns, the militias, had political power. Pluralism in the Lebanon of 1981 existed inasmuch as there was a plurality of party leaders and of little else. Subsequently, the limits of their power — both the territorial limits of their writ and the limits of their influence within their own groups — became apparent. From 1981 to 1987, their support fell from 54 to 30 per cent, to less than for the *zu`ama'*.

The politicians of the old school are a resilient social 'species'; unlike old soldiers they have not even faded away. In 1981, they were at their nadir, mentioned by just 6 per cent, eclipsed by Bashir Gemayel's rising star among the Christians, and Palestinian and Syrian power among the Muslims. By the end of 1982, Bashir Gemayel was dead, and the Palestinians and Syrians were out of Beirut. In Amin Gemayel, the presidency had a politician of the old school, and parliament again played a role. In 1984, 17 per cent named the *zu`ama'*, although at the time of the survey hopes of a return to normal political life had again been dashed, and in 1986 18 per cent named them. How can their subsequent jump to 38 per cent be explained? The prime reason was probably the deepening economic and social crisis. The *zu`ama'* might not be liked, but they do have business and administrative connections and in times of need can often place people or provide assistance, which, in turn, further augments their influence. In short: the *zu`ama'* remained a political force.

Assessments of power differed. Party leaders were named most often in Ras Beirut, the Metn and Jbeil, that is, in urban districts and regions in which the parties or militias had a strong presence. They were mentioned least often in the Bekaa, which the Syrian Army controls, and in East Beirut, where dissension within the Christian camp tarnished the prestige of party leaders. The renaissance of the *zu`ama'* varied by region. In Beirut it was strongest in Mseitbeh, Basta and Ashrafieh, and weakest in the Shi`i suburbs (30 per cent). It was also low around Nabatieh and especially in Akkar, regions in which the older leaders had been discredited long before the outbreak of war. Other strongholds of the *zu`ama'* were Baalbek and Hermel, the Chouf and Kisrawan.

Assessments of a group's power and influence is one thing, appreciation of the same another. Although the majority of respondents appreciated leaders of the new type, they were less likely to testify to their effective influence than they were to that of the old-school politicians. The social profiles of the supporters of the two types are very different. People on lower incomes, with less education and no property preferred the new leaders. People with higher incomes and property leant towards the old politicians. A majority of Shi`is (77 per cent) and Druze (69 per cent) approved of the new leaders. While the old politicians did not find a majority in any group, support for them was above average among the Maronites (49 per cent), the Greek Orthodox (41 per cent) and the Sunnis (40 per cent).

**Table 7.44**

|  | Agreement (%) |
|---|---|
| *'The time of the old politicians is finished. The new leaders represent the basic feeling in the country and function better.'* | 62 |
| *'The old politicians are better than the new generation. At least they are tolerant, moderate and realistic.'* | 37 |

The appeal of both types also varied in accordance with the respondent's psycho-social attitudes. Of those favouring the new leaders, most — a higher than average proportion — were open to change, would take risks, were dissatisfied with their occupation and working conditions,[45] were socially envious and regarded differences between rich and poor as the major conflict in Lebanon. The new leaders also enjoyed higher than average support among the non-religious minority. By contrast, supporters of politicians of the old school had high representation among those who were less inclined to risk-taking and tended to be satisfied with their occupations and working conditions,[46] believed success depended on their own efforts, were more religious,[47] had strong family and communal loyalties, preferred neighbours from the same group but had nothing against colleagues from other communities, did not think class cleavages were the most important cause of conflict and did not agree that religious differences were simply a guise for social differences.

In summary, it may be said that those who preferred the new leaders tended to be at an economic disadvantage and have a comparatively strong sense of economic deprivation. Their social attitudes were, in a nutshell, populistic; accordingly, they were susceptible to the populist style and populist programmes of the 'new leaders'. As a simplification, we shall refer to them as 'populists'. By

---

[45] Seventy-six per cent of the very dissatisfied but only 53 per cent of the satisfied support the new leaders.

[46] Only 22 per cent of the very dissatisfied, but 50 per cent of the satisfied thought the old-school politicians better.

[47] Twenty-three per cent of the non-religious prefer the old politicians, but 44 per cent of the very religious do so.

## Attitudes and Opinions of Economically Active Lebanese

contrast, those with fewer disadvantages and a weaker sense of deprivation were inclined to prefer the old politicians. Their social attitudes were essentially those of moderately conservative liberals. There are populists and liberals in all communities. But whereas liberals enjoyed considerable support among Maronites, Greek Orthodox and Sunnis, populism clearly had the upper hand among the Shi`is and Druze.

As shown, the proportion of those who preferred the new leaders is larger than the proportion of those who also regarded them as the most influential group. This raises the question of the respondents' 'politicization': were they willing to brave active politics, or did they feel that discretion was the better part of valour?

**Table 7.45**

|  | Agreement (%) |
|---|---|
| *'In the present situation every Lebanese needs strong political opinions and clear alternatives.'* | 82 |
| *'If you keep out of politics you have peace and a clear conscience.'* | 62 |
| *'Stretch your feet only to the edge of the carpet.'*[48] | 69 |

The reactions to these statements reveal a discrepancy. Over four-fifths approved of strong political opinions, yet almost two-thirds preferred to keep out of politics and a good two-thirds to keep their feet on the ground, that is, to avoid unrealistic demands. As people who disapprove of politics are seldom politically minded, and as political detachment correlates well with moderation in demands and aspirations, that means a bare quarter of respondents were prepared to participate in politics and to question the status quo.

There is a further consideration: the feeling that strong political convictions were necessary had weakened. In 1984 and 1986 almost all respondents affirmed it, in 1987 only four-fifths. What can we conclude from our synopsis? A majority preferred the new leaders and thought clear convictions important, but only a minority thought their influence could change anything and were prepared to take an active part in politics. These are clear symptoms of resignation.

However, resignation was neither common to all communities nor ubiquitous. Highly politicized groups can be precisely pinpointed, primarily the Druze and the Shi`is in West Beirut. Only 26 per cent of Druze and 38 per cent of Shi`is wanted

---

[48] A Lebanese proverb.

to keep out of politics. These respondents did not live in the Chouf, the south or the Bekaa but in the capital: in Ras Beirut 71 per cent did not want to keep out of politics, and 79 per cent did not want to keep their feet on the ground, in Tarik al-Jadideh 85 and 70 per cent respectively, in the Shi`i suburbs 75 and 69 per cent.[49] These are the districts in which fears of the future, powerlessness, dissatisfaction and perceptions of a conflict between rich and poor were strongest, where populist new leaders found greatest resonance and where people were most politicized and most prepared to act politically.

What significance did respondents accord foreign factors in the conflict that was tearing Lebanon apart, and how did they think the conflict would end if the Lebanese had to deal only with one another?

Table 7.46

|  | Agreement (%) |
|---|---|
| *'Even if foreigners stayed out of Lebanese affairs, it would be difficult to reach an understanding; it is possible that the fighting between hostile Lebanese groups would break out again.'* | 50 |
| *'If foreigners stayed out, conflicts in Lebanon would never end in victory or defeat for anyone.'* | 56 |

Under the prevailing circumstances both statements were hypothetical. Thus, one may assume that the standpoints expressed were not speculative assessments of the situation but rather reflections of real fears and wishes. Renewed conflict even in the absence of foreign interference was held as a possibility by a higher than average number of Greek Orthodox and Greek Catholics, that is, by members of two communities that did not have their own militia and had frequently been victims in past phases of the conflict. A majority in Basta, Ashrafieh and the Christian suburbs, the Metn, Kisrawan and Baalbek-Hermel shared this view, all districts and regions of relative quiet at the time of the survey. By contrast, this view was held much less frequently in areas in which at that time there was great tension and violent incidents: Bourj al-Barajneh and Nabatieh. This speaks in favour of interpreting the first finding as the fears of those who were then

---

[49] In crass contrast, 90 per cent of respondents in Mseitbeh and Basta prefer to 'keep their feet on the ground', and in Ashrafieh nearly everyone.

enjoying some peace, and the latter as the hopes of those who were acutely affected.[50]

The civil war of 1958 was settled on the formula 'neither victor nor vanquished'. The wish seems to have been father to the reactions to this formula — both agreement and disagreement. Fifty-six per cent of the Druze, 75 per cent of the respondents in the Chouf and 67 per cent in Baalbek-Hermel answered No, areas that have their victors, and where the victors were satisfied with what they had.[51] Yeses were frequent in the regions of Jbeil and Jezzine, regions that feared a new outbreak of inconclusive fighting. But the most interesting finding is another: 61 per cent of all Shi`i respondents answered Yes, and 70 per cent of the inhabitants of the Shi`i suburbs of Beirut; in Ras Beirut 63 per cent agreed and in Tarik al-Jadideh no fewer than 76 per cent. The members of the most mobilized community, the inhabitants of those very areas in the country where discontent and politicization was rampant, thought victory improbable — a sign of resignation, even there where one would most expect a combative spirit, but surely a sign too of the desire for an end to the fighting.

In 1987, the Lebanese viewed their political system with resignation and realism: that is the result of this section in a nutshell. The respondents distinguished precisely between what they wanted and what they thought was realistic. There was a strong populist ground swell, particularly among Shi`is, in favour of the new leaders, leaders of parties and militias, alongside the realization that the tide had turned against them. Only a minority, but a respectable one, supported the traditional politicians. Contrary to many predictions, they have not ended up on the trash heap of history and nor have their political beliefs, characterized by a traditional, conservatively inclined liberalism. The great majority wanted and held political convictions, but only one-quarter were prepared to engage actively in politics in the then prevailing circumstances. This minority of highly mobilized, willing activists lived almost exclusively in two districts of West Beirut and in the Shi`i suburbs. And even the majority of them thought decisive defeat or victory in the internal Lebanese conflicts unlikely. Resignation and realism were almost inseparable in 1987.

## Political tendencies

Because Lebanese politics are highly personalized, party preferences have never been an adequate indicator of political orientations and tendencies. Support for

---

[50] This is further supported by the fact that specifically in Bourj al-Barajneh and Nabatieh 'foreign intervention' was the main source of tension — the Palestinians in the former, the Israelis in the latter.

[51] It is revealing that two-thirds of those who expected some conclusive result also thought renewed internal fighting was likely.

individual politicians may reliably reflect a party preference, but this is not the case for the majority of politicians. Hence, respondents were asked to name the politician whose ideas and positions were closest to their own as well as the one with whom they had least in common. As most Lebanese newspapers take a clear political line, respondents' choice of newspapers is useful information. Respondents were also asked to name their ideal country. Such preferences give at least a rough idea of the social and political order each respondent favours. Who were the most popular politicians in 1980s?

**Table 7.47**

| Politician of choice | 1984[52] | 1986 | 1987 |
|---|---|---|---|
| No reply | 20 | 16 | 46 |
| None | 12 | 22 | 20 |
| Nabih Berri | 13 | 10 | 7 |
| Raymond Eddé | 8 | 4 | 3 |
| Walid Jumblatt | 4 | 7 | 3 |
| Bashir Gemayel | 6 | 8 | 2 |
| Camille Chamoun | 4 | 9 | 2 |
| Georges Hawi | 3 | 2 | 2 |
| Kamal Jumblatt | 2 | 3 | 1 |
| Amin Gemayel | 4 | 3 | 1 |
| Selim al-Hoss | 5 | 4 | 1 |
| Rashid Karami | 2 | 3 | 1 |
| Gamal Abdel Nasser | 1 | 1 | – |
| Mohamed Shamseddin | 2 | – | – |
| Imam Musa Sadr | 1 | 1 | – |
| Samir Geagea | – | 2 | 1 |
| Sheikh Fadlallah | 1 | 1 | 1 |
| Chafiq Wazzan | 1 | – | – |
| Elias Sarkis | – | – | 1 |
| Imam Khomeini | – | – | 1 |
| Others[53] | 11 | 3 | 7 |

Figures in %

---

[52] This question was not asked in 1981.
[53] Politicians mentioned by less than 1 per cent of the respondents.

*Attitudes and Opinions of Economically Active Lebanese* 497

The most important finding is that the proportion of respondents who claimed not to have a favourite politician or were not prepared to name one rose from one-third in 1984 to two-thirds in 1987. This is a considered political view, as will be shown below. Politicians lost support across the board.[54] The fact that every politician mentioned had more opponents than supporters underscores this point.

Who were the most unpopular politicians in 1987?

**Table 7.48**

|  | % |
|---|---|
| Amin Gemayel | 16 |
| Nabih Berri | 8 |
| Samir Geagea | 7 |
| Walid Jumblatt | 5 |
| Yassir Arafat | 2 |
| Hafez el-Assad | 2 |
| Pierre Gemayel | 1 |
| Sheikh Fadlallah | 1 |
| Imam Khomeini | 1 |
| Victor Qassir | 1 |
| Rashid Karami | 1 |
| Ronald Reagan | 1 |
| All politicians | 7 |
| No answer | 47 |

Former President Gemayel had far more enemies than supporters. The same holds for Geagea, the leader of the Lebanese Forces, and to a lesser extent for Walid Jumblatt and Berri, the respective leaders of the Druze and Shi`i militias. In brief, those who possessed and exercised effective power in (parts of) the country were generally more disliked than liked. Six per cent of the respondents loathed foreign politicians and 7 per cent the whole political class.

What political tendencies[55] do these preferences reveal, and how did they change over the period covered by the surveys?

---

[54] This holds both for deceased politicians — Bashir Gemayel, Kamal Jumblatt, Rashid Karami, Gamal Abdel Nasser and Camille Chamoun — and for those still living. One of the deceased, Elias Sarkis, is the only Lebanese politician named for the first time in 1987.

[55] The politicians mentioned were subsumed under the following categories: militant Christians (in or pro-Kata'ib, Lebanese Forces, National Liberal Party or Lebanese Front); moderate Christians (all other

**Table 7.49**

| Political tendencies | 1984 | 1986 | 1987 |
|---|---|---|---|
| No answer, none | 32 | 38 | 66 |
| Moderate Christian | 11 | 5 | 7 |
| Moderate Muslim | 9 | 7 | 3 |
| Militant Christian | 16 | 24 | 7 |
| Amal | 16 | 11 | 7 |
| PSP | 7 | 9 | 4 |
| Left | 3 | 2 | 2 |
| Islamic fundamentalists | 1 | 1 | 2 |
| Others | 5 | 3 | 2 |

Figures in %

The first point is that support for both the 'moderate', traditional leaders and the 'militant' politicians and parties or organizations declined considerably.

Despite the previously expressed — non-personalized — preference of 37 per cent of the respondents for politicians of the old school, only 10 per cent actually named a politician of this ilk. Sixty-two per cent had expressed a general preference for 'new leaders', leaders of parties and militias, but only 22 per cent named a specific leader in this category. In other words, in 1987 only one-fifth of all respondents still consciously supported politicians who — irrespective of their actual politics — may be termed radical.

If one subsumes supporters of Amal, PSP, the diverse left-wing organizations as well as the Islamic fundamentalists under a programme of militant, albeit divergent, rejection of the pre-1975 Lebanese status quo, this group enjoys the sympathies of 15 per cent of the respondents. If one regards all Christian politicians, moderate and militant, as a single group favouring this status quo, they enjoy roughly the same level of support.

What are the social profiles of the different tendencies? The largest group is the Lebanese version of the 'Non-voters' Party', a party that has doubled its support since 1984. It contains both populists and liberals in the sense defined above.

Christians); Amal (Berri, Shamseddin and others pro-Amal); Progressive Socialist Party — PSP (Walid and Kamal Jumblatt and other PSP); Leftists (CP, Organization for Communist Action in Lebanon, Syrian Social Nationalist Party — SSNP, Nasserites; respondents naming Soviet or other non-Lebanese socialist politicians were also counted as left-wing); Islamic fundamentalists (Fadlallah, Khomeini, Islamic Amal, other Islamist leaders); moderate Muslims (independent Muslims and zu'ama').

## Attitudes and Opinions of Economically Active Lebanese

Those who give 'no answer' tend to be populists: conservatively cautious, powerless, dissatisfied people with strong family ties, they regard the cleavages between rich and poor as more important than those between communities, want to refrain from politics and believe that neither side can win in the Lebanese conflict. On the whole, the picture is one of abstinence born of resignation. By contrast, those who say 'none of them' tend to be conservative liberals in the higher income and better educated strata, who are unafraid of the future, feel they can influence things, are satisfied with their occupation, value their own efforts and are free of social envy. They do not have strong family ties, are loyal to their community, yet accept members of other communities as neighbours. They do not think the cleavage between rich and poor is paramount, or that the new leaders are better. In short, this is the de luxe version of political abstinence.

Where does the 'Non-voters' Party' have most and least support? It has a three-quarters majority in Ashrafieh (84 per cent) and the Christian suburbs (75 per cent), equally divided between 'no answer' and 'none of them'. It is very strong in Basta too (82 per cent, of which 49 per cent 'none'). In Tarik al-Jadideh, 72 per cent gave no answer, as did 14 per cent in Mseitbeh, where 54 per cent did not like any politician. In the Shi'i suburbs, strongholds of populism, and in Ras Beirut between 52 and 62 per cent gave no answer.

The fluctuation in abstinence is much greater out of Beirut. In Sidon and Nabatieh almost no one gave an answer. Three-quarters of the respondents in Akkar and Baalbek-Hermel did not mention any name, and between 60 and 65 per cent in Koura, Zghorta, Jezzine, the central and western Bekaa as well as in the Chouf and the Metn; in the latter two regions most abstainers replied 'none of them'. 'Non-voters' were in the minority only in Kisrawan (44 per cent), Tripoli (41 per cent) and, above all, Jbeil (14 per cent).

Who are the adherents of the moderate Christians? Their social profile resembles that of the liberal 'non-voters': people in the upper income and educational strata, not conservatively cautious, satisfied with their occupations, religious, but with neither strong family nor communal ties. A higher than average number of them accept mixed marriages. They do not regard the conflict in Lebanon as a class conflict, think politicians of the old school better than the new leaders and doubt whether one party can gain a decisive victory in the conflict. Their stronghold is Jbeil, where they won the support of 45 per cent; here Raymond Eddé is virtually unassailable. In Tripoli, Zghorta, Koura, Batroun and in Kisrawan they receive between 15 and 22 per cent, in the Bekaa 13 per cent, in the Metn 10 per cent. Their strength lies in areas in which the Lebanese Forces do not call the tune or, as in Jbeil, are accepted with reluctance, and in predominantly Muslim areas with substantial Christian minorities.

The social profile of support for the moderate Muslims resembles that for the moderate Christians and that of the 'none-of-them' non-voters. Support is drawn mainly from the middle- and higher-income strata (with high representation among people with a technical education). Few are afraid of the future, most are satisfied with their jobs and working conditions and are not socially envious. Although predominantly religious too, in contrast to the moderate Christians' supporters, they tend to have strong family and communal loyalties. Few agree that the cleavage between rich and poor is a cause of the conflict or find the new leaders effective. Their strongholds are Basta and Mseitbeh in the capital, the Chouf, Aley and the north Metn regions (14 per cent) and, above all, Tripoli (23 per cent).

Supporters of the militant Christians are quite different. They predominate among younger respondents and the lower income groups, but their educational qualifications are above average. They tend to be religious with fairly weak family and strong communal ties. Nor do they see the Lebanese conflict as a class conflict. They agree that the old politicians are more tolerant, but think the new leaders more effective. They believe that the conflict will continue even without foreign interference. Among them, the representation of industrial workers is slightly higher. A substantial minority of 34 per cent of militant Christians' supporters are not conservatively cautious, and 15 per cent think they could be happy without believing in God. By background and income this tendency is a Christian form of populism. The strongholds of the militant Christians are Kisrawan, with the support of one-third of the respondents, the Metn and the eastern suburbs of Beirut, where they draw one-quarter. In both Jezzine and Jbeil they have 16 per cent.

The Muslim form of populism is support for Nabih Berri and other Amal leaders. They too have greater appeal for the young, the lower income strata and industrial workers, but, unlike their Christian counterparts, also for the less educated. Like the militant Christians, Amal supporters are predominantly religious. In contrast to the former, they are very dissatisfied with their jobs and working conditions and regard the Lebanese conflict primarily as one between rich and poor. They too think the new leaders are better. Their level of politicization is above average and they also believe that without foreign intervention any conflict in Lebanon must end inconclusively. The strongholds of Berri's supporters are Bourj al-Barajneh and Haret Hreik, both 30 per cent, Chiyah and Ghobeiri as well as Jnah, Ouzai and Hay al-Sellum, each 20 per cent; in Tarik al-Jadideh they make up 14 per cent, in Mseitbeh 11 per cent. Outside the capital, Berri is the preferred politician of one-fifth of the respondents in Baalbek-Hermel.

The adherents of the Jumblatts and the Progressive Socialist Party differ completely from those of the militant Christians and Amal. Their profile is not populist, but liberal-conservative. Their representation in the upper income groups is higher than average, among large landowners as well as among agricultural labourers. PSP supporters are generally satisfied with occupation and working conditions, do not believe that their children will be worse off than they are, foster no social envy and believe to a higher than average degree that Lebanese society is middle-class. They do not disapprove of mixed marriages, let alone of neighbours from other communities. They are politicized and believe victory is possible in Lebanon, but also that there would be no further conflicts is foreign interference ceased. The bastion of Jumblatt support is the Chouf, but it is also respectable in Ras Beirut and Mseitbeh (16 and 10 per cent respectively). In Akkar and the Bekaa they have 8 per cent, in the Koura and Batroun 7 per cent.

It is almost impossible to draw a social profile of the small group of Leftist respondents on the basis of their choice of politician. Their attitude profile, however, is very clear. The Left are open to change, are dissatisfied with occupation and employer, though they do see career prospects, believe in mutual support but not that employers are too powerful. Their religiousness, family and communal loyalties are below average. To them the Lebanese conflict is a class conflict, religion and community just excuses to divert attention from the fundamental cleavage. They favour the new leaders, are highly politicized, do not 'keep their feet on the ground' and believe in the possibility of victory. Their militancy differs from that of the Amal or Christian militants, who tend to lump together family loyalties, religiousness, sense of community and the class interests of relatively deprived strata. Their militancy is rooted in political convictions far removed from traditional ties. Their stronghold is Ras Beirut, where they were named by 16 per cent of the respondents. In Tarik al-Jadideh they reach 9 per cent, in Bourj al-Barajneh 8 per cent — the hard core of the once so powerful Left in the southern suburbs in the pre-and early war years. Out of Beirut they draw 5 per cent in Akkar and the Koura-Batroun-Zghorta region and 6 per cent in Sidon.[56]

Who supports the Islamic fundamentalists? Eighty per cent is drawn from the lowest income group, 42 per cent have not completed any formal education. Among them the sense of impotence predominates, as does dissatisfaction with occupation and working conditions. They are very religious and have strong family loyalties. They reject mixed marriage, as well as members of other communities as neighbours or colleagues. And they are highly politicized. They are best described as religious superpopulists. Their stronghold is the southern suburbs of Beirut: Chiyah with 11 per cent, followed by Haret Hreik with 9 per

---

[56] In Sidon these are mostly supporters of Mustapha Saad or his late father, who term themselves Nasserites. In many respects their profile resembles that of supporters of moderate Muslim politicians rather than the genuine Left.

cent and Bourj al-Barajneh with 8 per cent; in Tarik al-Jadideh they have 3 per cent. Out of Beirut their strength lies mainly in the Bekaa (5 per cent). What are the respective strengths of these different political tendencies in the different zones of military control in Lebanon?

Table 7.50 Zones of military control and political tendencies

| Political tendencies | Christian militias | Syrian army (Christian maj.) | Syrian army (Muslim maj.) | Druze militia | Shi`i militia | All respondents |
|---|---|---|---|---|---|---|
| No answer | 42 | 40 | 45 | 18 | 74 | 46 |
| No politician | 18 | 20 | 24 | 42 | 5 | 20 |
| Moderate Christians | 10 | 16 | 5 | 3 | – | 7 |
| Moderate Muslims | – | 3 | 5 | 7 | 1 | 3 |
| Militant Christians | 13 | 8 | 4 | 6 | 1 | 7 |
| Amal | 8 | 2 | 7 | 1 | 10 | 7 |
| PSP | 2 | 4 | 3 | 20 | – | 4 |
| Left | 3 | 4 | 2 | 1 | 2 | 2 |
| Islamic Fundamentalists | 1 | 1 | 3 | 1 | 3 | 2 |
| Others | 3 | 2 | 2 | 1 | 4 | 2 |

Figures in %

From the analysis so far, it is apparent that each tendency has its strongholds. This also applies to regions. Yet, each tendency has a wide spread of support. Geographically speaking, there are no political monopolies; support for all is ubiquitous, even if weak in places.

Perhaps not monopolies by territory; but by confession? The only true monopoly is Islamic fundamentalism — by its nature it could hardly be otherwise. But Amal is not far from being one either: its support is 96 per cent Shi`i and 98 per cent Muslim. Militant Christian support is almost as one-sided. Although its distribution by Christian denomination is considerably broader than Amal's by Muslim, its confessional support is 95 per cent Christian. The two moderate tendencies have somewhat broader support across the confessional divide: 14 per cent of Muslims do support moderate Christians; 7 per cent of Christians support moderate Muslims, though their overwhelming support is Sunni (91 per cent).

**Table 7.51** Political tendencies by religious community

| Religious community | 'Non-voters' no answers | Party' none | Moderate Christians | Moderate Muslims | Militant | Amal | PSP | Left | Islamic Fundam. | All respondents |
|---|---|---|---|---|---|---|---|---|---|---|
| Sunnis | 24 | 24 | 12 | 91 | 4 | 1 | 13 | 7 | 3 | 21 |
| Shi'is | 31 | 15 | 2 | 2 | – | 96 | 3 | 47 | 94 | 27 |
| Druze | 2 | 4 | – | – | 1 | 1 | 53 | – | 3 | 4 |
| Maronites | 19 | 25 | 63 | 3 | 64 | 2 | 26 | 12 | – | 25 |
| Greek Orthodox | 11 | 15 | 12 | 2 | 14 | – | 1 | 23 | – | 11 |
| Greek Catholic | 9 | 12 | 8 | – | 9 | 1 | 3 | 7 | – | 8 |
| Armenians | 4 | 5 | 3 | 2 | 8 | – | 1 | 4 | – | 4 |

Figures in %

Only the support for the PSP and the Left is truly multi-confessional. Although Druze alone make up a slight majority of all PSP support, 31 per cent is Christian. By denomination, support for the Left comes largely from Shi`is (47 per cent) and Greek Orthodox (23 per cent); the most multi-confessional tendency is a non- or anti-confessional tendency.

Finally, if the 'Non-voters' Party' actually existed, one could say much the same of it. Support for both wings is spread across all denominations, with Shi`i support strong for the populist wing (no answer) and lower than average for the liberal wing (none). What about the obverse of the above, the composition of the confessions by political tendency?

Table 7.52 Religious communities by political tendency

|  | Sunnis | Shi`is | Druze | Maronites | Greek Orthodox | Greek Catholics | Armenians |
|---|---|---|---|---|---|---|---|
| No answer | 52 | 53 | 27 | 35 | 47 | 49 | 46 |
| No politicians | 24 | 11 | 22 | 20 | 28 | 30 | 26 |
| Moderate Chr. | 4 | – | – | 17 | 8 | 6 | 5 |
| Moderate Musl. | 13 | – | – | – | 1 | – | 1 |
| Militant Chr. | 1 | – | 1 | 18 | 9 | 7 | 14 |
| Amal | – | 25 | 1 | – | – | 1 | – |
| PSP | 2 | – | 47 | 4 | 1 | 1 | 1 |
| Left | 1 | 4 | – | 1 | 5 | 2 | 3 |
| Islamic Fund. | – | 6 | 1 | – | – | – | – |
|  | 3 | 1 | – | 5 | 1 | 4 | 4 |

Figures in %

Although different political tendencies may draw their support overwhelmingly from one community, the reverse is not true. No community overwhelmingly supports one political tendency. Indeed, not one political tendency has the backing of the majority of any one community.

The PSP come closest to a majority — among the Druze. This highlights the nature of this political group. While the PSP is a fairly multi-denominational tendency, it is the Druze tendency. Only very small Druze minorities express support for politicians of other tendencies. Politically, the Druze are the most homogeneous community. Amal is an almost exclusively Shi`i tendency, but supported by only one-quarter of the Shi`i respondents. Practically all Islamic fundamentalists are Shi`i, but these make up only 6 per cent of the Shi`is, among whom the Left is almost as popular (4 per cent). Of the Maronites, 17 per cent prefer moderate and 18 per cent militant Christian politicians, that is, pretty even support, while 5 per cent support the PSP and the Left.

Nine per cent of the Greek Orthodox are for militant Christian politicians, 8 per cent for moderate and 5 per cent for the Left, while of the Greek Catholics 6 per cent are for moderate and 7 per cent militant Christians. Finally, hardly any Sunnis support militants; 13 per cent prefer moderate Muslim and 4 per cent moderate Christian politicians. Lowest support for militants, irrespective of confession, is found among communities that do not have their own militia. Four-fifths of the Greek-Catholics and three-quarters of the Greek Orthodox, the Sunnis and the Armenians did not express a preference for any political tendency. To summarize: militant political tendencies find the support of half the Druze, one-third of the Shi`is and almost one-quarter of the Maronites. But a majority in every community finds little appeal in political tendencies, let alone militant ones. Political militancy in Lebanon — even when measured by as long a yard-stick as the popularity of militant politicians — is a cause of a minority.

An analysis of newspaper readership provides further details on political tendencies and orientations. Over the period of the surveys readership of the leading newspapers has fluctuated as follows:

**Table 7.53**

| Newspapers | 1981 | 1984 | 1986 | 1987[57] |
|---|---|---|---|---|
| *An-Nahar* | 57 | 50 | 40 | 28 |
| *As-Safir* | 37 | 44 | 32 | 14 |
| *Al-'Amal* | 23 | 11 | 10 | 5 |
| *Al-Anwar* | 10 | 7 | 10 | 5 |
| *L'Orient-Le Jour* | 6 | 4 | 2 | 4 |
| *Le Reveil* | 3 | 1 | 2 | 2 |
| *An-Nida* | 7 | 14 | 11 | 7 |
| *Al-Ahrar* | 2 | 1 | 2 | 1 |
| *Al-Liwa* | 6 | 1 | 7 | 1 |
| *Amal* | – | 19 | 8 | 6 |

Figures in %

[57] Multiple answers allowed.

The first point to note is the decline in newspaper readership. In 1981 and 1984, respondents read on average 1.5 newspapers, in 1986 1.2 and in 1987 only 0.7. One reason for this is the rising cost of living. Another is disappointment with political developments and disenchantment with militant politics: the combined market share of the tendentious and radical papers has fallen more than that of the serious and factual press.

*An-Nahar* is the leading and most reputable newspaper in the country. Its approach is moderately liberal. It has a reputation for comprehensive and reliable reportage and considered editorial comment. The same holds for the French-language *L'Orient-Le Jour*, a newspaper closely associated with *an-Nahar*. They are read by a higher than average proportion of upper-income, well-educated respondents, *an-Nahar* by 55 per cent of university graduates, *L'Orient-Le Jour* by 15 per cent. *An-Nahar* is read primarily in Ashrafieh and the eastern suburbs of Beirut, the Metn, Kisrawan and, in particular, Jbeil, but also in the West Beirut districts of Mseitbeh and Basta as well as in Tripoli, Koura and Zghorta. *L'Orient-Le Jour* sells well in the Metn, Kisrawan, Jbeil and East Beirut, but scarcely at all in predominantly Muslim areas. It has a disproportionately high number of readers among Armenians. Since 1984, *an-Nahar* has lost fewer readers than the average of the Lebanese press, while *L'Orient-Le Jour* has held its own.

*As-Safir*, although originally left-wing, is not linked to any party or organization. Its stance has gradually become left-liberal. It also has a reputation for reliable, comprehensive coverage, but its editorial commentary takes greater account of the Muslim population than does that of *an-Nahar*. *As-Safir* too is read by members of the upper-income strata — 41 per cent of its readership is in the highest income group — though by education its readership is more average: technical and secondary school graduates are highly represented. Its areas of circulation, besides West Beirut, are the Chouf, Tripoli, Koura and Akkar; it is bought by only between 5 and 6 per cent of the respondents in the Christian and Shi`i suburbs. Among its readership Druze and Sunnis are highly represented (each one-quarter). Its readership has declined by about two-thirds since 1984.

*Al-'Amal* is the official organ of the Kata'ib Party. In the mid-1980s, the newspaper was a source of strife between the party and the Lebanese Forces; at times two different issues appeared. This may explain its higher than average decline in circulation. It is sold only in East Beirut and its hinterland. Its readers are mostly Maronite and Greek Orthodox; few Greek Catholics read it and no Muslims at all.

*Le Reveil* — a French-language newspaper formerly close to Amin Gemayel — may have profited from the difficulties suffered by *Al-'Amal*. It serves the same areas as *Al-'Amal*, with its best sales in the Metn. It is most popular among women and Armenians.

*Al-Anwar* is published in Hazmiyeh, a town controlled by the loyalist section of the Lebanese Army at the time of the survey. Its editorial policy follows the tradition of Chehabist reformism. It is read by members of the Christian communities, but also by Sunnis in Basta and in Tripoli. Its loss of readership is lower than average.

*An-Nida* is the official organ of the Communist Party. The well-educated are highly represented in its readership. It sells very well in Ras Beirut (35 per cent), in Mseitbeh (14 per cent) and Tarik al-Jadideh (12 per cent), and has average sales in the Shi`i suburbs; higher than average shares of its readership live in the Chouf and Akkar. By denomination, most of its readers are Druze, Shi`is and Greek Orthodox.

*Al-Liwa* is the mouthpiece of West Beirut political Sunni Islam. It is also sold in Tripoli and Sidon and has a small but faithful readership.

The same may be said of *Ahrar*, the newspaper of the National Liberal Party of former President Camille Chamoun. It is sold exclusively in East Beirut and Kisrawan.

*Amal* is the organ of the eponymous Shi`i movement. It is read in the southern suburbs of Beirut and the regions of Nabatieh and Baalbek-Hermel. Its readership is almost exclusively Shi`i; one-fifth of all Shi`i respondents claim to read it.

The opinion and readership profiles of the Lebanese newspapers allow a comparison between their readerships and support for the different political tendencies described above.

The portions of the Christian and the Shi`i militant populist tendencies correlate fairly well with the readership shares of the corresponding newspapers. The portion of readers of liberal, reformist and left-liberal newspapers, however, is about five times as large as the portion of declared supporters of moderate political tendencies.

Of course, care must be taken not to read too much into these differences: some respondents read several newspapers, including ones with whose editorial opinion they do not agree. But even allowing for such qualifications, the point may be taken that there are far more liberal-minded and reformist people, in the broad sense, than political tendencies indicate.

This is in keeping with the liberal attitude profile of those who said they did not like any of the politicians. In short: the number of liberals and progressive moderates is far greater than those who showed some enthusiasm for moderate politicians. In the Lebanon of 1987, dislike of politicians in general is not an indication of political apathy.

**Table 7.54** Political tendencies and newspaper readership

| Political tendencies | Supporters | Newspapers | | Readership |
|---|---|---|---|---|
| Militant Christians | 7 | militantly Christian | *Al-'Amal* | 5 |
| | | | *Le Reveil* | 2 |
| | | | *Al-Ahrar* | <u>1</u> |
| | | | | 8 |
| Amal supporters | 7 | Amal | *Amal* | 6 |
| PSP | 4 | Left (CP) | *An-Nida* | 7 |
| Left | <u>2</u> | | | |
| | 6 | | | |
| Moderate Christian | 7 | liberal, reformist | *An-Nahar* | 28 |
| Moderate Muslims | 3 | | *L'Orient-Le Jour* | 4 |
| | | | *Al-Anwar* | 5 |
| | | | *Al-Liwa* | 1 |
| | | liberal Left Muslim | *As-Safir* | 14 |
| | – | | | – |
| | 10 | | | 52 |

Figures in %

'Which country do you think comes closest to an ideal country?' An open question of this nature is to empirical social research what the discharge from a shotgun into thick undergrowth is to a hunter: both may scatter and hit nothing, but may fell a superb head of game. In the case of the Lebanon study it has produced results beyond expectation.

There have been significant developments over time. Admiration for Lebanon has declined strongly, as has that for Iran. The interest in countries welcoming immigrants has jumped. And democratic, neutral, prosperous countries have become the ideal of almost half the respondents.

**Table 7.55**

| Ideal country | 1984[58] | 1986 | 1987 |
|---|---|---|---|
| Switzerland, Austria, Scandinavian countries | 30 | 33 | 47 |
| France | 7 | 8 | 9 |
| USA | 4 | 6 | 6 |
| Other western countries | 10 | 8 | 10 |
| USSR and socialist countries | 10 | 7 | 5 |
| Iran | 7 | 3 | 2 |
| Arab labour-seeking states | 2 | 1 | – |
| Other Arab countries | 3 | 4 | – |
| Immigration countries | 1 | 2 | 12 |
| Lebanon | 15 | 8 | 4 |
| Israel | 1 | 1 | 1 |
| No country | 10 | 19 | 3 |

Figures in %

In 1984, just before the irretrievable collapse of their attempt to stabilize Lebanon with inadequate means, France and the USA had lost prestige; since then they have regained some of it. Maronites have a higher than average admiration of France, the country with which they have had contact for centuries; but even then it is only admired by 13 per cent of all Maronites. The Greek Orthodox in particular regard the USA as an almost ideal country; but, once again, only 13 per cent of them do so. Even in 1987, Muslims were not enamoured of the USA.

France is esteemed by those in favour of a separation of religion and politics. The principal attraction of France is its secular order, that of the USA the opportunities open to the industrious.

A number of other western countries were named by between 6 and 16 per cent of respondents from all communities, most frequently by the Greek Orthodox. Most of them were successful in their occupation, had no social envy, were not very religious and had no fears of the future — obviously a group who admire the social order of western industrial states.

[58] This question was not asked in 1981.

In 1987, the model of the socialist states still had a higher than average attraction for the Druze (27 per cent) and Armenians (15 per cent) as well as for respondents in the Chouf and northern Lebanon (each 12 per cent). These respondents tend to be non-religious, without strong family or communal loyalties, in favour of the new leaders, strongly politicized and free of fears of the future; they also think victory in the Lebanese conflict is possible. Their preference for a socialist country is one of political conviction, a phenomenon common among those who prefer left-wing politicians.

In 1987, the Arab oil-states dropped off the list. The Lebanese may appreciate the economic opportunities they offer, but no one regards them as ideal countries. The same applies to other Arab countries. Syria, the Arab brother country with the greatest influence on Lebanon's fate, was named by only 0.2 per cent of the respondents.

Despite the enormous love the Lebanese have for their country, evident to even the most casual visitor, it is not surprising that few regard it as an ideal country. To do so requires a patriotism of heroic proportions. Yet 4 per cent have it, a group who defy classification by social factors or attitudes.

In 1984, 7 per cent of the respondents admired Khomeini's Iran above all other countries, even then a modest showing for a sample with 26 per cent Shi`is. In 1987, just 11 per cent of the Shi`i respondents, or 2 per cent of the entire sample, thought Iran an ideal country. The presence in Lebanon of Pasdaran has undoubtedly enhanced the fighting abilities of the Hezbollah militia; it is doubtful whether it has done the same for the attractiveness of the Islamic state's political and social order. The case of the Islamic fundamentalists trenchantly demonstrates the gulf in Lebanon today between fighting power and might, on the one hand, and support and popularity among the population, on the other.

Which countries do appeal to Shi`is? Nineteen per cent of them mentioned western countries that still accept immigrants: Canada, Australia, Latin American countries and African countries too, in which tens of thousands of Lebanese — and in particular Shi`is — have found acceptance and a livelihood. These countries are also mentioned by 16 per cent of the Sunnis, about 11 per cent of each of the Maronites, Greek Catholics and Armenians as well as 7 per cent of the Greek Orthodox. All in all, they are admired by 12 per cent of the respondents, beyond doubt an indication of the dramatic rise in the wish to emigrate: in 1984 countries of immigration were named by only 1 per cent.

That it is not only a matter of wishful thinking but at times of very real conviction is revealed by the profile of those who name such countries. A higher than average number have technical skills, that is, qualifications such countries welcome. Most feel higher than average dissatisfaction with employer and earnings and with career prospects, and would also work as migrant labourers in the Gulf states. They regard the new leaders as an improvement but do not want to get involved in politics. These respondents exhibit all the characteristic attitudes of populist tendencies but do not believe that their wishes can be realized politically. The resigned populist thinks of emigrating.

The admirers of French secularism, American opportunities, western or eastern European, Arab and Iranian models of society and those hoping to find better prospects in a new country together comprise only half of the Lebanese. The largest group by far — 47 per cent — see their ideal in other countries: Switzerland, Austria, Sweden and the other Scandinavian countries. Switzerland alone was named by almost one-third of all respondents. These countries have many features in common. They are small, democratic, prosperous and, for the most part, neutral. It is more than just a desire for the old Lebanese magic formula, which saw in Lebanon the 'Switzerland of the Orient'. This formula may have been at the back of some minds. But even in 1984 these countries together were mentioned less often than Switzerland alone in 1987. It is more likely that the intensive discussion of the constitutional and social systems of comparable countries conducted in the Lebanese press since 1985 has made its mark. Circumstantial evidence in support of this surmise is the fact that admiration of these countries goes hand in hand with the level of education.

Be that as it may, the admirers of small, democratic and prosperous countries reveal a remarkably coherent attitude profile. Though satisfied and not envious, they perceive a widening social divide in Lebanon. They are religious, but do not regularly practise their religion. They regard politicians of the old school as more tolerant, but are not convinced of the need for 'strong political convictions', preferring to 'keep their feet on the ground' and themselves out of politics. A disproportionately large number are not afraid of the future. In short: the 'Swiss' ideal is the common political denominator of the optimistic liberals. They are more or less evenly spread across the communities, and in each they are the largest group.

In summary, although political orientations in the extraordinarily complex Lebanese society are exceptionally complex, it is possible to discern certain contours. The Lebanese are disappointed in their politicians. The surprising point is not the fact as such — in such circumstances which people would not be? — but its extent. In 1984 one-third could not identify themselves with any politician or gave no answer, in 1987 two-thirds. All politicians have lost popularity, and every single one has more opponents than supporters. Those who either find none of the politicians attractive or have not answered are either resigned populists — poor, dissatisfied, loyal to family and community, but disenchanted — or disgusted liberals.

Other liberals support moderate Christian (7 per cent) and Muslim politicians (3 per cent), together one-tenth of all respondents. Strongly politicized and predominantly religious populists are adherents of militant Christian and Shi`i politicians: each of these tendencies was preferred by 7 per cent of respondents. 'Superpopulists' support Islamic fundamentalism, a particularly impoverished, ill-educated, pious, dissatisfied and activist group comprising 2 per cent of the respondents, that is, a very small minority.

Jumblatt and his Progressive Socialists have a curious group of supporters. They are drawn from different communities, are liberal conservatives in terms of social characteristics and attitudes, yet express a political militancy akin to the populists. Four per cent of respondents professed a preference for this group in 1987. Two per cent of the respondents are convinced Leftists, a predominantly well-educated and thoroughly secular group drawn from all communities, from which they stand aloof.

Each of these political tendencies has its geographic strongholds, but none of them has an absolute majority anywhere, at best a relative one. All — with the exception of the Left — have strong support in specific communities: almost half the Druze support Jumblatt or the PSP, one-quarter of the Shi`is Berri or Amal, almost one-fifth of the Maronites the militant Christians. But none of these tendencies has a majority within a community. Seventy per cent of the members of communities that have no militia — Sunnis, Greek Orthodox, Greek Catholics and Armenians — gave either no name or no answer. Political militancy is a minority phenomenon in all communities, and, on the whole, the cause of a minority.

The analysis of newspaper readership by political tendencies, social characteristics and attitudes revealed that liberals and reformists, in the broad sense, are far more numerous than expressions of political preference lead one to believe.

Finally, the question of the country that most closely corresponds to respondents' ideals also provides insights. Iran and the Iranian model of an Islamic republic are the ideal of only one-tenth of the Shi`is, that is, the ideal of only a minority among the militant Shi`i populists. Socialist countries are the ideal of more respondents than professed support for left-wing Lebanese politicians, but even then they are the ideal of only one-third of the Leftists and radical progressives. Twelve per cent of the respondents, compared to only 1 per cent three years previously, see their ideal in countries of emigration. They are predominantly resigned and depoliticized populists, Shi`is in particular. That by 1987 more than one-tenth of all respondents appeared to have given up hope of a better future in their own country is a syndrome of grave crisis.

But this is more than balanced by a symptom of hope. In 1987, almost half of all respondents in all communities named as their ideal small, democratic, prosperous countries such as Switzerland, Austria or Sweden. Three years previously one-third fewer had.

## Religion and politics

Even in the pre-war period the Lebanese formula for regulating the relationship between religion and politics, between religious communities and power in the state, caused heated controversy. Opposition to the formula was not restricted to issues of the concrete division of power between the communities, the question of who gets how much. There were also objections of principle. As this formula proved incapable of preventing the war, objections of principle have grown. But they come from different quarters, and the proposals for redefining the relationship between religion and politics are as varied. One concept calls for the separation of religion and politics: the secularization of the state and legal order. A second calls for a decentralization that would give each religious community its own canton, where each would be free to order the relationship between religion and politics as it saw fit. Finally, in recent years there have been fundamentalist religious calls for just the opposite of secularization, namely to order the state and society more strictly by religious principles. What support do these various concepts enjoy among the respondents?

'One should not mix religion and politics.' Agreement with this very generally formulated statement of secularism has risen from 84 per cent in 1981 and 1984, through 87 per cent in 1986, to 93 per cent in 1987. But there was similar agreement with a more specific statement. 'There are very real differences between the religious communities in our country, but one should keep them out of politics.' Ninety-two per cent answered Yes. Agreement was lower only among the less educated strata and in parts of the Shi`i suburbs. In other words, there is broad disapproval of what has taken place in Lebanon since, at the latest, the outbreak of war, that is, the definition of politics in terms of religion and religious communities. However, it would be premature to equate this mood with approval of a precise concept of secularization, as the reactions to another statement show.

'The best solution to Lebanon's present dilemma is a completely secular state and society.' In 1984 75 per cent agreed, in 1986 only 52 per cent and in 1987 63 per cent. This wide fluctuation may be explained by politico-military developments. Nineteen eighty-six was a year of bitter conflicts. At any rate, all three surveys[59] produced a majority for the concept of comprehensive secularization. Who is for and against this concept?

---

[59] This question was not asked in 1981.

Approval is disproportionately high among the young and the better educated as well as the highest income group. There was considerable divergence by urban district and by region. Approval was strongest — three-quarters of the respondents — in Ashrafieh and the Christian suburbs, followed by Ras Beirut (69 per cent). Secularists are a minority in Chiyah, only 42 per cent. Out of Beirut approval is strongest in Jbeil (almost 90 per cent), followed by the Metn and the Chouf (both almost three-quarters). It is also above average in Koura, Akkar and Kisrawan. It is well below average in Nabatieh (40 per cent), Sidon (24 per cent) and Jezzine (22 per cent). There are also marked differences between the communities. The Druze are the most secularist (77 per cent), and the Maronites, Armenians (both 73 per cent) and Greek Orthodox (70 per cent) strongly in favour too. Lower than average approval was expressed by the Greek Catholics (60 per cent), the Sunnis (57 per cent) and the Shi`is (53 per cent). The widespread approval among the Druze is not surprising: their strongest political leaders have consistently championed this cause. But the majorities in the Christian communities are less self-evident. Leading Christian politicians too have long supported secularization, provided that it is a thorough-going secularization: that is, it does not stop at the abolition of political proportionality, but extends civil jurisdiction to personal status. The statement allows for this: 'secularization of state and society'. It is commonly assumed that this demand for complete secularization is purely tactical, intended to provoke rejection by the Muslim communities. Whether this is the case or not, the results show that in 1987 a clear majority of all Christians were prepared to accept full secularization. There were also majorities for secularization among the Sunnis and the Shi`is, though only just among the latter.

By attitude profile, two broad groups support secularization. One embraces the non-religious and people with weak family and communal loyalties. The other is those moderately religious people — a higher than average number — who are not conservatively cautious, are satisfied with their job, unafraid of the future and who do not feel impotent, that is, the optimistic liberals.

By political tendency, strongest support for secularization comes from supporters of the Left and of the PSP, from moderate Christians and those who dislike all politicians. The secularists' common political denominator is the dislike of two types of politicians: Islamic fundamentalists and militant Christians. These results may give adherents of secularization good grounds for optimism. But too much should not be read into them, as the reactions to another statement testify.

'Every Lebanese should have the right to join a secularized community that has the same rights as the other communities — personal status law, political representation, etc.' The respondents were fairly evenly divided on this proposal. The idea of creating a secular community which every citizen would be entitled to join — or to remain in their traditional communities — has been discussed in Lebanon for some time. It is conceived of as facilitating a voluntary, gradual and, hence, politically painless transition to secularization. This concept stops far short of full secularization, yet finds less approval. How can this be explained?

The social characteristics and attitudes of the advocates and opponents of this concept are similar to those of the more radical one. But the differences are less blurred. Respondents with higher levels of income and education, non-religious people, radical reformists and liberals have higher than average representation. Their political tendencies are Left, PSP and moderate Christian and Muslim. Islamic fundamentalists (91 per cent) and supporters of Berri and Amal (72 per cent) are opposed.

The geographic distribution of the Noes is as revealing: two-thirds of the respondents in Bourj al-Barajneh, Haret Hreik, Tarik al-Jadideh, Nabatieh and Jezzine, and 80 per cent in Chiyah, Jnah-Ouzai and Sidon.

Acceptance of secularization varies greatly by community.

Table 7.56

| Religious community | For a secular community | For secularization of state and society |
|---|---|---|
| Maronites | 65 | 73 |
| Armenians | 59 | 73 |
| Greek Orthodox | 58 | 70 |
| Greek Catholics | 56 | 60 |
| Druze | 49 | 77 |
| Sunnis | 47 | 57 |
| Shi`is | 31 | 53 |
| All respondents | 50 | 63 |

Figures in %

In all communities support was significantly greater for the 'secularization of state and society' than for a 'secular community'. The explanation may lie in formulation. The description of the secular community is far more concrete, elaborating on what secularization of state and society could entail: persons would have the right to withdraw from their religious community, that is, contract civil marriages and seek non-communal political representation. The more concrete the secularization, the fewer the secularists.

The loss of support is greater among the Muslim communities. This is hardly surprising; for secularization would mean that Muslims could opt for civil rather than Qur'anic marriage and inheritance laws, and that women could legally enter into mixed marriages.

The results on secularization as a whole give cause for scepticism. There may be a widespread general feeling that religion and politics do not mix well: 90 per cent of the respondents agree. A little short of a two-thirds majority approve of secularization of state and society. But once concrete consequences of secularization are elucidated — as under the most moderate hypothesis of individual volition — approval drops to just 50 per cent, and only 30 per cent among Shi`is.

Many Christians fear that their Muslim compatriots want political secularization without that of society and civil legislation. They perceive in this not only the loss of political power but the thin end of the Islamic legal wedge. Our findings will not help to disperse such fears. Christian fears of subjection to a non-secularized Muslim majority have given birth to concepts of economic and political decentralization intended to enable effective communal autonomy.

What are the opinions on such concepts?

**Table 7.57**

|  | Agreement (%) | | | |
|---|---|---|---|---|
|  | 1981 | 1984 | 1986 | 1987 |
| 'During the crisis[60] each region has had to get by on its own. Perhaps a decentralized economy is a good thing.' | 52 | 61 | 46 | 31 |
| 'Coexistence between the communities would be easier if each community had its own region.' | * | 23 | 25 | 18 |
| 'The identity and uniqueness of my community are more important to me than loyalty to the country.' | * | * | * | 12 |
| 'Most regions in Lebanon are mixed. All Lebanon is for all the Lebanese.' | * | 86 | 85 | 70 |

* Not asked

[60] Lebanese euphemism for war.

## Attitudes and Opinions of Economically Active Lebanese

There is even less approval for the concept of decentralization than for that of secularization. The small majority favourable to economic decentralization in 1981 had shrunk to less than one-third in 1987. One-quarter approved the wider concept of 'cantonalization' in 1986, but only 18 per cent in 1987. Only 12 per cent preferred the uncompromising formulation of communal over national interests.

The contrary thesis to decentralization and cantonalization also lost much support in 1987, a reflection of the fact that it was no longer supported in many places. However, it still has a broad majority.

Decentralization finds approval where it exists de facto, where people feel relatively secure and go about their business without too much disruption: in the Christian heartland of Jbeil (75 per cent), Kisrawan (57 per cent) and the Metn (56 per cent) and in East Beirut (43 per cent), in the Christian areas in the north — Koura, Zghorta and Batroun — (51 per cent) as well as in the Chouf (49 per cent) and the Syrian-controlled northern Bekaa (40 per cent). Regions of great insecurity and concomitant economic depression show little enthusiasm: southern Lebanon (14 per cent), the Shi`i suburbs of Beirut (8 per cent) and Ras Beirut (4 per cent).

Similarly, religious cantons find higher than average support where they exist de facto: in all areas controlled by Christian militias (greatest in Kisrawan with 41 per cent and least in Ashrafieh with 24 per cent, which is still above average), in the de facto Shi`i cantons of Baalbek and Nabatieh (both 28 per cent) and in the Chouf (22 per cent). By political tendency, 34 per cent of the militant and 22 per cent of the moderate Christians are in favour of cantonalization.

Who constitute the hard core of those who put the identity of their own community before loyalty to their country? They have higher than average representation in the Metn (25 per cent), in Basta (22 per cent) and above all in the eastern suburbs, where support reaches 30 per cent. By community they are most frequent among Armenians (17 per cent), Maronites and Greek Catholics (both 15 per cent). Their religiousness and family loyalties are higher than average. By political tendency they have higher than average representation among militant Christians (24 per cent) and Islamic fundamentalists (24 per cent).

Whereas approval of economic decentralization and denominational cantonalization is a product of the normative power of facts, preference for community over country, whether Christian or Shi`i fundamentalist, is an extreme position rooted in fear, in other words, a soft not a hard core.

Advocates of both forms of decentralization are minorities in virtually everywhere and in all communities. The great majority of respondents are of the opinion that Lebanon belongs to all Lebanese. Hence, decentralization is even less acceptable than secularization as a means of regulating the relationships between religion and politics in Lebanon. The antithesis of secularization is a religious stamp on state and society. What are opinions on this concept?

**Table 7.58**

|  | Agreement (%) | | | |
|---|---|---|---|---|
|  | 1981 | 1984 | 1986 | 1987 |
| 'The believer must return to his spiritual and cultural roots and seek the meaning in his religious destiny.' | 79 | 78 | 79 | 68 |
| 'Life in any society must be based on faith and religious values' | 67 | 62 | 68 | 55 |

The majority of those who desire a return to spiritual sources also want religious values to play a larger role in society. This is not a harmless pietistic position, but a fundamentalist one. It has stronger support than the secularist position. But it may have peaked: a decline of over 10 per cent within a year may be more than only statistically significant.[61] Who entertains these fundamentalist views? Their representation is higher than average among the less-educated strata, the very religious, very regular visitors of places of worship and people with strong family and communal loyalties. Their bastions are Kisrawan, Tripoli, Sidon and the Metn (all over 85 per cent).

Support is higher than average among Maronites and Sunnis, lower than average among Greek Catholics, Greek Orthodox and, above all, the Druze. By political tendency, they are Islamic fundamentalists and militant Christians (both nearly 90 per cent).

Lebanese 'fundamentalism' is a peculiar phenomenon. It is found among Shi`is; but this community, susceptible to fundamentalism as such anyway, is less affected than the Sunni and Maronite communities. But above all, it is a very Lebanese, that is, multi-confessional fundamentalism. As every community has its own variety of fundamentalism, the chances than any single one can carry the day are negligible. This increases the likelihood that each will seek ascendancy within the respective community. And indeed, since 1986, there has been a shift in armed conflict from between to within communities. Perhaps the decline in

[61] In both cases $p < 0.001$.

approval between 1986 and 1987 is best explained by precisely these internal conflicts.

The analysis of attitudes to concepts which present alternatives to the Lebanese formula for regulating relationships between religion and politics presents a very contradictory picture. The major contradiction is between 65 per cent for a secularization of state and society and 55 per cent for a society based on by religious beliefs and values. One-quarter of the respondents were both for and against secularization.[62] This may be illogical, but then so is social reality at times.

When none of the new concepts find the approval of the majority, are the respondents prepared to make do with what they have?

'It doesn't matter what our wishes are, there seems to be no chance that secularization can take place in Lebanon. Community membership is a reality that you have to accept.' Fifty-four per cent answered Yes. Who answered No? They tend to be younger, highly educated and, above all, Druze. They are particularly common in the southern suburbs, that is, among the urban Shi`is, and in Ashrafieh. They also have little fear of the future, are less religious, have fewer family and communal ties, and are highly politicized.

The profile of this group alone is sufficient guarantee that reality will not be accepted. The relationship between religion and religious community, on the one hand, and politics, state and society, on the other, is controversial not only between, but also within, all communities, and all the evidence suggests this state will persist.

## Forms of conflict regulation

Which political order do the Lebanese respondents think most suitable for regulating the conflicts in their country? The statements emphasize different points: the first, the necessity of overcoming existing divisions, agreement on this having risen from over 80 to over 90 per cent between 1981 and 1987; the second, a means to this end. This view too has a majority, but nothing approaching unanimity. In all four surveys at least two-thirds — in 1984 and 1986 considerably more — of the respondents felt that the country could be governed only if the communities worked together and their authentic representatives exercised power.

---

[62] This is still the case if one uses the more concrete option of a secular community.

**Table 7.59**

|  | Agreement (%) | | | |
|---|---|---|---|---|
|  | 1981 | 1984 | 1986 | 1987 |
| *'Lebanon won't have a united and strong government until the state overcomes the differences between the Lebanese people and the confessionalist factions.'* | 83 | 82 | 85 | 94 |
| *'Lebanon won't have a strong and united government until authentic representatives of the communities have a share in power.'* | 67 | 79 | 73 | 66 |

The remaining one-third either did not share this view or had difficulties with 'authentic representatives'. The former respondents will include less religious people with few family and communal ties, especially Leftists, people who do not want such a government. Because they reject confessionalism, they disapprove on principle of a political order based on communal power-sharing. But this group is only a minority of those who answered No. Most of the Noes are in the 'Non-voting Party'. By contrast, over 80 per cent of those with militant political views said Yes, they believe their representatives are authentic. If one recalls that in recent years militant groups and militias have endeavoured to present their leaders as the respective 'true' representatives, one may surmise that some of those who said No did so in protest against the specious claims of many contemporary aspirants, not against communal participation in government as such.

Be that as it may, the responses to the first statement show that almost all respondents react positively to the catch-phrase 'overcoming the differences between Lebanese and confessional factions'. Responses to the second show that the idea of a division of power between the communities appears acceptable to at least two-thirds.

In 1987 the respondents were presented with a number of detailed statements[63] on desirable political orders. An examination of their answers throws light on feasible forms of conflict regulation.

---

[63] The preamble read: 'Like ours, many countries have lots of different groups — language groups, religious groups, ethnic groups or others. These countries have many different forms of government and people have different opinions about how they should be governed. We should like to present some of these

## Table 7.60

|  | Agreement (%) |
|---|---|
| 'The country must be partitioned and each group should found its own state.' | 4 |
| 'The numerically strongest group should govern. The other groups must accept what this group decides.' | 6 |
| 'The strongest group should govern. The other groups must accept what the strongest group decides.' | 20 |
| 'One group should govern, and groups that don't like it must leave the country.' | 10 |
| 'Because of the nature of Lebanese society, important decisions need the agreement of all large without opposition.' | 35 |
| 'All vote for the party of their choice. The party or parties that win form the government, the other parties remain in the opposition.' | 71 |
| 'Because of the nature of Lebanese society, important decisions need the agreement of all large communities.'[64] | 80 |

A number of conclusions are immediately apparent. Participation is rejected more strongly than economic decentralization and cantonalization. Even rule by the numerically largest group is rejected out of hand. Yet one-fifth can accept the notion of domination by one group, and one-tenth accept it in the crass form of 'either join in or get out'. In other words, a substantial minority find extremely undemocratic forms of government quite acceptable.

There is greater acceptance of less extreme undemocratic solutions, such as a one-party state: 35 per cent answered Yes. Nonetheless: partition as well as all undemocratic forms of conflict regulation, be it rule by the strongest or largest group, be it a one-party state, are rejected by large majorities. Even after twelve years of war and civil war most Lebanese were still democrats.

There is a remarkable finding in respect of democratic forms of government. Seventy-one per cent of the respondents accept government by the majority pure and simple, yet four-fifths accept the necessity of consent by the major communi-

opinions. Please give us your opinion about each, whether you think it is acceptable or unacceptable for Lebanon.'

[64] This formulation was used in the 1981, 1984 and 1986 surveys. To enable a comparison over time it was retained unaltered.

ties to important political decisions, that is, the basic principle of consociational democracy.

Before similarities and, especially, dissimilarities in support for these two forms of democracy — majority government and consociation — are dealt with in detail, the profiles of support for each option will be briefly sketched.

Those who are for partition are also for economic decentralization and cantons, and, disproportionately for their numbers, are prepared to put community before country. These people are found in the Christian suburbs of Beirut and in the Metn, among Maronites, Greek Orthodox and Greek Catholics. They have higher than average fears of the future and want to have nothing to do with politics.

Respondents in favour of domination by the numerically strongest group are found predominantly in the lower educational strata, in Nabatieh, Baalbek-Hermel and Metn, but infrequently in the southern suburbs of Beirut. They are very religious, loyal to family and apolitical. They too put community before country and reject secularization. Their favourite politicians are Islamic fundamentalists as well as Berri. Of the Shi`i respondents, 11 per cent answered Yes, that is, only 11 per cent of what is probably the numerically strongest community.

The concept of domination by one group has a disproportionate appeal for older respondents. They have strong family and communal ties. They also tend to support militant Christian politicians and Jumblatt or reject all politicians. They also reject political commitment. They are found mainly in the Chouf, in Kisrawan and in Baalbek-Hermel, that is, in regions already dominated by one group. Their profile reveals rural, apolitical and satisfied optimists who think their community is the strongest and life under its dominance not bad.

The profile of those who favour an extreme form of group domination — that is, would welcome the departure of dissidents — is quite different. They usually have very little education, are very dissatisfied, religious, against secularization and highly politicized. Higher than average support came from the Shi`i suburbs, the Metn and Baalbek, and Islamic fundamentalists, Jumblatt's followers and militant Christians. Their support for denominational cantons is also higher than average. Thus, they are characterized by extreme populist militancy. They are found in areas in which efforts to expel other groups have been successful. If dominance and expulsion are impracticable in the country at large, then at least it can be managed in each group's own canton. The size of this group — 10 per cent of all respondents — gives some indication of the potential for conflict in Lebanon. It is small, but militant, and supports different, mutually hostile political tendencies. Its ideas and motivation are the stuff of which it takes only guns to make a civil war.

Those who accept a one-party state are people with low incomes in the old part of West Beirut and, above all, in the Christian suburbs. They tend to be young.

They give higher than average support to general secularization as well as a secular community. Supporters of the Left, militant Christians and, to a slightly lesser extent, Amal, have higher than average representation among them. Particularly interesting — and indicative of their approval of a one-party state — is their composition by community. In favour are primarily Greek Orthodox and Greek Catholics, against primarily Druze. Thus, support is drawn mainly from urbanized communities without their own militia. One single party open to all could give them at least a say, something they have lacked since the outbreak of war. By contrast, it is not difficult for the Druze to work out that in such a system they would have far less say than in plural forms of political organization. The differences in the reactions to the option of a one-party state throw the logic of the various communal interests into sharp relief; it appears as though a single unity party is perceived as a proportionally structured party.

The overlap between the support for simple majority and consociational democracy is so great, and both groups are so large that it is sensible to analyse them together. Seventy-eight per cent of those who find a pure majority democracy acceptable also accept the principle of consociation, and 72 per cent of those in favour of consociation also accept a pure majority democracy. What are the profiles of the three groups evident in this overlapping: those in favour of simple majority democracy alone, those in favour of consociational democracy alone and, finally, those, the majority, in favour of both. Seventeen per cent find only a simple majority acceptable, 23 per cent only consociation and 60 per cent both.

Simple majority democrats are not particularly satisfied, not religious, and not family and community oriented. They prefer the new leaders, in particular those of Amal, PSP and, above all, the Left. They admire socialist states and secular, centralized France. They want a secularized state and society. On the other hand, they reject a secular community, probably because they regard it as a fudge. It is in keeping with the logic of communal interests that greatest support is found among the Shi`is and Druze: in a first-past-the-post system the largest group has the best prospects, and a fairly small group generally has better prospects than under strict proportionality.

Pure consociational democrats are generally less well-off people in agriculture and manufacturing. Conservatively cautious people who dislike taking risks have higher than average representation. In common with majority democrats, they are dissatisfied with occupation and job. Like the majority of those who accept both forms of democracy, they have strong family and communal loyalties. They are not very active in politics and generally do not favour any politician. However, Islamic fundamentalists and militant Christians have higher than average representation. As they do not believe in ultimate victory in the Lebanese conflict and regard communities as a reality that must be accepted, they accept government by authentic representatives of all communities. What they do not want in any circumstances is a secularized state.

The majority of those who accept both the majority vote system and a system in which consensus of the large communities is obligatory on matters of general importance have higher than average representation in the upper income and educational groups. They do not want to get involved in contemporary politics. They do not believe any side can win the conflict. Like the pure consociationists, they accept the communities as reality, but think a secular community would make good sense. They include, above all, those who disapprove of the entire present political class, but also many supporters of moderate Christian and Muslim politicians.

The following table is a schematic summary of their social and attitude profiles.[65]

**Table 7.61**

|  | Only majority democracy | Only consociation | Both acceptable |
|---|---|---|---|
| Social characteristics | young<br>lower income<br>higher education<br>West Beirut<br>Northern Lebanon<br>Shi`is<br>Druze | lower income<br>lower education<br>Kisrawan, Jbeil<br>Tripoli, Sidon<br>East Beirut | higher income<br>East Beirut<br>Chouf, Aley<br>Kisrawan, Jbeil |
| Psycho-social attitudes | risk-takers | non-risk-takers<br>not open to change<br>fear of the future |  |
| Society and economy | social envy |  | no social envy |
| Religion and community | non-religious<br>weak family ties<br>no communal<br>solidarity | religious<br><br>communal<br>solidarity | <br><br>communal<br>solidarity |

[65] Only those characteristics for which there were significant differences between the groups have been included.

|  |  |  |  |
|---|---|---|---|
|  | pro mixed marriages | contra mixed marriages |  |
|  | rich against poor: main cause of conflict |  | rich against poor: not a cause of conflict |
| Political orientation | new leaders better Amal PSP | no politician militant Christians | no politician moderate Christians |
|  | Left | Islamic fundamentalist | moderate Muslims |
| Religion and politics | for secularization | against secular community against secularization |  |
|  | laicization possible | laicization impossible |  |
|  | community not more important than state |  |  |

As a simplification, it may be said that pure majority democrats are predominantly militant progressives, pure consociationists are thorough conservatives, and those who accept both types of democratic system are liberals. The finding that both a pure majority democracy as well as a form of consociation could command a majority in Lebanon is one of the most interesting and important results of the entire survey because it contradicts two views current in internal Lebanese politics, the one that the Lebanese want normal majority rule and nothing else, and the other that, if they were free to do so, the Lebanese would return to the status quo ante bellum. The finding is important because it could be the starting point for considerations about the form of a future political system that will command majority support, a system that avoids both inflexible majority voting and inflexible proportionality. It is important that this crucial finding that both forms of democracy command a majority is valid not only for the sample as a whole, but also for its chief sub-groups. This can be established by examining acceptance of the different forms of conflict regulation in a number of sub-groups against different social characteristics.

There are majorities for both majority democracy and consociation in all age groups. The widest acceptance of pure majority is among 21 to 25-year-olds (72 per cent), more than their acceptance of consociation (67 per cent); in all other categories consociation leads.

Table 7.62 Forms of conflict regulation by age

|   | Partition | strongest group rules | largest group rules | only one group rules | one-party state | majority demo-cracy | con-socia-tion[66] |
|---|---|---|---|---|---|---|---|
| 15-20 | 3 | 24 | 9 | 13 | 42 | 68 | 81 |
| 21-25 | 5 | 17 | 6 | 13 | 45 | 72 | 67 |
| 26-35 | 4 | 21 | 6 | 10 | 37 | 76 | 81 |
| 36-45 | 4 | 18 | 6 | 11 | 33 | 73 | 83 |
| 46+ | 3 | 30 | 8 | 10 | 33 | 75 | 90 |
| All respondents | 4 | 20 | 6 | 10 | 35 | 71 | 80 |

Figures in %

By income group, there are majorities for both forms of democracy. Consociation finds greater acceptance in all income groups. Acceptance of both forms rises in line with income.

By education, both consociation and majority vote are acceptable to a majority, the former more so; university graduates find the two forms equally acceptable, that is, support for majority vote is higher than average in this category.

By occupational groups, both forms of democracy are acceptable to a majority, with respondents in all categories favouring consociation.

There are majorities for both concepts in all parts of the country. In West Beirut the acceptance of majority democracy is 5 per cent greater than for consociation, in northern Lebanon 10 per cent. Elsewhere consociation has the edge.

[66] Differences between age groups significant only for consociation.

**Table 7.63** Forms of conflict regulation by income

|  | Partition | strongest group rules | largest group rules | only one group rules | one-party state | majority democracy[67] | consociation |
|---|---|---|---|---|---|---|---|
| 1 (lowest income) | 4 | 19 | 7 | 12 | 43 | 68 | 72 |
| 2 | 4 | 18 | 5 | 11 | 37 | 71 | 79 |
| 3 | 3 | 26 | 5 | 12 | 34 | 75 | 84 |
| 4 (highest income) | 4 | 21 | 3 | 8 | 34 | 82 | 84 |
| All respondents | 4 | 20 | 6 | 10 | 35 | 71 | 80 |

Figures in %

**Table 7.64** Forms of conflict regulation by education

|  | Partition | strongest group rules | largest group rules | only one group rules | one-party state | majority democracy[68] | consociation |
|---|---|---|---|---|---|---|---|
| none | 4 | 22 | 12 | 18 | 37 | 64 | 89 |
| primary | 3 | 23 | 7 | 10 | 31 | 78 | 81 |
| technical | 4 | 22 | 5 | 11 | 39 | 72 | 80 |
| secondary | 4 | 20 | 5 | 9 | 41 | 75 | 77 |
| university | 4 | 19 | 6 | 8 | 34 | 79 | 79 |
| All respondents | 4 | 20 | 6 | 10 | 35 | 71 | 80 |

Figures in %

---

[67] For both majority democracy and consociation, $\rho < 0.001$.
[68] For both democratic options, $\rho < 0.001$.

**Table 7.65** Forms of conflict regulation by area

|  | Partition | strongest group rules | largest group rules | only one group rules | one-party state | majority democracy[69] | consociation |
|---|---|---|---|---|---|---|---|
| East Beirut | 8 | 37 | 8 | 10 | 65 | 78 | 94 |
| West Beirut | 1 | 13 | 2 | 13 | 40 | 75 | 70 |
| Metn | 10 | 26 | 9 | 14 | 35 | 67 | 76 |
| Kisrawan, Jbeil | 5 | 24 | 7 | 9 | 27 | 69 | 91 |
| Chouf, Aley | 1 | 43 | 2 | 6 | 18 | 86 | 92 |
| Tripoli, Sidon | 3 | 12 | 3 | 8 | 29 | 67 | 89 |
| Southern Lebanon | 7 | 1 | 18 | 3 | 32 | 66 | 83 |
| Northern Lebanon | 7 | 26 | 11 | 10 | 39 | 80 | 70 |
| Bekaa | 2 | 32 | 7 | 13 | 28 | 73 | 83 |
| ALL RESPONDENTS | 4 | 20 | 6 | 10 | 35 | 71 | 80 |

Figures in %

A majority accept both concepts in the different districts of Beirut as well as in the different regions. Majority democracy leads in Ras Beirut, Tarik al-Jadideh, Haret Hreik, Bourj al-Barajneh and Jnah-Ouzai, and consociation elsewhere in Beirut and the rest of the country.

[69] For both democratic options, $\rho < 0.001$.

*Attitudes and Opinions of Economically Active Lebanese* 529

Table 7.66 Forms of conflict regulation by area: Beirut districts and regions

|  | Partition | strongest group rules | largest group rules | only one group rules | one-party state | majority democracy | consociation |
|---|---|---|---|---|---|---|---|
| Ras Beirut | 1 | 1 | 1 | 16 | 32 | 79 | 71 |
| Mseitbeh | 1 | 43 | 1 | 9 | 32 | 84 | 95 |
| Basta | 1 | 49 | 4 | 5 | 65 | 87 | 96 |
| Tarik al-Jadideh | – | – | – | 18 | 31 | 81 | 56 |
| Ashrafieh | 4 | 36 | 4 | 7 | 64 | 75 | 96 |
| Eastern suburbs | 13 | 37 | 13 | 13 | 67 | 81 | 92 |
| Chiyah | – | – | 3 | 22 | 44 | 60 | 69 |
| Haret Hreik | 2 | 2 | 2 | 9 | 37 | 69 | 56 |
| Bourj al-Barajneh | 6 | – | 3 | 10 | 34 | 64 | 59 |
| Al-Jnah | – | 2 | 5 | 19 | 48 | 70 | 52 |
| Metn | 10 | 26 | 9 | 14 | 35 | 67 | 76 |
| Kisrawan | 4 | 42 | 2 | 15 | 42 | 73 | 93 |
| Jbeil | 6 | 3 | 12 | 3 | 11 | 65 | 89 |
| Chouf, Aley | 1 | 43 | 2 | 6 | 18 | 86 | 92 |
| Sidon | – | 9 | 4 | 7 | 36 | 52 | 92 |
| Nabatieh | 8 | – | 29 | 3 | 27 | 68 | 79 |
| Jezzine | 5 | 3 | – | 3 | 40 | 62 | 90 |
| Bekaa | 2 | 22 | 1 | 10 | 35 | 71 | 80 |
| Baalbek, Hermel | 1 | 49 | 18 | 18 | 17 | 76 | 91 |
| Tripoli | 6 | 17 | 1 | 10 | 21 | 84 | 86 |
| Koura, Zghorta | 7 | 27 | 8 | 12 | 38 | 73 | 80 |
| ALL RESPONDENTS | 4 | 20 | 6 | 10 | 35 | 71 | 80 |

Figures in %

**Table 7.67** Forms of conflict regulation by religious community

|  | Partition | strongest group rules | largest group rules | only one group rules | one-party state | majority democracy | consociation[70] |
|---|---|---|---|---|---|---|---|
| Sunnis | 2 | 21 | 2 | 8 | 36 | 76 | 85 |
| Shi`is | 2 | 11 | 11 | 13 | 35 | 69 | 72 |
| Druze | 4 | 23 | 1 | 13 | 16 | 88 | 77 |
| Maronites | 7 | 27 | 6 | 10 | 39 | 76 | 85 |
| Gr.Orthodox | 5 | 31 | 6 | 13 | 50 | 73 | 85 |
| Gr.Catholic | 6 | 25 | 5 | 8 | 42 | 73 | 80 |
| Armenians | 3 | 29 | 7 | 4 | 34 | 72 | 76 |
| ALL RESPONDENTS | 4 | 20 | 6 | 10 | 35 | 71 | 80 |

Figures in %

By community, a majority of respondents in all groups accept both majority and consociational democracy. The Druze prefer majority vote to consociation (88 to 77 per cent); the reverses is true in the other communities.

There are some exceptions by political tendency. Leftist respondents — 2 per cent of the entire sample — reject consociation (23 per cent acceptance). Eighty-six per cent accept majority vote democracy, and 51 per cent a one-party state. Islamic fundamentalist respondents, on the other hand, show the greatest acceptance of consociation (91 per cent), but three-quarters of them reject majority vote democracy. Respondents of other political tendencies accept both forms with large majorities. Among PSP supporters more accept majority democracy than consociation, Amal supporters find them equally acceptable. All other political tendencies show a preference for consociation.

Finally, it should be noted that 52 per cent of militant Christians also find a one-party state acceptable and 39 per cent 'domination by the strongest group' — yet acceptance of consociation is higher than average.

[70] Differences between communities significant only for consociation.

## Attitudes and Opinions of Economically Active Lebanese

**Table 7.68** Forms of conflict regulation by political tendencies

|  | Partition | strongest group rules | largest group rules | only one group rules | one-party state | majority democracy | consociation[71] |
|---|---|---|---|---|---|---|---|
| no answer | 3 | 17 | 7 | 12 | 38 | 73 | 80 |
| no politician | 5 | 33 | 5 | 8 | 38 | 78 | 90 |
| moderate Christians | 4 | 17 | 7 | 5 | 30 | 79 | 83 |
| moderate Muslims | 3 | 28 | 2 | 7 | 21 | 77 | 90 |
| militant Christians | 8 | 39 | 8 | 12 | 52 | 64 | 84 |
| Amal | 3 | 13 | 11 | 4 | 40 | 65 | 65 |
| PSP | 7 | 26 | 4 | 13 | 20 | 86 | 68 |
| Left | 2 | 5 | 2 | 9 | 51 | 86 | 23 |
| Islamic Fundament. | 3 | 3 | 12 | 55 | 27 | 24 | 91 |
| others | 4 | 13 | 4 | 6 | 29 | 92 | 82 |
| ALL RESPONDENTS | 4 | 20 | 6 | 10 | 35 | 71 | 80 |

Figures in %

By zones of military control, both forms of democracy are acceptable to a majority. Only in the area controlled by the Druze militia is majority vote democracy (85 per cent) slightly more popular than consociation (83 per cent). In general, the acceptance of consociation does not vary significantly by military control. All in all, the crucial finding that both majority vote democracy and consociational democracy are acceptable to a majority is valid for all age- and income-groups, all levels of education, all occupations, in all regions, in all districts of Beirut and in all communities.

There are two exceptions among the sub-groups: Leftists reject consociation, and Islamic Fundamentalists reject majority vote democracy. Both reactions are plausible in terms of the profiles of these groups. Together, these groups comprise

---

[71] For both democratic options, $\rho < 0.001$.

only 4 per cent of the entire sample. Even if their overall support were twice or thrice this — for which there is no evidence — it would have little effect on the general conclusions.

Table 7.69 Forms of conflict regulation by zones of military control

|  | Partition | strongest group rules | largest group rules | only one group rules | one-party state | majority democracy | consociation |
|---|---|---|---|---|---|---|---|
| Christian militias & Lebanese Army | 5 | 20 | 5 | 10 | 40 | 73 | 78 |
| Syrian Army: Christian majority | 5 | 28 | 7 | 11 | 41 | 73 | 82 |
| Syrian Army: Muslim majority | 3 | 24 | 6 | 13 | 39 | 76 | 82 |
| Druze militia | 3 | 34 | 2 | 12 | 23 | 85 | 83 |
| Shi`i militia | 4 | 5 | 13 | 7 | 35 | 66 | 78 |
| ALL RESPONDENTS | 4 | 20 | 6 | 10 | 35 | 71 | 80 |

Figures in %

A second important result is the preference for the principle of consociation to that of majority vote, both in the sample as a whole and in most sub-groups. Exceptions are the 20- to 25-year-olds, certain districts of West Beirut (Ras Beirut, Tarik al-Jadideh, Haret Hreik, Bourj al-Barajneh and Jnah-Ouzai), the Druze community and the PSP and the left-wing political tendencies. But in all these sub-groups, apart from the Left, a majority also accepts consociation; differences in the levels of acceptance are minor.

In summary, these results must be adequately interpreted and their relevance acknowledged.

Virtually all Lebanese would like the divisions in their society to be bridged and a strong government that can act with general consent to be established. Two-thirds hold the opinion that a broadly based government is impossible unless it includes authentic community leaders. A part of the remaining one-third questions the claims of leaders either commonly presented as authentic or self-appointed. But another part categorically rejects the principle of communal representation in government, and this group is militant.

Every single undemocratic proposal for conflict regulation is acceptable only to a minority. Partition of the country is supported by a tiny, predominantly apolitical and fearful group. The idea that the numerically strongest group should rule is also supported by very few, mainly rural Shi`is, and is not seriously demanded by anybody. A one-party state is advocated by bare majorities of the militant Christians and the Left; but their visions of a one-party state can hardly coincide. Otherwise, this concept strikes an echo mainly among members of those Christian communities that have neither their own militias nor any power at present; but they too would prefer democratic solutions to the conflict. The acceptance of a one-party state by a good third of the respondents may be interpreted primarily as expression of a readiness to accept any solution that ends the war.

Acceptance of solutions which propound the domination of one group is potentially far more problematic. In part, this is the projection of regional dominance on to the whole country; thus it is wishful thinking and fairly harmless. But a group of 10 per cent accept a very harsh form of domination. This economically frustrated, highly militant group has no difficulties in imagining the expulsion of all opponents. This group is itself divided between opposing political tendencies that would obstruct any attempt to impose such a 'solution'. However, the presence of one or several groups with profiles of this nature are a godsend to any political force in or out of the country that has an interest in perpetuating tension. National domination by one group and the expulsion of those who do not submit to it may seem an improbable perspective, but it is reality in certain parts of the country and could become reality in others. There are enough players for such a game of terror, as acceptance by 10 per cent of the respondents shows.

In view of all the horrors perpetrated since the outbreak of war, the large majorities in favour of democratic forms of conflict regulation are impressive. As discussed, a militantly progressive group of 17 per cent are exclusively in favour of majority vote democracy, and a conservative minority of 23 per cent insists equally exclusively on the power of veto for the communities and a division of power between the existing groups. A liberal majority of all respondents would agree to either form of democracy. Given normal democratic processes in Lebanon — fair elections or referendums — one of these options would carry the day. The liberal majority could form a coalition with either the progressive or the conservative democratic groups, or seek support from both.

## Prospects of coexistence

How do the Lebanese themselves judge the prospects of ending the divisions? Do they think the different groups can coexist? Do they think change is possible? Do they think victory for one group is possible or improbable? Is coexistence probable after all that has happened? Are convictions and human relations strong enough to rebuild the fabric of the country, external circumstances permitting?

Their reactions to the possibility of coexistence between different groups in principle are ambivalent.

**Table 7.70**

| | Agreement (%) |
|---|---|
| 'Whether we like it or not: when different language, religious, ethnic or racial groups live in the same country, they must either dominate or be dominated.' | 53 |
| 'Very different religious, ethnic, language or racial groups can live together in the same country, accept each other and respect each other's rights.' | 70 |
| 'A country with groups with different traditions is wealthier for it and its society benefits.' | 64 |

More than half of the respondents thought domination by one group was inevitable. But two-thirds thought mutual respect for others' rights possible. And almost two-thirds thought coexistence between groups an enrichment. In other words, some of the respondents agreed with statements that are, logically, mutually exclusive. Does the first case reflect regrettable insight into the inevitable, the second express a desire?

Those who accept the thesis of the inevitability of domination tend to come from middle-income, but less educated groups, and live in the Chouf, Kisrawan and the Bekaa, that is, in regions in which one group already dominates. By community, Greek Orthodox and Greek Catholics have higher than average representation, groups that have experience of domination by others. It is characteristic that respondents living in regions controlled by the Syrian Army and, in particular, the Druze militia, moderate Muslims and people who do not prefer any politician are more likely to believe in domination than people living in Shi`i-controlled areas. In short: they are people who are resigned to their situation. But other groups also agreed: those open to change and unafraid of the future, satisfied with their economic situation, who believe victory is possible, support economic decentralization and religious cantons, place communal interests above those of the country and do not think all Lebanese territory is for all Lebanese. These are obviously people who not only accept domination but think it desirable. Islamic fundamentalists and militant Christians have higher than average representation.

Table 7.71

|  | Agreement (%) |
|---|---|
| 'The strength of the different communities makes fundamental long-term changes in the political system impossible.' | 52 |
| 'Perhaps it doesn't look like it, but it is possible that the political system can be changed in the near future.' | 35 |

Whereas the former group dislikes being dominated and only acquiesces, the latter enjoy dominating — or wish to do so.

The thesis of coexistence on the basis of mutual respect for others' rights is approved by respondents in all income groups, and disproportionately by the better educated. They do not have pronounced family and communal loyalties, show higher than average acceptance of mixed marriages and want secularization. They tend to live in urban districts and regions in which different communities do still coexist, for instance, in Ras Beirut and Tarik al-Jadideh, in the Metn and in Jbeil, but also in the cities and towns in the south and the north. Politically, they are, above all, Left and supporters of moderate Christians, but include Amal and PSP adherents.

People who have to deal with others in their daily life also believe that different traditions enrich the country: agreement is strongest in Ras Beirut, whose cosmopolitan past would appear not to have been completely forgotten, and in Jbeil. Agreement is lowest in Kisrawan and in the Chouf (33 and 31 per cent respectively), typical confessional monopolies.

The result on the whole is that a clear majority believes that coexistence is possible in principle. They are primarily liberals and secularists, as well as respondents living in mixed regions. The sceptics are those currently dominated, those who would like to dominate and those in regions without cultural variety — and the number of homogeneous regions has increased since the outbreak of war.

**Table 7.72**

|  | Agreement (%) |
|---|---|
| *'With the strength and determination of our group we will eventually achieve our goals.'* | 72 |
| *'Victory isn't worth the sacrifices and losses my community would suffer.'* | 62 |
| *'In the struggle between the different communities in our country we're all losers.'* | 77 |

Do the respondents think fundamental change is probable or not? Just under half the respondents think changes possible in the long term, but only one-third think changes are possible in the short term. The former attitude is conditioned largely by community and political orientation. Both agreement and disagreement seem to be wishful thinking. A higher than average number of Greek Orthodox and Maronites assume that the political system will not really change (70 and 63 per cent respectively), a view shared by only 26 per cent of the Druze and 40 per cent of the Shi`is. Most Leftists, PSP supporters, Islamic fundamentalists and Amal supporters believe in long-term change.

People with high incomes or university education tend to believe in change in the short term. They are especially common in the eastern suburbs of Beirut and in the Metn. A disproportionately high number of them are Druze or Maronites, moderate Muslims, supporters of Jumblatt or militant Christian politicians. Most are well-off, self-assured, secularist optimists who expect cantonalization will bring calm and economic recovery. This view finds almost no support in the southern suburbs of the capital and the areas of crisis in the south.

Thus, long-term perspectives of change or status quo are conditioned by desires and hopes that vary by community and political tendency, and short-term perspectives are conditioned primarily by regional and local security. Those in peaceful areas with fairly settled power relationships, and who have little to complain of, tend to assume that a new political system will soon assure these pleasant conditions, while those in insecure areas or not very well off tend to be pessimistic. The general view, though, is that there is little likelihood of a fundamentally different system in the near future.

How do Lebanese assess the prospects of victory and defeat, and do they see any sense in the sacrifices demanded of most of them? At first sight, the answers seem ambivalent. Almost three-quarters believe they will win, a little under two-thirds do not think such a victory is worth the cost, and over three-quarters think that in the end all will be losers.

Detailed analysis reveals that the contradictions are more apparent than real. Ninety per cent of the less-educated, the Druze and Shi`is are confident of victory. Most of them live in West Beirut and the Chouf. The majority are pessimistic populists: powerless, dissatisfied, religious, family-oriented and opposed to secularization. Over half of them doubt whether victory will be worthwhile, or worth the sacrifices and losses, and 90 per cent of them continue to believe in the possibility of coexistence. Almost three-quarters think all communities will be losers. In short: the majority of those seemingly confident of victory are putting on a brave face in what for most is a rotten situation.

However, there is a group of 15 per cent of all respondents whose proclaimed confidence of winning and acceptance of sacrifices and losses coincides with other characteristics of militancy. They tend to reject politicians of the old school, are highly politicized, do not want to 'keep their feet on the ground'; nor, for the most part, do they desire secularization, mixed marriages or neighbours from other communities. Politically, they support the Islamic fundamentalists, Amal, the PSP, the militant Christians and the Left.

The military activists of all persuasions form the hard core of those who profess confidence that they will win. A smaller majority are convinced that victory is not worth the sacrifices and losses. Their composition is different to that of the confident group, both genuine and apparent. They are Greek Orthodox (73 per cent), Sunni (68 per cent) and Greek Catholic (66 per cent) rather than Shi`i, Maronite and Druze. The former three, largely urbanized groups have suffered most in the war, and, as communities without their own militias, have little to gain from any group's victory.

Their political views vary considerably. There is higher than average support from supporters of moderate Christians and Muslims: they have prospects of winning. But two-thirds of Amal supporters also agree, though far fewer militant Christians (51 per cent), PSP supporters (46 per cent) and Islamic fundamentalists (only 24 per cent).

Finally, more than three-quarters of all respondents believe that all communities will be losers. Druze — in 1987 the only community to have gained from the war — show least agreement, but still 61 per cent of them express this view. Agreement in the south, particularly unsettled in 1987, is well above average.

How do the respondents judge those concrete possibilities of coexistence in Lebanon against the background of their relative hopes of victory and fears of losses?

**Table 7.73**

|  | Agreement (%)[72] | | |
| --- | --- | --- | --- |
|  | 1984 | 1986 | 1987 |
| *'In recent months horrible things have happened, I fear that this has made coexistence between the communities very difficult.'* | 48 | 44 | 21 |
| *'In spite of everything that has happened, the Lebanese would be able to reach agreement among themselves if foreign forces would stop interfering in our affairs.'* | 79 | 69 | 75 |
| *'In spite of the terrible events of the past few months, I believe that coexistence between the communities is still possible.'* | 82 | 79 | 86 |

After a trough from 1984 to 1986 belief in the possibility of Lebanese coexistence recovered strongly. Agreement on concrete Lebanese coexistence is even greater than on fundamental and general questions of coexistence, between groups in countries with different groups, analysed above. Interestingly, coexistence is thought more probable when the cessation of foreign interference is not a condition; obviously such intervention is not regarded only negatively.

The belief that coexistence has become more difficult is stronger among respondents in the lowest income group, most of them members of Christian communities in the south of the country: these strata and groups were the main victims of the heaviest conflicts in the years prior to 1987. Belief in agreement without foreign interference is far stronger among Christians and Sunnis, far weaker among Druze and Shi`is, both of whom have profited from foreign assistance since 1984. Ninety per cent of the Muslim communities believe straightforwardly in understanding and coexistence; the Christians are more sceptical, though over 80 per cent agree.

[72] These questions were not asked in 1981.

This belief in coexistence, despite all the contrasts and differences of opinion on numerous questions, runs through all social strata and all communities. It is rooted in certain fundamental assumptions and hopes which have survived the years of war virtually unscathed.

The statements on this point were first included in the 1981 survey. Agreement was so great that empirical social researchers would normally have dropped them from further surveys. They were retained because of the peculiarities of the Lebanese situation. One could never be sure whether opinion might not change after all. And above all, the statements reveal what holds Lebanon together.

Table 7.74

|  | Agreement (%) | | | |
| --- | --- | --- | --- | --- |
|  | 1981 | 1984 | 1986 | 1987 |
| 'Monotheistic religions like Christianity and Islam believe in the same God and teach similar ethical and social principles.' | 92 | 82 | 88 | 91 |
| 'The divisions between the Lebanese regions are unnatural; they will disappear as soon as the crisis is over.' | 87 | 90 | 92 | 74 |
| 'A good friend is a good friend, whether he is called George or George Mohammed | 96 | 96 | 96 | 98 |

The agreement on the similarities between the two religions was affected by the appearance of Islamic fundamentalism in Lebanon in 1984. But it soon became clear that for most Lebanese Muslims Islam and Islamic fundamentalism were not the same.[73]

Belief in the reunification of Lebanon was much less strong in 1987 than in 1981, 1984 and 1986, when the statement referred to the reunification not of Lebanon, but of Beirut.[74] Belief in reunification is lowest among respondents in the south, where people are very sceptical that effective separation of the extreme south, under Israeli control, will disappear, probably with justification. Human relationships across the community boundaries have obviously not been affected by the events of war during the period of the surveys. Finally, one of the axioms of

---

[73] Noes were disproprtionately highly represented among non-religious respondents.
[74] 'The division between "East" and "West" is unnatural.'

Lebanese political culture is the necessity of compromise on the basis of realistic assessments.

'In the present situation the strengths of the different communities make it necessary to search for a compromise and reach some agreement.' Ninety-two per cent of the respondents agreed. In summary, in 1987, even after twelve years of war the great majority of the Lebanese believed, that given the chance, their communities would coexist.

There are some signs of resignation. Over 50 per cent fear that in a society with several communities it is inevitable that one community will dominate. But only a minority desire domination. Two-thirds think coexistence with mutual respect is possible and that different traditions enrich the country. Almost half think long-term change in the political system is possible, but only one-third short-term change. In 1987, one could not speak of a revolutionary mood. Although two-thirds think they could win, the hard core of military activists on all sides is only about 15 per cent. Almost two-thirds believe that a victory will not be worth the cost in sacrifices and losses, and three-quarters believe that all communities will be losers.

Concerning the concrete situation in Lebanon, almost 90 per cent think coexistence between the communities is possible. Over 90 per cent see and welcome the similarities between the two large confessions and the possibilities of friendship across the community boundaries. Over 90 per cent also think compromises and understanding between the communities are necessary.

These findings show that majority acceptance of democracy and consociation are not isolated political opinions. They are rooted in a political culture of coexistence and compromise that has survived the long years of war intact.

## Coexistence under conditions of extreme crisis

The survey of 1984 was conducted between January and April. On February 7th of that year heavy fighting broke out in Beirut and its hinterland. The regular Lebanese Army disintegrated along more or less confessional lines. Beirut was once again divided along the 'green line'. If the term 'civil war' had not been quite appropriate in earlier phases of the war, it was now. From February 7th it was civil war — a traumatic day for the Lebanese. By February 6th, 270 interviews had been completed, that is, more than half the planned survey. The interviewers were willing to continue their work despite the fighting. This was a rare opportunity for empirical social research: the chance of a survey just before and just after the outbreak of an acute phase of civil war. Interviewing resumed on February 9th; the sample in the second phase was amended to include 500 respondents.

An analysis of the data by gender, age, occupation, education and community membership revealed no significant deviation in composition between the sample of 270 interviewed before February 7th and the 500 after that date. A before and after comparison was possible. It then transpired that, apart from community membership, there were no significant deviations by social characteristics between each month's interviews from February 7th to completion of the survey. It became possible to draw a comparison over months of crisis.[75]

How did the trauma of February 7th, 1984, and the subsequent period of fighting affect the attitudes of the Lebanese? Fear of the future before and after this date hardly changed: 69 and 64 per cent respectively of all respondents. The comparison over time, though, shows differences between the two groups.[76]

Table 7.75

| Fear of the future | January | February | March | April |
|---|---|---|---|---|
| Muslims | 68 | 54 | 72 | 57 |
| Christians | 69 | 81 | 64 | 61 |

Figures in %

Among Muslims, fear first decreased after February 7th — most markedly among Shi'is, down to 40 per cent — and then rose again in March. Among Christians fear increased considerably in February, before falling again. Feelings of social impotence have a similar pattern:

[75] To remove the deviation by community affiliation (Muslim respondents were under-represented in February and March), there are separate comparisons over time for Christians and Muslims. Other important deviations: in the Christian sub-samples secondary school graduates are under-represented in March, and respondents in northern Lebanon in March and April; in the Muslim sub-samples the oldest age group is over-represented in April.

In the following tables the before–after comparison is based on the interviews before (N=270) and after (N=507) February 7th. Comparisons over four months are separate for Christian and Muslim respondents:

|  | January and 1–7 February | | 7–28 February | | March | | April | | All respondents | |
|---|---|---|---|---|---|---|---|---|---|---|
|  | N | % | N | % | N | % | N | % | N | % |
| Muslims | 167 | 62 | 35 | 28 | 37 | 42 | 175 | 60 | 414 | 53 |
| Christians | 103 | 38 | 92 | 72 | 51 | 58 | 117 | 40 | 363 | 47 |
| N = | 270 | | 127 | | 88 | | 292 | | 777 | |

[76] Significance for Christians is at the 5 per cent level.

**Table 7.76**

| Social impotence | January | February | March | April |
|---|---|---|---|---|
| Muslims | 83 | 66 | 68 | 61 |
| Christians | 73 | 82 | 52 | 48[77] |

Figures in %

When Shi`i and Druze militias overran West Beirut, fear and impotence declined among Muslims, whereas this initially caused panic among Christians. In April fear had declined again, and both confessional groups felt themselves less impotent than in January: the Muslims were in charge in their regions and the Christians found consolation in the fact that they had been able to retain undisputed control over their regions.

The outbreak of civil war precipitated a decline in the exchange rate of the Lebanese pound and an economic crisis. All respondents were more sceptical about the economic situation after February 7th than before.

**Table 7.77**

| Economic situation | January | February | March | April |
|---|---|---|---|---|
| Muslims | 73 | 54 | 62 | 53 |
| Christians | 68 | 78 | 70 | 64 |

Figures in %

At the beginning of the crisis, Muslims are slightly more optimistic; by April they are considerably less optimistic ($p < 0.005$). The Christians' economic structure is less susceptible to crises. The Shi`is, though victors in West Beirut, are the most pessimistic group. Their positive assessment of the economic situation fell from 59 per cent in January to 41 per cent in April: their residential areas have suffered greatest damage.

The readiness to seek work in the Persian Gulf rises from 33 per cent before to 40 per cent after February 7th. The fluctuation in the monthly figures for and between the two groups are considerable:

---

[77] $p < 0.001$ for both Muslims and Christians.

**Table 7.78**

| Gulf states | January | February | March | April |
|---|---|---|---|---|
| Muslims | 35 | 43 | 57 | 48 |
| Christians | 31 | 23 | 46 | 34 |

Figures in %

Christians react only in March, Muslims as early as in February; in April readiness declines in both groups. The marked and immediate readiness of Muslims to seek work as migrants reflects their greater dismay at the incipient economic crisis. As a consequence of the new civil war, the Christians' belief in Lebanon's unique economic role in the Middle East falls from 85 to 74 per cent, whereas that of Muslims shows no significant change. After fear and impotence, the assessment of the economic situation mirrors the changes in opinion: in terms of power the Muslims feel themselves relative victors, economically the Christians do. In all cases, though, after violent swings in February and March, the reactions in April are more moderate.

Among both[78] groups the sense of communal loyalty rises from January to March, with some April figures sticking at high levels. 'It doesn't matter whether they are rich or poor, I feel very close to the members of my community.'

**Table 7.79**

| Communal solidarity | January | February | March | April |
|---|---|---|---|---|
| Muslim | 37 | 62 | 70 | 62 |
| Christians | 41 | 54 | 53 | 56 |

Figures in %

'It is good if there are no conflicts in a community.'

---

[78] Significant only for Muslims, $p < 0.001$.

**Table 7.80**

| No conflict in the community | January | February | March | April |
|---|---|---|---|---|
| Muslim | 61 | 85 | 81 | 79 |
| Christians | 54 | 59 | 75 | 57 |

Figures in %

With the outbreak of war, the need to have people from the same community as neighbours increased dramatically. The Christians reacted later than Muslims, whose neighbourhoods were at the centre of the fighting.

**Table 7.81**

| Neighbours | January | February | March | April |
|---|---|---|---|---|
| Muslim | 29 | 47 | 76 | 40 |
| Christians | 38 | 36 | 47 | 56 |

Figures in %

Among all respondents the desire for homogeneous residential areas remains higher (47 per cent) than it was before February 7th (32 per cent).[79] Immediately after the outbreak of fighting, perceptions of the character of the conflict also change: it is perceived less as a conflict between rich and poor:[80]

**Table 7.82**

| Rich-poor conflict | January | February | March | April |
|---|---|---|---|---|
| Muslims | 69 | 54 | 49 | 66 |
| Christians | 68 | 49 | 54 | 63 |

Figures in %

---

[79] $p < 0.001$.
[80] Only the changes among the Christians are significant at the 5 per cent level.

It is remarkable that at the height of the fighting in a confrontation that was unequivocally confessional, half of the respondents persist in seeing it primarily as one between rich and poor. In April this view is nearly as widespread as pre-February 7th. How does the crisis affect perceptions of the political system? There are considerable fluctuations in the assessment of influential groups.

**Table 7.83**

| Influential groups | January | February | March | April |
|---|---|---|---|---|
| zu`ama': | | | | |
| Muslims | 30 | 6 | 3 | 14 |
| Christians | 33 | 22 | 31 | 23 |
| party leaders: | | | | |
| Muslims | 43 | 51 | 57 | 57 |
| Christians | 46 | 66 | 45 | 49 |

Figures in %

The standing of the *zu`ama'* among Muslims, which had gradually improved after 1982, falls sharply in February, to recover slightly in April. Fluctuations in Christian views are no more than temporary. The prestige of the party leaders soars among Muslims: they are the victors of the February war. At the moment of greatest crisis party leaders have an even higher standing among Christians,[81] before falling back to their January level. The preference among Muslims for the new type of politician rises significantly[82] during the crisis, to settle down again in April:

**Table 7.84**

| New leaders better | January | February | March | April |
|---|---|---|---|---|
| Muslims | 58 | 89 | 92 | 69 |
| Christians | 53 | 41 | 62 | 51 |

Figures in %

[81] $p < 0.005$.
[82] $p < 0.001$.

In the overall before and after comparison differences are not significant. The prestige of two of the new leaders rises enormously as a consequence of February 7th: Nabih Berri and Walid Jumblatt, the victors in the battle for West Beirut. Berri's support among Muslims rises from 19 per cent in January to 34 per cent in April, Jumblatt's from 8 per cent in January to 27 per cent in March, to fall back to 11 per cent in April. Support for militant Christian leaders rises from 13 per cent in January to 33 per cent in February, to fall back to 19 per cent in April. Do Lebanese want to keep out of politics?

**Table 7.85**

| Keep out of politics | January | February | March | April |
|---|---|---|---|---|
| Muslims | 56 | 50 | 73 | 66 |
| Christians | 54 | 59 | 81 | 73 |

Figures in %

In February half the Muslim respondents, and some 62 per cent of the Shi`is, did not share this view. The high level of politicization soon falls, and among Christians significantly more strongly than among Muslims. In the sample as a whole, before February 7th, 55 per cent wanted to have nothing to do with politics, after this date 67 per cent.

Has the experience of direct civil war influenced the attitudes of the Lebanese on the relationship between religion and politics? Support for the concept of the secularization of state and society, as the most promising approach to the country's problems, suffers considerably in February, above all among Muslims:[83]

**Table 7.86**

| Secularized state | January | February | March | April |
|---|---|---|---|---|
| Muslims | 84 | 40 | 68 | 56 |
| Christians | 95 | 91 | 78 | 80 |

Figures in %

---

[83] The changes are highly significant, both among Muslims and Christians, $\rho < 0.001$.

Before February 7th, 88 per cent of the whole sample agreed, afterwards only 70 per cent. But this concept, too, recovers relatively rapidly from the shock of armed confrontation, as shown by reactions to another statement: 'It doesn't matter what we may want, secularization seems to have no chance in Lebanon. Community membership is a reality you have to accept.'

**Table 7.87**

| Laicization impossible | January | February | March | April |
|---|---|---|---|---|
| Muslims | 42 | 79 | 63 | 57 |
| Christians | 34 | 35 | 59 | 40 |

Figures in %

From February onwards the Muslim majority is lost, and from March that of the Christians. In April, Muslims are still sceptical, though less so, whereas Christian doubters are again in the minority.[84]

The reaction to the concept of religious cantons is similar. In the before and after comparison, approval rises from 18 to 27 per cent. But the comparison over time shows that, at least among Muslims, this is a temporary expression of fear:[85]

**Table 7.88**

| Religious cantons | January | February | March | April |
|---|---|---|---|---|
| Muslims | 16 | 37 | 35 | 13 |
| Christians | 20 | 24 | 42 | 37 |

Figures in %

In general, with the renewal of warfare, secularization seemed less attractive and cantons more so; conversely: once the worst was over, a reaction set in. But how does acute crisis affect fundamental attitudes to coexistence and their expression? One formulation in the 1984 questionnaire acquired a topicality that could not have been anticipated when devised:

---

[84] $\rho < 0.001$ among the Muslims, $\rho < 0.005$ among the Christians.
[85] $\rho < 0.001$ among the Muslims, $\rho < 0.005$ among the Christians.

'In recent months horrible things have happened in Lebanon. I fear that coexistence between the communities has become more difficult.' In the before-and-after comparison agreement rose from 39 to 54 per cent. But the comparison over time corrects the impression that the belief in coexistence had been permanently shaken:

**Table 7.89**

| Coexistence harder | January | February | March | April |
|---|---|---|---|---|
| Muslims | 38 | 80 | 83 | 43 |
| Christians | 42 | 51 | 67 | 50 |

Figures in %

Under the immediate impression of the fighting coexistence is thought to have become far more difficult,[86] but in April optimism is rising once again and the figures are approaching those for January. Responses to the question of a probable worsening of the conflict show the same pattern.

**Table 7.90**

| Conflict will worsen | January | February | March | April |
|---|---|---|---|---|
| Muslims | 50 | 71 | 76 | 56 |
| Christians | 47 | 55 | 75 | 66 |

Figures in %

The answer is yes: the February increase for Muslims is very significant, in March for both groups. In April, Muslims are almost back at their January level; the Christian reaction is also positive, but more gradual.[87] Whether more difficult or not, do the Lebanese think coexistence possible in principle, even in the middle of war? 'In spite of the terrible events of recent months, I believe that coexistence between the communities is still possible.'

---

[86] See previous note.
[87] Both for Muslims and Christians $p < 0.001$.

*Attitudes and Opinions of Economically Active Lebanese*

**Table 7.91**

| Coexistence possible | January | February | March | April |
|---|---|---|---|---|
| Muslims | 87 | 77 | 94 | 87 |
| Christians | 79 | 80 | 77 | 68 |

Figures in %

Even at the height of the fighting, both Christians and Muslims continued to believe in coexistence. Their opinions on coexistence in principle are not significantly influenced by events. Throughout the crisis both Muslims and Christians retained their consensus on the principle of consociation.

**Table 7.92**

| Consociation | January | February | March | April |
|---|---|---|---|---|
| Muslims | 93 | 91 | 75 | 87 |
| Christians | 82 | 89 | 90 | 72 |

Figures in %

In March one-quarter of Muslim and in April a good quarter of Christian respondents had doubts about this form of conflict regulation;[88] but at no time was it seriously questioned.

Finally, the fluctuations in the agreement with the main points of the Lebanese political credo are hardly significant, neither among Christians nor among Muslims, neither in the analysis by months nor in the overall comparison of responses before and after February 7th: in and throughout open civil war, the respondents believe that Islam and Christianity share one God and similar ethical and social principles, that friends and colleagues from other communities remain friends and remain welcome, and that the country will be reunited.

We can now draw up a balance of this detailed study, a study of an extremely violent, bloody and significant event in the Lebanese conflict. Feelings of fear and powerlessness rise, as is to be expected, in situations of actual fighting, and they change sides with the fortunes of war. The economic effects of the renewed

[88] $\rho < 0.001$ for the Christians, $\rho < 0.005$ for the Muslims.

warfare are soon felt. In acute crisis the Lebanese become more aware of their communal ties. They then have a greater desire to live among members of, and in territory controlled by, their own community. Nonetheless, even at the height of the fighting cantonalization did not appeal to a majority. Support for a secular state and society suffers a setback when Christians and Muslims start shooting at one another. But the feeling that they will never overcome the political barriers of confessionalism never lasts very long. Once the crisis has peaked the pendulum swings back.

When the guns speak, the established politicians, the political brokers in times of peace, lose standing and influence, and each side gathers round its warlords. As soon as the guns fall silent, the former slowly return and the star of the latter quickly sinks. When coexistence patently gives way to conflict, belief in the possibility of its success recedes — could it be otherwise? — but only for as long as the open conflict lasts. People's assessments of their own situation and the situation of the country as a whole are realistic. Attitudes and opinions betray war-shock. But they also show that people recover or adjust to it extraordinarily quickly. It is not necessary for the roar of cannon to cease — just to grow a little quieter, and the shells a little less frequent — for the Lebanese penchant for moderation to reassert itself.

The series of surveys between 1981 and 1987 show that fundamental elements of Lebanese political culture — a willingness to coexist, tolerance and the search for consensus in diversity — have survived the years of war more or less intact. The analysis of the months of January through April 1984, when the war irrevocably became civil war, strongly substantiate the general findings. The war and civil war in Lebanon were not the wars of the majority of the Lebanese. The majority of the Lebanese prefer to coexist — even in war.

# 8

## A Revocable Covenant
## A Preliminary Synopsis

We swear to be one People of true Brothers —
We swear that no Extremity shall part us,
We will be free, free as our Fathers left us,
Preferring Death in any shape, to Slavery.
We'll put our strong trust in the Highest God,
Nor fear what might of Man can do against us.

Friedrich Schiller

I understand, you're not prepared
for people such as I.
Well, I'm not going to disappear ...
When I come back
Under a redder moon, dear friends,
I'll come in a tank,
Talk with a cannon and
Blow you away.
Where my tank goes
Is the road.
What my cannon says
Is what I mean.

> And the only one
> I'll let off lightly is my brother;
> I'll just smash his face in.
>
> Bertold Brecht

The National Pact of 1943 was not the 'Rütli oath', that Swiss national myth celebrated by Schiller. The Lebanese of the independence era were not 'one people of true brothers', but members of different communities with different interests, whose contradictory expressions of self-awareness were rooted in their respective histories. The Lebanon within the borders of 1920 was not the first choice of any of the communities, though it was more acceptable to some than others. It was the second choice of all parties, and all Lebanon could get in 1943. Few accepted its finality. One half of the Lebanese continued to hope for circumstances conducive to their preference: a greater Syria or Arab unity. The other half continued to harbour mental reservations about the new republic: should the circumstances favourable to what the first half preferred ever obtain, they hoped to withdraw to Mount Lebanon. Indeed, many in this latter group always thought it a mistake not to have settled for just that in the first place.

Certainly, the Lebanese of 1943 all wanted to 'be free, free as our fathers left us'. But some saw their forefathers free of the French and others saw them free of other Arabs. The former hoped the latter's fear of their Arab brethren would diminish in time; the latter trusted in renewed help from abroad in the event of acute danger.

Lebanon was a confederation until dissolved by mutual agreement: a joint-stock company for mutual advantage, as it were, in which dividends were properly shared.

Second-best solutions can be very beneficial to those involved and, hence, very durable. The Lebanese alliance was convenient and sensible; until the early 1970s the partners were not dissatisfied with it. Most internal and external observers and analysts regarded it as a remarkable 'success story': a multi-communal state that peacefully regulated the coexistence of communities, was modernizing without revolutionary upheaval and increasing the prosperity of all its people, and all this in freedom and democracy. Proponents of consociational democracy saw in the Lebanese state proof that their model could work, that it was possible to create and maintain democratic stability under the difficult conditions existing in multi-communal states in non-European countries.[1]

---

[1] Arend Lijphart, *Democracy in Plural Societies: A comparative exploration* (New Haven and London, 1977), pp. 147ff.

Once the war had begun, growing numbers of analysts produced very different explanations of why the Lebanese experiment had always been doomed to failure: social tension found release in violent class conflict;[2] there were irreconcilable differences between the different national identities which the various Lebanese communities perceived themselves to have;[3] the Lebanese consociational system broke down because it functioned badly;[4] some even blamed the system as such.[5]

Finally, a number of authors sought to explain the war not in terms of domestic factors — tension between classes or communities or the inadequacy of the political system — but primarily or exclusively in terms of regional and international influences.[6]

We have considered the system of conflict regulation in pre-war Lebanon, seen how the country became the centre of the Middle Eastern storm, traced the phases and forms of the conflict and presented empirical material on the perceptions of leadership groups as well as on the opinions and attitudes of ordinary Lebanese. It is now time to make a synopsis of the different conflict factors.

To do so, it is necessary to distinguish between the context in which the war originated and the causes of its protraction.

## Lebanese against Lebanese

Lebanese shot at Lebanese in every year of the war. Regardless of the significance of non-Lebanese factors, there were always sufficient grounds for Lebanese strife

---

[2] E.g., Samih K. Farsoun and Walter Carroll, 'The Civil War in Lebanon: Sect, class, and imperialism', *Monthly Review* 28/2 (1976), pp. 12–37; Suad Joseph and Barbara L.K. Pillsbury, eds., *Muslim–Christian Conflicts: Economic, political and social origins* (Boulder and Folkestone, 1978).

[3] See Enver M. Koury, *The Crisis in the Lebanese System, Confessionalism and chaos (Foreign Affairs Studies, No. 38)* (Washington D.C., 1976).

[4] For instance, Richard H. Dekmejian, 'Consociational Democracy in Crisis: The case of Lebanon', *Comparative Politics* 10 (1978), pp. 251–65: Lijphart, *Democracy in Plural Societies*, p. 149, criticizes the 'inflexible institutionalization of consociational principles' in Lebanon.

[5] 'The confessional system itself — as the embodiment of a consociational model — was the root of the problem'; Michael C. Hudson, 'The Lebanese crisis: The limits of consociational democracy', *Journal of Palestine Studies* 5 (1976), p. 114. See also, Michael C. Hudson, *The Precarious Republic Revisited: Reflections on the collapse of pluralist politics in Lebanon. Contemporary Arab Studies, Seminar Paper No. 2* (Washington D.C., 1977). See also a more recent, extremely differentiated analysis, Michael C. Hudson, 'The problem of authoritative power in Lebanese politics: Why consociationalism failed', in Nadim Shehadi and Dana Haffar Mills, eds., *Lebanon: A history of conflict and consensus* (London, 1988), pp. 224–39; Hudson substantiates his view of why — even making adequate allowance for other factors — both the Lebanese system of consocation and Chehabist statism contributed to their own destruction.

[6] 'Indeed, it seems as if Lebanese democracy did not have any right to survive when its regional environment was not only lacking democratic institutions, but was even hostile to them ... it is this writer's belief that it would have survived one way or another had it not been for the unusual regional violence in which it was trapped'; Iliya Harik, 'The economic and social factors in the Lebanese crisis', *Journal of Arab Affairs* 1/2 (1982), p. 235.

within a wider war that was not pre-eminently Lebanese, grounds for a civil war within the war.

Social tension had worsened in the first half of the 1970s. Yet, the distribution of income in pre-war Lebanon was only moderately inequitable, on a par with that in France or Mexico. The mode of incorporation of strata and communities was moderately egalitarian. All communities had their privileged and deprived groups. The traditionally urban communities, the Sunnis and Greek Orthodox, were relatively better off, the later and latest urbanizers, the Maronites and Shi`is respectively, less so. On the whole, the Shi`i community was at the greatest disadvantage: the predominantly Shi`i areas of the country had been neglected longest: Shi`i notables paid little attention to Shi`i interests, and the rest of the country had virtually ignored the fact that from 1969 onwards warfare increasingly disrupted the south. The discrimination against the Shi`is was in part 'home-made', and in part already a product of war.

Largely as a result of the Chehabist social policies of the 1960s, income and educational inequalities between the communities had narrowed considerably since independence. However, these inequalities were more sharply perceived: 'There is less evil, but people are more aware it' (de Tocqueville). This paraphrase of what is known as relative deprivation in current socio-scientific terminology perfectly describes the development in Lebanon in the pre-war years. The abrupt break with Chehabist policies of social reform served to exacerbate perceptions of relative deprivation: rising expectations were disappointed.

The expansive educational policies of the 1960s produced more aspirants for jobs with good salaries than the labour market could absorb. Competition for jobs in the public service became very tough. As these posts were filled in accordance with communal quotas, the harsher competition brought the quota system itself into question.

Relatively deprived rural people and peripheral areas, together with numerous unemployable high-school and university graduates, are phenomena which create social strain in homogeneous societies too. The sense of relative deprivation is by no means unique to multi-communal states. In multi-communal Lebanon both absolute and relative deprivation were perceived less as phenomena of stratum or class, of region or age-group than of community. Objectively, there was some truth to this view, but only some. The important point is that in Lebanon whole communities felt themselves deprived; whether they were or not was irrelevant to the political consequences.

Two groups in particular were susceptible: those — for the most part Shi`is — forced from the land by economic processes or the war and those — Shi`is and Sunnis — who expected their education would improve their circumstances. Without putting too fine a point on it, the former were the future ranks of the militias, and in the latter the cadres. Generally overlooked before the war was the fact that many Maronites were similarly affected: some were forced to leave the land and others were disappointed in their expectations of social advancement. They too ultimately filled similar militia positions. However, in the pre-war period social protest was initially articulated as the political protest of the Muslim communities against the state — a state they perceived as dominated by Christians.

As explained, Christian dominance in pre-war Lebanon existed mainly on paper. In constitutional reality the position of the president was hardly more powerful than that of the prime minister: decisions required the consent of both. There was always parity in the cabinet. The Christian majority in parliament had been qualified by an electoral modus operandi that made far more Christian deputies dependent upon Muslim voters than vice versa. In the final instance, Christian ascendancy was symbolic: the head of state was a Christian, and Christians had a formal majority in the chamber of deputies.

Symbolic though it may have been, this 'dominance' did have one fundamental consequence: social demands were regarded not only as demands of deprived Muslims but as demands against a 'Christian-dominated' state. In popular usage of political campaigns this came to mean: against 'the Christians'.

Individual demands led to demands for changes in the division of power as practised, and ultimately in the National Pact itself.

Inevitably, the latter touched deep-seated fears among the Lebanese Christians. These pertained primarily to foreign policy — the question of Lebanese independence. The Christians knew that during the mandate the majority of Muslims had come to accept the idea of independence, and celebrated it in 1943. But as early as 1958 the Christians had felt that Lebanese independence had been endangered. From 1969 onwards, they perceived the threat as deadly: the Palestinians were taking Lebanon for granted as a base for their liberation struggle. This they pursued without regard for Lebanese interests, yet with the benevolent understanding, if not enthusiastic approval, of Lebanese Muslims. What to the Muslims was natural solidarity with other Arabs was to the Christians further proof of the Muslims' 'double standards of loyalty'. Lebanon's conflict of identity was clearer than ever. Dual loyalty was not a problem for Lebanese Muslims: they regarded themselves as Lebanese and as Arabs, and saw no contradiction. But most Christians insisted, as always, that Lebanese should be Lebanese, and Lebanese alone.

The Christian fear goes deeper. Even more than any 'anschluss', they fear minority status among a Muslim majority. Whether this be within a larger Arab state or in Lebanon itself is, to them, a matter only of degree; the nature of the threat is the same. Even before the war this fear drove the Christian parties to oppose any change whatsoever in the Lebanese status quo. Hence, in 1969, a party such as the Kata'ib, for years a pillar of Chehabist reforms, could make common cause with the opposition because it thought a strong front for the preservation of the political status quo more important than changes in the economic status quo.

Many Lebanese Muslims who felt themselves economically deprived strove to alter their situation by changing the political status quo. Conversely, many Christians now began to defend the economic status quo — or ceased actively seeking its reform — because they sought to defend the existing political system. When war broke out, the deprived on both sides trained their guns on the other.

Social conflicts, communal perception of them as intercommunal conflicts, symbolic Christian dominance, controversy over foreign policy as a reflection of a conflict of identity: can these together adequately explain why Lebanese started shooting at Lebanese? On balance, probably not. Lebanon had long lived with such conflicts and controversies without resorting to armed violence. Certainly, social conflicts worsened in the first half of the 1970s. But — in contradistinction to the tendency to treat them as conflicts between communities — they rarely took the form of intercommunal strife. The trade union movement was inter-confessional, as was the student movement. Christians as well as Muslims championed radical economic and political reform. Analysts of various political persuasions diagnosed incipient class consciousness. The labour movement had always had an uphill struggle against the fragmented structures of Lebanese business; nevertheless, they had employed peaceful means — strikes, demonstrations and negotiations — to considerable effect.

The political system had changed as well. Equality by quota had been practised in civil service appointments since 1958. During Franjieh's incumbency the traditional practice of reserving certain civil service posts to particular communities had been relaxed. The parliamentary elections of 1972 returned a record number of deputies with few ties to the old school of politicians. Notwithstanding this, considerable responsibility for the worsening domestic political strains lay with Lebanese politicians. Politicians of the Chehabist school had recognized the destructive potential of social inequalities; yet, as Jumblatt pointed out, they had little confidence in the people's common sense. Neither Chehab, nor his associates, nor his successor, seriously attempted to win support for their political objectives or methods by presenting them in a way people might understand. They preferred to implement whatever measures they thought right technocratically and autocratically. They manipulated the political system instead of trying to change it by democratic means. In doing so, they estranged many politicians who supported their reforms in principle, and failed to convince many voters they might have won over. Ultimately, this attempt to reform Lebanon was defeated by an extraordinarily heterogeneous coalition of anti-reformists, anti-militarist liberals and proponents of more rapid and more radical change. 'Reform from above' had failed by 1969.

The time of the 'foxes' had come again. They had many qualities: the sense to respect the mainstays of the country's equilibrium, a willingness to compromise and considerable resources of tolerance. A sense of social justice and an awareness of social change were not among them. After 1970, corruption and administrative incompetence flourished unchecked. Such deficiencies played right into the hands of the 'lions': turning growing discontent to account, they staked their political claims with roars of radicalism. The 'foxes' had to follow suit if they wanted to keep their following within their respective communities. The ravages of war seem to have spared the social insensibility of the old political class. In 1982/3 Amin Gemayel revealed just as little understanding as Suleiman Franjieh a dozen years before for social problems that by now needed far more urgent attention.

The social responsibility of the 'lions' was hardly better. They mobilized the poor not as poor but as members of particular communities. They exploited without restraint the communities' sense of relative communal deprivation. The leaders of the left-wing parties used another language; but once the effectiveness of confessional mobilization became apparent, they too resorted to it. In short: the 'lions' first sought the 'political kingdom', more or less trusting that the rest would be given to them. Kamal Jumblatt, who accused Chehab of having no confidence in the people, himself ultimately preferred violent to peaceful persuasion.

The old and the new leadership groups of the pre-war republic each contributed in its own way to its decline and fall.

This fact challenges the hypothesis that the Lebanese system of 1943 is itself the root of the Lebanese troubles. The anti-Pact politicians have had far fewer scruples about exploiting various communal identities and communal resentments than those who created and tried to preserve this system. The latters' efforts were not altruistic, but they were tempered by an awareness of the need to limit and regulate conflict. Numerous multi-communal states, including consociational and simple-majority systems, have had their 'lions' — as a rule, as many as there are communities — and many of them their intercommunal conflicts as well. It is conceivable that under a simple-majority system — without proportionality and quotas — relative deprivation would have emerged in Lebanon far earlier. For instance, if Lebanese civil servants had been appointed solely on merit, the Christian communities' traditional educational advantage alone would have ensured their predominance in the civil service for decades. In reality, until the late 1970s, the quota system functioned as a form of positive discrimination towards the Muslim communities.

Admittedly, in a greater number of multi-communal states 'law and order' has been maintained through domination by one community, and by one minority in Lebanon's Arab neighbours. Though, as Lehmbruch pointed out in 1967, there is no reason to believe that the political systems in these states are more efficient. The ascendancy of one community in Iraq, for instance, has not been able to prevent years of bloody civil war.

In Lebanon, in turn, years of war have proved that no single community could ever have dominated. The balance of power never did permit this, and, regarding only the domestic Lebanese balance of power, does not today either.

Lebanese consociationalism had its achievements: the inequalities inherited from Ottoman rule were considerably reduced; pre-war standards of living were higher than in any neighbouring state; above all, there was in Lebanon a degree of individual and collective freedom that citizens of neighbouring countries could only dream of. Freedom and democracy existed not in spite of, but because of, the country's multi-communal society: its equilibrium rendered authoritarian solutions impossible.

Pre-war Lebanon could have been socially and economically more equitable. The chance to experiment with a more democratic form of Chehabism was missed, for which both the old elite in their social blindness and the new in their radicalism and power-hunger must bear responsibility. These attitudes explain why Lebanese could start shooting at one another, but not why they actually did so.

## The militarization of the conflict

Might the Lebanese have resorted to internecine warfare even in the absence of the Palestinians? Perhaps, but it is improbable. In 1975 there was far less discord among the political elite than in 1958, at least as far as domestic matters were concerned.

A crucial factor in the militarization of the domestic Lebanese conflicts was the presence of an armed power within and contending with the state — the Palestinians. In terms of their own interests, their experience in Jordan and the logic of their self-preservation, they had no choice but to arm all groups prepared to act as their allies. Syria, for its part, had an interest in enabling the Palestinians to withstand the authority of the Lebanese state, though not, as subsequently became clear, in allowing them and their allies to destroy it. Israel had an interest in giving the Lebanese state — or, if it proved incapable, other armed groups — cause to act against the Palestinians. Lebanon became a surrogate battlefield for Palestine. It took a while before the war also became a civil war.

Lebanese are also to blame. Kamal Jumblatt and his left-wing allies could hardly have seized power on their own, but saw a chance with Palestinian support. The Kata'ib tried to provoke the Lebanese Army into moving against the Palestinians. The Muslim establishment hindered any army operations, preferring rather to take advantage of hostilities to effect limited changes in domestic distribution of power.

Notwithstanding the responsibility of various Lebanese groups, it is questionable whether Lebanon could have remained aloof from the Middle Eastern conflict. Jordan had no history of Christian-Muslim rivalries, a strong central authority, a functioning secret service and a homogeneous army, yet could not avoid a bloody war. Might an intact Chehabist system with the support of a stronger army have prevented a Lebanese-Palestinian war, or won it? A speculation, like another much discussed in Lebanon since 1986: if the Christians had not resisted the Palestinians, would the Shi`is — the community hardest hit by Palestinian activities — have done so later, as they have in recent years?

All that is certain is that war in Lebanon started as one between Palestinians and Christians, and that by arming and training their Lebanese allies, the Palestinians enabled them to fight a civil war. They militarized the Lebanese conflict. The conflict existed and was militarizable. But it was a secondary conflict, a consequence of the wars over Palestine that had been fought in Palestine itself and on Egyptian, Syrian and Jordanian territory. Since 1969 they have been fought on Lebanese territory too.

## Inconclusive interventions

What holds for the outbreak of war is also true of its course. Civil war was largely an epiphenomenon of conflicts to which Lebanon was incidental, but which took place on Lebanese territory. Of twenty-six distinct confrontations — excluding petty warfare — six involved only non-Lebanese parties. In nine cases Lebanese faced foreign forces and in three an alliance between foreigners and other Lebanese. Only nine confrontations were primarily inter-Lebanese, and six of these were not between but within the two major blocks.

The first of the three rounds of civil war across the religious divide lasted from the summer of 1975 to the autumn of 1976: the hostilities between the Christian parties and the allied forces of the Left, the Lebanese Arab Army and the Palestinians, of which the Palestinians were the main military force. The struggle for the Chouf between Christian and Druze militias was civil war, even if the Druze received Palestinian support in its final phase. The Druze and Shi`i conflict with the Lebanese government and army over the Lebanese-Israeli agreement was civil war par excellence; the anti-agreement party received Syrian support, the government American and French.

The remaining instances of exclusively civil war are conflicts within the confessional blocks: Christians against Christians, Shi`is against Druze, and Shi`is against Shi`is. From late 1985, most hostilities were of this nature, an unequivocal sign of stalemate between Christian and Muslim militias. The Christian militias lost all regions except the Christian heartland, where they faced no internal challenge.

The most numerous and heaviest conflicts involved foreign forces and powers. These 'supra-Lebanese' wars caused greatest loss of life, above all of Palestinians in 1976 and Palestinians, Syrians and Israelis in 1982. Foreign intervention has been a constant feature of the war, either to help one of the internal factions to victory or to establish external hegemony over Lebanon. Neither goal has yet been achieved; the attempts have foundered on either other foreign intervention or the resistance of one of the Lebanese parties.

The Palestinian attempt to help Kamal Jumblatt and his alliance to victory failed because of Syrian intervention, as did the earlier attempt of the Christian parties to crush the Palestinians. Syria tried to subordinate both Palestinians and Christians. It abandoned the former attempt in 1977 when it needed Palestinian support for its anti-Sadat policy. Vehement Christian resistance and the fear of Israeli reaction defeated the latter. Israeli intervention did drive the PLO out of Beirut. But it did not achieve its second objective, the ascendancy of pro-Israeli Lebanese forces; this was foiled by Syrian and Shi`i opposition. The Franco-American intervention between 1982 and 1984 was intended to restore the authority of the Lebanese state and obtain the withdrawal of all foreign troops. These aims were frustrated by Israeli obstruction, Syrian opposition and the Druze-Shi`i uprising against the central government, which precipitated the disintegration of the Lebanese Army.

The second attempt to establish Syrian hegemony — the Militia Agreement — failed because of opposition from Christians and the Christian part of the army. Iran's attempt to use fundamentalist Shi`i militias to gain a foothold in Lebanon met with the opposition of Amal, supported by Syria.

Not only did all Lebanese attempts to establish internal hegemony fail; foreign intervention to establish external hegemony failed too: no victoria Palestinensis and no pax Syriana, Israelica or Americana. There has been no peace at all, just war and more war, on a large scale and small.

The full force of the Middle Eastern storm moved to Lebanon when the USA began to seek a settlement to the Palestine question over the heads of first the PLO and then Syria too, and to the exclusion of the USSR. To wreck American policy, first the PLO and then Syria grasped every opportunity to demonstrate within

Lebanon and from Lebanese territory that a settlement in the Middle East was impossible without them, secure in the knowledge of Soviet approval and arms. Begin and Sharon thought victory in Lebanon would bring peace to Israel's northern border. Official US approval lasted as long as Haig was Secretary of State, though arm supplies continue. The superpowers had to learn to live with their respective clients' relative independence. The USSR was unable to prevent Syria from waging war on the PLO in 1976 and 1983. The USA could control Sharon's war on Syria in Lebanon, but could not prevent his successor from frustrating American peace initiatives in Lebanon. The USSR indicated that it was prepared to guarantee Syria's security interests, but that these did not necessarily include a Syrian presence in Lebanon; after initial hesitation, the USA accepted Israel's war against the PLO, but not against the Syrians in Lebanon. The superpowers had a mutual interest in preventing any direct clash between Syria and Israel in Lebanon that might have compelled them to fulfil their respective defence commitments.

Since 1982, both Syria and Israel have generally avoided direct hostilities in Lebanon. Israel returned to its 'red line' policy of 1976. For many years Syria respected this line: it attempted neither to advance beyond it nor to use its air force against recalcitrant Lebanese. Both regional powers preferred to let local Lebanese clients look after their interests. Israel has a small but reliable ally in the South Lebanese Army, which provides valuable, albeit limited, help in defending Israel's 'security zone'. Syria dominated most of Lebanon's territory. However, because of the unreliability of local allies it preferred to tolerate several of them, playing one off against the other. Its attempt to win over the Lebanese Forces failed when Hobeika lost power. In early 1986, Syrian intervention saved Amal from defeat at the hand of the Druze. But Syrian support for Amal was dosed so that Amal would not defeat Hezbollah in the intra-Shi`i struggle. Finally, Syria tolerated Amal's fight against the return of the Arafat wing of the PLO, while using Syrian-sponsored Palestinian organizations to control the Palestinians in Beirut.

As a consequence of the disappointing results of spectacular foreign interventions, the superpowers were reticent about greater involvement and pressed their clients, Syria and Israel, to practise similar caution. These clients, in turn, sought to maintain a controlled tension through their Lebanese sub-clients.

## The transformation of the Lebanese factions

The outbreak of war prompted a succession of communal mobilizations as one community after another felt its existence threatened: the Christians in 1975/6, the Druze in 1982 and the Shi`is in 1983. Not all communities mobilized, or organized militias of their own. The smaller Christian communities chose for the most part to join the Maronites, after experiencing that their adversaries seldom distinguished between Maronites and other Christians. As a result of their expulsion, non-Maronite Christians from the Bekaa, Aley, the Chouf and southern Lebanon became more militant than ever. Although the Sunnis in Beirut felt directly threatened after Shi`i militias took control of Sunni residential areas in 1984, by that time it was too late for effective mobilization.

The longer the war lasted, the stronger the trend became to replace the initial, largely spontaneous civil militias with professional militias. The Christians, Druze and Shi`i militias gained control over compact territories; they established their own civil administrations and financial autonomy through levies and customs duties in their own ports. To all intents and purposes, their leaders supplanted the civilian politicians.

Empirical surveys show that the three communities with powerful militias and demarcated 'cantons' have a pronounced sense of group identification and of solidarity. In political terms, however, the 'lions' among them had the support of only a minority in their communities. Hence, militiamen, militia commanders and militant politicians had an interest in maintaining at least some tension between the conflicting parties. Peace would diminish their influence. The interests of the regional powers in continuing tension in Lebanon was reinforced by those of the intra-Lebanese factions, an independent factor for hostilities. The war became a self-perpetuating phenomenon.

## Misperceptions of the interests of foreign allies

At one or other time all Lebanese factions placed their hopes of victory in foreign help. And all the factions fostered illusions to varying degrees about the interests and objectives of their respective allies. 'The search for eternal protection always ended badly for the protégés, who were used by the protector for as long as possible. No politico-military protector acts selflessly, and the price is often exorbitant.'[7] Before the war the Sunnis hoped that the Palestinians' power would serve to improve their own share of power. The Christians hoped to retain their power with Syrian help, increase it with Israeli help, and regain what they had lost with American help. They deluded themselves. Palestinians, Syrians and Israelis primarily pursued their own interests. The Americans were primarily interested in a settlement to the Palestine question; when Lebanon proved too hot a potato, they dropped it.

---

[7] Georges Corm, 'Quelques réflexions méthodologiques et historiques sur la perception de la société libanaise par les élites des communautés chrétiennes', in Joseph Abou Jaoude et al., *La nouvelle société libanaise dans la perception des Fa`aliyat des communautés chrétiennes*, vol. 3, *Etudes et Rapports* (Kaslik, 1984), p. 59.

The Druze under Walid Jumblatt were the shrewdest by far, using both Israeli and Syrian help to expand their sphere of influence considerably, and expediently changing sides. But once they had to rely on Syria alone, from 1986 onwards, they were deprived of the fruits of their recent military successes in West Beirut and lost exclusive dominance in their own canton.

The conflict between the Shi`i militias has been fanned by the rivalry between their protectors, Syria and Iran. Amal and Hezbollah each hoped that their respective ally would ultimately enable them to win. The signs were that they, too, would learn the bitter lesson taught the other communities.

The views of ordinary Lebanese reveal that many politicians of the old school are right in their opinion that the Lebanese, left alone, would reach agreement among themselves. Yet, pre-war, many of these same politicians, and most of the warlords since then, did not want to be left alone, but sought the next reversal of allegiance in the hope of riding to victory on the backs of others. At one time or another, every party to the war has called for the revocation of the Lebanese covenant — in vain.

## The intentions of Arab neighbours

Of all the foreign interests, only Syria exercised decisive influence in Lebanon. First Israel and then Syria disposed of the Palestinians. Syria was chiefly responsible for the failure of the American intervention and, through its client organizations, for Israel's decision to restrict itself to its immediate security interests in the south of the country. *Post hoc* accusations of Syrian long-term objectives reek of conspiracy theory. Such theories — as in this case — are seldom plausible. Syria does have long-term interests, and its leaders pursue them with patience and pertinacity. In the words of President Assad, Syria's policy towards all Arab states is one of 'interventionist nationalism', actively pursued whenever opportune. This certainly includes maximizing Syrian influence in Lebanon in the long term and controlling and instrumentalizing the Palestinian movement. Moreover, Syria feels it has strong security interests in Lebanon, which it regards as its soft underbelly in respect of Israel.[8]

Similarly, all evidence points to Syria operating without a 'general plan'. It grasps its opportunities as they arise. The confrontation that erupted between the Lebanese state and the PLO in 1968 gave Syria the opportunity to act as arbiter, and to acquire influence on both adversaries. It could best exercise and retain its

---

[8] See Daniel Pipes, 'Damascus and the claim to Lebanon, *Orbis* 30/4 (1987), pp. 663–81, and Elisabeth Picard, 'La politique de la Syrie au Liban: Les développements incontrôlables d'une stratégie ambitieuse', *Maghreb–Machrek* 116 (1987), pp. 5–34.

role by obstructing either side's victory. It saved the Palestinians from defeat by the Lebanese Army in 1969 and 1973 and by the Christian parties in 1975, and did the same for the Christians against the Palestinians and Jumblatt in 1976.

When President Sarkis assumed office, he believed that the Syrian leaders would help the Lebanese state to rebuild a tenable equilibrium, and to keep the Palestinians in check. He was soon expressing reservations.

His adviser, Karim Pakradouni, records him saying in 1976: 'Nasser only wanted Lebanon to adopt his foreign policy and Chehab wanted a free hand in his country's domestic policies. There was the possibility of reaching a satisfactory agreement. Chehab followed Nasser's line in foreign policy and Nasser supported Chehab's domestic policies.'[9] But Sarkis was no longer certain that Syria would allow him the same scope. In 1978 he was already despairing: 'Syria ... does not understand Lebanon and will never understand it, even if they are here for one hundred years. They want to apply their methods here and believe that the Lebanese president ought to govern the country their way.'[10] In 1979, the Syrian Vice-President, Khaddam, was quite open: 'Rest assured, Mr President, we shall stop shelling Beirut. We have other means and will hit elsewhere ... Other blows can also be lethal, not only those to the head. In future we will let the 20,000 Palestinians fight against the 20,000-strong Lebanese Forces.'[11] Syria did just that; it did use its own army to bring adversaries in Lebanon to heel, but also its client groups, and that more and more frequently.

When the Arafat wing of the PLO digressed from the Syrian line, Syria let dissident Palestinians, with Syrian logistic support, drive them out of Syrian-controlled Lebanon. When Amin Gemayel agreed to let Syria dictate his foreign policy he was rewarded with Syrian support against his Druze and Shi`i adversaries, who were bent on driving him from office.

It would appear that Syria had a notion that its neighbour owed it 'something' for its persistent involvement in conflicts and attempted settlements. The 1985 Agreement between Syria and the Christian, Druze and Shi`i militias was the first formal expression of what this 'something' might embrace: 'strategic complementarity' between the two countries, i.e. an identical foreign policy, a treaty on the stationing of Syrian troops in Lebanon and the 'rehabilitation' of the Lebanese Army under Syrian supreme command. These conditions did not amount to annexation, but went far further than the 'Finlandization' in respect of foreign policy that Chehab agreed with Nasser, and which Sarkis and Gemayel were

---

[9] Karim Pakradouni, *La paix manquée: Le mandat d'Elias Sarkis (1976–1982)*, 2nd edn (n.p., 1984), pp. 21f.
[10] Ibid., p. 146.
[11] Ibid., p. 191.

prepared to accept. Had the Agreement been ratified, the two states would have remained formally independent, and Syrian domination of Lebanon would have been guaranteed.

The Lebanese Forces reacted to the Agreement by getting rid of their commander. The Christian section of the army and the Lebanese president rejected it. The Shi`i and Druze militias stood by their consent.

At first, neither Syria nor its Lebanese allies seriously tried to break Christian resistance with armed force. Instead, they boycotted the country's political institutions. This policy would culminate in the dramatic circumstances surrounding the expiry of Amin Gemayel's term of office in the summer of 1988, to which we shall turn in the next chapter.

## The demise of a consociational democracy: The failure of the elite and the international crisis

In summary, the leadership groups failed the Lebanese consociational democracy at precisely the time the country was sliding into an international crisis. A crisis of this nature might well have drawn a homogeneous state into war, but not necessarily into a civil war. Pre-war Lebanon had survived social strains and cleavages between its religious communities. Changes in the modes of incorporation of strata and communities deepened the domestic crisis: they brought greater equality, but simultaneously heightened the sense of relative deprivation among the previously disadvantaged Muslim communities. When the traditional elites regained power from the technocratic reformists of the Chehabist era, they used it to disappoint rising expectations.

At the same time, Lebanon became the last bastion of the Palestinians. To secure it, the Palestinians armed any political group willing to support them. This militarized the internal conflicts. In most phases of the war, the civil war remained an epiphenomenon of the surrogate war over Palestine. But it prepared the ground for enormous changes in the Lebanese political system. Militant leaders replaced the traditional elites in all communities. After a decade and a half of fighting, both the international war and the civil war were unresolved. Regional as well as militant domestic parties had an interest in continued tension, making of the war a self-perpetuating phenomenon. The equilibrium of consociation gave way to an equilibrium of terror.

# 9

# The Disintegration of the State
# The Road to Dependence, 1988–1990

> The new Lebanon will not be independent; will not be unified; will not be democratic ... Syria will dominate Lebanon.
>
> Paul A. Jureidini and R.D. McLaurin

When made in 1984, this pessimistic prediction was already plausible.[1] Events in 1988 made it probable. Up to this time the attenuated Lebanese state had continued to exist in its institutions; after that it began to disintegrate. Efforts to resuscitate it ended in greater fragmentation, and greater dependence of each fragment on Syria.

## Lebanon without a president

Like all significant changes in Lebanon since 1967, the collapse of the state was heralded by events in other parts of the Middle East. Syria found itself increasingly isolated. In December 1987 the Palestinians of the West Bank and Gaza rose against Israeli occupation. At the end of July 1988 Jordan renounced its claims to the West Bank. The PLO proclaimed the independent state of Palestine. They announced they were prepared to recognize Israel and negotiate peace. The

---

[1] Paul A. Jureidini and R.D. McLaurin, 'Lebanon after the war of 1982' in Edward E. Azar et al., eds., *The Emergence of a New Lebanon: Fantasy or reality?* (New York, 1984), p. 29.

majority of the Arab states favoured a new attempt to regulate the Palestine question.[2] Syria alone pursued a policy of confrontation.

And alone of all Arab states, Syria had supported Iran in its war with Iraq. This war ended in late July 1988. Iraq was unbowed, powerful and bent on barely concealed revenge against the hostile regime in Damascus. Henceforth, it supplied Syria's opponents in Lebanon from its abundant arsenal: initially the Lebanese Forces, then units of the Lebanese Army stationed in the Christian heartland as well.

Syria reacted to the new threat in the east with greater efforts to secure its western front, i.e., finally to secure hegemony over Lebanon. A convenient opportunity was to hand: Amin Gemayel's term of office was about to expire. Under the Lebanese Constitution, a new president had to be elected by September 22nd, 1988. Until late July the run-up to the elections had followed Lebanese custom. Candidates were or had themselves proposed, militias and parties pronounced their 'veto' against this one and that one. And everyone was looking for the compromise candidate acceptable to all political forces. As in the past, the realities of power could not be disregarded. In 1958 Chehab had been elected with American and Egyptian approval, in 1976 Sarkis with that of Syria, in 1982 Bashir Gemayel with that of Israel and Amin Gemayel with that of America; this time potential candidates sought the approval of the Syrian government. It soon became clear that Syria sought not only to prevent the election of any candidate it felt unreliable, but also to secure the election of a vassal. Lebanese politicians returning from Damascus told of demands to present a written manifesto and commit themselves to it. They were left in no doubt that the support of the Syrian government depended on whether this manifesto agreed in content with the 1985 Militia Agreement of Damascus. Most candidates were not prepared to comply.

One who did officially announce his candidature was Suleiman Franjieh. Although he made no reference to a programme of reforms, the Syrian government immediately gave him their full support. They obviously placed greater value on reliability than reforms. Most Muslim politicians expressed their support for Franjieh, without enthusiasm but in acceptance of Syria's will. Opinion was divided among the Christians. Some traditional politicians felt that Franjieh, although pro-Syrian, was an unbending patriot and, hence, the person most likely to preserve the fabric of the state in the prevailing circumstances and prevent worse. The Lebanese Forces were bitterly opposed to the man who had expelled them from the north. But there were also moderate politicians who did not want to vote for the man who, as president from 1970 to 1976, had not stopped the drift

---

[2] Arnold Hottinger, 'Arafats Friedensangebot an Israel. Ein Durchbruch in der Palästinafrage?', *Europa Archiv* 44/2 (1989), pp. 39–46.

towards war, and since then had been regarded as the symbol of submission to Syria.

The Speaker of the Chamber of Deputies, Husseini, summoned the deputies to the Mansour Palace, which was accessible from both sides of the 'Green Line', on August 18th, 1988. Of the ninety-nine deputies elected in 1972, seventy-six were still alive. Twenty-eight of the thirty-five Muslim survivors took their seats, but only ten of the forty-one Christian, and of the twenty-one Maronites just two. The Lebanese Forces forcibly prevented some deputies from attending the session, others stayed away because they disapproved of the candidate or what he stood for. As there was no quorum the presidential election could not be held. For the first time in the Lebanon's history there was a distinct possibility that a president would not be elected within the period set by the Constitution. Supporters and opponents of Syria began to prepare themselves for this eventuality. Under Article 62 of the Constitution the cabinet exercises executive powers if the presidency is vacant. But for over a year there had been only a caretaker government. Prime Minister Karami had resigned on May 4th, 1987, and been assassinated four weeks later on June 1st. Gemayel had appointed the Minister of Education, Salim al-Hoss, acting premier until a new government was formed. Hoss now declared that he was withdrawing the government's resignation. His intention was obvious: should a president not be elected, a Hoss government would exercise executive powers. In a letter to Hoss, Gemayel pointed out that under the Constitution the resignation of the Karami government was final. Should a successor not have been elected by the time his term of office expired, he would appoint a new government before leaving office.

But matters had not reached that stage yet; efforts to elect a president were continuing. On September 15th, the American special envoy Murphy flew to Damascus. For three days he negotiated with the Syrian government. The result was a complete surprise: the American and Syrian governments jointly proposed the deputy Mikhail Daher. That two foreign powers should nominate a candidate — previous foreign interventions had at least been cloaked in diplomatic discretion — was as unusual and astonishing as the intention clear. Daher came from northern Akkar, a region that had had to come to an arrangement with the Syrians as early as 1975. He was better known as a lawyer than a politician. His loyalty to Syria was as unquestioned as Franjieh's, but, unlike the latter, he lacked both a political power base and personal standing. Syria had no interest in any compromise candidate, a second Elias Sarkis — a man willing to cooperate with the Syrians, but not to play their game. The next president of Lebanon had to be compliant.

The strongest western power desired Syrian help in freeing its citizens held hostage in Lebanon. It agreed to Syria's choice and presented it as their own.

Murphy went to Lebanon and told the Maronite Patriarch: 'The choice is between Daher and chaos.'

Anyone who still doubted that Syria and its Lebanese allies were determined to prevent the election of anyone else was soon taught otherwise. Husseini resummoned parliament, not to the 'neutral' Palais Mansour, but to the old parliament building abandoned at the start of the war, on the Place de l'Etoile, an area under Syrian control.

The reaction of Christian politicians, Church leaders and the military was unanimous. Deputies who voted for Franjieh were not prepared even to consider Daher. A group of twenty-seven parliamentarians visited the Maronite Patriarch to demand free elections in the Palais Mansour. The strongest objection came from the commander of the army, Aoun: as the army was sworn to upheld parliamentary democracy, it could not accept that America and Syria nominate the president.

On his penultimate day in office President Amin flew to Damascus for a last attempt at mediation. On the same day Aoun and Geagea had a meeting. The two men were not friends, as Aoun had never concealed his opinion that the only legitimate armed force in the country was the army and that therefore the militias had to disband. However, both feared that Gemayel might bow to Syrian pressure, a fear that proved all too true. On his return Gemayel, declared to deputies assembled at the seat of the Patriarch that he saw no other prospect but to elect Daher, which the deputies again rejected. On his last day in office, September 22nd, 1988, Gemayel tried to form a new government. But not one Muslim politician was prepared to join the cabinet in these circumstances. Late that evening Aoun and Geagea presented the president with an ultimatum to dismiss the caretaker Hoss government: 'Mr President, it is your constitutional right either to form a new government or not. Should you choose to do the latter, we will consider you a traitor from midnight.' At 23.45 Gemayel signed two decrees. The first dismissed the caretaker cabinet, the second appointed an interim government until the election of a new president. This government was composed of six officers, one each from the Maronite, Greek Orthodox, Greek Catholic, Sunni, Shi`i and Druze communities. Michel Aoun became Prime Minister.

There can be no doubt about the constitutional legality of this government. Article 53 states that the president appoints the ministers, 'one of whom he chooses as prime minister'. The premier does not have to resign; the president can dismiss him and appoint a new prime minister. Moreover, the Aoun government kept the rules of the National Pact. If the presidency is vacant the cabinet is the sole executive, and offices are distributed among the communities represented in the government. There was a precedent for this: in 1952, President Beshara al-Khoury appointed the commander of the army, Fouad Chehab, who was a

Maronite, Prime Minister of an interim government. In contrast to 1952, though, in September 1988 neither constitutionality nor respect for the rules of the National Pact could procure undivided recognition for a government. The Hoss and the Aoun cabinets both claimed to be the legal government. Aoun governed *de facto* in the Christian heartland, Hoss in the areas under the control of Muslim militias and Syrian forces. Neither government was representative of all communities in Lebanon as the three Muslim officers named as ministers in Aoun's cabinet did not assume office, and two of the three Christian ministers in the Hoss cabinet accepted that it had been dissolved and no longer observed their official duties.

The country had no president, but two governments that denied each other's legality and legitimacy. After October 18th, 1988 there was no speaker of the chamber of deputies either: Husseini's period of office expired. Parliament was not reconvened.

The split in the executive was soon mirrored in the administration and the army command. Aoun appointed new heads of the Deuxième Bureau, the Republican Guard and the Sûreté Générale; Hoss replied with counter-appointments. In early November, the minister of defence in the Hoss government demanded that Aoun 'cease his political activities', as these were incompatible with the post of army commander. As expected, Aoun did not comply, and Hoss appointed Brigadier-General Sami Khatib as commander-in-chief of the army. For their part, the Aoun cabinet replaced all army and garrisoned police officers who did not report to headquarters for duty, most of them Muslims, with officers drawn from the area under its control, most of them Christians. Civil servants in the ministries and subordinate authorities accepted their instructions from the government of the area in which they had their offices. One institution maintained its unitary character: the Central Bank financed the expenditures of both governments. Three months after the presidential elections broke down, the Lebanese state existed in little more than name.

After these events holders of office abandoned even the pretence of verbal restraint. At a congress in Mukhtara, attended also by representatives of the Baath, the SSNP, the CP and Hobeika's militia, Berri and Jumblatt, ministers in the Hoss government, declared that the National Pact was dead and demanded 'democracy by numbers alone'. Jumblatt went even further: he would prefer the 'national territories' to join Syria rather than reunify with a 'territory under the control of the West and the friends of Israel'. Both militia leaders rejected France's proposal to organize presidential elections under the auspices of UN troops and the Maronite Patriarch's offer to try again to find a compromise candidate. Shortly afterwards, the Syrian Vice-President, Khaddam, declared that every candidate would have to present a written manifesto for approval, which confirmed the earlier rumours. The two militia leaders and their Syrian patron could not have been more explicit. They called for fundamental change in Lebanon's political system and recognition of Syrian hegemony.

Aoun was equally explicit. He announced that henceforth his cabinet was the 'independent government' and continued: 'Are we an independent country or a province of Syria? ... The Syrians rule our country. They meddle in everything, large and small.' He suspected Syria's ultimate goal was the annexation of Lebanon — and he would resist it.

## General Aoun's attempt to restore the state

On January 12th, 1989 the Council of Ministers of the Arab League appointed a commission on the Lebanese crisis. The moving force behind this Arab initiative was Iraq. Its aim, as stated by the Iraqi foreign minister, was 'to prevent Syria gaining control of Lebanon by violence or intimidation'. Syria had consistently resisted any attempt to 'Arabize' or 'internationalize' the Lebanese question. But as it was now isolated in the Arab world, it grudgingly agreed to the commission. The chairman was the Kuwaiti foreign minister. The commission invited leading Lebanese to talks in Tunis, including Aoun, Hoss and Husseini. Hoss and Husseini stressed the need for political reforms in Lebanon. Aoun admitted that there were differences of opinion among the Lebanese. However, he himself would be able to settle them, once Syrian troops had withdrawn. This withdrawal and re-establishing the Lebanese state were his main objectives.

On his return from Tunis, Aoun's immediate task was to consolidate his government's authority in the Christian heartland. It was under increasing pressure from the Lebanese Forces. Aoun did not dispute the need for the militia, while the country faced foreign threat. But he would not sanction more than an auxiliary to the regular army. On no account could a militia presume to exercise functions of state. But this was precisely what the Lebanese Forces were doing to an increasing extent. They refused to hand over control of their ports to the state, continuing to collect 'excise duties' while the budget deficit grew for lack of such regular income. The militia competed with the army for recruits, offering higher pay than the army could. Finally, it created a 'development council' to pursue through the means of well-directed subsidies the militia's own social, educational and economic policies in opposition to the civil authorities.

After a number of incidents, heavy fighting broke out between the army and the militia on February 10th, 1989. Aoun accused the Lebanese Forces of preparing a coup d'état, and of behaving like the Mafia. He held it his duty to protect the rights of the legitimate government. The opposing forces were large — estimates put the strength of the army brigades under Aoun's command at 15,000, that of the militia at 10,000 — and both had been heavily armed by Iraq. The fighting took place in the Christian suburbs of Beirut, around some villages in the mountains and along the entire desert in the enclave. Both sides used tanks and artillery.[3] The Maronite Patriarch and a gathering of Christian politicians appealed for a cease-fire. Aoun agreed, after the militia had accepted the main demands of the government: to hand over to the army Dock Five in Beirut harbour — the most important customs post in the country — and the Bourbara road-block in the north of the Christian territory. The militiamen returned to their barracks. The state had regained control of its most important source of revenue.[4]

The Aoun government had shown that it was serious about restoring the authority of the state.[5] It had not hesitated to act forcibly against a militia in its 'own camp'. It now called on all other militias either to close 'their' ports or hand them over to the government. Franjieh's Marada militia formally acquiesced by handing over the port of Selaata to an army brigade stationed in the north of the country. But Berri and Jumblatt and their militias refused.

On March 3rd, 1989 Aoun issued an order to blockade the PSP and Amal ports of Khalde, Jiyeh and Ouzai. The Lebanese navy and helicopter units barred access to these ports.

## Bombardment and blockade

Prior to this the Syrian government had officially warned Aoun he might do as he wished in 'his' part of the country, but they would not tolerate any action against militias in other parts of the country. When Aoun stuck to his guns they reacted promptly and brutally. Syrian artillery in the upper Metn and PSP artillery in the Chouf bombarded the ports of Beirut and Jounieh. Aoun's army responded by bombarding the airport. All three facilities had to close.

---

[3] Casualties amounted to 77 dead and 200 wounded, most of them military.

[4] According to Aoun, the Lebanese Forces had revenues of LL400 million per day from 'custom duties' at the ports of Beirut and Jounieh and various levies: 2 per cent on the sale of buildings and property, 1 per cent on new buildings and inheritances, 4 per cent on turnover in the catering trade, $40–125 per traveller on the Larnaka ferry and LL20 on a litre of petrol. Under the new agreement, revenue of the Lebanese Forces would come from 'turnover tax' on catering and entertainment.

Dany Chamoun alleged that other sources of the Lebanese Forces income included prostitution and drug dealing.

After the agreement came into force the state's revenues from customs rose rapidly. Within a week the dollar fell from LL502 to LL450.

[5] Jihad Alam, 'Crise dans la crise, guerre dans la guerre', *Les Cahiers de l'Orient* 14/2 (1989), p. 41, comments: 'Pour la première fois, une autorité institutionelle tentait et réussissait, en partie, à mettre fin au règne des milices', and continues by saying that Aoun's action against the Lebanese Forces was very popular among both Christians and Muslims.

Aoun resorted to verbal escalation. On March 14th, 1989 he announced he had no choice but to declare a war of liberation against Syria. Certainly, Syria was stronger — otherwise it could not have occupied Lebanon. The Lebanese had no alternative but to rise against the occupying forces: Arab and non-Arab states alike, including Syria, insisted that the Lebanese state re-establish its authority: 'That's all I'm doing.'

Syria and its allied militias took escalation beyond words. On March 21st, they imposed a total blockade on the territory controlled by the Aoun government, closing all checkpoints along the demarcation line in Beirut, in the mountains and in the north. All ports of the Christian heartland were within range of Syrian artillery in the mountains; even the ferry service to Cyprus had to be temporarily suspended. Once again, the Syrians resorted to their tried tactic against Palestinian and Christian Lebanese resistance: long-range attrition bombardments of residential areas. They had learnt from experience: 240 mm mortars, incendiary bombs for the first time, and greater accuracy. The destruction was not only greater than previously but more telling: within a few days a power station and 80 per cent of the territory's reserves of petrol, diesel and gas had been destroyed.

Aoun's troops hit back hard. They were far better armed than Syria's opponents in any previous confrontation in Lebanon had been, apart from the Israelis. Long-range artillery hit Syrian positions in the Bekaa and destroyed Druze villages in the vicinity of PSP positions. Civilians in West Beirut suffered as much from Lebanese bombardments of Syrian positions as civilians in East Beirut from Syrian fire. Tens of thousands of people from West Beirut, especially residents of the Shi`i districts near the airport, fled to the south again.

The Syrians viewed the fighting as a renewal of the 'Lebanese civil war', in which their sole role was to support their allies. In part this was true. The Druze militia had joined the fighting on March 6th. Amal and Hezbollah had suspended their Shi`i war on January 25th, and did not intervene, apart from some shooting of little military consequence along the Green Line. But they gave political weight to the civil-war thesis by a joint statement declaring they would fight against Aoun until victory was theirs. The attitude of the regular army units loyal to the Hoss government was remarkable. Their participation in the fighting was at best symbolic, and there is evidence that Muslim officers passed information on Syrian Army positions on to colleagues loyal to Aoun. Now, as in some earlier phases of the war, civil war was an epiphenomenon of what was essentially a Syrian offensive against the remnant of an independent Lebanese state.

Bombardment and blockade had disastrous consequences for the small area in which the writ of this state still ran. Normal life and business came to a virtual standstill. Even on relatively 'quiet' days indiscriminate shooting kept the population in their cellars, and factories, schools, shops and offices shut. On April 13th,

1989, the anniversary of the outbreak of war, approximately 10,000 shells and rockets fell on the Christian enclave: the heaviest bombardment since the Israeli siege of West Beirut in 1982. Hospitals and grain silos went up in flames; power supplies were cut completely; and shortages of petrol and food appeared.

The other part of Lebanon suffered great loss of life and property too. Aoun's artillery pounded Syrian targets between Beirut and Baalbek as best they could. As always, there were fewer military than Lebanese civilian casualties.

Aoun's attempt to restore the Lebanese state had turned the demarcation lines into battle-fronts again.

## Onlookers

For years, ordinary Lebanese had dreamt of release from the despotism of local militias and foreign armies. When Aoun expressed these wishes as his policy, he could count on enthusiastic support. The ferocity of the Syrian reprisals caused many to question whether Aoun had chosen the right moment for his attempt and whether he had the means to achieve his aim. To the first question he replied: 'Better late than never'. As to the second question, he left no doubt that a war of liberation would require great sacrifices, and that Lebanon did not have the strength to liberate itself on its own. He evidently counted on outside support, both Arab and international.

Precisely this hope explains the speed and the violence of the Syrian reaction. Syria needed to break the new resistance before it could attract regional or international support. Support never came. The Arab League attempted to arrange a cease-fire; its statements on the crux of the issue, the withdrawal of Syrian troops from Lebanon, were sibylline. After lengthy vacillation the chairman of the League's Lebanon Committee, the Kuwaiti foreign minister, called for the withdrawal of 'Israeli and non-Israeli' troops. As Israel made its withdrawal conditional on Syria's, and Syria its conditional on Israel's, the formula remained a unfeasible. Saudi Arabia worked to prevent any statement that might displease Syria, for fear of strengthening Iraqi influence. Iraq favoured Syrian withdrawal, and continued to supply Aoun's army, though not with armaments — such as ground-to-ground missiles — that could reach Syrian territory. Lebanese sceptics feared that Iraq was prepared to fight Syria to the last Lebanese. Israel drew satisfaction from the fact that thousands of Lebanese sought refuge in the Israeli-controlled zone. Moreover, the events in Lebanon distracted international attention from the Palestinian intifada.

International reaction was equally disappointing for Aoun and his supporters. The new US administration made it clear that it had no intention of becoming involved in Lebanon again.[6] Leading officials pointedly demonstrated disinterest,[7] and intimated their continued displeasure with Aoun for thwarting the election of Mikhail Daher as president. They washed their hands of the affair by recommending a cease-fire.

At first the French government took a stronger line. Their special envoy, François Deniau, labelled Syria the aggressor in Lebanon.[8] Syria protested strongly, and Deniau's statement was officially interpreted as a 'private opinion'.[9] Similarly, after Syrian threats, a French gesture of political support for General Aoun — a hospital ship and a tanker laden with petrol — was re-interpreted as a purely humanitarian measure for the benefit of all Lebanese, irrespective of political leanings. France almost certainly retreated because Washington did not respond to the French foreign minister's plea for support. Nonetheless, France was the only foreign power to provide at least some help. Seriously injured Lebanese from both parts of Beirut were evacuated on French ships, and French oil supplies enabled Lebanon's power station to restore electricity.[10]

Despite American reluctance, France finally raised the issue of Lebanon in the UN Security Council. It was supported by the USSR, which let its disquiet about Syria's actions in Lebanon be known. The Security Council voted unanimously to instruct the Secretary-General, Pérez de Cuéllar, to establish 'contact with the different parties', to call for a cease-fire and to support the mediation of the Arab League. All in all, international reaction amounted to humanitarian aid from the former mandatory and offers of mediation from the Arab League and the United Nations. That could not impress Syria.

Syria alone was prepared, and determined, to use military force to pursue its political goals in Lebanon, and was, as always since it first intervened in Lebanon, in a position to do so at minimum cost to itself. Fighting has always taken place on Lebanese territory; no Syrian adversary has been strong enough to carry it into Syria. The Syrian Army has learnt from experience not to risk potentially costly mobile warfare. The war was one of bombardment. Syria risked the lives of a few soldiers, its opponents, though, risked the lives of the civilian population on both

---

[6] President Bush declared that there was no spectacular plan to bring peace to Lebanon.

[7] In a speech on American Middle-East policies to the Institut Français des Relations Internationales in April 1989 Murphy did not even mention Lebanon.

[8] Deniau tried to elicit greater involvement from the USA, in vain. Embittered, he pointed out that Syria tolerated the cultivation of opium poppies and the training of terrorists in the Bekaa Valley, practices the USA readily condemned elsewhere in the world.

[9] By Dumas, the Foreign Minister, and Kouchner, Secretary of State. Premier Rocard declared that France favoured the withdrawal of Syrian troops from Lebanon, but did not intend to go to war with Syria.

[10] The Federal Republic of Germany voted for a resolution of the European Council of Ministers that called for the withdrawal of all non-Lebanese troops from Lebanon. As a practical measure it continued its development aid projects in Syria.

sides of the front as well as what was left of the country's infrastructure. Syria could practise a 'scorched earth policy', a policy of scorched Lebanese earth. Arnold Hottinger wrote of 'General Aoun's gamble with death'.[11] In his view, Aoun speculated that reports of killing in Lebanon would provoke an international outcry and gain him international support. If indeed this was Aoun's 'gamble', it soon seemed that he had lost.[12]

The international outcry was subdued: repetition robs even horror stories of their news value. By April, the first cracks had appeared in the wall of political support for General Aoun. Some Christian politicians started wondering aloud whether it might not be wiser to accept the election of a pro-Syrian president, such as Franjieh or Daher, and thereby preserve the Lebanese state, albeit under Syrian hegemony, and hope for better times. Others accused Aoun of wanting to sacrifice Lebanese Christians to liberate the Lebanese Muslims; the latter should liberate themselves — a new variation on the argument for partition. Twenty-three Christian deputies conferred at the seat of the Maronite Patriarch and called for a ceasefire. They declared that 'to restore peace' they were ready to meet 'all parties and authorities concerned'.[13] The Maronite Patriarch remarked that the country had to be liberated by reason and dialogue. The deputies' initiative also provoked heavy protest. Thousands of young people demonstrated against the deputies and against the Patriarch, a novelty in the history of Christian Lebanon. Two opposed bodies of opinion emerged in the Christian enclave. One held that losses were already so high and the prospects of success were so slight that there was no point to further fighting. The other could not conceive of simply writing off these losses and returning to the status quo ante; for them there was no alternative to soldiering on.

Aoun disregarded the sceptical voices among the traditional politicians and religious hierarchy; for him there was no turning back. His strongest support came from the youth of the enclave, to whom he appealed with increasingly populist slogans: 'You are the liberation generation, you are the nation and the national will ... Tell the deputies you didn't elect them, so they've got no right to speak for you ... Tell the Church the reason you're here is to speak the truth ... The state is not the people; the people are the state.' His tone towards the West was also popular. 'Food parcels aren't enough, we want our political rights to be

---

[11] *Neue Zürcher Zeitung*, April 7th, 1989; similarly Joseph Maila, *Esprit* 150/5 (1989), p. 119: 'Il semble que le général Aoun mise sur une intervention des Puissances en faveur d'une internationalisation de la crise'.

[12] See Anders Andreas Rieck, 'Syriens beharrliche Strategie im Libanon', *Frankfurter Allgemeine Zeitung*, September 20th, 1989: 'His [Aoun's] most manifest failure was the United States. In contrast to 1982/3, it now seemed inclined to accept Lebanon as a Syrian sphere of influence, as a trade-off for Syrian compromise on Israel.'

[13] For the text of the declaration, see *Les Cahiers de l'Orient* 14 (1989), pp. 100f.

respected.' In April there was a youth demonstration in front of the American embassy to protest against 'the silence of the so-called democratic states concerning Syrian terrorism'.

Aoun may have got some sympathy outside the Christian enclave, but no support. The assassination of the Sunni Mufti of the Lebanese Republic, Sheikh Hassan Khaled, was understood as a warning to all prepared to meet or cooperate with Aoun: ever since the abortive presidential election the Mufti had been untiring in his efforts to mediate between the Aoun and Hoss governments. Claiming to be poorly armed, the predominantly Muslim units of the Lebanese Army did not support the Syrians and their allied militias against the enclave. But nor did they respond to the General's appeal to side with him in his war of liberation.

At the end of April Aoun showed himself to be more conciliatory. When an extraordinary meeting of the Arab League in Tunis called for a cease-fire, the lifting of the blockade of all ports, the airport and all roads, and the despatch of Arab observers to supervise the cease-fire, Aoun agreed. In other words, he would reverse his measures against the militias' illegal ports, that is, those measures that had precipitated the latest confrontation. On May 2nd, he gave his 'war of liberation' a new interpretation. Henceforth, it would be pursued by 'diplomatic means'.

The Syrian troops and their allies preferred less diplomatic means. For a few days they observed the cease-fire proclaimed by the Arab League. On May 2nd, they resumed their bombardment of the enclave; within a week it was as intense as ever.

## Mediators

The Arab League was not prepared to accept the Syrian affront. France and the USSR urged it to do something. The Arab summit conference in Casablanca opened on May 23rd, 1989. It agreed to appoint three heads of state, the kings of Saudi Arabia and Morocco and the president of Algeria, to attend to the Lebanese crisis, and laid down precise objectives. This 'troika', as the media dubbed it, was to convene the Lebanese parliament within six months, so that it could introduce political reforms, elect a president, form a government of national unity and 'restore the sovereignty of Lebanon over all its territory'. The resolution of Casablanca neither mentioned Syria by name nor condemned it,[14] but its resolution on Lebanese independence was a clear stand against what a number of Arab governments regarded as Syrian intentions. The troika's mandate to prepare a comprehensive settlement of Lebanon's domestic and foreign political problems

---

[14] For the text of the resolution, see *Les Cahiers de l'Orient* 14 (1989), p. 107.

was in effect the Arabization of the Lebanon question. Aoun's 'no-turning-back' policy appeared to be bearing fruit.

The troika went to work quickly. It established a general secretariat in Jedda, headed by the deputy Secretary-General of the League, the Algerian Lakhdar Ibrahimi. Ibrahimi was even more explicit than the summit conference. The troika's objective was not only to lift the blockade, but 'to liberate Lebanon from all regional hegemony and restore its national sovereignty'. The troika issued ultimatums to Syria and Iraq, the one to observe the cease-fire, the other to cease supplying Aoun and the Lebanese Forces with arms. Ibrahimi's negotiations with the conflicting Lebanese factions made rapid progress towards a compromise on internal reform. But Syria proved far more intractable in talks on restoring Lebanese sovereignty. To speed up matters, at the end of May the three heads of state invited the Lebanese parliament to convene outside Lebanon and prepare a document on national reconciliation.

Syria's reaction to these initiatives was to renew its bombardment of the Christian enclave and tighten the blockade. For the first time, Syrian warships, some equipped with new radar-controlled missiles, started patrolling the Lebanese coast to intercept sea traffic with the enclave. They sank a Maltese tanker and generally enforced the blockade more effectively. On June 5th, Presidents Gorbachev and Mitterand released a joint declaration welcoming the troika's efforts. The troika continued to negotiate, but encountered stubborn resistance from Syria. Every time an emissary visited Damascus or Beirut, every time the troika's foreign ministers met, Syria intensified its bombardments in Lebanon.

On July 31st, the troika announced that its efforts had failed and blamed the Syrian government in language unusually clear for Arab diplomatic documents. Its report[15] stressed the broad agreement between the Lebanese interlocutors on all important questions. All desired peace and coexistence, the overwhelming majority agreed to political reforms, to reactivating the offices and institutions of state — including presidential elections — and consented to parliament convening outside Lebanon. The Lebanese factions could not agree on the conditions of a cease-fire. The report holds Syria partly responsible: 'In spite of their promise to use their influence to open traffic routes and communications, the Syrians have done nothing in this regard; on the contrary, the sea blockade was maintained and violent actions increased.'

The report records serious differences of opinion between the troika and Syria on the question of Lebanese sovereignty and future Syro-Lebanese relations. The troika had proposed concentrating Syrian troops in the Bekaa Valley after a mutually acceptable interim period. Under the troika's aegis, Syria and Lebanon

---

[15] For the full text, see *Les Cahiers de l'Orient* 15 (1989), pp. 61–82.

would conclude a security treaty that would regulate matters of bases, troop strength and duration of stay. Syria rejected both proposals. President Assad himself had objected to Syrian troops being mentioned at all on the grounds that Syria was not an occupying power that had to be forced to withdraw. He also rejected any role for the troika in any treaty between Syria and Lebanon. Subsequently, the Syrian president refused to discuss these contentious issues and delegated further talks to his foreign minister. These too were inconclusive. 'In summary, our Syrian brothers have not changed their position.' The troika's overall conclusion was sober: 'In our view, the main obstruction was the differences in opinion between the Committee, on the one hand, and Syria, on the other hand, over extending sovereignty ...; because of the Syrian views, the others parts of the document of agreement cannot be realized either, as the document has been conceived as an indivisible whole.'

The Arab League's peace initiative had been frustrated, not by political differences between the Lebanese, but by the question of whether Lebanon should survive as an independent country. Syrian aims were now even clearer than they had been at the signing of the Militia Agreement of Damascus in 1985: Syrian troops to be stationed in Lebanon indefinitely and a treaty to be drawn up between Syria and Lebanon on 'special and privileged relations ... in all fields: politics, security, economics and others', without Arab mediation.

The Syrian government registered its disapproval of the troika's unequivocal report unofficially in a thirty-six hour bombardment of Beirut, and officially in a statement by the foreign minister: 'The Syrian Army will remain in Lebanon to continue its national mission and to defend the honour and dignity of the Lebanese people.'

On August 13th, 1989, Druze and Palestinian militiamen, supported by Syrian troops, attacked Souk al-Gharb. They tried to break through the positions of the Lebanese Army, apparently with the aim of advancing on the presidential palace at Baabda. After five hours of close combat, the Lebanese soldiers managed to beat off the attack. After this defeat, Druze and Syrians resumed their routine 'trench warfare' at artillery and rocket range.

The international reaction to these events was less equivocal than in previous months. Iraq called for another Arab summit. Jordan and the PLO demanded the withdrawal of Syrian troops, Saudi Arabia and the states of the European Community wanted a cease-fire. The Pope spoke of genocide in Lebanon. Earlier, on July 15th, the Security Council of the United Nations had called for a cease-fire and commended the efforts of the troika. Four days afterwards France had despatched an aircraft carrier, a frigate and a transporter equipped with landing craft to the Lebanese coast. Mitterand declared that the independence of Lebanon was under threat and had to be protected — but that the French fleet was being sent for humanitarian, not military purposes.[16]

Meanwhile, the obstruction and blockade continued. By the end of August, the four-and-a-half month confrontation had cost 1,000 lives and many more had been injured. One hundred and twenty factories had been destroyed, 400 damaged. Hundreds of thousands of Beirutis from both halves of the city had fled to other parts of the country, or abroad.

On September 7th, 1989, the situation took a surprising turn. The Arab troika resumed its work 'in response to the situation in Lebanon and the many Lebanese, Arab and international appeals'. On September 13th, it presented new proposals. Apart from a cease-fire with immediate effect and an end to the blockade, the Lebanese parliament should meet in Saudi Arabia on September 30th to discuss a document on national reconciliation prepared by the troika. This time the troika was successful. Within a few days the fighting and shooting had ceased, and ports, airport and the checkpoints between East and West Beirut were re-opened. France congratulated the troika and withdrew its fleet. The Lebanese pound rose against the dollar.

How can this sudden success be explained? Strong international protest had underlined Syria's isolation, which undoubtedly influenced the Syrian government.[17] More importantly, though, the troika had gone a long way towards accommodating Syrian views.

Its first concession was the creation of a security committee, to stop and search all ships approaching Lebanon for weapons obviously intended for Aoun. Ships carrying weapons were to be turned away. Land routes — along which Syrian supplies were sent — would not be patrolled. Further concessions were contained in the document on national reconciliation[18] presented to the Lebanese parliament. Initially, the troika had proposed a partial Syrian withdrawal after six months; the new document proposed two years' grace. Before this period began, certain conditions had to be met: the election of a new president, the formation of a government of national unity and the passage of constitutional reforms. All three were

---

[16] Assessments of what the French naval presence actually achieved vary. John Kelly, American Under-Secretary for Middle Eastern affairs, took the view that the fleet satisfied emotional and humanitarian needs but was inadequate for any military action. See *Les Cahiers de l'Orient* 15 (1989), p. 56. For a different view, see Anders Andreas Rieck, 'Syriens beharrliche Strategie im Libanon', *Frankfurter Allgemeine Zeitung*, July 29th, 1989: 'sending its fleet deterred the Syrians from drastic action in August'. The aircraft carrier Foch had Super-etendards armed with Exocet missiles on board. A marginal deterrence cannot be excluded — Syrian air-attacks, for instance. On the other hand, Syrian bombardments were no less heavy after the appearance of the French navy than before.

[17] The Soviet ambassador in Damascus issued a statement that the USSR intended to reduce its military aid to Syria.

[18] For the complete text, see *Les Cahiers de l'Orient* 15 (1989), pp. 83–91.

measures the Syrian government could influence or hinder. After the two years, Syrian troops would be stationed not only in the Bekaa Valley, as initially proposed, but also 'at the entrance to the western Bekaa from Dahr al-Baidar to a line running from Hammana along the Mdeirej ridge to Ain Dara, i.e., deep in the Lebanon Mountains, 'as well as at other points', which left all options open. Troop strength and duration should be settled by the Syrian and Lebanese governments; the troika would be willing 'to assist both states in this matter, if they so desire'. In effect, this left Arab mediation in matters of security to the whim of the Syrian government. There was no longer any mention of a role for the troika in Syro-Lebanese treaties governing 'privileged relations' in other fields. In a nutshell, the troika's new document presented compromise formulae that met Syrian demands on all previously contentious issues.

President Chadli of Algeria explained how and why it came to this.[19] Whereas one section of the Lebanese demanded the withdrawal of Syrians, the other opposed it. Because some Arab states were strongly in favour of withdrawal, the troika had initially made any settlement conditional on Syrian withdrawal. This, in turn, had displeased the Syrians, who rejected it. Thereupon, the troika had broken off its mediation. It had resumed it at the request of Arab and other states. The question then was whether Syrian withdrawal was indeed a prerequisite for an internal political settlement in Lebanon. It was doubtful whether any Lebanese force had both the power to guarantee security and the confidence of all Lebanese. Therefore, the troika had decided to deal with internal Lebanese issues first and treat the Syrian withdrawal as the last stage of any settlement. However, the troika put itself under obligation to the Lebanese to support them on the issue of withdrawal, but only when the conditions of internal reconciliation had been fulfilled. In short: the troika had abandoned its original linkage between internal Lebanese reconciliation and Syrian withdrawal because the Syrians rejected this linkage and had the strength to get their way.

Syria had good reasons to suspend the fighting — which it could resume at any time — and wait to see what the proposed parliamentary conclave produced.

It was far more difficult for General Aoun to accept the troika's new proposals. He had achieved something. For the first time in years the Arab League was making a serious effort to resolve the crisis in Lebanon. Parliament was going to meet at a neutral location, which raised the possibility of restoring the institutions of state. Had Aoun not insisted there was 'no turning back' this would never have happened. But he was no closer to liberating the country than when he proclaimed this goal. On the contrary, unless the troika's proposals were amended, parliament might accept, and the Arab League recognize, Syrian occupation for, in effect, an

---

[19] *L'Orient-Le Jour*, October 3rd, 1989.

undefined period. This would legalize Syrian ascendancy in Lebanon. Yet Aoun had little choice but to give the deputies a chance. After months of heavy fighting, the population longed for peace. Diplomatic pressure, even from foreign governments that approved of his stand, was enormous. He accepted, exhorting the deputies to insist on a fixed and unequivocal timetable for Syrian withdrawal.

Aoun's was not the only pressure on the deputies. The Shi`i militias made it clear that they were not interested in constitutional compromise. They wanted nothing less than one man one vote. The Druze militia announced that after years of sacrifice, tinkering with the old political system was not enough.

Those who dared to question the Syrian position on Lebanon were forewarned. The Sunni deputy for the Bekaa, Nazem Kadri, canvassed among his colleagues for Syrian withdrawal from the Bekaa on the ground that this region also belonged to Lebanon.[20] Ten days before the conclave he was murdered.

## Taif: The hour of the foxes

On October 1st, 1989, the Saudi foreign minister opened the conclave of Lebanese deputies in Taif in Saudi Arabia. The keynote of his address was 'failure is forbidden'. The objective was reconciliation and peace. If achieved, Syrian troops would have no grounds to remain. Saudi Arabia would act as 'moral guarantor' that once the Lebanese parties were agreed and reconciled the Syrian withdrawal would begin.[21] The troika had good reasons to entrust this task to the deputies. In 1985 the militias' attempt at an accord, the Militia Agreement of Damascus, had failed. There was no longer a president, and neither of the two governments was representative. The only constitutional organ left whose legitimacy was not in doubt was the Chamber of Deputies. Sixty-two deputies had come to Taif from Lebanon or from exile in France, Switzerland and Iraq. One half were Christians, the other half Muslims. The former speaker of parliament, Husseini, acted as chairman.

Conclave is the apposite term.[22] In Taif the deputies were received royally, and immediately isolated. Journalists, staff and advisers were kept away from them; their only contact with the outside world was by telephone. The foreign ministers of the troika attended the deliberations from start to finish. A three-day conclave had been planned; it lasted twenty-three days. The veterans of pre-war Lebanese politics knew that this was their first opportunity in many years decisively to

---

[20] Statement of Deputy Abdel Magid al-Rafii during the Taif conclave.
[21] Prince Saud al-Faisal assured the deputies that Syria would not agree to a withdrawal in writing, as this would give the impression it had backed down to Aoun. He affirmed — as had President Chadli before him — that the troika, in particular Saudi Arabia, would give Lebanon their full support should Syria create difficulties; *L'Orient-Le Jour*, October 3rd, 1989.
[22] The account that follows is reconstructed from interviews with a number of Lebanese deputies who wish to remain anonymous. They were conducted between December 1989 and February 1990.

influence Lebanese politics, and grasped it. The deliberations opened with a general debate, trenchant expressions of all the differing views on domestic and foreign policy. The deputies from the Christian enclave demanded a guarantee of linkage between political reforms and the withdrawal of the Syrian Army. Muslim deputies rejected even a partial withdrawal before agreement was reached on constitutional reform and army reorganization, and before southern Lebanon was liberated from Israeli occupation. Different groups expected different things from constitutional reform. The deputies of the Lebanese Front wanted to retain the strong executive of the existing Constitution. Deputies close to Jumblatt demanded that all real power should be vested in the government. A number of deputies wanted to replace proportional confessional representation with one man one vote. But communal interests soon came to the fore. The Sunnis wanted a more powerful premier, the Shi`is a powerful speaker of the chamber of deputies, and the only surviving Druze deputy wanted a senate with a Druze speaker. Initially, agreement had seemed impossible, but gradually it became evident that only a small minority wanted really radical political change; a large majority would accept limited reforms.

A committee of seventeen, reflecting as usual communal strengths, was chosen to draft an outline for constitutional reform. As working papers, they had a document from the troika as well as proposals that Husseini and the Maronite Patriarch had agreed on in advance. What emerged was a complete revision of the constitutional section of the 'document of national reconciliation'. In the words of one committee member, 'everyone was dissatisfied, but almost everyone found it acceptable'.

The document[23] opens with statements of principle on the character and identity of Lebanon:

> A sovereign, free and independent nation, a definitive fatherland for all its sons in the unity of country, people and institutions, within the borders laid down in the Lebanese Constitution and internationally recognized.
> Lebanon is an Arab country, both by kinship and identity ... Lebanon is a democratic and parliamentary republic, founded on the principles of respect for civil liberties, for freedom of expression and of religion, and of equal rights and duties for all citizens without distinction. All power and sovereignty derives from the people; they exercise their rights through the

[23] For the full text see *L'Orient-Le Jour*, October 24th, 1989 and 'L'Accord de Taëf, Document d'entente pour le Liban', *Les Cahiers d'Orient* 16–17/1 (1990), pp. 115–28. This volume also contains a detailed critical appraisal by Joseph Maila, 'Le "Document d'Entente Nationale": Un commmentaire', pp. 135–217.

constitutional institutions. The system is based on the principle of the division of powers.

These statements are both an unequivocal rejection of dependence in any form, of non-democratic and non-secular forms of government and of partition, and a profession of loyalty to the National Pact of 1943. Indeed, the general principle implicit in the National Pact is explicitly stated: Lebanon is an Arab country without any qualification, and it is a definitive fatherland.

This is followed by statements on the economic and social order: 'The economy is a free enterprise system based on individual initiative and private property. The balanced development of the regions ... is a pillar of the state and its stability. The state must try to establish full social justice through financial, economic and social reforms.' In this respect the document goes far beyond the Constitution. It postulates a free-market economy in conjunction with adequate state welfare, and gives particular weight to reducing the disparities between living conditions in different parts of the country. Probably the most important statement in the document reads: 'Power cannot be recognized as lawful unless it is in agreement with the pact of coexistence.'

The National Pact of 1943 was an unwritten agreement. In the Taif Agreement, coexistence between the religious communities is solemnly affirmed, declared the foundation of Lebanese legality and, more explicitly than ever before, recognized as the both the state's raison d'étre and its objective. What the document does change is the existing formula for the division of power. The constitution of parliament would be reformed. 'While honouring the principles of coexistence', a new electoral law would have to be drawn up. So long as parliament did not pass an electoral law that 'transcends the confessional system', the seats in the chamber of deputies 'will be distributed as follows: the same number for Christians and Muslims, with proportional representation for the communities within each group and proportional representation between the regions'. Thus, parity would replace the Christians' existing numerical superiority of 6:5. Provision was also made for future developments. 'The first time a non-confessional parliament is elected' a senate would have to be created that represents 'all spiritual families', with powers restricted 'to matters of vital concern'. This is the outline of a bicameral system: a chamber of deputies without confessional proportionality or parity, and a senate that preserves representation by religious community for matters of fundamental importance. The new parliament with equal group representation would have to give its consent to a bicameral system.

Two provisions for the period of transition were particularly controversial in Taif: the increase in the number of seats in parliament, and the right of a government of national unity to appoint deputies to new as well as to vacant seats. To achieve parity between Christians and Muslims the number of seats had to be changed. The troika had proposed raising it from 99 to 128. The majority in Taif vehemently opposed this. They feared this would enable too many militia leaders and warlords — and Syrian clients — to enter parliament, especially if seats were filled by appointment.[24] Some deputies objected to appointment, even as a one-off measure, on principle. Finally, a compromise was reached. As the situation in the country rendered imminent elections unlikely, the deputies accepted appointment and raised the number of parliamentary seats to 108, the minimum number needed to create parity without depriving the Christians of existing seats.

The reforms the conclave decided for the executive went even further than those for the legislature. Although not expressly stated, the existing distribution of the major offices of state by community was retained: a Maronite president, a Sunni prime minister, a Shi`i speaker of the chamber of deputies and a cabinet with confessional parity. But their powers were modified.

The presidency was reduced to a largely ceremonial office. The president would no longer be the head of the executive, but 'head of state and symbol of unity'. He remained supreme commander of the army and chairman of the defence council, though bound by cabinet decisions. He would no longer regularly chair cabinet meetings, but only 'when he so wishes'; nor would he have a vote. He would have only a suspensive veto against cabinet decisions. He would nominate the prime minister only after 'obligatory consultations' with the deputies, and would not be able to dismiss him.

By contrast, the powers of the prime minister were considerably increased. Henceforth, he would chair cabinet meetings, be 'responsible for implementing the general policies of the council of ministers' and sign all decrees except the one appointing him. He could be dismissed only by parliament.

The speaker of the chamber of deputies also gained powers. His term of office was extended from one year to a full parliament.[25] Furthermore, as chairman ex officio at the president's 'obligatory consultations' with the deputies prior to nominating a prime minister, he would, as in the election of the president, have the role of 'kingmaker'.

'Executive power resides in the Council of Ministers.' The most significant increase in power was reserved to the government as a collective body. Whereas previously it shared the right to introduce bills with the president, in future this would be its exclusive prerogative. It would oversee the implementation of laws, control the administration and appoint civil servants. As symbolic expression of

---

[24] These fears were fuelled by the 1985 Militia Agreement of Damascus, which proposed raising the number of seats to no less than 198.

[25] The speaker can be dismissed after two years, but only by a two-thirds majority.

the new importance of the council of ministers, a separate seat of government — distinct from those of the president and the prime minister — would be created. As a rule, cabinet decisions should be taken 'by mutual agreement'.[26] Should this prove impossible, it would be necessary to vote. 'Issues of vital concern' would require a two-thirds majority. These 'vital issues' were defined as: general mobilization, declaration of war and conclusion of peace, international treaties, the budget, long-term development plans, the appointment of senior civil servants,[27] administrative reform, the dissolution of parliament, the electoral law, the law on nationality, laws on personal status and the dismissal of ministers. If more than one-third of the cabinet resigned, the government would be deemed to have resigned.[28] The intention of these provisions as a whole was to ensure the government functioned as a collective executive in accordance with the principles of consociation.

The reforms agreed to in Taif altered both the powers of the most important organs of state and, implicitly, the division of power between the communities. Parliament became more powerful, and was constituted on parity. The speaker of parliament and the head of government gained additional powers at the expense of the head of state: the highest political representatives of the Shi`is and Sunnis became more influential than that of the Maronites, who retained only symbolic precedence. A collective organ drawn from all communities and constrained by institutional provisions to decisions by consensus replaced the Maronite-Sunni duumvirate as the centre of power: the cabinet became the strongest constitutional organ. The fundamental difference between the new coexistence pact of Taif and the National Pact of 1943 lay in the distribution of power. The old pact was a matter between two communities, the new one was between all communities on the basis of parity between Christians and Muslims.

The Taif Agreement records the 'renewal of the contract between the Lebanese communities'.[29] The statement elsewhere in the document that 'the abolition of confessionalism' is 'a vital national objective' is an apparent contradiction. However, practical measures proposed to this latter purpose are tentative: a 'national council' chaired by the president and including the prime minister, the speaker of parliament and 'eminent people in the socio-political, cultural and academic fields'. The council's task is 'to abolish confessionalism in stages'.

---

[26] The Arab text uses the word tawafuqiyyan, which, in modern Arab political science is the equivalent of 'concordance', or the 'amicabilis compositio' of the Peace of Westphalia.

[27] Category I under the Lebanese Civil Service Law, roughly equivalent to politically appointed civil servants or government officials.

[28] The cabinet also resigns on the election of the president, the opening of a new parliament and the resignation or death of the prime minister.

[29] Maila, 'Document d'Entente Nationale', p. 175.

However, it does not have a timetable. Nor is there a timetable for the introduction of a bicameral system, a system which, contrary to 'abolishing confessionalism', i.e., communal representation, would preserve it in a senate.

Two concrete measures should take effect during a 'transitional period'. Firstly, appointment by communal representation in the lower and middle-level ranks of the civil service would be abolished, whereas parity between Christians and Muslims in the senior ranks, as well as among army officers, was reaffirmed. Secondly, identity cards would in future not record communal affiliation or religion.[30]

Joseph Maila has pertinently described the idea of 'abolishing confessionalism' as 'a Utopia typical of multi-communal societies'.[31] As he points out, this Utopia — both the hope of its gradual realization and the absence of any timetable — was already present in Riad Solh's famous speech of October 7th, 1943, in which he explained the National Pact. Forty-six years later the conclave of Taif still clung to this Utopia, and adjourned its realization ad Calendas Libanicas. Both in 1943 and in 1989 an 'interim' proved the suitable form of compromise between dream and socio-political reality.

As for as the domestic section of the Taif Agreement, the conclave was a moment of glory for the 'foxes' of Lebanese politics. Once again, realism, tolerance and an ability to compromise proved to be the strongest qualities of the old, elected political class. The Christian deputies were prepared to abandon untenable positions, and their Muslim colleagues avoided immoderate demands. The symbolic privileges of the Christians had long had little substance, and were abolished. The old proportionality had become questionable, based as it was on insubstantial demographic or pseudo-demographic arguments. It was replaced by a parity based on the existence of two religious groups.

These reforms had their weak points. Saudi support for the Lebanese Sunnis was particularly telling in Taif. The community obtained a share of power out of proportion to its real social importance. Along the broad divide, the Maronite presidency lost power, whereas the Sunni premiership gained greatly and the Shi`i speakership a little less so. But these shifts are qualified by the enormous increase in the powers of the collective cabinet representing all communities.

Finally, decisions to introduce a social market system and to pursue a regionally balanced development policy showed that the deputies had learnt from previous mistakes. All in all, the Taif decisions on domestic politics are a remark-

---

[30] The importance of this reform must be seen against the background of the countless 'identity-card murders' in the first years of the war.

[31] Maila, 'Document d'Entente Nationale', p. 176.

able achievement: a realistic attempt with broad support to regulate that part of the Lebanese conflict that was a civil war.

The conclave at Taif dealt not only with internal Lebanese conflicts. It also had to consider the question of military and political relations between Lebanon and Syria. It soon became clear that on this matter there was little for the deputies to negotiate. Before the conclave the troika had discussed the paragraphs in question word for word with the Syrian government. Where opinions had differed, the Syrian view had ultimately prevailed. The foreign ministers of the troika assured the deputies that they were not in a position to achieve more. Thus, as far as the section of the document dealing with international relations was concerned, the conclave had to decide on the text as it stood.

The text sanctioned the role of the Syrian Army as 'helping the Lebanese government to restore its authority', for a period of two years after the domestic reforms had been introduced; gave legal recognition to the stationing of Syrian troops in the Bekaa, in the mountains and 'in other places' for an indefinite period that the Syrian and Lebanese governments would determine at a later stage without the mediation of the troika; formally 'thanked' the Syrian Army for its assistance; and committed Lebanon and Syria to bilateral treaties establishing 'privileged relationships in all fields'.

It was not for the deputies to negotiate these issues: they could either accept or reject this diktat. The likely consequence of rejection was the immediate resumption of shelling. Nonetheless, many, especially Christian, deputies insisted on more precise conditions for Syrian withdrawal. Joseph Skaff, in particular, a Greek Catholic deputy for Zahle, and thus directly affected by the Syrian presence, demanded improvements to the text with great pertinacity. The Saudi foreign minister travelled to Damascus to make a last attempt. After two meetings with President Assad, the second lasting six hours, he returned with marginal concessions. Assad had consented to a parliament of 108 instead of 128 deputies, a matter of domestic Lebanese politics. As for the 'Syrian' section of the document, it might include the empty phrase 'within the limits of each country's sovereignty and independence', a concession not without irony.

Prince Saud al-Faisal told the deputies they had to decide; the text as it stood was their last chance. He reminded them of the rejection of the United Nations plan for the partition of Palestine in 1947; the Palestinians were still searching for a bit of land. The Lebanese, too, were in danger of becoming a homeless people. Should the war be resumed, the consequence would be devastation and emigration. 'We have been unable to get anything better from the Syrians, and we cannot do any more.' The members of the troika then tried to point out the advantages of the proposed settlement. There was nothing to prevent the Lebanese stationing more soldiers in the Bekaa than the Syrians. Then Syria would no longer have any reason to remain in Lebanon. And when Syria withdrew its troops, Israel could be induced to withdraw. This was the only way to break the Israeli-Syrian habit of using the other's presence in Lebanon to justify its own. The Saudi foreign minister concluded — in the presence of his monarch and the Moroccan and Algerian foreign ministers — with a promise of aid for Lebanon, if the document was accepted.

After lengthy vacillation, a majority emerged in favour of accepting the fait accompli. One deputy's reasoning will have held for many: 'It's not a question of deciding whether the Syrians invade or not. They're already there; they control 80 per cent of the country and they control some militias. Compared with that, the Agreement is a serious attempt to get rid of them. They've agreed to disarm the militias within six months, and they've accepted the principle of withdrawal in two phases. For the first time the Arabs are on our side. I see the risks; I don't see the Agreement as an ideal solution, but it's the best we can get at present. Compared with a hopeless military struggle, compromise is a better solution.'

On the twenty-third day of consultations the conclave voted. Fifty-six of sixty-two deputies were in favour; two were in favour on condition that a date was set for Syrian withdrawal; three put on record that they favoured the complete abolition of confessionalism. Four deputies abstained. The new coexistence pact was passed, and, by the same token, the Syrian occupation was declared legal.

## Presidential election and assassination

The results of the Taif conclave found broad international approval. The United Nations Security Council, the USA, the states of the European Community, Egypt and even Iraq welcomed them as a chance to end to war in Lebanon.

The troika took immediate steps to put the agreement into effect. It asked the speaker of the chamber of deputies to summon the Lebanese parliament in Beirut on November 7th officially to accept the Agreement at a properly constituted sitting and to elect a president. Ibrahimi flew to Beirut to get Aoun to agree.

However, Aoun refused. He declared that he had no difficulties with the political reforms, though he would have preferred something more radical. But it was impossible for him to consent to legalizing the Syrian presence in Lebanon because that meant relinquishing Lebanese independence. The deputies had the right to pass reforms, but no constitutional powers to conclude international treaties, and certainly none to surrender the sovereignty of the country. Should they persist in their course, he would be forced to dissolve parliament.

Aoun's radical refusal soon isolated him from the great majority of Lebanese political leaders. The deputies stood by their decision. The Maronite Patriarch celebrated a Te Deum, and defended the deputies.[32] The Lebanese Forces discreetly indicated acceptance of the Taif Agreement. For the first time in months it seemed they had a chance of escaping from Aoun's shadow and re-establishing their influence in the Christian heartland.

But Aoun was not isolated among the Christian population. Almost all followed the call for a general strike against the decisions of Taif. Tens of thousands attended a demonstration in front of the presidential palace at Baabda and acclaimed Aoun. This was a new phenomenon. For the first time in Lebanon's history a large body of Christians no longer heeded their traditional political and spiritual leaders' calls for moderation, but were prepared to support the man who took a clear stand in simple language.

Aoun had the right personality for this mass phenomenon. He came from farming stock and had made good by his own efforts. He was born in 1936, in Haret Hreik, at that time a small Maronite village on the southern edge of Beirut. The fate of this village, the first 'Christian pocket' overrun by the Palestinians in 1975, may well have conditioned his aversion to any military and political role for foreigners in Lebanon. His career is atypical of army officers. He first read law at the Jesuit University, intermittently interrupting his studies to earn enough money to continue. After graduation he entered the Military Academy, and was the best student of his year. His political preference was the Bloc National. Embittered by the army's ineffectualness when war broke out, he wanted to resign. Raymond Eddé advised him to stay. In 1976 he planned the attack on Tel al-Za`tar. Sarkis gave him the opportunity to build a new army unit of both Muslims and Christians. In 1983 and 1984 he commanded it in the fight for Souk al-Gharb. Afterwards there was broad political agreement to appoint him commander-in-chief of the army. His experience with his Muslim soldiers rendered him immune to ideas of Christian separatism and strengthened his Lebanese patriotism. A 'son of the people', who had struggled to build a successful career, shown personal courage under fire, had an affection for all Lebanon, liked talking but — in contrast to old-school politicians — always spoke his mind: it was an extraordinarily attractive mixture.

Convinced that the provisions on future Syro-Lebanese relations accepted in Taif would be fatal for Lebanon and encouraged by open mass support, Aoun crossed the Rubicon. On November 4th, 1989, by Decree 420, he dissolved parliament. 'The situation is comparable with that of de Gaulle and Pétain, the

---

[32] On this point he was in harmony with the Vatican, which was reported as taking the view that when faced with two evils one sometimes had to accept the lesser.

one the representative of the free France, the other of the occupied ... We will resist a treaty concluded under the shadow of occupation.' That Aoun's government was the lawful executive after the failure to elect a president in September 1988 is constitutionally virtually indisputable. The dissolution of parliament by an interim executive is anything but. Raymond Eddé thought it incontestable under Article 55 of the Lebanese Constitution;[33] he has referred to himself ever since as a 'former deputy'. The Speaker of parliament, Husseini, consulted the French constitutional lawyer Georges Vedel. Vedel came to a different conclusion. If the presidency is vacant, the government does exercise the executive functions of this office under Article 62 of the Constitution; but it may not dissolve parliament as this would prolong the interim. A dissolution of parliament by an interim government would leave the government as the only remaining constitutional organ, in flagrant violation of the fundamental principle of the division of powers.

Apart from the legal considerations, the wisdom of Aoun's step was questionable politically. Parliament was the only constitutional office recognized by all sides, and conditions in Lebanon at the end of 1989 made the prospect of elections illusory.[34]

Husseini ignored the decree of dissolution and convened parliament at the Koleyat air-force base in the extreme north of Lebanon, seven kilometres from the Syrian border. After the conclave, most Christian deputies had not returned to the area under Aoun's control but had gone to Paris so that Aoun could not prevent them from attending a sitting of parliament. Husseini flew to Paris and persuaded twenty-five of them to go to Koleyat, where they were taken in the private aircraft of the Lebanese millionaire Hariri. Deputies from West Beirut arrived by road. The fifty-eight deputies who came constituted a quorum and parliament convened on November 5th, 1989.

It re-elected Husseini as speaker and — the absent — Albert Moukheiber as his deputy. Then an official vote was taken on the Taif Agreement.[35] All the deputies

---

[33] If the Cabinet agrees and he gives reasons, the President of the Republic can dissolve the Chamber of Deputies before its legal term expires. In this event the electorate must be called upon in terms of Article 25, and the new chamber must convene fifteen days after the results of the election are announced. By Article 25, parliamentary elections must be held within three months of the dissolution of parliament. As Decree 420 of the Aoun government set January 1990 as the date for elections, and as Aoun gave his reasons for dissolving parliament, Eddé regarded the decree as constitutional.

[34] At the beginning of 1990 Aoun found himself forced to postpone the elections for an indefinite period. It proved impossible to organize elections even in those areas of Lebanon not occupied by foreign troops.

[35] The legality of this vote is disputable. Article 75 of the Lebanese Constitution reads: 'When the Chamber meets to elect the President of the Republic, it meets solely as an elective body and not as a consultative assembly. It must proceed to elect the Head of State without delay and discussion.' The vote on the Taif Agreement preceded the election of the president because the Muslim deputies had made their participation in the election conditional on the acceptance of the reforms.

present agreed to this procedure, though nine recorded objections. The election of the president followed immediately. René Moawad, Deputy for Zghorta, was elected on the second ballot with fifty-two votes and six abstentions.[36]

The fifty-four-year-old René Moawad came from one of the 'great families' of the Maronite north. A lawyer, Deputy since 1957, he epitomized the cultivated, astute *za`im* of the old school. As the mind behind innumerable political compromises, he was regarded as an ideal candidate. Neither he nor his supporters had taken part in the war, nor did he have a militia. He appealed to many Lebanese nationalists because he had voted for Bashir Gemayel in 1982. He was acceptable to the pro-Syrian forces because he had never left any doubt about his view that a settlement in Lebanon was only possible in agreement with Syria.

Numerous ambassadors had attended Moawad's election, which was welcomed by almost all Arab states, the USA, the USSR and France.[37] After well over a year, Lebanon again had an elected president, one who had not been elected under foreign coercion, but in a classic Lebanese compromise, a president of the 'foxes'.

This election would not have been possible without Aoun's obduracy. But Aoun's concern was not solely, or even mainly, a presidential election; he wanted a Syrian withdrawal. As the decisions at Taif had not attained this — in his view they legalized the Syrian presence — by his own logic he had to reject what his efforts had achieved. As he had dissolved parliament because it would put its seal of approval on the Taif Agreement, he did not recognize Moawad's election by this parliament. The election of Moawad, however, left him isolated. Previously he had enjoyed at least *de facto* recognition as one of two heads of government. Now in the eyes of most Arab and other governments he was simply a rebellious general. He might continue to compare himself with the de Gaulle of 1940, but unlike the latter, he did not have the support of a major power. Rather, he was a de Gaulle who ruled only Dunkirk. But he still had the support of the masses in the Christian enclave. On the evening the president was elected, demonstrators stormed the Maronite patriarchate in Bkirke, manhandled the Patriarch and forced him to kiss a photograph of Aoun. There were bomb attacks on the homes of numerous Christian deputies. Aoun expressed only equivocal disapproval of these attacks, and 'understanding for the anger of the people'. His statements became increasingly strident: 'I am the president of free and sovereign Lebanon. Those on the other side are collaborators. Together with the government, I

---

[36] On the first ballot Moawad had received thirty-five votes, George Saade, the president of the Kataib, sixteen and Elias Hrawi, deputy for Zahle, five. Suleiman Franjieh and Mikhail Daher, the Syrian candidate in 1988, withdrew their candidacies before the ballot.

[37] Iran's reaction was negative: Moawad's election 'reaffirmed the confessional system'. The Iraqi reaction was reserved: the situation in Lebanon remained complicated as long as the occupation by foreign troops, 'above all Syrian,' continued.

exercise the privileges of the president and my legitimacy comes from the people ... René Moawad is just a former deputy, that's all.'

Moawad adopted quite a different tone. He appealed to all Lebanese to join in creating peace. 'To bring reconciliation between Lebanese of different tendencies and orientations is the great challenge of my life. No one is excluded from this reconciliation, not even those who insist on excluding themselves.' The only demonstrations for the new president took place in his home town, Zghorta. But the Lebanese showed in other ways that they hoped he would succeed: there were traffic jams in Beirut — a sign of normalization — shops and restaurants were full and the dollar exchange rate rose from 534 to 420 Lebanese pounds.

Former president Helou and other Maronite notables tried to establish a dialogue between Moawad and Aoun. However, Aoun rejected all overtures. He called on the deputies to dissociate themselves from the decisions of Taif, promising, if they did so, to rescind his dissolution of parliament. Any Christian deputy who dared to join a government under Moawad and Hoss would lose his right to live in the free areas of the country.

Although Berri and Jumblatt were also opposed to Taif, though for other reasons than Aoun's, they recognized Moawad and declared themselves prepared to serve in the government. But Moawad was unable to persuade any representative Christian politicians to join his government of national unity. The idea of an interim government was broached. Moawad refused even to consider using force against Aoun and the area under his control: 'I want to win the east with dialogue, not by arms.'

The Syrian government had offered to help him 'eliminate the obstacle Aoun', and showed their annoyance at Moawad's persistence in reaching a compromise. A Syrian newspaper published a purported interview with Moawad. The Lebanese president was reported as saying what the Syrians would have liked to hear from him: 'The privileged relationship between Lebanon and Syria is based on historical and geographic circumstances ... on the bonds of kinship and on the common struggle against French colonialism ... Lebanon and Syria are one people in two states, part of one Arab nation dismembered by the colonial powers.'[38] The office of the president stated that he had given no interviews, nor had he made any statements.[39]

Tension was rising as Lebanon celebrated its forty-sixth Day of Independence on November 22nd, 1989. While Moawad was once again stressing the need to implement the decisions of Taif, Aoun was labelling the same decisions 'treason

---

[38] The Syrian newspaper *Thawra*, quoted in the Lebanese papers of November 8th, 1989.

[39] A few days later this occurrence was repeated in the form of an 'interview' with the wife of the Lebanese president. She likewise denied having given one.

and a failure'. As President Moawad was driving back home after the reception for the accredited ambassadors at the government house, a large bomb exploded along the route. Fourteen people were killed, among them the new president. The Syrian minister of defence accused Israel, Iraq and Aoun of having organized the assassination. East Beirut newspapers pointed out that the attack occurred in an area controlled exclusively by the Syrian Army. As in so many other earlier political murders in Lebanon, the identity of the murderers will probably never be known for certain. 'Cui bono?' may not help to pin down the perpetrators in a country in which many people are in the position to carry out such a deed, and many might be willing. But, as in the cases of the assassinations of Kamal Jumblatt, Bashir Gemayel, Mohammed Shukair, Hassan Khaled and Nazem Kadri, there was one clear winner: Syria. This became clear two days later.

## Syria's man as Lebanon's president

By Lebanese custom, a successor is not chosen until the predecessor has been buried. This period of respect was not observed after Moawad's assassination. On the night of November 22nd, Speaker Husseini went to Damascus to consult with the Syrian Vice-President, Khaddam. By next morning thirty-nine deputies had gathered in the Park Hotel in Chtaura, the headquarters of the Syrian military intelligence. Other deputies were once again flown in from Paris in Hariri's private aircraft. Parliament sat the next day, protected from journalists by a special unit of Syrian troops. The fifty-three deputies present were a quorum. Radio Damascus announced the result before the presidential election had taken place.[40] The only candidate was Elias Hrawi. He was elected on the second ballot by forty-seven votes, with five abstentions. Immediately afterwards parliament extended its own life for another four years. The new president called on the Lebanese 'to reflect, instead of letting themselves get mixed up in political adventures', to be realistic, 'instead of listening to slogans that turned dreams to nightmares and hopes to tears'.

Hrawi himself is undoubtedly a realist: by conviction and in his own interest he is Syria's man. For years he has championed the view that Lebanon must come to some arrangement with Syria. 'Under the present circumstances the shortest route is via Damascus. In international relations nothing is ever final. One can make treaties and modify them later.' Nor is Hrawi less Maronite than the Maronites of the Christian heartland, like Gemayel, or of the Christian north, like Moawad. But he is a Maronite of the Bekaa, which has been under Syrian control since 1976. As such he has no time for politics that neglect the interests of the Christian

---

[40] Reported in most Lebanese newspapers on November 25th, 1989.

periphery. The Lebanese Forces' expedition to Zahle in 1980/1 taught him how costly it can be for Christians to challenge Syria in this region. His convictions and experience dovetail with his interests. He is a large landowner, and his lands lie in the Bekaa. A son of the Syrian Vice-President, Khaddam, has an interest in his canning factory. His agribusiness exports mainly to the Arab world. In a nutshell: he has made a lot of money out of Syria, believes he can do political business with them, and is utterly convinced that at present any business or politics against Syrian interests is doomed. He has a strong aversion to what he regards as political adventurism. In his eyes Bashir Gemayel was an adventurer, and Michel Aoun is one too.

Hence, in contrast to Moawad, Hrawi was determined to deal quickly with Aoun, if necessary with the help of the Syrian Army. The day after his election he dismissed Aoun as commander-in-chief of the army and gave him forty-eight hours to leave the presidential palace at Baabda, or face the consequences. 'We have not been elected to start a new war. But should there be a new outbreak of violence, it will take only a few hours to deal with those who have no legitimacy. I am determined to rule from Baabda ... even if there is only one room left standing.' A military action that would destroy heavily fortified Baabda 'in a few hours' had to include the Syrian air force. But the ultimatum ran out without anything happening. A few hours after Hrawi had issued his threat, tens of thousands of people, a large proportion of them children and teenagers, gathered round the palace at Baabda. Tents were put up and a sit-in started that was to last weeks. Speakers, singers, poets and musicians entertained the crowds; political rallies in support of Aoun alternated with dancing. The permanent festival meant any air-attack would have been premeditated massacre.

Hrawi had to lower his sights. The Maronite Patriarch, no friend of Aoun's, advised against using force, as did the USA, the USSR, France and the Vatican. The commander of the Israeli air force warned Syria that sending in Syrian planes could lead to 'unfortunate confrontations' with Israeli planes, which regularly patrolled the Lebanese skies.[41] Moreover, Iraqi supplies of ground-to-air missiles enabled Aoun to strengthen the anti-aircraft defences around Baabda. Through all this, what Aoun's opponents called the 'Baabda carnival' went on. A spontaneous outpouring was now an organized event[42] and a means of political mobilization. Within a few weeks the initial demonstrations against the Taif decisions had developed into a broad pro-Aoun movement with strong elements of a personality

---

[41] By doing so, Israel reaffirmed that it considered Lebanese airspace as a 'Red Line' area it would not allow Syria to transgress. By contrast, Israel had not protested against the Syrian naval blockade of the Christian enclave.

[42] The schools in the enclave took it in turns to send delegations to Baabda.

cult.[43] A considerable part of the youth in the Christian enclave seemed to have found a common cause in rejection of the traditional parliamentary system and its representatives, in admiration for a political figure perceived as offering leadership for their time, and in an eagerness for all-Lebanese unity and liberation.[44] If Hrawi had intended to solve the 'Aoun problem' with force quickly, he had missed his opportunity. On December 14th, 1989, he declared that he had never given Aoun an ultimatum and did not contemplate a military attack on Baabda. He had other, more subtle means of achieving his end.

Immediately after the presidential election, Salim Hoss was asked to form a government. The Muslim ministers appointed by Hoss, including the militia leaders Berri and Jumblatt, assumed office, as did the Christian ministers from Syrian occupied areas. Two Christian ministers from the Christian enclave hesitated: Michel Sassine remained in Paris and Georges Saade, leader of the Kata'ib, vacillated between acceptance and refusal. It was a flawed version of the 'government of national unity' called for in the Taif Agreement. However, Hrawi and Hoss quickly exploited whatever opportunities the administrative apparatus offered to isolate Aoun further. Civil servants were ordered to leave ministries and other government offices located in the area under Aoun's control. Anyone who did not obey received no pay. A shake-up in the foreign ministry rid it of pro-Aoun diplomats. Finally, the government appointed a new commander-in-chief of the army, the Maronite general, Emile Lahoud. The new commander called on all officers and soldiers to accept his command. All this had few immediate consequences. But in the traditionally apolitical Lebanese officers' corps some began to think about where their loyalties lay.[45]

Aoun's most pressing problem arose from the Hoss government's instruction to the central bank to cease all payments to the army and civil service in the enclave. Aoun could retaliate by refusing to deposit state revenues collected in the enclave with the Central Bank, using them instead to pay the soldiers and civil servants under his authority. But state expenditure in the enclave, as in the rest of the country, had long exceeded state revenues. The budget deficit was financed by

---

[43] Popular chants included: 'We want to sacrifice ourselves body and soul for you, General' and 'We don't need God's help, we have our own help' (Aoun in Arabic means help).

[44] A survey of demonstrators in Baabda in early 1990 showed that 35 per cent were under 18 and a further 40 per cent between 19 and 39. Ninety-six per cent were for a united Lebanon, 95 per cent for direct election of the president, 85 per cent for a new electoral law and against the existing parties. Ninety-five per cent said they were against the Taif decisions. (The author thanks Professor Labaki for this information from a still unpublished survey.)

[45] On January 3rd, 1990 Aoun had three officers who had been negotiating with General Lahoud arrested for allegedly planning to place the Amchit garrison under Lahoud's command and advance southwards.

loans and the printing press. And only a government in charge of the Central Bank in West Beirut had these possibilities, i.e., Hrawi and Hoss, not Aoun.

Aoun's only way out of this dilemma was to increase state revenues in the enclave, at the expense of the Lebanese Forces, who had kept only part of their promise of February 1989 and still collected considerable amounts in 'taxes' and 'customs duties'. The militia was able to pay its civil and military personnel as well as its militiamen far better than Aoun could pay his civil servants, officers and soldiers. This situation had long been a thorn in Aoun's side. When the Central Bank stopped payment it became a matter of necessity to change it. The Hoss government's financial sanctions put Aoun on a collision course with the Lebanese Forces.

## War between the army and militia in the Christian heartland

This was not only a fight over money. A year earlier Aoun had launched his campaign to restore the authority of the state by clipping the wings of the Lebanese Forces. He had been only partially successful. Both the Lebanese Forces and Aoun knew that this had not settled the fundamental issue between them: Who was in charge, the state or the militia?

Aoun claimed to represent the state. The Lebanese Forces saw their right to existence in the defence of the 'Christian people', as their ideologues put it, or of the 'eastern regions', to use Samir Geagea's term. Aoun's ideal was the restoration of the centralized Lebanese state, Geagea's a loose federation with far-reaching autonomy for the Christian part. For him, his militia was the legitimate guardian of the interests of this semi-state. Aoun wanted to liberate the entire country; Geagea had always said that the Muslim Lebanese had to liberate themselves, if they so wished. In the meantime, all that mattered was the right to self-determination in the eastern regions.

Their different goals reflect their different assessments of the situation. Geagea saw no point in challenging superior Syrian power, and, accordingly, none in Aoun's war of liberation either. During the Syrians' war against the enclave, the Lebanese Forces had fought alongside the army because the survival of the region they regarded as their own was at stake. Geagea did not make a public statement for months. But once the immediate military threat to the Christian heartland receded, he saw no cause for unconditional solidarity with Aoun. The Kata'ib, in which the militia had been calling the shots for some years, was represented at Taif by its leader, Saade. On December 17th, Geagea broke his long silence to declare that Taif should be given a chance. Feelers were immediately put out among Hrawi and the Lebanese Forces. For Aoun this was tantamount to treason. Henceforth the conflict was not only economic but also political.

The rivalry was all the greater as the competition was for the hearts of the Christian population. Geagea's popularity was a shadow of that of Bashir Gemayel ten years previously. Owing to its methods of collecting money and other arbitrary practices, the militia had become more unpopular from year to year, and was hated in many areas. Aoun, on the other hand, had become an idol of the people almost overnight. The overwhelming majority of the population preferred his civil servants and disciplined soldiers.

In January 1990, both parties prepared for battle. Their arsenals were well-stocked with Iraqi supplies. The militia stationed troops in the vicinity of army barracks. Fighting started on January 27th. Aoun's government had decided that a school building the militia had requisitioned in Fourn al-Chebbak should be returned to the ministry of education. The school lay at a strategic point on the Damascus road between Baabda and East Beirut. When the militia refused to withdraw, the army opened fire. Within hours heavy fighting had broken out in many places. The army was stronger.[46] However, as a large part of the army was permanently stationed on the borders of the enclave, facing Syrian troops, only a limited number of soldiers was available for other duties at any one time. The Lebanese Forces had prepared themselves well. They attacked the relatively lightly defended garrisons on the coast. On January 31st, the Amchit garrison capitulated, as did the Sarba garrison and the naval base at Jounieh on February 2nd. A smaller unit stationed in Beirut harbour withdrew to West Beirut and placed itself under General Lahoud's command. Within a few days Geagea controlled the entire coast of the enclave.

The army launched a counteroffensive on February 6th. After heavy fighting it took Dbayeh, where the militia had several barracks and its department of finance, and reached the coast near Antelyas. As a relief attack, the militia encircled the Adma helicopter base in Kisrawan. Aoun lost almost his entire helicopter fleet. Although outnumbered by the militia, the army commando unit in Adma resisted desperately, until an agreement was reached which allowed the commandos to withdraw with their weapons. On February 10th, the militia started an advance on the army position of Kleiat[47] in the mountains, but it soon ground to a halt. On the same day Colonel Paul Farès, who had quit the army a few weeks previously, declared himself commander of a 'neutral army'; the surviving soldiers of the garrisons that had capitulated to the militia put themselves under his command.

A day later the army attacked the eastern suburbs of Beirut. After extremely intense and bitter close combat, the army took Ain al-Rummaneh on February

---

[46] Aoun's part of the army had about 15,000 men, of which 9,000 were combat forces. The Lebanese Forces numbered about 10,000 militiamen, half of whom were ready for combat.

[47] From here the army had made a futile attempt to send reinforcements to the Adma garrison.

16th. The Lebanese Forces withdrew — via West Beirut — to Ashrafieh, the centre of East Beirut. Geagea issued a statement asking 'the legal authorities', i.e., Hrawi and the Hoss government, for help. As a gesture of goodwill towards this government, he transferred the four Fuga-Magister army aircraft, which had been captured when the militia took the Halat military airport, to Lahoud's Koleyat air base. Hrawi replied that he would provide assistance only if Geagea unconditionally accepted the Taif Agreement and the authority of the government.

As the army started to advance on the suburbs of Sin el-Fil and Nabaa on March 1st, they seemed to have gained the upper hand. Yet Aoun's soldiers were soon in difficulties. Streets and houses had been mined, militiamen put up bitter resistance, and the army began to run out of ammunition.

Just over a month of mobile warfare ended in stalemate. The Christian heartland was criss-crossed with demarcation lines as effective as the 'Green Line' dividing East and West Beirut. The Lebanese Forces were in possession of the Jbeil and Kisrawan regions and had kept the central districts of East Beirut: Ashrafieh and Karantina, though these were now isolated from the rest of their territory and accessible only by sea. Aoun's army held the Metn and the narrow coastal strip between Beirut and the Dog River as well as the eastern suburbs of Beirut, including the area around Baabda and a small section of Kisrawan.

In military terms this war left the army in an extremely unfavourable position. It had failed to subject the militia and had lost control over two-thirds of the territory in the Christian enclave. Aoun and his staff had miscalculated badly. The garrisons on the coast had not been properly fortified; some officers had gone over to the militia;[48] with the loss of ports and some coastal munitions depots, the army had eventually run out of ammunition; and the army had underestimated the militia's fighting strength and morale.

The best units of the Lebanese Army had been taught the same lesson other conventional troops had learnt fighting determined militiamen. To wrest a built-up area from a militia one had more or less to destroy it, and then fight from house to house. The Lebanese Army had the additional 'disadvantage' of showing as much consideration as possible for the population. The militia did not; and as its losses mounted, the army, too, showed less and less.

The fighting was more intense and bitter than any Lebanon had experienced since the outbreak of war; the worst could still be bettered. Heavy artillery, tanks and rockets were used in the most densely populated part of the country. For the first time there had been a lot of mobile warfare. In consequence, the loss of life on both sides was exceptionally high; that of the militia was supposedly three to

---

[48] The Fifth Brigade especially proved relatively unreliable; since Bashir Gemayel's time it had had close ties with the militia.

four times that of the army. All in all, this war between Christians probably took a higher toll in lives than the Syrian bombardment of the enclave in the previous year.

The Lebanese Forces' utter disregard for their 'own' people knew no bounds.[49] They chose their positions without consideration, shot from schools, convents and hospitals, and practised a 'scorched earth' policy: a Reuters correspondent entering Ain al-Rummaneh with the army reported it looked 'like an earthquake had hit it'. The hard core of the militia comprised around 1,000 fighters recruited among refugees from northern Lebanon, Geagea's most devoted troops. They were deployed mainly in Beirut and 'fought as in a foreign land'.[50] The resentment of homeless villagers against city-dwellers and of have-nots against relative haves fuelled assault, looting and violence. Pupils and schoolchildren, almost all of whom had taken part in the Baabda demonstrations, were favourite targets. Members of army officers' families were taken hostage and captured soldiers occasionally shot dead, as were militiamen who did not want to go on fighting. The militia did nothing to arrange food and water for the populace, indeed at times obstructed supplies. Some observers came to the conclusion that the militia wanted to punish the population for their own unpopularity and Aoun's popularity. The Lebanese Forces became known as the 'securitate'.

With such an adversary it is not surprising that Aoun and his army continued to enjoy wide sympathy. But the belief that they might be successful had been badly knocked. In mid-March Aoun offered to negotiate with President Hrawi, since the recent battles had shown that 'conflict cannot be solved by violence, only by dialogue'. Hrawi rejected talks until Aoun accepted the Taif Agreement.

The Lebanese Forces kept the port Aoun had built in Antelyas under fire, in order to discourage traffic, and Aoun replied by firing on the ports controlled by the militia: the Christian adversaries inside the enclave prolonged the blockade that Syria had imposed in 1989. Both sides were too exhausted for further mobile warfare, and expressed their animosity in small-scale commando raids, shelling and sporadic fighting along the demarcation lines in East Beirut and in Kisrawan. The Vatican mediated a cease-fire that took effect on May 21st, and held primarily because of mutual exhaustion. It remained precarious and the reciprocal hatred undiminished.

---

[49] On the following, see Union des Jeunes Européens, *Livre Blanc du conflit Armée-Forces Libanaises* (Paris, 1990).
[50] Interview with an eye-witness.

## Loss of credibility

Five years previously Geagea had opposed Amin Gemayel on the ground that his policies would leave Lebanon dependent on Syria. Shortly afterwards, Geagea made approaches to Syria, though with little success. In 1989 Aoun had declared a 'war of liberation' against Syria, and in 1990 ordered the attack on Geagea's militia because the latter was prepared to accept the Taif Agreement, and therewith dependence on Syria. When his attempt to establish his authority throughout the Christian enclave failed, he too sought Syrian support.

With few supply lines to the outside world and a low stock of armaments, Aoun accepted petrol and munitions from Hobeika's pro-Syrian militia and the SSNP, allowing them to resume their political activities in the Metn in exchange. Syrian designs in providing limited aid were obvious. Syria had as little interest in Geagea's victory and the reunification of the Christian enclave under the Lebanese Forces as it had in Aoun's victory; its interest lay in a war of attrition between the Christian nationalist forces. Moreover, Syria was in no hurry to initiate the process — and the time schedule — foreseen in the Taif Agreement. Finally, a weakened Aoun in the presidential palace at Baabda reminded President Hrawi and Premier Hoss that Syria alone was in a position to help them realize their plans.

After the intra-Christian cease-fire, Hrawi and his government made desperate attempts to find a peaceful, generally acceptable solution. On July 11th, 1990, they solemnly appealed to all political forces in the country 'to side with legality', 'without excluding anybody or granting anybody a monopoly on the representation of a community or a region', and proposed a plan of action. The first step would be the withdrawal of all militias from both halves of Beirut. The appeal drew the approval and support of the Arab troika; the Saudi Foreign Minister, Prince Saud al-Faisal, and envoy Ibrahimi had already obtained the agreement of the Syrian government. France, the Vatican and the Maronite Patriarch also supported the government's initiative.

Geagea agreed, provided that Aoun handed Baabda and Yarze to the government. Aoun rejected the appeal out of hand, because it issued 'from illegal offices'. Notwithstanding this rejection, the troika asked Ibrahimi to make another attempt to convince Aoun to accept the Taif Agreement. He proposed forming a government of national unity that would include both Aoun and Geagea. He met Aoun no fewer than four times. Although Aoun did not reject Ibrahimi's proposal directly, he made a number of demands: no appointed deputies; stronger powers for the president vis-à-vis the prime minister; dissolution of the militias and parliamentary elections prior to ratification of the constitutional amendments agreed in Taif. In effect, these demands called into question all the domestic political compromises of Taif. Geagea and a number of politicians pointed out that during the Taif conference Aoun had taken the view that the political system and organization meant nothing to him, he was solely interested in the country's sovereignty; 'but now he no longer speaks of sovereignty, only of the president's powers'. Ibrahimi commented, 'I do not understand whom or what the general is in favour of', and Aoun replied, 'The general and the people decide together.' In the summer of 1990 there was mounting evidence that Aoun was losing touch with reality. He waited in his palace, and again took to frequently addressing crowds of fervent supporters, who continued to support him despite all set-backs. His rejection of Taif grew more intense; he even went as far as establishing contacts with Hezbollah, with which he had only the rejection of Taif in common. It seemed that he placed his hopes in Syria: because Syria had no interest in implementing the Taif process, it would support him against his Christian as well as his other Lebanese opponents. The former protagonist of the struggle for liberation made increasingly direct approaches to Syria. At the end of July he went as far as to describe express Syrian-Lebanese relations in terms customarily heard in Damascus: 'As regards customs, tradition and culture, we are a single people. Why should we not have closer ties than neighbourly and privileged relations?' Damascus certainly had no objection to closer ties. But it would soon make it plain that the unsuccessful and isolated general was not its favoured partner.

## Divided and ruled

In the summer of 1990, after fifteen years of war, the situation in Lebanon was more desperate than ever. There was sporadic fighting in many parts of the country. In the south, the vicious circle of commando raids in the Israeli 'security zone' and 'punitive expeditions', usually air-attacks, continued throughout 1989 and the first half of 1990. The power struggle between the Lebanese Shi`is was as unresolved as the struggle for hegemony in the Christian heartland. Amal and Hezbollah resumed their armed conflict in December 1989, after Hezbollah militiamen from the Bekaa infiltrated through the zone controlled by the South Lebanon Army into the hinterland of Sidon. Interrupted by cease-fires, the two militias fought over a few villages in Iklim al-Touffah. PLO troops in the camps near Sidon tried in vain to separate the fighters, and made minor territorial gains in the process. The animosity between the two Shi`i organizations was as bitter as that between the adversaries in the Christian enclave. Berri accused Hezbollah of not having any genuinely Lebanese policy, of being the playthings of extreme Iranian tendencies. He was undoubtedly right; all the same, Hezbollah's military muscle continued to improved. By May 1990, the fundamentalist organization was strong enough to attack Amal in the heart of West Beirut. Once again the Syrians intervened and restored order, without helping one or other side to victory. As in the case of the Lebanese Christians, a Shi`i stalemate best served Syrian interests: attenuation by attrition.

As vehicles for politics, the large Lebanese communities had completely broken down. The Sunnis had lost their military power right at the beginning of the war. The Maronites and Shi`is were tearing themselves to pieces. The Arab initiative had given the country a president and a government. But the peace process initiated in Taif was bogged down. Those dissatisfied with their treatment under the proposed dispensation, above all the Shi`is, and the declared opponents of Taif, above all Aoun and his followers, had been weakened by intra-communal opponents. But this had not strengthened the central government.

By mid-1990, Lebanon had disintegrated into a number of small territories controlled by different politico-military forces, some in condominium with Syria or Israel, and all at daggers drawn with every neighbouring territory. Syria maintained order in the far north as well as in Tripoli, where Sunni fundamentalist movements occasionally contested it. In the Christian north, the Franjiehs — Suleiman (Slimmy), son of the assassinated Tony, took power from his uncle Robert in August 1990 — had been able to retain some autonomy under Syrian suzerainty, and were very appreciative of Syrian protection against potential Islamic militancy in Tripoli and, in particular, against the deadly enemy to the south, Geagea and his militia. In the Bekaa the Syrian Army maintained a balance between different Shi`i Islamic fundamentalist groups, Palestinians and Hobeika's Zahle-based Christian militia. In mid-1990 the 'hottest' internal borders were the demarcation lines between the Lebanese Forces and Aoun's army. South of the old 'Green Line', Amal and Hezbollah feuded in West Beirut and the southern suburbs, under the watchful eye of the Syrians, and further south, where the eye was Palestinian. Since 1983 Jumblatt's Druze had been worried about Shi`i or Palestinian incursions into their enlarged but underpopulated territory. In Sidon, Sunni Popular Nasserites shared power with Arafat's PLO, which had rebuilt much of its military infrastructure in the camps on the edge of the city.[51] The Amal militia controlled the hinterland of Sidon. Although it detested the Palestinians, Amal was unable to thwart their comeback because Hezbollah posed an even greater threat. Finally, the demarcation lines between the area under Lahad's South Lebanon Army and the Israeli 'security zone' had become a hotbed of organizations dedicated to liberating Palestine by military means.

This splintering of the country meant that the vast majority of Lebanese, irrespective of area, were forced to live under militia rule, in other words, life

---

[51] The PLO forces in southern Lebanon even held 'manoeuvres' in February 1990.

under a greater or lesser degree of despotism. If there had been any identification between Lebanese civilians and 'their' respective militia in earlier years, it had since evaporated. As they became more unpopular, the militias had to resort to more ruthless methods. The progressive impoverishment of the country exacerbated this tendency, so that in time the militias became an enormous financial burden on their respective areas. All the militias seemed determined to hold their own not only against one another, but also against the populace they claimed to be protecting. The Lebanese were a people held hostage, held hostage by the various militias.

The war in Lebanon had taken a terrible toll in lives and economic destruction. Precise figures for recent years are not available. It is estimated that casualties in each of Aoun's two wars against the Syrians and against the Lebanese Forces amounted to 1,000 dead and 3,500 wounded. About 25,000 houses and flats were destroyed. 1989[52] and 1990 proved to be the worst years ever for the economy. GDP declined by 20 per cent in 1989 and a further 10 per cent in 1990. Most power plants, power lines and water mains were damaged or destroyed, and manufacturing virtually ceased. Capital continued to drain out of the country.

The militias collected far more in levies and dues than the state. In 1990 the budget deficit reached 65 per cent of GDP. Current revenue was barely enough to service the existing debt; to cover current expenditure the government resorted to the printing press.

In such a situation it is hardly surprising that emigration rose dramatically: 150,000 Lebanese are thought to have left the country in 1989-90. Anyone with the means — money or education — left a country that offered only war, oppression and poverty. Those who remained could not afford to leave: they were hostages in a poorhouse.

---

[52] See the full report of the Beirut Chamber of Commerce in *ad-Diyar*, April 11th, 1990.

## Armies and militias, mid-1990

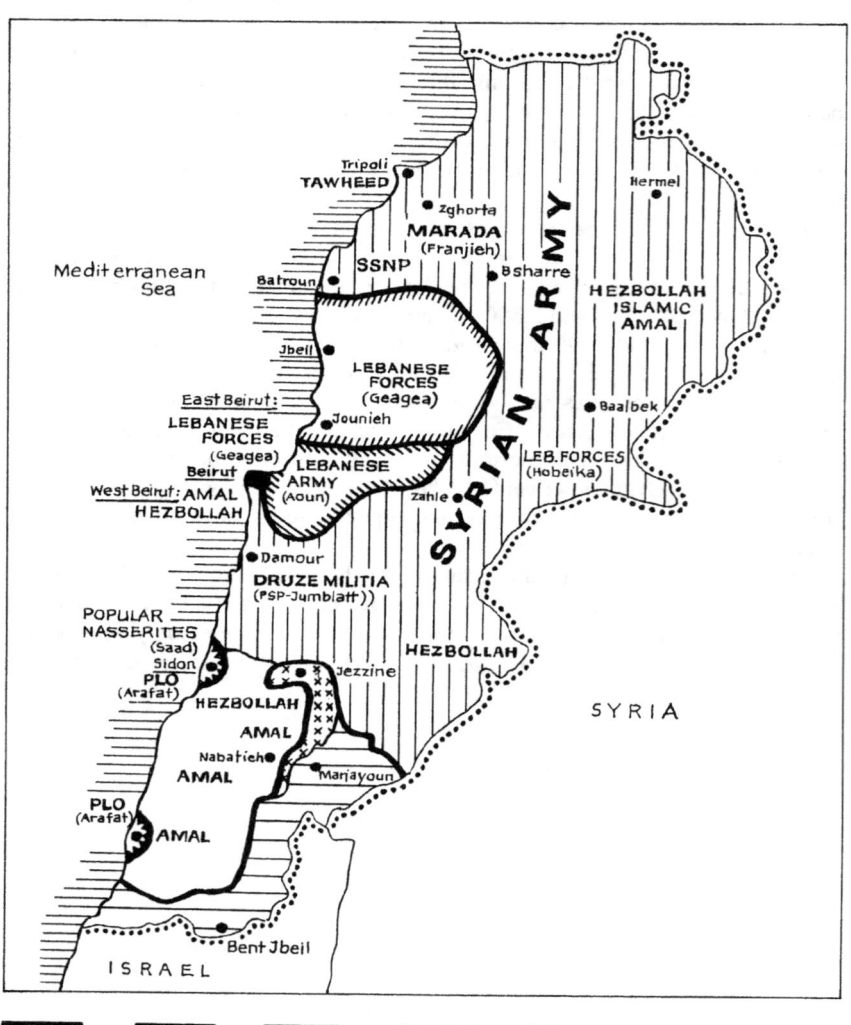

# 10

## The Two Faces of the Second Republic
## Trappings of Sovereignty, 1990–1992

C'est à l'homme de la Nation qui réunit le plus de suffrages et de moyens, que passe l'autorité. Mais avant tout, il doit obtenir l'agrément des Turks, dont il devient le vassal et le tributaire. Il arrive même qu'à raison de leur suzeraineté, ils peuvent nommer le Hakem contre le gré de la Nation ...; mais cet état de contrainte ne dure qu'autant qu'il est maintenu par la violence qui l'établit.

Volney, *Voyage en Syrie et en Egypte* 1790

As a rule, the Lebanese vassals acted independently on the domestic level ... The Egyptians, the Assyrians, the Babylonians recorded their advent by the chisel on the rock of the foot of the mountain; the Romans, the Byzantines, the Crusaders signalized their presence by monumental structures which now lie in ruins; the Persians, the Saljuqs, the Mongols hardly left a trace. There was no reason to believe that the new upstarts would leave much of an impression — though they might stay for four centuries.

Philip Hitti, 1957

To all those who are sceptical and doubtful I say: do not worry. Lebanon, with the will of all, is a final nation for all the Lebanese. It is too solid to melt and too shiny to be eclipsed.

Elias Hrawi

As long as there was disagreement over how to reconstitute a Lebanese state, Lebanon slid ever deeper into violence. Despite enormous reservations, the deputies in Taif had legalized the presence of Syrian troops, so as to set formal geographic restrictions and time-limits to this presence. They wanted to end the war, disband the militias and, through concessions, obtain Syrian cooperation in the hope that, once re-established, a state would restore complete sovereignty in the medium or long term. General Aoun and his supporters felt that before any state could be re-established, it first had to be liberated from Syria. The conclave of Taif decided to pledge the state's sovereignty so as to redeem it in more favourable times. Aoun, fearing that Syria would not honour the redemption, wanted to re-establish sovereignty by force.

Aoun failed. In mid-1990 it seemed that his failure might also block the road from Taif too. The Syrian government had never been really happy with the Taif Agreement; the troika had taken months to obtain Syria's consent. The status quo in mid-1990 worked in Syria's favour: a weak Lebanese government and extremely splintered political and military forces. Citing the incapability of the Lebanese, Syria could have let the Taif process stagnate unfinished and followed an inexpensive policy of divide and rule. This seemed to be their preference in the first half of 1990.

Then, in August 1990, crucial changes in the Middle East precipitated, as so often in the past, change in Lebanon.

## In the shadow of the Kuwait conflict

On August 2nd, 1990, Iraq invaded Kuwait. Within a short time a powerful anti-Iraqi international coalition had formed under the leadership of the USA. The Arab states could not avoid taking sides. For Syria the choice was comparatively easy: Saddam Hussein's Iraq had been Syria's enemy for years. But Syria had a more fundamental reason to join the anti-Iraqi coalition. Hafez el-Assad had grasped the significance for the Middle East of the 1989 changes in eastern Europe more quickly than other Arab leaders. The USSR was no longer willing or able to act as a counterweight to American power in the region, which left the USA as crucial power broker. Whereas Saddam Hussein drew false conclusions from America's 1984 debacle in Lebanon, Hafez el-Assad, unsentimental as always, quietly trimmed his sails and cautiously tacked towards the USA.

This required a correction to his Lebanese policy too. In view of the international indignation over Iraq's annexation of Kuwait, it was advisable to counter comparisons between Syria's role in Lebanon and Iraq's in Kuwait, or Israel's on the West Bank, comparisons Saddam Hussein drew all too readily in his speeches. The most elegant way was to resume the Taif process, a resumption Saudi Arabia, the patron power of Taif and America's most important regional ally, had long desired. Resumption was all the easier for Syria in that its position in Lebanon had, if anything, improved since 1989: Aoun and Geagea had weakened each other, but the Hrawi-Hoss administration still could not deal with Aoun and the militias without Syrian assistance.

Aoun had not read the signs of the times so well. He was on bad terms with the Americans — the American embassy had been closed after demonstrations by his supporters — and doing nothing to improve them. His militant speeches had annoyed the Israelis; he could expect neither aid nor a good word from that quarter. After August 2nd, 1990, his alliance with Iraq angered not only Syria, but the USA as well. For months France and the Vatican had been trying to persuade Aoun to compromise with Hrawi, and were tired of his obstinacy. In short: Aoun presented himself as the first political victim of the Gulf War. Whether the USA actually gave Syria the go-ahead is irrelevant: their interests coincided.

Another politician who grasped the potential of the new international and regional constellation quickly was Elias Hrawi. His direct appeals and his offers of compromise via Arab and international mediators had fallen on deaf ears. Even Syria's response to his request for military assistance was reserved. But when the situation changed, Syria's renewed interest in the Taif process strengthened Hrawi's hand *vis-à-vis* his neighbour. Those in Lebanon and elsewhere who had underestimated Hrawi would be taught a lesson in the coming months. Hrawi offered to realize the Taif Agreement in accordance with the letter of the text, and Syria accepted. He then acted with remarkable energy and speed.

## Constitutional amendment

In mid-August parliament was presented with constitutional amendments which gave precise constitutional expression to the principles and institutional reforms agreed upon in Taif. The opening paragraph of the Taif Agreement — the fundamental declaration on the character and the identity of Lebanon — was adopted unaltered as the preamble to the Constitution. The institutional reforms are reflected in amendments to thirty articles of the Constitution, which, in content, are identical to the agreements made at Taif.[1]

Parliament convened on August 26th, 1990: of the fifty-one deputies present, twenty-six were Christians and twenty-five Muslims. There were forty-eight votes for and one against the constitutional amendments, with two abstentions. The timetable set in Taif came into effect on the date of this vote: six months for the disbandment of the militias, two years for all Syrian troops to withdraw to the Bekaa. The Taif process had begun in earnest.

The reactions to the new constitutional amendments were similar to those in 1989. The Sunnis, in particular Saeb Salam, expressed great satisfaction. Sheikh Shamseddin expressed the Shi`is' relative dissatisfaction with an 'agreement by necessity and not free choice'. Walid Jumblatt was realistic: 'There is no alternative to Taif. It will be hard to revise because that could lead to new wars.' Aoun spoke of a comedy in several acts: parliament had been dissolved by the legal government on November 4th, 1989 and any subsequent decisions were null and void.

The government made Aoun a final offer: he should hand Baabda over to General Lahoud; the Lebanese Forces would withdraw from Ashrafieh; and Aoun himself would be appointed a minister of state. On September 13th, the general declined all dialogue with the 'puppets in West Beirut' and declared: 'I embody the solution'. There would be no further attempts at compromise.

On September 21st, Hrawi promulgated the revised Constitution and broadcast to the nation: 'Today I present to you a Constitution that shall form the basis of the Second Republic ... We will form a government that shall include all parties, end the war, disband the militias, restore the authority of the state and its laws throughout the territory of all Lebanon, deal with the economic crisis ... and at the same time, create a lasting foundation for brotherly relations with Syria ... I hope that we shall be able to hold parliamentary elections in the near future. To those who demand immediate elections in the present circumstances, we say that they have been answered by those of us who left Lebanon to protest against those who have maltreated, murdered and kidnapped and destroyed homes and livelihoods.'

Even supporters of Aoun, above all in the traditionally legalistic Lebanese military, began to question whether the general's position was still legal and legitimate. Three of Aoun's predecessors as army commander, Emile Boustani, Victor Khoury and Ibrahim Tannous, appealed to Aoun's soldiers to recognize the authority of General Lahoud, and a number of officers did.

---

[1] For a French translation of the preamble and the modified articles of the constitution, see *Libanoscopie* 88 (1990), p. 26.

## Aoun's defeat

On September 28th, troops under Lahoud's command tightened the economic blockade by taking control of all checkpoints on the borders of the area controlled by Aoun. As in the autumn of 1989, Aoun's supporters replied with daily demonstrations at Baabda and at the checkpoints. Even outside the enclave the blockade had little support, for the populace rather than Aoun's soldiers bore the brunt of it. On the evening of October 1st, demonstrators with lighted candles marched to the demarcation line between Ashrafieh and the eastern suburbs, where troops of the Lebanese Army as well as militiamen of the Lebanese Forces had taken up position. As demonstrators gathered on the bridge over the Nahr al-Mott, the Dead River, machine guns and artillery opened fire, killing thirteen people and injuring ninety. The demonstrations continued, but the belief in non-violent resistance had taken a knock.

At the beginning of October, elite Syrian troops took up positions on the borders of Aoun's enclave. On October 11th, in accordance with a cabinet decision, President Hrawi wrote to President Assad requesting military support for the Lebanese Army under the terms of the Taif Agreement. On that and the next day Syrian fighters buzzed Baabda, without intervention of the Israeli air force: the 'Red Line' in the air seemed to have disappeared.

At seven o'clock on the morning of October 13th, the Syrian air force began to bomb Baabda, and Syrian and Lebanese tanks advanced from the mountains and West Beirut. The previous evening Aoun had said he would fight to the finish. Two and a half hours after the attack started he sought refuge in the French Embassy, called on his troops to recognize General Lahoud's authority, and asked France for political asylum.

The appeal came too late for some of his troops: they were already in battle. Others decided to ignore Aoun's capitulation and resist. Yet others were confused; in Araya, Aoun's soldiers raised a white flag, and then shot at the advancing Syrians. Although most of Aoun's forces did not fight, Syrian casualties were heavy, estimated at about four hundred killed. What resistance there was was followed by revenge: Syrian troops executed approximately one hundred captured Aoun soldiers, and killed fifteen villagers in Bsous, where civilians had fired on the Syrians.[2]

During the Syrian attack the Lebanese Forces shelled Baabda and the Metn. Hezbollah units advanced into the Christian village of Hadeth, but were soon beaten back by Hobeika's pro-Syrian militia.

---

[2] On this and the following, see Foundation for Human and Humanitarian Rights, *The October Debacle: Report on Lebanon, Fall of 1990* (n.p. [Beirut], November 4th, 1990).

The fighting was over in just eight hours. Some of Aoun's closest associates also took refuge in the French Embassy. Syrian troops arrested about twenty high-ranking officers — mainly in military intelligence, on Aoun's general staff or commanders of the brigades that had resisted — and took them to the Syrian headquarters at Anjar in the Bekaa or to Syria. The archives of the presidential palace at Baabda, the Ministry of Defence and army headquarters at Yarze were seized by Syrian troops; there was probably nothing that the Syrians did not learn about the Lebanese Army.

For a few days, until officers restored discipline, the population in Aoun's former enclave had to suffer humiliating searches, confiscations and looting by the victorious troops and, above all, the militias on their heels. Syrian units took up positions at strategic points and Lebanese and Syrian troops carried out joint controls and patrols. Though low-profile, the signals of the new order were unmistakeable: resistance would not be tolerated, but otherwise the Syrian Army was just helping the Lebanese government to re-establish its authority in an area liberated from rebels. Contrary to widespread expectations, Aoun's supporters were not hounded. Their civilian arm, the 'National Coordination Office' was soon able to resume its political activities. Although France granted Aoun political asylum — a 'matter of honour' for Mitterand — the Lebanese government would not allow him to leave the country.

President Hrawi went to Damascus to thank his Syrian colleague for their assistance.

The Christians, traumatized both by the speed and severity of the blow against Aoun and by his inglorious capitulation, had expected worse. His capitulation was sensible as it prevented further loss of blood; a day earlier, though, and no blood would have been spilt at all. The shock was all the greater coming as it did after months of euphoria generated by the constant demonstrations in support of Aoun. But that was not the end of it: on October 21st, Dany Chamoun, his wife and their two small sons were murdered. Chamoun had been a critical supporter of Aoun, and opposed to the Syrian presence in Lebanon.[3] After this, no one dared to criticize Syria's ascendancy openly.

The Lebanese Forces gained little by Aoun's fall. Their hopes of becoming the sole representatives of Christian Lebanon were short-lived. The Syrian and Lebanese armies kept them, unlike Hobeika's pro-Syrian militia — arch-enemies of Geagea's — and the SSNP, out of the general's ex-territory. Politically, they were being side-lined: Aoun's supporters hated them more than ever for collaborating

---

[3] Many quarters, including the German information service, *Terrorismus* 1 (1991), pp. 6f., blame the murder on Syria. Although Chamoun's death did help to stabilize Syria's position in Lebanon, the eradication of an entire family is indicative of a militia vendetta.

with Hrawi and Syria, and the latter still did not trust them, despite their compliance in Aoun's defeat.

The only people who benefited from Aoun's fall were the convinced proponents of the Taif process, and they lost no time capitalizing on it.

## Militia-free Beirut

Prior to October 13th, General Lahoud commanded 6,000 men. By incorporating most of Aoun's units, the size of the official Lebanese Army doubled. Aoun's soldiers may have been demoralized, but they were well-trained, well-armed and anti-militia, irrespective of leanings. Thus, the new army was strong enough and motivated enough for the government's next task: to rid Beirut of militias.

Before the government announced its 'security plan' for Beirut it cleared all details with Syria. The heavy Syrian deployments in West Beirut and the Metn could, if necessary, underscore the government's intentions. On November 17th, Lebanese troops took up positions at numerous points in the capital, and the government ordered all militias out. Amal withdrew to the south of the country immediately and the PSP militia withdrew to the Chouf. Hezbollah left three days later. The Lebanese Forces agreed to leave on condition that pro-Syrian militias left the Metn, that the Kata'ib got back its offices and institutions and that the soldiers stationed in Ashrafieh had not fought for Aoun. The government was conciliatory: the Kata'ib got its offices[4] back and the soldiers assigned to Ashrafieh were drawn from the Sarba garrison, which, for the most part, had remained neutral in the intra-Christian struggle. With a military parade to demonstrate their strength, the Lebanese Forces began to withdraw on November 23rd, and were gone from Beirut by December 3rd, apart from 300 militiamen left behind in the militia's headquarters in Karantina and at the harbour.

The next day the army began to remove the barricades along the 'Green Line': Beirut was re-united for the first time since February 1984, and (virtually) free of militiamen for the first time since 1975. On December 6th, Hrawi was able to visit Ashrafieh for the first time since taking office.

Success bred success. After lengthy Syrian and Iranian mediation, Amal and Hezbollah ordered their militiamen to withdraw from the bitterly disputed Iklim al-Touffah. Five officers who had remained loyal to Aoun left the French Embassy and submitted to General Lahoud. In mid-December an Arab head of state visited Beirut for the first time in years: President Chadli of Algeria, who promised military aid to help rebuild the Lebanese Army.

---

[4] But not the institutions that the Lebanese Forces had confiscated from Amin Gemayel in 1988, 'Maison du Futur' and the daily *Le Réveil*; these were provisionally taken over by the army.

## Government of national unity

Salim Hoss, Prime Minister under several presidents, had always preferred small cabinets of qualified technocrats rather than pure politicians. President Hrawi, himself a politician of the old school, was not particularly fond of these preferences or of the premier. Hoss, in the letter and spirit of the revised Constitution, insisted on his prerogatives as head of the executive. Since taking office, Hrawi had acted like a president of the First Republic. Conflicts between the two men were inevitable. Hrawi got his way: what he had lost through the constitutional amendments he made up for in Syrian support. Of this he could be sure since opting unequivocally for manifest and close collaboration. Constitution and constitutional reality began to diverge at a very early stage in the history of the Second Republic.

The composition of the new government was settled de facto between Hrawi and the Syrian government. The new powers of the speaker, like those of the prime minister, were largely ignored: the parliamentary consultations he led ex officio were purely formal. On December 15th, Hrawi negotiated in Damascus without Hoss and Husseini; Hoss resigned on December 19th, and the next day Omar Karami was asked to form a government, which he presented on December 24th.

The new premier had a lot in common with the president. Both came from the Lebanese periphery; accordingly, it was natural for them to take Syria into account. Both were also personally in favour of close collaboration with Syria. Finally, both belonged to the pragmatic school of politics.

Their cabinet was the largest in Lebanese history: an enormous coalition, thirty ministers representing all political parties and leanings except Hezbollah, the National Liberals, Aoun supporters and the Communists. No less than seven militia leaders were ministers of state without portfolio: Berri, Jumblatt, Geagea, Hobeika, Slimmy Franjieh, Abdallah el-Amin (pro-Syrian Baath Party) and Assad Hardan (SSNP militia). Karami came straight to the point: the fact that these warlords were members of the government meant they were prepared to disband their militias. In addition to their leaders, Amal, PSP, the Lebanese Forces and Kata'ib each got two cabinet posts. Besides the representatives of the Baath Party and the SSNP, one other minister was utterly committed to promoting Syrian interests. A large majority of the cabinet was drawn from old political families. Hrawi had no compunction in appointing his son-in-law and two prominent business associates as ministers.

The composition of the cabinet was a manifesto in itself. There were only three strongly anti-Syrian ministers, those of the Lebanese Forces and the Kata'ib. Three others were unreservedly pro-Syrian. The rest were prepared to work closely with Syria, be it by conviction or necessity. The militant 'lions' had been included, but the traditional 'foxes' of Lebanese politics were in the majority. In short: it was a cabinet for the Taif process.

The most vehement protest against the cabinet came from the ranks of the Lebanese Forces. They demanded a 'more balanced' government, and thought the Christian ministers unrepresentative. In a smaller cabinet it would probably have been easier to find the votes for the one-third blocking minority; this was precisely what Hrawi wanted to avoid. Geagea tried to get ten Christian ministers to resign with him, but only the other two from his own group would join him. Premier Karami declared the government would, if necessary, do without them.

The vote of confidence was taken on January 9th, 1991. The circumstances surrounding the formation of the government were strongly criticized, but in the end thirty-four of the forty deputies present voted for the new cabinet.

The government's declaration contained the entire Taif programme: to send the army into the illegal ports and then into the south; to disband the militias and integrate a large proportion of the militiamen into the army, the police force and other government services; to fill the vacant and new parliamentary seats; to conclude the treaties with Syria provided for in the Agreement; to prepare for the return of all refugees and expellees; to start rebuilding the country.

## Disarming the militias

In mid-January, the government ordered the army to act against the remaining militiamen in greater Beirut. Even after large numbers of militiamen had departed, taking their heavy weapons, some militias tried to retain control of parts of Beirut. The government now prohibited the carrying of all weapons and the wearing of uniforms. The army was instructed to search for caches of weapons, to prevent identity checks or 'tax' collection by militiamen and to break up unauthorized demonstrations. It proceeded to search militia offices, raid suspect places and arrest any armed persons, now always referred to as 'gunmen', a term devoid of glory.

The most vehement protests came from the Lebanese Forces; Geagea spoke of the 'danger of a new civil war'. The army was cautioned not to cross a 'Red Line' around the headquarters of the Lebanese Forces. The Defence Minister, Michel Murr, replied that there would be no more 'islands' beyond the writ of the army. On March 9th, the army occupied the headquarters of the Lebanese Forces, Amal, the PSP and Hezbollah, and confiscated arms caches in East and West Beirut. On March 11th, the army entered the militias' ports: Dock Five in Beirut harbour, Dbayeh, Ouzai and Khalde. Four days later the port of Beirut was re-opened for normal business.

The militia leaders, bound by cabinet discipline, were disempowering themselves. Jumblatt tendered his resignation, but later withdrew it.[5] The ministers from the Lebanese Forces and the Kata'ib boycotted cabinet meetings, yet without tendering their resignations. Karami gave them an ultimatum; only Geagea resigned, and was replaced by Roger Dib, a close associate. Hrawi's gamble had paid off: the militia leaders grumbled, but did not seriously oppose the government's policy, or give up their seats in the cabinet.

At their summit meeting on Martinique in mid-March, Bush and Mitterand expressly supported the Taif process. The USA resumed arms shipments to the Lebanese Army, which they had suspended in 1984.

On March 20th, the government took the momentous decision that all militias had to disband by the end of April. It was one thing to leave Beirut with heavy weaponry and fall back on strongholds in Kisrawan, the Chouf or the south. It was quite another thing to surrender these strongholds and cease to exist as armed organizations. The cabinet's decision was unequivocal: all arms were to be handed over to the army within a month and all intelligence services disbanded. If necessary, this decision would be enforced with the help of 'the brotherly Syrian Army'. Hrawi declared: 'The days of the militias are numbered, the peace process cannot be stopped.'

The cabinet meetings that followed drew up plans for the future of the militiamen. It was out of the question that young people who had learnt nothing but martial arts would easily find a job in civilian life. Unemployed, they would be a dangerous potential for social and political unrest. It was agreed that the state would start training and assessing 20,000 militiamen immediately, and pay them $100 per month. At the end of this period, they would get permanent jobs in the army, the security service, the police or the civil service.

Once again, the Lebanese Forces protested strongly. Geagea again evoked the threat of a new war and called for a referendum on the disbandment of the militias. There were demonstrations in favour of the militias in Kisrawan and Jbeil. But these were rearguard actions. In the second half of April, the Lebanese Forces started shipping heavy equipment abroad. Jumblatt announced that he would hand over his arms only to the Syrian, not the Lebanese Army. Arguments soon broke out over the distribution of posts: which militia would get what posts in which organization? Of the total, 6,500 had been allocated to the Lebanese Forces, 2,800 each to Amal and the PSP, and the rest divided among the other militias.

---

[5] Contrary to the Syrian position, Jumblatt had expressed some sympathy for Saddam Hussein. Depressed by having to apologize in Damascus and cooperate in depriving his militia of power, he decided to withdraw from politics completely. He changed his mind only at the urging of his community.

At the end of April, army units occupied Zghorta, Koura and Batroun, on May 1st, they occupied Jbeil, Kisrawan and the Chouf. At the same time, the army occupied the last of the militia ports. The occupation of the most important militia strongholds had passed off without incident. The Lebanese Army had conducted the entire operation without Syrian support, after settling, as was now usual, all details with the Syrian Army.

The government made some concessions on the surrender of heavy weapons. The PSP handed over theirs to the Syrian Army. The Lebanese Forces returned the heavy weaponry that it had taken from the Lebanese Army previously: tanks, helicopters and heavy artillery. The government allowed them to store heavy weaponry obtained elsewhere, until it could be shipped abroad. The militias' arsenals were so well stocked that the hand-over took longer than planned. The government gave up collecting slight arms, as there were just too many of them.

Thus the militias were not completely disarmed. Some may have kept part of their heavy weaponry hidden. Nevertheless, on May 1st, 1991, the rule of the large militias ended, in general and in their strongholds as well. The government also hoped that after losing their ports, i.e., their most important source of revenue, the militias would not be able to maintain militiamen in civilian dress and light weapons. At the beginning of June, the army opened its rehabilitation and training camps for ex-militiamen.

## Treaty of brotherhood, cooperation and coordination with Syria

Regardless of the skill of the Lebanese government and the determination of the Lebanese Army, the militias could not have been disarmed without the agreement of the Syrian government and its willingness to support the Lebanese Army if required. Syria had fulfilled one of its most important undertakings under the Taif Agreement without reservation or hesitation. Now it was the turn of the Lebanese government to fulfil a Lebanese undertaking without reservation or hesitation: the treaty with Syria.

Like the constitutional amendments, the text of the treaty[6] was drafted quickly: the principles had been agreed in Taif. The two countries would seek 'the highest levels of cooperation in all fields, including political, economic, educational, scientific and others', 'within the framework of their respective sovereignty and independence' (Article 1). Security was important: 'Lebanon will not become a transit or a base for any power, state or organization which seeks to undermine Syria's security, while Syria, keen to preserve Lebanon's security, unity and

---

6 For an English translation of the text, see *Middle East Reporter* 66/727 (1991), pp. 218-20.

independence, will not allow any action that would constitute a threat or danger to Lebanon's security.' (Article 3). Both countries 'will seek maximum coordination in formulating Arab and foreign policies and coordinate their stands and positions in Arab and international organizations' (Article 5). The treaty reaffirmed that, in keeping with the timetable agreed on in Taif, the two governments would decide on 'the redeployment of Syrian troops in the Bekaa Valley, the entrance to the western Bekaa, Dahr al-Baidar all the way to Hammana, Mdeirej, and Ain Dara, and should the need arise in other points' (Article 4).

A series of organs was created to carry out the provisions of the treaty: a Higher Council comprising the presidents, premiers, their deputies and the speakers of parliament of both countries, which would meet once a year; a Follow-up and Coordination Committee, comprising the prime ministers and the appropriate ministers for the topics on the agenda, which would meet twice a year; ministerial committees for foreign affairs, economic affairs and defence, which would meet in bi-monthly rotation; and a General Secretariat. The treaty also stipulated bilateral agreements in all areas mentioned in the treaty.

Opinion on the treaty, as on the Taif Agreement, was divided. The Maronite Patriarch expressed the main point of the opponents: 'A treaty between unequal partners means that one will dominate the other.' Minister Marouan Hamade put a new argument for the supporters: in signing the treaty, Syria formally recognized Lebanon. Whatever the arguments, the die had been cast. On May 15th, the government accepted the treaty without dissent; two ministers, Dib and Saade of the Lebanese Forces and the Kata'ib respectively, abstained. On May 22nd it was signed in Damascus. In their speeches, the presidents emphasized different points: Hafez el-Assad repeated the formula of 'one people in two separate states'. Hrawi spoke of the treaty as 'the best option for Lebanon, better than persisting in the previous situation ... The treaty does not diminish the nationhood of the country recovering from sixteen years of civil war.'

## Filling the Chamber of Deputies

In early May, parliament had amended the Constitution in accordance with the Taif Agreement. The number of deputies was raised to 108, half of them Christians and half Muslims, with proportional representation by community within each. Of the nine new Muslim seats, three went to the Shi`is (the South, Baalbek and Baabda) and two each to the Sunnis (Beirut and Tripoli), the Druze (Hasbaya and Beirut) and, for the first time, the Alawites (Tripoli and Akkar).

Government appointment of deputies to new and vacant seats had been hotly disputed in the conclave; now it was hotly disputed in public. A fundamental objection was that it made a mockery of the principle of the separation of powers.

Others took it as an insult to elected deputies; as Walid Jumblatt put it: 'One can't appoint just anybody to fill Kamal Jumblatt's seat.' Yet others feared the government would make too many concessions to Syria and the militias. The proponents argued that it would be impossible to hold normal elections in the near future, and parliament was slowly dying away: of the ninety-nine deputies elected in 1972, only sixty-eight were alive in 1991. The most cogent argument for appointment was the urgent need to apply the letter of the Taif Agreement.

Be that as it may: 384 candidates were proposed. On June 7th, the government 'elected' forty deputies, all of them with large majorities. The problematic nature of the proceedings as an exercise in democracy is best demonstrated by the fact that thirteen of the forty were cabinet ministers: almost half the government elected themselves to parliament.

Politically, the new deputies reflected the composition of the government, though the proportion of unreservedly pro-Syrian members was higher, viz. one-quarter. Many of these represented parties that had seldom if ever held a seat: the SSNP, the pro-Syrian Baath Party (three deputies), Amal and the Alawite parties. All the old parties — Kata'ib, PSP, Tashnag — regained the seats they had held previously, with two glaring exceptions: Pierre Gemayel's former seat went to Hobeika, and Camille Chamoun's to the openly pro-Syrian Jean Obeid, deliberate swipes at the militantly Christian parties.[7] Over half the new deputies came from or were close associates of old political families: fourteen of the forty were sons or close relatives of deceased deputies.

The seats for the 'new' parties were more than a gesture towards loyal supporters of Syria. It was felt that it was better to have these factions represented in parliament than on the loose as an extra-parliamentary opposition.

All in all, amendment and appointments were carried out in the same spirit as the formation of the Karami government: as a step in the Taif process. Those co-opted were pro-Taif and the majority of them *zu'ama'*.

## Disarming the PLO

After its expulsion, the Arafat wing of the PLO had gradually rebuilt a power-base in and around the Palestinian camps at Sidon and Tyre. The Palestinians were not mentioned in the Taif Agreement, but tacitly subsumed under 'militias', who were to be disarmed. Consequently, the PLO did not expect anything good of Taif and sided with the opponents of the Agreement, especially Aoun. After his fall, Palestinian fears for their future in Lebanon grew. The PLO demanded a new agreement with the Lebanese government on Palestinian status in Lebanon. None of the

---

[7] The late deputies' sons, Amin Gemayel and Dory Chamoun, are said to have had first refusal.

representative political groupings showed any interest. Most Lebanese were convinced that their tragedy started with the Cairo Agreement of 1969. Parliament's decision to declare the Agreement null and void was one of the few issues on which the Lebanese could agree in May 1987. No one was prepared even to consider a new agreement.

Hrawi had made this clear in November 1990: the PLO's military presence would have to end within six months. Karami's inaugural speech affirmed that the decision on disbandment applied to both 'Lebanese and non-Lebanese militias'. The PLO repeated its view that it was not a militia, but an army for the liberation of Palestine that had nothing to do with domestic politics in Lebanon. To which Speaker Husseini replied: 'Abu Ammar and Abu Iyad seem to be living in 1982.' Lebanon intended to adhere strictly to the 1948 cease-fire agreement with Israel. Only the army and UNIFIL were responsible for security in the south. In future, the Palestinians and their camps in Lebanon would be treated in the same way as in all other Arab states.

Tension between the Lebanese and Palestinians rose sharply when the anti-Iraqi coalition went on the offensive in the Gulf War. At the end of January 1991, the PLO in southern Lebanon tried 'to open a second front' to support Saddam Hussein. They fired Grad missiles and Katyusha rockets into northern Israel and the 'security zone'. Israel and the USA responded with shelling and helicopter attacks. The Lebanese Army was forced to act. On February 6th, an army brigade was ordered to the south 'to silence all guns in the region', as Defence Minister Murr put it. This provoked a struggle between those Palestinian units that wanted to accept the Lebanese ultimatum and those that did not. The former got their way. At the end of March, the argument over the Palestinians' status flared up again. The Palestinians insisted they were not a militia and, consequently, would not let themselves be disarmed.

The Lebanese reaction was unanimous. Hrawi stated that the Palestinians were not allowed to carry arms in public. Berri demanded that the same laws apply to Lebanese and Palestinians. Interior Minister al-Khatib declared that the cloak of resistance was no excuse for a state within a state. Foreign Minister Boueiz confirmed that the government did not intend to sign a new agreement with the Palestinians. The Syrian Defence Minister Tlass underscored the Lebanese consensus by announcing that all militias, Lebanese and non-Lebanese, had to disappear.

The Palestinians wanted nothing more than they had achieved in 1969 and 1975: the right to make war on Israel from Lebanese territory. However, in 1991 they found no allies among the Lebanese. Not only had the Palestinians not liberated an inch of Palestinian territory in the previous fifteen years, but, in contrast to 1969 and 1975, the Arafat wing of the PLO could no longer count on the support of Syria.

On April 20th, 1991, Lebanese soldiers detained guerrillas of the Popular Front on a commando raid in the south. In mid-May there were gun-fights between the Lebanese Army and Palestinians near Tyre. In June, the Lebanese went on the offensive. The government ordered the PLO to hand over positions they held outside the camps as well as their heavy weaponry. The PLO leadership in Tunis ordered the Palestinian troops around Sidon not to comply.

Six thousand Palestinians faced an equal number of Lebanese soldiers in units composed of Christians and Muslims. Unlike the Palestinians, these units had not yet fought together. Artillery and rocket duels opened the fighting on July 1st. The next day the Lebanese attacked Palestinian positions. Twelve hours later the Palestinians had lost all their positions outside the camps: a 'sweeping victory', in the words of Defence Minister Murr. On July 4th, the Palestinians announced they would hand over their heavy and medium-calibre weapons. The army also disarmed the Lebanese militias in Sidon. A few days later, Lebanese troops surrounded the Palestinian camps at Tyre, and the Palestinians capitulated. Arafat tried to make a grand exit by 'donating' all arms to the Lebanese Army; previously, this might have made an impression, but the Lebanese of 1991 were in no mood for poor comedy after their tragedy.

This did not affect the result. The Palestinians had been driven out of Beirut by the Israelis in 1982 and out of Tripoli by the Syrians in 1985; their last autonomous units capitulated to the Lebanese in 1991. The Arafat-led PLO was now an army in exile.

## Dereliction of the Taif Agreement

The Second Republic emerged because international and regional circumstances had changed. President Hrawi grasped the opportunity to rescue the Taif Agreement from the quicksands of squabbling and doggedly pursued its realization.

A realist, Hrawi was convinced that Lebanon's only option lay in implementing the Taif Agreement. As he regarded General Aoun as the principal obstacle in this process, he did not hesitate to remove him with the help of the Syrian Army, despite the risk involved of alienating large sections of the Christian community.

The results appeared to bear out his success. By mid-1991 most Lebanese were relieved that militia rule was over and security re-established in civilian life and happy that their country was reunited, and even took a little pride in their army's victory over the remnants of the PLO. People began to wonder seriously whether, despite repeated disillusionment, they should not give peace another chance. As a pragmatic reflection of this mood, the inflow of capital swelled appreciably in the summer of 1991.

This success was possible because both Syria and Lebanon fulfilled their obligations under the Taif Agreement to the letter. The Lebanese government did not take a single important decision without consulting the Syrian government, and Syria then gave these decisions its loyal support. This close coordination made it possible to end the wars and restore security.

The price of success was restrictions on Lebanese sovereignty, as codified in the 'Treaty of Brotherhood' between the two states. The coordination mechanisms laid down in this treaty differ little from those in the Franco-German Treaty of Friendship or the Single European Act. What distinguishes Syro-Lebanese from Franco-German or European cooperation is the extreme imbalance of power between the partners and, in particular, the provision of the treaty which gives the stronger partner the right to station troops on the territory of the weaker for an indefinite period.

Janus is an apposite symbol of the Second Republic: one face is the restoration of the Lebanese state, the restrictions on its sovereignty the other. This double-facedness is rooted in the Taif Agreement. The price of the initial successes soon proved to be much higher than anticipated in Taif. Hard on the heels of the restrictions on Lebanon's sovereignty came others, namely, restrictions on democracy and on the rule of law. In Taif the conclave had connived in making a mockery of the division of powers by bowing to Syrian pressure and agreeing to let the government 'elect' the deputies. The 'election' two years later was also at Syria's insistence. However, in Taif there had been no mention at all of restrictions on the freedom of expression and the freedom of the press. It was bad enough that with spreading censorship and self-censorship the Lebanese newspapers grew duller and duller. More ominous was the practice from the summer of 1991 onwards of arresting supporters — usually young — of Aoun without a warrant, and detaining them without a proper trial.

The composition of the Karami government reflected the letter of the Taif Agreement, but not the spirit. The record number of ministers in this government were indeed drawn equally from the communities. But as a majority of the Christian ministers were political lightweights without much support among the Christians, the most important political forces in Christian Lebanon found themselves deprived of the one-third blocking minority guaranteed them in Taif. This crass violation of the principle of consensus could be justified as long as it was seen as a means of advancing the rapid implementation of the Taif process.

The seriousness of this violation became apparent from the summer of 1991 onwards, as first Syria and then the Lebanese government began to postpone putting further provisions of the Taif Agreement into effect, and then to contravene not only the spirit but also the letter of the compact.

As so often in the history of independent Lebanon, dereliction of the Agreement arose not so much from Lebanese as from regional developments. The USA had initiated another attempt to resolve the Palestine conflict and negotiate a comprehensive peace settlement for the Middle East. The first round of talks had removed all illusions that the negotiations would be anything but difficult and protracted. It was crucial to the Western initiative that Syria be included in all serious negotiations. To accommodate this new interest, it was politic for the Western powers to moderate their scrutiny of Syria's Lebanon policy, a development which widened the potential scope for this policy. From Syria's point of view, any strengthening of its influence in Lebanon was an improvement in its negotiating position.

Once again, southern Lebanon was Syria's chosen terrain: without any danger to its own territory, Syria could remind Israel that without Syrian cooperation peace on its northern border was a chimera. This time the PLO could not be instrumentalized in Syria's interest: with Syrian consent and support, the Lebanese Army had mopped up the PLO's residual military outposts.

But there was a substitute to hand: Hezbollah. Whereas the PLO had always striven for at least a degree of independence from Syria — initially with fluctuating fortunes, then increasingly in vain — Hezbollah was held to be more predictable because, as an organization, it was thought to be more dependent upon Syria.

The Taif Agreement made provision for the disarming of all militias, both Lebanese and non-Lebanese. In the general euphoria over the accomplishment of the former and, in the form of the PLO, the partial accomplishment of the latter, many Lebanon-watchers overlooked the fact, or failed to notice, that Hezbollah had not been disarmed, neither in the areas bordering on the Israeli 'security zone' nor in its bases in Syrian-controlled northern Bekaa. In May 1991, the Syrian Vice-President, Khaddam, had declared that so long as Israel had not withdrawn from southern Lebanon, resistance to it had to to continue.[8]

After concluding its operations against the PLO, the Lebanese Army wanted to extend its control to other areas south of the Litani River, and sought Syrian

---

[8] Ahmad Beydoun has drawn attention to the fact that both President Hrawi and Walid Jumblatt as well as the general secretary of the Lebanese Baath Party initially opposed further activity on the part of resistance groups in Lebanon. The local people in southern Lebanon were also hostile because of the inevitable consequences. The Syrians, however, 'plus sensibles aux considérations stratégiques qu'aux réactions locales' and respecting Iran's wishes, were of a different opinion. Vice-President Khaddam 'désavoua donc ses amis libanais'; President Hrawi, who had issued a strongly-worded statement against new military operations, 'fut obligé de la nuancer'. Ahmed Beydoun, 'Le Liban pacifié. Dissolution des milices? Renaissance de la société civile?', in Centre d'Action et d'Information pour le Liban, ed., *Perspectives et réalités du Liban* (Paris, n.d. [1993]), pp. 70f.

consent — in vain. In the summer, Hezbollah and allied organizations stepped up their attacks on Lahad's South Lebanese Army and Israeli troops in the 'security zone', and, true to form, Israel stepped up its reprisals.

The hopes of a peaceful future kindled by the early successes of the Second Republic suffered a dramatic setback in autumn 1991. As a result of the new fighting in the south and the obvious disregard for parts of the Taif Agreement, the confidence of potential investors was undermined: within a few months the inflow of capital dried up completely.

In January 1992, the Lebanese government presented a budget with a projected borrowing requirement equal to half the gross domestic product. This precipitated a flight into dollars, which continued even though the government withdrew its budget proposals. The Lebanese Central Bank tried to support the currency, but, after spending one-third of its foreign-currency reserves, finally capitulated on February 29th. By the beginning of May, one US dollar bought 2,000 Lebanese pounds, a dismal record.

To protest against the rapidly worsening economic situation, a general strike was called for May 6th, which paralyzed the country, and at times took on shades of a popular uprising. The prime minister's office, the finance minister's home, a hotel owned by the speaker and petrol stations owned by the president's son were attacked and devastated. In many places the anti-Syrian tone of the demonstrations could not be ignored.

The government could not be saved: Karami felt obliged to tender his resignation. Even more openly than previously, the new cabinet was formed in Damascus . And the predominance of Syrian frontmen was more pronounced than ever. Certain ministers who had been prepared to accept close, but not unconditional, collaboration with Syria were retired. The new premier, Rashid Solh, returned from Damascus and announced new elections.

This reversed the sequence and priority of the measures agreed to in Taif. The Agreement provided for the creation of a constitutional court, the return of all displaced persons to their places of origin and, above all, the partial withdrawal of the Syrian Army two years after the beginning of the Taif process, a step due in September 1992.

Elections at short notice meant elections before it was possible to determine whether the new electoral law was constitutional or not, elections in regions to which a large part of the population had not yet returned, elections in a country completely controlled by occupying forces.

Subsequent events were to show that this is exactly what was intended.

## Gerrymandering

Less than two months after it had been sworn in, the Solh government presented an electoral bill. After brief resistance, parliament passed it on July 16th. Only one deputy spoke out fearlessly, the aged Albert Moukheiber, for many years Deputy Speaker. It was, to quote his succinct summing up, 'imported and imposed'.

The electoral law was tailored to the advantage of those who approved of full cooperation without qualification, and to the disadvantage of those who might be expected to resist being forced into line. Among those favoured were both Christians and Muslims, but mainly Muslims; among those disfavoured were both Christians and Muslims, but mainly Christians.

The Taif Agreement was being broken not only in political practice or by altered priorities, but also in law.

After lengthy debates, wrangling and negotiations with Damascus, the conclave in Taif had settled a chamber of 108 deputies. The new electoral law[9] made provision for 128 deputies. The regional distribution of the additional seats was grossly uneven. The number of deputies from the Bekaa rose by more than half, from northern Lebanon by 40 per cent and from the south by 25 per cent. The number of seats for Beirut and Mount Lebanon was increased by less than one-fifth. Two-thirds of the new deputies were to be elected from the Lebanese periphery. In other words, those regions gained most where the Syrian Army had been stationed for fifteen years, and even in the event of a partial withdrawal would still be stationed.[10]

The new distribution led to distortions. In future, a deputy from the Bekaa would represent 16,000 voters, compared with a countrywide average of 18,500.[11]

The second blatant violation of the Taif Agreement concerned the size of the constituencies. In Taif the deputies had agreed that constituencies would henceforth be based on provinces (muhafazat); under the old electoral law they had been based on districts (qaza). The decision had been taken after judicious consideration. Small constituencies were more susceptible to domination by one community, which, in turn, helped to create and entrench confessional monopolies. The hope in Taif was that larger constituencies would encourage intercommunal alliances and, thus, favour politicians who were acceptable not only to their own group, but also to members of other groups.

---

[9] For an extract in English, see *Lebanon Report* 3/8 (1992), p. 4.

[10] Cf. map of constituencies, Chapter 2, p. 83.

[11] The Interior Ministry published statistics on the electoral roll. See *as-Safir*, April 30th, 1992. Moreover, the 14,379 registered Alawite voters have two seats, whereas the 26,250 registered voters of other minorities (Protestants, Syrian Orthodox, Latin Christians, Chaldeans and Jews) share a single seat.

Table 10.1 Table of Constituencies

| Governorate | Constituency | District | No. of seats | Sunni | Shi'i | Druze | Alawite | Maronite | Greek Catholic | Greek Orthodox | Anglican | Armenian Catholic | Armenian Orthodox | Minorities |
|---|---|---|---|---|---|---|---|---|---|---|---|---|---|---|
| Beirut | Beirut city | Beirut | 19 | 6 | 2 | 1 | | 1 | 1 | 2 | 1 | 1 | 3 | 1 |
| Mount Lebanon | Jbeil | Jbeil | 3 | | 1 | | | 2 | | | | | | |
| | Kisrawan | Kisrawan | 5 | | | | | 5 | | | | | | |
| | Metn | Metn | 8 | | | | | 4 | 1 | 2 | | | 1 | |
| | Baabda | Baabda | 6 | | 2 | 1 | | 3 | | | | | | |
| | Aley | Aley | 5 | | | 2 | | 2 | | 1 | | | | |
| | Chouf | Chouf | 8 | 2 | | 2 | | 3 | 1 | | | | | |
| Southern Lebanon & Nabatieh | Southern Lebanon | Sidon city | 2 | 2 | | | | | | | | | | |
| | | Sidon district | 3 | | 2 | | | | 1 | | | | | |
| | | Nabatieh | 3 | | 3 | | | | | | | | | |
| | | Tyre | 4 | | 4 | | | | | | | | | |
| | | Bent Jbeil | 3 | | 3 | | | | | | | | | |
| | | Marjayoun & Hasbaya | 5 | 1 | 2 | 1 | | | | 1 | | | | |

*The Two Faces of the Second Republic* 627

| Governorate | Constituency | District | No. of seats | Sunni | Shi'i | Druze | Alawite | Maronite | Greek Catholic | Greek Orthodox | Anglican | Armenian Catholic | Armenian Orthodox | Minorities |
|---|---|---|---|---|---|---|---|---|---|---|---|---|---|---|
| | | Jezzine | 3 | | | | | 2 | 1 | | | | | |
| The Bekaa | Zahle | Zahle | 7 | 1 | 1 | | | 1 | 2 | 1 | | | 1 | |
| | Baalbek/ Hermel | Hermel | 10 | 2 | 6 | | | 1 | 1 | | | | | |
| | West Bekaa | West Bekaa & Rashaya | 6 | 2 | 1 | 1 | | 1 | | 1 | | | | |
| Northern Lebanon | Northern Lebanon | Tripoli city | 8 | 5 | | | 1 | 1 | | 1 | | | | |
| | | Tripoli district | | | | | | | | | | | | |
| | | Akkar | 7 | 3 | | | 1 | 1 | | 2 | | | | |
| | | Zghorta | 3 | | | | | 3 | | | | | | |
| | | Koura | 3 | | | | | | | 3 | | | | |
| | | Bsharre | 2 | | | | | 2 | | | | | | |
| | | Batroun | 2 | | | | | 2 | | | | | | |
| TOTAL | | | 128 | 27 | 27 | 8 | 2 | 34 | 8 | 14 | 1 | 1 | 5 | 1 |

The new electoral law chose neither uniformly small nor uniformly large constituencies. It laid down a hybrid system: Beirut, northern and southern Lebanon had large constituencies, Mount Lebanon and the Bekaa small ones. There was a small Muslim majority in the Beirut constituency, a large one in southern Lebanon and more or less parity in the north. In these constituencies Muslim voters would, for the most part, henceforth be able to determine the Christian deputies. In Mount Lebanon there was an overwhelming Christian majority, which, had the region been treated as a single constituency, would have determined who were elected as Muslim deputies. To prevent this, the province was divided into six small constituencies. In consequence, the overall Christian majority counted for little, and Jumblatt, in particular, was freed of the need to court Christian voters in his Chouf constituency. The Bekaa was divided into three constituencies, each of which corresponded to the stronghold of a powerful politician of the Second Republic: Zahle for President Hrawi, Baalbek-Hermel for Speaker Husseini and west Bekaa/Rashaya for Interior Minister Khatib.

The purpose of this uneven treatment was obvious. It was not a question of local representation, as under the previous system of small constituencies, nor one of intercommunal alliances and preference for moderate politicians, as decided in Taif. Constituencies were large or small depending on whether this could help pro-Syrian candidates and prominent champions of the Second Republic, and harm their opponents.

The motive for this system of advantage and disadvantage was primarily political. The conjunction of the regional distribution of the additional seats and the drawing of the constituencies produced an enormous disequilibrium between Muslim and Christian Lebanon.

As discussed above, the political sting of the earlier Christian parliamentary majority of six to five had been largely assuaged by the fact that more Christian deputies were elected with Muslim votes than vice versa. Taif had settled on parliamentary parity between Christians and Muslims. The new electoral law effectively undermined this equality. Not only did more Christian deputies depend on Muslim votes than ever before, whereas few Muslims did, but the provisions of the new electoral law also ensured that the number of Christian deputies elected by Christian majorities would not constitute a blocking minority of one-third of all deputies. Instead of the parity envisaged in Taif, Muslims would in effect dominate the new parliament.

A high Christian turnout would not have altered matters. However, other provisions of the electoral law effectively prevented a good turnout. The return of all displaced persons to their places of origin, as agreed to in Taif, had not yet taken place, so that about one-third of all voters would not be able to vote in their home constituencies. (In Beirut polling booths were organized for refugees from the Chouf and Aley constituencies, but not for refugees from Bsharre and Akkar in the north, the Bekaa or southern Lebanon.)

Above all, the electoral law did not extend the right to vote to Lebanese living abroad, estimated at about one-third of all voters. In 1992 almost 2,400,000 Lebanese were on the electoral roll, equally divided between Christians and Muslims.[12] According to various estimates,[13] there were only 2,300,000 Lebanese in the country altogether (many of whom were not old enough to vote), 1,300,000 Muslims and 1,000,000 Christians. In the last years of the fighting, including Aoun's 'War of Liberation', a disproportionate number of Christians had sought refuge and work abroad, but had retained their domicile in Lebanon and, hence, their voting rights.

It is more likely that the Lebanese abroad were deprived of their right to vote for political than for confessional reasons. Many of Aoun's supporters lived abroad, and there, unlike in Lebanon, they could and did express their views vociferously. The government had not the least interest in allowing them to take part in the elections. Whatever the political motivation, excluding the voters abroad compounded the already grave electoral disequilibrium between Muslims and Christians.

The new electoral law constituted a complete break with the Taif Agreement. Conceived primarily as an instrument to safeguard and consolidate a pro-Syrian policy, it profoundly disturbed the equilibrium between Christians and Muslims.

This view was also widely shared in Lebanese political circles, including those basically pro-government and favourable to cooperation with Syria. The foreign minister — President Hrawi's son-in-law — resigned in protest. The opposition to elections under these conditions spread well beyond the Christian parties — the National Liberal Party, the National Bloc, the Lebanese Forces and the Kata'ib — to numerous independent deputies, not least among them Muslims. Salim Hoss declared that national unity was more important than elections.

The Maronite Patriarch, supported by his entire synod, became the most important spokesman for the opposition. He rejected elections until all displaced people had returned, the Lebanese abroad were allowed to vote and the occupation was ended. The call for a general strike on July 23rd in protest against the elections was followed in all parts of the country free from Syrian troops.

The government paid no attention to the opposition. It set about drawing up 'slates', lists of 'government candidates', for each constituency, helped more or

---

[12] *As-Safir*, April 30th, 1992. These were all Lebanese nationals domiciled in Lebanon. The roll did not include Lebanese nationals not domiciled in Lebanon - the Lebanese abroad in the proper sense.

[13] Estimates of Saudi-Aid/Hariri Foundation, Université Laval and Université St. Joseph. See also Salma Husseini, 'Redistribution de la population du Liban pendant la guerre civile (1975-1988)', Unpublished dissertation, Ecole des Hautes Etudes en Science Sociales, Paris, 1992.

less discreetly by the representatives of the Syrian powers. And it was by and large successful. In the southern Lebanon constituency, Berri formed a broad coalition between his Amal and Hezbollah, Communists, the SSNP, some members of old and prominent Shi`i and Christian families and, in the person of Rafiq Hariri's sister, a representative of the new moneyed aristocracy. He was opposed by a list put together by Kamal Assad, whose support was concentrated in the Israeli 'security zone'. On the whole, the south was prepared to take part in the elections.

So was northern Lebanon. The 'government slate' was an alliance of old political families from Tripoli and Zghorta, plus two Sunni Islamic fundamentalists and two Alawites.

Interior Minister Khatib headed the 'state list' in the west Bekaa seat, Hrawi's son the list in Zahle, and Speaker Husseini that in Baalbek-Hermel, a seat contested by Hezbollah.

Beirut was not quite so easy for the pro-government forces. Prime Minister Rashid Solh stood, as did Salim Hoss, who overcame his initial reluctance after a lengthy talk with Syrian Vice-President Khaddam. Saeb Salam and his son Tamam, however, did not give in. Jumblatt and his PSP represented the government in the Chouf and Aley constituencies. In the other constituencies in Mount Lebanon the government had great difficulty finding candidates, and had to resort to SSNP and Hobeika supporters, hardly political assets in this region.

The opposition decided not to campaign, and called for a boycott of the elections. Because the electoral law rendered it impossible for them to attain even a blocking minority in parliament, the opposition adopted a policy of turning the elections into a referendum against the elections.

None of the Christian parties put up candidates: a flying visit from Amin Gemayel ended the Kata'ib's hesitation. Nor did any of the leading independent Christian *zu`ama'* in Mount Lebanon stand. The government could find just one candidate for the five seats in the Kisrawan constituency.

Thus, even before the campaign began it was obvious that the elections could hardly produce representative results. Just how unrepresentative would depend on the success or otherwise of the boycott.

## A minority to the polls

Irregularities in varying degrees have been the rule rather than the exception in Lebanese elections. People long deceased made a habit of casting their vote, the government authorities interfered, votes were bought and sold. Nevertheless, apart from the 1947 elections, certain minimum standards were always respected. The election campaigns were utterly free, the ballot was secret, the returning officers were civil servants, results were published in detail and could be challenged, even if there was little likelihood of success. The parliamentary elections in 1992 fell well short of these traditional standards.[14] The election campaign was unusually short. Opposition candidates were obstructed in their electioneering. When Kamal Assad held an election meeting in Tibnin, roadblocks were set up to prevent people attending; about 20,000 still managed to get through. After the rally one of his assistants, the lawyer Nabih Khoury, was kidnapped. Despite a strike by the Bar, at the end of 1992 he had still not been released. Numerous young supporters of Aoun canvassing for the boycott were arrested without a warrant.

The electoral roll could not be brought up to date. Therefore, people were entitled to vote on the strength of their birth certificate, a concession open to abuse.[15]

In many constituencies polling stations were improperly staffed. In the west Bekaa constituency they were run by officials from the ministry of the interior; the government candidate was the minister of the interior. Many polling stations were without ballot boxes. It took almost a week to count the votes in the constituencies in the Bekaa and northern Lebanon. The final results had still not been published at the end of 1992.

As the prime political concern was the voter turnout, the provisional official results probably erred on the high rather than the low side.[16]

The highest turnout, 40 per cent of the registered voters, was recorded in the northern Bekaa and southern Lebanon, and that was approximately one-third below the last parliamentary elections in 1972. In the largest cities, Beirut and Tripoli, 10.1 per cent and 15 per cent respectively voted, compared with 47.2 per cent and 59.6 per cent in 1972. The lowest turnout was in the predominantly Maronite constituencies in Mount Lebanon. In Jbeil it was all of 6.5 per cent, and one candidate, Maha Assad, was elected to parliament on forty-one votes. In Kisrawan the elections had to be repeated for lack of candidates. The turnout for the bye-elections in October was 20.9 per cent, compared with 57 per cent twenty years previously. For the country as a whole, the turnout was less than 20 per cent.

Even assuming that one-third of the electorate was abroad, and therefore not allowed to vote, and working only on the two-thirds in the country, the turnout was still less than one-third, compared with around 60 per cent in earlier elections.

---

[14] On the following, see Joseph Maila, 'Liban: Des élections sous influence', *Les Cahiers de l'Orient* (in the press).

[15] A sociology student in one of the Bekaa constituencies assured the author that ten people had used her birth certificate to vote.

[16] *L'Orient-Le Jour* published the provisional results in full. The Center for Policy Studies in Beirut is preparing a detailed study of the results.

The election boycott was an enormous success: as a referendum, the result of the elections was an unequivocal vote against the electoral law and against elections in the prevailing circumstances.

If the opposition had hoped their campaign would force the elections to be annulled, they underestimated the pertinacity — and cynicism — of the leaders of the Second Republic and their operators in Damascus.

The newly elected parliament might be the least representative in Lebanese history, and it might lack democratic legitimacy, but its legality was beyond dispute. After all, gerrymandering is a common enough practice in numerous political systems, which, nonetheless, continue to be regarded as democracies.[17]

The immediate effect of the new electoral law and the electoral boycott was on the composition of the new parliament, which was quite different from any previous one. There was least change in the parliamentary representation of northern Lebanon. The 'government slate' won every seat, which returned Karami and eight of his supporters, representatives of the Maronite political dynasties in Zghorta and two new deputies, a Sunni Islamic fundamentalist and two Alawites. The political affiliations of the new representatives from southern Lebanon were radically different from the old. Kamal Assad's supporters in the 'security zone' were unable to vote, because Israel would not let anyone cross its demarcation line on election day. The 'government slate' headed by Berri was in effect unchallenged. Despite this, a comparatively respectable 37 per cent of the voters went to the polls,[18] even though the turnout in the overwhelmingly Christian villages of Jezzine was below 5 per cent. Mustapha Saad ran as an independent in Sidon, and was returned by the Sunni population. Berri celebrated his success as a 'victory over four hundred years of feudalism'.

Under the circumstances, it was not surprising that the slate of the Minister of the Interior, Khatib, won in the west Bekaa/Rashaya constituency. But there was a considerable upset in the neighbouring Baalbek-Hermel constituency: the Hezbollah slate defeated that of the former speaker, Husseini. Husseini himself was elected, but only because Hezbollah had put up one candidate fewer than Shi`i seats. Husseini was initially outraged, alleged electoral fraud and announced his resignation, which he withdrew after a Syrian rebuke. Hezbollah candidates may have benefited from the fact that many polling stations were supervised by Hezbollah members instead of civil servants. Yet many observers agreed that on account of its commitment to social work and a multitude of other efforts in the

---

[17] Protest came from the ranks of the European Parliament and from the Democratic presidential candidate, Bill Clinton, who said the Lebanese elections were 'not free and not fair'.

[18] The relativeness of the 37 per cent turnout is illustrated by the comparison with the turnout of 60 per cent in 1972.

interests of the population, support for the Islamic organization extends well beyond the circle of ideological adherents. Husseini, on the other hand, gave more attention to the power struggles in Beirut than to his constituency. A further argument for Hezbollah's genuine success was the turnout of 40 per cent, the highest in the country.

There were surprises in Zahle, too. In the president's former constituency only 31 per cent of the electorate bothered to vote. The president's son was not elected, a clear sign that voters were not prepared to vote for the 'government slate' en bloc. Mohsen Dalloul, known for his very strong Syrian connections, just scraped into parliament. By contrast, Elie Skaff, the son of Joseph Skaff, a critic of Syria's policy in Lebanon, won easily.

Because Salam, as well as respected Maronite and Orthodox politicians, did not stand, the turnout in Beirut was extremely low. Salim Hoss's slate won most votes; the Prime Minister, Rashid Solh barely won his seat. The Maronite seat went to an SSNP candidate.

Only one person on the anti-government slate was elected in the Chouf and Aley constituencies: Emir Faisal Arslan, head of one of the two Druze political dynasties. The Chouf produced the highest turnout in Mount Lebanon: the Druze and the Sunnis went to the polling booths and the Christians stayed at home. In the Baabda constituency only 12 per cent of the electorate cast their vote. The Maronite seats fell to pro-Syrian candidates, among them Elie Hobeika, who won about 3 per cent of the potential votes. In the Metn, 14 per cent of the voters elected Nassib Lahoud and August Bakkos, two independent, though pro-government notables, as well as the pro-Syrian Michel Murr. As mentioned, the turnout in Jbeil was a derisory 6.5 per cent. The Kisrawan bye-elections were won by the slate of the former and future foreign minister, Boueiz, who agreed to stand so as to prevent one of Hobeika's men or the SSNP taking the seat.

All in all, there was a considerable shift in the relative importance of the factions in parliament. No fewer than nineteen deputies could be regarded as Syria's men, among them Khatib, Murr, Hobeika and the SSNP and Baath members. The strongest uniform parliamentary faction was Berri's, with seventeen deputies, followed by Hezbollah with fourteen, to which could be added the two Sunni Islamic fundamentalists. Hrawi's faction was eleven strong, Salim Hoss and Walid Jumblatt commanded ten votes each, Karami nine and Slimmy Franjieh six.

In respect of Lebanese domestic politics, there were two major changes. On the one hand, the Shi`i representation changed radically: from traditional notables to Amal and Hezbollah. In view of the relatively high turnout in Shi`i regions, these deputies, unlike many others, could be regarded as genuine representatives. On the other hand, the major Christian political tendencies were not represented at all, a consequence of the electoral law and the boycott. Michel Aoun, Amin Gemayel, Raymond Eddé and Dory Chamoun were not in parliament, but in exile. Apart from the Zghorta faction, all important Christian groups constituted an extra-parliamentary opposition. Half the deputies were indeed Christians, but the Christian deputies represented a minority of the Lebanese Christians, as the extremely low turnout in Christian strongholds amply testified.

Syrian influence on the Lebanese parliament grew enormously. The majority of the surviving deputies of the parliament elected in 1972 were moderate, but resolute champions of an independent Lebanon, without reservation. Necessity rather than inclination had persuaded them to cooperate with Syria. The 1991 'elections' to fill new and vacant seats swept in the first wave of unconditional pro-Syrian deputies. The elections of 1992 considerably increased their numbers. With the support of that group which traditionally favoured close cooperation with Syria, those members who were pro-Syrian by conviction now commanded a majority in the chamber of deputies. This gave Syria a legal basis for its policies in Lebanon.

In short: The Lebanese winners in the 1992 elections were the more militant Shi`i factions; the effective losers were the Christians. But the real winner was Syria.

The electoral law and the election results rocked that internal Lebanese equilibrium that constituted the basis of the Taif Agreement. Dependence upon Syria had already been accepted in part in Taif. Violations of the Agreement greatly extended this dependence and entrenched it in the Lebanese political system. Belatedly, the costs of ending the war and reconstituting the Lebanese state rose considerably.

## Evolving in dependence

The new government formed at the end of October 1982 broke with custom: it was not parliament in miniature. Its composition was so different that it could be seen as a deliberate and novel counterweight intended to reconcile those who had boycotted the elections with the state.

Rafiq Hariri, billionaire and patron of various causes, holder of both Lebanese and Saudi Arabian nationality, but not of a seat in parliament, was appointed Prime Minister. Many of his ministers — successful business people and respected technocrats — were not deputies either. His government programme emphasised reconstruction and economic growth: policies for infrastructural renewal and administrative reform, for modernizing education, for agricultural development and urban planning, and, above all, for new jobs.

The prime minister and his closest advisers inspired confidence. On the day of his appointment the US dollar cost 2,200 Lebanese pounds, a fortnight after he was sworn in 1,900 Lebanese pounds. Many Lebanese felt that at last they had a government capable of providing economic growth.

The formation of the new government encouraged a mood of cautious optimism, which, in turn, facilitated non-government contacts and overtures between very different political groups. Hezbollah supporters talked to Kata'ib representatives, Geagea met Hobeika, and Jumblatt called on all Christians from the Chouf, including former members of the Lebanese Forces, to return to their home region.

In spite of these favourable signs, the inflow of capital was very sluggish. The Lebanese abroad were the obvious source, but experience had taught them to wait and watch. For, the formation alone of a government that was more competent and inspired greater confidence than its predecessors removed none of the major obstacles to investment.

Southern Lebanon was still in the grip of Hezbollah attacks and Israeli reprisals. But even in the rest of the country the rule of law was precarious. Active Aoun supporters and members of the Lebanese Forces were still being arrested.[19] And youths were hauled before military courts for printing and distributing leaflets.

Moreover, even in Hariri's cabinet strongly pro-Syrian ministers were in charge of all departments that exercised real power.[20] In his inaugural speech Hariri promised to observe the Syro-Lebanese treaty of brotherhood, and stressed that the relationship between Syria and Lebanon was a concern solely of these two states, a pre-emptive rejection of potential Arab or international offers of mediation.

Hariri himself had excellent contacts in the governments of Saudi Arabia and the USA, and enjoyed their goodwill; but this had little effect on his country's dependence upon Syria.

The composition of his government made it abundantly clear that Hariri was allowed considerable autonomy in economic matters, but not in crucial questions of power and of relations between Syria and Lebanon. An improvement in Lebanon's economic and social situation was in Syria's interest, if only to preclude a repetition of the economic unrest of 1991. If a more competent government could achieve this, fine; but there could be no question of Syria

---

[19] In December 1992 Amnesty International reported that approximately 200 supporters of Aoun had been arrested in the previous months, and expressed concern about reports of ill-treatment and torture.

[20] As principal author of the electoral law, Sami Khatib had become a liability, and was replaced as Interior Minister by Beshara Merhej, originally a member of the pro-Iraqi Ba'ath Party who later switched his support to Syria. The new Defence Minister, Mohsen Dalloul, only just scraped in in Zahle, but has the complete trust of Damascus.

relaxing its political grip. The Hariri government could flex economic muscles in political and military shackles.

These limits were soon brought home to him. On November 26th, Hariri won a vote of confidence with a large majority. But before this the deputies had thrown out his more radical proposals for reform, by refusing both to grant him authority to rule by decree for a limited period and to suspend the immunity of civil servants, an indispensable step for administrative reform. Hariri had the great fortune to be utterly independent: he did not live at the expense of the state, but covered state expenditures out of his own pocket. He could afford to ignore deputies coveting cabinet seats, the scourge of non-parliamentary cabinets in the past.

Hariri could expect little effective support from the extraparliamentary opposition. Although the boycott had demonstrated the opposition's numerical strength, it was united on nothing else. Unable to get the elections annulled, and deprived of a parliamentary platform, the opposition coalition splintered.[21]

The extent of their impotence was revealed when Syria and its Lebanese allies again wielded the most effective instrument for keeping the Christians in particular in their place: the call for the abolition of 'political confessionalism', i.e., parliamentary elections without regard for parity or proportionality.

The new Article 95 of the Constitution made provision for this development, but did not set any date. In his inaugural speech on November 10th, 1992, however, the new speaker, Nabih Berri, set a date in so far as he expressed the hope that this parliament would be the last to be elected on a confessional basis. Hezbollah took up the demand for deconfessionalization. One month later, the Syrian Vice-President, Khaddam, declared that before Syria could consider a partial withdrawal of its troops, Lebanon would have to be deconfessionalized. Ten days later a Syro-Lebanese summit meeting was held in Damascus. The communiqué made absolutely no mention of any Syrian withdrawal, although by the terms of the Taif Agreement this was due in September 1992. On December 8th, President Hrawi declared that deconfessionalization would be based on consensus, the Taif Agreement and the Constitution.

This was, so to speak, a new ball game, another blatant violation of the Taif Agreement, but no less effective for that. Partial Syrian withdrawal would follow the abolition of parity and proportionality; if people did not like that — and few Christians did — they should learn to like the Syrian Army.

This political deal strengthened Syria's position as arbiter over Lebanon's future, and Lebanon's dependence on Syria's goodwill, as never before.

---

[21] A power struggle broke out in the Kata'ib between the civilian wing led by Georges Saadé and Karim Pakradouni and former members of the Lebanese Forces led by Samir Geagea.

# 11

## The Emergence of a Nation
## Epilogue and Conjectures

The excesses committed during the combat ... have increased intercommunity distrust and hatred to levels unknown for at least a century ... The last decade of sordid violence has ... taken a heavy toll on tolerance, the sine qua non for pluralism.

> Paul A. Jureidini and R.D. McLaurin, 1984

A crowd of men suddenly turned up then
Who wanted to talk to the military men
But the military talked with bren and sten
And the men never said anything again.

> Bertold Brecht

Protectorat: Système juridique qui place un état sous la dépendance d'un autre, en ce qui concerne notamment sa politique étrangère et sa défense militaire.

> Larousse, *Dictionnaire du français contemporain*

> Why are negative predictions so common? Because it is very easy to say that things will go wrong and very easy for people to understand.
>
> Karl W. Deutsch

> A nation is a number of people who either share a fallacy about common origins or dislike the same neighbours.
>
> Bohemian saying

Michael C. Hudson called Lebanon a 'precarious nation' a decade before war broke out. After sixteen years of war and civil war and internal strife can one still speak of a Lebanese nation? Have not, as Jureidini and McLaurin assert, all too many excesses committed by all too many groups taken a heavy toll on tolerance, without which no multi-communal state can be a nation?

There is a stark contrast between the opinions and desires of the majority of Lebanese in the survey and the everyday reality of the war years: separation, impoverishment and death. Does this support a contentious hypothesis in social research that the opinions and desires of individuals are one thing, behaviour, in particular group behaviour, another? Might the individual Lebanese be Dr Jekyll, whereas Lebanese in groups behave like Mr Hyde? The answer is clear. The overwhelming majority of Lebanese want peace, coexistence and national unity. They have expressed this not only as individuals in anonymous interviews, but also as groups in mass demonstrations over the years of war, repeatedly, whenever they had the opportunity.

## Peace and unity movements

The first demonstration took place in November 1975. On his own initiative, the television announcer Sharif Akhawi called for a demonstration against the fighting. Tens of thousands of East and West Beirutis responded to his appeal. The militiamen resumed their shooting only after the demonstrators had returned home. The fighters prevented further demonstrations by staging heavy artillery duels hours before the announced time of any demonstration, forcing the civilian population off the streets.

When the Israelis besieged West Beirut in 1982, an estimated 100,000 inhabitants — Christian and Muslim — found refuge in East Beirut. The reception Gemayel and Karami received from the people of Sidon on their joint visit after the Israeli troops had withdrawn was a spectacular demonstration of the desire for reconciliation.

Organized mass protest against the war and for national unity really got going in 1985. A peace movement 'Women Against War', marched on parliament and the presidential palace. Protesting war cripples marched on crutches or in wheelchairs from Tripoli to Beirut. Professional associations and societies defeated militia attempts to divide them. In the 1988 board elections of the Lebanese Association of Lawyers, Kata'ib and Amal candidates were defeated by anti-war and anti-polarization candidates. In the board elections of the Medical Association not one of the candidates associated with militias or warring factions was successful. To spare themselves further disgrace the militias forced the Association of Engineers to postpone their elections.

The most representative protest against the war came from the trade unions. The Confédération Générale des Travailleurs Libanais (CGTL) maintained its non-confessional stance throughout the war. In 1988 the trade unions had approximately 55,000 paid-up members, that is, about one-quarter of the total workforce, more or less the level in the USA and Mexico. The CGTL comprises 165 separate unions of various types, some restricted to specific trades or industries, others with a general membership. Some are strictly apolitical, others strongly politicized; there are trade unionists of every shade of opinion, from Communists to Phalangists. Trade unions and the confederation have consociational structures. As an informal and flexible arrangement, there are equal numbers of Christians and Muslims on union executives. The federations have the same number of seats at confederation conferences, which also ensures political proportionality. All important decisions are taken in consensus. Until the mid-1980s the trade unions concentrated on wages, working conditions and labour legislation. By doing so, the CGTL became one of the truly representative organizations in the country.

The economic crisis involved it in politics. Between 1977 and 1982 the CGTL was able to get wage increases at least equal to the rate of inflation. With recession this became impossible. As real incomes fell, the CGTL turned its attention to the causes of economic decline: the war and the *de facto* partition of the country.

In 1986 it called a strike for the first time. Workers walked out in all parts of the country — to the chagrin of all politico-military leaders. This was followed by a series of increasingly political strikes in April, July, August, September and November 1987, April 1988 and May 1990. These were not strikes in the usual sense, but mass demonstrations that drew support from far beyond trade-union circles. Reformist intellectuals who had taken part in the student movement of the 1960s started to involve themselves in trade-union activities. The CGTL newspaper, 'The Voice of Unity', called for an end to the war and for renewed coexistence among the Lebanese. November 1987 was a high point of political activism. The trade-union-backed peace movement organized huge demonstrations in Tripoli, Jbeil, Sidon and Tyre. The largest took place in Beirut, where, according to police estimates, 60,000 demonstrators from East and West Beirut gathered at the Museum checkpoint chanting 'East and West united' and 'national unity'. The president of the CGTL, Antoine Bechara, was carried shoulder-high from the Museum in East Beirut across to West Beirut and back. This popular response annoyed the various militias; Bechara in East Beirut and his communist deputy in West Beirut received threats against their lives. In protest against these and similar practices two trade unionists resigned from the executive of the Jumblatt's Progressive Socialist Party.

Strikes did not change the political situation, as the trade unions had hoped. As Brecht wrote: many wanted to talk with the military, but were silenced by machine-guns. However, the trade unions gave tens of thousands of Lebanese workers and innumerable others the chance to demonstrate that they rejected the slogans of all warring factions.

In the spring of 1990 the Lebanese demonstrated yet again their willingness to help one another, irrespective of religious affiliation, in times of distress. Just as during the Israeli siege eight years earlier West Beirutis had found refuge in the eastern section, so as Aoun's army fought the Lebanese Forces tens of thousands of East Beirutis found refuge in West Beirut.

## The foundations of a new consensus

Demonstrations for peace and coexistence in the presence of heavily armed militiamen express the desire for a new consensus as clearly as any survey. After all that has happened since 1975, there is less hate and more tolerance among the Lebanese that might be expected; and after so many years of apparent disunity, the desire for unity is stronger than might be assumed. The Lebanese are not a Hobbesian society in which each community regards the others as packs of wolves. The obstacle to a new consensus was not fanatic masses but short-sighted or power-hungry elites. Surveys and protests show that consociation is deeply rooted in people's attitudes. Only a cartel of hostile elites obstructed its practice: the 'lions' — mercenary leaders, warlords and, above all, a band of non-Lebanese lion-tamers who set 'their' lions against one another as and when required.

There has been no lack of constitutional blueprints for restructuring or reconstructing Lebanon. Proposals for a unitary, deconfessionalized state hope to encourage a uniform nation; this attempt to equate the will of the majority with the will of the nation is a guise to subordinate opponents. The contrary assumption that the communities or religious groups are nations treats the country as a

*The Emergence of a Nation*

territory of separate nations. Such attempts at political engineering underestimate the political maturity of Lebanese society.

The surveys have revealed that the majority of Lebanese have little difficulty in reconciling communal identity and national identity. People think of themselves as Maronite or Sunni or Shi`i, and, at the same time, as Lebanese, much as the Welsh or the Scots see themselves as Welsh or Scots as well as British, and Bavarians and Rheinlanders are also Germans. Lebanese do have a strong sense of communal affiliation. But only a small minority feel that this is more important than their Lebanese nationality. Most people want to stay what they are and accept that others feel the same way; and all want to live in peace with each other in the same country.[1]

The new coexistence pact, that part of the Taif Agreement that deals with domestic policy, is remarkably close to the wishes of the population revealed in the survey.

A large majority accepts a political system based on power-sharing between the communities. A majority almost as large would also accept a simple one-man-one-vote system. These findings suggest that the Lebanese would prefer a system combining elements of consociation and majority voting, as practised in Switzerland, for instance. This would, on the one hand, give each community the same entrenched rights, and, on the other hand, allow for alternating majorities in all matters that did not affect the existence and identity of the communities. In their new pact the Lebanese deputies have provided for the transition to a hybrid system of this kind. There is greater consensus on this point than either Jacobins or separatists like.

Did such a consensus exist before the war? Perhaps; there are no comparable empirical data for the pre-war period. But it is more plausible that this consensus is a product of the war. To share the unsociable view of the Bohemian saying at the head of the chapter, war experiences have probably helped it emerge.

The old consensus of 1943 was based on good economic sense and a common desire for independence: from France, in the case of the Muslims, and Syria, in the case of the Christians. The new consensus is more solid. It is rooted in common suffering, a common yearning for peace and a common desire for independence from everybody. Less than one per cent of Lebanese respondents expressed sympathy or admiration for Israel, but no more than one per cent welcomed Syria's fraternal embrace either. This finding has been confirmed by

---

[1] The drift of the above is confirmed in an opinion poll the Lebanese MASS Institute and the French market research firm OPTEM conducted in September and October 1989. See MASS and OPTEM, *Les Libanais et le Liban* (Paris, October 1989). The crucial item reads: 'Despite the crisis, a strong sense of community unites the Lebanese, which makes it possible to rebuild the country.' 73 per cent of the respondents agreed.

subsequent developments. The low turnout in the 1992 parliamentary elections demonstrated the attenuated standing of candidates on the pro-Syrian government slates, with the relative exception of southern Lebanon, where Berri had built up his own solid constituency. By contrast, the overwhelming success of the election boycott must be interpreted as an unequivocal rejection of an 'imported and imposed' system. There is one thing the Lebanese do not want to be: dependent on others.

## A nation too late?

Some small nations have never had the state they want, and others have lost the one they had. The Lebanese had an independent state. But they became a nation only when the state was in mortal danger. Has the Lebanese nation emerged too late to save the independence of the state?

Regardless of the likes and dislikes of the Lebanese people, their state has grown more and more dependent on Syria, and this is unlikely to change in the foreseeable future. But just how dependent Lebanon will be is difficult to judge.

The satellization of Lebanon is already at an advanced stage. In 1992 a Syro-Lebanese summit was held every forty days on average, and ministers and top civil servants made hundreds of trips to Damascus. Syria's leaders settle internal Lebanese disputes between the president, prime minister and speaker of the chamber of deputies. Parliamentary candidates prior to the election and deputies since then vie with each other for the patronage of various groups close to the centre of power in Syria. In Damascus the careers of Lebanese Army officers and civil servants are made or broken. This dependent political system has evolved its own client-patron structures, in which the Syrian government has assumed the role of the supreme *za'im*, keeping order among both traditional *zu'ama'* and warlords turned politicians.[2] New identities of interest gain permanence; for systems of patronage are concerned not only with fame but also with fortune.

---

[2] Joseph Maila has a fine grasp of the situation: 'Le retour de la vieille culture politique s'est doublé cependant d'un élément nouveau, inquiétant: celui de l'inféodation de la classe politique libanaise, dans sa grande majorité, à l'ordre syrien. On pouvait, certes, penser, sur un plan de strict droit international, que la quatrième partie de l'Accord de Taëf prévoyant l'aménagement des relations avec la Syrie, créait une structure de servitude. On ne pouvait penser qu'elle susciterait aussi rapidement une culture de servilité. Attentifs aux suggestions syriennes, perméables à ses pressions, dociles à ses commandements, la classe dirigéante va au-delà des désirs de Damas dans sa volonté de se maintenir en place et de gouverner. L'ordre proconsulaire qui règne aujourd'hui au Liban en aura été facilité.'; 'L'accord de Taëf: Deux ans après', in Centre d'Action et d'Information pour le Liban, ed., *Perspectives et réalités du Liban* (Paris, n.d. [1993]), p. 56.

Tacit acceptance of linkage between 'deconfessionalization' and a partial Syrian withdrawal has rendered any withdrawal improbable. The Hariri government itself is a concession to placate the Lebanese — on the calculation that the economic carrot will sweeten the political stick — and it took riots and an election boycott to win even this.

Is new prosperity conceivable without effective political sovereignty? Will Lebanese invest in Lebanon if proper legal protection cannot be enforced? Will the Lebanese abroad return with their capital before they are sure they can exercise their cultural freedoms and civil rights, in particular the freedom of expression?

If the answers to the above are negative, the prospects for the future are economic stagnation, renewed emigration of skilled and qualified people and a gradual 'Syrianization' not only of the state, but also of Lebanese society.

However, in early 1993 there is no definite answer to these questions yet. The Hariri government may succeed in restoring Lebanon as a centre for commerce and finance, and possibly also for agricultural and manufacturing industries able to adapt quickly to the needs of the Gulf states. It is also conceivable that the Lebanese educational system and cultural life will return to their former standards and variety. If all this were to come about, it might be attractive for Lebanese to leave the low-growth economies of the western industrialized states and return to Lebanon with their families and capital, instead of subjecting themselves or their children to increasingly complex naturalization procedures in Europe, North America and Australia. Above all, it could put an end to emigration.

Rebuilding a flourishing economy would also put an end to a situation in which many Lebanese live from day to day. However, to judge by the experience of numerous other societies, renewed prosperity will hardly be conducive to political apathy. On the contrary, it will almost certainly nourish a new drive for political freedom.

## The neighbour's uncertain future

Lebanon's future path does not really depend on the Lebanese themselves, and only to a limited extent on the Lebanese government. It will be largely determined by their large neighbour. Predictions about Syria, however, are immensely difficult.

This is partly due to the Syrian political system, in which one man has the final say. This man voices his intentions only when he thinks it necessary. His long rule has amply demonstrated a remarkable perseverance in pursuit of his goals, and an equally remarkable ability to recognize changing circumstances and modify his goals, strategies and tactics accordingly. Among his predecessors there was scarcely one who wanted to accept the existence of an independent Lebanon. Lebanese politicians were long puzzled by Hafez el-Assad's objectives in Lebanon. Since 1985 at the latest these objectives have been clear: not primitive annexation, as Saddam Hussein later attempted in Kuwait, but unreserved recognition of Syrian ascendancy in a formally independent Lebanon. This objective was achieved with the signing of the 'Treaty of Brotherhood' in 1991, and entrenched at the heart of the Lebanese system in 1992 by the election of a Lebanese parliament dominated by Syrian clients.

In matters of foreign and security policy Lebanon is a vassal state, both by the terms of the treaty and in practice. As the Syrians have already penetrated much of the Lebanese system, this link will not be broken soon.

To what extent the current Syrian leadership expects conformity in cultural and economic affairs remains to be seen. Traditionally, the Syrian Baath Party has had a predilection for cultural policies that encourage Arab uniformity and for state intervention in the economy. The diversity of the Lebanese educational system at all levels, and the consequent bi- and multi-lingualism of large sections of the Lebanese population, had always been a thorn in the flesh of Baath Party ideologists. No less so was the anarchic, successful Lebanese economy, which adapted to the war so well so long, and inevitably gave Syrians cause for unwelcome comparisons. Yet it is unlikely that ideology will determine Syrian economic policy. For years Syria has been dependent on foreign economic aid. To improve its economic performance, it has considerably liberalized the economy. Instead of forcing Lebanon to conform to economic policies it itself is abandoning, it would be in Syria's interest to profit from Lebanon as much as possible. Lebanese like to talk about a 'Hong Kong scenario': Lebanon as a flourishing international commercial and financial centre, with a substantial share of the benefits accruing to Syria. What the Lebanese have in mind is the fairly independent Hong Kong without a sell-by date. The less ideological Syrian politicians think along similar lines, though with far more political control. The Hariri government may be regarded as an experiment with this model.

How consistent will Syrian policy towards Lebanon be in the medium and long term? The present Syrian regime has proved remarkably stable in a once notoriously unstable country. This stability is primarily the achievement of one man of exceptional ability. The greater the power concentrated in his hands, the greater is the likelihood of a struggle for succession when he departs. The jockeying in Damascus during Hafez el-Assad's illness in 1984 may have been a foretaste of events in post-Assad Syria. He is said to be preparing his son to succeed him, and there are signs that members of the president's entourage are once again vying for influence. Hafez el-Assad's imminent death has often been reported; and absolute power has often proved an elixir of life.

There is no reason why the post-Assad leaders in Syria should see their interests in Lebanon in a different light. What is questionable is whether they will be able to pursue these policies with Assad's brilliance. In the event of a lengthy struggle for power, Syria may have to cut back on its current powerful position in Lebanon, or even withdraw. But it is unlikely that any post-Assad government will voluntarily abandon Assad's Lebanon policy; this policy has always been an element of a wider, regional policy.

For the Syrian leaders, Lebanon's social and economic make-up has always been secondary to the country's potential as a pawn and as a card in the Middle East poker game of war and peace. Until there is a comprehensive Middle East peace settlement — and even more so when one is in the offing — Syria sets great store by as great a control over Lebanon as possible. One effect of Lebanon's dependence on Syria is that now it is more susceptible to developments elsewhere in the Orient than it already was in 1967.

## 'Drifting dunes'

Yassir Arafat has compared the constellations of power in the Middle East with drifting dunes: one never can tell in which direction the wind will blow them. Since 1967 several 'dunes' have drifted into each other in Lebanon and threatened to bury the country. Dunes neither respect borders nor keep direction. Their shapes alter, merge, blur, dissolve.

Predicting medium and long term developments in Middle Eastern politics is like predicting changes in a sea of sand. Anything is possible, nothing is too extraordinary or too unlikely.

There could be localized whirlwinds restricted to Lebanon or parts of the country. Until Syria and Israel come to some agreement, there is always the possibility of proxy war in southern Lebanon. If Hezbollah's actions excessively provoke or hurt Israel, Israel might decide to extend the 'security zone' or retaliate by attacking bases deeper in Lebanese territory.

There could be heavy storms. Failure to reach an agreement on autonomy for the Palestinians in the occupied territories will almost certainly intensify the intifada and encourage Islamic fundamentalists to oust the PLO and change the nature of the Palestine conflict. This could, in turn, promote the cause of those in Israel who have long preached that the best solution is radical 'population transfers'. In this event, it would be virtually impossible for Jordan and Syria to stand by idly. And Lebanon would again be a likely battleground.

Iraq could cause new turbulence. The second Gulf War did not utterly crush Iraq's military potential. Fearful of Iran, some Gulf states have already taken tentative steps to improve their relations with Iraq. It is extremely unlikely that

Saddam Hussein would repeat his adventure in Kuwait, whose independence is guaranteed by Western powers. But he could return to his previous practice of attempting to subvert his Arab adversaries and supporting opposition movements against them. A potential target would be a Syria embroiled in fighting over the Assad succession. Whether this would widen or narrow Lebanon's scope is impossible to predict.

Nor can a general change of climate in the Middle East be excluded. A considerable number of Israelis disapprove of dominating the Palestinians in the occupied territories, and reject 'transfers' as morally indefensible. On the other hand, the PLO has dropped its maximum demands, and seems ready to accept less than an independent Palestinian state. Thus, the prospect of peace in Palestine is no longer totally unrealistic. This would greatly facilitate a rapprochement between Syria and Israel.

Whether Lebanon would benefit from such a development is by no means certain. It might result in the implementation of Security Council Resolution 425, involving the withdrawal of both Syria and Israel from Lebanon. On the other hand, Israel — and the Western states — might succumb to the temptation of buying Syria's signature to a Middle East settlement with Lebanon's freedom. This would seal Lebanon's fate as an independent state.

None of the possible political developments sketched above holds particularly good prospects for Lebanon. But probabilities are not certainties. One should not underestimate the country's power to resist being absorbed by its larger neighbour. In recent years many small states whose existence had been all but forgotten have regained their independence.

Notwithstanding separation, expulsion and massacre, among the Lebanese there is now greater consensus on the need to preserve Lebanon than there was at the time of independence. This new consensus is a consequence not so much of the cost-benefit considerations of a small elite as of the experiences of the people as a whole. It is easier to create a state than a nation. Their most recent history has taught the Lebanese that they are a nation and that they want to remain a nation. Their sense of democracy and love of freedom are deeply rooted. It is not very likely that such a nation will stop aspiring to effective self-determination as a fully sovereign state.

# Bibliography

## A Books

Abdel-Malek, Anouar, *Egypte, Société militaire*, Paris, 1962

Abouchdid, Eugénie E., *Thirty Years of Lebanon and Syria (1917–1947)*, Beirut, 1948

Abou Jaoudé, Joseph et al., *La nouvelle société libanaise dans la perception des Fa`aliyat (decision-makers) des communautés chrétiennes*, 3, Etudes et Rapports, Kaslik, 1984

Abou Rjaily, Khalyl and Boutros Labaki, *Les paroisses déplacées des églises du Liban*, Paris and Beirut, 1987

Accaoui, Selim and Magida Salman, *Comprendre le Liban* (Culture Critique 12), Paris, 1976

Aggiouri, René, *Le conflit de Palestine dans le jeu des puissances (1950–1967)*, Beirut, 1968

Ajami, Fouad, *The Vanished Imam. Musa al Sadr and the Shia of Lebanon*, London, 1986

—— *The Arab Predicament: Arab political thought and practice since 1967*, Cambridge, 1981

Al-Khuri, Bisharah, *Haqa'iq lubnaniyyah (Lebanese Realities)*, 3 vols., Beirut, 1960

Allemann, Fritz René (ed.), *Die arabische Revolution. Nasser über seine Politik*, Frankfurt, 1988

Almond, Gabriel and James S. Coleman, *The Politics of the Developing Areas*, Princeton, 1960

—— and Sidney Verba, *The Civic Culture*, Princeton, 1963

—— and G. Bingham Powell, *Comparative Politics: A developmental approach*, Boston, 1966
Amos II, John W., *Palestinian Resistance. Organization of a Nationalist Movement*, New York, 1980
Antonius, George, *The Arab Awakening: The story of the Arab national movement*, New York, 1946
Antoun, Richard and Iliya Harik (eds.), *Rural Politics and Social Change in the Middle East*, Bloomington and London, 1972
Apter, David E., *The Politics of Modernization*, Chicago, 1965
Asad, Muhammad, *The Principles of State and Government in Islam*, Berkeley and Los Angeles, 1961
Azar, Edward E. et al. (eds.), *The Emergence of a New Lebanon. Fantasy or reality?*, New York, 1984

Banton, Michael, *Race Relations*, London, 1967
Barakat, Halim, *Lebanon in Strife. Student preludes to the civil war*, Austin and London, 1977
Barth, Frederik (ed.), *Ethnic Groups and Boundaries. The social organization of culture difference*, Boston, 1969
Barudio, Günter, *Der Teutsche Krieg 1618–1648*, Frankfurt, 1985
Bash, Harry H., *Sociology, Race and Ethnicity. A critique of American ideological intrusions upon sociological theory*, New York, 1979
Bauberot, Jean et al. (eds.), *Palestine et Liban. Promesses et mensonges de l'Occident*, Paris, 1977
Bauer, Otto, *Die Nationalitätenfrage und die Sozialdemokratie*, Vienna, 1924
Baz, Selim, *Pièces diplomatiques relatives aux événements de 1860 au Liban*, Beirut, 1978
Benassar (alias Gabriel Menassa), *Anatomie d'une guerre et d'une occupation. Evénements du Liban de 1975 à 1978*, Paris, 1978
Benedict, Ruth, *Patterns of Culture*, London, 1961
Bergstraesser, Arnold, *Die Macht als Mythos und als Wirklichkeit*, Freiburg, 1965
—— and Wilhelm Cornides (eds.), *Die Internationale Politik 1955. Eine Einführung in das Geschehen der Gegenwart*, Munich, 1958
Berting, Jan et al. (eds.), *Problems in International Comparative Research in the Social Sciences*, Oxford, 1979
Betts, Robert Brenton, *Christians in the Arab East. A political study*, Athens, 1975
Beydoun, Ahmad, *Identité confessionnelle et temps social chez les historiens libanais contemporains*, Beirut, 1984

Biegel, L.C., *Minderheden in het Midden-Oosten. Hun betekenis als politieke factor in de Arabische wereld*, Deventer, 1972
Binder, Leonard (ed.), *Politics in Lebanon*, New York, 1966
Binswanger, Karl, *Untersuchungen zum Status der Nichtmuslime im Osmanischen Reich des 16. Jahrhunderts. Mit einer Neudefinition des Begriffs "Dhimma"*, Munich, 1977
Blechman, Barry M. and Stephen S. Kaplan (eds.), *Force without War. The use of the armed forces as a political instrument*, Washington, 1978
Braude, Benjamin and Bernard Lewis, *Christians and Jews in the Ottoman Empire. The functioning of a plural society*, 2 vols., New York and London, 1982
Brinton, Crane, *The Anatomy of Revolution*, New York, 1938
Brockelmann, Carl, *Geschichte der arabischen Literatur*, Leiden, 1942
Büren, Rainer, *Ein palästinensischer Teilstaat? Zur internen regionalen und internationalen Dimension der Palästinafrage*, Baden-Baden, 1982
Bulloch, John, *Death of a Country. The civil war in Lebanon*, London, 1977
—— *Final Conflict. The war in the Lebanon*, London, 1983

Campbell, Ernest Queener (ed.), *Racial Tensions and National Identity*, Nashville, Tenn., 1972
Carre, Oliver (ed.), *L'Islam et l'Etat dans le monde d'aujourd'hui*, Paris, 1982
—— et al. (eds.), *Radicalismes islamiques*, I, Paris, 1985
Carstens, Karl et al. (eds.), *Die Internationale Politik 1966–67*, Munich, 1973
Catroux, Georges, *Dans la bataille de la Méditerranée*, Paris, 1949
CEMAM-Report, *Religion. State and Ideology* (Center for the Study of the Modern Arab World, Saint-Joseph's University). Reports 1975, 3, Beirut, 1976
CEMAM-Report, *Islamic Law and Change in Arab Society* (Center for the Study of the Modern Arab World, Saint Joseph's University). Reports 1976, 4, Beirut, 1978
Chamoun, Camille, *Crise au Moyen-Orient*, Paris, 1963
—— *Crise au Liban*, Beirut, 1977
—— *Mémoires et souvenirs*, Beirut, 1979
Chamussy, René, *Chronique d'une guerre. Liban 1975–1977. En postface: Les doutes de l'après-guerre*, Paris, 1978
Charaf, Georges, *Communautés et pouvoir au Liban*, Beirut, 1981
Charles-Roux, François, *La France et les chrétiens d'Orient*, Paris, 1939
Charon, Cyrille, *Histoires des patriarcats Melkites*, 2 vols., Rom 1910–1911
Chevallier, Dominique (ed.), *La société du Mont Liban à l'époque de la révolution industrielle en Europe*, Paris, 1971
—— (ed.), *L'espace social de la ville arabe*, Paris, 1979

Chiha, Michel, *Visage et présence du Liban*, Beirut, 1964

Cobban, Alfred, *The Nation-State and National Self-Determination*, New York, 1969

Cohen, Abner, *Two-Dimensional Man. An essay on the anthropology of power and symbolism in complex society*, Berkeley, 1974

—— (ed.), *Urban Ethnicity*, London, 1974

Copeland, Miles, *The Game of Nations. The amorality of power politics*, London, 1969

Corm, Georges, *Le Proche-Orient eclaté. De Suez à l'invasion du Liban, 1956–1982*, Paris, 1983

—— *Géopolitique du conflit libanais. Etude historique et sociologique*, Paris, 1986

Couland, Jacques, *Le Mouvement Syndical au Liban 1919–1946. Son évolution pendant le mandat français de l'occupation à l'évacuation et au Code du Travail*, Paris, 1970

Cox, Oliver C., *Caste, Class and Race: A study in social dynamics*, New York, 1948

Cudsi, Alexander S. and Ali E. Hillal Dessouki (eds.), *Islam and Power*, London, 1981

Curtis, Michael (ed.), *Religion and Politics in the Middle East*, Boulder, Col., 1981

Dahdah, Nagib, *Evolution historique du Liban*, Beirut, 1967

Dawisha, Adeed J., *Syria and the Lebanese Crisis*, London and Basingstoke, 1980

Dekmejian, Hrair Richard, *Egypt under Nasir. A study in political dynamics*, New York, 1971

Desjardins, Thierry, *Le martyre du Liban*, Paris, 1976

Despres, Leo A. (ed.), *Ethnicity and Resource Competition in Plural Societies*, The Hague, 1975

Deutsch, Karl W., *Nationalism and Social Communication: An inquiry into the foundations of nationality*, Cambridge, Mass., 1962

—— and William Foltz (eds.), *Nation-Building*, New York, 1966

Dib, Pedro, *L'église maronite*, Paris, 1930

Dibs, Joseph, *Les maronites du Liban*, Paris, 1875

—— *Perpétuelle orthodoxie des maronites*, Arras, 1896

Döring, Peter A. et al. (eds.), *Bildung in sozio-ökonomischer Sicht*, Cologne and Vienna, 1989

Douglas, Mary, *Purity and Danger*, London, 1966

Dubar, Claude and Salim Nasr, *Les classes sociales au Liban*, Paris, 1976

Dupuy, Trevor Nevitt, *Elusive Victory: The Arab-Israeli wars, 1947–74*, Indianapolis, 1977

Eckstein, Harry (ed.), *Internal War. Problems and approaches*, London, 1964
Edwards, R.C. et al. (eds.), *Labor Market Segmentation*, Lexington, Mass., 1975
Eisenstadt, S.N., *Modernization: Protest and change*, Englewood Cliffs, N.J., 1966
Emerson, Rupert, *From Empire to Nation. The rise to self-assertion of Asian and African peoples*, Cambridge, Mass., 1960
Ende, Werner and Udo Steinbach (eds.), *Der Islam in der Gegenwart*, Munich, 1984
Entelis, John P., *Pluralism and Party Transformation in Lebanon — Al Kata'ib, 1936–1970*, Leiden, 1974
Esman, Milton J. (ed.), *Ethnic Conflict in the Western World*, Ithaca, N.J., 1977
—— and Itamar Rabinovich (eds.), *Ethnicity, Pluralism and the State in the Middle East*, Ithaca and London, 1988
Etteldorf, Raymond, *Catholic Churches in the Middle East*, New York, 1955
Evans-Pritchard, E.E., *Witchcraft, Oracles and Magic among the Azande*, Oxford, 1937
Evron, Yair, *War and Intervention in Lebanon. The Israeli-Syrian deterrence dialogue*, Baltimore, 1987

Fattal, Antoine, *Le statut légal des Non-Musulmans en pays d'Islam*, Beirut, 1958
Fawaz, Leila Tarazi, *Merchants and Migrants in Nineteenth Century Beirut*, Cambridge and London, 1983
Fischhof, Adolph, *Österreich und die Bürgschaften seines Bestandes*, Vienna, 1869
Flores, Alexander, *Intifada, Aufstand der Palästinenser*, Berlin, 1988
Fondation Libanaise, Fondation libanaise pour la paix civile permanente (ed.), *Le droit à la mémoire*, Beirut, 1988
Francis, Emmerich K., *Interethnic Relations*, New York, 1976
Freedman, Robert O., *Soviet Policy toward the Middle East since 1970*, New York, 1978
Furnival, J.S., *Netherlands India. A study of plural economy*, Cambridge, 1939
—— *Colonial Policy and Practice. A comparative study of Burma and Netherlands India*, New York, 1956

Gardet, Louis, *La cité musulmane*, Paris, 1954
Geertz, Clifford (ed.), *Old Societies and New States. The quest for modernity in Asia and Africa*, London, 1963

Gellner, Ernest and John Waterbury (eds.), *Patrons and Clients in Mediterranean Societies*, London, 1977

Gemayel, Amine, *L'offense et le pardon*, Paris, 1988

Gibb, H.A.R. and J.H. Kramers (eds.), *Shorter Encyclopedia of Islam*, Leiden, 1953

Glazer, Nathan and Daniel Patrick Moynihan, *Beyond the Melting Pot*, Cambridge, Mass., 1963

Golan, Galia, *Yom Kippur and After. The Soviet Union and the Middle East crisis*, Cambridge, 1977

Goria, Wade R., *Sovereignty and Leadership in Lebanon 1943–1976*, London, 1985

Gurr, Ted Robert, *Why Men Rebel*, Princeton, N.Y., 1970

Hacke, Christian, *Amerikanische Nahostpolitik. Kontinuität und Wandel von Nixon bis Reagan*, Bonn, 1985

Haddad, Wadi D., *Lebanon. The politics of revolving doors*, New York, 1985

Hajjar, Joseph, *L'Europe et les destinées du Proche-Orient (1815–1848)*, Paris, 1970

Haley, P. Edward and Lewis W. Snider (eds.), *Lebanon in Crisis. Participants and issues*, Syracuse and New York, 1979

Hammel, Eric, *The Root. The Marines in Beirut. August 1982–February 1984*, San Diego, 1985

Hanf, Theodor, *Erziehungswesen in Gesellschaft und Politik des Libanon*, Bielefeld, 1969

—— Heribert Weiland and Gerda Vierdag, *South Africa: The prospects of peaceful change. An empirical enquiry into the possibility of democratic conflict regulation*, London, 1981

Harik, Iliya F., *Politics and Change in a Traditional Society: Lebanon, 1711–1845*, Princeton, 1968

Harkabi, Yehoshafat, *Arab Strategies and Israel's Response*, New York, 1977

Hartmann, Klaus-Peter, *Untersuchungen zu Sozialgeographie christlicher Minderheiten im Vorderen Orient* (Beihefte zum Tübinger Atlas des Vorderen Orients. Reihe B., 43), Wiesbaden, 1980

Hechter, Michael, *Internal Colonialism: The celtic fringe in British national development 1536–1966*, London, 1975

Hershlag, Zvi Yehuda, *Introduction to the Modern Economic History of the Middle East*, Leiden, 1964

Herzog, Chaim, *The War of Atonement*, London, 1975

Hirst, David, *The Gun and the Olive Branch. The roots of violence in the Middle East*, London, 1977

Hitti, Philip K., *Lebanon in History. From the earliest times to the present*, London, 1967
Homsy, Basile, *Les capitulations et la protection des chrétiens au Proche-Orient aux XVIe, XVIIe et XVIIIe siècles*, Harissa, 1956
Honigmann, John J. (ed.), *Handbook of Social and Cultural Anthropology*, Chicago, 1974
Horowitz, Donald L., *Ethnic Groups in Conflict*, Berkeley, 1985
Hourani, Albert H., *Minorities in the Arab World*, London, 1947
—— *Syria and Lebanon. A political essay*, London, 1954
—— *Arabic Thought in the Liberal Age 1798–1939*, London, 1962
Hudson, Michael C., *The Precarious Republic. Political modernization in Lebanon*, New York, 1968

Isaacs, Harold Robert, *Idols of the Tribe. Group identity and political change*, New York, 1975
*Israel in Lebanon*, Report of the International Commission to enquire into reported violations of International Law by Israel during its invasion of the Lebanon (London, 28 August 1982–29 November 1982), London, 1983
Ismail, Adel, *Histoire du Liban du XVIIème siècle à nos jours*, 2 vols., Paris, 1955

Johnson, Michael, *Class and Client in Beirut. The Sunni Muslim community and the Lebanese State 1840–1985* (Political Studies of the Middle East Series, 28), London, 1986
Joumblatt, Kamal, *Pour le Liban*, Paris, 1978
Jureidini, Paul A. and William E. Hazen, *The Palestinian Movement in Politics*, Lexington, Mass., 1976

Kaiser, Karl et al. (eds.), *Die Internationale Politik 1968–69*, Munich, 1974
—— and Udo Steinbach (eds.), *Deutsch-Arabische Beziehungen*, Munich, 1981
Karpat, Kemal H., *Political and Social Thought in the Contemporary Middle East*, London, 1968
Kazziha, Walid W., *Revolutionary Transformation in the Arab World. Habbash and his comrades from Nationalism to Marxism*, London, 1975
—— *Palestine in the Arab Dilemma*, London, 1979
Kepel, Gilles, *Le prophète et le pharaon. Les mouvements islamistes dans l'Egypte contemporaine*, Paris, 1984
Kerr, Malcolm H., *Lebanon in the Last Years of Feudalism, 1840–1868* (Oriental Series, 33), Beirut, 1959
Kewenig, Wilhelm, *Die Koexistenz der Religionsgemeinschaften im Libanon*, Berlin, 1965

Khadduri, Majid, *War and Peace in the Law of Islam*, Baltimore, 1955
Khadduri, Walid, *International Documents on Palestine*, Beirut, 1969
Khalaf, Samir, *Persistence and Change in 19th Century Lebanon*, Beirut, 1979
—— *Lebanon's Predicament*, New York, 1987
Khalid, Detlev, *Islam und politischer Extremismus: Einführung und Dokumentation*, Hamburg, 1985
Khalidi, Walid, *Conflict and Violence in Lebanon: Confrontation in the Middle East*, Cambridge, 1979
Khoury, Enver M., *The Crisis in the Lebanese System. Confessionalism and Chaos* (Foreign Affairs Study, 38), Washington D.C., 1976
Khuri, Fuad I., *From Village to Suburb. Order and change in Greater Beirut*, Chicago, 1975
Khuri, Yüsif Q. (ed.), *at-ta'ifiah fi lubnan: min khilal munaqashat maglis annuwab 1923–1987 (Confessionalism in Lebanon. Parliamentary Debates 1923–1987)*, Beirut, 1989
Kirk, George E., *Contemporary Arab Politics. A concise history*, London, 1961
Kissinger, Henry, *Years of Upheaval*, Boston, 1982
Kodmani-Darwish, Bassma (ed.), *Liban: Espoirs et réalités*, Paris, 1987
Köhler, Wolfgang, *Die Vorgeschichte des Krieges im Libanon*, Wiesbaden, 1980
Kraemer, Gudrun, *Arabismus und Nationalstaatlichkeit: Syrien als nahöstliche Regionalmacht*, Ebenhausen, 1987
Kramer, Martin (ed.), *Shi'ism, Resistance and Revolution*, Boulder, Col. and London, 1987
Kriener, Gustav-Adolf, *Geschichte der evangelischen Gemeinde zu Beirut*, Beirut, 1958
Kuderna, Michael, *Christliche Gruppen im Libanon. Kampf um Ideologie und Herrschaft in einer unfertigen Nation*, Wiesbaden, 1983
Kuper, Leo and M.G. Smith (eds.), *Pluralism in Africa*, Berkeley and Los Angeles, 1969

Labaki, Boutros, *Introduction à l'histoire économique du Liban. Soie et commerce extérieur en fin de période ottomane (1840–1914)*, Beirut, 1984
Labaki, Kesrouan, *Des idées pour le Liban*, Antelias, 1984
Lammens, Henri, *L'évolution historique de la nationalité syrienne*, Alexandria, 1919
Landau, Jacob M. et al. (eds.), *Electoral Politics in the Middle East. Issues, voters and elites*, London, 1980
Laqueur, Walter Z., *Communism and Nationalism in the Middle East*, London, 1956

—— (ed.), *The Israel-Arab Reader. A documentary history of the Middle East conflict*, New York, 1969
—— *Confrontation: The Middle East war and world politics*, London, 1974
Laurent, Annie and Antoine Basbous, *Guerres secrètes au Liban*, Paris, 1987
Leftwich, Adrian (ed.), *South Africa. Economic growth and political change. With comparative studies of Chile, Sri Lanka and Malaysia*, London and New York, 1974
Legum, Colin et al. (eds.), *Middle East Contemporary Survey*, V, 1980–81, New York and London, 1982
—— (ed.), *Middle East Contemporary Survey*, VI, 1981–82, New York and London, 1984
Lehmbruch, Gerhard, *Proporzdemokratie: Politisches System und politische Kultur in der Schweiz und in Österreich*, Tübingen, 1967
Lenin, W.I., *Über die nationale und die koloniale nationale Frage*, East Berlin, 1960
Lerner, Daniel, *The Passing of Traditional Society. Modernizing the Middle East*, Glencoe, 1962
Lijphart, Arend, *The Politics of Accommodation. Pluralism and democracy in the Netherlands*, Berkeley, 1975
—— *Democracy in Plural Societies. A comparative exploration*, New Haven and London, 1977
—— *Power-sharing in South Africa*. Institute of International Studies, Berkeley, 1985
Lipset, Seymour Martin, *The First New Nation*, New York, 1963
Longrigg, Stephen H., *Syria and Lebanon under French Mandate*, London, 1958
Lutsky, V., *Modern History of the Arab Countries*, Moscow, 1969

Magubane, Bernhard, *The Political Economy of Race and Class in South Africa*, New York, 1979
Mahdi, Muhsin, *Die geistigen und sozialen Wandlungen im Nahen Osten*, Freiburg i.Br., 1961
Malinowski, Bronislaw, *A Scientific Theory of Culture and Other Essays*, Chapel Hill, 1944
Ma'oz, Moshe (ed.), *Palestinian Arab Politics*, Jerusalem, 1975
—— and Avner Yaniv (eds.), *Syria under Assad. Domestic constraints and regional risks*, London, 1986
Marx, Karl and Friedrich Engels, *Werke*, 6, East Berlin, 1959
—— *Werke*, 15, East Berlin, 1961
Mason, Philip, *Patterns of Dominance*, London, 1970
—— *Race Relations*, London, 1970

McLaurin, Ronald D. (ed.), *The Political Role of Minority Groups in the Middle East*, New York, 1979
—— Mohammed Mughisuddin and Abraham R. Wagner, *Foreign Policy Making in the Middle East. Domestic influences on policy in Egypt, Iraq, Israel and Syria*, New York, 1977
Meo, Leila M.T., *Lebanon. Improbable nation. A study in political development*, Bloomington, 1965
Messarra, Antoine Nasri, *La structure sociale du parlement libanais*, Beirut, 1977
—— *Le modèle politique libanais et sa survie. Essai sur la classification et l'aménagement d'un système consociatif*, Beirut, 1983
Miller, Aaron David, *The PLO and the Politics of Survival*, (Washington Papers, 11–99), New York, 1983
Mokdessi, Toufic and Lucien George, *Les partis politiques*, Beirut, 1959
*Moslem Lebanon Today*, Beirut, 1976

Nantet, Jacques, *Histoire du Liban*, Paris, 1963
Nasr, Salim and Theodor Hanf (eds.), *Urban Crisis and Social Movements. Arab and European perspectives*, Beirut, 1987
Nasser, Gamal Abdel, 'Philosophie der Revolution', in Fritz René Allemann (ed.), *Die arabische Revolution. Nasser über seine Politik*, Frankfurt, 1958
Nordlinger, Eric A., *Conflict Regulation in Divided Societies*, Cambridge, Mass., 1972
Norton, Augustus Richard, *Amal and the Shi'a. Struggle for the soul of Lebanon*, Austin, Tex., 1987

*La Nouvelle Société Libanaise dans La Perception des Fa`aliyat (decision-makers) des Communautés Chrétiennes*, 3 vols., Kaslik, 1984
O'Ballance, Edgar, *Arab Guerilla Power, 1967–1972*, London, 1974
Oberschall, Anthony, *Social Conflict and Social Movements*, Englewood Cliffs, N.J., 1973
Odeh, B.J., *Lebanon: Dynamics on Conflict. A modern political history*, London, 1985
O'Neill, Bard, *Revolutionary Warfare in the Middle East; Israelis versus Fadayeen*, Colorado, 1974
Owen, Roger (ed.), *Essays on the Crisis in Lebanon*, London, 1976

Pakradouni, Karim, *La paix manquée. Le mandat d'Elias Sarkis (1976–1982)*, Ohne Ort, 1984
Pareto, Vilfredo, 'The Mind and Society. A treatise on general sociology', 4, *The General Form of Society*, New York, 1963

Perlmutter, Amos, *Egypt. The praetorian state*, New Brunswick, 1974
Peroncel-Hugoz, Jean-Pierre, *Une croix sur le Liban*, Paris, 1984
Petran, Tabitha, *The Struggle over Lebanon*, New York, 1987
Picard, Elizabeth, *Liban, état de discorde. Des fondations aux guerres fratricides*, Paris, 1988
Pohl-Schöberlein, Monika, *Die schiitische Gemeinschaft des Südlibanon (Gabal, Amil) innerhalb des libanesischen konfessionellen Systems*, Berlin, 1975
Pryce-Jones, David, *The Face of Defeat, Palestinian Refugees and Guerillas*, London, 1974
Pye, Lucian, *Aspects of Political Development*, Boston, 1966

Quandt, William B., *Decade of Decisions. American policy toward the Arab Israeli conflict, 1967–1976*, Berkeley, 1977
—— Fuad Jabber and Ann Mosely Lesch, *The Politics of Palestinian Nationalism*, Berkeley, 1973
Qubain, Fahim I., *Crisis in Lebanon*, Washington, 1961

Rabbath, Edmond, *La formation historique du Liban politique et constitutionnel. Essai de synthèse*, Beirut, 1973
Rabinovich, Itamar, *The War for Lebanon, 1970–1983*, Ithaca and London, 1984
Rabuschka, Alvin, *A Theory of Racial Harmony*, Columbia, 1974
—— and Kenneth A. Shepsle, *Politics in Plural Societies. A theory of democratic instability*, Columbus, Ohio, 1972
Raphael, Pierre, *Le role du Collège Maronite Romain dans l'orientalisme aux XVIIème et XVIIIème siècles*, Beirut, 1950
Raymond, André et al. (eds.), *La Syrie d'aujourd'hui*, Paris, 1980
Renner, Karl, *Das Selbstbestimmungsrecht der Nationen, in besonderer Anwendung auf Österreich*, Leipzig and Vienna, 1918
Republique libanaise, Ministère du Plan, Direction Centrale de la Statistique. *Enquête par sondage sur la population active au Liban*, 2 vols., Beirut, 1972
—— Ministère du Plan, *Mission IRFED-Liban 1960–61*, Beirut, n.d.
Rieck, Andreas, *Die Schiiten und der Kampf um den Libanon. Politische Chronik 1958–1988*, Hamburg, 1989
Ristelhueber, René, *Les traditions françaises au Liban*, Paris, 1918
Rondot, Pierre, *Les institutions politiques du Liban*, Paris, 1947
Rothschild, Joseph, *Ethnopolitics. A conceptual framework*, New York, 1981

Sadat, Anwar, *Revolt on the Nile*, London, 1957
Safa, Elie, *L'émigration libanaise*, Beirut, 1960

Salem, Elie, *Modernization without Revolution. Lebanon's experience*, Bloomington, 1973

Salibi, Kamal S., *Crossroads to Civil War. Lebanon 1958–1976*, New York, 1976

—— *The Modern History of Lebanon*, London, 1977 (reprint)

—— *A House of Many Mansions. The history of Lebanon reconsidered*, London, 1988

Samne, Georges, *La Syrie*, Paris, 1920

Saunders, Harold H., *The Other Walls. The politics of the Arab–Israeli peace process*. American Enterprise Institute for Public Policy Research (A.E.I.), Washington, 1985

Sayegh, Raymond, *Les conflits dans les zones de crise: Le Proche-Orient et le Liban*, Ohne Ort, 1985

Scheffler, Thomas, *Ethnischreligiöse Konflikte und gesellschaftliche Integration im Vorderen und Mittleren Orient*, Literaturbericht, Berlin, 1982

Schiff, Ze'ev, *October Earthquake: Yom Kippur 1973*, Tel Aviv, 1974

—— and Ehud Ya`ari, *Israel's Lebanon War*, London and Sydney, 1984

Schiller, David Thomas, *Der Bürgerkrieg im Libanon. Entstehung, Verlauf, Hintergründe*, Munich, 1979

—— *Palästinenser zwischen Terrorismus und Diplomatie. Die paramilitärische palästinensische Nationalbewegung von 1918 bis 1981*, Munich, 1982

Schmucker, Werner, *Krise und Erneuerung im libanesischen Drusentum*, Bonn, 1979

Shaked, Haim and Itamar Rabinovich (eds.), *The Middle East and the United States*, New Brunswick, 1980

Sharabi, Hisham, *Palestine and Israel: The lethal dilemma*, New York, 1969

—— *Neopatriarchy. A theory of distorted change in Arab society*, New York and Oxford, 1988

Sharaf, Shamil, *Die Palästinenser. Geschichte der Entstehung eines nationalen Bewußtseins*, Vienna, 1983

Shehadi, Nadim and Dana Haffar Mills (eds.), *Lebanon: A history of conflict and consensus*, London, 1988

Shils, Edward, *Political Development in the New States*, The Hague, 1965

Shwadran, B., *Jordan: A state of tension*, New York, 1959

Smith, M.G., *The Plural Society in the British West Indies*, Berkeley, 1965

Sou'al (Viermonatszeitschrift), Sondernummer, *L'islamisme aujourd'hui*, Paris, 1985

Spagnolo, John P., *France and Ottoman Lebanon, 1861–1914*, London, 1977

Springer, Rudolf (Pseudonym für Karl Renner), *Der Kampf der österreichischen Nationen um den Staat*, Leipzig and Vienna, 1902

Srinivas, M.N., *Caste in Modern India and other Essays*, London, 1962

—— *Social Change in Modern India*, Berkeley, 1967
Stein, Gustav and Udo Steinbach (eds.), *The Contemporary Middle Eastern Scene*, Opladen, 1979
Steinbach, Udo and Rüdiger Robert (eds.), *Der Nahe und Mittlere Osten. Politik, Gesellschaft, Wirtschaft, Geschichte, Kultur*, 2 vols., Opladen, 1988
Suad, Joseph and Barbara L.X. Pillsbury (eds.), *Muslim-Christian Conflicts: Economic, political and social origins*, Boulder, Col. and Folkstone, 1978
Suleiman, Michael W., *Political Parties in Lebanon. The challenge for a fragmental political culture*, Ithaca and New York, 1967
Sweet, Louise E. (ed.), *Peoples and Cultures of the Middle East. An anthropolitical reader*, 2 vols., Garden City, N.Y., 1970

Taqi Ad-Din, S., *al-tatawur at-taribi lilmushkilah al-lubnaniyyah (The historical development of the Lebanese problem)*, Beirut, 1977
Thompson, Dennis L. and Dov Ronen (eds.), *Ethnicity. Politics and Development*, Boulder, Col., 1986
Tibi, Bassam, *Die Krise des modernen Islams. Eine vorindustrielle Kultur im wissenschaftlich-technischen Zeitalter*, Munich, 1981
—— *Der Islam und das Problem der kulturellen Bewältigung sozialen Wandels*, Frankfurt, 1985
—— *Vom Gottesreich zum Nationalstaat. Islam und panarabischer Nationalismus*, Frankfurt, 1987
Tocqueville, Alexis de, *Der alte Staat und die Revolution*, Hamburg, 1969
Toufik, Touma, *Paysans et institutions féodales chez les druzes et les maronites du Liban du XVIIème siècle à 1914*, Beirut, 1971
Tueni, Ghassan, *Une guerre pour les autres*, Paris, 1985
Tyan, Emile, *Histoire de l'organisation judiciaire en pays d'Islam*, Paris, 1938

Universite Libanaise, Institut des Sciences Sociales (ed.), *La politique de la population au Liban*, Beirut, 1982

Vallaud, Pierre, *Le Liban au bout du fusil. Avant-propos de Jean Lacouture*, Paris, 1976
Van Dam, Nikolaos, *The Struggle for Power in Syria. Sectarianism, regionalism and tribalism in politics, 1961–1978*, London, 1979
Van Den Berghe, Pierre L., *The Ethnic Phenomenon*, New York and Oxford, 1981

Wahba, Mourad (ed.), *Youth, Violence, Religion. Secularization and desecularization*, Cairo, 1983

Weber, Max, *Wirtschaft und Gesellschaft. Grundriß der verstehenden Soziologie*, 1(I), Tübingen, 1976
Whetten, Lawrence C., *The Canal War: Four-power conflict in the Middle East*, Cambridge, Mass., 1974
Winkler, Heinrich August (ed.), *Nationalismus in der Welt von heute*, Göttingen, 1982
Wym, W., *Nasser of Egypt. The search for dignity*, Cambridge, Mass., 1959

Yaari, Ehud, *Strike Terror. The story of Fatah*, New York, 1970
Yamak, Labib Zuwiyya, *The Syrian Social Nationalist Party: An ideological analysis*, Cambridge, Mass., 1966
Yaniv, Avner, *Dilemmas of Security Politics, Strategy, and the Israeli Experience in Lebanon*, New York and Oxford, 1987
*The Yearbook of Education*, London, 1949
Younes, Riad, *Politik und Proporzsystem in einer südlibanesischen Dorfgemeinschaft. Eine empirisch sozio-politische Untersuchung*, Munich, 1975
Young, Crawford, *The Politics of Cultural Pluralism*, Madison, Wisc., 1976

Zamir, Meir, *The Formation of Modern Lebanon*, London, 1985
Zapf, Wolfgang (ed.), *Theorien des sozialen Wandels*, Cologne and Berlin, 1969
Ziadeh, Nicola Abdo, *Syria and Lebanon*, Beirut, 1968

# B Articles

Ahmed, Naveed, 'The Lebanese Crisis: The role of the PLO', *Pakistan Horizon*, 29:1 (1976) pp. 31–46
Alam, Jihad, 'Crise dans la Crise, Guerre dans la Guerre', *Les Cahiers de l'Orient*, 14:2 (1989) pp. 35–48
Al-Azmeh, Aziz, 'The Progressive Forces', in Roger Owen (ed.), *Essays on the Crisis in Lebanon*, London, 1976, pp. 59–72
Alem, Jean-Pierre, 'Troubles insurrectionnels au Liban', *Orient*, 2:6 (1958) pp. 37–47
Almond, Gabriel, 'Comparative Political Systems', *The Journal of Politics*, 18 (1956) p. 397
Ansari, Hamied N., 'The Islamic Militants in Egyptian Politics', *International Journal of Middle East Studies*, 16 (1984) pp. 123–44
Aucagne, Jean, 'L'Imam Moussa Sadr et la communauté chiite', *Travaux et Jours*, 53 (1974) pp. 31–51
Avi-Ran, Reuven, 'The Syrian Military-Strategic Interests in Lebanon', *The Jerusalem Quarterly*, 46 (1988) pp. 131–44

Azar, Edward E. and Kate Shnayerson, 'United States — Lebanese Relations: A pocketful of paradoxes', in Edward E. Azar et al. (eds.), *The Emergence of a New Lebanon*, New York, 1984, pp. 219–75

Bagley, Christopher, 'Racialism and Pluralism: A dimensional analysis of forty-eight countries', *Race*, 13:3 (1972) pp. 347–54
Bailey, Clinton, 'Lebanon's Shi'is after the 1982 War' in Martin Kramer (ed.), *Shi'ism, Resistance and Revolution*, Boulder, Col. and London, 1987, pp. 219–36
Barakat, Halim, 'Social and Political Integration in Lebanon: A case of social mosaic', *Middle East Journal*, 27 (1973) pp. 301–18
Baron, H. M., 'Racial Domination in Advanced Capitalism: A theory of nationalism and divisions in the labor market', in R.C. Edwards et al. (eds.), *Labor Market Segmentation*, Lexington, Mass., 1975, pp. 173–216
Basile, Antoine, 'Contraintes et perspectives de l'économie libanaise', in Joseph Abou Jaoude et al., *La nouvelle société libanaise dans la perception des Fa`aliyat (decision-makers) des communautés chrétiennes*, 3, Etudes et Rapports, Kaslik, 1984, pp. 263–86
Bentley, G. Carter, 'Theoretical Perspectives on Ethnicity and Nationality', *Sage Race Relations Abstracts*, 8:2 (1983) pp. 1–53
Berner, Wolfgang, 'Die Nah- und Mittelostpolitik der UdSSR', in Udo Steinbach and Rüdiger Robert (eds.), *Der Nahe und Mittlere Osten. Politik, Gesellschaft, Wirtschaft, Geschichte, Kultur*, 1, Opladen, 1988, pp. 711–78
Beydoun, Ahmad, 'Le Liban pacifié. Dissolution des milices? Renaissance de la société civile?', in Centre d'Action et d'Information pur le Liban (ed.), *Perspectives et réalitiés du Liban*, Paris, (1993) pp. 70ff
Bödigheimer, Walter, 'Die arabischen Gipfelkonferenzen von Riad und Kairo. Ein Versuch zur Lösung der Libanon-Krise', *Europa-Archiv*, 32:2 (1977) pp. D 48–D 54
Bourgey, André, 'Beyrouth. ville éclatée', *Hérodote*, 17:1 (1980) pp. 5–30
Bryer, David, 'The Origins of the Druze Religion' *Der Islam*, 52 (1975) pp. 47–84 and 53 (1976) pp. 4–27
Büttner, Friedemann, 'Der Islam und die Entfaltung der arabischen politischen Ideen', in Karl Kaiser and Udo Steinbach (eds.), *Deutsch–Arabische Beziehungen*, Munich, 1981, pp. 27–43
Burawoy, M., 'Race, Class and Colonialism', *Social and Economic Studies*, 23 (1974) pp. 521–60

Carra De Vaux, B., 'Druzes', in H.A.R. Gibb and J.H. Kramers (eds.), *Shorter Encyclopedia of Islam*, Leiden, 1953, p. 94

Carré, Olivier, 'Le mouvement idéologique ba`thiste', in André Raymond et al. (eds.), *La Syrie d'aujourd'hui*, Paris, 1980, pp. 185–224

Ceroc, 'Le droit à la différence pour plus de justice et de liberté'. Centre d'Etudes de Recherches sur l'Orient Chrétien, First Colloquium, Beirut, 1985

Chaoul, Melhem, 'Le dispositif de la guerre au Liban, fonction de réduction', in Fondation Libanaise pour la Paix Civile Permanente (ed.), *Le droit à la mémoire*, Beirut, 1988, pp. 60–39 (Arab pagination)

Coakley, John, 'National Territories and Cultural Frontiers: Conflicts of principle in the formation of states in Europe', *West European Politics*, 5 (1982) pp. 34–49

Collins, James F., 'The Soviet Union', in P. Edward Haley and Lewis W. Snider (eds.), *Lebanon in Crisis. Participants and Issues*, Syracuse and New York, 1979, pp. 209–23

Connor, Walker, 'Self Determination. The new phase', *World Politics*, 20 (1967) pp. 30–53

—— 'Nation Building or Nation Destroying', *World Politics*, 24:3 (1972) pp. 319–55

—— 'A Nation is a Nation, is a State, is an Ethnic Group, is a... ', *Ethnic and Racial Studies*, 1:4 (1978) pp. 377–400

Cooley, John K., 'The Palestinians', in P. Edward Haley and Lewis W. Snider (eds.), *Lebanon in Crisis. Participants and issues*, Syracuse and New York, 1979, pp. 21–54

Corm, Georges, 'Quelques réflexions méthodologiques et historiques sur la perception de la société libanaise par les élites des communautés chrétiennes', in Joseph Abou Jaoude et al., *La nouvelle société libanaise dans la perception des Fa`aljyat (decision-makers) des communautés chrétiennes*, 3, Etudes et Rapports, Kaslik, 1984, pp. 45–61

Crow, Ralph E., 'Religious Sectarianism in the Lebanese Political System', *The Journal of Politics*, 24:3 (1962) pp. 489–520

Daalder, Hans, 'The Consociational Democracy Theme', *World Politics*, 26:4 (1974) pp. 604–21

Davies, James C., 'Toward a Theory of Revolution', *American Sociological Review*, 27 (1962) pp. 5–19

Dawisha, Adeed, J., 'The Transnational Party in Regional Politics: The Arab Ba`th Party', *Asian Affairs*, 61:1 (1974) pp. 23–31

—— 'The Impact of External Actors on Syria's Intervention in Lebanon', *Journal of South Asian and Middle Eastern Studies*, 2:1 (1978) pp. 22–43

Dekmejian, Hrair Richard, 'Consociational Democracy in Crisis: The case of Lebanon', *Comparative Politics*, 10 (1978) pp. 251–65

Delprat, Raymond, 'Blocages économiques et crise sociale au Liban', *Etudes des cahiers de l'orient contemporain*, 26 (April, 1969) pp. 5–12
Deutsch, Karl W., 'Social Mobilization and Political Development', *American Political Science Review*, 55:3 (1961) pp. 493–514
—— 'External Involvement in Internal War', in Harry Eckstein (ed.), *Internal War. Problems and approaches*, London, 1964, pp. 100–10

El-Solh, Alia, 'Nommer le mal', *Le Monde*, 25 April 1989
Ende, Werner, 'Imam Musa as Sadr', *Orient*, 14:3 (1973) p. 103
Entelis, John P., 'Ethnic Conflict and the Reemergence of Radical Christian Nationalism in Lebanon', in Michael Curtis (ed.), *Religion and Politics in the Middle East*, Boulder, Col., 1981, pp. 227–45
Esman, Milton J., 'The Management of Communal Conflict', *Public Policy*, 21 (1973) pp. 49–78
—— 'Two Dimensions of Ethnic Politics: Defense of homelands, immigrant rights', *Ethnic and Racial Studies*, 8:3 (1985) pp. 438–40

Faour, Ali, 'The Displacement Crisis and Force Migration in Beirut in 1984', in Salim Nasr and Theodor Hanf (eds.), *Urban Crisis and Social Movements. Arab and European perspectives*, Beirut, 1987, pp. 165–98
Farsoun, Samih K., 'Family Structure and Society in Modern Lebanon', in Louise E. Sweet (ed.), *Peoples and Cultures of the Middle East. An anthropological reader*, 2 vols., Garden City, N.Y., 1970, pp. 257–307
—— and Walker Caroll, 'The Civil War in Lebanon: Sect, class, and imperialism', *Monthly Review*, 28:2 (1976) pp. 12–37
Franz, Erhard, 'Religiöse und periphere Minderheiten', in Udo Steinbach and Rüdiger Robert (eds.), *Der Nahe und Mittlere Osten. Politik, Gesellschaft, Wirtschaft. Geschichte, Kultur*, 1, Opladen, 1988, pp. 67–78

Gabir, H., 'as-sultah wat-tawazun fi lubnan' (Herrschaft und Gleichgewicht im Libanon), *shu'un falastniyyah*, 50–51, Beirut, n.d.
Gammer, Moshe, 'The War in Lebanon: The course of hostilities', in Colin Legum et al. (eds.), *Middle East Contemporary Survey*, VI, 1981–82, New York and London, 1984, pp. 128–57
Geertz, Clifford, 'The Integrative Revolution: Primordial sentiments and civil politics in the new states', in idem (ed.), *Old Societies and New States. The quest for modernity in Asia and Africa*, London, 1963, pp. 105–57
Grimblat, Francis, 'La communauté chiite libanaise et le mouvement national palestinien 1967–1986', *Guerres mondiales et conflicts contemporains*, 151 (1988) pp. 71–91

Hakim, Georges, 'The Economic Basis of Lebanese Polity', in Leonard Binder (ed.), *Politics in Lebanon*, New York, 1966, pp. 57–68

Hamade, Marwan, 'L'Islam libanais, du nassérisme à la participation', *Travaux et Jours*, 53 (1974) pp. 5–12

Hanf, Theodor, 'Le comportement politique des étudiants libanais', *Travaux et Jours*, 46 (1973) pp. 5–52

—— 'The "Political Secularization" Issue in Lebanon', *Annual Review of the Social Sciences of Religion*, 5 (1981) pp. 225–53

—— 'Die christlichen Gemeinschaften im gesellschaftlichen Wandel des arabischen Vorderen Orients', *Orient*, 22:1 (1981) pp. 29–49

—— 'Arabismus und Islamismus', in Heinrich August Winkler (ed.), *Nationalismus in der Welt von heute*, Göttingen, 1982, pp. 157–76

—— 'Beirut. Konflikt und Koexistenz in einer geteilten Stadt', *Geographische Rundschau*, 37:9 (1985) pp. 454–61

—— 'The Prospects of Accommodation in Communal Conflicts: A comparative study', in Peter A. Döring et al. (eds.), *Bildung in sozio-ökonomischer Sicht*, Cologne and Vienna, 1989, pp. 313–32

Harik, Iliya F., 'Lebanon', in Jacob M. Landau et al. (eds.), *Electoral Politics in the Middle East. Issues, voters and elites*, London, 1980, pp. 145–71

—— 'The Economic and Social Factors in the Lebanese Crisis', *Journal of Arab Affairs*, 1:2 (1981–1982) pp. 209–44

Harris, William W., 'La politique libanaise de Hafez el-Hassad', in Bassma Kodmani-Darwish (ed.), *Liban: Espoirs et réalités*, Paris, 1987, pp. 91–117

Hottinger, Arnold, 'An Eye-Wittness Report on Iraq', *Swiss Review of World Affairs*, 9 (1959) pp. 12–16

—— 'Zu`ama and Parties in the Lebanese Crisis of 1958', *The Middle East Journal*, 15:2 (1961) pp. 127–40

—— 'Zu`ama in Historical Perspective', in Leonard Binder (ed.), *Politics in Lebanon*, New York, 1966, pp. 85–105

—— 'How the Arab Bourgeoisie Lost Power', *Journal of Contemporary History*, 3 (1968) pp. 111–28

—— 'Syrische Wünsche nach Gleichschaltung im Libanon', *Neue Zürcher Zeitung*, 8 January 1986

—— 'Verfassungsentwurf Teherans für Libanon — Über die Ausbreitung der iranischen Revolution', *Neue Zürcher Zeitung*, 6 April 1987

—— 'Dreißigjähriger Krieg der Araber?', *Neue Zürcher Zeitung*, 24 November 1987

—— 'Arafats Friedensangebot an Israel. Ein Durchbruch in der Palästinafrage?', *Europa-Archiv*, 44:2 (1989) pp. 39–46

Hourani, Albert H., 'Ideologies of the Mountain and the City', in Roger Owen (ed.), *Essays on the Crisis in Lebanon*, London, 1976, pp. 33–41
Hudson, Michael C., 'Review of Chamoun, Crise au Moyen-Orient', *Middle East Journal*, 18:2 (1964) p. 245
—— 'The Lebanese Crisis: The Limits of consociational democracy', *Palestine Studies*, 5 (1976) pp. 109–22
—— 'The Problem of Authoritative Power in Lebanese Politics. Why consociationalism failed', in Nadim Shehadi and Dana Haffar Mills (eds.), *Lebanon: A history of conflict and consensus*, London, 1988, pp. 224–39
Huntington, Samuel P., Preface to Eric A. Nordlinger, *Conflict Regulation in Divided Societies*, Cambridge, Mass., 1972

Jupp, James, 'Ceylon and Malaysia', in Adrian Leftwich (ed.), *South Africa. Economic growth and political change. With comparative studies of Chile, Sri Lanka and Malaysia*, London and New York, 1974, pp. 187–211
Jureidini, Paul A., 'Lebanon's Regional Policy', in Edward E. Azar et al. (eds.), *The Emergence of a New Lebanon. Fantasy or reality?*, New York, 1984, pp. 207–18
—— and R.D. McLaurin, 'Lebanon after the War of 1982', in Edward E. Azar et al. (eds.), *The Emergence of a New Lebanon. Fantasy or reality?*, New York, 1984, pp. 3–35

Karpat, Kemal H., 'The Ottoman Ethnic and Confessional Legacy in the Middle East', in Milton J. Es Man and Itamar Rabinovich (eds.), *Ethnicity Pluralism, and the State in the Middle East*, Ithaca and London, 1988, pp. 35–53
Kassir, Samir, 'L'affirmation des chiites libanais', *Le Monde Diplomatique*, May, 1985, p. 12
Kerr, Malcolm H., 'Rezension zu Qubain', *Middle East Journal*, 16:1 (1962) p. 96
Keyes, Charles F., 'Towards a New Formulation of the Concept of the Ethnic Groups', *Ethnicity*, 3 (1976) pp. 202–13
Khalaf, Samir, 'On Entrapment and Escalation of Violence', *American Arab Affairs*, 24 (Spring, 1988) pp. 14–18
Khalaf, Tewfik, 'The Phalange and the Maronite Community: From Lebanonism to Maronitism', in Roger Owen (ed.), *Essays on the Crisis in Lebanon*, London, 1976, pp. 43–57
Khalid, Detlev, 'Nabih Berri (Nabih Birri)', *Orient*, 26 (1985) pp. 141–46
Khouri, Fred J., 'The Arab-Israeli Conflict', in P. Edward Haley and Lewis W. Snider (eds.), *Lebanon in Crisis. Participants and issues*, Syracuse and New York, 1979, pp. 161–77

Khuri, Fuad I, 'Sectarian Loyalty among Rural Migrants in Two Lebanese Suburbs: A stage between family and national allegiance', in Richard Antoun and Iliya Harik (eds.), *Rural Politics and Social Change in the Middle East*, Bloomington and London, 1972, pp. 198–213

Kiwan, Fadia, 'Stratification sociale et identification politique à Bourj el Barajneh' (Social stratification and political identity in a Beirut suburban village), *L'Afrique et l'Asie Modernes*, 115:4 (1977) pp. 15–27

Kodmani-Darwish, Bassma, 'Frankreich, ein zuverlässiger Verbündeter Libanons', *Beiträge zur Konfliktforschung*, 14:3 (1984) pp. 77–91

—— 'L'Iran, nouvel acteur fort au Liban?', in idem (ed.), *Liban: Espoirs et réalités*, Paris, 1987, pp. 153–64

Kurani, Habib, 'Lebanon, Educational Reform', in *The Yearbook of Education*, London, 1949

Labaki, Boutros, 'Structuration communautaire, rapports de force entre minorités et guerres au Liban', *Guerres mondiales et conflits contemporains*, 151 (1981) pp. 43–70

—— 'L'économie politique du Liban indépendant 1943–1975', in Nadim Shehadi and Dana Haffar Mills (eds.), *Lebanon: A History of Conflict and Consensus*, London, 1988, pp. 166–80

Lechleitner, Herwig, 'Konfessionsgruppen und Wirtschaftsleben im Libanon', *Geographische Rundschau*, 24:6 (1972) pp. 213–18

Lehmbruch, Gerhard, 'Konkordanzdemokratie im politischen System der Schweiz', *Politische Vierteljahresschrift*, 9 (1968) pp. 443–59

—— 'Consociational Democracy in the International System', *European Journal of Political Research*, 3:4 (1975) pp. 377–91

List, Harald, 'Antoine Lahad', *Orient*, 29:2 (1988) pp. 179–87

Maila, Joseph, 'Le "Document d'Entente Nationale"'. Un commentaire, *Les Cahiers de l'Orient*, 16–17:1 (1990) pp. 135–217

—— 'L'accord de Taëf: Deux ans après', in Centre d'Action at d'Information pour le Liban (ed.), *Perspectives et réalités du Liban*, Paris, (1993) p. 56

—— 'Liban: Les élections sous influence', *Les Cahiers de l'Orient*, in press

Marshall, Susan E., 'Paradoxes of Change: Culture crisis, islamic revival, and the reactivation of patriarchy', *Journal of Asian and African Studies* 19:1–2 (1984) pp. 1–17

Mayer, Thomas, 'Lebanese Politics and the 'Missile Crises', in Colin Legum et al. (eds.), *Middle East Contemporary Survey*, V, 1980–81, New York and London, 1982, pp. 675–76

McDonald, D.B., 'Dhimma', in H.A.R. Gibb and J.H. Kramers (eds.), *Shorter Encyclopedia of Islam*, Leiden, 1953, pp. 55f

McKay, James, 'An Exploratory Synthesis of Primordial and Mobilizationist Approaches to Ethic Phenomena', *Ethnic and Racial Studies*, 5:4 (1982) pp. 395–420

McLaurin, Ronald D., 'Lebanon and its Army: Past, present and future', in Edward E. Azar et al. (eds.), *The Emergence of a New Lebanon. Fantasy or reality?*, New York, 1984, pp. 79–114

Mertz, Robert Anton, 'Why George Habbash Turned Marxist', *Mideast Magazine*, 10:4 (1970) pp. 31–6

Messarra, Antoine Nasri, 'Un modèle consociatif au Proche-Orient arabe: Approche comparative du système politique libanais', *Droit, institutions et système politique*, Paris, 1987

Nahas, Dunia, 'L'évolution des organisations palestiniennes', *Travaux et Jours*, 52 (1974) pp. 77–99

Nasr, Salim, 'Pour éclairer la guerre civile au Liban. Jalons pour une position des rapports entre confessions et société libanaise', in Jean Bauberot et al. (eds.), *Palestine et Liban. Promesses et mensonges de l'Occident*, Paris, 1977, pp. 144–59

—— 'Les formes de regroupement traditionnel dans la société de Beyrouth', in Dominique Chevallier (ed.), *L'espace social de la ville arabe*, Paris, 1979, pp. 145–98

—— 'L'Islam politique et l'Etat libanais (1920–1975)', in Olivier Carre (ed.), *L'Islam et l'Etat dans le monde d'aujourd'hui*, Paris, 1982, pp. 31–43

—— 'Mobilisation communautaire et symbolique religieuse: L'imam Sadr et les chiites du Liban (1970–1975)', in Mourad Wahba (ed.), *Youth, Violence, Religion. Secularization and de-secularization*, Cairo, 1983, pp. 384–403

—— 'Beyrouth: Remarques sur les acteurs d'un drame urbain', in Salim Nasr and Theodor Hanf (eds.), *Urban Crisis and Social Movements. Arab and European perspectives*, Beirut, 1987, pp. 141–46

—— 'A New Approach to the Conflict: The social dynamics of an internal war', *American-Arab Affairs*, 24 (Spring, 1988) pp. 19–21

Nasr, Marlène and Salim, 'Morphologie sociale de la banlieue-est de Beyrouth', *Maghreb-Machrek* 73 (1976) pp. 78–88

Nasr, Nafhat and Monte Palmer, 'Alienation of Political Participation in Lebanon', *International Journal of Middle East Studies*, 8 (1977) pp. 493–516

Norton, Augustus Richard, 'Harakat Amal', in Edward E. Azar et al. (eds.), *The Emergence of a New Lebanon. Fantasy or reality?*, New York, 1984, pp. 162–204

—— 'Waiting for the Nadir', *American Arab Affairs*, 24 (Spring, 1988) pp. 21–5

Olmert, Yosef, 'Lebanon', in Colin Legum et al. (eds.), *Middle East Contemporary Survey*, VI, 1981–82, London and New York, 1984, pp. 702–33

Olson, Mancur, 'Rapid Growth as a Destabilizing Force', *Journal of Economic History*, 23 (1963) pp. 529–52

Picard, Elizabeth, 'La politique de la Syrie au Liban', *Maghreb-Machrek*, 116 (1987) pp.6–34

—— 'Political Identities and Communal Identities: Shifting mobilization among the Lebanese Shi'a through ten years of war, 1975–1985', in Dennis L. Thompson and Dov Ronen (eds.), *Ethnicity, Politics and Development*, Boulder, Col., 1986, pp. 159–78

Pipes, Daniel, 'Damascus and the Claim to Lebanon', *Orbis*, 30:4 (1987) pp. 663–81

Porat, Yehoshua, 'The Peasant Revolt of 1858–61 in Kisrawan', *Asian and African Studies*, 2 (1966) pp. 77–157

Quandt, William B., 'Lebanon, 1958, and Jordan, 1970', in Barry M. Blechman and Stephen S. Kaplan (eds.), *Force without War. The use of the armed forces as a political instrument*, Washington, 1978, pp. 222–88

—— 'Reagan's Lebanon Policy: Trial and error', *The Middle East Journal*, 38:2 (1984) pp. 237–54

Rabinovich, Itamar, 'The Limits of Military Power: Syria's role', in P. Edward Haley and Lewis W. Snider (eds.), *Lebanon in Crisis. Participants and issues*, Syracuse and New York, 1979, pp. 55–73

'Le Rapport du Père Lebret', *Le Commerce du Levant*, 1:3 (1960) p. 25

Reissner, Johannes, 'Säkularisierung des Libanon? Äußerungen von Muslimen zum neuen Schlagwort ."Almana"', *Orient*, 17:3 (1976) pp. 13–37

—— 'Die militant-islamischen Gruppen', in Werner Ende and Udo Steinbach (eds.), *Der Islam in der Gegenwart*, Munich, 1984, pp. 470–86

Rieck, Andreas, 'Syriens beharrliche Strategie im Libanon', *Frankfurter Allgemeine Zeitung*, 29 July 1989

Rondot, Pierre, 'Les nouveaux problèmes de l'état libanais', *Revue Française de Science Politique*, 2 (1954) pp. 326–56

—— 'Les chrétiens d'Orient', *Cahiers de l'Afrique et de l'Asie*, 4, (1955)

—— 'L'expérience du collège unique dans le système représentatif libanais', *Revue Française de Science Politique*, 7, (1957) pp. 67ff

—— 'Quelques réflexions sur les structures du Liban', *Orient*, 2:6 (1958) pp. 23–36
—— 'Le Liban devant la résistance palestinienne', *Revue de la Défense Nationale*, 25 (1969) pp. 1410–32
Ross, Jeffrey A., 'Urban Development and the Politics of Ethnicity: A conceptual approach', *Ethnic and Racial Studies*, 5:4 (1982) pp. 440–56
Rozat, G. and R. Bartra, 'Racism and Capitalism', *Sociological Theories. Race and colonialism*, Paris, 1980

Saba, Paul, 'The Creation of the Lebanese Economy – economic growth in the nineteenth and twentieth centuries', in Roger Owen (ed.), *Essays on the Crises in Lebanon*, London, 1976, pp. 1–22
Said, Edward W., 'Palestinians in the Aftermath of Beirut', *Journal of Palestine Studies*, 12:46 (1983) pp. 3–9
Salem, Elie, 'Cabinet Politics in Lebanon', *The Middle East Journal*, 21:4 (1967) pp. 488–502
Salibi, Kamal S., '"Right" and "Left" in Lebanon', in Gustav Stein and Udo Steinbach (eds.), *The Contemporary Middle Eastern Scene*, Opladen, 1979, pp. 97–104
—— 'Lebanon since the Crisis of 1958', *The World Today*, 17:1 (1961) pp. 32–42
—— 'L'historiographie libanaise, histoire de vanité', *L'Orient*, 25 May 1965
—— 'The Personality of Lebanon in Relation to the Modern World', in Leonard Binder (ed.), *Politics in Lebanon*, New York, 1966, pp. 263–70
Sanan, Fernand, 'Notes sur la répartition du revenu au Liban', *L'économie des pays arabes, étude mensuelle*, 20:222 (1977) pp. 9–15
Sayigh, Rosemary, 'The Struggle for Survival. The economic conditions of palestinian camp residents in Lebanon', *Journal of Palestine Studies*, 7:2 (1978) pp. 101–19
Schiff, Ze`ev, 'The Green Light', *Foreign Policy*, 50:1 (1983) pp. 73–85
Schlicht, Alfred, 'The Role of Foreign Powers in the History of Lebanon and Syria from 1799 to 1861', *Journal of Asian History*, 14:2 (1980) pp. 97–126
Schölch, Alexander, 'Der libanesische Bürgerkrieg', *Aus Politik und Zeitgeschichte* (Beilage zu Das Parlament), 9 April 1977, pp. 3–21
Seurat, Michel, 'Identité communautaire, violence urbaine, déréliction du politique: un quartier populaire de Tripoli au Liban', in Salim Nasr and Theodor Hanf (eds.), *Urban Crises and Social Movements. Arab and European Perspectives*, Beirut, 1987, pp. 193–98
Shapira, Shimon, 'The Origins of Hizbollah', *The Jerusalem Quarterly*, 46 (1988) pp. 115–30

Shils, Edward, 'Primordial, Personal, Sacred, and Civic Ties', *British Journal of Sociology*, 8 (1957) pp. 130–45

Sicking, Thom, 'Dépérissement d'un village libanais', *Travaux et Jours*, 47 (1973) pp. 5–21

Sirhan, Bassem, 'Palestinian Refugee Camp Life in Lebanon', *Journal of Palestine Studies*, 4:2 (1975) pp. 91–107

Smith, Anthony D., 'Towards a Theory of Ethnic Separatism', *Ethnic and Racial Studies*, 2:1 (1979) pp. 21–37

Smith, M.G., 'Institutional and Political Conditions of Pluralism', in Leo Kuper and M.G. Smith (eds.), *Pluralism in Africa*, Berkeley and Los Angeles, 1969, pp. 27–66

Smooha, Sammy, 'Pluralism and Conflict. A theoretical exploration', *Plural Societies*, 6:3 (1975) pp. 69–89

Snider, Lewis W. et al., 'Israel', in P. Edward Haley and Lewis W. Snider (eds.), *Lebanon in Crisis. Participants and issues*, Syracuse and New York, 1979, pp. 91–112

—— 'The Lebanese Forces: Wartime origins and political significance', in Edward E. Azar et al. (eds.), *The Emergence of a New Lebanon. Fantasy or reality?*, New York, 1984, pp. 117–61

Spagnolo, John P., 'Constitutional Change in Mount Lebanon: 1861–1864', *Middle Eastern Studies*, 7:1 (1971) pp. 25–48

Steinbach, Udo, 'Ideengeschichte im Zeichen von Kolonialismus, Unabhängigkeitsbewegung und Modernisierung', in idem and Rüdiger Robert (eds.), *The Contemporary Middle Eastern Scene*, 1, Opladen, 1979, pp. 135–84

—— 'Israelisch-arabischer Konflikt', in idem and Rüdiger Robert (eds.), *The Contemporary Middle Eastern Scene*, Opladen, 1, 1979, pp. 639–61

Stemer-Picard, Elisabeth, 'Le Liban et la résistance palestinienne', *Revue Française de Science Politique*, 25:1 (1975) pp. 5–22

Steppat, Fritz, 'Die arabischen Staaten zwischen Ost und West', in Arnold Bergstraesser and Wilhelm Cornides (eds.), *Die Internationale Politik 1955. Eine Einführung in das Geschehen der Gegenwart*, Munich, 1958, pp. 619–54

—— 'Nassers Revolution', *Europa-Archiv*, 17 (1962) pp. 163–73

—— 'Internationale Politik am Mittelmeer', in Karl Carstens et al. (eds.), *Die Internationale Politik 1966–67*, Munich, 1973, pp. 207–305

—— 'Der Mittelostkonflikt nach dem Krieg von 1967', in Karl Kaiser et al. (eds.), *Die Internationale Politik 1968–69*, Munich, 1974, pp. 227–34

Stoakes, Frank, 'The Supervigilantes: The Lebanese Kataeb Party as a builder, surrogate and defender of the State', *Middle Eastern Studies*, 11:3 (1975) pp. 215–36

Stookley, Robert W., 'The United States', in P. Edward Haley and Lewis W. Snider (eds.), *Lebanon in Crisis. Participants and issues*, Syracuse and New York, 1979, pp. 225–48

Suleiman, Michael W., 'Crisis and Revolution in Lebanon', *The Middle East Journal*, 26:1 (1972) pp. 11–24

Tabbarah, Riad, 'Background to the Lebanese Conflict', *International Journal of Comparative Sociology*, 20:1–2 (1979) pp. 101–21

—— 'Le développement arabe et les ressources humaines libanaises', in Université Libanaise. Institut des Sciences Sociales (ed.), *La politique de la population au Liban*, Beirut, 1982

Tabet, Jad, 'Images de Beyrouth', in Salim Nasr and Theodor Hanf (eds.), *Urban Crisis and Social Movements. Arab and European perspectives*, Beirut, 1987, pp. 129–39

Terrill, W. Andrew, 'Low Intensity Conflict in Southern Lebanon: Lessons and dynamics of the Israeli Shi'ite War', *Conflict Quarterly*, 7:3 (1987) pp. 22–35

Tibi, Bassam, 'Naher Osten — Nach dem Sechs-Tage-Krieg 1967 begann eine neue Epoche. Die regionalen und internationalen Folgen eines militarisierten Konflikts', *Beiträge zur Konfliktforschung*, 17:4 (1987) pp. 69–98

Van Dam, Nikolaos, 'Middle Eastern Political Clichés: 'Takriti' and 'Sunni' Rule in Iraq; 'Alawi Rule' in Syria. A critical appraisal', *Orient*, 21 (1980) pp. 42–57

Van Den Berghe, Pierre L., 'The Present State of Comparative Race and Ethnic Studies', in Jan Berting et al. (eds.), *Problems in International Comparative Research in the Social Sciences*, Oxford, 1979, pp. 23–36

—— 'Pluralism', in John J. Honigmann (ed.), *Handbook of Social and Cultural Anthropology*, Chicago, 1974, pp. 959–77

Wallerstein, Imanuel, 'Social Conflict in Post-Independence Black Africa: The concepts of race and status-groups reconsidered', in E. Campbell (ed.), *Racial Tensions and National Identity*, Nashville, Tenn., 1972, pp. 207–26

Wolpe, Harold, 'The "White Working Class" in South Africa', *Economy and Society*, 5 (1976) pp. 197–240

Zuwiyya Yamak, Labib, 'Party Politics in the Lebanese Political System', in Leonard Binder (ed.), *Politics in Lebanon*, New York, 1966, pp. 143–66

## C Pamphlets, dissertations and unpublished manuscripts

Abou Rjaily, Khalyl and Boutros Labaki, *Bilan de treize ans de guerres au Liban: Les pertes*. 1ère édition provisoire, Beirut, October, 1987 (unpublished manuscript)

Aggiouri, René, *Les problèmes actuels du Proche-Orient*, Beirut, 1960
Al-Hafiz, Yasin, 'qira'ah naqdiyyah liba`d turuhat al-harb fi Lubnan' (Eine Kritik gewisser Thesen über den Libanonkrieg), in *Lubnan ad-dimuqrati al-`arabi al-`almani*, 8, Beirut, 1981
Assaf, Georges, September, 1983: '*Bain de sang' dans la Montagne à la suite du brusque retrait des troupes israéliennes*, Middle East Council of Churches (ed.), Beirut, 1983
—— *Rapport sur la situation dans les deux districts du Chouf et d'Aley depuis l'invasion israélienne*, Middle East Council of Churches (ed.), n.d.
Association Libanaise du Planning Familial. *La famille au Liban*, mimeographed, Beirut, 1971
As-Sulh, M., *al-maruniyyah as-siasiyyah sirah datiyyah (Der politische Maronitismus – selbsterfahrene Geschichte)*, Beirut, 1978
Atiyah, Najla, *The Attitude of the Lebanese Sunnis Toward the State of Lebanon*, dissertation, University of London, 1973

Boustany, Fouad E., *Le problème du Liban*, Kaslik, 1978

Chamie, Joseph, *Religious Fertility Differentials in Lebanon*, dissertation, University of Michigan, 1976
Connor, Walker, *Ethnonational Versus Other Forms of Group Identity: The problem of terminology*, Paper presented to the Conference on Pluralism, Cape Town, May, 1977
Conseil Superieur Des Interets Communs, *Recueil des Statistiques de la Syrie et du Liban*, Beirut, 1942–1943
*La Crise libanaise dans ses principales dimensions*, 1976
Crow, Ralph E., *Interest Groups in the Lebanese Political Process*, Beirut, 1962

Delprat, Raymond, *Liban: L'évolution du niveau de vie en milieu rural 1960–1970*, Beirut, 1970

Foundation For Human And Humanitarian Rights, T*he October Debacle: Report on Lebanon*, Fall, 1990. (Beirut) 4 November, 1990

*Genocide au Liban*, 1976
Great Britain, *The Covenant of the League of Nations*, H.M.S.O., London, 1935

Hanf, Theodor and Salim Nasr, *Gewerkschaftliche Konkordanz im Libanon. Bestimmungsfaktoren gewerkschaftlicher Einheit in einer kulturell und politisch*

*fragmentierten Gesellschaft. Eine empirische Untersuchung.* Forschungsbericht des DIPF, Frankfurt, 1982
Hudson, Michael C., *The Precarious Republic Revisited. Reflections on the collapse of pluralist politics in Lebanon*, Contemporary Arab Studies Seminar Paper No. 2, Georgetown University, Washington, 1977
Husseini, Salma, *Redistribution de la population du Liban pendant la guerre civile (1975–1988)*, unpublished dissertation, École des Hautes Études en Science Sociales, Paris, 1992

Joumblatt, Kamal, 'La démocratie économique', *Cénacle libanais*, Beirut, 1950
—— 'La démocratie sociale', *Cénacle libanais*, Beirut, 1953

Khalife, Issam, *A la recherche d'une politique ou d'un concept de sécularisation dans le Liban multiconfessionnel 1958–1975*, dissertation, University of Paris-Sorbonne, 1982
Kramer, Martin, *The Moral Logic of Hizbollah*, Occasional Papers 101, Shiloah Institute, Tel Aviv, 1987

Labaki, Boutros, *Rapports de force intercommunautaires et genèse des conflits internes au Liban*, Paper delivered at the Congress of the European Consortium for Political Research, Freiburg im Breisgau, 1983
—— *From Extended Family to the Community in Lebanon*, mimeographed, Beirut, 1988
—— *L'économie politique de la crise libanaise. Impact et enjeux*, Faculty of Arts and Human Sciences, St. Joseph's University, mimeographed, Beirut, 1988
Laurent, Annie and Antoine Basbous, *Le Liban et son voisinage*, dissertation, Université de Droit, d'Économie et de Sciences Sociales, Paris, 1986
Lebanese National Movement, *Merip Reports*, 61 (1977)
Lebret Report, cf. Republique Libanaise, Ministère du Plan, Mission IRFED-Liban
Lehmbruch, Gerhard, *A Non-Competitive Pattern of Conflict Management in Liberal Democracies. The case of Switzerland, Austria and Lebanon* (Paper delivered at the 7th Congress of the International Political Science Association), Brussels, 1967
*Le Liban que nous voulons bâtir*, Texte du document diffusé par le Front Libanais en date du 23 décembre à Deir Aoukar, 1980
Liban 1975–1976. *Qu'avons-nous fait et que faire?*, 1976
List, Harald, *Die südlibanesische Armee und ihr Territorium*, unpublished manuscript, Freiburg im Breisgau, 1988
*Lumieres franches sur la question libanaise*, 1975

Mallat, Chibli, *Shi'i Thought from the South of Lebanon* (Papers on Lebanon 7), Oxford, 1988

Mandate for Syria and Lebanon, 24 July 1922, *League of Nations Official Journal*, August, 1922

Mass and Optem, *Les Libanais et le Liban*, Paris, 1989

Naccache, Georges, *Un nouveau style: Le chéhabisme*, Beirut, 1961

Nasr, Salim, 'The Crisis of Lebanese Capitalism', in *Merip Reports*, 73 (1978) pp. 3–13

—— *Redrawing the Social Geography of Lebanon*. Research report, Fletcher School of Law and Diplomacy, Tufts University, Cambridge, Mass., 1988

*Note sur la question libanaise*, 1975

*Note explicative sur la situation au Liban*, 1976

Picard, Elizabeth, *From Community-Class to Patriotic Struggle. An Attempt at an Analysis of the Role and Significance of the Shi'a in the Lebanese Political System (1970–1984)*, Paper delivered at the MESA Conference, San Francisco, 1984

*Rapport de l'IRFED*, Beirut and Paris, 1962, Dokumente I–1–13,38 and 36

*Rapport analytique sur l'attitude des musulmans du Liban depuis le 13 avril 1975*, 1976

Republique Française, *Rapport sur la situation en Syrie et au Liban à la Commission de Tutuelle de la Société des Nations*, Paris, 1926–1939 (table 3)

Resumé mensuel des travaux de la Société des Nations, 10:7, July, 1930

Sa`ad Ed-Din, Ibrahim, *Anatomy of Egypt's Militant Islamic Groups*, Paper presented at the Congress of the Middle East Studies Association, Washington, November, 1980

Salam, Nawaf, *L'insurrection de 1958 au Liban*, dissertation, University of Paris-Sorbonne, 1979

—— *The Agony of Lebanon: Scenarios and Solutions*, Harvard University, Center for International Affairs, mimeographed, Cambridge, 1982

—— *Prospects for Lebanon. An essay on political opportunities and constraints*, Oxford, 1987

Salibi, Kamal S., *Lebanon and the Middle Eastern Question*, Oxford, 1988

Schemeil, Yves, *Sociologie du système politique libanais, dissertation*, University of Grenoble, 1976

Schiller, David Thomas, *Entstehung und Verlauf des libanesischen Bürgerkrieges*, diploma dissertation, Berlin, 1978

Smith, M.G., *The Nature and Variety of Plural Units, Yale University*, mimeographed, New Haven, 1982

Stoldt, Jürgen, *Das Scheitern einer politischen Modernisierung: Säkularisierungsinitiativen im Libanon 1920–1976*, M.A. thesis, University of Freiburg im Breisgau, 1986

*Temoignages vivants sur la crise qui traverse le Liban*, 1975

*Union Des Jeunes Européens*, Livre Blanc du conflit Armée-Forces Libanaises, Paris, n.d.

Younes, Riad, *Die libanesische internationale Migrationsbewegung. Eine Literaturstudie*, Freiburg im Breisgau, 1976

# Selected Annotated Literature in Arabic on the Conflict in Lebanon

Al-Hafiz, Yasin, qira'ah naqdiyyah li ba`d turuhat al-harb fi Lubnan (*A Critique of Certain Theses on the War in Lebanon*), in: Lubnan ad-dimuqrati al-`arabi al-`almani, No. 8, Beirut 1981.
   The author, a secular Arab nationalist from a Shiite background, criticizes some of the standard theses of the 'National Movement'. He takes the view that the Lebanese Left utterly misjudged the phenomenon of community. Denying the existence of minorities worsened the conflicts. The concept of 'communities as classes', in particular, is untenable: the Lebanese Maronites do not in a position of socio-economic dominance. Most Christians who took part in the fighting came from the lower, not the middle class. He regards the concept of 'political laicization' as political fraud, as another term for confessional hegemony. Any attempt to use the Palestinians to re-establish Sunnite hegemony and force the Maronites to capitulate will only split Lebanon and the Arab world.

Al-Magdub, Muhammad, masir Lubnan fi mashari` (*Various Proposals on the Future of Lebanon*), Beirut 1978.
   The author, a professor at the Lebanese University, was a confidant of several prime ministers. He discusses different proposals for changing Lebanon's political structures and weighs up their advantages and disadvantages: the Swiss example of a federal state with cantons; administrative decentralization; an internationalization of the crisis in Lebanon, and the neutralization of the country. He pleads for an constructive dialogue, and is convinced that unity is possible, despite all that has happened.

`Amil, Mahdi, an-nazariyyah fi al-mumarasah as-siasiyyah, bahth fi asbab al-harb al-ahliyyah fi Lubnan (*Theory in Political Practice. A study of the causes of the crisis in Lebanon*), Beirut 1979.

The author, a Shiite, is professor of philosophy at the Lebanese University and a member of the Communist Party. The first section of his book deals with the Arab factors of the conflict in Lebanon. These include, above all, the distance between the 'bourgeois leaders of the Arab national liberation movement' and the masses and the effect on Lebanon of the 'crisis in the revolutionary alternative'. The second part deals with the 'contradictions in Lebanese social structures' in the light of the crises since independence. He concludes with an analysis of the role of class and the Communist Party.

At-ta`ayush al-islami–al-masihi. kaif wa `ala ayy assaas? (*Islamic-Christian Coexistence. On what basis?*), Beirut 1981.

Issued by the 'Union of the Forces of the Working People', a Nasserite organization, this publication stresses that Christianity is a religion, not a nationalism. It examines the differences between Christianity and Zionism and pays tribute to the cultural role played by Arab Christians. The book concludes with a dialogue in articles between a Nasserite journal and a radical Maronite publication.

`Atiyyah, Nagla, lubnan: al-mushkilah wal-ma'sat (*Lebanon: Problem and Drama*), Beirut 1977.

The author, a Greek Orthodox political scientist, analyses the weaknesses of the Lebanese political system: confessionalism, the fears of the Christians and the frustrations of the Muslims. She identifies the question of 'participation', social tensions, the traditionalism of the political leaders, the Left and the Palestinian resistance movement as critical factors. Then she turns to the 'drama': the weakness, inflexibility and disequilibrium of the state; the coalition between political Islam, the Left and the Palestinians against the state, and the resulting paralysis; the reorganization of the Christians outside the structures of the state; and, finally, the war between the two factions. The author considers three possibilities: continued fighting, partition and the search for a new formula for coexistence. She discusses three variants for the last: complete secularization, 'political secularization' and a modification of the old formula. She feels the third option is most plausible, as it allows for realistic reconciliation and modernization of the state.

`Awn, Fu'ad, wa-yabqa al-gaish huwa al-hall (*The Army is Still the Solution*), Beirut 1988.

The author is deputy Chief of Staff of the lebanese army. He first gives a history of the army: its pre-war development, its disintegration in 1976, the periods of reconstruction from 1976 to1982 and 1982 to 1984 and its second disintegration in 1984. The author then discusses the measures introduced by the new army command since 1984 as well as possible ways in which the army might help to solve the crisis.

Bustani, Jules Fu'ad, aqdar wa tawaqqu`at (*Fates and Predictions*), Beirut 1979.

The author was a military intelligence officer. He deals with regional and international factors of the war in Lebanon: the Arab–Israeli conflict, American and Soviet strategy, terrorism, and changes in the Arab world. The author also analyses key events in the history of the Lebanese army.

Faris, Walid, al-fikr al-masihi al-lubnani ad-dimuqrati fi muwagahat utruhat at-ta`rib wat-tadwib (*Christian Democratic Thinking versus the Theses of Arabism and Disintegration*), n.p. 1980.

A radical, militant Maronite intellectual presents his view of the contrast between Arabism and secularism, on the one hand, and pluralism, on the other. He champions pluralism as a prerequisite for democracy and unity in Lebanon and decentralization as a solution to the conflict.

Hizb al-kutlah al-wataniyyah, maslahat tullab kisruwan-al-futuh (*Kisrawan Student Section of the National Bloc*) (ed.), at-taqsim. al-azamah al-lubnaniyyah `ala daw' at-tagarib al-`alamiyyah (*Partition. The Lebanon crisis in the light of international experience*), n.p., 1976.

A group of student supporters of Raymond Edde's National Bloc analyse the background to separatist movements: Katanga, Biafra, Quebec, Occitania, Brittany, Gascogne, Corsica, Belgium, Northern Ireland and Bangla Desh. After considering the motives of the movements and the emergence of separatist ideologies, the study concludes with an account of the difficulties modern separatist movements face in gaining recognition.

Hoss, Salim, nafidah `ala al-mustaqbal (*A Window on the Future*), Beirut 1979.

The author, an economics professor and long-serving prime minister, weighs up internal and external factors of conflict and comments on various proposed solutions. The second part deals with perspectives for Lebanese reconstruction and development, all of which, he feels, depend on restoring national unity and a joint Arab aid programme.

Idem, as-silm al-ahli al-barid, Lubnan al-mugtama` wad-dawlah (1964-1967) (*The Cold Peace. Lebanon: Society and state 1964-1967*), 2 vols., Beirut 1980.

This comprehensive and detailed account of Lebanon's political economy is written with great understanding. This is particularly true of the second volume, which deals with the social and political crises of the post-Chehab era. The analysis of various economic sectors demonstrates that 'Lebanese society hungers for a state'. The crisis in agriculture, oligopolistic practices in the professions and the resulting restrictions on graduates' upward mobility are treated as political neuralgic points. Finally, the author examines the relationship between community and social stratum and how intercommunal conflict distracts from social conflict.

Khalid, Hasan (ash-shaih), al-muslimun fi Lubnan wal-harb al-ahliyyah, mahadir igtima` at qimmat `aramun athna' al-harb al-ahliyyah (*The Muslims in Lebanon and the Civil War*, Papers delivered at the summit meetings at Aramun during the civil war), Beirut 1978.

This volume published by the Mufti of the Lebanese Republic is an important source on developments in political Islam between 1973 and 1978. It contains speeches and statements of the Mufti as well as an account of the deliberations of leading political and religious dignitaries at the 'summit meetings' at Aramun, the seat of the Mufti, at which at attempt was made to coordinate Muslim politics during the fighting in 1975–1976. Yassir Arafat often attended. Whereas in 1974/75 the meetings emphasized 'Islamic demands': constitutional amendments, abolition of confessionalism, census, etc., in late1975 they concentrated on dissociating themselves from the Left and rejecting full secularization, and in 1976 to efforts to settle the conflict between the Syrians and Palestinians. Although the Mufti continued to oppose laicization in 1977 and 1978, he also declared that Lebanon should not have a theocratic form of government.

Khalifah, `Isam, fi mu`tarak al-qadiyyah al-lubnaniyyah (*Unravelling the Lebanon Question*), Beirut 1985.

The author, a secular Maronite, is professor of history at the Lebanese University and a leading member of the Lebanese Federation of Trade Unions. He criticizes the ideologies underpinning the most common explanations of the conflict in Lebanon — 'communities as classes' and 'pluralism through civilization' — as well as the historistic attempts to justify them. He also examines how such ideologies exacerbate conflict.

Khalifah, Nabil, Lubnan wal-khiyar al-`arabi: al-hiyad wat-tahiyid (*Lebanon and the Fourth Option: Neutrality and Neutralization*), in: silsilat al-fikr as-siasi, No. 9, Jbeil and Beirut 1984.

The author, a moderate Maronite journalist, first examines the failure of the Syrian, Israeli and American options, and then considers different concepts of neutrality as potential solutions to the crisis in Lebanon. He draws on Lebanese policies of neutrality as implemented in practice as well as proposals of contemporary politicians. He concludes by comparing the main characteristics of various neutral states and shows how well these apply in the case of Lebanon.

Lahhud, Fu'ad, ma'sat gaish Lubnan (*The Drama of the Lebanese Army*), Baabda 1976.

The author was commander of the Lebanese armoured division, then deputy for the National Liberal Party and, until his death, chairman of the Chamber's Defence Committee. His book is a history of the Lebanese army since independence. His analyses of start of the 1972 crisis and the disintegration of the army in 1972 are particularly interesting.

Lubnan al-akhar, mu'tamar hawl al-`almanah wal-huwwiyyah al-`arabiyyah, mu'assasat ad-dirasat wal-abhath al-lubnaniyyah (*The Other Lebanon. Congress on Secularism and Arab Identity*). Institute of Lebanese Studies and Research, Beirut 1976.

These proceedings of a congress held in February 1976 constitute, as it were, a charter for a secular and Arab Lebanon. Muslim speakers demand secularism, Christians emphasize the Arab nature of Lebanon. The driving force behind the conference was the former minister, Nagib Abu-Haidar.

Lubnan al-gadid, dirasah `ilmiyyah tanqud al-barnamag al-marhali lil-ahzab al-yasariyyah fi Lubnan wa-tatrah al-barnamag al-badil libina' Luban al-gadid kama tarah wa-turiduh al-kata'ib al-lubnaniyyah. bi-qalam muhallil al-`amal as-siasi, manshurat dar al-`amal (*The New Lebanon. A scientific study of the criticism of the programmes of the parties of the Left in Lebanon. Proposal for a constructive programme, 'The New Lebanon', as viewed and desire by the Lebanese Kata'ib. (Written by the political editor of the newspaper al-`Amal.)*), Beirut 1977.

The author (Nabil Khalife) first discusses the programmes of the Lebanese Left and accuses them of contradictions between tactic and strategy in particular. A separate chapter is devoted to the Syrian Socialist National Party, whose founder, Antoun Saadé, he accuses of creating a new political religion that will eventually merge with Islam. The author contrasts this with the Kata'ib option, a democratic and secular solution. The Lebanese nation needs to be united through social equality, education and a consistent development policy.

Muhsin, Ibrahim, al-harb wa-tagribat al-harakah al-wataniyyah al-lubnaniyyah (*The War and the Experience of Lebanese National Movement*), Beirut 1983.

The leader of the Organization for Communist Action in Lebanon studies the different phases of the war since 1975. His analysis includes both Lebanese and regional factors of the conflict and, in this context, discusses the emergence and development of his organization.

Nagi, Amin, lan na'isha dimmiyyin (*We do not want to be anyone's wards*), Beirut 1979.

Amin Nagi is the pseudonym of Antoine Najm, a member of the Kata'ib's politburo, and one of the party's leading theoreticians. He sees the cause of the war in irreconciliable objectives of Muslims and Christians. The Muslims want a Muslim country and a Muslim president, the Christians refuse to become wards of Islam, and do not regard Lebanon as a Muslim country. The first section of the book deals with Muslim attitudes towards the Lebanese state: rejection of the state during the mandate, acceptance of the National Pact so as to get rid of the French, and, since then, numerous alliances with foreign groups against their Christian fellow-citizens. The author then presents a history of the Christians' position under Islam from the 'Charter of Omar' to the Ottoman Empire. He concludes that Muslim believers neither can nor want to abandon the goal of an Islamic state. For this reason, Arabism will always be an illusion. While Christians strive for secular Arabism, Muslims regard simply as 'Islam for modern times' (Ch. V). Secularism and Islam are irreconcilable, and attemps to create secular Muslim states have either failed or only scratched the surface. The dominant tendency in Islam now clearly rejects any form of secularism. In conclusion, he recommends that Lebanese Christians reject second-class status as wards of Islam.

Nasr, G.A., mihnat lubnan fi thawrat al-yasar (*The Lebanese Crisis in the Revolution of the Left*), Beirut 1977.

The author is close to the Kata'ib. He examines different positions of the Lebanese Left: defend the PLO, reforms, defend the Muslims oppressed by the Lebanese system, oppose partition and defend the Arab nature of Lebanon. He points out contradictions between these different positions and the political tendencies supporting them.

Nasr, Nuqula, harb lubnan ... wa madaha! (*The War in Lebanon ... and its Environment!*), Beirut 1977.

The book presents the Kata'ib's view of the 'Two Year War' (1975–1977), and draws a contrast between the interpretations of the 'Islamo-progressive' coalition and the Lebanese Front. The author draws up a list of each side's casualties. He emphasizes the responsibilities of the Arab League and the United Natoins. Finally, he presents proposals for a national solution as well as for relations between Lebanon and the Arab states and the rest of the world.

Qabbani, `Abd al-`aziz, Lubnan was-sigah al-ma'sat (*Lebanon and the Drama Formula*), Beirut 1982.
The author, a Sunnite lawyer, was close to the National Movement. The book discusses the positions of the leaders of the Lebanese Front, deals with the fundamental political attitudes of the Lebanese Christians as well as problems of regional development, and concludes with a critique of the National Pact of 1943.

Qabbani, Khalid, al-lamarkaziyyah wa-mas'alat tatbiqiha fi Lubnan (*On Decentralization and the Problems of Applying it in Lebanon*), Beirut and Paris 1981.
The author, professor of law and administration at the Lebanese University and a member of the State Council, has served as an adviser to several prime ministers. This work opens with a history of political administration in Lebanon from Ottoman rule to the present. The author then deals with the concepts of Christian parties and institutions for political decentralization and the counterproposals of the Left and of Islamic organizations for greater centralization. In conclusion, he recommends administrative, but not political decentralization.

Shararah, Waddah, hurub al-istitba`, Lubnan al-harb al-ahliyyah ad-da'imah (The Successive Wars in Lebanon: A permanent civil war), Beirut 1979.
The author, professor of philosophy at the Lebanese University, is a leading, politically independent Shiite intellectual. Of particular interest are his analyses of the Lebanese student movement and its reformist nature (Ch. IV), the eradication of Chehabism (Ch. I) and the development of the Shiite movement

Tarabulsi, Fawwaz, qadiyyat Lubnan al-wataniyyah wad-dimuqratiyyah (*Nationhood and Democracy in Lebanon*), Beirut 1978.
This collection of editorials and commentaries by the leading mind of the Organization for Communist Action in Lebanon appeared in the journal al-Hurriyah between 1973 and 1976. The author analyses confessionalism as a system that benefits the elites but not the masses; the National Pact is a 'tribal pact'; the confessional conflict as dividing the working class; and the prospects of complete secularization.

Yakan, Fathi, al-mas'alah al-lubnaniyyah min manzur islami (*The Lebanon Question from the Islamic Point of View*), Beirut 1979.

The author is one of the leaders of a Sunnite fundamentalist group. He discusses the emergence of the Lebanese state, and analyses the structures of the country's communities and political parties and presents and comments on the various explanations for the outbreak of war. In his opinion, one major cause is the Maronites' political and economic privileges; others include the conflicts between Arab states and the Palestine question. Finally, he examines proposals for a solution and expresses himself in favour of that proposed by the Islamic fundamentalists.

# Questionnaire 1984, 1986, 1987

One man says: 'I'd rather work hard, build up my own business and take risks to get ahead and make a lot of money.'

Another says: 'I'd rather have a safe job with a regular income so that I don't have to think about the future.'

Do you agree with the first or the second man?

Whom do you trust?
- Close relatives
- Friends
- Colleagues
- Neighbours
- Employers
- Nobody

In your opinion, which of the following factors counts most for success in life?
- Experience
- Education/Training
- Connections
- Luck
- Astuteness
- Inheritance

Most regions in Lebanon are mixed. All Lebanon is for all Lebanese.

The best solution to Lebanon's present dilemma is a completely secular state and society.

In spite of the terrible events of the past few months, I believe that coexistence between the communities is still possible.

If foreigners stayed out, conflicts in Lebanon would never end in victory or defeat for anyone.

Which politician's ideas and positions can you most agree with?

Which country do you think is the most perfect country?

Every Lebanese should have the right to join a secularized community that has the same rights as the other communities — own efforts, personal status, law, political representation, etc.

It doesn't matter what the workers do, they can never win against the bosses.

Before you start something, you should know whether it will work or not.

Whatever the political solution, Lebanon must remain a single economic entity.

When you start changing things, they usually get worse.

The services that Lebanon provides for the region are unique. Despite the crisis, Lebanon has consolidated its position.

Even ordinary people can get ahead if they help one another and act together.

One should not mix religion and politics.

The monotheistic religions like Christianity and Islam believe in the same God and teach similar ethical and social principles.

During the crisis each region has had to get by on its own. Perhaps a decentralized economy is a good thing.

Coexistence between the communities would be easier if each community had its own region.

It doesn't matter what anyone wants, secularization seems to have no chance in Lebanon. Community membership is a reality you have to accept.

In your opinion, which of the following groups has the greatest influence in Lebanon?
- Large landowners
- Religious leaders
- Bankers
- Zu`ama
- Merchants
- Party leaders
- Industrialists
- Ministers
- Military officers

If I could, I'd like to have a different occupation.

Which politician's ideas and positions do you agree with least?

On the whole, I'm satisfied with my boss.

Of course, everyone would like to earn more, but I'm satisfied with my salary.

If I could, I'd like to work in the Gulf.

It's a pity, but I don't have any prospects in my job.

I don't want to work for someone else all my life; some day I want to be my own boss.

If my colleagues are honest and cooperative, I don't mind what group they belong to.

If my family disagrees with the strongest political tendency in my community, I'll side with my family.

I prefer neighbours who have the same background as myself.

I believe in a life after death, in which the righteous will be rewarded and the wicked will be punished.

I try to live by the teachings of my religion.

I often visit a place of worship.

It doesn't matter whether they are rich or poor, I feel close to all members of my community.

I can be happy and enjoy life even if I don't believe in God.

People like me can't do anything to improve people's lives.

Compared to how my parents lived, I think I'm much better off.

I fear my children won't have it as good as me.

When I see people from the wealthy parts of town I think to myself that's how I want to live, and I have a right to live like that.

When I think of the future, I feel uncertain and afraid.

Even if foreigners stayed out of Lebanese affairs, it would be hard to reach an understanding; it is possible that the conflicts between hostile Lebanese groups would break out again.

Imagine you won some money in the national lottery. What is the first thing you would do with it?
- Buy a house or property
- Buy a car or new furniture
- Start my own business
- Put the money in a good investment with the bank

The believer must return to his spiritual and cultural roots and seek the meaning of his religious destiny.

The identity and uniqueness of my community are more important to me than loyalty to my country.

Life in any society must be based on faith and religious values.

It is good if there are no conflicts between the sons of the same community.

The division of Lebanon into different regions is unnatural, and will disappear as soon as the crisis is over.

A good friend is a good friend, whether he is called Georges or Mohammed.

Because of the nature of Lebanese society, important decisions need the agreement of all large communities.

The differences between the social groups have widened since 1975.

In Lebanon a rich minority is buying up everything, and the large majority is losing out.

Very different religious, ethnic, language or racial groups can live together in the same country, accept each other and respect each other's rights.

In the present situation every Lebanese needs strong political opinions and clear alternatives.

In recent months horrible things have happened. I fear that this has made coexistence between the communities very difficult.

The time of the old politicians is finished. The new leaders represent the basic feeling in the country and function better.

There are very real differences between the religious communities in our country, but one should keep them out of politics.

Lebanon won't have a strong and united government until authentic representatives of the communities have a share in power.

Of course there are political and religious differences in this country. But the differences between rich and poor are more important.

In spite of all that has happened, the Lebanese could reach an agreement among themselves if foreign forces would stop interfering in our affairs.

Whether we like it or not: when different language, religious, ethnic or racial groups live in the same country, they must either dominate or be dominated.

Lebanon won't have a united and strong government until the state overcomes the differences between the Lebanese people and between the confessionalist factions.

If you keep out of politics you have peace and quiet and have a clear conscience.

The old politicians are better than the new generation. At least they are tolerant, moderate and realistic.

In Lebanon the majority of people are middle-class, with only a few rich people and not very many poor people.

People who try to exploit differences between the communities in politics do this to hide the real differences between rich and poor.

A country with groups with different traditions is wealthier for it and its society benefits.

One man says: 'It is not so important if my daughter marries a man with a different religion, as long as she loves him.'
A second man says: 'Marriages between people of different religions are not good and are often unhappy. I don't want my daughter to marry someone with a different religion.'
Do you agree with the first man or the second man?

Think of the situation in Lebanon. Could you please look at the following forms of government and tell us for each whether you think it is acceptable or unacceptable for Lebanon:
- The strongest group should govern. The other groups must accept what this group decides.
- The numerically strongest group should govern. The other groups must accept what this group decides.
- One group should govern, and groups that don't like it must leave the country.
- One single party that everybody can join should govern without an opposition.
- Everybody votes for the party of their choice. The party or parties that win form the government, the other parties remain in the opposition.
- The country must be partitioned and each group should found its own state.

# Questionnaire

- Which of these do you think is the best solution for our country?

The strength of the different communities makes fundamental long-term change in the the political system impossible.

Perhaps it doesn't look like it, but it is possible that the political system can be changed in the near future.

In the present situation, given the strength of the different communities, it is necessary to search for a compromise and come to some agreement.

Victory isn't worth the sacrifices and losses my community would suffer.

In the struggle between the different communities in our country we're all losers.

With the strength and determination of our group we will eventually achieve our goals.

'Stand by your brother, be he oppressor or oppressed.'

'Stretch your feet only to the edge of the carpet.'

Statistics
- Date of interview
- Month of interview
- Year of interview

Age:
- 15–20 years
- 21–25 years
- 26–35 years
- 36–45 years
- 46–55 years
- over 55 years

Religious community:
- Sunni
- Shi`i
- Druze
- Maronite

- Greek Orthodox
- Greek Catholic
- Armenian
- Other Christian

Gender:
- male
- female

Marital status:
- single
- married
- widowed or divorced

- Number of children
- Number of persons dependent on your wage/salary
- Monthly income
- Other income (monthly or annual)

Respondent's occupation:
- large landowner, industrialist
- self-employed
- civil servant, white-collar worker
- artisan
- farmer
- blue-collar worker
- tertiary sector
- farm worker

Formal education:
- none
- primary school
- technical school (brevet)
- secondary school
- university

- Father's occupation (see Respondent's occupation)
- Place of origin
- place of residence
- place of work

Do you own:
- a house
- a piece of property

In which economic sector do you work?
- state and para-statal companies
- agriculture
- manufacturing
- building and construction
- commerce
- banking and insurance
- transport
- education
- other service industries

Which newspapers do you read regularly?
- An-Nahar
- As-Safir
- Al-`Amal
- An-Anwar
- L'Orient-Le Jour
- Le Reveil
- An-Nida
- Al-Ahrar
- Al-Liwa
- Amal

# Index of Names

Abdel Nasser, Gamal 111, 115–18, 120, 123, 128, 144–6, 148, 152–4, 158, 160, 182, 186, 362, 397–8, 401–2, 415, 428, 496, 564
Abi Nader, Fouad 297
Abi-Lama, Emire 55
Abu Iyad 1, 147, 204, 216, 386, 620
Abu Jaude, Michel 419–20
Abu Jihad 147
Abu Musa 215, 294, 302–3, 312–13, 318
Abu Nidal 259
Abu Rjaily, Khalil 339
Abu Shakra 285
el-Achkar, Assad 87
Acton, Lord 45
Aflak, Michel 77
Aggiouri, René 72, 163
Ahdabj, Aziz 214
Akhawi, Sharif 638
Ali, Muhammad 51–2, 57
Ali, Sleiman 219
el-Amin, Abdallah 614
Ammar, Abu 620
Aoun, Michel 296, 570–9, 581–3, 590–605, 608–14, 619, 621, 629, 634–5, 640
Arab, Issam 187
Arafat, Yassir 147, 149, 151, 160, 166, 168, 170, 174, 185–6, 204–6, 213, 215–20, 225, 228–9, 264, 293–5, 303–5, 312–13, 318, 497, 561, 619
Arens, Moshe 275, 283
Arslan, Faisal 427, 633
Arslan, Majid 267
al-Assad, Hafez 138, 173, 182–4, 192, 210, 214, 216–19, 224, 231, 234, 246, 266, 288, 292, 294, 497, 563, 580, 589, 618, 644
Assad, Kamel 116, 123, 266
Assad, Maha 631
Aziz, Jean 406

Bakkos, August 633
Barakat, Halim 41
Basbous, Antoine 279
Bashir II, Chehab 55, 57–8, 64
Bashir III 58
Bauer, Otto 30
Bechara, Antoine 640
Begin, Menachem 182, 229, 233, 248, 250, 263, 265, 268, 560
Berri, Nabih 190, 193, 245, 267, 280–2, 289, 293, 303, 307, 310, 312–13, 315–17, 319, 380, 426–7, 496–7, 500, 512, 515, 522, 546, 571, 573, 594, 597, 603, 614, 620, 630, 632–3, 636
Bertoli, Cardinal 210
Betts, Robert Benton 89
Beydoun, Ahmad 40
Binder, Leonard 40
Bitar, Salah 77

Boueiz 620, 630
Boulos, Jawad 191
Boustani, Emile 123, 166, 367, 610
Boustani, Fouad Ephrem 191, 233
Boutros, Fouad 252, 363–4, 368, 378, 403, 420
Brecht, Bertold 552, 637, 640
Brown, Dean 218
Bush, George 616

Carter, James 228
Catroux, General 71
Chadli, Benjedid 582, 613
Chakib Effendi 59
Chamoun, Camille 78, 111, 114–18, 121–3, 128–9, 191–2, 205–6, 208, 211–12, 214, 222, 232, 234, 237, 240, 246, 248, 287, 293, 309, 319, 368, 393, 402, 408, 413, 415, 431, 496, 619
Chamoun, Dany 248, 612, 634
Chamran, Mustapha 245
Chamussy, René 41
Chatila, Kamal 187
Chehab, Emire 55–7
Chehab, Fouad 58, 94–5, 98, 114, 117–24, 129, 130, 139, 146, 188, 323, 362–3, 367–9, 374, 556–7, 564
Cheito, Ibrahim 376
Chemali, Fouad 385, 415, 419
Chiha, Michel 70, 74, 163
Corm, Georges 142
Couve de Murville, Maurice 210

Daher, Mikhail 569–70, 576–7
Dalloul, Mohsen 633
Daoud, Daoud 317
al-Darazi 52
de Giringeau 240
Delprat, Raymond 101
Deniau, François 576
Deutsch, Karl 180, 638
Dib, Roger 616, 618
Dubar, Claude 40, 97, 103
Dudin, Hassan 388

Eddé, Emile 69, 123, 422
Eddé, Raymond 78, 121–3, 125, 127, 166, 174, 193–4, 208, 219, 267, 365, 367, 369, 375, 377, 406, 409, 418, 420, 496, 499, 591–2, 634
Eitan, Rafael 259

Fadlallah, Mohammad Hussein (Sheikh) 496
Faisal, Emir 8
Fakhr al-Din II 55–6, 64
Farès, Paul 599
Farhat, Albert 381
Farroukh, Omar 364–5, 370
Fattal, Antoine 179
Franjieh, Suleiman 116–17, 123–5, 127–9, 163, 167, 170–1, 173–4, 191–2, 205, 207–10, 210, 212, 214–15, 219, 224, 232, 234–7, 248, 267, 269, 283–4, 286–7, 293, 297, 299, 309, 334, 368, 375, 377, 406, 409, 413, 556, 568–70, 573, 577, 604, 614, 633
Franjieh, Tony 125, 167
Freije, Musa de 377

Geagea, Samir 237, 278, 299–302, 306–7, 309, 311, 318, 415, 432, 496, 570, 598–604, 635
Gemayel, Amin 193, 269–71, 273, 281, 286–7, 289, 292, 297–8, 299–300, 302, 313, 315, 319, 408, 496, 557, 564, 568–70, 595, 602, 630, 634, 638
Gemayel, Bashir 168, 193, 231–2, 237, 247–8, 251–2, 257–9, 266–8, 276, 300, 385, 430, 438, 490, 496, 568, 593, 595–6, 599
Gemayel, Pierre 116, 118–19, 122–3, 138, 162, 173, 191–2, 204, 208, 214–15, 232, 272, 287, 293, 298, 368, 371, 497, 619
Ghanem, Iskandar 170, 208
Ghanem, Shukri 64
Gorbachev, Mikhail 579
Goria, Wade 41
Gouraud, General 65

Habash, George 145, 147, 150, 164, 170, 186
Habib, Philip 251–2, 259, 263–4, 268, 271, 274, 283, 286
Haddad, Gregoire 189

## Index of Names

Haddad, Saad 227–8, 230, 241–2, 244, 252, 273, 298, 320
el–Hafez, Ziad 379
al-Hafiz, Yasin 97
Haig, Alexander 248, 250, 257, 263, 560
Hakim, Adnan 364, 366
Hamade, Marouan 618
Hannash 249
Hardan, Assad 614
Hariri, Rafiq 592, 595, 630, 634–6
Hartmann, Klaus-Peter 87–9
Hawatmeh, Nayef 150
Hawi, Georges 496
Hayek, Boutros 64
Helou, Charles 121–4, 165, 367, 372, 415, 594
Hitti, Philip 607
Hobeika, Elie 300, 306–7, 309–12, 318, 328, 561, 571, 602, 604, 610, 614, 619, 633, 635
al-Hoss, Selim 226, 231, 304, 310, 315, 320, 496, 569, 570–2, 574, 578, 594, 597–8, 600, 602, 609, 614, 629–30, 633
Hottinger, Arnold 577
Hrawi, Elias 595–8, 600–2, 608–16, 618, 620–1, 628–30, 636
Hudson, Michael C. 40, 638
Huntington, Samuel P. 13
al-Husri, Sati 145
Hussein, King 146, 151, 182, 190
Hussein, Saddam 608, 620
Husseini, Hussein 190, 245, 283, 296, 380, 569–72, 584, 592, 595, 614, 620, 626, 628, 630–1

Ibrahim, Pasha 57–60
Ibrahimi, Lakhdar 579, 590

Jadid, Salah 183
Jalloud, Abdel-Salam 219
Jibril, Ahmed 150, 170
Johnson, Michael 41
Jumblatt, Kamal 81, 114, 116–17, 119, 122–4, 126, 133, 136, 138–40, 164–6, 168, 172, 174, 189, 193, 204–5, 207–8, 213, 216–19, 222–3, 231, 242, 256, 275–7, 323, 366, 368–9, 391–3, 399, 402, 496, 556–7, 560, 595, 614, 616, 619
Jumblatt, Walid 189, 270, 277, 279, 284, 289, 293, 299, 307, 310, 315, 319–20, 334, 343, 407, 426, 496, 501, 512, 522, 562, 571, 573, 594, 604, 610, 619, 628, 630, 633, 635
Jureidini, Paul 567, 637

Kadri, Nazem 583, 595
Karamé, Elie 298, 309
Karami, Omar 614
Karami, Rashid 117–18, 122–3, 128–9, 164–6, 187, 193–4, 205–7, 209–10, 212, 214, 235, 283–4, 287, 293, 295–6, 310, 319–20, 363–4, 370, 372, 398, 421, 496, 569, 614–16, 624, 638
Kassem, General 146
Kerr, Malcolm 289
Kewenig, Wilhelm 40, 47
Khaddam, Abdel Halim 208, 212, 251, 286–7, 400, 564, 571, 595–6, 623, 630, 636
Khalaf, Salah, (see Abou Iyad
Khalaf, Samir 40
Khaled, Hassan 172, 331, 578, 595
Khalidi, Walid 41
al-Khatib, Ahmedl 214, 620, 628, 632–3
Khatib, Sami 571
Khomeini, Ayatollah 280, 428, 496
al-Khoury, Beshara 70–1, 91, 114, 570
Khoury, Fuad 41
Khoury, Nabil 631
Khoury, Victor 241, 610
Kissinger, Henry 141, 159, 173, 175–6, 181, 206, 377, 391
Köhler, Wolfgang 41
Kohn, Hans 7
Kosygin, Aleksej 220
Kourani, Habib 53
Kuderna, Michael 41

Labadi, Mahmoud 386
Labaki, Boutros 70, 97, 102, 339
Lahad, Antoine 298, 302, 320, 604, 624
Lahoud, Emile 597, 599–600, 610–11,

613
Lahoud, Nassib 633
Lebret, Louis-Joseph 98, 363
Lehmbruch, Gerhard 45, 141, 558
Lenin, Vladimir I. 30, 45
Lijphart, Arend 33
Lubrani, Uri 283

Maan, Emire 55
Maila, Joseph 588
Malek, Charles 1, 116, 118, 191, 384, 431–2
Marx, Karl 12, 20, 232
Massad, Boulos 59
Méouchy, Pierre Paul 117
Messarra, Antoine 41
Mitterand, François 579, 580, 612, 616
Moarbès, Antoine 383
Moawad, René 593–6
Mohsen, Zuhair 148, 213
Moukheiber, Albert 592, 625
Moussavi, Hussein 280
Mufti of the Republic, (see Khaled, Hassan
Muqaddam, Farouk 187
Murphy 569
Murr, Michel 615, 620, 633

Naccache, Georges 113
Najjar, Ibrahim 383, 431
Naaman, Boulos 191, 297, 385
Nasr, Marlène 105
Nasr, Salim 40, 86, 97, 103, 105, 395
Nasser, See Abdel Nasser
Norton, Augustus Richard 41

Obeid, Jean 619

Pakradouni, Karim 306, 310, 564
Pareto, Vilfredo 361
Peres, Shimon 298
Pérez de Cuéllar, Javier 576
Pharaon, Henri 70–1, 73, 117, 376, 423
Picard, Elizabeth 41

Qaddafi, Muammar 264, 315
Qassir, Victor 497
Qassis, Charbel 191

Quandt, William 179
Qulaylat, Ibrahim 187, 297

Raad, Inam 369, 372, 380, 408
Rabbath, Edmond 209
Rabinovich, Itamar 41
el-Rafai, Abdel-Majid 77, 583
Reagan, Ronald 144, 248, 257, 263–5, 271–5, 288, 291–2, 496
Renen, Ernest 7
Renner, Karl 30
Rifai, Nureddine 205
Rondot, Pierre 47

Saad, Maarouf 167, 173
Saad, Mustapha 187, 632
Saade, Georges 597–8, 618
Saadé, Antoun 76
Sadat, Anwar 144, 154, 158, 173–4, 183–4, 228
al-Sadr, Musa 85, 108, 127–8, 138, 172, 189, 190, 205, 207, 223, 244–5, 282, 327, 332, 366–7, 394, 496
Said, Hanna 208, 214
Salam, Saeb 113, 116–17, 122–9, 170, 172, 187, 193–4, 208–9, 256, 264, 266, 268, 283–4, 287, 319, 367, 377, 398, 402, 411, 610, 630, 633
Saleh, Sobhi 403, 425–6
Salem, Elie 179
Salem, Tamam 630
Salibi, Kamal 40–1, 47, 49, 57
Samné, Georges 84
Saqr, Etienne 382
Sarkis, Elias 119, 123–4, 219, 223–4, 231, 234, 239–42, 252, 266–7, 270–1, 306, 315, 375, 378, 420, 496, 564, 568–9, 591
Sartawi, Issam 294, 387, 417, 419–20
Sassine, Michel 597
Saud al-Faisal 589, 602
Schemeil, Yves 41, 101, 126
Schiller, David 41
Schiller Wallenstein, Friedrich von 323, 362
Sfeir, Nasrallah 310, 577, 584, 591, 593, 596, 602
Shaban, Said 294

## Index of Names

Shamseddin, Mohammad 190, 281, 496, 610
Sharon, Ariel 182, 257–9, 262, 264, 272, 274–5, 283, 300, 560
Shukair, Mohammed 319, 375, 403, 595
Shukairi, Ahmad 148–9, 158
Shulz, George 263, 265, 274, 283
Skaff, Elie 631
Skaff, Joseph 589
Slim, Mohsin 368
Solh, Rashid 205, 624, 630, 633
Solh, Riad 70–2, 76, 114–15, 117
Solh, Sami 114–16
Solh, Takieddine 373

Tabbara, Riad 396
Takla, Philippe 206
Tannous, Ibrahim 610
Tehini, Fouad 376
Tell, Wasfi 141

Tlass 620
Tönnies, Ferdinand 12
Traboulsi, Fawaz 382, 410
Tuéni, Ghassan 209

Usayran, Adel 287, 375

van den Berghe, Pierre 13
Vance, Cyrus 228
Vedel, Georges 592

Wakim, Najah 187
Wazzan, Chafiq 251–2, 264, 270, 281–4, 287, 289, 496
Weber, Max 11
Weinberger, Caspar 288
Weizmann, Ezer 248

Yafi, Abdallah 116, 209
Younes, Manuel 423, 431–2

# Index of Places

Adma 599
Aichieh 227, 344,
Ain al-Rummaneh 201, 204, 215, 223, 234, 239, 243, 248, 286, 600–1
Ain Assad 343
Ain Dara 582, 618
Ain al-Helweh 164, 195
Ain Waraqa 56
Aintoura 56, 215
Akkar 47, 64, 102, 108–10, 161, 197, 207, 211, 220, 222, 227, 318, 327, 344, 347, 446, 454–6, 469–70, 478, 485, 488, 491, 499, 501, 506–7, 514, 569, 629
Aley 83, 197, 210, 224, 260, 275–6, 278, 284, 328, 343, 347, 446, 452–4, 469, 529, 629, 633 (see also Chouf
Amchit 599
Anjar 106, 612
Antelyas 210, 599, 601
Aramoun 65
Araya 611
Arkoub 164–5, 168
Ashrafieh 201, 233, 239, 246, 268, 291, 297, 300, 311, 446, 453–4, 460, 463, 466, 469, 478, 484, 491, 494, 499, 506, 514, 517, 519, 529, 600, 611
Awali 298–9

Baabda 83, 215, 253, 260, 272, 319, 580, 591, 596–7, 599–602, 610–11, 633
Baal Mohsen 305
Baalbek 48, 128, 195, 249, 280, 347, 358
Baalbek-Hermel 280, 445–6, 454–5, 460, 462–3, 469, 476, 486–7, 491, 494–5, 499–500, 507, 517, 529, 628, 630, 632
Badawi 195
Barouk 172
Basta 446, 453–4, 463, 466, 469–70, 478, 482, 484, 491, 494, 499–500, 506–7, 517, 529
Batroun 83, 237, 344, 347, 617
Beaufort 242
Beirut 47–8, 50, 54, 58, 60–4, 66, 72, 78, 85, 97–8, 103, 106, 112, 116, 127, 145, 147, 155, 160–1, 164–5, 168, 170, 172–3, 187, 194–5, 197, 199, 200–2, 208–11, 214, 219–20, 222, 224–7, 236–7, 242–7, 249–53, 255–6, 258–60, 262–4, 266–70, 275–7, 279, 281, 283–6, 289, 291–300, 302–5, 307, 310, 312–14, 317–19, 321, 326, 328, 333, 336–8, 344–6, 350, 353, 358–9, 364, 366, 377, 388, 395–6, 400, 412, 430, 433, 443, 445–6, 449,

453–4, 456, 460, 462–3, 466, 469–70, 478–9, 482, 484, 486–9, 491, 495, 499–502, 506–7, 514, 517, 522, 528–9, 531, 539–40, 628–31
— east, 117, 174, 195, 197, 202, 205, 210, 215, 223, 231, 233–5, 237, 239–40, 242, 244–5, 251, 266, 281, 283, 292, 296, 310–12, 328, 344–7, 357, 411, 440, 442–6, 449, 452–4, 460, 462, 466, 469–70, 476, 482, 484, 486, 491, 506–7, 517, 524, 528–9, 615
— west, 117, 120, 122, 171, 187, 202, 209–10, 215, 220, 223–4, 242, 245–6, 253, 255, 258, 260, 262–4, 266–9, 281, 284, 286, 289, 291–6, 304–6, 310–12, 314–15, 327, 329–30, 334, 338–40, 344–7, 357, 440, 444, 449, 452, 454, 460, 462–3, 470, 476, 478–9, 482, 484, 488, 493, 495, 506–7, 522, 524, 526, 528, 532, 537, 542, 546, 610–11
Beit Eddine 58, 240, 251
Beit Meri 240
Beit Millat 207
Bekaa 47–8, 52, 55, 58, 60, 64, 66, 85, 102, 106, 110, 127–8, 131, 164–5, 171, 174, 195, 197, 205, 207, 210–11, 219–20, 222, 224, 239, 241, 246, 249, 250–1, 253, 260, 262, 267, 280, 285, 288, 294, 298, 311, 315, 317, 327, 332, 336, 343–4, 346–7, 356, 366, 377, 383, 388, 395, 400, 435, 440, 443, 446, 449, 452, 454, 463, 469–70, 478–91, 494, 499, 501–2, 517, 528–9, 534, 574, 579, 582–3, 589, 595–6, 603–4, 610, 618, 623, 625, 628–9, 631–2
Bshara 83, 323
Bhamdoun 225, 260, 285, 289
Bikfaya 215–16, 240, 283, 310
Bireh 285
Bkerke 593
Bourbara 573
Bourj Abou Haidar (see Basta'
Bourj al-Barajneh 195, 201, 211, 223, 303–4, 313, 318, 345, 446,

453, 463, 469, 478, 487, 494, 500–1, 502, 515, 528–9, 532
Bourj el-Shemali 196
Bouss 611
Broumanna 240
el–Buss 195

Chatila 173, 195, 201, 268–9, 271–2, 274, 281, 300, 303, 307, 313, 318
Chekka 222–3, 235–6, 294
Chiyah 201, 204, 215, 223, 234, 243, 286, 317, 345, 445–6, 453, 463, 469, 478, 486–7, 500–1, 514–15, 529
Chouf 53, 56, 58–9, 62, 78, 116–17, 187, 197, 222, 231, 260, 266, 273, 275–8, 282–5, 289, 291–2, 297–9, 301–3, 328, 332, 334, 336, 340, 343, 345–7, 438, 440, 443–6, 449, 452–4, 460–3, 467, 469, 476, 478, 484–8, 491, 494–5, 499–501, 506–7, 510, 514, 517, 522, 524, 528–9, 534–5, 537, 613, 617, 629–33
Chtaura 48, 173, 224, 595

Dahr el-Beidar 582, 618
Damour 211–12, 214, 223, 259, 268–9, 299, 332, 343
Dayr Ashayer 170
Dbayeh 197, 211, 599, 615
Deir al–Qamar 58, 197, 222, 285, 297
Dekwaneh 168, 201

Ehden 236–7, 299

Fakhani 252
Fayadiye 215, 233–4, 241, 267
Fourn el-Chebbak 599

Ghobeiri, (see Chiyah

Hadeth 611
Halat 600
Hama 2, 305
Hammana 582, 618
Hamra 201, 295, 314, 345
Haret Hreik 204, 345, 446, 454, 463,

469, 478, 485, 487, 500–1, 515, 528–9, 532, 591
Hasbaya 83, 163, 170
Hay Salloum, (see Jnah
Hazmiyeh 211
Hermel 83, 347 (see also Baalbek and Hermel)
Hermon 48, 52
Hoch Omara 343

Iklim al–Kharroub 299, 302, 312, 343, 347
Iklim al–Touffah 603, 613

Jabal Amel 64
Jabal Druze 275
Jbeil 83, 197, 440, 442–3, 445–6, 449, 452–3, 454, 463, 469, 477–8, 482, 485, 491, 495, 499–500, 506, 514, 517, 524, 528–9, 535, 617, 631, 633
Jezzine 83, 197, 220, 222, 260, 299, 301–2, 321, 344–5, 347, 445–6, 453, 456, 460, 463, 466–7, 469–70, 476, 478–9, 482, 486, 488, 495, 499–500, 514–15, 529, 632
Jisr al–Pasha 195, 201, 211, 222
Jiyeh 211, 573
Jnah, Ouzai 445–6, 453, 463, 469, 485, 500, 515, 528–9, 532
Jounieh 58, 197, 216, 218, 240, 258, 283, 573, 599

Kafur 251
Kahhale 167–8, 210, 284
Kantari 201, 209
Karantina 197, 201, 211–12, 223, 269, 309, 600, 613
Kaslik 232, 297
Kaukaba 242
Kfar Chouba 173
Kfar Falous 302
Khalde 303, 315, 573, 615
Khiam 345
Kisrawan 52–3, 56, 59, 78, 440, 442–3, 445–6, 449, 452–3, 460, 462–3, 467, 469, 478, 482, 485–6, 491, 494, 499–500, 506–7, 514,
517–18, 522, 524, 528–9, 534–5, 599, 617, 630–1, 633
Kleiat 599
Kobayat 197
Koleyat 592, 600
Koura 83, 222, 237, 297, 344, 347, 445–6, 454, 456, 469–70, 478, 485, 499, 501, 506, 514, 517, 529, 617
Koura and Zghorta 83, 222, 237, 297, 344, 347, 445–6, 454–6, 469–70, 478, 485, 499, 501, 506, 514, 517, 529

Laqlouq 347
Litani 48, 119, 131, 227, 230, 255, 257, 623
Louweize 56

Madfoun 237
Maghdousheh 313
Marjayoun 83, 227, 242, 344
Maslakh 201, 211
Masnaa 214
Maysalun 8
Mazra (see Mseitbeh)
Mdeirej 582, 618
Melkart 171, 173
Metn 83, 210, 215, 219, 222, 224, 235, 262, 278, 283, 300, 312, 318, 343–4, 347, 440, 442–6, 449, 452–4, 463, 469, 476–8, 485–6, 491, 494, 499–500, 506, 514, 517–18, 522, 528–9, 535–6, 573, 611, 633
Mieh-Mieh 195, 301, 321
Mreij 286, 345
Mseitbeh 453–4, 463, 466, 469–70, 478, 484, 491, 499–501, 506–7, 529
Mtein 215
Mukhtara 571

Nabaa 195, 201, 205, 223, 244, 327, 345, 600
Nabatieh 83, 195, 252, 255, 347, 445–6, 453, 456, 460, 462, 466–7, 469–70, 479, 487–8, 491, 494, 499, 507, 514–15, 517, 522, 529
Nahr el-Bared 195

Nahr el-Kalb (Dog River) 600
Nahr el-Mott 611
Naqqoura 321
North Lebanon 235, 238, 262, 344, 347, 445, 452, 461, 625, 628, 630–1

Ouzai 573, 615 (see also Jnah)

Qaa 205, 239, 343
Qannoubin 56

Ras-Beirut 201 345, 446, 453–4, 466, 469–70, 478, 484, 486–8, 491, 494–5, 499, 501, 507, 514, 517, 528–9, 532, 535
Rashaya 165, 347, 628, 632
Rashidieh 195, 313
Rayak 220

Saadiyat 211–12
Sabra 195, 201, 268–9, 271–2, 274, 281, 300, 303, 307
Sadnayel 344
Salima 225
Sannine 250
Sarba 599
Selaata 573
Sidon 47, 54, 66, 83, 131, 167, 170, 174, 195, 204, 220, 252, 255, 260, 299, 302, 318, 337, 340, 347, 363, 395, 440, 443, 446, 453, 456, 460, 462–3, 466–7, 469–70, 476, 478–9, 482, 486–8, 499, 501, 507, 514–15, 518, 524, 528–9, 603–4, 619, 621, 632
Sin el–Fil 20, 600
Sofar 220, 315
Souk el-Gharb 276, 284–6, 289, 295–6, 304, 310, 580, 591
South Lebanon 64, 102, 123, 161, 226–8, 242, 245, 273, 275, 281–2, 312, 315–16, 318, 321, 335, 343–4, 347, 440, 443–4, 449, 452, 476, 479, 517, 528, 623, 628–30, 635

Taalabaya 210, 343
Tarchiche 215
Tel al-Mirr 222
Tel al-Za'tar 195, 201, 211–12, 224, 591
Tibnin 170, 631
Tarik al-Jadideh 312, 446, 453–4, 463, 469–70, 485, 488, 494–5, 499–502, 507, 515, 528–9, 532, 535
Tripoli 47, 54, 64, 66, 77, 98, 110, 117, 164, 187, 195, 197, 204–5, 207, 214, 218, 220, 222–4, 235, 237, 253, 255, 294–5, 297, 305–6, 332, 340, 344, 346, 435, 443, 445–6, 452, 454–6, 460–1, 469–70, 477–8, 482, 486, 488, 499–500, 506–7, 518, 524, 528–9, 604, 630–1
Tyre 47, 83, 164, 173–4, 195, 197, 204, 230, 255, 259, 313, 318, 323, 619

Uyun Al–Siman 216

Wadi Abu Jamil 282
Wavell 195

Yarze 233, 253, 260, 612

Zahle 47, 50, 58, 83, 197, 207, 209, 211, 249–52, 255, 262, 301, 305, 306, 338, 343–4, 358, 454, 469, 589, 596, 604, 628, 633
Zahrani 83, 227, 255, 344
Zghorta 83, 124, 167, 191, 205, 207, 214, 223, 236, 282, 446, 469, 529, 617, 630, 632 (see also Koura
Zokak el–Blat (see Basta)

# Index of Subjects

Abu Musa faction of the PLO 312
agriculture 74, 100
Ahrar 505, 507
Ain al-Rummaneh incident 204
*Al-Anwar* 505, 507
*Al-Liwa* 505, 507–8
Alawites 2, 153, 294–5, 305, 618–19, 629, 632
Amal 128, 207, 244–5, 255, 265–6, 270, 280–6, 289, 296–8, 302–4, 312–19, 321, 329, 334, 337, 345–6, 380, 391, 406, 426, 462, 498, 500–2, 504, 508, 512, 515, 523, 525, 530–1, 535–7, 562–3, 573, 583, 603, 613–14, 616, 619, 630
American University of Beirut 61, 125, 147, 583, 603,
Aministrative Council (of Mount Lebanon) 61
*An-Nahar* 505–6, 508
*An-Nida* 505, 507–8
Arab Democratic Panthers (Pink Panthers) 294, 305
Arab League, Arab States 111, 114, 162, 173, 205, 222, 225–6, 251, 274, 303, 572, 575, 578, 580
Arab Liberation Front (ALF) 150, 160, 245, 255
Arab National Movement (Habash) 145, 147
Arab Peace Force 222, 225, 234, 240

Arab Socialism 146
Armenians 50, 57, 66, 76, 79, 105, 199, 201, 349, 441, 454, 456–8, 472, 474, 476, 482, 484–6, 488–9, 505–6, 510, 512, 514–15, 517, 530
Army, Israeli 149, 164, 303, 321, 338, 340
Army, Lebanese 164–7, 170–3, 204, 213, 222, 227, 233–4, 236, 241–2, 245, 250, 252–3, 255–6, 265, 269, 278, 280–2, 284–6, 289, 298–9, 303, 309–13, 321, 340, 345, 353, 559, 570, 572, 574–5, 597, 599–601, 605
Army, Syrian 220, 222, 224–5, 228, 233–4, 239, 241–2, 246, 251, 255, 262, 276, 294–5, 304–5, 314, 317, 338, 340, 343, 574, 576, 580, 589, 596, 604
As–Safir 505–6, 508
Ashoura 279
Assyrians 50, 89
Austria 57, 60, 511
Austro Marxists 30
Autonomy of Mount Lebanon 63

Baath Party 75, 77–8, 85, 122, 145–8, 152, 169, 216, 218, 220, 231, 280, 283, 294, 308, 427, 571, 614, 619, 633
Baghdad Pact 116, 144

balance of payments 353
banking 102–3, 115
Beit Eddine conference 240, 251
bicameral system 595, 598
Black September 3, 151, 158, 168–9, 172
bombings 330, 341
budget deficit 353–4, 572, 597, 605
Byzantium 51

Cabinet 118–19, 121–2, 125–6, 569–72, 586–8, 616
Cairo Agreement 123, 166–8, 170–1, 195, 212–13, 223, 225, 251, 320, 620
Camp David Agreements 183–4, 239, 257, 264–5
cantonalization, see federalism
capital losses 351
capitulations 57
Census 65, 69, 86–90, 96–7, 115, 307
Central Bank 571, 598, 623
Chehabists, Chehabism 123–4, 129, 369, 375, 554, 556, 558–9, 565
Christians, Lebanese 3–5, 272, 301, 313, 338, 346, 382–3, 387, 398, 404, 414–15, 428, 438, 440–2, 452, 454, 456–8, 462–3, 466, 474–5, 485–6, 488, 491, 498–502, 504–5, 507–8, 512, 514–18, 522–5, 530–3, 535–8, 541–50, 555, 612, 622, 625, 628–30, 634, 636
city warfare 336
civil service 69, 72–3, 93–4, 556, 588, 630
civil society, secular society 134, 513–15
civil status 69
civil war 5, 37–8, 59, 111, 113, 117, 119, 121, 193, 206–9, 226–7, 234, 237, 241, 275, 278, 284–5, 291–3, 295–8, 301–3, 305, 311, 314–15, 317–18, 320, 436, 438, 495, 521–2, 540, 542–3, 546, 549–500, 554, 556, 558–9, 565, 574, 588, 615, 638
class, class conflict 15, 18, 20–1, 24, 28, 31, 49, 62–3, 78, 97–8, 100, 103–6, 109–10, 115, 130–1, 459, 468, 480, 487–9, 492, 497, 499–501, 524
co-existence 7–8, 11, 13, 27, 29, 32, 34, 38, 40, 43, 435–7, 452, 486–7, 516, 534–40, 547–50, 579, 585, 587, 590, 641
Communist Party (CP) 75, 107, 133, 169, 187, 305, 571
communities, Lebanese 41, 58, 113, 138, 140
— geographical distribution 194, 470
— income distribution 100–1, 440, 456
— occupation distribution 456
— religious distribution 86
communities 21–2, 24, 32, 35–7
community identity, consciousness 20, 112, 365, 379, 584, 640
compromise 37, 70–4, 421–2
consociation 29, 40, 73–4, 130, 134, 160, 177, 522–6, 528, 530–32, 540, 549, 553, 557–8, 565, 639–40
conspiracy theory, plot theory 181, 391, 417, 563
Constitution, Lebanese Republic 68
crime 329–30

Damascus Agreement 212–13, 215, 311
deaths 339, 605
decentralization 516–17, 521–2,
democracy optimists 27
democracy pessimists 27
Democratic Front for the Liberation of Palestine (DFLP) 150, 169, 185, 204, 390
Deprivation, symbolic, cultural 30, 35
Deprivation, relative 23–4, 459, 468, 470, 478, 488, 554, 557, 565
Destour 70
Deuxième Bureau 119, 122, 125, 127, 129, 162, 169, 187, 368–9, 375, 380, 571
Development Council 572

## Index of Subjects

development policies 122, 125, 374, 588
Dhimma 3–4, 53, 414, 432
document of national reconciliation 581–2
dominance 36, 522, 533
Druze 5, 127, 133, 137, 139, 188–9, 197, 210, 217, 266–7, 270, 273, 275–8, 282–6, 289, 292–3, 296–7, 299, 302–6, 308, 314–15, 321, 325, 328–9, 332, 334, 336–7, 343, 386, 392, 400, 404, 406, 408, 416, 420, 426, 429, 432, 441, 453, 456–8, 460, 462–3, 470, 472, 474, 476, 478–9, 482, 484–5, 487–9, 491, 493, 495, 497, 504–7, 510, 512, 514–15, 518–19, 523–4, 530, 532, 536–8, 542, 618, 633
Druze militia (PSP) 266, 275–6, 314, 438, 466, 476, 502, 531–2, 574, 580, 583
Duumvirate, president–premier 91–2, 96, 118, 587

Eastern question 38
economic policies 100, 107, 372
education 31–2, 47, 54, 56, 62, 66, 69, 94, 98, 358, 430, 438–42, 444–9, 457–63, 465–6, 468–70, 472, 474–5, 481, 484, 487, 491, 499–501, 506, 511, 515, 522, 524, 526–7, 531, 536, 541, 554, 557
Egypt 50, 52, 57–58, 62, 89, 111, 116, 118, 143–8, 152, 154–5, 157–60, 162, 173–5
Ehden incident 236–7
Eisenhower Doctrine 111, 116, 118
electoral system, electoral law 68–9, 73, 82, 90, 115, 623, 629, 634
emigration, expatriate Lebanese 62, 89, 103, 348–9, 354, 371, 411, 605, 643
ethnicity 13–15, 18
evacuation of the PLO from Beirut 264, 293
expulsions 330, 332, 334, 342, 345–6
extended families 56, 60, 77, 79, 80–1, 124

family associations 80
family business 81
family solidarity 483
Fatah 169–70, 172, 177, 185–7, 195, 205, 213, 215, 218, 220, 223, 245, 253, 255, 294, 318
Fayadiye incident 234,
federalism, cantonalization 307, 404, 517, 521, 536, 550
fertile crescent 76
feudalism, see taxation
Flag War 305
flight, refugees 346, 355, 359
France 28, 39, 116, 124, 180, 217–18, 284, 291, 310, 449, 509, 523, 571, 576, 578, 580–1, 583, 591, 593, 596, 602, 609, 611–12
Free Lebanon 242, 321

Geneva Peace Conference 158, 174, 228, 287–8, 293
GNP 352
government lending 569, 571
Great Britain 57, 60, 116, 142
Greater Lebanon, Grand Liban 64–6, 68–9, 86–7, 97, 132
Greek Catholics, see also Melchites 57, 71, 90, 94, 106, 133, 139, 199, 249, 285, 441–2, 453–4, 456–8, 460, 470, 472, 474, 476, 478, 482, 484, 486, 488, 494, 504–6, 510, 512, 514–15, 517–18, 522–3, 534, 537
Greek Orthodox 57, 59, 63–4, 70–1, 76–7, 84–5, 88, 90, 93, 106, 133, 139, 186, 193, 199, 201, 207, 209, 249, 267, 285, 296, 435, 441–2, 454, 456–8, 460, 466, 470, 474, 476, 479, 482, 486, 488, 492–4, 504–7, 509–10, 512, 514–15, 518, 522–3, 534, 536–7, 554
Greek Orthodox Council 84
green line 215, 223, 242–3, 295–6, 302, 304, 310–11, 318, 540, 569, 574, 600, 604
Guardians of the Cedars 191, 247

Gulf war 155, 184, 568, 609

Haddad militia, South Lebanon Army (Lahad) 298, 321, 561, 603–4
Hapsburg Empire 7, 10, 30
Hentshag Party 79
Hezbollah 156, 281–2, 297, 304, 315–18, 321, 329, 334, 337, 358, 561, 563, 574, 603–4, 611, 613, 623, 630, 632–3, 635–6
Holy Spirit University 232

Identity card murders 327
Income disparities 100–2, 130, 345, 554
Incorporation 18, 21–3, 97–8, 103, 105, 110, 130–1, 554, 565
Industry 66, 74, 97, 99, 103, 109, 120, 366
Inflation 348, 350, 354–5
Interim government 570, 592
Iran 155, 257, 280, 303, 316–18, 508–10, 512, 560, 563, 568
Iraq 159–60, 177, 184, 218, 225, 257, 568, 572–3, 575, 579–80, 583, 590, 595, 608–9
IRFED 99–100, 363
Islamic Amal 280
Islamism, Islamic fundamentalism 152, 156, 161, 365, 414, 498, 501–2, 504, 510, 512, 514–15, 517–18, 522–3, 525, 530–31, 535–7, 539, 630, 632–3
Israel 3–4, 162–5, 168, 171–5, 181–2, 184–5, 205–6, 208, 218, 226, 228–33, 235, 240, 242, 248, 250–3, 256–60, 262–5, 269, 271–5, 277–9, 282, 287–9, 292–3, 298, 300, 304, 307–8, 313, 316, 320–2, 324–5, 333–4, 338, 357, 509, 558–63, 567–8, 571, 575, 589, 595, 604, 609, 620, 623–4, 632, 645–6
Israeli invasion 1982 228, 234, 241, 244, 258, 265–6, 280, 289, 293, 303, 315, 322
Israeli–Arab wars 114, 116, 122, 127, 145–50, 152, 154, 156, 158–9, 163, 172–3, 175

Israeli–Lebanese Agreement 271, 273–5, 277, 279, 282–9, 292–3, 295, 297, 303–4
Italy 264, 285

Jacobinism 28–9, 31, 35–6, 38, 73
Jacobites 50, 89, 105
Jordan 141, 145–8, 150–1, 153, 157–60, 163, 168, 171, 174–5, 177

Kata'ib, Phalangists 70, 72, 77–9, 112, 116–18, 123, 128, 134–5, 190–1, 193, 204–6, 208–10, 215–16, 222–3, 231, 235–7, 247–9, 268–9, 272, 276, 282, 284, 296–7, 299–300, 302, 306, 309, 325, 328, 334, 337, 344, 365, 383, 394, 406, 411, 414, 419, 422, 431, 597–8, 613–14, 618–19, 629–30, 635
kidnappings 330, 345
Kurds 89, 99, 199, 201, 304, 344
Kuwait 251, 609

L'Orient-Le Jour 505–6, 508
Lausanne conference of National Reconciliation 295, 297
*Le Reveil* 505–6, 508
Lebanese Arab Army 214–15, 227, 611–13, 617, 623
Lebanese forces 190–1, 193, 204–6, 208–10, 215–16, 222–3, 231, 235–7, 247–9, 268–9, 272, 276, 282, 284, 296–7, 299–300, 302, 306, 309, 325, 328, 334, 337, 344, 364–5, 383, 394, 406, 411, 414, 419, 422, 431, 568–9, 572, 579, 582, 591, 596–602, 604–5, 610–11, 613–18, 629, 635
Lebanese Front 190–3, 211, 213, 219, 222–7, 231–4, 236–7, 240–1, 243, 246–52, 269, 276, 287, 309, 584
left, Lebanese 185–7, 189, 213, 269, 280, 311, 314, 487–8, 498, 501–2, 504–5, 508, 512, 514–15, 523, 525, 531–3, 535, 537, 571
Libya 184–5, 190, 219–20, 225, 245

# Index of Subjects

majority democracy 73, 317, 426, 523–33, 557, 584, 586, 641
Makassed 84, 136–7
Mandate 8, 65, 75
Marada, Franjieh militia 191, 235, 297, 573
Maronite League 84
Maronite patriarch 571, 577, 618, 629
Maronites 50–2, 56–7, 60, 64–6, 70–2, 78–9, 85, 88, 89, 91–5, 100, 105–6, 108, 117, 122, 132–3, 139, 199, 201, 207, 216–17, 235, 249, 259, 277–8, 285, 296, 320, 376, 379–80, 382, 386–7, 391, 393, 395, 399, 404, 406–11, 416, 419–20, 426, 453–4, 456–8, 460–1, 464, 466, 472, 474, 476–9, 484–7, 489, 492–3, 505, 509–10, 512, 514–15, 517–18, 522, 530, 536, 554–5, 561, 569, 587, 595
Marxism 15, 370
massacres 222–3, 268, 285, 303, 330, 342
Melchites 51, see also Greek Catholics
Melkart Agreement 171
Militia Agreement of Damascus (Tripartite Agreement) 306, 319, 560, 568, 580, 583, 590, 605
militia financing 333
militias, paramilitary organization 78, 117, 120, 122, 128, 181–2, 184, 188, 190–1, 205–6, 208, 210–15, 218, 222, 227, 231, 233–5, 239–49, 255–6, 270, 273, 281, 285–6, 286, 289, 295–9, 302–7, 309, 311, 314, 317, 462, 561–3, 590, 604, 617, 639
misery belt 318
missing persons 339
mixed marriage 81, 137, 396, 485–6
mobility, professional 449–50
mobility, geographical 451–2
mobilization, political 18, 28–9, 33–4, 41, 495
modernization 12, 15, 17, 24, 27, 34–5, 62, 67, 79, 110

Mount Lebanon 60, 625, 628, 630–1
mountain war 215, 276, 323
Mourabitoun 187–8, 209–10, 215, 242, 284, 291, 295, 297, 304, 312, 314, 379, 390, 398, 402, 425–6
Movement of the 24th October 187
Movement of the Deprived 108, 128, 189
Multinational Force (MNF) 264, 269, 275, 284–7, 291, 315
Muslim brotherhood 152, 155–6, 246
Muslims, Lebanese 65, 69, 112, 116, 118, 128, 132, 207, 216, 255, 541–3, 549, 625, 628–9

Najjade 70, 72, 77–9, 85
Nation building 9, 11–12, 27–8
Nation-state 12
national bloc 123, 128, 629
National Dialogue Committee 208–10
National Liberal Party (NLP) see also Chamoun 78, 167, 190, 614, 629
National Movement see PSP, CP, OCAL, SSNP, Lebanese Left
National Pact 71, 73–4, 82, 98, 110–13, 117–18, 121, 127, 129, 133–4, 140, 188, 192–3, 205–7, 209–10, 212, 232, 316, 319–20, 366–7, 376, 385, 413, 421, 423, 552, 555, 570, 585, 587–8
nationalism, Arab 8, 143, 145–7, 152
nationalism, Lebanese (nationalists) 61, 70, 76, 79, 130, 132–3, 138–9, 364
nationalism, greater Syria 70
nationalism 7–8, 10–11, 29, 35
newspapers 505–7
notables (see also zu'ama) 54, 56, 58–60, 65, 70, 75, 79, 81, 84–5, 108, 114–15, 119–20, 123, 127–9, 191, 193, 209–10, 213, 289, 305, 316, 376, 379, 383, 401, 403, 406, 410, 422, 425, 427

one-party state 521–3, 530, 533

Operation Litani 230
Organization for Communist Action in Lebanon (OCAL) 75, 169, 382–4
Ottoman Empire 8, 10, 53, 61, 63, 142–3

Palestine Liberation Organization (PLO) 148, 165, 168, 175, 185–7, 206, 226, 228–9, 242, 256, 293–4, 297, 302–3, 312–13, 318, 334, 580, 603–4, 619–21, 623, 646
Palestinian camps 148, 170, 204, 211, 220, 222, 237, 253, 255, 258, 268, 295, 312, 315, 318, 325, 620
Palestinian Liberation Army (PLA) 148, 171, 210–11, 215, 220, 242, 295
Palestinians, military organizations (see also PLO) 141–2, 187, 195, 209–11, 213–14, 218–19, 223, 241–2, 244, 252, 604
Palestinians (see also PLO) 3, 5, 99, 112, 120, 123, 127, 148, 371, 374–6, 387–9, 391, 394, 397–400, 403–4, 409, 416–19, 420, 423, 425, 428, 558, 568, 619, 621, 636
parity 92–3, 95, 119, 585, 587–8
Parliament 68, 79, 90, 96, 114, 119, 123, 166, 185, 212–14, 234, 266, 269, 278, 283, 300, 307, 312, 320, 367, 570–1, 578, 582, 585, 590–1, 595, 604, 610
Parliamentary elections 71, 85, 90, 114, 116, 122–3, 125
Parliamentary Speaker 571, 586
parties 68, 75, 77–9, 82, 84–5, 92, 94, 96, 107–8, 122, 124, 126–9, 133, 136
Partition 27, 32, 192, 207–8, 210, 212, 217–18, 224, 307, 377, 379, 413, 421, 423, 428, 431, 433, 521–2, 526–8
peace movements 638–40
per capita income 355
plural societies 14
Popular Front for the Liberation of Palestine (PFLP) (Habbash) 150, 158–9, 164, 167, 169–70, 173, 185, 187, 195, 302–3, 621
Popular Nasserite Organization (Sidon) 187, 299, 301, 604
Population Movements by religion 347
Population statistics 86
President of the Republic 72, 86, 90, 586
Presidential elections 123, 248, 259, 569, 592, 595
Prime minister 71–2, 76, 91–2, 114–16, 119, 121–2, 125, 129, 586, 634–5
privileges 58, 61–2, 67, 96, 127, 130, 376, 379, 380–2, 390, 410, 424–5, 428
Progressive Socialist Party (PSP) 77–9, 119, 127, 133, 135, 187, 189, 276, 278, 283–4, 292, 497, 500, 514, 525, 531–2, 535–7, 613–14, 616–17, 619, 630
proportion 61, 73–4, 86, 96, 109, 307, 584–5, 588, 636
Protein Company 173
protocol of Alexandria 114
proxy war 39

Ramgavar Party 79
Reagan Plan 264–6, 272–3, 275, 292, 294
red line 218, 226–9, 231, 244, 250, 561, 596, 611,615
Reglement Chakib Effendi 59
Rejectionist Front 173, 206
religiosity 480–2
religious, heads of the community 84
religious communities, (see communities)
revolution 7, 12, 23, 26, 28, 59–62, 110, 114, 188–19, 126, 129, 133
Revolutionary Guards (Pasdaran) 280
Rosewater Revolution 114
Russia 45, 142

Saint Joseph's University 61, 366
Saiqa 148, 150–1, 164–5, 167, 169,

## Index of Subjects

171, 173, 185, 187, 205, 211, 213, 215, 220
Saudi Arabia 143, 150, 155, 171, 177, 205, 209, 240, 251, 263, 265, 575, 578, 580–1, 583, 609, 635
secularization 11, 135–8, 513–17, 587–8
secularization of state and society 514–16, 519, 523, 546
secularization, political 137, 139, 213, 423, 433
security policy, Lebanese 161, 371
security zone, Israeli 302, 321, 604, 623–4, 630, 632
Senate 588
Shi'a 4, 51–4, 56, 58–60, 76, 71, 76–7, 84–5, 87–8, 92–4, 98–9, 105–10, 122–3, 126–7, 131, 133, 136, 139, 155, 161, 170, 172, 189–90, 193, 197, 199, 201–2, 204–5, 207, 210, 223, 226–7, 243–6, 255, 258, 265, 267–8, 270, 273, 278–89, 291–3, 296–8, 301–6, 312–13, 315–18, 321, 327–9, 331–2, 334, 340, 342, 344–6, 366–7, 375–6, 380, 383, 386, 395–6, 398, 400, 406–8, 410, 412, 416–17, 420–2, 427, 429, 460–1, 466, 470, 472, 474, 476–8, 482, 484, 487, 489–91, 494–5, 503–06, 510–12, 514–19, 522–3, 530, 533, 537, 554, 564, 584, 588, 603–4, 610, 618, 630, 634, 644–46
Siege of West Beirut 263, 267
silk production 56
Sinai Disengagement Agreement (Sinai II) 159, 183, 206
social conflict 107–10, 361, 389, 391
social distinctions 13, 17–19, 21, 33, 98–102, 477–84, 544–5
Soviet Union (USSR) 75, 144, 176, 181–2, 251, 260, 305, 509, 560, 578, 581, 593, 596, 608
strategic consensus 257, 263
street fighting 337
student movement 96, 109
Sudan 222, 234
Sunnis 5, 52–4, 56, 59–60, 68–71, 76–8, 84–6, 88, 91–3, 99–100, 106, 108–9, 113–15, 118, 122, 126, 128–9, 132–3, 136, 139–40, 147, 150, 153, 161, 165, 172, 174, 183, 187, 193, 197, 199, 201, 205, 207, 210, 212, 214, 235, 245–6, 251, 253, 255 258, 267, 269–70, 275, 278, 280, 282, 284, 287, 291, 294–6, 299–302, 304–5, 309–10, 312–14, 318–19, 331–2, 334, 336, 343–5, 364, 366, 375, 379, 383, 386, 394–5, 398, 400–3, 406, 408, 410, 415, 417, 421–2, 426–7, 429, 432–3, 470–1, 473–4, 476–7, 479, 482, 484, 486, 488–9, 491, 493, 503–5, 510, 512, 514–16, 518, 530 537–8, 553, 562, 584, 587–8, 604, 618, 633
Supreme Shi'i Council 108, 131, 189–90
Switzerland 509, 511
Syria 4, 49–50, 57–8, 64–6, 70–2, 75–8, 89, 103, 110–11, 116, 125, 133, 138, 141, 144–6, 148, 151–60, 162–3, 165–6, 171–6, 181–5, 190, 195, 205–6, 208–9, 211–13, 215–20, 223–5, 227–9, 231–4, 237, 239–43, 246, 248–53, 255–60, 262–3, 265, 267, 270–5, 277–8, 280, 283–9, 291–5, 297–8, 300–1, 303–9, 311–15, 317–19, 330, 335, 338–9, 349, 377, 382–4, 387–8, 390, 397, 399–400, 408, 410, 413, 417, 425, 427–8, 432, 509, 560, 563–5, 569, 572, 574, 576–8, 589, 593–4, 601–2, 608–9, 614, 617–19, 622–3, 634–6, 643–6
Syrian Peoples' Party (SPP) (see SSNP)
Syrian Social National Party (SSNP) 70, 75–78, 85, 107, 114, 117, 120–21, 187, 192, 205, 222, 283, 294–5, 297, 305, 310, 318, 345, 612, 614, 619, 630, 633

Taef Agreement 585, 587–8, 591–3, 597, 600–2, 608–9, 621–3, 625, 634, 636
Tanzim 191, 223, 247, 385, 415

www.ingramcontent.com/pod-product-compliance
Lightning Source LLC
Chambersburg PA
CBHW071428300426
44114CB00013B/1353